Michael Parkin

Introduction to Microeconomics

Sixteenth Custom Edition for Indiana University Bloomington
Prepared for Professor Self's Economics E201 Course

Taken from:
Microeconomics, Eleventh Edition
by Michael Parkin

Microeconomics, Fifth Edition
by R. Glenn Hubbard and Anthony Patrick O'Brien

D1288225

Cover Art: Courtesy of Pearson Learning Solutions.

Taken from:

Microeconomics, Eleventh Edition
by Michael Parkin
Copyright © 2014, 2012, 2010 by Pearson Education, Inc.
Upper Saddle River, New Jersey 07458

Microeconomics, Fifth Edition
by R. Glenn Hubbard and Anthony Patrick O'Brien
Copyright © 2015, 2013, 2010 by Pearson Education, Inc.
Upper Saddle River, New Jersey 07458

Pearson Learning Solutions, 501 Boylston Street, Suite 900, Boston, MA 02116
A Pearson Education Company
www.pearsoned.com

Printed in the United States of America

1 2 3 4 5 6 7 8 9 10 v092 17 16 15 14

000200010271915870

JH

ISBN 10: 1-269-94373-1
ISBN 13: 978-1-269-94373-4

Prepared for use in Professor Self's

Introduction to Microeconomics E201

Fall 2014 Semester, Sections 7662 And 7663

You should bring this syllabus/guide to the first day of class and refer to it throughout the semester.

Contents

Introduction to Microeconomics E201

Instructor Name and Contact Information

Instructor Name: James K. Self, Ph.D.[1]
Office: Wylie Hall 345
Phone: (812) 855-7590
Office hours: Tuesdays and Thursdays 8:00am to
    9:00am, Wednesdays 9:00a.m. to 01:00p.m, or
    by appointment
E-mail: jkself@indiana.edu

Class Webpage

The class Oncourse webpage is the primary mode of communication for all class information, exam information, homework, etc. You will need to visit the site regularly throughout the semester. You can access Oncourse by using this web address https://oncourse
.iu.edu/portal

You should be able to log on to the Oncourse system by using your Indiana University's username and password. Once in the system you should see this class in your menu of classes. If you do not see this class in your menu, you should check with the Oncourse help desk. Help desk contact information is found on the same webpage (if you just added the class, then give a day for the system to cycle). You should also ensure that you are registered for the class. Oncourse loads information from the official class rosters and if you are not listed on the official roster, you will not see this course in your Oncourse menu of classes.

Finishing an Incomplete

If you are trying to finish an incomplete grade from a previous semester by taking this course, you will need to see me. If there is room in the class and it

is in agreeable with the instructor that you received the incomplete from, I will allow you to complete your work in this class. I will need to add you to the Oncourse roster and it is your responsibility to co-ordinate with your original instructor to ensure that your incomplete is removed from your transcript.

Required Textbook and Material

The required materials for this class are the items listed below. You should purchase the custom book package for this class. If you purchase a used version, you may not have active subscription to MyLabsPlus listed in the optional materials or the package of scantron sheets. In the package, you will find the following[2],

1. Selected chapters and pages from Microeconomics, 11th Edition, by Michael Parkin
2. Chapter 5 from Microeconomics, 5th Edition, by Glenn Hubbard and Anthony P. O'Brien
3. Package of scantron sheets (you will need around 30 and is included with the package or you can purchase separately at the bookstores)

Optional Material

- A subscription MyEconLab (included in the package as MyLabsPlus)
- Wall Street Journal

Prerequisites

None. However, a basic understanding of high school algebra, geometry, and graphical presentation is expected.

Course Description

This course is designed to give you a familiarity with the language common to economics, an elementary ability to analyze various microeconomic problems common in our economy and society, along with

---

[1]You may call me "Professor Self" or "Dr. Self" or informally "Jim." I will normally address you by your first name unless you tell me that you prefer me to address you in a formal manner (i.e. Mr. and last name or Ms. and last name). For those unfamiliar with university etiquette general practiced in the United States, when writing or addressing an instructor with a doctorate-level degree, such as a Ph.D., is to use the term Doctor (Dr.) and not Mr. or Ms. The word Doctor is a designation for a person who has obtained a doctorate-level degree. It is not appropriate to address an instructor without a Ph.D. (or other doctorate-level degree) with the term Doctor. It is always considered acceptable etiquette to use the informal term professor when addressing instructors, in general, regardless of the instructor's actual academic rank (professor is an academic rank also).

---

[2]I designed this package to provide a text that will physically (order of topics as you turn the pages) follow the topics of the course, in the order that I will cover them. I also wanted to eliminate material that we will not cover. My intent was to provide you a lower cost book that is inclusive of all additional items needed for the course, but does not include excessive additional readings that are not covered in the class. You may notice my name appears on the package. I want it to be clear that I do not receive any royalties for this package. Any money that would normally be extended to me as a result of this package is directly donated to the Indiana University Foundation and is used to help fund varies student activities.

being able to think through everyday microeconomic problems. Models and theories studied will help you to understand how producers could best allocate scarce resources to produce goods and services. Likewise, you will gain insight into what drives consumers to give up resources to obtain goods and services produced by others. Upon completion of this course, you should be able to apply learnt tools not only to business situations but also to problems and situations in your everyday life. You will find that the tools of economic reasoning are extremely useful in a multitude of everyday situations that require decisions on how to allocate your time and resources. My hoped is that you use economic reasoning throughout your life and not think of it as only a tool of business.

Desired Learning Outcome

The primary learning outcome of this course is that you are able to apply economic reasoning to both everyday choices and business decisions. In addition, you should have the ability to apply basic economic models to various problems and situations in the micro setting.

Course Learning Objects

Have an understanding and ability to apply, at an elementary level, each of the following concepts and models.

1. **Note-taking skills in an economics class**

   a) Be able to take notes about a class lecture and capture the main points discussed and presented.

   b) Be able to take notes from the textbook and be able to capture the main points discussed.

   c) Be able to form questions on various economic concepts that aid in your understanding.

2. **Introductory concepts**

   a) Overview of economic systems: resource allocation with scarcity

   b) Illustration of basic concepts using the production possibilities frontier (PDF)

   c) Comparative advantage and gains from trade

3. **Price Determination in Competitive Markets**

   a) Demand curves and demand shifters

   b) Supply curves and supply shifters

   c) Determination of competitive market equilibrium price and trading volume

   d) Comparative statistics exercises: changes in market equilibrium

   e) Government intervention—price controls and taxes

4. **Elasticity**

   a) Price elasticity of demand: definition, formula, numerical calculation using the midpoint formula

   b) Relationship between price elasticity, consumer expenditures (seller revenues)

   c) Factors that influence the observed price elasticity of demand

   d) Price elasticity of supply: definition, formula, numerical calculation

   e) Factors that influence the observed price elasticity of supply

5. **Economics of Consumer Choice**

   a) The consumer's constrained optimization problem

   b) Budget constraint

   c) Total and marginal utility

   d) Law of diminishing marginal utility

   e) Utility maximization rule and consumer equilibrium

   f) Consumer equilibrium responses to price changes

   g) Individual consumer demand curve and market demand curve

6. **Economics of Production**

   a) The production function

   b) Fixed vs. variable inputs: short-run vs. long-run

   c) Total Product and Marginal Product

7. **The Firm's Cost Curves**

   a) Fixed and Variable costs, explicit and implicit costs

   b) Short-run total, average, and marginal cost curves

   c) Economies and diseconomies of scale using the long-run average cost curve

8. **Perfect Competition**

   a) Competitive firm's demand and revenue curves

   b) Short-run profit maximization and loss minimization

   c) Short-run supply curve of the firm and industry

   d) Long-run equilibrium and long-run adjustment dynamics

9. **Imperfect Competition**

   a) Characteristics of Pure Monopoly and Monopolistic Competition

   b) Demand and revenue curves under imperfect competition

   c) Profit maximization/loss minimization for a firm with monopoly power

10. **Introduction to Welfare Economics**

    a) Net social welfare (consumer surplus + producer surplus) maximization rule

    b) The competitive ideal

    c) Welfare effect of exercising monopoly power

    d) External costs in a competitive market (negative externalities)

    e) External benefits in a competitive market (positive externalities)

    f) Public Goods

Attendance Policy

You are required to bring a scantron sheet, marked with a number two pencil, to each lecture and turn it in to a class assistant. I will use this for attendance record keeping purposes. On the scantron sheet, you need to fill in your Indiana University identification number, in the identification number box, in the name box your last name, a space, and your first name, along with the lecture date in the birth date section. It is your responsibility to attend all class sessions, show up on time, and turn in a correctly filled out scantron sheet.

A class assistant will be located at the door, at the end of the period to collect your scantron sheet. The class assistant will only accept one sheet from each student. If you turn in more than one sheet, you and the student(s) that you are turning in a sheet for will both (all) be considered to have breached the university's Student Conduct Code. Your properly documented attendance will be rewarded with a maximum of (6) extra credit points. Each recorded attendance will count as .25 points (you can earn a maximum of (6) extra credit points in this manner). There will be no extra credit given for attendance if you are not in class for any reason, or if you forget to turn in a properly filled out scantron sheet.

If you are not able to attend class or attend class but do not turn-in a properly filled out scantron sheet, you will not receive the extra credit for that day. There is no makeup for attendance regardless of the reason.

Last Day to Withdraw with an Automatic "W"

The last day to withdraw from the class and receive an automatic "W" is Sunday, October 26. This is also the last day to get a withdrawal slip signed without a special petition. After this date, you can obtain a late withdrawal from a course only by first receiving special permission from the dean of the college. Such permission is **VERY** difficult to get. University rules specify that permission for late withdrawals is "given only for urgent reasons relating to extended illness or equivalent distress" to a student who is "**passing** the course on the date of withdrawal."

Students with Disabilities

If you desire classroom/testing accommodations for a disability, contact me outside of class and present to me the written supporting memorandum of accommodation from the Office of Disability Services for Students (http://studentaffairs.iub.edu/dss/). Requests for accommodations for disability must be received and authorized by me, in written form, no less than **two weeks** in advance of your need. This is required to allow adequate time to review and make appropriate arrangements. Simply having a memorandum and/or a belief that you should be given special arrangements does not entitle you to them. None of these arrangements is costless. It must first be determined what the Office of disability Services is recommending and if resources are available to accommodate your request. No accommodation should be assumed until authorized by me.

General Course requirements

You are expected to attend all class periods, read the lecture material prior to class, participate in the class, and take notes as required. Class lectures will cover materiel in your textbook and some material that is not in your textbook. You are responsible for textbook and supplemental material on course examinations. Your course grade is calculated from your performance on three in term semester examinations and your final examination. In addition, you will have the opportunity to participate in Collaborative Learning sessions (discussed later) and given an opportunity to earn extra credit attendance points (discussed above).

Student Learning Design

The course is designed around the class lectures. However, lectures are only a part of the learning process. Each part of the course, homework, reading assignments, and Collaborative Learning are designed to complement each other and no part should be considered a substitute for the other.

Each part of the course design is important to help you learn the course topics and earn a good grade. The homework (discussed in detail later) is structured to complement the lectures, as are the reading assignments.

During the lecture, terms, concepts, and use of concepts will be discussed. However, you should have already read the particular chapter from the text that discusses the lecture material, and you should be familiar with the various definitions and concepts that are planned to be discussed during the lectures.

The lecture itself will be a traditional format with some in-class problems to help you fully grasp the material. I will use an overhead transparency projector and you can find lecture note guides on the course webpage (you should go to the tool section of the Oncourse webpage for these note guides). I will generally not use PowerPoint presentations since they are better suited for business presentations and not as conducive to class learning. Instead, I will use a mix of PowerPoint type presentation, overhead projection slides, and class handouts.

I must emphasis that I do not intent to entertain you during the lecture and you should not expect to be entertained. Please set your expectation with the purpose of trying to understand the foundations of economics. Once you appreciate this and immerse yourself in the subject I believe you will find it very interesting and enjoy the lectures from an academic perspective.

Once Collaborative Learning (discussed later) starts Thursday of the third week there will be a summary Collaborative Learning (weekly) homework assignment that will give you a good overview of what we covered during the week. It will also provide an opportunity to practice using the concepts study during the week. The first Weekly home assignment will cover material covered in the first two weeks of lectures. The figure on the next page shows the relationship of the course requirements for a typical week in the semester.

Examination Format

The three semester exams will be a mixture of multiple choice, true/false, matching, short answer, fill in the blank type questions. A particular exam may or may not include each of these five types of questions. The final exam covers all topics covered in the course and it will consist of all multiple choice type questions.

Exam Dates

- Exam 1: Tuesday, September 23, during the regularly scheduled classroom
- Exam 2: Tuesday, October 21, during the regularly scheduled classroom
- Exam 3: Tuesday, November 18, during the regularly scheduled classroom
- Final Exam: 10:15 a.m. to 12:15 p.m., **Monday**, December 15, room will be announced later

Your schedule must permit you to be free to take the final exam at the time listed above. There are no alternatives to taking the final exam at this time and date. If you are enrolled in two or more of the following courses you have a conflict—Economics E201, Mathematics M212, Mathematics T101, and Mathematics V118. Drop all but one of these conflicting courses now, unless you can resolve the conflict with your instructor(s) in the other course(s). Please do not ask if you may have an alternative time for the Economics E201 final—your request will be denied (this is the department policy and I do not have the authority to change the time unilaterally). Please consult the final exam schedule to avoid additional conflicts.

Makeup Policy for Final Exam

Only under extraordinary circumstance such as a documented medical emergency will I grant you permission for a make-up final. If you miss the final exam without proper documentation or approval from me, you will generally not be allowed to take a make-up final. Under some circumstances, I may allow you to take a make-up final for non-document reasons. However, your make-up final will be worth only 80 % of the available points allocated to your final exam, if the reason is not properly documented. If I give you permission for a make-up final, I will assign you an incomplete for the course and the make-up final will be administered in the next semester (Spring 2015). You must see me and sign a removal of incomplete document to receive the incomplete or you will receive a zero on your final exam. If you do not take the final exam, you will receive a grade of zero for your final exam grade. It is university policy, general, not to allow make-up finals unless there are extreme circumstances (oversleeping is not an extreme circumstance)—in other words **DO NOT** miss the final.

A Typical Week's Study Plan

Saturday-Monday

- Review weekly home assignment and attend your CL session if it is scheduled for Friday.

- Read Tuesday's Lecture reading assignment and attend your CL session if it is scheduled for Monday.

Weekly Study Activities

You should plan to spend a minimum of (10) hours per non-test week for E201. This is an estimate and some students will require more. Very few students will require less.

(3) Hours for lecture
(1) Hour for CL session (or additional study if you opt out of CL)
(4) Hours homework/quizzes
(2) Hours reading and study

Friday

- **Attend lecture** in a well-rested state
- Finish weekly home assignment and attend you CL session if it is scheduled for Thursday

Tuesday

- **Attend lecture** in a well-rested state
- Ask questions about any item you do not understand

Thursday

Wednesday

- Read Thursday's Lecture reading assignment and start your weekly home assignment

Makeup Policy for Semester Exams

There will not be any make-ups given for any of the semester exams. If you must miss a schedule semester exam and have approval from me, the final exam course weight will be increased by the amount of course points that your approved missed exam is worth. It is not in your best interest to miss an exam. You should only request an approved miss of an exam if you truly are unable to take the schedule semester exam. Your missed exam grade will be credited in proportion to the percent score earned answering the questions on the final exam.

> For example if you have approval to miss one semester exam and earn 80 % on the questions on the final examination then you will also earn 80% of the 80 points on the semester exam (or 64 points).

You may only receive one approved miss in the semester. If you must miss two or more exams, you will be considered for an incomplete grade of "I" for the course. To receive an incomplete you will need to be approved by me and meet the university policy on incompletes grades.

If it is necessary to miss any exam, you must contact me (prior to the exam if possible) via e-mail or phone if you are unable to access your email. In general, I will not grant you permission for the "approved miss" if one class meeting passes after the schedule exam date before you contact me.

> For example, the Semester exam is scheduled on Saturday and you have an unexpected illness immediately before the exam and miss the exam. If you contact me before the Tuesday's class, then I will give you an approved miss and the exam points will be moved to your final exam. However, I reserve the option to require you to provide documentation supporting your request. If you wait and contact me after Tuesday's class then you will not be given approval and you will receive zero points for that exam. All attempts should be made to contact me prior to the exam. The best way to contact me is via email; however, you are responsible to ensure conformation of your request since email is not completely reliable.

Collaborative Learning (CL) Sessions

CL sessions are an hour per week. They are offered at various times on Mondays, Thursdays and Fridays. Participation in CL is strictly voluntary, but is highly recommended. It is your responsibility to attend your CL sessions regularly and participate actively. Complete participation earns you a full credit of 6 % of your course grade, which is 24 course points. These points are subtracted from the course points allocated to your final exam and re-allocated to CL. This means that CL reduces the course weight of your final exam from 120 course points out of 400 to 96 course points out of 400. Partial participation earns you partial credit, full participation implies you attend regularly, bring prepared assignments, and participate in discussions in a mature and professional manner. You should consider the first and second CL weeks as a "trial period" for CL, allowing you to participate and judge whether you want to continue participating in CL.

The first CL sessions are scheduled for Thursdays, Fridays, and Mondays. Various sections will be available on these days. You will need to sign up for your top three preferred CL section times and submit your choices to me no later than the end of class on Tuesday, September 2. You will be given an opportunity to fill out and turn in your sign-up sheet during class on Thursday, August 28.

- The form will be posted on the class webpage along with times of each CL section by Friday of the first week of class. It is my hoped that I can give your first or second preference but I cannot guarantee this.
- No later than the Wednesday before the first CL session, you will see your assigned CL section in a grade book posted in Post'em found in the tool section of the Oncourse class web page. The grade book will be called "CL". Your assigned section will be found in the first column of this grade book.
- If you need to find out where your CL session meets, after you know which session you are assigned in, go to the class web page in Oncourse, there is a tab called "CL Leaders and times" click on it and read the table.

There will be no makeup work allowed for CL. If you need to be absent from your CL session, you are allowed to miss at most 4 CL sessions which will be recorded as an "approved miss" and the 2 points allocated for that day will be reallocated back to your final. If you miss more than four CL sessions, you will be considered to be not participating in CL and all points will be reallocated back to your final exam regardless of how many CL sessions you participated in throughout the semester. If you miss five or more CL sessions for any reason, you will not receive CL credit and your final exam will retain its full weight of 120 course points. Please choose the CL sessions wisely that you decide to miss. Once you miss a CL session for any reason, it is missed.

The below examples are provided to give you an idea how your course points will be allocated for CL and your final exam under different circumstances. The initial course point allocation for the final exam is 120 course points without consideration for CL.

- Example 1: If you chose the CL option and have no missed CL sessions, then the point allocation is 96 course points for your final and 24 course points for your CL

- Example 2: If you chose the CL option and missed three of the CL sessions, then your course point allocation will be 102 course points for the final exam and 18 course points for CL.

- Example 3: If you chose the not to participate in CL or you missed more than four CL sessions, then your final exam will be worth 120 course points.

- General reallocation formula: Final exam course points equal 120 – Earned CL points. All earned CL points are earned at a 100% (i.e., earned points 19 out of 19 possible and your final exam is worth 101 course points).

Course Outline

Tentatively the material covered during the semester will be chapters 1 through 6, 8, 10–13, and 18 from Parkin, along with chapter 5 from Hubbard and O'Brien. Please note that your text has been re-ordered to the order according to the sequence of topics cover in this course. Most chapters will be covered in their entirety with some of the chapters covered only partially. All changes to text coverage will be announced via the class webpage. A tentative reading list and lecture schedule is provided at the end. This document will be updated throughout the semester on the Oncourse class webpage. The schedule can be found by selecting the announcement tab, in Oncourse, and then clicking on the hyperlink in the announcement list for lecture schedule.

Reading Assignments

Reading assignments and lecture topic schedule is given at the end of this syllabus and the syllabus is posted on the class webpage. In additions, I recommend that you read a daily paper such as the *Wall Street Journal* for general information on the economy and current issues in today's world.

Non-graded Weekly Home Assignments

If you choose to participate in CL, you should bring your completed (or at least attempted) weekly home assignment to your CL session. If you choose not participating in CL, you should still work through the assignments. The homework is the summary assignment discussed in the Student Learning Design that is intended to serve as a summary account of the learning objectives covered during the week. Weekly home assignment will be posted on the class webpage (on Oncourse) on the Tuesday proceeding the intended CL session. Answers to the non-graded Weekly home assignment problems will be posted on the class webpage the following week of the date it was assigned.

There will be 12 CL sessions and Weekly home assignment assignments throughout the semester. See the below table for the dates of CL.

CL Number	Dates (Thursday/Friday/Monday)	CL Number	Dates (Thursday/Friday/Monday)
1	September 4/5/8	7	October 23/24/27
2	September 11/12/15	8	October 30/31/November 3
3	September 18/19/22	9	November 6/7/10
4	September 25/26/29	10	November 13/14/17
5	October 2/3/6	11	November 20/21/December 1 (the Monday after Thanksgiving break)
Fall Break October 10-12 (No CL)		**November 23 through November 30 is Thanksgiving Break (No CL)**	
6	October 16/17/20	12	December 4/5/8

Please go to the class Oncourse webpage to see the listing of Weekly home assignment (posted via a tool link in on the class Oncourse webpage). I strongly encourage you to do these assignments each week and not wait until the day or week before an exam.

Extra Credit

There is no extra credit offered for this course other than the already mentioned attendance points and some possible extra questions on the examinations. Please do not ask for additional extra credit; the answer will be—NO.

Student Conduct

You will be held to the university's "Code of Student Rights, Responsibilities, and Conduct." Any cheating will be dealt with in accordance with university policy. I follow the policy in the IU Academic Handbook with regard to cheating and academic dishonesty. At a minimum, a grade of zero will be given for any assignment or examination on which you are found to be cheating. All incidents will be reported to the Dean of Student's Office.

Basic classroom etiquette requires that you be quiet and attentive in class. This means that, except when we are engaged in-group work, only one person will be talking in the classroom at any time. Everyone in the room will give respectful attention to the sole speaker. Students creating disruptions in class will be asked to leave the class and will still be responsible for any material missed. Continued disruptions will be dealt with in accordance with university policy.

Any level of "chatting" with friends, reading newspapers, leaving early, and/or eating in class are disruptive and rude to your classmates and me. If for some reason you have to leave early on a particular day, please sit in the back of the class, leave quietly, and notify the class assistants of this need. This will be allowed as long as it is of an infrequent nature. Use the time in class wisely, appropriately, and efficiently.

When emailing please remember that that email is a means of communication and you should be always be respectful in your writings. Once you send the email, it is too late.

Course Grade Calculation

To calculate your course grade add together all earned course points from the semester exams, collaborative learning points, attendance points, final examination, and extra credit attendance points (see the description of attendance points in the attendance section of this syllabus). Once the total earned points for the semester are calculated, a course grade can be determined by using the table below. I may or may not adjust a particular test and/or final course grade. Any grade adjustment given will never make it more difficult for you to earn a particular grade.

- Term Examinations 1 is worth 80 points and exams 2 and 3 are each worth 100 course points.
- *Final exam is worth 120 course points minus any earned CL points.*

For example, you wish to determine your course grade and you have the follow scores.

- Went to 11 of the 12 CLs and earned 22 CL points
- Earned 80% on exam one
- Earned 72% on exam two
- Earned 75% on exam three
- Earned 72% on the final exam
- Earned 5.5 extra credit course points for attendance

To figure your grade you first need to determine how many course points you earned.

a) For test 1 you earned 64 course points $[64 = .8*80]$
b) For test 2 you earned 72 course points $[72 = .72*100]$
c) For test 3 you earned 75 course points $[75 = .75*100]$
d) For CL you earned 22 out of 22 course points 22 (CL points are always earned at 100%)
e) For the final exam you earned 70.56 course points $[70.56 = .72*(120 - 22)]$
f) For your extra credit attendance you earned 5.5

By summing (a) through (f), you find that you have earned 309.06 course points out of 400 or 77.27%. Using the chart below, you find that your course grade is a "B-." Notice that your grade without CL and the extra credit attendance would have only been a C+ for the course.

Tracking your grades

- It is your responsibility to keep track of your grades by regularly checking your Oncourse grade books. Attendance will be recorded in the Oncourse grade book and all other grades, such as exams, CL, et cetera, will be posted in Post'em within Oncourse. If you have a discrepancy, you will need to alert the appropriate class assistant in order to see if there is a mistake.

- If you have any discrepancies with your attendance records you will need to contact Your Head Class Assistant (contact information will be posted on Oncourse in the announcements)
- If you have any discrepancies with your test grades, you will need to see me (Dr. Self) during my office hours.
- If you have any discrepancies with your CL grades, you will need to contact your CL leader within one week of the posted grade. (contact information will be posted on Oncourse)
  - ➢ Your head CL leader is the manager of the your CL grade and if you believe your grade is incorrect you should follow the below process for correction:

(1) you inform your CL leader via email (save this email and response),
(2) your CL leader makes a determination as to if there is a CL grading mistake,
(3) your CL leader sends the correction to the Head CL leader, and
(4) the Head CL leader makes the correction on Oncourse.
  - ➢ Grades will be posted no later than the Wednesday evening following CL. The Wednesday of the next week following this posting is your **discrepancy deadline**.

Use the below chart to determine your letter grade on any exam and your final course grade.

Total Points Earned			Total Points Earned as a Percentage			Grade
400.0	through	388	100.0%	through	97%	A+
387.6	through	366	96.9%	through	91.5%	A
365.6	through	356	91.4%	through	89%	A–
355.6	through	342	88.9%	through	85.5%	B+
341.6	through	326	85.4%	through	81.5%	B
325.6	through	308	81.4%	through	77%	B–
307.6	through	294	76.9%	through	73.5%	C+
293.6	through	270	73.4%	through	67.5%	C
269.6	through	266	67.4%	through	66.5%	C–
265.6	through	254	66.4%	through	63.5%	D+
253.6	through	238	63.4%	through	59.5%	D
237.6	through	220	59.4%	through	55%	D–
219.6	through	0	54.9%	through	0.0%	F

Lecture Reading Assignments and General Schedule

Fall 2014, E201 sections 7662 and 7663
Lecture Reading Assignments and General Schedule as of May 21, 2014

Lecture		Reading assignment *(There are overlaps in the reading assignments. This is due to material coverage beginning and ending in different lectures.)*
Day	**Date**	
Tuesday	Aug 26	Class syllabus and begin PARKIN Chapter 1: What is Economics
Thursday	Aug 28	PARKIN Chapter 1
Tuesday	Sep 2	PARKIN Chapter 1 and begin PARKIN Chapter 2: The Economic Problem (including PPF, comparative advantage)
Thursday	Sep 4	PARKIN Chapter 2 *(CL sessions start)*
Tuesday	Sep 9	PARKIN Chapter 2
Thursday	Sep 11	PARKIN Chapter 3: Demand and Supply
Tuesday	Sep 16	PARKIN Chapter 3
Thursday	Sep 18	PARKIN Chapter 4 Elasticity (through page 93)
Tuesday	**Sep 23**	**Exam One, in Class**
Thursday	Sep 25	PARKIN Chapter 4 Elasticity (page 94 through end of chapter)
Tuesday	Sep 30	PARKIN Chapter 5: Efficiency
Thursday	Oct 2	PARKIN Chapter 5: Efficiency
Tuesday	Oct 7	PARKIN Chapter 6: Government Actions in Markets
Thursday	Oct 9	PARKIN Chapter 6
Tuesday	Oct 14	PARKIN Chapter 6
Thursday	Oct 16	PARKIN Chapter 8: Utility and Demand (through page 184)
Tuesday	**Oct 21**	**Exam Two, in Class**
Thursday	Oct 23	PARKIN Chapter 8: Utility and Demand
Tuesday	Oct 28	PARKIN Chapter 10: Organizing Production (will not be responsible for measures of concentration)
Thursday	Oct 30	PARKIN Chapter 11: Output and Costs
Tuesday	Nov 4	PARKIN Chapter 11
Thursday	Nov 6	PARKIN Chapter 12: Perfect Competition
Tuesday	Nov 11	PARKIN Chapter 12
Thursday	Nov 13	PARKIN Chapter 12
Tuesday	**Nov 18**	**Exam Three, in Class**
Thursday	Nov 20	PARKIN Chapter 13: Monopoly
November 23 through November 30 is Thanksgiving Break		
Tuesday	Dec 2	PARKIN Chapter 13: Monopoly
Thursday	Dec 4	PARKIN Chapter 13: Monopoly and start HUBBARD Chapter 5
Tuesday	Dec 9	HUBBARD Chapter 5: Externalities, Environmental Policy, and Public Goods
Thursday	Dec 11	HUBBARD Chapter 5
Monday	Dec 15	**Final Exam: 10:15 a.m. to 12:15 p.m., location to be determined**

"PARKIN" refers to Microeconomics (11TH Edition), by Michael Parkin and "HUBBARD" refers to Microeconomics (5TH Edition), by Glenn Hubbard and Anthony P. O'Brien

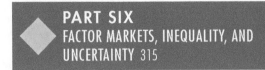
Chapters 1–11, 13, and Glossary taken from *Microeconomics*, Eleventh Edition by Michael Parkin
Chapter 12 taken from *Microeconomics*, Fifth Edition by R. Glenn Hubbard and Anthony Patrick O'Brien

The future is always uncertain. But at some times, and now is one such time, the range of possible near-future events is enormous. The major source of this great uncertainty is economic policy. There is uncertainty about the way in which international trade policy will evolve as protectionism is returning to the political agenda. There is uncertainty about exchange rate policy as competitive devaluation rears its head. There is extraordinary uncertainty about monetary policy with the Fed having tripled the quantity of bank reserves and continuing to create more money in an attempt to stimulate a flagging economy but providing no guidance about its eventual exit strategy from stimulus. And there is uncertainty about fiscal policy as a one trillion dollar deficit approaches a fiscal cliff and interacts with an aging population and rising health-care costs to create a national debt time bomb.

In the five years since the subprime mortgage crisis of August 2007 moved economics from the business report to the front page, justified fear has gripped producers, consumers, financial institutions, and governments.

Even the *idea* that the market is an efficient mechanism for allocating scarce resources came into question. Many thoughtful people worried about rising income inequality and some political leaders called for the end of capitalism and the dawn of a new economic order in which tighter regulation reigned in unfettered greed.

Rarely do teachers of economics have such a rich feast on which to draw. And rarely are the principles of economics more surely needed to provide the solid foundation on which to think about economic events and navigate the turbulence of economic life.

Although thinking like an economist can bring a clearer perspective to and deeper understanding of today's events, students don't find the economic way of thinking easy or natural. *Microeconomics* seeks to put clarity and understanding in the grasp of the student through its careful and vivid exploration of the tension between self-interest and the social interest, the role and power of incentives—of opportunity cost and marginal benefit—and demonstrating the possibility that markets supplemented by other mechanisms might allocate resources efficiently.

Parkin students begin to think about issues the way real economists do and learn how to explore difficult policy problems and make more informed decisions in their own economic lives.

The Eleventh Edition Revision

Thoroughly updated, stripped of technical detail where possible, extensively illustrated with well-chosen photographs, enlivened with new applications features that focus on issues at play in today's world, responsive to the suggestions of reviewers and users, and seamlessly integrated with MyEconLab: These are the hallmarks of this eleventh edition of *Microeconomics*.

This comprehensive revision builds on the solid foundation of the previous edition and retains its thorough and careful presentation of the principles of economics, its emphasis on real-world examples and applications, its development of critical thinking skills, its diagrams renowned for pedagogy and clarity, and its path-breaking technology.

Most chapters have been thoroughly reworked to achieve even greater clarity and to place greater emphasis on applications to current issues. Some sections of chapters have been removed and other sections added to cover new issues, particularly those that involve current policy problems.

Current issues organize each chapter. News stories about today's major economic events and debates tie each chapter together, from new abbreviated chapter-opening vignettes to *Reading Between the Lines* and end-of-chapter problems and applications and online practice.

A new feature, Economics in the News, is aimed at better motivating students and showing them how to use the economic toolkit to understand the events and issues they are confronted with in the media. It also helps them to work the related *Economics in the News* end-of-chapter problems and applications.

A second new feature, At Issue, shows two sides of a controversial issue and helps students to apply the economic way of thinking to clarify and debate the issues.

Among the many issues covered in one or more of the two new features described above are:

- Capitalism and its critics in Chapter 1
- Energy independence in Chapter 2
- The relentlessly rising cost of college in Chapter 3
- Price gouging in Chapter 5
- The monopoly power of the NCAA in Chapter 13

Highpoints of the Revision

Most topics are well explained in the previous edition and are hard to improve on. So the highpoints of the current revision are the new *Economics in the News* and *At Issue* features. Nonetheless, three topics have been substantially revised. They are:

- Price discrimination
- Carbon emissions and climate change externalities
- Education and health care

Price Discrimination The key idea we want our students to understand about price discrimination is that it converts consumer surplus into producer surplus and economic profit. To strengthen this insight, I now begin with a brief explanation of the relationship between producer surplus and economic profit. I then use a carefully constructed model of two separated markets to show how discrimination between them can increase producer surplus. I build on this model to show how perfect price discrimination, if it were possible, would grab the entire consumer surplus and convert it to producer surplus. I illustrate the attempt to move toward perfect price discrimination with applications to Microsoft's pricing of Windows and Disney's pricing of tickets to its theme parks.

Carbon Emissions and Climate Change Externalities What Nicholas Stern has called the greatest market failure and what some climate-change skeptics see as a problem that markets will eventually solve gets a thoroughly new treatment. I begin by contrasting the success story of local air quality in the major U.S. cities with the unrelenting rise in atomospheric carbon concentration. I then explain the three methods of coping with environmental externalities: property rights, mandating the use of clean technologies, and taxing or pricing emissions. I explore the ability of each method to achieve an effcient outcome. I also explore the special challenge that arises from the global rather than national scope of carbon emission.

Education and Health Care These two large items of public expenditure are not *public goods* but are examples of goods that have large *positive externalities*. I have expanded and revised my explanation of the problem of delivering an efficient quantity of these goods with an emphasis on the potential role for vouchers in both markets. I also have a new discussion of charter schools and the role they can play. U.S. health-care service and expenditures are placed in a global perspective.

Economics in the News

Complementing *Economics in the News* questions, which have appeared daily in MyEconLab and in end-of-chapter problems in previous editions, a series of new *Economics in the News* boxes help students to answer news-based questions (see an example below). The topics covered by these boxes are:

- The invisible hand and entrepreneurship at work
- The fragile global economy in 2013
- Rising global food costs
- Energy independence cost and inefficiency
- The market for college education
- The market for gasoline
- Elasticities of demand for peanut butter
- The changing market for coat hangers
- The principal–agent problem at JPMorgan Chase
- Cost curves at the checkout line
- Record stores exit
- The falling cost of sequencing DNA
- Microsoft monopoly
- Boeing versus Airbus
- The choice of college major and job prospects

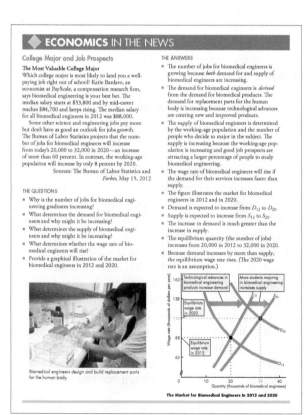

At Issue

Seven new *At Issue* boxes engage the student in debate and controversy. An *At Issue* box (see below) introduces an issue and then presents two opposing views. It leaves the matter unsettled so that the student and instructor can continue the argument in class and reach their own conclusions.

The goal of *At Issue* is to motivate the student to think about the opposing arguments and to take a stand on the issues.

The seven issues covered by this feature are:

- The protest against capitalism and the Occupy Wall Street movement
- Do we need a law against price gouging?
- Does the minimum wage cause unemployment?
- Is offshore outsourcing good or bad for America?
- Is Obamacare the solution to U.S. health-care problems?
- Should we be doing more to limit carbon emissions?
- Monopoly power at NCAA: Is it good or bad?

Features to Enhance Teaching and Learning

The new features that I have just described are additions to an already powerful teaching and learning package. Here, I briefly review the features retained from the previous edition.

Reading Between the Lines

This Parkin hallmark helps students think like economists by connecting chapter tools and concepts to the world around them. In *Reading Between the Lines*, which appears at the end of each chapter, students apply the tools they have just learned by analyzing an article from a newspaper or news Web site. Each article sheds additional light on the questions first raised in the Chapter Opener. Questions about the article also appear with the end-of-chapter problems and applications.

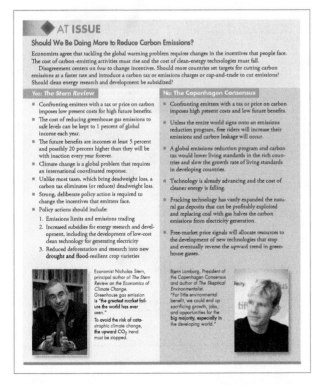

Economics in the News

34. After you have studied *Reading Between the Lines* on pp. 74–75, answer the following questions.
    a. What happened to the price of peanut butter in 2011?
    b. What substitutions do you expect might have been made to decrease the quantity of peanut butter demanded?

Diagrams That Show the Action

Through the past ten editions, this book has set new standards of clarity in its diagrams; the eleventh edition continues to uphold this tradition. My goal has always been to show "where the economic action is." The diagrams in this book continue to generate an enormously positive response, which confirms my view that graphical analysis is the most powerful tool available for teaching and learning economics.

Because many students find graphs hard to work with, I have developed the entire art program with the study and review needs of the student in mind.

The diagrams feature:

- Original curves consistently shown in blue
- Shifted curves, equilibrium points, and other important features highlighted in red
- Color-blended arrows to suggest movement
- Graphs paired with data tables
- Diagrams labeled with boxed notes
- Extended captions that make each diagram and its caption a self-contained object for study and review.

Economics in Action Boxes

This feature uses boxes within the chapter to address current events and economic occurrences that highlight and amplify the topics covered in the chapter. Instead of simply reporting the current events, the material in the boxes applies the event to an economics lesson, enabling students to see how economics plays a part in the world around them as they read through the chapter.

Some of the many issues covered in these boxes include the best affordable choice of recorded music, movies and DVDs, the cost of selling a pair of shoes, how Apple doesn't make the iPhone, opposing trends in air pollution and carbon concentration, information-age monopolies, is the American dream still alive, and how is income redistributed. A complete list can be found on the inside back cover.

Chapter Openers

Each chapter opens with a student-friendly vignette that raises questions to motivate the student and focus the chapter. This chapter-opening story is woven into the main body of the chapter and is explored in the *Reading Between the Lines* feature that ends each chapter.

Key Terms

Highlighted terms simplify the student's task of learning the vocabulary of economics. Each highlighted term appears in an end-of-chapter list with its page number, in an end-of-book glossary with its page number, boldfaced in the index and in MyEconLab in the interactive glossary and the Flash Cards.

In-Text Review Quizzes

A review quiz at the end of each major section enables students to determine whether a topic needs further study before moving on. This feature includes a reference to the appropriate MyEconLab study plan to help students further test their understanding.

REVIEW QUIZ

1 What is the distinction between a money price and a relative price?
2 Explain why a relative price is an opportunity cost.
3 Think of examples of goods whose relative price has risen or fallen by a large amount.

You can work these questions in Study Plan 3.1 and get instant feedback.   MyEconLab

End-of-Chapter Study Material

Each chapter closes with a concise summary organized by major topics, a list of key terms with page references, and problems and applications. These learning tools provide students with a summary for review and exam preparation.

Interviews with Economists

Each part closes with an overview of the chapters and a teaser of an interview with a leading economist whose work correlates to what the student is learning. These interviews explore the education and research of these prominent economists and their advice for those who want to continue the study of economics. All past and present interviews I have conducted are available in full in MyEconLab.

◆ For the Instructor

This book enables you to focus on the economic way of thinking and choose your own course structure in your principles course:

Focus on the Economic Way of Thinking

As an instructor, you know how hard it is to encourage a student to think like an economist. But that is your goal. Consistent with this goal, the text focuses on and repeatedly uses the central ideas: choice; tradeoff; opportunity cost; the margin; incentives; the gains from voluntary exchange; the forces of demand, supply, and equilibrium; the pursuit of economic rent; the tension between self-interest and the social interest; and the scope and limitations of government actions.

Flexible Structure

You have preferences for how you want to teach your course. I have organized this book to enable you to do so. The flexibility chart on p. xi illustrates the book's flexibility. By following the arrows through the chart you can select the path that best fits your preference for course structure. Whether you want to teach a traditional course that blends theory and policy, or one that takes a fast-track through either theory or policy issues, *Microeconomics* gives you the choice.

Instructor's Supplemental Resources

The supplements for instructors are:

- Instructor's Manual
- Solutions Manual
- Test Item Files
- PowerPoint Resources

Instructor's Manual The Instructor's Manual for *Microeconomics* integrates the teaching and learning resources and serve as a guide to all the supplements. Written by Laura A. Wolff of Southern Illinois University Edwardsville, the Instructor's Manual is available in hard copy and electronically on the Instructor's Resource Disk.

Each chapter contains an overview, a list of what's new in the eleventh edition, and ready-to-use lecture notes, which enable a new user of Parkin to walk into a classroom and deliver a polished lecture.

Solutions Manual The comprehensive solutions manual for *Microeconomics* provides instructors with solutions to the Review Quizzes and the end-of-chapter Problems and Applications as well as additional problems and the solutions to these problems. Written by Mark Rush of the University of Florida and reviewed for accuracy by Jeannie Gillmore of the University of Western Ontario, the Solutions Manual is available in hard copy and electronically on the Instructor's Resource Disk, or downloaded from MyEconLab or the Instructor Resource Center.

Test Item Files Three separate Test Item Files with nearly 6,500 questions, provide multiple-choice, true/false, numerical, fill-in-the-blank, short-answer, and essay questions. Mark Rush reviewed and edited all the questions to ensure their clarity and consistency.

New questions were written by Rebecca Stein of the University of Pennsylvania, Svitlana Maksymenko of the University of Pittsburgh, and James K. Self of the University of Indiana, Bloomington.

Questions follow the style and format of the end-of-chapter text problems. End-of-part tests contain integrative questions that cover all the chapters in the part. New to the eleventh edition are news based application questions for each chapter of the text.

Fully networkable and available for Windows® and Macintosh®, TestGen's graphical interface enables instructors to view the Test Item Files, edit and add questions; transfer questions to tests; and print different forms of tests. Tests can be formatted as in any word-processing document with varying fonts, styles, margins, headers, and footers. Search and sort features let the instructor quickly locate questions and arrange them in a preferred order. QuizMaster, working with your school's computer network, automatically grades exams, stores the results, and allows the instructor to view or print a variety of reports.

PowerPoint Resources A set of full-color Microsoft® PowerPoint Presentations for each chapter.

Each chapter contains:

- Lecture notes with all the textbook figures animated, tables from the textbook, and speaking notes from the Instructor's Manuals
- Large-scale versions of all the figures and tables in the textbook, animated for instructors to incorporate into their own slide shows
- Clicker-ready multiple-choice quizzes that test important concepts

The presentations can be used electronically in the classroom or can be printed to create hard copy transparency masters. This item is available for Macintosh and Windows.

In addition, a separate set of PowerPoint lecture notes is available for students in MyEconLab.

Getting Your Instructor's Resources

Instructor's Resource Disk Compatible with Windows and Macintosh, the Instructor's Resource Disk contains electronic files of every instructor supplement for the eleventh edition. Files included are: Microsoft® Word and Adobe® PDF files of the Instructor's Manual, Solutions Manual, Test Item Files; the Computerized TestGen® Test Item Files; and the PowerPoint resources. Add this useful resource to your exam copy bookbag, or locate your local Pearson Education sales representative at www.pearsonhighered.educator to request a copy.

Instructors can download supplements from a secure, instructor-only source via the Pearson Higher Education Instructor Resource Center Web page (www.pearsonhighered.com/irc).

BlackBoard and WebCT BlackBoard and WebCT ready conversions of the TestGen Test Item Files are available for download from www.pearsonhighered.com/irc.

Study Guide

The eleventh edition Study Guide by Mark Rush is coordinated with the text, MyEconLab, and the Test Item Files. Each chapter contains key concepts, helpful hints, true/false/uncertain questions, multiple-choice questions, and short-answer questions. Each part allows students to test their cumulative understanding with questions that go across chapters and to work a sample midterm examination. The student is encouraged to explain some common misconceptions as if he or she were the teacher.

MYECONLAB MyEconLab

MyEconLab works hand-in-hand with *Microeconomics*. Robin Bade and I, assisted by Jeannie Gillmore, Laurel Davies, and Sharmistha Nag, have authored and overseen all of the MyEconLab content for *Microeconomics*. Our team has worked hard to ensure that the Parkin MyEconLab is tightly integrated with the book's content and vision.

With comprehensive homework, quiz, test, and tutorial options, instructors can manage all assessment needs in one program.

- All of the Review Quiz questions and end-of-chapter Problems and Applications are assignable and automatically graded in MyEconLab.
- All the Review Quiz questions and end-of-chapter Study Plan Problems and Applications are available for students to work in Study Plan.
- All the end-of-chapter Additional Problems and Applications are not available to students in MyEconLab unless assigned by the instructor.
- Many of the problems and applications are algorithmic, draw-graph, and numerical exercises.
- Test Item File questions are available for assignment as MyEconLab quizzes, tests, or homework.
- The Custom Exercise Builder enables instructors to create their own problems for assignment as test or homework questions.
- The powerful Gradebook records each student's performance and time spent on tests, the study plan, and homework and generates reports by student or by chapter.

Enhanced Pearson eText The enhanced Pearson eText, the entire textbook with animated figures that include audio narration is available online in MyEconLab textbook resources. For MyEconLab users, the eText is available offline via an iPad/Android app. Instructors and students can highlight the text, bookmark, search the glossary, and take notes.

Economics in the News *Economics in the News* is a turn-key solution to bringing daily news into the classroom. Updated daily during the school year, I upload a microeconomic article and provide links for further information and questions that may be assigned for homework or for classroom discussion.

Auto-Graded *Economics in the News* New to the eleventh edition are auto-graded *Economics in the News* exercises updated weekly throughout the school year. Each week I upload a multi-part microeconomic exercise with links to the relevant article.

Experiments in MyEconLab Experiments are a fun and engaging way to promote active learning and mastery of important economic concepts. Pearson's experiments program is flexible and easy for instructors and students to use.

- Single-player experiments allow your students to play against virtual players from anywhere at any time with an Internet connection.
- Multiplayer experiments allow you to assign and manage a real-time experiment with your class.

Pre- and post-questions for each experiment are available for assignment in MyEconLab.

For a complete list of available experiments, visit www.myeconlab.com.

AACSB and Learning Outcomes All end-of-chapter and Test Item File questions are tagged in two ways: to AACSB standards and to discipline-specific Learning Outcomes. These two separate tagging systems allow instructors to build assessments around desired departmental and course outcomes and track results in MyEconLab's gradebook.

Visit www.myeconlab.com for more information and an online demonstration of instructor and student features.

◆ Acknowledgments

I thank my current and former colleagues and friends at the University of Western Ontario who have taught me so much. They are Jim Davies, Jeremy Greenwood, Ig Horstmann, Peter Howitt, Greg Huffman, David Laidler, Phil Reny, Chris Robinson, John Whalley, and Ron Wonnacott. I also thank Doug McTaggart and Christopher Findlay, co-authors of the Australian edition, and Melanie Powell and Kent Matthews, co-authors of the European edition. Suggestions arising from their adaptations of earlier editions have been helpful to me in preparing this edition.

I thank Rebecca Stein for her thoughtful suggestions and constructive criticism that brought the extensive revision to my treatment of price discrimination. And I thank Yoram Bauman for careful and helpful reviews of my new coverage of environmental externalities.

I thank the several thousand students whom I have been privileged to teach. The instant response that comes from the look of puzzlement or enlightenment has taught me how to teach economics.

It is a special joy to thank the many outstanding editors, media specialists, and others at Pearson who contributed to the concerted publishing effort that brought this edition to completion. Denise Clinton, Publisher of MyEconLab has played a major role in the evolution of this text since its third edition, and her insights and ideas can still be found in this new edition. Donna Battista, Editor-in-Chief for Economics and Finance, is hugely inspiring and has provided overall direction to the project. As ever, Adrienne D'Ambrosio, Executive Acquisitions Editor for Economics and my sponsoring editor, played a major role in shaping this revision and the many outstanding supplements that accompany it. Adrienne brings intelligence and insight to her work and is the unchallengeable pre-eminent economics editor. Sarah Dumouchelle, Editorial Project Manager, provided a steady hand throughout the revision process, managing our immense supplements program, keeping the supplements authors' contributions on track, and working with rights and permissions advisors. Nancy Freihofer, Senior Production Project Manager, oversaw the production and design process and coordinated the photo research program. Susan Schoenberg, Director of Media, directed the development of MyEconLab; Noel Lotz, Content Lead for MyEconLab, managed a complex and thorough reviewing process for the content of MyEconLab; and Melissa Honig, Senior Media Producer ensured that all our media assets were correctly assembled. Lori Deshazo, Executive Marketing Manager, provided inspired marketing strategy and direction. Catherine Baum provided a careful, consistent, and intelligent copy edit and accuracy check. Jonathan Boylan designed the cover and package and yet again surpassed the challenge of ensuring that we meet the highest design standards. Joe Vetere provided endless technical help with the text and art files. And Heather Johnson with the other members of an outstanding editorial and production team at Integra-Chicago kept the project on track on an impossibly tight schedule.

I thank all of these wonderful people. It has been inspiring to work with them and to share in creating what I believe is a truly outstanding educational tool.

I thank our talented eleventh edition supplements authors and contributors—Laurel Davies, Jeannie Gillmore, Svitlana Maksymenko, Sharmistha Nag, Jim Self, Rebecca Stein, and Laurie Wolff.

I especially thank Mark Rush, who yet again played a crucial role in creating another edition of this text and package. Mark has been a constant source of good advice and good humor.

I thank the many exceptional reviewers who have shared their insights through the various editions of this book. Their contribution has been invaluable.

I thank the people who work directly with me. Jeannie Gillmore provided outstanding research assistance on many topics, including the *Reading Between the Lines* news articles. Richard Parkin created the electronic art files and offered many ideas that improved the figures in this book. Laurel Davies managed an ever-growing and ever more complex MyEconLab database. And Sharmistha Nag has helped me to create *Economics in the News* questions for MyEconLab.

As with the previous editions, this one owes an enormous debt to Robin Bade. I dedicate this book to her and again thank her for her work. I could not have written this book without the tireless and unselfish help she has given me. My thanks to her are unbounded.

Classroom experience will test the value of this book. I would appreciate hearing from instructors and students about how I can continue to improve it in future editions.

Michael Parkin
London, Ontario, Canada
michael.parkin@uwo.ca

Reviewers

Eric Abrams, Hawaii Pacific University
Christopher Adams, Federal Trade Commission
Tajudeen Adenekan, Bronx Community College
John T. Addison, University of South Carolina
Syed Ahmed, Cameron University
Frank Albritton, Seminole Community College
Milton Alderfer, Miami-Dade Community College
William Aldridge, Shelton State Community College
Donald L. Alexander, Western Michigan University
Terence Alexander, Iowa State University
Stuart Allen, University of North Carolina, Greensboro
Sam Allgood, University of Nebraska, Lincoln
Neil Alper, Northeastern University
Alan Anderson, Fordham University
Lisa R. Anderson, College of William and Mary
Jeff Ankrom, Wittenberg University
Fatma Antar, Manchester Community Technical College
Kofi Apraku, University of North Carolina, Asheville
John Atkins, University of West Florida
Moshen Bahmani-Oskooee, University of Wisconsin, Milwaukee
Donald Balch, University of South Carolina
Mehmet Balcilar, Wayne State University
Paul Ballantyne, University of Colorado
Sue Bartlett, University of South Florida
Jose Juan Bautista, Xavier University of Louisiana
Klaus Becker, Texas Tech University
Valerie R. Bencivenga, University of Texas, Austin
Ben Bernanke, Chairman of Federal Reserve
Radha Bhattacharya, California State University, Fullerton
Margot Biery, Tarrant County College, South
John Bittorowitz, Ball State University
David Black, University of Toledo
Kelly Blanchard, Purdue University
S. Brock Blomberg, Claremont McKenna College
William T. Bogart, Case Western Reserve University
Giacomo Bonanno, University of California, Davis
Tan Khay Boon, Nanyard Technological University
Sunne Brandmeyer, University of South Florida
Audie Brewton, Northeastern Illinois University
Baird Brock, Central Missouri State University
Byron Brown, Michigan State University
Jeffrey Buser, Columbus State Community College
Alison Butler, Florida International University
Colleen Callahan, American University
Tania Carbiener, Southern Methodist University
Kevin Carey, American University
Scott Carrell, University of California at Davis
Kathleen A. Carroll, University of Maryland, Baltimore County
Michael Carter, University of Massachusetts, Lowell
Edward Castronova, California State University, Fullerton

Francis Chan, Fullerton College
Ming Chang, Dartmouth College
Subir Chakrabarti, Indiana University-Purdue University
Joni Charles, Texas State University
Adhip Chaudhuri, Georgetown University
Gopal Chengalath, Texas Tech University
Daniel Christiansen, Albion College
Kenneth Christianson, Binghamton University
John J. Clark, Community College of Allegheny County, Allegheny Campus
Cindy Clement, University of Maryland
Meredith Clement, Dartmouth College
Michael B. Cohn, U. S. Merchant Marine Academy
Robert Collinge, University of Texas, San Antonio
Carol Condon, Kean University
Doug Conway, Mesa Community College
Larry Cook, University of Toledo
Bobby Corcoran, retired, Middle Tennessee State University
Kevin Cotter, Wayne State University
James Peery Cover, University of Alabama, Tuscaloosa
Erik Craft, University of Richmond
Eleanor D. Craig, University of Delaware
Jim Craven, Clark College
Jeremy Cripps, American University of Kuwait
Elizabeth Crowell, University of Michigan, Dearborn
Stephen Cullenberg, University of California, Riverside
David Culp, Slippery Rock University
Norman V. Cure, Macomb Community College
James D'Angelo, University of Cincinnati
Dan Dabney, University of Texas, Austin
Andrew Dane, Angelo State University
Joseph Daniels, Marquette University
Gregory DeFreitas, Hofstra University
David Denslow, University of Florida
Shatakshee Dhongde, Rochester Institute of Technology
Mark Dickie, University of Central Florida
James Dietz, California State University, Fullerton
Carol Dole, State University of West Georgia
Ronald Dorf, Inver Hills Community College
John Dorsey, University of Maryland, College Park
Eric Drabkin, Hawaii Pacific University
Amrik Singh Dua, Mt. San Antonio College
Thomas Duchesneau, University of Maine, Orono
Lucia Dunn, Ohio State University
Donald Dutkowsky, Syracuse University
John Edgren, Eastern Michigan University
David J. Eger, Alpena Community College
Harold W. Elder, University of Alabama
Harry Ellis, Jr., University of North Texas
Ibrahim Elsaify, Goldey-Beacom College
Kenneth G. Elzinga, University of Virginia
Patrick Emerson, Oregon State University
Tisha Emerson, Baylor University

Monica Escaleras, Florida Atlantic University

Antonina Espiritu, Hawaii Pacific University

Gwen Eudey, University of Pennsylvania

Barry Falk, Iowa State University

M. Fazeli, Hofstra University

Philip Fincher, Louisiana Tech University

F. Firoozi, University of Texas, San Antonio

Nancy Folbre, University of Massachusetts, Amherst

Kenneth Fong, Temasek Polytechnic (Singapore)

Steven Francis, Holy Cross College

David Franck, University of North Carolina, Charlotte

Mark Frank, Sam Houston State University

Roger Frantz, San Diego State University

Mark Frascatore, Clarkson University

Alwyn Fraser, Atlantic Union College

Marc Fusaro, East Carolina University

James Gale, Michigan Technological University

Susan Gale, New York University

Roy Gardner, Indiana University

Eugene Gentzel, Pensacola Junior College

Kirk Gifford, Brigham Young University-Idaho

Scott Gilbert, Southern Illinois University, Carbondale

Andrew Gill, California State University, Fullerton

Robert Giller, Virginia Polytechnic Institute and State University

Robert Gillette, University of Kentucky

James N. Giordano, Villanova University

Maria Giuili, Diablo College

Susan Glanz, St. John's University

Robert Gordon, San Diego State University

Richard Gosselin, Houston Community College

John Graham, Rutgers University

John Griffen, Worcester Polytechnic Institute

Wayne Grove, Syracuse University

Robert Guell, Indiana State University

William Gunther, University of Southern Mississippi

Jamie Haag, Pacific University, Oregon

Gail Heyne Hafer, Lindenwood University

Rik W. Hafer, Southern Illinois University, Edwardsville

Daniel Hagen, Western Washington University

David R. Hakes, University of Northern Iowa

Craig Hakkio, Federal Reserve Bank, Kansas City

Bridget Gleeson Hanna, Rochester Institute of Technology

Ann Hansen, Westminster College

Seid Hassan, Murray State University

Jonathan Haughton, Suffolk University

Randall Haydon, Wichita State University

Denise Hazlett, Whitman College

Julia Heath, University of Memphis

Jac Heckelman, Wake Forest University

Jolien A. Helsel, Kent State University

James Henderson, Baylor University

Doug Herman, Georgetown University

Jill Boylston Herndon, University of Florida

Gus Herring, Brookhaven College

John Herrmann, Rutgers University

John M. Hill, Delgado Community College

Jonathan Hill, Florida International University

Lewis Hill, Texas Tech University

Steve Hoagland, University of Akron

Tom Hoerger, Fellow, Research Triangle Institute

Calvin Hoerneman, Delta College

George Hoffer, Virginia Commonwealth University

Dennis L. Hoffman, Arizona State University

Paul Hohenberg, Rensselaer Polytechnic Institute

Jim H. Holcomb, University of Texas, El Paso

Robert Holland, Purdue University

Harry Holzer, Georgetown University

Gary Hoover, University of Alabama

Linda Hooks, Washington and Lee University

Jim Horner, Cameron University

Djehane Hosni, University of Central Florida

Harold Hotelling, Jr., Lawrence Technical University

Calvin Hoy, County College of Morris

Ing-Wei Huang, Assumption University, Thailand

Julie Hunsaker, Wayne State University

Beth Ingram, University of Iowa

Jayvanth Ishwaran, Stephen F. Austin State University

Michael Jacobs, Lehman College

S. Hussain Ali Jafri, Tarleton State University

Dennis Jansen, Texas A&M University

Andrea Jao, University of Pennsylvania

Barbara John, University of Dayton

Barry Jones, Binghamton University

Garrett Jones, Southern Florida University

Frederick Jungman, Northwestern Oklahoma State University

Paul Junk, University of Minnesota, Duluth

Leo Kahane, California State University, Hayward

Veronica Kalich, Baldwin-Wallace College

John Kane, State University of New York, Oswego

Eungmin Kang, St. Cloud State University

Arthur Kartman, San Diego State University

Gurmit Kaur, Universiti Teknologi (Malaysia)

Louise Keely, University of Wisconsin, Madison

Manfred W. Keil, Claremont McKenna College

Elizabeth Sawyer Kelly, University of Wisconsin, Madison

Rose Kilburn, Modesto Junior College

Amanda King, Georgia Southern University

John King, Georgia Southern University

Robert Kirk, Indiana University-Purdue University, Indianapolis

Norman Kleinberg, City University of New York, Baruch College

Robert Kleinhenz, California State University, Fullerton

John Krantz, University of Utah

Joseph Kreitzer, University of St. Thomas

Patricia Kuzyk, Washington State University

David Lages, Southwest Missouri State University

W. J. Lane, University of New Orleans

Leonard Lardaro, University of Rhode Island

Kathryn Larson, Elon College

Luther D. Lawson, University of North Carolina, Wilmington

Elroy M. Leach, Chicago State University

Jim Lee, Texas A & M, Corpus Christi

Sang Lee, Southeastern Louisiana University

Robert Lemke, Florida International University

Mary Lesser, Iona College

Philip K. Letting, Harrisburg Area Community College

Jay Levin, Wayne State University

Arik Levinson, University of Wisconsin, Madison

Tony Lima, California State University, Hayward

William Lord, University of Maryland, Baltimore County

Nancy Lutz, Virginia Polytechnic Institute and State University

Brian Lynch, Lakeland Community College

Murugappa Madhavan, San Diego State University

K. T. Magnusson, Salt Lake Community College

Svitlana Maksymenko, University of Pittsburgh

Mark Maier, Glendale Community College

Jean Mangan, Staffordshire University Business School

Denton Marks, University of Wisconsin, Whitewater

Michael Marlow, California Polytechnic State University

Akbar Marvasti, University of Houston

Wolfgang Mayer, University of Cincinnati

John McArthur, Wofford College

Katherine McClain, University of Georgia

Amy McCormick, Mary Baldwin College

Russ McCullough, Iowa State University

Catherine McDevitt, Central Michigan University

Gerald McDougall, Wichita State University

Stephen McGary, Brigham Young University-Idaho

Richard D. McGrath, Armstrong Atlantic State University

Richard McIntyre, University of Rhode Island

John McLeod, Georgia Institute of Technology

Mark McLeod, Virginia Polytechnic Institute and State University

B. Starr McMullen, Oregon State University

Sandra McPherson, Millersville University

Mary Ruth McRae, Appalachian State University

Kimberly Merritt, Cameron University

Charles Meyer, Iowa State University

Peter Mieszkowski, Rice University

John Mijares, University of North Carolina, Asheville

Richard A. Miller, Wesleyan University

Judith W. Mills, Southern Connecticut State University

Glen Mitchell, Nassau Community College

Jeannette C. Mitchell, Rochester Institute of Technology

Khan Mohabbat, Northern Illinois University

Bagher Modjtahedi, University of California, Davis

Michael A. Mogavero, University of Notre Dame

Shahruz Mohtadi, Suffolk University

Barbara Moore, University of Central Florida

W. Douglas Morgan, University of California, Santa Barbara

William Morgan, University of Wyoming

James Morley, Washington University in St. Louis

William Mosher, Clark University

Joanne Moss, San Francisco State University

Nivedita Mukherji, Oakland University

Francis Mummery, Fullerton College

Edward Murphy, Southwest Texas State University

Kevin J. Murphy, Oakland University

Kathryn Nantz, Fairfield University

William S. Neilson, Texas A&M University

Bart C. Nemmers, University of Nebraska, Lincoln

Melinda Nish, Orange Coast College

Anthony O'Brien, Lehigh University

Norman Obst, Michigan State University

Constantin Oglobin, Georgia Southern University

Neal Olitsky, University of Massachusetts, Dartmouth

Mary Olson, Tulane University

Terry Olson, Truman State University

James B. O'Neill, University of Delaware

Farley Ordovensky, University of the Pacific

Z. Edward O'Relley, North Dakota State University

Donald Oswald, California State University, Bakersfield

Jan Palmer, Ohio University

Michael Palumbo, Chief, Federal Reserve Board

Chris Papageorgiou, Louisiana State University

G. Hossein Parandvash, Western Oregon State College

Randall Parker, East Carolina University

Robert Parks, Washington University

David Pate, St. John Fisher College

James E. Payne, Illinois State University

Donald Pearson, Eastern Michigan University

Steven Peterson, University of Idaho

Mary Anne Pettit, Southern Illinois University, Edwardsville

William A. Phillips, University of Southern Maine

Dennis Placone, Clemson University

Charles Plot, California Institute of Technology, Pasadena

Mannie Poen, Houston Community College

Kathleen Possai, Wayne State University

Ulrika Praski-Stahlgren, University College in Gavle-Sandviken, Sweden

Edward Price, Oklahoma State University

Rula Qalyoubi, University of Wisconsin, Eau Claire

K. A. Quartey, Talladega College

Herman Quirmbach, Iowa State University

Jeffrey R. Racine, University of South Florida

Ramkishen Rajan, George Mason University

Peter Rangazas, Indiana University-Purdue University, Indianapolis

Vaman Rao, Western Illinois University

Laura Razzolini, University of Mississippi

Rob Rebelein, University of Cincinnati

J. David Reed, Bowling Green State University

Robert H. Renshaw, Northern Illinois University

Javier Reyes, University of Arkansas

Jeff Reynolds, Northern Illinois University

Rupert Rhodd, Florida Atlantic University

W. Gregory Rhodus, Bentley College

Jennifer Rice, Indiana University, Bloomington

John Robertson, Paducah Community College

Malcolm Robinson, University of North Carolina, Greensboro

Richard Roehl, University of Michigan, Dearborn

Carol Rogers, Georgetown University

William Rogers, University of Northern Colorado

Thomas Romans, State University of New York, Buffalo

David R. Ross, Bryn Mawr College

Thomas Ross, Baldwin Wallace College

Robert J. Rossana, Wayne State University

Jeffrey Rous, University of North Texas

Rochelle Ruffer, Youngstown State University

Mark Rush, University of Florida

Allen R. Sanderson, University of Chicago

Gary Santoni, Ball State University

Jeffrey Sarbaum, University of North Carolina at Chapel Hill

John Saussy, Harrisburg Area Community College

Don Schlagenhauf, Florida State University

David Schlow, Pennsylvania State University

Paul Schmitt, St. Clair County Community College

Jeremy Schwartz, Hampden-Sydney College

Martin Sefton, University of Nottingham

James K. Self, Indiana University

Esther-Mirjam Sent, University of Notre Dame

Rod Shadbegian, University of Massachusetts, Dartmouth

Neil Sheflin, Rutgers University

Gerald Shilling, Eastfield College

Dorothy R. Siden, Salem State College

Mark Siegler, California State University at Sacramento

Scott Simkins, North Carolina Agricultural and Technical State University

Jacek Siry, University of Georgia

Chuck Skoro, Boise State University

Phil Smith, DeKalb College

William Doyle Smith, University of Texas, El Paso

Sarah Stafford, College of William and Mary

Rebecca Stein, University of Pennsylvania

Frank Steindl, Oklahoma State University

Jeffrey Stewart, New York University

Allan Stone, Southwest Missouri State University

Courtenay Stone, Ball State University

Paul Storer, Western Washington University

Richard W. Stratton, University of Akron

Mark Strazicich, Ohio State University, Newark

Michael Stroup, Stephen F. Austin State University

Robert Stuart, Rutgers University

Della Lee Sue, Marist College

Abdulhamid Sukar, Cameron University

Terry Sutton, Southeast Missouri State University

Gilbert Suzawa, University of Rhode Island

David Swaine, Andrews University

Jason Taylor, Central Michigan University

Mark Thoma, University of Oregon

Janet Thomas, Bentley College

Kiril Tochkov, SUNY at Binghamton

Kay Unger, University of Montana

Anthony Uremovic, Joliet Junior College

David Vaughn, City University, Washington

Don Waldman, Colgate University

Francis Wambalaba, Portland State University

Sasiwimon Warunsiri, University of Colorado at Boulder

Rob Wassmer, California State University, Sacramento

Paul A. Weinstein, University of Maryland, College Park

Lee Weissert, St. Vincent College

Robert Whaples, Wake Forest University

David Wharton, Washington College

Mark Wheeler, Western Michigan University

Charles H. Whiteman, University of Iowa

Sandra Williamson, University of Pittsburgh

Brenda Wilson, Brookhaven Community College

Larry Wimmer, Brigham Young University

Mark Witte, Northwestern University

Willard E. Witte, Indiana University

Mark Wohar, University of Nebraska, Omaha

Laura Wolff, Southern Illinois University, Edwardsville

Cheonsik Woo, Vice President, Korea Development Institute

Douglas Wooley, Radford University

Arthur G. Woolf, University of Vermont

John T. Young, Riverside Community College

Michael Youngblood, Rock Valley College

Peter Zaleski, Villanova University

Jason Zimmerman, South Dakota State University

David Zucker, Martha Stewart Living Omnimedia

Supplements Authors

Luke Armstrong, Lee College

Sue Bartlett, University of South Florida

Kelly Blanchard, Purdue University

James Cobbe, Florida State University

Carol Dole, Jacksonville University

Karen Gebhardt, Colorado State University

John Graham, Rutgers University

Jill Herndon, University of Florida

Gary Hoover, University of Alabama

Patricia Kuzyk, Washington State University

Sang Lee, Southeastern Louisiana University

Svitlana Maksymenko, University of Pittsburgh
Robert Martel, University of Connecticut
Katherine McClain, University of Georgia
Russ McCullough, Iowa State University
Barbara Moore, University of Central Florida
James Morley, Washington University in St. Louis
William Mosher, Clark University
Constantin Ogloblin, Georgia Southern University

Edward Price, Oklahoma State University
Mark Rush, University of Florida
James K. Self, University of Indiana, Bloomington
Rebecca Stein, University of Pennsylvania
Michael Stroup, Stephen F. Austin State University
Della Lee Sue, Marist College
Nora Underwood, University of Central Florida
Laura A. Wolff, Southern Illinois University, Edwardsville

1

WHAT IS ECONOMICS?

After studying this chapter, you will be able to:

♦ Define economics and distinguish between microeconomics and macroeconomics

♦ Explain the two big questions of economics

♦ Explain the key ideas that define the economic way of thinking

♦ Explain how economists go about their work as social scientists and policy advisers

Is economics about money: How people make it and spend it? Is it about business, government, and jobs? Is it about why some people and some nations are rich and others poor? Economics is about all these things. But its core is the study of *choices* and their *consequences*.

Your life will be shaped by the choices that you make and the challenges that you face. To face those challenges and seize the opportunities they present, you must understand the powerful forces at play. The economics that you're about to learn will become your most reliable guide. This chapter gets you started by describing the questions that economists try to answer and looking at how economists think as they search for the answers.

1

Definition of Economics

A fundamental fact dominates our lives: We want more than we can get. Our inability to get everything we want is called **scarcity**. Scarcity is universal. It confronts all living things. Even parrots face scarcity!

Not only do I want a cracker—we all want a cracker!

Think about the things that *you* want and the scarcity that *you* face. You want to go to a good school, college, or university. You want to live in a well-equipped, spacious, and comfortable home. You want the latest smart phone and the fastest Internet connection for your laptop or iPad. You want some sports and recreational gear—perhaps some new running shoes, or a new bike. You want much more time than is available to go to class, do your homework, play sports and games, read novels, go to the movies, listen to music, travel, and hang out with your friends. And you want to live a long and healthy life.

What you can afford to buy is limited by your income and by the prices you must pay. And your time is limited by the fact that your day has 24 hours.

You want some other things that only governments provide. You want to live in a safe neighborhood in a peaceful and secure world, and enjoy the benefits of clean air, lakes, rivers, and oceans.

What governments can afford is limited by the taxes they collect. Taxes lower people's incomes and compete with the other things they want to buy.

What *everyone* can get—what *society* can get—is limited by the productive resources available. These resources are the gifts of nature, human labor and ingenuity, and all the previously produced tools and equipment.

Because we can't get everything we want, we must make *choices*. You can't afford *both* a laptop *and* an iPhone, so you must *choose* which one to buy. You can't spend tonight *both* studying for your next test *and* going to the movies, so again, you must *choose* which one to do. Governments can't spend a tax dollar on *both* national defense *and* environmental protection, so they must *choose* how to spend that dollar.

Your choices must somehow be made consistent with the choices of *others*. If you choose to buy a laptop, someone else must choose to sell it. Incentives reconcile choices. An **incentive** is a reward that encourages an action or a penalty that discourages one. Prices act as incentives. If the price of a laptop is too high, more will be offered for sale than people want to buy. And if the price is too low, fewer will be offered for sale than people want to buy. But there is a price at which choices to buy and sell are consistent.

Economics is the social science that studies the *choices* that individuals, businesses, governments, and entire societies make as they cope with *scarcity* and the *incentives* that influence and reconcile those choices.

The subject has two parts:

- Microeconomics
- Macroeconomics

Microeconomics is the study of the choices that individuals and businesses make, the way these choices interact in markets, and the influence of governments. Some examples of microeconomic questions are: Why are people downloading more movies? How would a tax on e-commerce affect eBay?

Macroeconomics is the study of the performance of the national economy and the global economy. Some examples of macroeconomic questions are: Why is the U.S. unemployment rate so high? Can the Federal Reserve make our economy expand by cutting interest rates?

REVIEW QUIZ

1 List some examples of the scarcity that you face.
2 Find examples of scarcity in today's headlines.
3 Find an example of the distinction between microeconomics and macroeconomics in today's headlines.

You can work these questions in Study Plan 1.1 and get instant feedback.   MyEconLab

Two Big Economic Questions

Two big questions summarize the scope of economics:

- How do choices end up determining *what, how,* and *for whom* goods and services are produced?
- Do the choices that people make in the pursuit of their own *self-interest* unintentionally promote the broader *social interest*?

What, How, and For Whom?

Goods and services are the objects that people value and produce to satisfy wants. *Goods* are physical objects such as cell phones and automobiles. *Services* are tasks performed for people such as cell-phone service and auto-repair service.

What? *What* we produce varies across countries and changes over time. In the United States today, agriculture accounts for 1 percent of total production, manufactured goods for 22 percent, and services (retail and wholesale trade, health care, and education are the biggest ones) for 77 percent. In contrast, in China today, agriculture accounts for 10 percent of total production, manufactured goods for 47 percent, and services for 43 percent. Figure 1.1 shows these numbers and also the percentages for Brazil, which fall between those for the United States and China.

What determines these patterns of production? How do choices end up determining the quantities of cell phones, automobiles, cell-phone service, auto-repair service, and the millions of other items that are produced in the United States and around the world?

How? *How* we produce is described by the technologies and resources that we use. The resources used to produce goods and services are called **factors of production**, which are grouped into four categories:

- Land
- Labor
- Capital
- Entrepreneurship

Land The "gifts of nature" that we use to produce goods and services are called **land**. In economics, *land* is what in everyday language we call *natural resources*. It includes land in the everyday sense

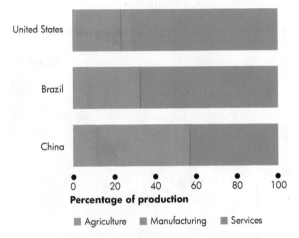

FIGURE 1.1 What Three Countries Produce

United States

Brazil

China

0   20   40   60   80   100
Percentage of production

■ Agriculture ■ Manufacturing ■ Services

Agriculture and manufacturing are small percentages of production in rich countries such as the United States and large percentages of production in poorer countries such as China. Most of what is produced in the United States is services.

Source of data: CIA Factbook 2012, Central Intelligence Agency.

—— MyEconLab animation ——

together with minerals, oil, gas, coal, water, air, forests, and fish.

Our land surface and water resources are renewable and some of our mineral resources can be recycled. But the resources that we use to create energy are nonrenewable—they can be used only once.

Labor The work time and work effort that people devote to producing goods and services is called **labor**. Labor includes the physical and mental efforts of all the people who work on farms and construction sites and in factories, shops, and offices.

The *quality* of labor depends on **human capital**, which is the knowledge and skill that people obtain from education, on-the-job training, and work experience. You are building your own human capital right now as you work on your economics course, and your human capital will continue to grow as you gain work experience.

Human capital expands over time. Today, 88 percent of the adult population of the United States have completed high school and 30 percent have a college or university degree. Figure 1.2 shows these measures of human capital in the United States and its growth over the past 110 years.

FIGURE 1.2   A Measure of Human Capital

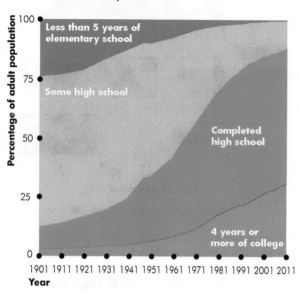

In 2011, 30 percent of the population had 4 years or more of college, up from 2 percent in 1901. A further 58 percent had completed high school, up from 10 percent in 1901.

Source of data: U.S. Census Bureau, *Statistical Abstract of the United States,* 2012.

————— MyEconLab animation —————

Capital The tools, instruments, machines, buildings, and other constructions that businesses use to produce goods and services are called **capital.**

In everyday language, we talk about money, stocks, and bonds as being "capital." These items are *financial capital.* Financial capital plays an important role in enabling businesses to borrow the funds that they use to buy physical capital. But financial capital is not used to produce goods and services and it is not a factor of production.

Entrepreneurship The human resource that organizes labor, land, and capital is called **entrepreneurship.** Entrepreneurs are the drivers of economic progress. They develop new ideas about what and how to produce, make business decisions, and bear the risks that arise from these decisions.

What determines how the factors of production are used to produce each good and service?

For Whom? *Who* consumes the goods and services that are produced depends on the incomes that people earn. People with large incomes can buy a wide range of goods and services. People with small incomes have fewer options and can afford a smaller range of goods and services.

People earn their incomes by selling the services of the factors of production they own:

- Land earns **rent.**
- Labor earns **wages.**
- Capital earns **interest.**
- Entrepreneurship earns **profit.**

Which factor of production earns the most income? The answer is labor. In 2011, wages were 68 percent of total income and the incomes from land, capital, and entrepreneurship 32 percent. These shares have been remarkably constant over time.

Knowing how income is shared among the factors of production doesn't tell us how it is shared among individuals. And the distribution of income among individuals is extremely unequal. You know of some people who earn very large incomes: Angelina Jolie earns $10 million per movie; and the New York Yankees pays Alex Rodriguez $27.5 million a year.

You know of even more people who earn very small incomes. Servers at McDonald's average around $7.25 an hour; checkout clerks, cleaners, and textile and leather workers all earn less than $10 an hour.

You probably know about other persistent differences in incomes. Men, on average, earn more than women; whites earn more than minorities; college graduates earn more than high-school graduates.

We can get a good sense of who consumes the goods and services produced by looking at the percentages of total income earned by different groups of people. The 20 percent of people with the lowest incomes earn about 5 percent of total income, while the richest 20 percent earn close to 50 percent of total income. So on average, people in the richest 20 percent earn more than 10 times the incomes of those in the poorest 20 percent. There is even huge inequality within the richest 20 percent and the top 1 percent earns almost 15 percent of total income.

Why is the distribution of income so unequal?

Economics provides some answers to all these questions about *what, how,* and *for whom* goods and services are produced and much of the rest of this book will help you to understand those answers.

We're now going to look at the second big question of economics: Does the pursuit of self-interest unintentionally promote the social interest?

Does the Pursuit of Self-Interest Unintentionally Promote the Social Interest?

Every day, you and 314 million other Americans, along with 6.7 billion people in the rest of the world, make economic choices that result in *what, how*, and *for whom* goods and services are produced. These choices are made by people who are pursuing their self-interest.

Self-Interest You make a choice in your **self-interest** if you think that choice is the best one available for you. All the choices that people make about how to use their time and other resources are made in the pursuit of self-interest. When you allocate your time or your budget, you do what makes the most sense to you. You might think about how your choices affect other people and take into account how you feel about that, but it is how *you* feel that influences your choice. You order a home delivery pizza because you're hungry, not because the delivery person needs a job. And when the pizza delivery person shows up at your door, he's not doing you a favor. He's pursuing *his* self-interest and hoping for a tip and another call next week.

The big question is: Is it possible that all the choices that each one of us makes in the pursuit of self-interest could end up achieving an outcome that is best for everyone?

Social Interest An outcome is in the **social interest** if it is best for society as a whole. It is easy to see how you decide what is in *your* self-interest. But how do you decide if something is in the social interest? To help you answer this question, imagine a scene like that in *Economics in the News* on the next page.

Ted, an entrepreneur, creates a new business. He hires a thousand workers and pays them $20 an hour, $1 an hour more than they earned in their old jobs. Ted's business is extremely profitable and his own earnings increase by $1 million per week.

You can see that Ted's decision to create the business is in his self-interest—he gains $1 million a week. You can also see that the decisions to work for Ted are in the self-interest of the workers—they gain $1 an hour (say $40 a week). And the decisions of Ted's customers must be in their self-interest otherwise they wouldn't buy from him. But is this outcome in the social interest?

The economist's answer is "Yes." It is in the social interest because it makes everyone better off. There are no losers.

Efficiency and the Social Interest Economists use the everyday word "efficient" to describe a situation that can't be improved upon. Resource use is **efficient** if it is *not* possible to make someone better off without making someone else worse off. If it *is* possible to make someone better off without making anyone worse off, society can be made better off and the situation is not efficient.

In the Ted story everyone is better off, so it improves efficiency and the outcome is in the social interest. But notice that it would also have been efficient if the workers and customers had gained nothing and Ted had gained even more than $1 million a week. But would that efficient outcome be in the social interest?

Many people have trouble seeing the outcome in which Ted is the only winner as being in the social interest. They say that the social interest requires Ted to share some of his gain either with his workers in higher wages or with his customers in lower prices, or with both groups.

Fair Shares and the Social Interest The idea that the social interest requires "fair shares" is a deeply held one. Think about what you regard as a fair share. To help you, imagine the following game.

I put $100 on the table and tell someone you don't know and who doesn't know you to *propose* a share of the money between the two of you. If you *accept* the proposed share, you each get the agreed upon shares. If you don't accept the proposed share, you both get nothing.

It would be efficient—you would both be better off—if the proposer offered to take $99 and leave you with $1 and you accepted that offer.

But would you accept the $1? If you are like most people, the idea that the other person gets 99 times as much as you is just too much to stomach. "No way" you say and the $100 disappears. That outcome is inefficient. You have both given up something.

When the game I've just described is played in a classroom experiment, about a half of the players reject offers of below $30.

So fair shares matters. But what is *fair*? There isn't a crisp definition of fairness to match that of efficiency. Reasonable people have a variety of views about it. Almost everyone agrees that too much inequality is unfair. But how much is too much? And inequality of what: income, wealth, or the *opportunity* to work, earn an income, and accumulate wealth?

You will examine efficiency again in Chapter 2 and efficiency and fairness in Chapter 5.

Questions about the social interest are hard ones to answer and they generate discussion, debate, and disagreement. Four issues in today's world put some flesh on these questions. The issues are:

- Globalization
- Information-age monopolies
- Climate change
- Economic instability

Globalization The term *globalization* means the expansion of international trade, borrowing and lending, and investment.

When Nike produces sports shoes, people in Malaysia get work; and when China Airlines buys new airplanes, Americans who work at Boeing in Seattle build them. While globalization brings expanded production and job opportunities for some workers, it destroys many American jobs. Workers across the manufacturing industries must learn new skills, take service jobs, which are often lower-paid, or retire earlier than previously planned.

Globalization is in the self-interest of those consumers who buy low-cost goods and services produced in other countries; and it is in the self-interest of the

multinational firms that produce in low-cost regions and sell in high-price regions. But is globalization in the self-interest of the low-wage worker in Malaysia who sews your new running shoes and the displaced shoemaker in Atlanta? Is it in the social interest?

◆ ECONOMICS IN THE NEWS

The Invisible Hand

From Brewer to Bio-Tech Entrepreneur
Kiran Mazumdar-Shaw trained to become a master brewer and learned about enzymes, the stuff from which bio-pharmaceuticals are made. Discovering it was impossible for a woman in India to become a master brewer, the 25-year-old Kiran decided to create a bio-pharmaceutical business.

Kiran's firm, Biocom, employed uneducated workers who loved their jobs and the living conditions made possible by their high wages. But when a labor union entered the scene and unionized the workers, a furious Kiran fired the workers, automated their jobs, and hired a smaller number of educated workers. Biocom continued to grow and today, Kiran's wealth exceeds $1 billion.

Kiran has become wealthy by developing and producing bio-pharmaceuticals that improve people's lives. But Kiran is sharing her wealth in creative ways. She has opened a cancer treatment center to help thousands of patients who are too poor to pay and created a health insurance scheme.

Source of information: Ariel Levy, "Drug Test"
The New Yorker, January 2, 2012

THE QUESTIONS
- Whose decisions in the story were taken in self-interest?
- Whose decisions turned out to be in the social interest?
- Did any of the decisions harm the social interest?

THE ANSWERS
- All the decisions—Kiran's, the workers', the union's, and the firm's customers'—are taken in the pursuit of self-interest.
- Kiran's decisions serve the social interest: She creates jobs that benefit her workers and products that benefit her customers. And her charitable work brings yet further social benefits.
- The labor union's decision might have harmed the social interest because it destroyed the jobs of uneducated workers.

Kiran Mazumdar-Shaw, founder and CEO of Biocom

Information-Age Monopolies The technological change of the past forty years has been called the *Information Revolution.*

Gordon Moore, who founded the chip-maker Intel, and Bill Gates, a co-founder of Microsoft, held privileged positions in this revolution. For many years, Intel chips were the only available chips and Windows was the only available operating system for the original IBM PC and its clones. The PC and Mac competed, but the PC had a huge market share.

An absence of competition gave Intel and Microsoft the power and ability to sell their products at prices far above the cost of production. If the prices of chips and Windows had been lower, many more people would have been able to afford a computer and would have chosen to buy one.

The information revolution has clearly served your self-interest: It has provided your cell phone, laptop, loads of handy applications, and the Internet. It has also served the self-interest of Bill Gates of Microsoft and Gordon Moore of Intel, both of whom have seen their wealth soar.

But did the information revolution best serve the social interest? Did Microsoft produce the best possible Windows operating system and sell it at a price that was in the social interest? Did Intel make the right quality of chips and sell them in the right quantities for the right prices? Or was the quality too low and the price too high? Would the social interest have been better served if Microsoft and Intel had faced competition from other firms?

Climate Change Climate change is a huge political issue today. Every serious political leader is acutely aware of the problem and of the popularity of having proposals that might lower carbon emissions.

Burning fossil fuels to generate electricity and to power airplanes, automobiles, and trucks pours a staggering 28 billion tons—4 tons per person—of carbon dioxide into the atmosphere each year.

Two thirds of the world's carbon emissions comes from the United States, China, the European Union, Russia, and India. The fastest growing emissions are coming from India and China.

The amount of global warming caused by economic activity and its effects are uncertain, but the emissions continue to grow and pose huge risks.

Every day, when you make self-interested choices to use electricity and gasoline, you contribute to carbon emissions; you leave your carbon footprint. You can lessen your carbon footprint by walking, riding a bike, taking a cold shower, or planting a tree.

But can each one of us be relied upon to make decisions that affect the Earth's carbon-dioxide concentration in the social interest? Must governments change the incentives we face so that our self-interested choices are also in the social interest? How can governments change incentives? How can we encourage the use of wind and solar power to replace the burning of fossil fuels that brings climate change?

Economic Instability The years between 1993 and 2007 brought remarkable economic stability, so much so that they've been called the *Great Moderation.* During those years, the U.S. and global economies were on a roll. Incomes in the United States increased by 30 percent and incomes in China tripled. Even the economic shockwaves of 9/11 brought only a small dip in the strong pace of U.S. and global economic expansion.

Flush with funds and offering record low interest rates, banks went on a lending spree to home buyers. Rapidly rising home prices made home owners feel well off and they were happy to borrow and spend. Home loans were bundled into securities that were sold and resold to banks around the world.

◆ AT **ISSUE**

The Protest against Market Capitalism

Market capitalism is an economic system in which individuals own all the land and capital and are free to buy and sell land, capital, and goods and services in markets. Billions of self-interested choices and their coordination in markets determine what, how, and for whom goods and services are produced. There is no supreme planner guiding the use of scarce resources and the outcome is unintended and unforeseeable.

Centrally planned socialism is an economic system in which the government owns all the land and capital, directs workers to jobs, and decides what, how, and for whom to produce. The Soviet Union, several Eastern European countries, and China have used this system in the past but have now abandoned it.

Our economy today is a **mixed economy**, which is market capitalism with government regulation.

The **Protest**

The protest against market capitalism takes many forms. Historically, **Karl Marx** and other communist and socialist thinkers wanted to replace it with *socialism* and *central planning*. Today, thousands of people who feel let down by the economic system want less market capitalism and more government regulation. The **Occupy Wall Street** movement is a visible example of today's protest. Protesters say:

- Big corporations (especially big banks) have too much power and influence on governments.
- Democratically elected governments can do a better job of allocating resources and distributing income than uncoordinated markets. More regulation in the social interest is needed—to serve "human need, not corporate greed."
- In a market, for every winner, there is a loser. Big corporations are the winners. Workers and unemployed people are the losers.

An Occupy Wall Street protester

The **Economist's Response**

Economists agree that market capitalism isn't perfect. But they argue that it is the best system available and while some government intervention and regulation can help, it is equally likely to harm the social interest. **Adam Smith** (see p. 53) gave the first systematic account of how market capitalism works. He says:

- The self-interest of big corporations is *maximum profit*. But an *invisible hand* leads decisions made in pursuit of self-interest to *unintentionally* promote the social interest.
- Politicians are ill-equipped to regulate corporations or to intervene in markets and those who think they can improve on the market outcome are most likely wrong.
- In a market, buyers get what they want for less than they would be willing to pay and sellers earn a profit. Both buyers and sellers gain. A market transaction is a "win-win" event.

"It is not from the benevolence of the butcher, the brewer, or the baker that we expect our dinner, but from their regard to their own interest."
The Wealth of Nations,
1776

Adam Smith

In 2006, as interest rates began to rise and the rate at which home prices were rising slowed, borrowers defaulted on their loans. What started as a trickle became a flood. As more people defaulted, banks took losses that totaled billions of dollars by the summer of 2007. Financial markets are global and a bank in France was the first to feel the pain that soon gripped the entire global financial system.

Banks take in deposits from people and businesses and get more funds by borrowing from each other and from other firms. Banks use these funds to make loans. All the banks' choices to borrow and lend and the choices of people and businesses to lend to and borrow from banks are made in self-interest. But does this lending and borrowing serve the social interest? Is there too much borrowing and lending or too little?

ECONOMICS IN THE NEWS

A Fragile Global Economy

Global Economy Recovering, but Major Risks Remain
In mid-2007, the U.S. mortgage market crashed and triggered a global financial and economic crisis. In mid-2012, the global economy, still recovering from that crisis, remained in a fragile state with more than 1 in 10 people unemployed in Europe. Another global crisis, this time starting in Europe, was feared.

Source: *OECD Press Release*, May 22, 2012

THE DATA

Unemployment Rates
(percentage of labor force)

	United States	Euro Area	OECD
2012	8.1	10.8	8.0
2013	7.9	11.1	7.9

THE QUESTIONS

- With the information provided in the news clip and the data table, what caused the financial and economic crisis of 2007?
- Has the world fully recovered from that crisis?
- Where is the greatest unemployment? Where is unemployment falling and where is it rising?
- Why does the existence of persistent high unemployment present a puzzle for economists?

THE ANSWERS

- Problems in the U.S. mortgage market brought the global economy crashing in 2007.
- Even 5 years later in 2012, the recovery was incomplete and a second crisis was feared.
- Europe has the greatest unemployment. Unemployment is falling a bit in the United States and the OECD as a whole but is rising in Europe.
- Unemployment is a puzzle because it is in no one's self-interest. It seems to be a waste of resources and doesn't seem to contribute to overcoming scarcity.

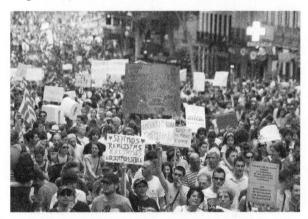

In Spain, 1 in 4 people who want a job can't find one.

When the banks got into trouble, the Federal Reserve (the Fed) bailed them out with big loans backed by taxpayer dollars. Did the Fed's bailout of troubled banks serve the social interest? Or might the Fed's rescue action encourage banks to repeat their dangerous lending in the future?

Banks weren't the only recipients of public funds. General Motors was saved by a government bailout. GM makes its decisions in its self-interest. The government bailout of GM also served the firm's self-interest. Did the bailout also serve the social interest?

We've looked at four topics and asked many questions that illustrate the big question: Can choices made in the pursuit of self-interest also promote the social interest? We've asked questions but not answered them because we've not yet explained the economic principles needed to do so.

REVIEW QUIZ

1 Describe the broad facts about *what, how*, and *for whom* goods and services are produced.
2 Use headlines from the recent news to illustrate the potential for conflict between self-interest and the social interest.

You can work these questions in Study Plan 1.2 and get instant feedback.   MyEconLab

By working through this book, you will discover the economic principles that help economists figure out when the social interest is being served, when it is not, and what might be done when it is not being served. We will return to each of the unanswered questions in future chapters.

◆ The Economic Way of Thinking

The questions that economics tries to answer tell us about the *scope of economics,* but they don't tell us how economists *think* and go about seeking answers to these questions. You're now going to see how economists go about their work.

We're going to look at six key ideas that define the *economic way of thinking.* These ideas are

- A choice is a *tradeoff.*
- People make *rational choices* by comparing *benefits* and *costs.*
- *Benefit* is what you gain from something.
- *Cost* is what you *must give up* to get something.
- Most choices are *"how-much"* choices made at the *margin.*
- Choices respond to *incentives.*

A Choice Is a Tradeoff

Because we face scarcity, we must make choices. And when we make a choice, we select from the available alternatives. For example, you can spend Saturday night studying for your next economics test or having fun with your friends, but you can't do both of these activities at the same time. You must choose how much time to devote to each. Whatever choice you make, you could have chosen something else.

You can think about your choices as tradeoffs. A **tradeoff** is an exchange—giving up one thing to get something else. When you choose how to spend your Saturday night, you face a tradeoff between studying and hanging out with your friends.

Making a Rational Choice

Economists view the choices that people make as rational. A **rational choice** is one that compares costs and benefits and achieves the greatest benefit over cost for the person making the choice.

Only the wants of the person making a choice are relevant to determine its rationality. For example, you might like your coffee black and strong but your friend prefers his milky and sweet. So it is rational for you to choose espresso and for your friend to choose cappuccino.

The idea of rational choice provides an answer to the first question: *What* goods and services will be produced and in what quantities? The answer is those that people rationally choose to buy!

But how do people choose rationally? Why do more people choose an iPod rather than a Zune? Why has the U.S. government chosen to build an interstate highway system and not an interstate high-speed railroad system? The answers turn on comparing benefits and costs.

Benefit: What You Gain

The **benefit** of something is the gain or pleasure that it brings and is determined by **preferences**—by what a person likes and dislikes and the intensity of those feelings. If you get a huge kick out of "Guitar Hero," that video game brings you a large benefit. And if you have little interest in listening to Yo Yo Ma playing a Vivaldi cello concerto, that activity brings you a small benefit.

Some benefits are large and easy to identify, such as the benefit that you get from being in school. A big piece of that benefit is the goods and services that you will be able to enjoy with the boost to your earning power when you graduate. Some benefits are small, such as the benefit you get from a slice of pizza.

Economists measure benefit as the most that a person is *willing to give up* to get something. You are willing to give up a lot to be in school. But you would give up only an iTunes download for a slice of pizza.

Cost: What You *Must* Give Up

The **opportunity cost** of something is the highest-valued alternative that must be given up to get it.

To make the idea of opportunity cost concrete, think about *your* opportunity cost of being in school. It has two components: the things you can't afford to buy and the things you can't do with your time.

Start with the things you can't afford to buy. You've spent all your income on tuition, residence fees, books, and a laptop. If you weren't in school, you would have spent this money on tickets to ball games and movies and all the other things that you enjoy. But that's only the start of your opportunity cost. You've also given up the opportunity to get a job. Suppose that the best job you could get if you weren't in school is working at Citibank as a teller earning $25,000 a year. Another part of your opportunity cost of being in school is all the things that you could buy with the extra $25,000 you would have.

As you well know, being a student eats up many hours in class time, doing homework assignments, preparing for tests, and so on. To do all these school activities, you must give up many hours of what would otherwise be leisure time spent with your friends.

So the opportunity cost of being in school is all the good things that you can't afford and don't have the spare time to enjoy. You might want to put a dollar value on that cost or you might just list all the items that make up the opportunity cost.

The examples of opportunity cost that we've just considered are all-or-nothing costs—you're either in school or not in school. Most situations are not like this one. They involve choosing *how much* of an activity to do.

How Much? Choosing at the Margin

You can allocate the next hour between studying and chatting online with your friends, but the choice is not all or nothing. You must decide how many minutes to allocate to each activity. To make this decision, you compare the benefit of a little bit more study time with its cost—you make your choice at the **margin**.

The benefit that arises from an increase in an activity is called **marginal benefit**. For example, your marginal benefit from one more night of study before a test is the boost it gives to your grade. Your marginal benefit doesn't include the grade you're already achieving without that extra night of work.

The *opportunity cost* of an *increase* in an activity is called **marginal cost**. For you, the marginal cost of studying one more night is the cost of not spending that night on your favorite leisure activity.

To make your decisions, you compare marginal benefit and marginal cost. If the marginal benefit from an extra night of study exceeds its marginal cost, you study the extra night. If the marginal cost exceeds the marginal benefit, you don't study the extra night.

Choices Respond to Incentives

Economists take human nature as given and view people as acting in their self-interest. All people— you, other consumers, producers, politicians, and public servants—pursue their self-interest.

Self-interested actions are not necessarily *selfish* actions. You might decide to use your resources in ways that bring pleasure to others as well as to yourself. But a self-interested act gets the most benefit for *you* based on *your* view about benefit.

The central idea of economics is that we can predict the self-interested choices that people make by looking at the *incentives* they face. People undertake those activities for which marginal benefit exceeds marginal cost; and they reject options for which marginal cost exceeds marginal benefit.

For example, your economics instructor gives you a problem set and tells you these problems will be on the next test. Your marginal benefit from working these problems is large, so you diligently work them. In contrast, your math instructor gives you a problem set on a topic that she says will never be on a test. You get little marginal benefit from working these problems, so you decide to skip most of them.

Economists see incentives as the key to reconciling self-interest and social interest. When our choices are *not* in the social interest, it is because of the incentives we face. One of the challenges for economists is to figure out the incentives that result in self-interested choices being in the social interest.

Economists emphasize the crucial role that institutions play in influencing the incentives that people face as they pursue their self-interest. Laws that protect private property and markets that enable voluntary exchange are the fundamental institutions. You will learn as you progress with your study of economics that where these institutions exist, self-interest can indeed promote the social interest.

REVIEW QUIZ

1 Explain the idea of a tradeoff and think of three tradeoffs that you have made today.
2 Explain what economists mean by rational choice and think of three choices that you've made today that are rational.
3 Explain why opportunity cost is the best forgone alternative and provide examples of some opportunity costs that you have faced today.
4 Explain what it means to choose at the margin and illustrate with three choices at the margin that you have made today.
5 Explain why choices respond to incentives and think of three incentives to which you have responded today.

You can work these questions in Study Plan 1.3 and get instant feedback.   MyEconLab

Economics as Social Science and Policy Tool

Economics is both a social science and a toolkit for advising on policy decisions.

Economist as Social Scientist

As social scientists, economists seek to discover how the economic world works. In pursuit of this goal, like all scientists, economists distinguish between positive and normative statements.

Positive Statements A *positive* statement is about what *is*. It says what is currently believed about the way the world operates. A positive statement might be right or wrong, but we can test it by checking it against the facts. "Our planet is warming because of the amount of coal that we're burning" is a positive statement. We can test whether it is right or wrong.

A central task of economists is to test positive statements about how the economic world works and to weed out those that are wrong. Economics first got off the ground in the late 1700s, so it is a young science compared with, for example, physics, and much remains to be discovered.

Normative Statements A *normative* statement is about what *ought to be*. It depends on values and cannot be tested. Policy goals are normative statements. For example, "We ought to cut our use of coal by 50 percent" is a normative policy statement. You may agree or disagree with it, but you can't test it. It doesn't assert a fact that can be checked.

Unscrambling Cause and Effect Economists are particularly interested in positive statements about cause and effect. Are computers getting cheaper because people are buying them in greater quantities? Or are people buying computers in greater quantities because they are getting cheaper? Or is some third factor causing both the price of a computer to fall and the quantity of computers bought to increase?

To answer such questions, economists create and test economic models. An **economic model** is a description of some aspect of the economic world that includes only those features that are needed for the purpose at hand. For example, an economic model of a cell-phone network might include features such as the prices of calls, the number of cell-phone users, and the volume of calls. But the model would ignore cell-phone colors and ringtones.

A model is tested by comparing its predictions with the facts. But testing an economic model is difficult because we observe the outcomes of the simultaneous change of many factors. To cope with this problem, economists look for natural experiments (situations in the ordinary course of economic life in which the one factor of interest is different and other things are equal or similar); conduct statistical investigations to find correlations; and perform economic experiments by putting people in decision-making situations and varying the influence of one factor at a time to discover how they respond.

Economist as Policy Adviser

Economics is useful. It is a toolkit for advising governments and businesses and for making personal decisions. Some of the most famous economists work partly as policy advisers.

For example, Jagdish Bhagwati of Columbia University, whom you will meet on p. 54, has advised governments and international organizations on trade and economic development issues.

Alan B. Krueger of Princeton University is on leave and serving as the chief economic adviser to President Barack Obama and head of the President's Council of Economic Advisers.

All the policy questions on which economists provide advice involve a blend of the positive and the normative. Economics can't help with the normative part—the policy goal. But for a given goal, economics provides a method of evaluating alternative solutions—comparing marginal benefits and marginal costs and finding the solution that makes the best use of the available resources.

REVIEW QUIZ

1 Distinguish between a positive statement and a normative statement and provide examples.
2 What is a model? Can you think of a model that you might use in your everyday life?
3 How do economists try to disentangle cause and effect?
4 How is economics used as a policy tool?

You can work these questions in Study Plan 1.4 and get instant feedback.   MyEconLab

SUMMARY

Key Points

Definition of Economics (p. 2)

- All economic questions arise from scarcity—from the fact that wants exceed the resources available to satisfy them.
- Economics is the social science that studies the choices that people make as they cope with scarcity.
- The subject divides into microeconomics and macroeconomics.

Working Problem 1 will give you a better understanding of the definition of economics.

Two Big Economic Questions (pp. 3–9)

- Two big questions summarize the scope of economics:

  1. How do choices end up determining *what, how,* and *for whom* goods and services are produced?
  2. When do choices made in the pursuit of *self-interest* also promote the *social interest?*

Working Problems 2 and 3 will give you a better understanding of the two big questions of economics.

The Economic Way of Thinking (pp. 10–11)

- Every choice is a tradeoff—exchanging more of something for less of something else.
- People make rational choices by comparing benefit and cost.
- Cost—*opportunity cost*—is what you must give up to get something.
- Most choices are "how much" choices made at the *margin* by comparing marginal benefit and marginal cost.
- Choices respond to incentives.

Working Problems 4 and 5 will give you a better understanding of the economic way of thinking.

Economics as Social Science and Policy Tool (p. 12)

- Economists distinguish between positive statements—what is—and normative statements—what ought to be.
- To explain the economic world, economists create and test economic models.
- Economics is a toolkit used to provide advice on government, business, and personal economic decisions.

Working Problem 6 will give you a better understanding of economics as social science and policy tool.

Key Terms

Benefit, 10
Capital, 4
Economic model, 12
Economics, 2
Efficient, 5
Entrepreneurship, 4
Factors of production, 3
Goods and services, 3
Human capital, 3
Incentive, 2

Interest, 4
Labor, 3
Land, 3
Macroeconomics, 2
Margin, 11
Marginal benefit, 11
Marginal cost, 11
Microeconomics, 2
Opportunity cost, 10
Preferences, 10

Profit, 4
Rational choice, 10
Rent, 4
Scarcity, 2
Self-interest, 5
Social interest, 5
Tradeoff, 10
Wages, 4

STUDY PLAN PROBLEMS AND APPLICATIONS

MyEconLab   You can work Problems 1 to 6 in MyEconLab Chapter 1 Study Plan and get instant feedback.

Definition of Economics (Study Plan 1.1)

1. Apple Inc. decides to make iTunes freely available in unlimited quantities.
   a. Does Apple's decision change the incentives that people face?
   b. Is Apple's decision an example of a microeconomic or a macroeconomic issue?

Two Big Economic Questions (Study Plan 1.2)

2. Which of the following pairs does not match?
   a. Labor and wages
   b. Land and rent
   c. Entrepreneurship and profit
   d. Capital and profit

3. Explain how the following news headlines concern self-interest and the social interest.
   a. Starbucks Expands in China
   b. McDonald's Moves into Gourmet Coffee
   c. Food Must Be Labeled with Nutrition Data

The Economic Way of Thinking (Study Plan 1.3)

4. The night before an economics test, you decide to go to the movies instead of staying home and working your MyEconLab Study Plan. You get 50 percent on your test compared with the 70 percent that you normally score.
   a. Did you face a tradeoff?
   b. What was the opportunity cost of your evening at the movies?

5. **Costs Soar for London Olympics**
   The regeneration of East London, the site of the 2012 Olympic Games, is set to add extra £1.5 billion to taxpayers' bill.
   Source: *The Times*, London, July 6, 2006
   Is the cost of regenerating East London an opportunity cost of hosting the 2012 Olympic Games? Explain why or why not.

Economics as Social Science and Policy Tool
(Study Plan 1.4)

6. Which of the following statements is positive, which is normative, and which can be tested?
   a. The United States should cut its imports.
   b. China is the largest trading partner of the United States.
   c. If the price of antiretroviral drugs increases, HIV/AIDS sufferers will decrease their consumption of the drugs.

ADDITIONAL PROBLEMS AND APPLICATIONS

MyEconLab   You can work these problems in MyEconLab if assigned by your instructor.

Definition of Economics

7. **Hundreds Line up for 5 p.m. Ticket Giveaway**
   By noon, hundreds of Eminem fans had lined up for a chance to score free tickets to the concert.
   Source: *Detroit Free Press*, May 18, 2009
   When Eminem gave away tickets, what was free and what was scarce? Explain your answer.

Two Big Economic Questions

8. How does the creation of a successful movie influence *what, how*, and *for whom* goods and services are produced?

9. How does a successful movie illustrate self-interested choices that are also in the social interest?

The Economic Way of Thinking

10. Before starring in *Iron Man*, Robert Downey Jr. had appeared in 45 movies that grossed an average of $5 million on the opening weekend. In contrast, *Iron Man* grossed $102 million.
    a. How do you expect the success of *Iron Man* to influence the opportunity cost of hiring Robert Downey Jr.?
    b. How have the incentives for a movie producer to hire Robert Downey Jr. changed?

11. What might be an incentive for you to take a class in summer school? List some of the benefits and costs involved in your decision. Would your choice be rational?

Economics as Social Science and Policy Tool

12. Look at today's *Wall Street Journal*. What is the leading economic news story? With which of the big economic questions does it deal and what tradeoffs does it discuss or imply?

13. Provide two microeconomic statements and two macroeconomic statements. Classify your statements as positive or normative. Explain why.

APPENDIX

Graphs in Economics

After studying this appendix, you will be able to:

◆ Make and interpret a scatter diagram

◆ Identify linear and nonlinear relationships and relationships that have a maximum and a minimum

◆ Define and calculate the slope of a line

◆ Graph relationships among more than two variables

▶ Graphing Data

A graph represents a quantity as a distance on a line. In Fig. A1.1, a distance on the horizontal line represents temperature, measured in degrees Fahrenheit. A movement from left to right shows an increase in temperature. The point 0 represents zero degrees Fahrenheit. To the right of 0, the temperature is positive. To the left of 0, the temperature is negative (as indicated by the minus sign). A distance on the vertical line represents height, measured in thousands of feet. The point 0 represents sea level. Points above 0 represent feet above sea level. Points below 0 represent feet below sea level (indicated by a minus sign).

In Fig. A1.1, the two scale lines are perpendicular to each other and are called *axes*. The vertical line is the *y*-axis, and the horizontal line is the *x*-axis. Each axis has a zero point, which is shared by the two axes and called the *origin*.

To make a two-variable graph, we need two pieces of information: the value of the variable *x* and the value of the variable *y*. For example, off the coast of Alaska, the temperature is 32 degrees—the value of *x*. A fishing boat is located at 0 feet above sea level—the value of *y*. These two bits of information appear as point *A* in Fig. A1.1. A climber at the top of Mount McKinley on a cold day is 20,320 feet above sea level in a zero-degree gale. These two pieces of information appear as point *B*. On a warmer day, a climber might be at the peak of Mt. McKinley when the temperature is 32 degrees, at point *C*.

We can draw two lines, called *coordinates*, from point *C*. One, called the *x*-coordinate, runs from *C* to the vertical axis. This line is called "the *x*-coordinate"

FIGURE A1.1   Making a Graph

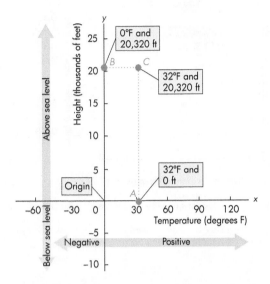

Graphs have axes that measure quantities as distances. Here, the horizontal axis (*x*-axis) measures temperature, and the vertical axis (*y*-axis) measures height. Point *A* represents a fishing boat at sea level (0 on the *y*-axis) on a day when the temperature is 32°F. Point *B* represents a climber at the top of Mt. McKinley, 20,320 feet above sea level at a temperature of 0°F. Point *C* represents a climber at the top of Mt. McKinley, 20,320 feet above sea level at a temperature of 32°F.

MyEconLab animation

because its length is the same as the value marked off on the *x*-axis. The other, called the *y*-coordinate, runs from *C* to the horizontal axis. This line is called "the *y*-coordinate" because its length is the same as the value marked off on the *y*-axis.

We describe a point on a graph by the values of its *x*-coordinate and its *y*-coordinate. For example, at point *C*, *x* is 32 degrees and *y* is 20,320 feet.

A graph like that in Fig. A1.1 can be made using any quantitative data on two variables. The graph can show just a few points, like Fig. A1.1, or many points. Before we look at graphs with many points, let's reinforce what you've just learned by looking at two graphs made with economic data.

Economists measure variables that describe *what, how,* and *for whom* goods and services are produced. These variables are quantities produced and prices. Figure A1.2 shows two examples of economic graphs.

FIGURE A1.2   Two Graphs of Economic Data

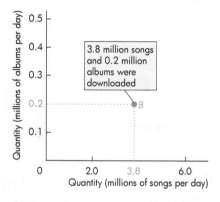

The graph in part (a) tells us that in 2010, 3.8 million songs per day were downloaded at an average price of $1.37 per song.

The graph in part (b) tells us that in 2010, 3.8 million songs per day and 0.2 million albums per day were downloaded.

(a) Singles downloads: quantity and price   **(b) Downloads: singles and albums**

MyEconLab animation

Figure A1.2(a) is a graph about song downloads in 2010. The *x*-axis measures the quantity of songs downloaded per day and the *y*-axis measures the price of a song. Point *A* tells us what the quantity and price were. You can "read" this graph as telling you that in 2010, 3.8 million songs a day were downloaded at an average price of $1.37 per song.

Figure A1.2(b) is a graph about song and album downloads in 2010. The *x*-axis measures the quantity of songs downloaded per day and the *y*-axis measures the quantity of albums downloaded per day. Point *B* tells us what these quantities were. You can "read" this graph as telling you that in 2010, 3.8 million songs a day and 0.2 million albums were downloaded.

The three graphs that you've just seen tell you how to make a graph and how to read a data point on a graph, but they don't improve on the raw data. Graphs become interesting and revealing when they contain a number of data points because then you can visualize the data.

Economists create graphs based on the principles in Figs. A1.1 and A1.2 to reveal, describe, and visualize the relationships among variables. We're now going to look at some examples. These graphs are called scatter diagrams.

Scatter Diagrams

A **scatter diagram** is a graph that plots the value of one variable against the value of another variable for a number of different values of each variable. Such a graph reveals whether a relationship exists between

two variables and describes their relationship.

The table in Fig. A1.3 shows some data on two variables: the number of tickets sold at the box office and the number of DVDs sold for nine of the most popular movies in 2011.

What is the relationship between these two variables? Does a big box office success generate a large volume of DVD sales? Or does a box office success mean that fewer DVDs are sold?

We can answer these questions by making a scatter diagram. We do so by graphing the data in the table. In the graph in Fig. A1.3, each point shows the number of box office tickets sold (the *x* variable) and the number of DVDs sold (the *y* variable) of one of the movies. There are nine movies, so there are nine points "scattered" within the graph.

The point labeled *A* tells us that *Fast Five* sold 27 million tickets at the box office and 2 million DVDs. The points in the graph form a pattern, which reveals that larger box office sales are associated with larger DVD sales. But the points also tell us that this association is weak. You can't predict DVD sales with any confidence by knowing only the number of tickets sold at the box office.

Figure A1.4 shows two scatter diagrams of economic variables. Part (a) shows the relationship between income and expenditure, on average, during a ten-year period. Each point represents income and expenditure in a given year. For example, point *A* shows that in 2006, income was $33,000 and expenditure was $31,000. This graph shows that as income increases, so does expenditure, and the relationship is a close one.

FIGURE A1.3 A Scatter Diagram

Movie	Tickets	DVDs
	(millions)	
Harry Potter and the Deathly Hallows: Part II	48	5.8
Transformers: Dark of the Moon	44	2.6
The Hangover Part II	32	2.6
Pirates of the Caribbean: On Stranger Tides	30	1.0
Fast Five	27	2.0
Cars 2	24	4.4
Thor	23	1.2
Rise of the Planet of the Apes	22	1.5
Captain America: The First Avenger	22	1.4

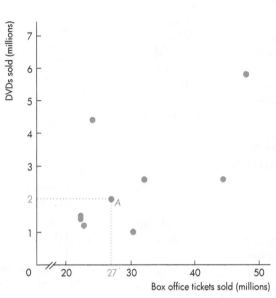

The table lists the number of tickets sold at the box office and the number of DVDs sold for nine popular movies.

The scatter diagram reveals the relationship between these two variables. Each point shows the values of the two variables for a specific movie. For example, point A shows the point for *Fast Five*, which sold 27 million tickets at the box office and 2 million DVDs.

The pattern formed by the points shows that there is a tendency for large box office sales to bring greater DVD sales. But you couldn't predict how many DVDs a movie would sell just by knowing its box office sales.

MyEconLab animation

Figure A1.4(b) shows a scatter diagram of U.S. inflation and unemployment from 2001 through 2011. Here, the points show no relationship between the two variables, but 2010 had a high unemployment rate and low inflation rate.

You can see that a scatter diagram conveys a wealth of information, and it does so in much less space than we have used to describe only some of its features. But you do have to "read" the graph to obtain all this information.

FIGURE A1.4 Two Economic Scatter Diagrams

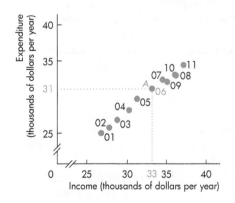

(a) Income and expenditure

(b) Unemployment and inflation

The scatter diagram in part (a) shows the relationship between income and expenditure from 2001 to 2011. Point A shows that in 2006, income was $33 (thousand) on the x-axis and expenditure was $31 (thousand) on the y-axis. This graph shows that as income rises, so does expenditure and the relationship is a close one.

The scatter diagram in part (b) shows a weak relationship between unemployment and inflation in the United States during most of the years.

MyEconLab animation

Breaks in the Axes The graph in Fig. A1.4(a) has breaks in its axes, as shown by the small gaps. The breaks indicate that there are jumps from the origin, 0, to the first values recorded.

The breaks are used because the lowest values of income and expenditure exceed $25,000. If we made this graph with no breaks in its axes, there would be a lot of empty space, all the points would be crowded into the top right corner, and it would be difficult to see whether a relationship exists between these two variables. By breaking the axes, we are able to bring the relationship into view.

Putting a break in one or both axes is like using a zoom lens to bring the relationship into the center of the graph and magnify it so that the relationship fills the graph.

Misleading Graphs Breaks can be used to highlight a relationship, but they can also be used to mislead—to make a graph that lies. The most common way of making a graph lie is to put a break in the axis and either to stretch or compress the scale. For example, suppose that in Fig. A1.4(a), the *y*-axis that measures expenditure ran from zero to $35,000 while the *x*-axis was the same as the one shown. The graph would now create the impression that despite a huge increase in income, expenditure had barely changed.

To avoid being misled, it is a good idea to get into the habit of always looking closely at the values and the labels on the axes of a graph before you start to interpret it.

Correlation and Causation A scatter diagram that shows a clear relationship between two variables, such as Fig. A1.4(a), tells us that the two variables have a high correlation. When a high correlation is present, we can predict the value of one variable from the value of the other variable. But correlation does not imply causation.

Sometimes a high correlation is a coincidence, but sometimes it does arise from a causal relationship. It is likely, for example, that rising income causes rising expenditure (Fig. A1.4a) and that high unemployment makes for a slack economy in which prices don't rise quickly, so the inflation rate is low (Fig. A1.4b).

You've now seen how we can use graphs in economics to show economic data and to reveal relationships. Next, we'll learn how economists use graphs to construct and display economic models.

Graphs Used in Economic Models

The graphs used in economics are not always designed to show real-world data. Often they are used to show general relationships among the variables in an economic model.

An *economic model* is a stripped-down, simplified description of an economy or of a component of an economy such as a business or a household. It consists of statements about economic behavior that can be expressed as equations or as curves in a graph. Economists use models to explore the effects of different policies or other influences on the economy in ways that are similar to the use of model airplanes in wind tunnels and models of the climate.

You will encounter many different kinds of graphs in economic models, but there are some repeating patterns. Once you've learned to recognize these patterns, you will instantly understand the meaning of a graph. Here, we'll look at the different types of curves that are used in economic models, and we'll see some everyday examples of each type of curve. The patterns to look for in graphs are the four cases in which

- Variables move in the same direction.
- Variables move in opposite directions.
- Variables have a maximum or a minimum.
- Variables are unrelated.

Let's look at these four cases.

Variables That Move in the Same Direction

Figure A1.5 shows graphs of the relationships between two variables that move up and down together. A relationship between two variables that move in the same direction is called a **positive relationship** or a **direct relationship**. A line that slopes upward shows such a relationship.

Figure A1.5 shows three types of relationships: one that has a straight line and two that have curved lines. All the lines in these three graphs are called curves. Any line on a graph—no matter whether it is straight or curved—is called a *curve*.

A relationship shown by a straight line is called a **linear relationship**. Figure A1.5(a) shows a linear relationship between the number of miles traveled in

FIGURE A1.5   Positive (Direct) Relationships

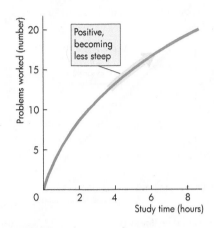

(a) Positive linear relationship   **(b) Positive, becoming steeper**   **(c) Positive, becoming less steep**

Each part shows a positive (direct) relationship between two variables. That is, as the value of the variable measured on the x-axis increases, so does the value of the variable measured on the y-axis. Part (a) shows a linear positive relationship—as the two variables increase together, we move along a straight line.

Part (b) shows a positive relationship such that as the two variables increase together, we move along a curve that becomes steeper.

Part (c) shows a positive relationship such that as the two variables increase together, we move along a curve that becomes flatter.

MyEconLab animation

5 hours and speed. For example, point A shows that you will travel 200 miles in 5 hours if your speed is 40 miles an hour. If you double your speed to 80 miles an hour, you will travel 400 miles in 5 hours.

Figure A1.5(b) shows the relationship between distance sprinted and recovery time (the time it takes the heart rate to return to its normal resting rate). This relationship is an upward-sloping one that starts out quite flat but then becomes steeper as we move along the curve away from the origin. The reason this curve becomes steeper is that the additional recovery time needed from sprinting an additional 100 yards increases. It takes less than 5 minutes to recover from sprinting 100 yards but more than 10 minutes to recover from 200 yards.

Figure A1.5(c) shows the relationship between the number of problems worked by a student and the amount of study time. This relationship is an upward-sloping one that starts out quite steep and becomes flatter as we move along the curve away from the origin. Study time becomes less productive as the student spends more hours studying and becomes more tired.

Variables That Move in Opposite Directions

Figure A1.6 shows relationships between things that move in opposite directions. A relationship between variables that move in opposite directions is called a **negative relationship** or an **inverse relationship**.

Figure A1.6(a) shows the relationship between the hours spent playing squash and the hours spent playing tennis when the total time available is 5 hours. One extra hour spent playing tennis means one hour less spent playing squash and vice versa. This relationship is negative and linear.

Figure A1.6(b) shows the relationship between the cost per mile traveled and the length of a journey. The longer the journey, the lower is the cost per mile. But as the journey length increases, even though the cost per mile decreases, the fall in the cost per mile is smaller the longer the journey. This feature of the relationship is shown by the fact that the curve slopes downward, starting out steep at a short journey length and then becoming flatter as the journey length increases. This relationship arises because some of the costs are fixed, such as auto insurance, and the fixed costs are spread over a longer journey.

FIGURE A1.6   Negative (Inverse) Relationships

(a) Negative linear relationship   **(b) Negative, becoming less steep**   **(c) Negative, becoming steeper**

Each part shows a negative (inverse) relationship between two variables. Part (a) shows a linear negative relationship. The total time spent playing tennis and squash is 5 hours. As the time spent playing tennis increases, the time spent playing squash decreases, and we move along a straight line.

Part (b) shows a negative relationship such that as the journey length increases, the travel cost decreases as we move along a curve that becomes less steep.

Part (c) shows a negative relationship such that as leisure time increases, the number of problems worked decreases as we move along a curve that becomes steeper.

MyEconLab animation

Figure A1.6(c) shows the relationship between the amount of leisure time and the number of problems worked by a student. Increasing leisure time produces an increasingly large reduction in the number of problems worked. This relationship is a negative one that starts out with a gentle slope at a small number of leisure hours and becomes steeper as the number of leisure hours increases. This relationship is a different view of the idea shown in Fig. A1.5(c).

Variables That Have a Maximum or a Minimum

Many relationships in economic models have a maximum or a minimum. For example, firms try to make the maximum possible profit and to produce at the lowest possible cost. Figure A1.7 shows relationships that have a maximum or a minimum.

Figure A1.7(a) shows the relationship between rainfall and wheat yield. When there is no rainfall, wheat will not grow, so the yield is zero. As the rainfall increases up to 10 days a month, the wheat yield increases. With 10 rainy days each month, the wheat yield reaches its maximum at 40 bushels an acre (point *A*). Rain in excess of 10 days a month starts to lower the yield of wheat. If every day is rainy, the wheat suffers from a lack of sunshine and the yield decreases to zero. This relationship is one that starts out sloping upward, reaches a maximum, and then slopes downward.

Figure A1.7(b) shows the reverse case—a relationship that begins sloping downward, falls to a minimum, and then slopes upward. Most economic costs are like this relationship. An example is the relationship between the cost per mile and the speed of the car. At low speeds, the car is creeping in a traffic snarl-up. The number of miles per gallon is low, so the cost per mile is high. At high speeds, the car is traveling faster than its efficient speed, using a large quantity of gasoline, and again the number of miles per gallon is low and the cost per mile is high. At a speed of 55 miles an hour, the cost per mile is at its minimum (point *B*). This relationship is one that starts out sloping downward, reaches a minimum, and then slopes upward.

FIGURE A1.7   Maximum and Minimum Points

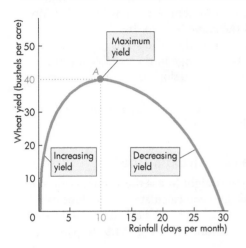

(a) Relationship with a maximum

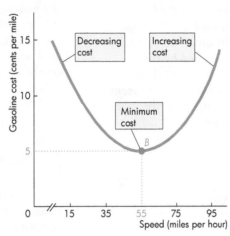

(b) Relationship with a minimum

Part (a) shows a relationship that has a maximum point, *A*. The curve slopes upward as it rises to its maximum point, is flat at its maximum, and then slopes downward.

Part (b) shows a relationship with a minimum point, *B*. The curve slopes downward as it falls to its minimum, is flat at its minimum, and then slopes upward.

MyEconLab animation

Variables That Are Unrelated

There are many situations in which no matter what happens to the value of one variable, the other variable remains constant. Sometimes we want to show the independence between two variables in a graph, and Fig. A1.8 shows two ways of achieving this.

In describing the graphs in Fig. A1.5 through Fig. A1.7, we have talked about curves that slope upward or slope downward, and curves that become less steep or steeper. Let's spend a little time discussing exactly what we mean by *slope* and how we measure the slope of a curve.

FIGURE A1.8   Variables That Are Unrelated

(a) Unrelated: *y* constant

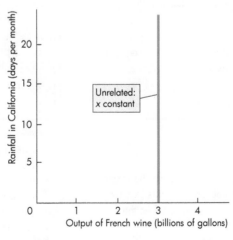

(b) Unrelated: *x* constant

This figure shows how we can graph two variables that are unrelated. In part (a), a student's grade in economics is plotted at 75 percent on the *y*-axis regardless of the price of bananas on the *x*-axis. The curve is horizontal.

In part (b), the output of the vineyards of France on the *x*-axis does not vary with the rainfall in California on the *y*-axis. The curve is vertical.

MyEconLab animation

The Slope of a Relationship

We can measure the influence of one variable on another by the slope of the relationship. The **slope** of a relationship is the change in the value of the variable measured on the y-axis divided by the change in the value of the variable measured on the x-axis. We use the Greek letter Δ (*delta*) to represent "change in." Thus Δy means the change in the value of the variable measured on the y-axis, and Δx means the change in the value of the variable measured on the x-axis. Therefore the slope of the relationship is

$$\text{Slope} = \frac{\Delta y}{\Delta x}.$$

If a large change in the variable measured on the y-axis (Δy) is associated with a small change in the variable measured on the x-axis (Δx), the slope is large and the curve is steep. If a small change in the variable measured on the y-axis (Δy) is associated with a large change in the variable measured on the x-axis (Δx), the slope is small and the curve is flat.

We can make the idea of slope clearer by doing some calculations.

The Slope of a Straight Line

The slope of a straight line is the same regardless of where on the line you calculate it. The slope of a straight line is constant. Let's calculate the slope of the positive relationship in Fig. A1.9. In part (a),

FIGURE A1.9   The Slope of a Straight Line

(a) Positive slope

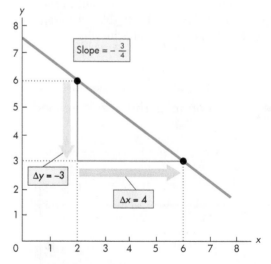

(b) Negative slope

To calculate the slope of a straight line, we divide the change in the value of the variable measured on the y-axis (Δy) by the change in the value of the variable measured on the x-axis (Δx) as we move along the line.

    Part (a) shows the calculation of a positive slope. When x increases from 2 to 6, Δx equals 4. That change in x

brings about an increase in y from 3 to 6, so Δy equals 3. The slope (Δy/Δx) equals 3/4.

    Part (b) shows the calculation of a negative slope. When x increases from 2 to 6, Δx equals 4. That increase in x brings about a decrease in y from 6 to 3, so Δy equals −3. The slope (Δy/Δx) equals −3/4.

when x increases from 2 to 6, y increases from 3 to 6. The change in x is +4—that is, Δx is 4. The change in y is +3—that is, Δy is 3. The slope of that line is

$$\frac{\Delta y}{\Delta x} = \frac{3}{4}.$$

In part (b), when x increases from 2 to 6, y decreases from 6 to 3. The change in y is *minus* 3— that is, Δy is −3. The change in x is *plus* 4—that is, Δx is 4. The slope of the curve is

$$\frac{\Delta y}{\Delta x} = \frac{-3}{4}.$$

Notice that the two slopes have the same magnitude (3/4), but the slope of the line in part (a) is positive (+3/+4 = 3/4) while that in part (b) is negative (−3/+4 = −3/4). The slope of a positive relationship is positive; the slope of a negative relationship is negative.

The Slope of a Curved Line

The slope of a curved line is trickier. The slope of a curved line is not constant, so the slope depends on where on the curved line we calculate it. There are two ways to calculate the slope of a curved line: You can calculate the slope at a point, or you can calculate the slope across an arc of the curve. Let's look at the two alternatives.

Slope at a Point   To calculate the slope at a point on a curve, you need to construct a straight line that has the same slope as the curve at the point in question. Figure A1.10 shows how this is done. Suppose you want to calculate the slope of the curve at point A. Place a ruler on the graph so that the ruler touches point A and no other point on the curve, then draw a straight line along the edge of the ruler. The straight red line is this line, and it is the tangent to the curve at point A. If the ruler touches the curve only at point A, then the slope of the curve at point A must be the same as the slope of the edge of the ruler. If the curve and the ruler do not have the same slope, the line along the edge of the ruler will cut the curve instead of just touching it.

Now that you have found a straight line with the same slope as the curve at point A, you can calculate the slope of the curve at point A by calculating the slope of the straight line. Along the straight line, as x

FIGURE A1.10   Slope at a Point

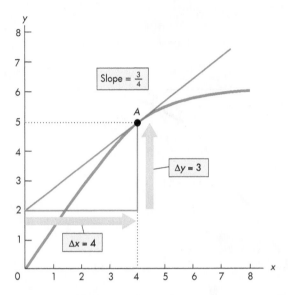

To calculate the slope of the curve at point A, draw the red line that just touches the curve at A—the tangent. The slope of this straight line is calculated by dividing the change in y by the change in x along the red line. When x increases from 0 to 4, Δx equals 4. That change in x is associated with an increase in y from 2 to 5, so Δy equals 3. The slope of the red line is 3/4, so the slope of the curve at point A is 3/4.

——— MyEconLab animation ———

increases from 0 to 4 (Δx is 4) y increases from 2 to 5 (Δy is 3). Therefore the slope of the straight line is

$$\frac{\Delta y}{\Delta x} = \frac{3}{4}.$$

So the slope of the curve at point A is 3/4.

Slope Across an Arc   An arc of a curve is a piece of a curve. Fig. A1.11 shows the same curve as in Fig. A1.10, but instead of calculating the slope at point A, we are now going to calculate the slope across the arc from point B to point C. You can see that the slope of the curve at point B is greater than at point C. When we calculate the slope across an arc, we are calculating the average slope between two points. As we move along the arc from B to C, x increases from 3 to 5 and y increases from 4.0 to 5.5. The change in x is 2 (Δx is 2), and the change in y is 1.5 (Δy is 1.5).

FIGURE A1.11   Slope Across an Arc

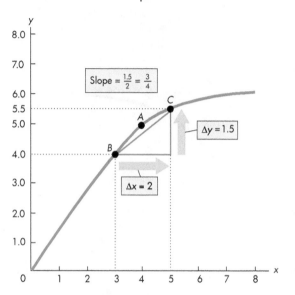

To calculate the average slope of the curve along the arc *BC*, draw a straight line from point *B* to point *C*. The slope of the line *BC* is calculated by dividing the change in *y* by the change in *x*. In moving from *B* to *C*, the increase in *x* is 2 (Δ*x* equals 2) and the change in *y* is 1.5 (Δ*y* equals 1.5). The slope of the line *BC* is 1.5 divided by 2, or 3/4. So the slope of the curve across the arc *BC* is 3/4.

— MyEconLab animation —

Therefore the slope is

$$\frac{\Delta y}{\Delta x} = \frac{1.5}{2} = \frac{3}{4}.$$

So the slope of the curve across the arc *BC* is 3/4.

This calculation gives us the slope of the curve between points *B* and *C*. The actual slope calculated is the slope of the straight line from *B* to *C*. This slope approximates the average slope of the curve along the arc *BC*. In this particular example, the slope across the arc *BC* is identical to the slope of the curve at point *A*, but the calculation of the slope of a curve does not always work out so neatly. You might have fun constructing some more examples and a few counter examples.

You now know how to make and interpret a graph. So far, we've limited our attention to graphs of two variables. We're now going to learn how to graph more than two variables.

◆ Graphing Relationships Among More Than Two Variables

We have seen that we can graph the relationship between two variables as a point formed by the *x*- and *y*-coordinates in a two-dimensional graph. You might be thinking that although a two-dimensional graph is informative, most of the things in which you are likely to be interested involve relationships among many variables, not just two. For example, the amount of ice cream consumed depends on the price of ice cream and the temperature. If ice cream is expensive and the temperature is low, people eat much less ice cream than when ice cream is inexpensive and the temperature is high. For any given price of ice cream, the quantity consumed varies with the temperature; and for any given temperature, the quantity of ice cream consumed varies with its price.

Figure A1.12 shows a relationship among three variables. The table shows the number of gallons of ice cream consumed each day at two different temperatures and at a number of different prices of ice cream. How can we graph these numbers?

To graph a relationship that involves more than two variables, we use the *ceteris paribus* assumption.

Ceteris Paribus

Ceteris paribus (often shortened to *cet par*) means "if all other relevant things remain the same." To isolate the relationship of interest in a laboratory experiment, a scientist holds everything constant except for the variable whose effect is being studied. Economists use the same method to graph a relationship that has more than two variables.

Figure A1.12 shows an example. There, you can see what happens to the quantity of ice cream consumed when the price of ice cream varies but the temperature is held constant.

The curve labeled 70°F shows the relationship between ice cream consumption and the price of ice cream if the temperature remains at 70°F. The numbers used to plot that curve are those in the first two columns of the table. For example, if the temperature is 70°F, 10 gallons are consumed when the price is $2.75 a scoop and 18 gallons are consumed when the price is $2.25 a scoop.

The curve labeled 90°F shows the relationship between ice cream consumption and the price of ice cream if the temperature remains at 90°F. The

FIGURE A1.12   Graphing a Relationship Among Three Variables

Price (dollars per scoop)	Ice cream consumption (gallons per day)	
	70°F	90°F
2.00	25	50
2.25	18	36
2.50	13	26
2.75	**10**	**20**
3.00	7	14
3.25	5	10
3.50	3	6

Ice cream consumption depends on its price and the temperature. The table tells us how many gallons of ice cream are consumed each day at different prices and two different temperatures. For example, if the price is $2.75 a scoop and the temperature is 70°F, 10 gallons of ice cream are consumed.

To graph a relationship among three variables, the value of one variable is held constant. The graph shows the relationship between price and consumption when temperature is held constant. One curve holds temperature at 70°F and the other holds it at 90°F.

A change in the price of ice cream brings a movement along one of the curves—along the blue curve at 70°F and along the red curve at 90°F.

When the temperature *rises* from 70°F to 90°F, the curve that shows the relationship between consumption and price *shifts* rightward from the blue curve to the red curve.

MyEconLab animation

numbers used to plot that curve are those in the first and third columns of the table. For example, if the temperature is 90°F, 20 gallons are consumed when the price is $2.75 a scoop and 36 gallons are consumed when the price is $2.25 a scoop.

When the price of ice cream changes but the temperature is constant, you can think of what happens in the graph as a movement along one of the curves. At 70°F there is a movement along the blue curve and at 90°F there is a movement along the red curve.

When Other Things Change

The temperature is held constant along each of the curves in Fig. A1.12, but in reality the temperature

changes. When that event occurs, you can think of what happens in the graph as a shift of the curve. When the temperature rises from 70°F to 90°F, the curve that shows the relationship between ice cream consumption and the price of ice cream shifts rightward from the blue curve to the red curve.

You will encounter these ideas of movements along and shifts of curves at many points in your study of economics. Think carefully about what you've just learned and make up some examples (with assumed numbers) about other relationships.

With what you have learned about graphs, you can move forward with your study of economics. There are no graphs in this book that are more complicated than those that have been explained in this appendix.

MATHEMATICAL NOTE
Equations of Straight Lines

If a straight line in a graph describes the relationship between two variables, we call it a linear relationship. Figure 1 shows the *linear relationship* between a person's expenditure and income. This person spends $100 a week (by borrowing or spending previous savings) when income is zero. Out of each dollar earned, this person spends 50 cents (and saves 50 cents).

All linear relationships are described by the same general equation. We call the quantity that is measured on the horizontal axis (or *x*-axis) *x,* and we call the quantity that is measured on the vertical axis (or *y*-axis) *y*. In the case of Fig. 1, *x* is income and *y* is expenditure.

A Linear Equation

The equation that describes a straight-line relationship between *x* and *y* is

$$y = a + bx.$$

In this equation, *a* and *b* are fixed numbers and they are called *constants*. The values of *x* and *y* vary, so these numbers are called *variables*. Because the equation describes a straight line, the equation is called a *linear equation.*

The equation tells us that when the value of *x* is zero, the value of *y* is *a*. We call the constant *a* the *y*-axis intercept. The reason is that on the graph the straight line hits the *y*-axis at a value equal to *a*. Figure 1 illustrates the *y*-axis intercept.

For positive values of *x*, the value of *y* exceeds *a*. The constant *b* tells us by how much *y* increases above *a* as *x* increases. The constant *b* is the slope of the line.

Slope of Line

As we explain in the chapter, the *slope* of a relationship is the change in the value of *y* divided by the change in the value of *x*. We use the Greek letter Δ (delta) to represent "change in." So Δy means the change in the value of the variable measured on the *y*-axis, and Δx means the change in the value of the variable measured on the *x*-axis. Therefore the slope of the relationship is

$$\text{Slope} = \frac{\Delta y}{\Delta x}.$$

To see why the slope is *b*, suppose that initially the value of *x* is x_1, or $200 in Fig. 2. The corresponding value of *y* is y_1, also $200 in Fig. 2. The equation of the line tells us that

$$y_1 = a + bx_1. \tag{1}$$

Now the value of *x* increases by Δx to $x_1 + \Delta x$ (or $400 in Fig. 2). And the value of *y* increases by Δy to $y_1 + \Delta y$ (or $300 in Fig. 2).

The equation of the line now tells us that

$$y_1 + \Delta y = a + b(x_1 + \Delta x). \tag{2}$$

Figure 1 **Linear Relationship**

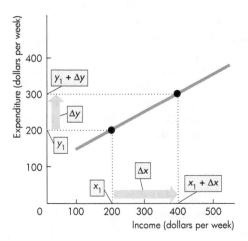

Figure 2 **Calculating Slope**

To calculate the slope of the line, subtract equation (1) from equation (2) to obtain

$$\Delta y = b\Delta x \qquad (3)$$

and now divide equation (3) by Δx to obtain

$$\Delta y/\Delta x = b.$$

So the slope of the line is b.

Position of Line

The y-axis intercept determines the position of the line on the graph. Figure 3 illustrates the relationship between the y-axis intercept and the position of the line. In this graph, the y-axis measures saving and the x-axis measures income.

When the y-axis intercept, a, is positive, the line hits the y-axis at a positive value of y—as the blue line does. Its y-axis intercept is 100. When the y-axis intercept, a, is zero, the line hits the y-axis at the origin—as the purple line does. Its y-axis intercept is 0. When the y-axis intercept, a, is negative, the line hits the y-axis at a negative value of y—as the red line does. Its y-axis intercept is -100.

As the equations of the three lines show, the value of the y-axis intercept does not influence the slope of the line. All three lines have a slope equal to 0.5.

Positive Relationships

Figure 1 shows a positive relationship—the two variables x and y move in the same direction. All positive relationships have a slope that is positive. In the equation of the line, the constant b is positive. In this example, the y-axis intercept, a, is 100. The slope b equals $\Delta y/\Delta x$, which in Fig. 2 is 100/200 or 0.5. The equation of the line is

$$y = 100 + 0.5x.$$

Negative Relationships

Figure 4 shows a negative relationship—the two variables x and y move in the opposite direction. All negative relationships have a slope that is negative. In the equation of the line, the constant b is negative. In the example in Fig. 4, the y-axis intercept, a, is 30. The slope, b, equals $\Delta y/\Delta x$, which is $-20/2$ or -10. The equation of the line is

$$y = 30 + (-10)x$$

or

$$y = 30 - 10x.$$

Example

A straight line has a y-axis intercept of 50 and a slope of 2. What is the equation of this line?
The equation of a straight line is

$$y = a + bx$$

where a is the y-axis intercept and b is the slope. So the equation is

$$y = 50 + 2x.$$

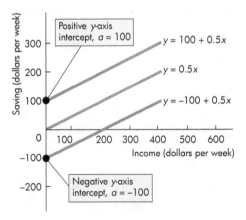

Figure 3 The y-Axis Intercept

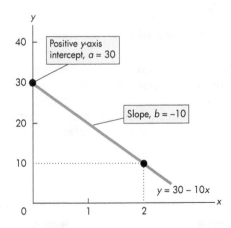

Figure 4 Negative Relationship

REVIEW QUIZ

1 Explain how we "read" the three graphs in Figs. A1.1 and A1.2.
2 Explain what scatter diagrams show and why we use them.
3 Explain how we "read" the three scatter diagrams in Figs. A1.3 and A1.4.
4 Draw a graph to show the relationship between two variables that move in the same direction.
5 Draw a graph to show the relationship between two variables that move in opposite directions.
6 Draw a graph to show the relationship between two variables that has (i) a maximum and (ii) a minimum.

7 Which of the relationships in Questions 4 and 5 is a positive relationship and which is a negative relationship?
8 What are the two ways of calculating the slope of a curved line?
9 How do we graph a relationship among more than two variables?
10 Explain what change will bring a *movement along* a curve.
11 Explain what change will bring a *shift* of a curve.

You can work these questions in Study Plan 1.A and get instant feedback.   MyEconLab

SUMMARY

Key Points

Graphing Data (pp. 15–18)

■ A graph is made by plotting the values of two variables x and y at a point that corresponds to their values measured along the x-axis and the y-axis.
■ A scatter diagram is a graph that plots the values of two variables for a number of different values of each.
■ A scatter diagram shows the relationship between the two variables. It shows whether they are positively related, negatively related, or unrelated.

Graphs Used in Economic Models (pp. 18–21)

■ Graphs are used to show relationships among variables in economic models.
■ Relationships can be positive (an upward-sloping curve), negative (a downward-sloping curve), positive and then negative (have a maximum point), negative and then positive (have a minimum point), or unrelated (a horizontal or vertical curve).

The Slope of a Relationship (pp. 22–24)

■ The slope of a relationship is calculated as the change in the value of the variable measured on the y-axis divided by the change in the value of the variable measured on the x-axis—that is, $\Delta y/\Delta x$.
■ A straight line has a constant slope.
■ A curved line has a varying slope. To calculate the slope of a curved line, we calculate the slope at a point or across an arc.

Graphing Relationships Among More Than Two Variables (pp. 24–25)

■ To graph a relationship among more than two variables, we hold constant the values of all the variables except two.
■ We then plot the value of one of the variables against the value of another.
■ A *cet par* change in the value of a variable on an axis of a graph brings a movement along the curve.
■ A change in the value of a variable held constant along the curve brings a shift of the curve.

Key Terms

STUDY PLAN PROBLEMS AND APPLICATIONS

MyEconLab   You can work Problems 1 to 11 in MyEconLab Chapter 1A Study Plan and get instant feedback.

Use the following spreadsheet to work Problems 1 to 3. The spreadsheet provides data on the U.S. economy: Column A is the year, column B is the inflation rate, column C is the interest rate, column D is the growth rate, and column E is the unemployment rate.

	A	B	C	D	E
1	2001	1.6	3.4	1.1	4.7
2	2002	2.4	1.6	1.8	5.8
3	2003	1.9	1.0	2.5	6.0
4	2004	3.3	1.4	3.5	5.5
5	2005	3.4	3.2	3.1	5.1
6	2006	2.5	4.7	2.7	4.6
7	2007	4.1	4.4	1.9	4.6
8	2008	0.1	1.5	-0.3	5.8
9	2009	2.7	0.2	-3.5	9.3
10	2010	1.5	0.1	3.0	9.6
11	2011	3.0	0.1	1.7	9.0

1. Draw a scatter diagram of the inflation rate and the interest rate. Describe the relationship.
2. Draw a scatter diagram of the growth rate and the unemployment rate. Describe the relationship.
3. Draw a scatter diagram of the interest rate and the unemployment rate. Describe the relationship.

Use the following news clip to work Problems 4 to 6.
Avengers **Shatters More Records:**

Movie	Theaters (number)	Revenue (dollars per theater)
Marvel's The Avengers	4,349	$23,696
Dark Shadows	3,755	$7,906
Think Like a Man	2,052	$2,834
The Hunger Games	2,531	$1,780

Source: boxofficemojo.com, Data for weekend of May 11–12, 2012

4. Draw a graph of the relationship between the revenue per theater on the *y*-axis and the number of theaters on the *x*-axis. Describe the relationship.
5. Calculate the slope of the relationship between 3,755 and 2,052 theaters.
6. Calculate the slope of the relationship between 2,052 and 2,531 theaters.

7. Calculate the slope of the following relationship.

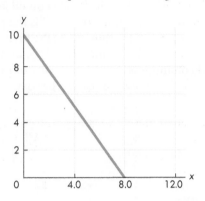

Use the following relationship to work Problems 8 and 9.

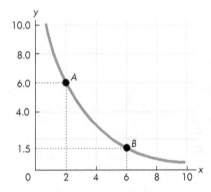

8. Calculate the slope of the relationship at point *A* and at point *B*.
9. Calculate the slope across the arc *AB*.

Use the following table to work Problems 10 and 11. The table gives the price of a balloon ride, the temperature, and the number of rides a day.

Price (dollars per ride)	Balloon rides (number per day)		
	50°F	70°F	90°F
5	32	40	50
10	27	32	40
15	18	27	32

10. Draw a graph to show the relationship between the price and the number of rides, when the temperature is 70°F. Describe this relationship.
11. What happens in the graph in Problem 10 if the temperature rises to 90°F?

ADDITIONAL PROBLEMS AND APPLICATIONS

MyEconLab   You can work these problems in MyEconLab if assigned by your instructor.

Use the following spreadsheet to work Problems 12 to 14. The spreadsheet provides data on oil and gasoline: Column A is the year, column B is the price of oil (dollars per barrel), column C is the price of gasoline (cents per gallon), column D is U.S. oil production, and column E is the U.S. quantity of gasoline refined (both in millions of barrels per day).

	A	B	C	D	E
1	2001	26	146	5.8	8.6
2	2002	26	139	5.7	8.8
3	2003	31	160	5.7	8.9
4	2004	42	190	5.4	9.1
5	2005	57	231	5.2	9.2
6	2006	66	262	5.1	9.3
7	2007	72	284	5.1	9.3
8	2008	100	330	5.0	9.0
9	2009	62	241	5.4	9.0
10	2010	79	284	5.5	9.0
11	2011	95	358	5.7	8.7

12. Draw a scatter diagram of the price of oil and the quantity of U.S. oil produced. Describe the relationship.
13. Draw a scatter diagram of the price of gasoline and the quantity of gasoline refined. Describe the relationship.
14. Draw a scatter diagram of the quantity of U.S. oil produced and the quantity of gasoline refined. Describe the relationship.

Use the following data to work Problems 15 to 17. Draw a graph that shows the relationship between the two variables x and y:

x	0	1	2	3	4	5
y	25	24	22	18	12	0

15. a. Is the relationship positive or negative?
    b. Does the slope of the relationship become steeper or flatter as the value of x increases?
    c. Think of some economic relationships that might be similar to this one.
16. Calculate the slope of the relationship between x and y when x equals 3.
17. Calculate the slope of the relationship across the arc as x increases from 4 to 5.
18. Calculate the slope of the curve in the figure in the next column at point A.

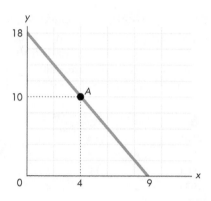

Use the following relationship to work Problems 19 and 20.

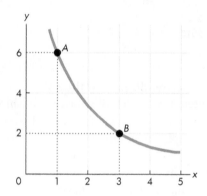

19. Calculate the slope at point A and at point B.
20. Calculate the slope across the arc AB.

Use the following table to work Problems 21 to 23. The table gives information about umbrellas: price, the number purchased, and rainfall in inches.

Price (dollars per umbrella)	Umbrellas (number purchased per day)		
	0 inches	1 inch	2 inches
20	4	7	8
30	2	4	7
40	1	2	4

21. Draw a graph to show the relationship between the price and the number of umbrellas purchased, holding the amount of rainfall constant at 1 inch. Describe this relationship.
22. What happens in the graph in Problem 21 if the price rises and rainfall is constant?
23. What happens in the graph in Problem 21 if the rainfall increases from 1 inch to 2 inches?

2

THE ECONOMIC PROBLEM

After studying this chapter, you will be able to:

◆ Define the production possibilities frontier and use it to calculate opportunity cost

◆ Distinguish between production possibilities and preferences and describe an efficient allocation of resources

◆ Explain how current production choices expand future production possibilities

◆ Explain how specialization and trade expand production possibilities

◆ Describe the economic institutions that coordinate decisions

Is producing ethanol from corn driving up the cost of food? How do we know when we are using our resources efficiently? How can we become more productive? Is it really true that both buyers and sellers gain from trade?

In this chapter, you study an economic model that answers these questions.

At the end of the chapter, in *Reading Between the Lines*, we'll apply what you've learned to understanding why food costs more today than it did a few years ago and how producing ethanol *is* one of the sources of higher food costs.

Production Possibilities and Opportunity Cost

Every working day, in mines, factories, shops, and offices and on farms and construction sites across the United States, 142 million people produce a vast variety of goods and services valued at $60 billion. But the quantities of goods and services that we can produce are limited by our available resources and by technology. And if we want to increase our production of one good, we must decrease our production of something else—we face a tradeoff. You are now going to study the limits to production.

The **production possibilities frontier** (*PPF*) is the boundary between those combinations of goods and services that can be produced and those that cannot. To illustrate the *PPF*, we look at a *model economy* in which the quantities produced of only two goods change, while the quantities produced of all the other goods and services remains the same.

Let's look at the production possibilities frontier for cola and pizza, which represent *any* pair of goods or services.

Production Possibilities Frontier

The *production possibilities frontier* for cola and pizza shows the limits to the production of these two goods, given the total resources and technology available to produce them. Figure 2.1 shows this production possibilities frontier. The table lists combinations of the quantities of pizza and cola that can be produced in a month and the figure graphs these combinations. The *x*-axis shows the quantity of pizzas produced, and the *y*-axis shows the quantity of cola produced.

The *PPF* illustrates *scarcity* because the points outside the frontier are *unattainable*. These points describe wants that can't be satisfied.

We can produce at any point *inside* the *PPF* or *on* the *PPF*. These points are *attainable*. For example, we can produce 4 million pizzas and 5 million cans of cola. Figure 2.1 shows this combination as point *E* and as possibility *E* in the table.

Moving along the *PPF* from point *E* to point *D* (possibility *D* in the table) we produce more cola and less pizza: 9 million cans of cola and 3 million pizzas. Or moving in the opposite direction from point *E* to point *F* (possibility *F* in the table), we produce more pizza and less cola: 5 million pizzas and no cola.

FIGURE 2.1   Production Possibilities Frontier

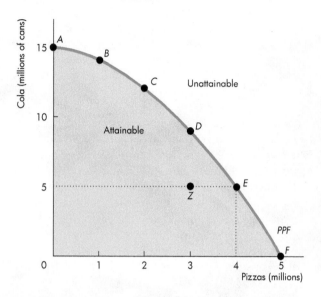

Possibility	Pizzas (millions)		Cola (millions of cans)
A	0	and	15
B	1	and	14
C	2	and	12
D	3	and	9
E	4	and	5
F	5	and	0

The table lists six production possibilities for cola and pizzas. Row *A* tells us that if we produce no pizzas, the maximum quantity of cola we can produce is 15 million cans. Points *A*, *B*, *C*, *D*, *E*, and *F* in the figure represent the rows of the table. The curve passing through these points is the production possibilities frontier (*PPF*).

The *PPF* separates the attainable from the unattainable. Production is possible at any point *inside* the orange area or *on* the frontier. Points outside the frontier are unattainable. Points inside the frontier, such as point *Z*, are inefficient because resources are wasted or misallocated. At such points, it is possible to use the available resources to produce more of either or both goods.

MyEconLab animation

Production Efficiency

We achieve **production efficiency** if we produce goods and services at the lowest possible cost. This outcome occurs at all the points *on the PPF*. At points *inside* the *PPF*, production is inefficient because we are giving up more than necessary of one good to produce a given quantity of the other good.

For example, at point *Z* in Fig. 2.1, we produce 3 million pizzas and 5 million cans of cola, but we have enough resources to produce 3 million pizzas and 9 million cans of cola. Our pizzas cost more cola than necessary. We can get them for a lower cost. Only when we produce *on the PPF* do we incur the lowest possible cost of production.

Production inside the *PPF* is *inefficient* because resources are either *unused* or *misallocated* or both.

Resources are *unused* when they are idle but could be working. For example, we might leave some of the factories idle or some workers unemployed.

Resources are *misallocated* when they are assigned to tasks for which they are not the best match. For example, we might assign skilled pizza chefs to work in a cola factory and skilled cola workers to cook pizza in a pizzeria. We could get more pizzas *and* more cola if we reassigned these workers to the tasks that more closely match their skills.

Tradeoff Along the *PPF*

A choice *along* the *PPF* involves a *tradeoff*. Tradeoffs like that between cola and pizza arise in every imaginable real-world situation in which a choice must be made. At any given time, we have a fixed amount of labor, land, capital, and entrepreneurship and a given state of technology. We can employ these resources and technology to produce goods and services, but we are limited in what we can produce.

When doctors want to spend more on AIDS and cancer research, they face a tradeoff: more medical research for less of some other things. When Congress wants to spend more on education and health care, it faces a tradeoff: more education and health care for less national defense or homeland security. When an environmental group argues for less logging, it is suggesting a tradeoff: greater conservation of endangered wildlife for less paper. When you want a higher grade on your next test, you face a tradeoff: spend more time studying and less leisure or sleep time.

All the tradeoffs you've just considered involve a cost—an opportunity cost.

Opportunity Cost

The **opportunity cost** of an action is the highest-valued alternative forgone. The *PPF* makes this idea precise and enables us to calculate opportunity cost. Along the *PPF*, there are only two goods, so there is only one alternative forgone: some quantity of the other good. To produce more pizzas we must produce less cola. The opportunity cost of producing an additional pizza is the cola we *must* forgo. Similarly, the opportunity cost of producing an additional can of cola is the quantity of pizza we must forgo.

In Fig. 2.1, if we move from point *C* to point *D*, we produce an additional 1 million pizzas but 3 million fewer cans of cola. The additional 1 million pizzas *cost* 3 million cans of cola. Or 1 pizza costs 3 cans of cola.

Opportunity Cost Is a Ratio

Opportunity cost is a ratio. It is the decrease in the quantity produced of one good divided by the increase in the quantity produced of another good as we move along the production possibilities frontier.

Because opportunity cost is a ratio, the opportunity cost of producing an additional can of cola is equal to the *inverse* of the opportunity cost of producing an additional pizza. Check this proposition by returning to the calculations we've just worked through. When we move along the *PPF* from *C* to *D*, the opportunity cost of a pizza is 3 cans of cola. The inverse of 3 is 1/3. If we decrease the production of pizza and increase the production of cola by moving from *D* to *C*, the opportunity cost of a can of cola must be 1/3 of a pizza. That is exactly the number that we calculated for the move from *D* to *C*.

Increasing Opportunity Cost

The opportunity cost of a pizza increases as the quantity of pizzas produced increases. The outward-bowed shape of the *PPF* reflects increasing opportunity cost. When we produce a large quantity of cola and a small quantity of pizza—between points *A* and *B* in Fig. 2.1—the frontier has a gentle slope. An increase in the quantity of pizzas costs a small decrease in the quantity of cola—the opportunity cost of a pizza is a small quantity of cola.

When we produce a large quantity of pizzas and a small quantity of cola—between points *E* and *F* in Fig. 2.1—the frontier is steep. A given increase in the quantity of pizzas *costs* a large decrease in the quantity of cola, so the opportunity cost of a pizza is a large quantity of cola.

ECONOMICS IN THE NEWS

Cost of Global Food Up Again

The cost of global food has increased by 8 percent since December 2011. All key food items cost more, except for rice. Asia's strong demand for food imports has contributed to this increase, notwithstanding bumper harvests.

Source: *Food Price Watch*, World Bank, April 2012

THE QUESTIONS

- How does the *PPF* illustrate the effect of Asia's strong demand for food imports on the cost of food?
- How does the *PPF* illustrate the effect of a bumper harvest?

THE ANSWERS

- The figure shows the global *PPF* for food and other goods and services.
- Before the bumper harvest, the *PPF* is PPF_0 and before Asia's strong demand for food, the world is producing at point *A*.
- Asia's strong demand for food brings an increase in food production and a decrease in the production of other goods and services, which is illustrated as a movement along the *PPF* from point *A* to point *B*.
- At point *B*, the *PPF* slope is steeper than at point *A*, which means that the opportunity cost of food is higher at point *B* than at point *A*.

- A bumper harvest increases the production of food at each level of production of other goods and services.
- The *PPF* illustrates the effects of a bumper harvest as an outward shift of the *PPF* from PPF_0 to PPF_1 in the figure.
- The bumper harvest lowered the opportunity cost of food, but the news clip says that this effect was not sufficient to offset the rise in opportunity cost resulting from Asia's strong demand.

PPF for Food and Other Goods and Services

The *PPF* is bowed outward because resources are not all equally productive in all activities. People with many years of experience working for PepsiCo are good at producing cola but not very good at making pizzas. So if we move some of these people from PepsiCo to Domino's, we get a small increase in the quantity of pizzas but a large decrease in the quantity of cola.

Similarly, people who have spent years working at Domino's are good at producing pizzas, but they have no idea how to produce cola. So if we move some of these people from Domino's to PepsiCo, we get a small increase in the quantity of cola but a large decrease in the quantity of pizzas. The more of either good we try to produce, the less productive are the additional resources we use to produce that good and the larger is the opportunity cost of a unit of that good.

How do we choose among the points on the *PPF*? How do we know which point is the best?

REVIEW QUIZ

1 How does the production possibilities frontier illustrate scarcity?
2 How does the production possibilities frontier illustrate production efficiency?
3 How does the production possibilities frontier show that every choice involves a tradeoff?
4 How does the production possibilities frontier illustrate opportunity cost?
5 Why is opportunity cost a ratio?
6 Why does the *PPF* bow outward and what does that imply about the relationship between opportunity cost and the quantity produced?

You can work these questions in Study Plan 2.1 and get instant feedback.   MyEconLab

Using Resources Efficiently

We achieve *production efficiency* at every point on the *PPF*, but which point is best? The answer is the point on the *PPF* at which goods and services are produced in the quantities that provide the greatest possible benefit. When goods and services are produced at the lowest possible cost and in the quantities that provide the greatest possible benefit, we have achieved **allocative efficiency**.

The questions that we raised when we reviewed the four big issues in Chapter 1 are questions about allocative efficiency. To answer such questions, we must measure and compare costs and benefits.

The *PPF* and Marginal Cost

The **marginal cost** of a good is the opportunity cost of producing one more unit of it. We calculate marginal cost from the slope of the *PPF*. As the quantity of pizzas produced increases, the *PPF* gets steeper and the marginal cost of a pizza increases. Figure 2.2 illustrates the calculation of the marginal cost of a pizza.

Begin by finding the opportunity cost of pizza in blocks of 1 million pizzas. The cost of the first million pizzas is 1 million cans of cola; the cost of the second million pizzas is 2 million cans of cola; the cost of the third million pizzas is 3 million cans of cola, and so on. The bars in part (a) illustrate these calculations.

The bars in part (b) show the cost of an average pizza in each of the 1 million pizza blocks. Focus on the third million pizzas—the move from *C* to *D* in part (a). Over this range, because 1 million pizzas cost 3 million cans of cola, one of these pizzas, on average, costs 3 cans of cola—the height of the bar in part (b).

Next, find the opportunity cost of each additional pizza—the marginal cost of a pizza. The marginal cost of a pizza increases as the quantity of pizzas produced increases. The marginal cost at point *C* is less than it is at point *D*. On average over the range from *C* to *D*, the marginal cost of a pizza is 3 cans of cola. But it exactly equals 3 cans of cola only in the middle of the range between *C* and *D*.

The red dot in part (b) indicates that the marginal cost of a pizza is 3 cans of cola when 2.5 million pizzas are produced. Each black dot in part (b) is interpreted in the same way. The red curve that passes through these dots, labeled *MC*, is the marginal cost curve. It shows the marginal cost of a pizza at each quantity of pizzas as we move along the *PPF*.

FIGURE 2.2   The *PPF* and Marginal Cost

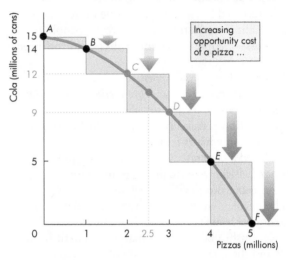

(a) *PPF* and opportunity cost

(b) Marginal cost

Marginal cost is calculated from the slope of the *PPF*. As the quantity of pizzas produced increases, the *PPF* gets steeper and the marginal cost of a pizza increases. The bars in part (a) show the opportunity cost of pizza in blocks of 1 million pizzas. The bars in part (b) show the cost of an average pizza in each of these 1 million blocks. The red curve, *MC*, shows the marginal cost of a pizza at each point along the *PPF*. This curve passes through the center of each of the bars in part (b).

— MyEconLab animation —

Preferences and Marginal Benefit

The **marginal benefit** from a good or service is the benefit received from consuming one more unit of it. This benefit is subjective. It depends on people's **preferences**—people's likes and dislikes and the intensity of those feelings.

Marginal benefit and *preferences* stand in sharp contrast to *marginal cost* and *production possibilities*. Preferences describe what people like and want and the production possibilities describe the limits or constraints on what is feasible.

We need a concrete way of illustrating preferences that parallels the way we illustrate the limits to production using the *PPF*.

The device that we use to illustrate preferences is the **marginal benefit curve**, which is a curve that shows the relationship between the marginal benefit from a good and the quantity consumed of that good. Note that the *marginal benefit curve* is *unrelated* to the *PPF* and cannot be derived from it.

We measure the marginal benefit from a good or service by the most that people are *willing to pay* for an additional unit of it. The idea is that you are willing to pay less for a good than it is worth to you but you are not willing to pay more: The most you are willing to pay for something is its marginal benefit.

It is a general principle that the more we have of any good or service, the smaller is its marginal benefit and the less we are willing to pay for an additional unit of it. This tendency is so widespread and strong that we call it a principle—the *principle of decreasing marginal benefit*.

The basic reason why marginal benefit decreases is that we like variety. The more we consume of any one good or service, the more we tire of it and would prefer to switch to something else.

Think about your willingness to pay for a pizza. If pizza is hard to come by and you can buy only a few slices a year, you might be willing to pay a high price to get an additional slice. But if pizza is all you've eaten for the past few days, you are willing to pay almost nothing for another slice.

You've learned to think about cost as opportunity cost, not as a dollar cost. You can think about marginal benefit and willingness to pay in the same way. The marginal benefit, measured by what you are willing to pay for something, is the quantity of other goods and services that you are willing to forgo. Let's continue with the example of cola and pizza and illustrate preferences this way.

FIGURE 2.3   Preferences and the Marginal Benefit Curve

Possibility	Pizzas (millions)	Willingness to pay (cans of cola per pizza)
A	0.5	5
B	1.5	4
C	2.5	3
D	3.5	2
E	4.5	1

The smaller the quantity of pizzas available, the more cola people are willing to give up for an additional pizza. With 0.5 million pizzas available, people are willing to pay 5 cans of cola per pizza. But with 4.5 million pizzas, people are willing to pay only 1 can of cola per pizza. Willingness to pay measures marginal benefit. A universal feature of people's preferences is that marginal benefit decreases.

—— MyEconLab animation ——

Figure 2.3 illustrates preferences as the willingness to pay for pizza in terms of cola. In row *A*, with 0.5 million pizzas available, people are willing to pay 5 cans of cola per pizza. As the quantity of pizzas increases, the amount that people are willing to pay for a pizza falls. With 4.5 million pizzas available, people are willing to pay only 1 can of cola per pizza.

Let's now use the concepts of marginal cost and marginal benefit to describe allocative efficiency.

FIGURE 2.4 Efficient Use of Resources

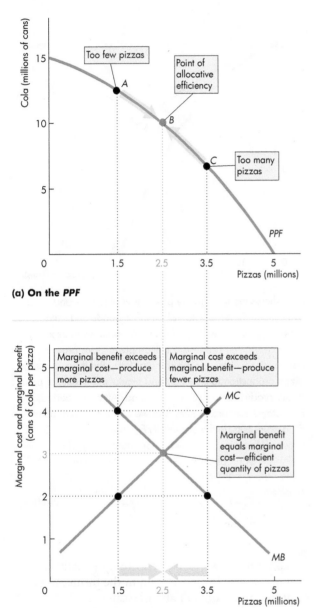

(a) On the PPF

(b) Marginal benefit equals marginal cost

The greater the quantity of pizzas produced, the smaller is the marginal benefit (MB) from pizza—the less cola people are willing to give up to get an additional pizza. But the greater the quantity of pizzas produced, the greater is the marginal cost (MC) of a pizza—the more cola people must give up to get an additional pizza. When marginal benefit equals marginal cost, resources are being used efficiently.

MyEconLab animation

Allocative Efficiency

At *any* point on the *PPF*, we cannot produce more of one good without giving up some other good. At the *best* point on the *PPF*, we cannot produce more of one good without giving up some other good that provides greater benefit. We are producing at the point of allocative efficiency—the point on the *PPF* that we prefer above all other points.

Suppose in Fig. 2.4, we produce 1.5 million pizzas. The marginal cost of a pizza is 2 cans of cola, and the marginal benefit from a pizza is 4 cans of cola. Because someone values an additional pizza more highly than it costs to produce, we can get more value from our resources by moving some of them out of producing cola and into producing pizza.

Now suppose we produce 3.5 million pizzas. The marginal cost of a pizza is now 4 cans of cola, but the marginal benefit from a pizza is only 2 cans of cola. Because the additional pizza costs more to produce than anyone thinks it is worth, we can get more value from our resources by moving some of them away from producing pizza and into producing cola.

Suppose we produce 2.5 million pizzas. Marginal cost and marginal benefit are now equal at 3 cans of cola. This allocation of resources between pizzas and cola is efficient. If more pizzas are produced, the forgone cola is worth more than the additional pizzas. If fewer pizzas are produced, the forgone pizzas are worth more than the additional cola.

REVIEW QUIZ

1 What is marginal cost? How is it measured?
2 What is marginal benefit? How is it measured?
3 How does the marginal benefit from a good change as the quantity produced of that good increases?
4 What is allocative efficiency and how does it relate to the production possibilities frontier?
5 What conditions must be satisfied if resources are used efficiently?

You can work these questions in Study Plan 2.2 and get instant feedback.   MyEconLab

You now understand the limits to production and the conditions under which resources are used efficiently. Your next task is to study the expansion of production possibilities.

Economic Growth

During the past 30 years, production per person in the United States has doubled. The expansion of production possibilities is called **economic growth**. Economic growth increases our *standard of living*, but it doesn't overcome scarcity and avoid opportunity cost. To make our economy grow, we face a trade-off—the faster we make production grow, the greater is the opportunity cost of economic growth.

The Cost of Economic Growth

Economic growth comes from technological change and capital accumulation. **Technological change** is the development of new goods and of better ways of producing goods and services. **Capital accumulation** is the growth of capital resources, including *human capital*.

Technological change and capital accumulation have vastly expanded our production possibilities. We can produce automobiles that provide us with more transportation than was available when we had only horses and carriages. We can produce satellites that provide global communications on a much larger scale than that available with the earlier cable technology. But if we use our resources to develop new technologies and produce capital, we must decrease our production of consumption goods and services. New technologies and new capital have an opportunity cost. Let's look at this opportunity cost.

Instead of studying the *PPF* of pizzas and cola, we'll hold the quantity of cola produced constant and examine the *PPF* for pizzas and pizza ovens. Figure 2.5 shows this *PPF* as the blue curve PPF_0. If we devote no resources to producing pizza ovens, we produce at point *A*. If we produce 3 million pizzas, we can produce 6 pizza ovens at point *B*. If we produce no pizza, we can produce 10 ovens at point *C*.

The amount by which our production possibilities expand depends on the resources we devote to technological change and capital accumulation. If we devote no resources to this activity (point *A*), our *PPF* remains the blue curve PPF_0 in Fig. 2.5. If we cut the current pizza production and produce 6 ovens (point *B*), then in the future, we'll have more capital and our *PPF* will rotate outward to the position shown by the red curve PPF_1. The fewer resources we use for producing pizza and the more resources we use for producing ovens, the greater is the expansion of our future production possibilities.

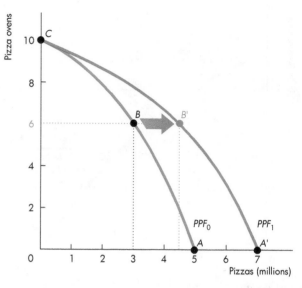

FIGURE 2.5   Economic Growth

PPF_0 shows the limits to the production of pizzas and pizza ovens, with the production of all other goods and services remaining the same. If we devote no resources to producing pizza ovens and produce 5 million pizzas, our production possibilities will remain the same at PPF_0. But if we decrease pizza production to 3 million and produce 6 ovens, at point *B*, our production possibilities expand. After one period, the *PPF* rotates outward to PPF_1 and we can produce at point *B'*, a point outside the original PPF_0. We can rotate the *PPF* outward, but we cannot avoid opportunity cost. The opportunity cost of producing more pizzas in the future is fewer pizzas today.

MyEconLab animation

Economic growth brings enormous benefits in the form of increased consumption in the future, but it is not free and it doesn't abolish scarcity.

In Fig. 2.5, to make economic growth happen we must use some resources to produce new ovens, which leaves fewer resources to produce pizzas. To move to *B'* in the future, we must move from *A* to *B* today. The opportunity cost of more pizzas in the future is fewer pizzas today. Also, on the new *PPF*, we still face a tradeoff and opportunity cost.

The ideas about economic growth that we have explored in the setting of the pizza industry also apply to nations. Hong Kong and the United States provide a striking case study.

Economics in Action

Hong Kong Catching Up to the United States

In 1969, the production possibilities per person in the United States were more than four times those in Hong Kong (see the figure). The United States devotes one fifth of its resources to accumulating capital and in 1969 was at point *A* on its *PPF*. Hong Kong devotes one third of its resources to accumulating capital and in 1969, Hong Kong was at point *A* on its *PPF*.

Since 1969, both countries have experienced economic growth, but because Hong Kong devotes a bigger fraction of its resources to accumulating capital, its production possibilities have expanded more quickly.

By 2011, production possibilities per person in Hong Kong had reached 94 percent of those in the United States. If Hong Kong continues to devote more resources to accumulating capital than the United States does (at point *B* on its 2011 *PPF*), it will continue to grow more rapidly. But if Hong Kong decreases its capital accumulation (moving to point *D* on its 2011 *PPF*), then its rate of economic growth will slow.

Hong Kong is typical of the fast-growing Asian economies, which include Taiwan, Thailand, South Korea, China, and India. Production possibilities

Economic Growth in the United States and Hong Kong

expand in these countries by between 5 percent and almost 10 percent a year.

If such high economic growth rates are maintained, these other Asian countries will continue to close the gap between themselves and the United States, as Hong Kong is doing.

A Nation's Economic Growth

The experiences of the United States and Hong Kong make a striking example of the effects of our choices about consumption and capital accumulation on the rate of economic growth.

If a nation devotes all its factors of production to producing consumption goods and services and none to advancing technology and accumulating capital, its production possibilities in the future will be the same as they are today.

To expand production possibilities in the future, a nation must devote fewer resources to producing current consumption goods and services and some resources to accumulating capital and developing new technologies. As production possibilities expand, consumption in the future can increase. The decrease in today's consumption is the opportunity cost of tomorrow's increase in consumption.

You can work these questions in Study Plan 2.3 and get instant feedback.   MyEconLab

REVIEW QUIZ

1 What generates economic growth?
2 How does economic growth influence the production possibilities frontier?
3 What is the opportunity cost of economic growth?
4 Why has Hong Kong experienced faster economic growth than the United States?
5 Does economic growth overcome scarcity?

Next, we're going to study another way in which we expand our production possibilities—the amazing fact that *both* buyers and sellers gain from specialization and trade.

Gains from Trade

People can produce for themselves all the goods and services that they consume, or they can produce one good or a few goods and trade with others. Producing only one good or a few goods is called *specialization*. We are going to learn how people gain by specializing in the production of the good in which they have a *comparative advantage* and trading with others.

Comparative Advantage and Absolute Advantage

A person has a **comparative advantage** in an activity if that person can perform the activity at a lower opportunity cost than anyone else. Differences in opportunity costs arise from differences in individual abilities and from differences in the characteristics of other resources.

No one excels at everything. One person is an outstanding pitcher but a poor catcher; another person is a brilliant lawyer but a poor teacher. In almost all human endeavors, what one person does easily, someone else finds difficult. The same applies to land and capital. One plot of land is fertile but has no mineral deposits; another plot of land has outstanding views but is infertile. One machine has great precision but is difficult to operate; another is fast but often breaks down.

Although no one excels at everything, some people excel and can outperform others in a large number of activities—perhaps even in all activities. A person who is more productive than others has an **absolute advantage**.

Absolute advantage involves comparing productivities—production per hour—whereas comparative advantage involves comparing opportunity costs.

A person who has an absolute advantage does not have a *comparative* advantage in every activity. John Grisham is a better lawyer and a better author of fast-paced thrillers than most people. He has an absolute advantage in these two activities. But compared to others, he is a better writer than lawyer, so his *comparative* advantage is in writing.

Because ability and resources vary from one person to another, people have different opportunity costs of producing various goods. These differences in opportunity cost are the source of comparative advantage.

Let's explore the idea of comparative advantage by looking at two smoothie bars: one operated by Liz and the other operated by Joe.

Liz's Smoothie Bar Liz produces smoothies and salads. In Liz's high-tech bar, she can turn out either a smoothie or a salad every 2 minutes—see Table 2.1. If Liz spends all her time making smoothies, she can produce 30 an hour. And if she spends all her time making salads, she can also produce 30 an hour. If she splits her time equally between the two, she can produce 15 smoothies and 15 salads an hour. For each additional smoothie Liz produces, she must decrease her production of salads by one, and for each additional salad she produces, she must decrease her production of smoothies by one. So

> Liz's opportunity cost of producing 1 smoothie is 1 salad,

and

> Liz's opportunity cost of producing 1 salad is 1 smoothie.

Liz's customers buy smoothies and salads in equal quantities, so she splits her time equally between the two items and produces 15 smoothies and 15 salads an hour.

Joe's Smoothie Bar Joe also produces smoothies and salads, but his bar is smaller than Liz's. Also, Joe has only one blender, and it's a slow, old machine. Even if Joe uses all his resources to produce smoothies, he can produce only 6 an hour—see Table 2.2. But Joe is good at making salads. If he uses all his resources to make salads, he can produce 30 an hour.

Joe's ability to make smoothies and salads is the same regardless of how he splits an hour between the two tasks. He can make a salad in 2 minutes or a smoothie in 10 minutes. For each additional smoothie

---

TABLE 2.1   Liz's Production Possibilities

Item	Minutes to produce 1	Quantity per hour
Smoothies	2	30
Salads	2	30

TABLE 2.2   Joe's Production Possibilities

Item	Minutes to produce 1	Quantity per hour
Smoothies	10	6
Salads	2	30

Joe produces, he must decrease his production of salads by 5. And for each additional salad he produces, he must decrease his production of smoothies by 1/5 of a smoothie. So

> Joe's opportunity cost of producing 1 smoothie is 5 salads,

and

> Joe's opportunity cost of producing 1 salad is 1/5 of a smoothie.

Joe's customers, like Liz's, buy smoothies and salads in equal quantities. So Joe spends 50 minutes of each hour making smoothies and 10 minutes of each hour making salads. With this division of his time, Joe produces 5 smoothies and 5 salads an hour.

Liz's Comparative Advantage In which of the two activities does Liz have a comparative advantage? Recall that comparative advantage is a situation in which one person's opportunity cost of producing a good is lower than another person's opportunity cost of producing that same good. Liz has a comparative advantage in producing smoothies. Her opportunity cost of a smoothie is 1 salad, whereas Joe's opportunity cost of a smoothie is 5 salads.

Joe's Comparative Advantage If Liz has a comparative advantage in producing smoothies, Joe must have a comparative advantage in producing salads. Joe's opportunity cost of a salad is 1/5 of a smoothie, whereas Liz's opportunity cost of a salad is 1 smoothie.

Achieving the Gains from Trade

Liz and Joe run into each other one evening in a singles bar. After a few minutes of getting acquainted, Liz tells Joe about her amazing smoothie business. Her only problem, she tells Joe, is that she would like to produce more because potential customers leave when her lines get too long.

Joe is hesitant to risk spoiling his chances by telling Liz about his own struggling business, but he takes the risk. Joe explains to Liz that he spends 50 minutes of every hour making 5 smoothies and 10 minutes making 5 salads. Liz's eyes pop. "Have I got a deal for you!" she exclaims.

Here's the deal that Liz sketches on a paper napkin. Joe stops making smoothies and allocates all his time to producing salads; Liz stops making salads and allocates all her time to producing smoothies. That is, they both specialize in producing the good in which they have a comparative advantage. Together they produce 30 smoothies and 30 salads—see Table 2.3(b).

They then trade. Liz sells Joe 10 smoothies and Joe sells Liz 20 salads—the price of a smoothie is 2 salads—see Table 2.3(c).

After the trade, Joe has 10 salads—the 30 he produces minus the 20 he sells to Liz. He also has the 10 smoothies that he buys from Liz. So Joe now has increased the quantities of smoothies and salads that he can sell to his customers—see Table 2.3(d).

TABLE 2.3   Liz and Joe Gain from Trade

(a) Before trade	Liz	Joe
Smoothies	15	5
Salads	15	5

(b) Specialization	Liz	Joe
Smoothies	30	0
Salads	0	30

(c) Trade	Liz	Joe
Smoothies	sell 10	buy 10
Salads	buy 20	sell 20

(d) After trade	Liz	Joe
Smoothies	20	10
Salads	20	10

(e) Gains from trade	Liz	Joe
Smoothies	+5	+5
Salads	+5	+5

Liz has 20 smoothies—the 30 she produces minus the 10 she sells to Joe. She also has the 20 salads that she buys from Joe. Liz has increased the quantities of smoothies and salads that she can sell to her customers—see Table 2.3(d). Liz and Joe both gain 5 smoothies and 5 salads an hour—see Table 2.3(e).

To illustrate her idea, Liz grabs a fresh napkin and draws the graphs in Fig. 2.6. The blue *PPF* in part (a) shows Joe's production possibilities. Before trade, he is producing 5 smoothies and 5 salads an hour at point *A*. The blue *PPF* in part (b) shows Liz's production possibilities. Before trade, she is producing 15 smoothies and 15 salads an hour at point *A*.

Liz's proposal is that they each specialize in producing the good in which they have a comparative advantage. Joe produces 30 salads and no smoothies at point *B* on his *PPF*. Liz produces 30 smoothies and no salads at point *B* on her *PPF*.

Liz and Joe then trade smoothies and salads at a price of 2 salads per smoothie or 1/2 a smoothie per salad. Joe gets smoothies for 2 salads each, which is less than the 5 salads it costs him to produce a smoothie. Liz gets salads for 1/2 a smoothie each, which is less than the 1 smoothie that it costs her to produce a salad.

With trade, Joe has 10 smoothies and 10 salads at point *C*—a gain of 5 smoothies and 5 salads. Joe moves to a point *outside* his *PPF*.

With trade, Liz has 20 smoothies and 20 salads at point *C*—a gain of 5 smoothies and 5 salads. Liz moves to a point *outside* her *PPF*.

Despite Liz being more productive than Joe, both of them gain from specializing—producing the good in which they have a comparative advantage—and trading.

FIGURE 2.6   The Gains from Trade

(a) Joe

(b) Liz

Initially, Joe produces at point *A* on his *PPF* in part (a), and Liz produces at point *A* on her *PPF* in part (b). Joe's opportunity cost of producing a salad is less than Liz's, so Joe has a comparative advantage in producing salads. Liz's opportunity cost of producing a smoothie is less than Joe's, so Liz has a comparative advantage in producing smoothies.

If Joe specializes in making salads, he produces 30 salads and no smoothies at point *B* on his *PPF*. If Liz specializes

in making smoothies, she produces 30 smoothies and no salads at point *B* on her *PPF*. They exchange salads for smoothies along the red "Trade line." Liz buys salads from Joe for less than her opportunity cost of producing them. Joe buys smoothies from Liz for less than his opportunity cost of producing them. Each goes to point *C*—a point outside his or her *PPF*. With specialization and trade, Joe and Liz gain 5 smoothies and 5 salads each with no extra resources.

ECONOMICS IN THE NEWS

Energy Independence

Is U.S. Energy Independence Finally Within Reach?
"Energy self-sufficiency is now in sight," says energy economist Phil Verleger.... Small energy companies using such controversial techniques as hydraulic fracturing, along with horizontal drilling, are unlocking vast oil and natural gas deposits trapped in shale in places like Pennsylvania, North Dakota, and Texas.

Source *NPR*, March 7, 2012

THE DATA

Energy Production and Consumption
(quadrillion Btu)

	Production	Imports	Consumption
Coal	22	−1	21
Natural gas	25	0	25
Oil	12	24	36
Nuclear	8	0	8
Renewables	8	0	8
Total	75	23	98

THE QUESTIONS

- What energy sources does the United States buy from other countries?
- Why is the United States *not* energy independent? Use a *PPF* graph to explain your answer.
- How can it become efficient for the United States to be energy independent?

THE ANSWERS

- The data table shows that the United States imports oil—buys oil from other countries. Oil imports are double U.S. oil production and two thirds of oil consumed.
- The United States is not energy independent because other countries have a comparative advantage in energy production. It costs less to buy some of our energy from other countries than to produce it all ourselves.
- The figure shows the U.S. *PPF* for energy and all other goods and services. We produce on the *PPF* at point *A*.
- To produce 60 quadrillion Btu, the production of other goods and services falls from 100 units to 90 units. The opportunity cost of 60 quadrillion Btu of energy is 10 units of other goods and services.
- The figure also shows a red "Trade line." The United States can buy (or sell) energy along that line. (It is like the trade line in Fig. 2.6). We can move along the trade line and consume at point *B*,

by buying (importing) 20 quadrillion Btu of energy at a cost of 10 units of other good and services.

- To be energy independent, we would forgo 30 units of other goods and services and produce and consume at point *C*.
- At point *C*, the United States consumes the same amount of energy as at point *B*, but the opportunity cost of the energy is higher than the opportunity cost of imported energy.
- For it to become efficient for the United States to be energy independent, the *PPF* must shift outward and the opportunity cost of energy must fall.
- Technological advances in hydraulic fracturing (fracking) and horizontal drilling and opening more gas wells will shift the *PPF* outward and lower the opportunity cost of energy.

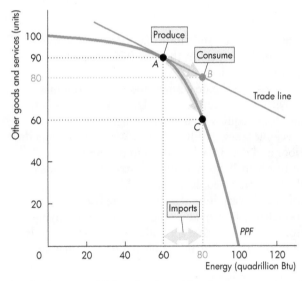

PPF for Energy and Other Goods and Services

REVIEW QUIZ

1 What gives a person a comparative advantage?
2 Distinguish between comparative advantage and absolute advantage.
3 Why do people specialize and trade?
4 What are the gains from specialization and trade?
5 What is the source of the gains from trade?

You can work these questions in Study Plan 2.4 and get instant feedback.   MyEconLab

◆ Economic Coordination

For 7 billion people to specialize and produce millions of different goods and services, individual choices must somehow be coordinated. Two competing coordination systems have been used: central economic planning and markets (see *At Issue*, p. 8).

Central economic planning works badly because economic planners don't know people's production possibilities and preferences, so production ends up *inside* the *PPF* and the wrong things are produced.

Decentralized coordination works best but to do so it needs four complementary social institutions. They are

- Firms
- Markets
- Property rights
- Money

Firms

A **firm** is an economic unit that hires factors of production and organizes them to produce and sell goods and services.

Firms coordinate a huge amount of economic activity. For example, Wal-Mart buys or rents large buildings, equips them with storage shelves and checkout lanes, and hires labor. Wal-Mart directs the labor and decides what goods to buy and sell.

But Sam Walton would not have become one of the wealthiest people in the world if Wal-Mart produced everything that it sells. He became rich by specializing in providing retail services and buying from other firms that specialize in producing goods (just as Liz and Joe did). This trade needs markets.

Markets

In ordinary speech, the word *market* means a place where people buy and sell goods such as fish, meat, fruits, and vegetables.

In economics, a **market** is any arrangement that enables buyers and sellers to get information and to do business with each other. An example is the world oil market, which is not a place but a network of producers, consumers, wholesalers, and brokers who buy and sell oil. In the world oil market, decision makers make deals by using the Internet. Enterprising individuals and firms, each pursuing their own self-interest, have profited by making markets—by standing ready to buy or sell items in which they specialize. But markets can work only when property rights exist.

Property Rights

The social arrangements that govern the ownership, use, and disposal of anything that people value are called **property rights**. *Real property* includes land and buildings—the things we call property in ordinary speech—and durable goods such as plant and equipment. *Financial property* includes stocks and bonds and money in the bank. *Intellectual property* is the intangible product of creative effort. This type of property includes books, music, computer programs, and inventions of all kinds and is protected by copyrights and patents.

Where property rights are enforced, people have the incentive to specialize and produce the goods and services in which they have a comparative advantage. Where people can steal the production of others, resources are devoted not to production but to protecting possessions.

Money

Money is any commodity or token that is generally acceptable as a means of payment. Liz and Joe don't need money. They can exchange salads and smoothies. In principle, trade in markets can exchange any item for any other item. But you can perhaps imagine how complicated life would be if we exchanged goods for other goods. The "invention" of money makes trading in markets much more efficient.

Circular Flows Through Markets

Trading in markets for goods and services and factors of production creates a circular flow of expenditures and incomes. Figure 2.7 shows the circular flows. Households specialize and choose the quantities of labor, land, capital, and entrepreneurial services to sell or rent to firms. Firms choose the quantities of factors of production to hire. These (red) flows go through the *factor markets*. Households choose the quantities of goods and services to buy, and firms choose the quantities to produce. These (red) flows go through the *goods markets*. Households receive incomes and make expenditures on goods and services (the green flows).

How do markets coordinate all these decisions?

FIGURE 2.7   Circular Flows in the Market Economy

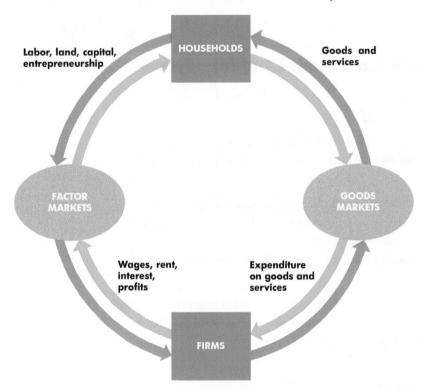

Labor, land, capital, entrepreneurship

Goods and services

FACTOR MARKETS

HOUSEHOLDS

GOODS MARKETS

Wages, rent, interest, profits

Expenditure on goods and services

FIRMS

Households and firms make economic choices and markets coordinate these choices.

Households choose the quantities of labor, land, capital, and entrepreneurial services to sell or rent to firms in exchange for wages, rent, interest, and profits. Households also choose how to spend their incomes on the various types of goods and services available.

Firms choose the quantities of factors of production to hire and the quantities of goods and services to produce.

Goods markets and factor markets coordinate these choices of households and firms.

The counterclockwise red flows are real flows—the flow of factors of production from households to firms and the flow of goods and services from firms to households.

The clockwise green flows are the payments for the red flows. They are the flow of incomes from firms to households and the flow of expenditure on goods and services from households to firms.

— MyEconLab animation —

Coordinating Decisions

Markets coordinate decisions through price adjustments. Suppose that some people who want to buy hamburgers are not able to do so. To make buying and selling plans the same, either more hamburgers must be offered for sale or buyers must scale down their appetites (or both). A rise in the price of a hamburger produces this outcome. It encourages producers to offer more hamburgers for sale and encourages some people to change their lunch plans. When the price is right, buying plans and selling plans match.

Alternatively, suppose that more hamburgers are available than people want to buy. In this case, more hamburgers must be bought or fewer hamburgers must be offered for sale (or both). A fall in the price of a hamburger achieves this outcome. It encourages people to buy more hamburgers and it encourages firms to produce a smaller quantity of hamburgers.

REVIEW QUIZ

1 Why are social institutions such as firms, markets, property rights, and money necessary?
2 What are the main functions of markets?
3 What are the flows in the market economy that go from firms to households and the flows from households to firms?

You can work these questions in Study Plan 2.5 and get instant feedback.   MyEconLab

◆ You have now begun to see how economists approach economic questions. You can see all around you the lessons you've learned in this chapter. *Reading Between the Lines* on pp. 46–47 provides an opportunity to apply the *PPF* model to deepen your understanding of why food costs more today than it did a few years ago.

The Rising Opportunity Cost of Food

U.S. Farmers' Corn Drive Set to Curtail Land for Soybeans

Financial Times
March 31, 2012

Food commodity prices were sent gyrating after U.S. farmers signaled plans to sow the most corn in 75 years, leaving less land for soybeans, which are facing a fall in supplies due to droughts in South America.

A U.S. government survey of 84,500 farm operators indicated they would plant 95.9m acres (38.4m hectares) with corn this spring, 4 percent more than last year, the most since 1937 and above expectations. Plantings of soybeans, often rotated with corn, would fall 1 percent from last year to 73.9m acres (29.6m hectares), with declines in such fertile states as Iowa, Missouri, and Nebraska.

The United States is the world's leading exporter of corn and vies with Brazil in soybean exports, so decisions made there are vital to global food markets. A growing world population and rising incomes in emerging economies have driven greater appetites for the crops, used in products from pig feed to vegetable oil. ...

"This is the annus horribilis for South American grain production. La Niña hit all the wrong places. ..." said Nick Higgins, commodity analyst at Rabobank, the Dutch bank that is one of the biggest lenders to the agribusiness industry. ...

Corn peaked at a record of almost $8 a bushel last June as growers sought to meet demand from livestock producers and the U.S. ethanol industry. If farmers follow through with planting intentions and yields are good, this year's crop could break records, helping ease concerns about food prices. ...

ESSENCE OF THE STORY

- U.S. farmers plan to sow the most corn in 75 years, leaving less land for soybeans.

- Farms will plant 95.9 million acres with corn in the 2012 spring, 4 percent more than in 2011 and the most since 1937.

- Corn production in South America was hit by drought (La Niña).

- The price of corn hit a record of almost $8 a bushel last June as growers sought to meet demand from livestock producers and the U.S. ethanol industry.

ECONOMIC ANALYSIS

- Ethanol is made from corn, so biofuel and food compete to use the same resources.

- As a consequence of the Energy Policy Act 2005, which mandated a steady increase in the production of ethanol, farmers have been increasing the number of acres devoted to corn production.

- By 2012, the amount of farmland in the United States devoted to corn production had increased to its highest level since 1937.

- Figure 1 shows the U.S. production possibilities frontier, PPF, for corn and other goods and services (including soybeans).

- The increase in the production of corn is illustrated by a movement along the PPF in Fig. 1 from point A in 2010 to point B in 2012.

- In moving from point A to point B, the United States incurs a higher opportunity cost of producing corn, as the greater slope of the PPF at point B indicates.

- In other regions of the world, despite the fact that more land was devoted to corn production, the amount of corn produced didn't change.

- The reason is that droughts in South America and Eastern Europe lowered the crop yield per acre in those regions.

- Figure 2 shows the rest of the world's PPF for corn and other goods and services in 2010 and 2012.

- The increase in the amount of land devoted to producing corn is illustrated by a movement along PPF_{10}.

- With a decrease in the crop yield, production possibilities decreased and the PPF rotated inward.

- The rotation from PPF_{10} to PPF_{12} illustrates this decrease in production possibilities.

- The opportunity cost of producing corn in the rest of the world increased for two reasons: the movement along its PPF and the inward rotation of the PPF.

- With a higher opportunity cost of producing corn, the cost of both biofuel and food increases.

Figure 1 U.S. PPF

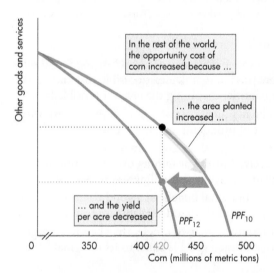

Figure 2 Rest of the World PPF

Key Points

Production Possibilities and Opportunity Cost
(pp. 32–34)

- The production possibilities frontier is the boundary between production levels that are attainable and those that are not attainable when all the available resources are used to their limit.
- Production efficiency occurs at points on the production possibilities frontier.
- Along the production possibilities frontier, the opportunity cost of producing more of one good is the amount of the other good that must be given up.
- The opportunity cost of all goods increases as the production of the good increases.

Working Problems 1 to 3 will give you a better understanding of production possibilities and opportunity cost.

Using Resources Efficiently (pp. 35–37)

- Allocative efficiency occurs when goods and services are produced at the least possible cost and in the quantities that bring the greatest possible benefit.
- The marginal cost of a good is the opportunity cost of producing one more unit of it.
- The marginal benefit from a good is the benefit received from consuming one more unit of it and is measured by the willingness to pay for it.
- The marginal benefit of a good decreases as the amount of the good available increases.
- Resources are used efficiently when the marginal cost of each good is equal to its marginal benefit.

Working Problems 4 to 10 will give you a better understanding of the efficient use of resources.

Economic Growth (pp. 38–39)

- Economic growth, which is the expansion of production possibilities, results from capital accumulation and technological change.
- The opportunity cost of economic growth is forgone current consumption.
- The benefit of economic growth is increased future consumption.

Working Problem 11 will give you a better understanding of economic growth.

Gains from Trade (pp. 40–43)

- A person has a comparative advantage in producing a good if that person can produce the good at a lower opportunity cost than everyone else.
- People gain by specializing in the activity in which they have a comparative advantage and trading with others.

Working Problems 12 and 13 will give you a better understanding of the gains from trade.

Economic Coordination (pp. 44–45)

- Firms coordinate a large amount of economic activity, but there is a limit to the efficient size of a firm.
- Markets coordinate the economic choices of people and firms.
- Markets can work efficiently only when property rights exist.
- Money makes trading in markets more efficient.

Working Problem 14 will give you a better understanding of economic coordination.

Key Terms

Absolute advantage, 40	Marginal benefit, 36	Preferences, 36
Allocative efficiency, 35	Marginal benefit curve, 36	Production efficiency, 33
Capital accumulation, 38	Marginal cost, 35	Production possibilities frontier, 32
Comparative advantage, 40	Market, 44	Property rights, 44
Economic growth, 38	Money, 44	Technological change, 38
Firm, 44	Opportunity cost, 33	

STUDY PLAN PROBLEMS AND APPLICATIONS

MyEconLab   You can work Problems 1 to 20 in MyEconLab Chapter 2 Study Plan and get instant feedback.

Production Possibilities and Opportunity Cost

(Study Plan 2.1)

Use the following information to work Problems 1 to 3. Brazil produces ethanol from sugar, and the land used to grow sugar can be used to grow food crops. Suppose that Brazil's production possibilities for ethanol and food crops are as follows

Ethanol (barrels per day)		Food crops (tons per day)
70	and	0
64	and	1
54	and	2
40	and	3
22	and	4
0	and	5

(handwritten: ↓ ↑ next to 54/40; ↑ ↓ next to 2/3)

1. a. Draw a graph of Brazil's *PPF* and explain how your graph illustrates scarcity.
   b. If Brazil produces 40 barrels of ethanol a day, how much food must it produce to achieve production efficiency?   *3 tons of food crop/day*
   c. Why does Brazil face a tradeoff on its *PPF*?

2. a. If Brazil increases its production of ethanol from 40 barrels per day to 54 barrels per day, what is the opportunity cost of the additional ethanol?   *3-2/54-40 = 1/14*
   b. If Brazil increases its production of food crops from 2 tons per day to 3 tons per day, what is the opportunity cost of the additional food?   *54-40/3-2=14*
   c. What is the relationship between your answers to parts (a) and (b)?   *The OC of 1 Ethanol is 1/14 Food crops. The OC of 1 Food crop is 14 Ethanol*

3. Does Brazil face an increasing opportunity cost of ethanol? What feature of Brazil's *PPF* illustrates increasing opportunity cost?   *from 0→22 Ethanol, OC=1/22 ; from 22-40 Ethanol OC = 1/18 . 1/18 > 1/22 graph outward, increasing.*

Using Resources Efficiently (Study Plan 2.2)

Use the above table to work Problems 4 and 5.

4. Define marginal cost and calculate Brazil's marginal cost of producing a ton of food when the quantity produced is 2.5 tons per day.   *54-40/3-2 = 14.*

5. Define marginal benefit, explain how it is measured, and explain why the data in the table does not enable you to calculate Brazil's marginal benefit from food.

6. Distinguish between *production efficiency* and *allocative efficiency*. Explain why many production possibilities achieve production efficiency but only one achieves allocative efficiency.

Use the following graphs to work Problems 7 to 10. Harry enjoys tennis but wants a high grade in his economics course. The graphs show his *PPF* for these two "goods" and his *MB* curve from tennis.

7. What is Harry's marginal cost of tennis if he plays for (i) 3 hours a week; (ii) 5 hours a week; and (iii) 7 hours a week?   *(i) 78-75/4-2 = 1.5 ; (ii) 75-70/6-4=2.5 (iii) 70-60/8-6=5*

8. a. If Harry uses his time to achieve allocative efficiency, what is his economics grade and how many hours of tennis does he play?
   b. Explain why Harry would be worse off getting a grade higher than your answer to part (a).

9. If Harry becomes a tennis superstar with big earnings from tennis, what happens to his *PPF*, *MB* curve, and his efficient time allocation?

10. If Harry suddenly finds high grades in economics easier to attain, what happens to his *PPF*, his *MB* curve, and his efficient time allocation?

[handwritten: wheat (graph with curves labeled PPF₀, PPF₁, Pork)]

Economic Growth (Study Plan 2.3)

11. A farm grows wheat and produces pork. The marginal cost of producing each of these products increases as more of it is produced.

   [handwritten: 11.c: increased (用 Δy-Δx)]

   a. Make a graph that illustrates the farm's *PPF*. *[handwritten: (PPF₀)]*

   b. The farm adopts a new technology that allows it to use fewer resources to fatten pigs. Use your graph to illustrate the impact of the new technology on the farm's *PPF*. *[handwritten: (PPF₁)]*

   [handwritten: d: no necessarily efficiency (if 在technology improve 之前用 的就是PPF₀上 的点, 那么 efficiency 将不变)]

   c. With the farm using the new technology described in part (b), has the opportunity cost of producing a ton of wheat increased, decreased, or remained the same? Explain and illustrate your answer.

   d. Is the farm more efficient with the new technology than it was with the old one? Why?

Gains from Trade (Study Plan 2.4)

12. In an hour, Sue can produce 40 caps or 4 jackets and Tessa can produce 80 caps or 4 jackets.

   a. Calculate Sue's opportunity cost of producing a cap. *[handwritten: 60/40 × 4/60 = 0.1 jacket]*

   b. Calculate Tessa's opportunity cost of producing a cap. *[handwritten: 60/80 × 4/60 = 0.075 jacket]*

   c. Who has a comparative advantage in producing caps? *[handwritten: Tessa]*

   d. If Sue and Tessa specialize in producing the good in which each of them has a comparative advantage, and they trade 1 jacket for 15 caps, who gains from the specialization and trade?

13. Suppose that Tessa buys a new machine for making jackets that enables her to make 20 jackets an hour. (She can still make only 80 caps per hour.)

   a. Who now has a comparative advantage in producing jackets? *[handwritten: Tessa]*

   b. Can Sue and Tessa still gain from trade?

   c. Would Sue and Tessa still be willing to trade 1 jacket for 15 caps? Explain your answer.

Economic Coordination (Study Plan 2.5)

14. For 50 years, Cuba has had a centrally planned economy in which the government makes the big decisions on how resources will be allocated.

   a. Why would you expect Cuba's production possibilities (per person) to be smaller than those of the United States?

   b. What are the social institutions that Cuba might lack that help the United States to achieve allocative efficiency?

Economics in the News (Study Plan 2.N)

Use the following data to work Problems 15 to 17. Brazil produces ethanol from sugar at a cost of 83 cents per gallon. The United States produces ethanol from corn at a cost of $1.14 per gallon. Sugar grown on one acre of land produces twice the quantity of ethanol as the corn grown on an acre. The United States imports 5 percent of the ethanol it uses and produces the rest itself. Since 2003, U.S. ethanol production has more than doubled and U.S. corn production has increased by 45 percent. *[handwritten: a. Brazil did.]*

15. a. Does Brazil or the United States have a comparative advantage in producing ethanol?

   b. Sketch the *PPF* for ethanol and other goods and services for the United States.

   c. Sketch the *PPF* for ethanol and other goods and services for Brazil.

16. a. Do you expect the opportunity cost of producing ethanol in the United States to have increased since 2003? Explain why.

   b. Do you think the United States has achieved production efficiency in its manufacture of ethanol? Explain why or why not.

   c. Do you think the United States has achieved allocative efficiency in its manufacture of ethanol? Explain why or why not.

17. Sketch a figure similar to Fig. 2.6 on p. 42 to show how both the United States and Brazil can gain from specialization and trade.

Use this news clip to work Problems 18 to 20.

Time for Tea

Americans are switching to loose-leaf tea for its health benefits. Tea could be grown in the United States, but picking tea leaves would be costly because it can only be done by workers and not by machine.

Source: *The Economist,* July 8, 2005

18. a. Sketch *PPF*s for the production of tea and other goods and services in India and in the United States.

   b. Sketch marginal cost curves for the production of tea in India and in the United States.

19. a. Sketch the marginal benefit curves for tea in the United States before and after Americans began to appreciate the health benefits of loose tea.

   b. Explain how the quantity of loose tea that achieves allocative efficiency has changed.

   c. Does the change in preferences toward tea affect the opportunity cost of producing tea?

20. Explain why the United States does not produce tea and instead imports it from India.

ADDITIONAL PROBLEMS AND APPLICATIONS

MyEconLab   You can work these problems in MyEconLab if assigned by your instructor.

Production Possibilities and Opportunity Cost

Use the following table to work Problems 21 and 22. Suppose that Yucatan's production possibilities are

Food (pounds per month)		Sunscreen (gallons per month)
300	and	0
200	and	50
100	and	100
0	and	150

21. a. Draw a graph of Yucatan's *PPF* and explain how your graph illustrates a tradeoff.

    b. If Yucatan produces 150 pounds of food per month, how much sunscreen must it produce if it achieves production efficiency?

    c. What is Yucatan's opportunity cost of producing 1 pound of food?

    d. What is Yucatan's opportunity cost of producing 1 gallon of sunscreen?

    e. What is the relationship between your answers to parts (c) and (d)?

22. What feature of a *PPF* illustrates increasing opportunity cost? Explain why Yucatan's opportunity cost does or does not increase.

Using Resources Efficiently

23. In problem 21, what is the marginal cost of a pound of food in Yucatan when the quantity produced is 150 pounds per day? What is special about the marginal cost of food in Yucatan?

24. The table describes the preferences in Yucatan.

Sunscreen (gallons per month)	Willingness to pay (pounds of food per gallon)
25	3
75	2
125	1

    a. What is the marginal benefit from sunscreen and how is it measured?

    b. Draw a graph of Yucatan's marginal benefit from sunscreen.

Use the following news clip to work Problems 25 and 26.

Malaria Eradication Back on the Table

In response to the Gates Malaria Forum in October 2007, countries are debating the pros and cons of eradication. Dr. Arata Kochi of the World Health Organization believes that with enough money malaria cases could be cut by 90 percent, but he believes that it would be very expensive to eliminate the remaining 10 percent of cases. He concluded that countries should not strive to eradicate malaria.

    Source: *The New York Times*, March 4, 2008

25. Is Dr. Kochi talking about *production efficiency* or *allocative efficiency* or both?

26. Make a graph with the percentage of malaria cases eliminated on the *x*-axis and the marginal cost and marginal benefit of driving down malaria cases on the *y*-axis. On your graph:

    (i) Draw a marginal cost curve that is consistent with Dr. Kochi's opinion.

    (ii) Draw a marginal benefit curve that is consistent with Dr. Kochi's opinion.

    (iii) Identify the quantity of malaria eradicated that achieves allocative efficiency.

Economic Growth

27. Capital accumulation and technological change bring economic growth, which means that the *PPF* keeps shifting outward: Production that was unattainable yesterday becomes attainable today; production that is unattainable today will become attainable tomorrow. Why doesn't this process of economic growth mean that scarcity is being defeated and will one day be gone?

Gains from Trade

Use the following data to work Problems 28 and 29. Kim can produce 40 pies or 400 cakes an hour. Liam can produce 100 pies or 200 cakes an hour.

28. a. Calculate Kim's opportunity cost of a pie and Liam's opportunity cost of a pie.

    b. If each spends 30 minutes of each hour producing pies and 30 minutes producing cakes, how many pies and cakes does each produce?

    c. Who has a comparative advantage in producing pies? Who has a comparative advantage in producing cakes?

29. a. Draw a graph of Kim's *PPF* and Liam's *PPF*.

    b. On your graph, show the point at which each produces when they spend 30 minutes of each hour producing pies and 30 minutes producing cakes.

    c. On your graph, show what Kim produces and what Liam produces when they specialize.

d. When they specialize and trade, what are the total gains from trade?

e. If Kim and Liam share the total gains equally, what trade takes place between them?

Use the following information to work Problems 30 and 31.

Before the Civil War, the South traded with the North and with England. The South sold cotton and bought manufactured goods and food. During the war, one of President Lincoln's first actions was to blockade the ports and prevent this trade. The South increased its production of munitions and food.

30. In what did the South have a comparative advantage?

31. a. Draw a graph to illustrate production, consumption, and trade in the South before the Civil War.

b. Was the South consuming inside, on, or outside its *PPF*? Explain your answer.

c. Draw a graph to show the effects of the Civil War on consumption and production in the South.

d. Did the Civil War change any opportunity costs in the South? If so, did the opportunity cost of everything increase? Did the opportunity cost of any items decrease? Illustrate your answer with appropriate graphs.

Use the following information to work Problems 32 and 33.

He Shoots! He Scores! He Makes Movies!

NBA All-star Baron Davis and his school friend, Cash Warren, premiered their first movie *Made in America* at the Sundance Festival in January 2008. The movie, based on gang activity in South Central Los Angeles, received good reviews.

Source: *The New York Times*, February 24, 2008

32. a. Does Baron Davis have an absolute advantage in basketball and movie directing and is this the reason for his success in both activities?

b. Does Baron Davis have a comparative advantage in basketball or movie directing or both and is this the reason for his success in both activities?

33. a. Sketch a *PPF* between playing basketball and producing other goods and services for Baron Davis and for yourself.

b. How do you (and people like you) and Baron Davis (and people like him) gain from specialization and trade?

Economic Coordination

34. Indicate on a graph of the circular flows in the market economy, the real and money flows in which the following items belong:

a. You buy an iPad from the Apple Store.

b. Apple Inc. pays the designers of the iPad.

c. Apple Inc. decides to expand and rents an adjacent building.

d. You buy a new e-book from Amazon.

e. Apple Inc. hires a student as an intern during the summer.

Economics in the News

35. After you have studied *Reading Between the Lines* on pp. 46–47, answer the following questions.

a. How has an Act of the United States Congress increased U.S. production of corn?

b. Why would you expect an increase in the quantity of corn produced to raise the opportunity cost of corn?

c. Why did the cost of producing corn increase in the rest of the world?

d. Is it possible that the increased quantity of corn produced, despite the higher cost of production, moves the United States closer to allocative efficiency?

36. **Lots of Little Screens**

Inexpensive broadband access has created a generation of television producers for whom the Internet is their native medium. As they redirect the focus from TV to computers, cell phones, and iPods, the video market is developing into an open digital network.

Source: *The New York Times*, December 2, 2007

a. How has inexpensive broadband changed the production possibilities of video entertainment and other goods and services?

b. Sketch a *PPF* for video entertainment and other goods and services before broadband.

c. Show how the arrival of inexpensive broadband has changed the *PPF*.

d. Sketch a marginal benefit curve for video entertainment.

e. Show how the new generation of TV producers for whom the Internet is their native medium might have changed the marginal benefit from video entertainment.

f. Explain how the efficient quantity of video entertainment has changed.

Your Economic Revolution

Three periods in human history stand out as ones of economic revolution. The first, the *Agricultural Revolution,* occurred 10,000 years ago. In what is today Iraq, people learned to domesticate animals and plant crops. People stopped roaming in search of food and settled in villages, towns, and cities where they specialized in the activities in which they had a comparative advantage and developed markets in which to exchange their products. Wealth increased enormously.

Economics was born during the *Industrial Revolution,* which began in England during the 1760s. For the first time, people began to apply science and create new technologies for the manufacture of textiles and iron, to create steam engines, and to boost the output of farms.

You are studying economics at a time that future historians will call the *Information Revolution.* Over the entire world, people are embracing new information technologies and prospering on an unprecedented scale.

During all three economic revolutions, many have prospered but many have been left behind. It is the range of human progress that poses the greatest question for economics and the one that Adam Smith addressed in the first work of economic science: What causes the differences in wealth among nations?

Many people had written about economics before **Adam Smith***, but he made economics a science. Born in 1723 in Kirkcaldy, a small fishing town near Edinburgh, Scotland, Smith was the only child of the town's customs officer. Lured from his professorship (he was a full professor at 28) by a wealthy Scottish duke who gave him a pension of £300 a year—ten times the average income at that time—Smith devoted ten years to writing his masterpiece:* An Inquiry into the Nature and Causes of the **Wealth of Nations***, published in 1776.*

Why, Adam Smith asked , are some nations wealthy while others are poor? He was pondering these questions at the height of the Industrial Revolution, and he answered by emphasizing the power of the division of labor and free markets in raising labor productivity.

To illustrate his argument, Adam Smith described two pin factories. In the first, one person, using the hand tools available in the 1770s, could make 20 pins a day. In the other, by using those same hand tools but breaking the process into a number of individually small operations in which people specialize—by the division of labor—ten people could make a staggering 48,000 pins a day. One draws

Every individual who intends only his own gain is led by an invisible hand to promote an end (the public good) which was no part of his intention.

ADAM SMITH
The Wealth of Nations

out the wire, another straightens it, a third cuts it, a fourth points it, a fifth grinds it. Three specialists make the head, and a fourth attaches it. Finally, the pin is polished and packaged.

But a large market is needed to support the division of labor: One factory employing ten workers would need to sell more than 15 million pins a year to stay in business!

JAGDISH BHAGWATI is University Professor at Columbia University. Born in India in 1934, he studied at Cambridge University in England, MIT, and Oxford University before returning to India. He returned to teach at MIT in 1968 and moved to Columbia in 1980. A prolific scholar, Professor Bhagwati also writes in leading newspapers and magazines throughout the world. He has been much honored for both his scientific work and his impact on public policy. His greatest contributions are in international trade but extend also to developmental problems and the study of political economy.

Michael Parkin talked with Jagdish Bhagwati about his work and the progress that economists have made in understanding the benefits of economic growth and international trade since the pioneering work of Adam Smith.

Professor Bhagwati, what attracted you to economics?

When you come from India, where poverty hits the eye, it is easy to be attracted to economics, which can be used to bring prosperity and create jobs to pull up the poor into gainful employment.

I learned later that there are two broad types of economist: those who treat the subject as an arid mathematical toy and those who see it as a serious social science.

If Cambridge, where I went as an undergraduate, had been interested in esoteric mathematical economics, I would have opted for something else. But the Cambridge economists from whom I learned—many among the greatest figures in the discipline—saw economics as a social science. I therefore saw the power of economics as a tool to address India's poverty and was immediately hooked.

After Cambridge and MIT, you went to Oxford and then back to India. What did you do in India?

I joined the Planning Commission in New Delhi, where my first big job was to find ways of raising the bottom 30 percent of India's population out of poverty to a "minimum income" level.

And what did you prescribe?

My main prescription was to "grow the pie." My research suggested that the share of the bottom 30 percent of the pie did not seem to vary dramatically with differences in economic and political systems. So growth in the pie seemed to be the principal (but not the only) component of an anti-poverty strategy. To supplement growth's good effects on the poor, the Indian planners were also dedicated to education, health, social reforms, and land reforms. Also, the access of the lowest-income and socially disadvantaged groups to the growth process and its benefits was to be improved in many ways, such as extension of credit without collateral.

Today, this strategy has no rivals. Much empirical work shows that where growth has occurred, poverty has lessened. It is nice to know that one's basic take on an issue of such central importance to humanity's well-being has been borne out by experience!

> My main prescription was to "grow the pie." ... Much empirical work shows that where growth has occurred, poverty has lessened.

*Read the full interview with Jagdish Bhagwati in MyEconLab.

3

DEMAND AND SUPPLY

After studying this chapter, you will be able to:

◆ Describe a competitive market and think about a price as an opportunity cost

◆ Explain the influences on demand

◆ Explain the influences on supply

◆ Explain how demand and supply determine prices and quantities bought and sold

◆ Use the demand and supply model to make predictions about changes in prices and quantities

In 2011, the price of peanut butter rose by 40 percent. Another price that just keeps rising is that of attending college—tuition. Why do some prices rise? And why do some prices fall, and some fluctuate?

This chapter answers these questions. The demand and supply model that you're about to study is the main tool of economics. It explains how prices are determined and how they guide the use of resources to influence What, How, and For Whom goods and services are produced.

We'll return to the rise in the price of peanut butter at the end of the chapter, in *Reading Between the Lines*. We'll also apply the demand and supply model to the market for college and explain why tuition keeps rising.

Markets and Prices

When you need a new pair of running shoes, want a bagel and a latte, plan to upgrade your cell phone, or need to fly home for Thanksgiving, you must find a place where people sell those items or offer those services. The place in which you find them is a *market*. You learned in Chapter 2 (p. 44) that a market is any arrangement that enables buyers and sellers to get information and to do business with each other.

A market has two sides: buyers and sellers. There are markets for *goods* such as apples and hiking boots, for *services* such as haircuts and tennis lessons, for *factors of production* such as computer programmers and earthmovers, and for other manufactured *inputs* such as memory chips and auto parts. There are also markets for money such as Japanese yen and for financial securities such as Yahoo! stock. Only our imagination limits what can be traded in markets.

Some markets are physical places where buyers and sellers meet and where an auctioneer or a broker helps to determine the prices. Examples of this type of market are the New York Stock Exchange and the wholesale fish, meat, and produce markets.

Some markets are groups of people spread around the world who never meet and know little about each other but are connected through the Internet or by telephone and fax. Examples are the e-commerce markets and the currency markets.

But most markets are unorganized collections of buyers and sellers. You do most of your trading in this type of market. An example is the market for basketball shoes. The buyers in this $3 billion-a-year market are the 45 million Americans who play basketball (or who want to make a fashion statement). The sellers are the tens of thousands of retail sports equipment and footwear stores. Each buyer can visit several different stores, and each seller knows that the buyer has a choice of stores.

Markets vary in the intensity of competition that buyers and sellers face. In this chapter, we're going to study a **competitive market**—a market that has many buyers and many sellers, so no single buyer or seller can influence the price.

Producers offer items for sale only if the price is high enough to cover their opportunity cost. And consumers respond to changing opportunity cost by seeking cheaper alternatives to expensive items.

We are going to study how people respond to *prices* and the forces that determine prices. But to pursue these tasks, we need to understand the relationship between a price and an opportunity cost.

In everyday life, the *price* of an object is the number of dollars that must be given up in exchange for it. Economists refer to this price as the **money price**.

The *opportunity cost* of an action is the highest-valued alternative forgone. If, when you buy a cup of coffee, the highest-valued thing you forgo is some gum, then the opportunity cost of the coffee is the *quantity* of gum forgone. We can calculate the quantity of gum forgone from the money prices of the coffee and the gum.

If the money price of coffee is $1 a cup and the money price of gum is 50¢ a pack, then the opportunity cost of one cup of coffee is two packs of gum. To calculate this opportunity cost, we divide the price of a cup of coffee by the price of a pack of gum and find the *ratio* of one price to the other. The ratio of one price to another is called a **relative price**, and a *relative price is an opportunity cost.*

We can express the relative price of coffee in terms of gum or any other good. The normal way of expressing a relative price is in terms of a "basket" of all goods and services. To calculate this relative price, we divide the money price of a good by the money price of a "basket" of all goods (called a *price index*). The resulting relative price tells us the opportunity cost of the good in terms of how much of the "basket" we must give up to buy it.

The demand and supply model that we are about to study determines *relative prices,* and the word "price" means *relative* price. When we predict that a price will fall, we do not mean that its *money* price will fall—although it might. We mean that its *relative* price will fall. That is, its price will fall *relative* to the average price of other goods and services.

REVIEW QUIZ

1   What is the distinction between a money price and a relative price?
2   Explain why a relative price is an opportunity cost.
3   Think of examples of goods whose relative price has risen or fallen by a large amount.

You can work these questions in Study Plan 3.1 and get instant feedback.   MyEconLab

Let's begin our study of demand and supply, starting with demand.

◆ Demand

If you demand something, then you

1. Want it.
2. Can afford it.
3. Plan to buy it.

Wants are the unlimited desires or wishes that people have for goods and services. How many times have you thought that you would like something "if only you could afford it" or "if it weren't so expensive"? Scarcity guarantees that many—perhaps most—of our wants will never be satisfied. Demand reflects a decision about which wants to satisfy.

The **quantity demanded** of a good or service is the amount that consumers plan to buy during a given time period at a particular price. The quantity demanded is not necessarily the same as the quantity actually bought. Sometimes the quantity demanded exceeds the amount of goods available, so the quantity bought is less than the quantity demanded.

The quantity demanded is measured as an amount per unit of time. For example, suppose that you buy one cup of coffee a day. The quantity of coffee that you demand can be expressed as 1 cup per day, 7 cups per week, or 365 cups per year.

Many factors influence buying plans, and one of them is the price. We look first at the relationship between the quantity demanded of a good and its price. To study this relationship, we keep all other influences on buying plans the same and we ask: How, other things remaining the same, does the quantity demanded of a good change as its price changes?

The law of demand provides the answer.

The Law of Demand

The **law of demand** states:

> Other things remaining the same, the higher the price of a good, the smaller is the quantity demanded; and the lower the price of a good, the greater is the quantity demanded.

Why does a higher price reduce the quantity demanded? For two reasons:

- Substitution effect
- Income effect

Substitution Effect When the price of a good rises, other things remaining the same, its *relative* price—its opportunity cost—rises. Although each good is unique, it has *substitutes*—other goods that can be used in its place. As the opportunity cost of a good rises, the incentive to economize on its use and switch to a substitute becomes stronger.

Income Effect When a price rises, other things remaining the same, the price rises *relative* to income. Faced with a higher price and an unchanged income, people cannot afford to buy all the things they previously bought. They must decrease the quantities demanded of at least some goods and services. Normally, the good whose price has increased will be one of the goods that people buy less of.

To see the substitution effect and the income effect at work, think about the effects of a change in the price of an energy bar. Several different goods are substitutes for an energy bar. For example, an energy drink could be consumed instead of an energy bar.

Suppose that an energy bar initially sells for $3 and then its price falls to $1.50. People now substitute energy bars for energy drinks—the substitution effect. And with a budget that now has some slack from the lower price of an energy bar, people buy even more energy bars—the income effect. The quantity of energy bars demanded increases for these two reasons.

Now suppose that an energy bar initially sells for $3 and then the price doubles to $6. People now buy fewer energy bars and more energy drinks—the substitution effect. And faced with a tighter budget, people buy even fewer energy bars—the income effect. The quantity of energy bars demanded decreases for these two reasons.

Demand Curve and Demand Schedule

You are now about to study one of the two most used curves in economics: the demand curve. You are also going to encounter one of the most critical distinctions: the distinction between *demand* and *quantity demanded.*

The term **demand** refers to the entire relationship between the price of a good and the quantity demanded of that good. Demand is illustrated by the demand curve and the demand schedule. The term *quantity demanded* refers to a point on a demand curve—the quantity demanded at a particular price.

Figure 3.1 shows the demand curve for energy bars. A **demand curve** shows the relationship between the quantity demanded of a good and its price when all other influences on consumers' planned purchases remain the same.

The table in Fig. 3.1 is the demand schedule for energy bars. A *demand schedule* lists the quantities demanded at each price when all the other influences on consumers' planned purchases remain the same. For example, if the price of a bar is 50¢, the quantity demanded is 22 million a week. If the price is $2.50, the quantity demanded is 5 million a week. The other rows of the table show the quantities demanded at prices of $1.00, $1.50, and $2.00.

We graph the demand schedule as a demand curve with the quantity demanded on the *x*-axis and the price on the *y*-axis. The points on the demand curve labeled *A* through *E* correspond to the rows of the demand schedule. For example, point *A* on the graph shows a quantity demanded of 22 million energy bars a week at a price of 50¢ a bar.

Willingness and Ability to Pay Another way of looking at the demand curve is as a willingness-and-ability-to-pay curve. The willingness and ability to pay is a measure of *marginal benefit*.

If a small quantity is available, the highest price that someone is willing and able to pay for one more unit is high. But as the quantity available increases, the marginal benefit of each additional unit falls and the highest price that someone is willing and able to pay also falls along the demand curve.

In Fig. 3.1, if only 5 million energy bars are available each week, the highest price that someone is willing to pay for the 5 millionth bar is $2.50. But if 22 million energy bars are available each week, someone is willing to pay 50¢ for the last bar bought.

A Change in Demand

When any factor that influences buying plans changes, other than the price of the good, there is a **change in demand**. Figure 3.2 illustrates an increase in demand. When demand increases, the demand curve shifts rightward and the quantity demanded at each price is greater. For example, at $2.50 a bar, the quantity demanded on the original (blue) demand curve is 5 million energy bars a week. On the new (red) demand curve, at $2.50 a bar, the quantity demanded is 15 million bars a week. Look closely at the numbers in the table and check that the quantity demanded at each price is greater.

FIGURE 3.1   The Demand Curve

	Price (dollars per bar)	Quantity demanded (millions of bars per week)
A	0.50	22
B	1.00	15
C	1.50	10
D	2.00	7
E	2.50	5

The table shows a demand schedule for energy bars. At a price of 50¢ a bar, 22 million bars a week are demanded; at a price of $1.50 a bar, 10 million bars a week are demanded. The demand curve shows the relationship between quantity demanded and price, other things remaining the same. The demand curve slopes downward: As the price falls, the quantity demanded increases.

The demand curve can be read in two ways. For a given price, the demand curve tells us the quantity that people plan to buy. For example, at a price of $1.50 a bar, people plan to buy 10 million bars a week. For a given quantity, the demand curve tells us the maximum price that consumers are willing and able to pay for the last bar available. For example, the maximum price that consumers will pay for the 15 millionth bar is $1.00.

─── MyEconLab animation ───

FIGURE 3.2   An Increase in Demand

Original demand schedule Original income		New demand schedule New higher income	
Price (dollars per bar)	**Quantity demanded** (millions of bars per week)	**Price** (dollars per bar)	**Quantity demanded** (millions of bars per week)
A 0.50	22	A' 0.50	32
B 1.00	15	B' 1.00	25
C 1.50	10	C' 1.50	20
D 2.00	7	D' 2.00	17
E 2.50	5	E' 2.50	15

A change in any influence on buying plans other than the price of the good itself results in a new demand schedule and a shift of the demand curve. A change in income changes the demand for energy bars. At a price of $1.50 a bar, 10 million bars a week are demanded at the original income (row C of the table) and 20 million bars a week are demanded at the new higher income (row C'). A rise in income increases the demand for energy bars. The demand curve shifts *rightward*, as shown by the shift arrow and the resulting red curve.

—————MyEconLab animation—————

Six main factors bring changes in demand. They are changes in

- The prices of related goods
- Expected future prices
- Income
- Expected future income and credit
- Population
- Preferences

Prices of Related Goods The quantity of energy bars that consumers plan to buy depends in part on the prices of substitutes for energy bars. A **substitute** is a good that can be used in place of another good. For example, a bus ride is a substitute for a train ride; a hamburger is a substitute for a hot dog; and an energy drink is a substitute for an energy bar. If the price of a substitute for an energy bar rises, people buy less of the substitute and more energy bars. For example, if the price of an energy drink rises, people buy fewer energy drinks and more energy bars. The demand for energy bars increases.

The quantity of energy bars that people plan to buy also depends on the prices of complements with energy bars. A **complement** is a good that is used in conjunction with another good. Hamburgers and fries are complements, and so are energy bars and exercise. If the price of an hour at the gym falls, people buy more gym time *and more* energy bars.

Expected Future Prices If the expected future price of a good rises and if the good can be stored, the opportunity cost of obtaining the good for future use is lower today than it will be in the future when people expect the price to be higher. So people retime their purchases—they substitute over time. They buy more of the good now before its price is expected to rise (and less afterward), so the demand for the good today increases.

For example, suppose that a Florida frost damages the season's orange crop. You expect the price of orange juice to rise, so you fill your freezer with enough frozen juice to get you through the next six months. Your current demand for frozen orange juice has increased, and your future demand has decreased.

Similarly, if the expected future price of a good falls, the opportunity cost of buying the good today is high relative to what it is expected to be in the future. So again, people retime their purchases. They buy less of the good now before its price is expected to fall, so the demand for the good decreases today and increases in the future.

Computer prices are constantly falling, and this fact poses a dilemma. Will you buy a new computer now, in time for the start of the school year, or will you wait until the price has fallen some more? Because people expect computer prices to keep falling, the current demand for computers is less (and the future demand is greater) than it otherwise would be.

Income Consumers' income influences demand. When income increases, consumers buy more of most goods; and when income decreases, consumers buy less of most goods. Although an increase in income leads to an increase in the demand for *most* goods, it does not lead to an increase in the demand for *all* goods. A **normal good** is one for which demand increases as income increases. An **inferior good** is one for which demand decreases as income increases. As incomes increase, the demand for air travel (a normal good) increases and the demand for long-distance bus trips (an inferior good) decreases.

Expected Future Income and Credit When expected future income increases or credit becomes easier to get, demand for a good might increase now. For example, a salesperson gets the news that she will receive a big bonus at the end of the year, so she goes into debt and buys a new car right now, rather than waiting until she receives the bonus.

Population Demand also depends on the size and the age structure of the population. The larger the population, the greater is the demand for all goods and services; the smaller the population, the smaller is the demand for all goods and services.

For example, the demand for parking spaces or movies or just about anything that you can imagine is much greater in New York City (population 7.5 million) than it is in Boise, Idaho (population 150,000).

Also, the larger the proportion of the population in a given age group, the greater is the demand for the goods and services used by that age group.

For example, during the 1990s, a decrease in the college-age population decreased the demand for college places. During those same years, the number of Americans aged 85 years and over increased by more than 1 million. As a result, the demand for nursing home services increased.

TABLE 3.1   The Demand for Energy Bars

The Law of Demand

The quantity of energy bars demanded

Decreases if:	Increases if:
■ The price of an energy bar rises	■ The price of an energy bar falls

Changes in Demand

The demand for energy bars

Decreases if:	Increases if:
■ The price of a substitute falls	■ The price of a substitute rises
■ The price of a complement rises	■ The price of a complement falls
■ The expected future price of an energy bar falls	■ The expected future price of an energy bar rises
■ Income falls*	■ Income rises*
■ Expected future income falls or credit becomes harder to get*	■ Expected future income rises or credit becomes easier to get*
■ The population decreases	■ The population increases

*An energy bar is a normal good.

Preferences Demand depends on preferences. *Preferences* determine the value that people place on each good and service. Preferences depend on such things as the weather, information, and fashion. For example, greater health and fitness awareness has shifted preferences in favor of energy bars, so the demand for energy bars has increased.

Table 3.1 summarizes the influences on demand and the direction of those influences.

A Change in the Quantity Demanded Versus a Change in Demand

Changes in the influences on buying plans bring either a change in the quantity demanded or a change in demand. Equivalently, they bring either a movement along the demand curve or a shift of the demand curve. The distinction between a change in the quantity demanded and a change in demand is the same as that between a movement along the demand curve and a shift of the demand curve.

A point on the demand curve shows the quantity demanded at a given price, so a movement along the demand curve shows a **change in the quantity demanded**. The entire demand curve shows demand, so a shift of the demand curve shows a *change in demand*. Figure 3.3 illustrates these distinctions.

Movement Along the Demand Curve If the price of the good changes but no other influence on buying plans changes, we illustrate the effect as a movement along the demand curve.

A fall in the price of a good increases the quantity demanded of it. In Fig. 3.3, we illustrate the effect of a fall in price as a movement down along the demand curve D_0.

A rise in the price of a good decreases the quantity demanded of it. In Fig. 3.3, we illustrate the effect of a rise in price as a movement up along the demand curve D_0.

A Shift of the Demand Curve If the price of a good remains constant but some other influence on buying plans changes, there is a change in demand for that good. We illustrate a change in demand as a shift of the demand curve. For example, if more people work out at the gym, consumers buy more energy bars regardless of the price of a bar. That is what a rightward shift of the demand curve shows—more energy bars are demanded at each price.

In Fig. 3.3, there is a *change in demand* and the demand curve shifts when any influence on buying plans changes, other than the price of the good. Demand *increases* and the demand curve *shifts rightward* (to the red demand curve D_1) if the price of a substitute rises, the price of a complement falls, the expected future price of the good rises, income increases (for a normal good), expected future income or credit increases, or the population increases. Demand *decreases* and the demand curve *shifts leftward* (to the red demand curve D_2) if the price of a substitute falls, the price of a complement rises, the expected future price of the good falls, income decreases (for a normal good), expected future income or credit decreases, or the population decreases. (For an inferior good, the effects of changes in income are in the opposite direction to those described above.)

FIGURE 3.3   A Change in the Quantity Demanded Versus a Change in Demand

When the price of the good changes, there is a movement along the demand curve and *a change in the quantity demanded*, shown by the blue arrows on demand curve D_0. When any other influence on buying plans changes, there is a shift of the demand curve and a *change in demand*. An increase in demand shifts the demand curve rightward (from D_0 to D_1). A decrease in demand shifts the demand curve leftward (from D_0 to D_2).

—— MyEconLab animation ——

◆ REVIEW QUIZ

1 Define the quantity demanded of a good or service.
2 What is the law of demand and how do we illustrate it?
3 What does the demand curve tell us about the price that consumers are willing to pay?
4 List all the influences on buying plans that change demand, and for each influence, say whether it increases or decreases demand.
5 Why does demand not change when the price of a good changes with no change in the other influences on buying plans?

You can work these questions in Study Plan 3.2 and get instant feedback.   MyEconLab

◆ Supply

If a firm supplies a good or service, the firm

1. Has the resources and technology to produce it.
2. Can profit from producing it.
3. Plans to produce it and sell it.

A supply is more than just having the *resources* and the *technology* to produce something. *Resources and technology* are the constraints that limit what is possible.

Many useful things can be produced, but they are not produced unless it is profitable to do so. Supply reflects a decision about which technologically feasible items to produce.

The **quantity supplied** of a good or service is the amount that producers plan to sell during a given time period at a particular price. The quantity supplied is not necessarily the same amount as the quantity actually sold. Sometimes the quantity supplied is greater than the quantity demanded, so the quantity sold is less than the quantity supplied.

Like the quantity demanded, the quantity supplied is measured as an amount per unit of time. For example, suppose that GM produces 1,000 cars a day. The quantity of cars supplied by GM can be expressed as 1,000 a day, 7,000 a week, or 365,000 a year. Without the time dimension, we cannot tell whether a particular quantity is large or small.

Many factors influence selling plans, and again one of them is the price of the good. We look first at the relationship between the quantity supplied of a good and its price. Just as we did when we studied demand, to isolate the relationship between the quantity supplied of a good and its price, we keep all other influences on selling plans the same and ask: How does the quantity supplied of a good change as its price changes when other things remain the same?

The law of supply provides the answer.

The Law of Supply

The **law of supply** states:

> Other things remaining the same, the higher the price of a good, the greater is the quantity supplied; and the lower the price of a good, the smaller is the quantity supplied.

Why does a higher price increase the quantity supplied? It is because *marginal cost increases.* As the quantity produced of any good increases, the marginal cost of producing the good increases. (See Chapter 2, p. 35 to review marginal cost.)

It is never worth producing a good if the price received for the good does not at least cover the marginal cost of producing it. When the price of a good rises, other things remaining the same, producers are willing to incur a higher marginal cost, so they increase production. The higher price brings forth an increase in the quantity supplied.

Let's now illustrate the law of supply with a supply curve and a supply schedule.

Supply Curve and Supply Schedule

You are now going to study the second of the two most used curves in economics: the supply curve. You're also going to learn about the critical distinction between *supply* and *quantity supplied*.

The term **supply** refers to the entire relationship between the price of a good and the quantity supplied of it. Supply is illustrated by the supply curve and the supply schedule. The term *quantity supplied* refers to a point on a supply curve—the quantity supplied at a particular price.

Figure 3.4 shows the supply curve of energy bars. A **supply curve** shows the relationship between the quantity supplied of a good and its price when all other influences on producers' planned sales remain the same. The supply curve is a graph of a supply schedule.

The table in Fig. 3.4 sets out the supply schedule for energy bars. A *supply schedule* lists the quantities supplied at each price when all the other influences on producers' planned sales remain the same. For example, if the price of an energy bar is 50¢, the quantity supplied is zero—in row *A* of the table. If the price of an energy bar is $1.00, the quantity supplied is 6 million energy bars a week—in row *B*. The other rows of the table show the quantities supplied at prices of $1.50, $2.00, and $2.50.

To make a supply curve, we graph the quantity supplied on the *x*-axis and the price on the *y*-axis. The points on the supply curve labeled *A* through *E* correspond to the rows of the supply schedule. For example, point *A* on the graph shows a quantity supplied of zero at a price of 50¢ an energy bar. Point *E* shows a quantity supplied of 15 million bars at $2.50 an energy bar.

FIGURE 3.4   The Supply Curve

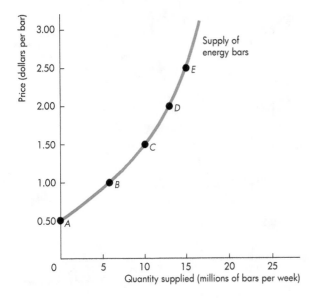

The table shows the supply schedule of energy bars. For example, at a price of $1.00, 6 million bars a week are supplied; at a price of $2.50, 15 million bars a week are supplied. The supply curve shows the relationship between the quantity supplied and the price, other things remaining the same. The supply curve slopes upward: As the price of a good increases, the quantity supplied increases.

A supply curve can be read in two ways. For a given price, the supply curve tells us the quantity that producers plan to sell at that price. For example, at a price of $1.50 a bar, producers are planning to sell 10 million bars a week. For a given quantity, the supply curve tells us the minimum price at which producers are willing to sell one more bar. For example, if 15 million bars are produced each week, the lowest price at which a producer is willing to sell the 15 millionth bar is $2.50.

———— MyEconLab animation ————

Minimum Supply Price The supply curve can be interpreted as a minimum-supply-price curve—a curve that shows the lowest price at which someone is willing to sell. This lowest price is the *marginal cost.*

If a small quantity is produced, the lowest price at which someone is willing to sell one more unit is low. But as the quantity produced increases, the marginal cost of each additional unit rises, so the lowest price at which someone is willing to sell an additional unit rises along the supply curve.

In Fig. 3.4, if 15 million bars are produced each week, the lowest price at which someone is willing to sell the 15 millionth bar is $2.50. But if 10 million bars are produced each week, someone is willing to accept $1.50 for the last bar produced.

A Change in Supply

When any factor that influences selling plans other than the price of the good changes, there is a **change in supply**. Six main factors bring changes in supply. They are changes in

- The prices of factors of production
- The prices of related goods produced
- Expected future prices
- The number of suppliers
- Technology
- The state of nature

Prices of Factors of Production The prices of the factors of production used to produce a good influence its supply. To see this influence, think about the supply curve as a minimum-supply-price curve. If the price of a factor of production rises, the lowest price that a producer is willing to accept for that good rises, so supply decreases. For example, during 2008, as the price of jet fuel increased, the supply of air travel decreased. Similarly, a rise in the minimum wage decreases the supply of hamburgers.

Prices of Related Goods Produced The prices of related goods that firms produce influence supply. For example, if the price of energy gel rises, firms switch production from bars to gel. The supply of energy bars decreases. Energy bars and energy gel are *substitutes in production*—goods that can be produced by using the same resources. If the price of beef rises, the supply of cowhide increases. Beef and cowhide are *complements in production*—goods that must be produced together.

Expected Future Prices If the expected future price of a good rises, the return from selling the good in the future increases and is higher than it is today. So supply decreases today and increases in the future.

The Number of Suppliers The larger the number of firms that produce a good, the greater is the supply of the good. As new firms enter an industry, the supply in that industry increases. As firms leave an industry, the supply in that industry decreases.

Technology The term "technology" is used broadly to mean the way that factors of production are used to produce a good. A technology change occurs when a new method is discovered that lowers the cost of producing a good. For example, new methods used in the factories that produce computer chips have lowered the cost and increased the supply of chips.

The State of Nature The state of nature includes all the natural forces that influence production. It includes the state of the weather and, more broadly, the natural environment. Good weather can increase the supply of many agricultural products and bad weather can decrease their supply. Extreme natural events such as earthquakes, tornadoes, and hurricanes can also influence supply.

Figure 3.5 illustrates an increase in supply. When supply increases, the supply curve shifts rightward and the quantity supplied at each price is larger. For example, at $1.00 per bar, on the original (blue) supply curve, the quantity supplied is 6 million bars a week. On the new (red) supply curve, the quantity supplied is 15 million bars a week. Look closely at the numbers in the table in Fig. 3.5 and check that the quantity supplied is larger at each price.

Table 3.2 summarizes the influences on supply and the directions of those influences.

A Change in the Quantity Supplied Versus a Change in Supply

Changes in the influences on selling plans bring either a change in the quantity supplied or a change in supply. Equivalently, they bring either a movement along the supply curve or a shift of the supply curve.

A point on the supply curve shows the quantity supplied at a given price. A movement along the supply curve shows a **change in the quantity supplied**. The entire supply curve shows supply. A shift of the supply curve shows a *change in supply*.

FIGURE 3.5   An Increase in Supply

Original supply schedule Old technology			New supply schedule New technology		
	Price (dollars per bar)	Quantity supplied (millions of bars per week)		Price (dollars per bar)	Quantity supplied (millions of bars per week)
A	0.50	0	A'	0.50	7
B	1.00	6	B'	1.00	15
C	1.50	10	C'	1.50	20
D	2.00	13	D'	2.00	25
E	2.50	15	E'	2.50	27

A change in any influence on selling plans other than the price of the good itself results in a new supply schedule and a shift of the supply curve. For example, a new, cost-saving technology for producing energy bars changes the supply of energy bars. At a price of $1.50 a bar, 10 million bars a week are supplied when producers use the old technology (row *C* of the table) and 20 million energy bars a week are supplied when producers use the new technology (row *C'*). An advance in technology *increases* the supply of energy bars. The supply curve shifts *rightward*, as shown by the shift arrow and the resulting red curve.

MyEconLab animation

Figure 3.6 illustrates and summarizes these distinctions. If the price of the good changes and other things remain the same, there is a *change in the quantity supplied* of that good. If the price of the good falls, the quantity supplied decreases and there is a movement down along the supply curve S_0. If the price of the good rises, the quantity supplied increases and there is a movement up along the supply curve S_0. When any other influence on selling plans changes, the supply curve shifts and there is a *change in supply*. If supply increases, the supply curve shifts rightward to S_1. If supply decreases, the supply curve shifts leftward to S_2.

TABLE 3.2   The Supply of Energy Bars

The Law of Supply

The quantity of energy bars supplied

Decreases if:	Increases if:
■ The price of an energy bar falls	■ The price of an energy bar rises

Changes in Supply

The supply of energy bars

Decreases if:	Increases if:
■ The price of a factor of production used to produce energy bars rises	■ The price of a factor of production used to produce energy bars falls
■ The price of a substitute in production rises	■ The price of a substitute in production falls
■ The price of a complement in production falls	■ The price of a complement in production rises
■ The expected future price of an energy bar rises	■ The expected future price of an energy bar falls
■ The number of suppliers of bars decreases	■ The number of suppliers of bars increases
■ A technology change decreases energy bar production	■ A technology change increases energy bar production
■ A natural event decreases energy bar production	■ A natural event increases energy bar production

FIGURE 3.6   A Change in the Quantity Supplied Versus a Change in Supply

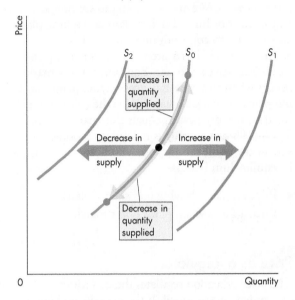

When the price of the good changes, there is a movement along the supply curve and a *change in the quantity supplied*, shown by the blue arrows on supply curve S_0. When any other influence on selling plans changes, there is a shift of the supply curve and a *change in supply*. An increase in supply shifts the supply curve rightward (from S_0 to S_1), and a decrease in supply shifts the supply curve leftward (from S_0 to S_2).

MyEconLab animation

◆ REVIEW QUIZ

1 Define the quantity supplied of a good or service.
2 What is the law of supply and how do we illustrate it?
3 What does the supply curve tell us about the producer's minimum supply price?
4 List all the influences on selling plans, and for each influence, say whether it changes supply.
5 What happens to the quantity of cell phones supplied and the supply of cell phones if the price of a cell phone falls?

You can work these questions in Study Plan 3.3 and get instant feedback.   MyEconLab

Now we're going to combine demand and supply and see how prices and quantities are determined.

Market Equilibrium

We have seen that when the price of a good rises, the quantity demanded *decreases* and the quantity supplied *increases*. We are now going to see how the price adjusts to coordinate buying plans and selling plans and achieve an equilibrium in the market.

An *equilibrium* is a situation in which opposing forces balance each other. Equilibrium in a market occurs when the price balances buying plans and selling plans. The **equilibrium price** is the price at which the quantity demanded equals the quantity supplied. The **equilibrium quantity** is the quantity bought and sold at the equilibrium price. A market moves toward its equilibrium because

- Price regulates buying and selling plans.
- Price adjusts when plans don't match.

Price as a Regulator

The price of a good regulates the quantities demanded and supplied. If the price is too high, the quantity supplied exceeds the quantity demanded. If the price is too low, the quantity demanded exceeds the quantity supplied. There is one price at which the quantity demanded equals the quantity supplied. Let's work out what that price is.

Figure 3.7 shows the market for energy bars. The table shows the demand schedule (from Fig. 3.1) and the supply schedule (from Fig. 3.4). If the price is 50¢ a bar, the quantity demanded is 22 million bars a week but no bars are supplied. There is a shortage of 22 million bars a week. The final column of the table shows this shortage. At a price of $1.00 a bar, there is still a shortage but only of 9 million bars a week.

If the price is $2.50 a bar, the quantity supplied is 15 million bars a week but the quantity demanded is only 5 million. There is a surplus of 10 million bars a week.

The one price at which there is neither a shortage nor a surplus is $1.50 a bar. At that price, the quantity demanded equals the quantity supplied: 10 million bars a week. The equilibrium price is $1.50 a bar, and the equilibrium quantity is 10 million bars a week.

Figure 3.7 shows that the demand curve and the supply curve intersect at the equilibrium price of $1.50 a bar. At each price *above* $1.50 a bar, there is a surplus of bars. For example, at $2.00 a bar, the surplus is 6

FIGURE 3.7   Equilibrium

Price (dollars per bar)	Quantity demanded	Quantity supplied	Shortage (−) or surplus (+)
	(millions of bars per week)		
0.50	22	0	−22
1.00	15	6	−9
1.50	10	10	0
2.00	7	13	+6
2.50	5	15	+10

The table lists the quantity demanded and the quantity supplied as well as the shortage or surplus of bars at each price. If the price is $1.00 a bar, 15 million bars a week are demanded and 6 million bars are supplied. There is a shortage of 9 million bars a week, and the price rises.

If the price is $2.00 a bar, 7 million bars a week are demanded and 13 million bars are supplied. There is a surplus of 6 million bars a week, and the price falls.

If the price is $1.50 a bar, 10 million bars a week are demanded and 10 million bars are supplied. There is neither a shortage nor a surplus, and the price does not change. The price at which the quantity demanded equals the quantity supplied is the equilibrium price, and 10 million bars a week is the equilibrium quantity.

MyEconLab animation

million bars a week, as shown by the blue arrow. At each price *below* $1.50 a bar, there is a shortage of bars. For example, at $1.00 a bar, the shortage is 9 million bars a week, as shown by the red arrow.

Price Adjustments

You've seen that if the price is below equilibrium, there is a shortage and that if the price is above equilibrium, there is a surplus. But can we count on the price to change and eliminate a shortage or a surplus? We can, because such price changes are beneficial to both buyers and sellers. Let's see why the price changes when there is a shortage or a surplus.

A Shortage Forces the Price Up Suppose the price of an energy bar is $1. Consumers plan to buy 15 million bars a week, and producers plan to sell 6 million bars a week. Consumers can't force producers to sell more than they plan, so the quantity that is actually offered for sale is 6 million bars a week. In this situation, powerful forces operate to increase the price and move it toward the equilibrium price. Some producers, noticing lines of unsatisfied consumers, raise the price. Some producers increase their output. As producers push the price up, the price rises toward its equilibrium. The rising price reduces the shortage because it decreases the quantity demanded and increases the quantity supplied. When the price has increased to the point at which there is no longer a shortage, the forces moving the price stop operating and the price comes to rest at its equilibrium.

A Surplus Forces the Price Down Suppose the price of a bar is $2. Producers plan to sell 13 million bars a week, and consumers plan to buy 7 million bars a week. Producers cannot force consumers to buy more than they plan, so the quantity that is actually bought is 7 million bars a week. In this situation, powerful forces operate to lower the price and move it toward the equilibrium price. Some producers, unable to sell the quantities of energy bars they planned to sell, cut their prices. In addition, some producers scale back production. As producers cut the price, the price falls toward its equilibrium. The falling price decreases the surplus because it increases the quantity demanded and decreases the quantity supplied. When the price has fallen to the point at which there is no longer a surplus, the forces moving the price stop operating and the price comes to rest at its equilibrium.

The Best Deal Available for Buyers and Sellers
When the price is below equilibrium, it is forced upward. Why don't buyers resist the increase and refuse to buy at the higher price? The answer is because they value the good more highly than its current price and they can't satisfy their demand at the current price. In some markets—for example, the markets that operate on eBay—the buyers might even be the ones who force the price up by offering to pay a higher price.

When the price is above equilibrium, it is bid downward. Why don't sellers resist this decrease and refuse to sell at the lower price? The answer is because their minimum supply price is below the current price and they cannot sell all they would like to at the current price. Sellers willingly lower the price to gain market share.

At the price at which the quantity demanded and the quantity supplied are equal, neither buyers nor sellers can do business at a better price. Buyers pay the highest price they are willing to pay for the last unit bought, and sellers receive the lowest price at which they are willing to supply the last unit sold.

When people freely make offers to buy and sell and when demanders try to buy at the lowest possible price and suppliers try to sell at the highest possible price, the price at which trade takes place is the equilibrium price—the price at which the quantity demanded equals the quantity supplied. The price coordinates the plans of buyers and sellers, and no one has an incentive to change it.

◆ REVIEW QUIZ

1 What is the equilibrium price of a good or service?
2 Over what range of prices does a shortage arise? What happens to the price when there is a shortage?
3 Over what range of prices does a surplus arise? What happens to the price when there is a surplus?
4 Why is the price at which the quantity demanded equals the quantity supplied the equilibrium price?
5 Why is the equilibrium price the best deal available for both buyers and sellers?

You can work these questions in Study Plan 3.4 and get instant feedback.   MyEconLab

Predicting Changes in Price and Quantity

The demand and supply model that we have just studied provides us with a powerful way of analyzing influences on prices and the quantities bought and sold. According to the model, a change in price stems from a change in demand, a change in supply, or a change in both demand and supply. Let's look first at the effects of a change in demand.

An Increase in Demand

If more people join health clubs, the demand for energy bars increases. The table in Fig. 3.8 shows the original and new demand schedules for energy bars as well as the supply schedule of energy bars.

The increase in demand creates a shortage at the original price and to eliminate the shortage, the price must rise.

Figure 3.8 shows what happens. The figure shows the original demand for and supply of energy bars. The original equilibrium price is $1.50 an energy bar, and the equilibrium quantity is 10 million energy bars a week. When demand increases, the demand curve shifts rightward. The equilibrium price rises to $2.50 an energy bar, and the quantity supplied increases to 15 million energy bars a week, as highlighted in the figure. There is an *increase in the quantity supplied* but *no change in supply*—a movement along, but no shift of, the supply curve.

A Decrease in Demand

We can reverse this change in demand. Start at a price of $2.50 a bar with 15 million energy bars a week being bought and sold, and then work out what happens if demand decreases to its original level. Such a decrease in demand might arise if people switch to energy gel (a substitute for energy bars). The decrease in demand shifts the demand curve leftward. The equilibrium price falls to $1.50 a bar, the quantity supplied decreases, and the equilibrium quantity decreases to 10 million bars a week.

We can now make our first two predictions:

1. When demand increases, the price rises and the quantity increases.
2. When demand decreases, the price falls and the quantity decreases.

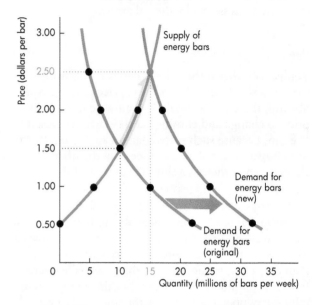

FIGURE 3.8   The Effects of a Change in Demand

Price (dollars per bar)	Quantity demanded (millions of bars per week)		Quantity supplied (millions of bars per week)
	Original	New	
0.50	22	32	0
1.00	15	25	6
1.50	**10**	20	**10**
2.00	7	17	13
2.50	5	15	15

Initially, the demand for energy bars is the blue demand curve. The equilibrium price is $1.50 a bar, and the equilibrium quantity is 10 million bars a week. When more health-conscious people do more exercise, the demand for energy bars increases and the demand curve shifts rightward to become the red curve.

At $1.50 a bar, there is now a shortage of 10 million bars a week. The price of a bar rises to a new equilibrium of $2.50. As the price rises to $2.50, the quantity supplied increases—shown by the blue arrow on the supply curve—to the new equilibrium quantity of 15 million bars a week. Following an increase in demand, the quantity supplied increases but supply does not change—the supply curve does not shift.

MyEconLab animation

ECONOMICS IN THE NEWS

The Market for College Education

Obama Decries Rising Cost of College Education
President Obama told colleges, "You can't assume that you'll just jack up tuition every single year. ... In the coming decade, 60 percent of new jobs will require more than a high school diploma...Higher education is not a luxury. It's an economic imperative that every family in America should be able to afford."
Source: *The Associated Press*, January 27, 2012

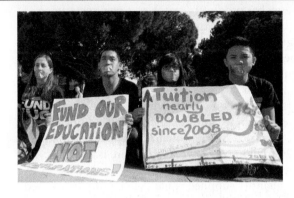

THE DATA

The scatter diagram provides data on college enrollments and tuition from 1981 through 2010.

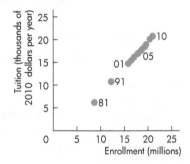

THE QUESTIONS

- What does the scatter diagram tell us?
- Why has college tuition increased? Is it because demand increased or supply increased?

THE ANSWERS

- The scatter diagram tells us that both tuition and enrollments have increased every year.
- An increase in demand brings a rise in the price (tuition) and an increase in the quantity (enrollments).
- An increase in supply brings a fall in the price and an increase in the quantity.
- Because both the price (tuition) and quantity (enrollments) have increased, the demand for college education has increased.
- The figure shows the market for college education.
- The supply curve of college education, S, slopes upward because the principle of increasing opportunity cost applies to college education just as it does to other goods and services.

- In 2001, the demand for college education was D_{2001}. The equilibrium tuition was \$15,000 and 16 million students were enrolled in college.
- Between 2001 and 2010:
  1) Income per person increased
  2) Population increased, and
  3) More new jobs required higher education.
- These (and possibly other) factors increased the demand for a college education. The demand curve shifted rightward to D_{2010}. Equilibrium tuition increased to \$21,000 and the quantity supplied increased to 21 million students.

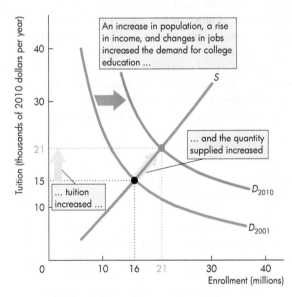

The Market for College Education

An Increase in Supply

When Nestlé (the producer of PowerBar) and other energy bar producers switch to a new cost-saving technology, the supply of energy bars increases. Figure 3.9 shows the new supply schedule (the same one that was shown in Fig. 3.5). What are the new equilibrium price and quantity? The price falls to $1.00 a bar, and the quantity increases to 15 million bars a week. You can see why by looking at the quantities demanded and supplied at the old price of $1.50 a bar. The new quantity supplied at that price is 20 million bars a week, and there is a surplus. The price falls. Only when the price is $1.00 a bar does the quantity supplied equal the quantity demanded.

Figure 3.9 illustrates the effect of an increase in supply. It shows the demand curve for energy bars and the original and new supply curves. The initial equilibrium price is $1.50 a bar, and the equilibrium quantity is 10 million bars a week. When supply increases, the supply curve shifts rightward. The equilibrium price falls to $1.00 a bar, and the quantity demanded increases to 15 million bars a week, highlighted in the figure. There is an *increase in the quantity demanded* but *no change in demand*—a movement along, but no shift of, the demand curve.

A Decrease in Supply

Start out at a price of $1.00 a bar with 15 million bars a week being bought and sold. Then suppose that the cost of labor or raw materials rises and the supply of energy bars decreases. The decrease in supply shifts the supply curve leftward. The equilibrium price rises to $1.50 a bar, the quantity demanded decreases, and the equilibrium quantity decreases to 10 million bars a week.

We can now make two more predictions:

1. When supply increases, the price falls and the quantity increases.
2. When supply decreases, the price rises and the quantity decreases.

You've now seen what happens to the price and the quantity when either demand or supply changes while the other one remains unchanged. In real markets, both demand and supply can change together. When this happens, to predict the changes in price and quantity, we must combine the effects that you've just seen. That is your final task in this chapter.

FIGURE 3.9   The Effects of a Change in Supply

Price (dollars per bar)	Quantity demanded (millions of bars per week)	Quantity supplied (millions of bars per week)	
		Original	New
0.50	22	0	7
1.00	15	6	15
1.50	10	10	20
2.00	7	13	25
2.50	5	15	27

Initially, the supply of energy bars is shown by the blue supply curve. The equilibrium price is $1.50 a bar, and the equilibrium quantity is 10 million bars a week. When the new cost-saving technology is adopted, the supply of energy bars increases and the supply curve shifts rightward to become the red curve.

At $1.50 a bar, there is now a surplus of 10 million bars a week. The price of an energy bar falls to a new equilibrium of $1.00 a bar. As the price falls to $1.00, the quantity demanded increases—shown by the blue arrow on the demand curve—to the new equilibrium quantity of 15 million bars a week. Following an increase in supply, the quantity demanded increases but demand does not change—the demand curve does not shift.

MyEconLab animation

The Market for Gasoline

Gas Prices: Down and Headed Lower
The price of gasoline has been falling for more than a
month. With oil prices also falling, more falls at the
pump are expected.

Source: CNN Money, May 4, 2012

THE DATA

	Quantity (millions of gallons per week)	Price (dollars per gallon)
April 6, 2012	365	4.00
May 4, 2012	372	3.85

THE QUESTIONS

- What does the data table tell us?
- Why did the price of gasoline decrease? Is it
  because demand changed or because supply
  changed, and in which direction?

THE ANSWERS

- The data table tells us that between April and May
  2012, the quantity of gasoline used increased and
  the price of gasoline fell.
- An increase in demand brings an increase in the
  quantity and a rise in the price.
- An increase in supply brings an increase in the
  quantity and a fall in the price.
- Because the quantity of gasoline used increased
  and the price of gasoline fell, there must have been
  in increase in the supply of gasoline.
- The supply of gasoline increases if the price of a
  factor of production used to produce gasoline falls.
  The news clip says the price of oil, which is used
  to produce gasoline, is falling. So the fall in the
  price of oil is the source of the increase in the supply.
- The figure illustrates the market for gasoline in 2012.
- The demand curve D_{April} shows the demand. In
  early April, the supply curve was S_0, the price was
  $4.00 per gallon, and the quantity used was 365
  million gallons per day.
- By the end of April and early May, the lower price
  of oil had increased the supply of gasoline to S_1.
  The price fell to $3.85 per gallon and the quantity
  used increased to 372 million gallons per day.

The Market for Gasoline in April 2012

- The lower price brought an increase in the quantity
  of gasoline demanded, which is shown by the
  movement along the demand curve.

All the Possible Changes in Demand and Supply

Figure 3.10 brings together and summarizes the effects of all the possible changes in demand and supply. With what you've learned about the effects of a change in *either* demand or supply, you can predict what happens if *both* demand and supply change together. Let's begin by reviewing what you already know.

Change in Demand with No Change in Supply The first row of Fig. 3.10, parts (a), (b), and (c), summarizes the effects of a change in demand with no change in supply. In part (a), with no change in either demand or supply, neither the price nor the quantity changes. With an *increase* in demand and no change in supply in part (b), both the price and quantity increase. And with a *decrease* in demand and no change in supply in part (c), both the price and the quantity decrease.

Change in Supply with No Change in Demand The first column of Fig. 3.10, parts (a), (d), and (g), summarizes the effects of a change in supply with no change in demand. With an *increase* in supply and no change in demand in part (d), the price falls and quantity increases. And with a *decrease* in supply and no change in demand in part (g), the price rises and the quantity decreases.

Increase in Both Demand and Supply You've seen that an increase in demand raises the price and increases the quantity. And you've seen that an increase in supply lowers the price and increases the quantity. Fig. 3.10(e) combines these two changes. Because either an increase in demand or an increase in supply increases the quantity, the quantity also increases when both demand and supply increase. But the effect on the price is uncertain. An increase in demand raises the price and an increase in supply lowers the price, so we can't say whether the price will rise or fall when both demand and supply increase. We need to know the magnitudes of the changes in demand and supply to predict the effects on price. In the example in Fig. 3.10(e), the price does not change. But notice that if demand increases by slightly more than the amount shown in the figure, the price will rise. And if supply increases by slightly more than the amount shown in the figure, the price will fall.

Decrease in Both Demand and Supply Figure 3.10(i) shows the case in which demand and supply *both decrease*. For the same reasons as those we've just reviewed, when both demand and supply decrease, the quantity decreases, and again the direction of the price change is uncertain.

Decrease in Demand and Increase in Supply You've seen that a decrease in demand lowers the price and decreases the quantity. And you've seen that an increase in supply lowers the price and increases the quantity. Fig. 3.10(f) combines these two changes. Both the decrease in demand and the increase in supply lower the price, so the price falls. But a decrease in demand decreases the quantity and an increase in supply increases the quantity, so we can't predict the direction in which the quantity will change unless we know the magnitudes of the changes in demand and supply. In the example in Fig. 3.10(f), the quantity does not change. But notice that if demand decreases by slightly more than the amount shown in the figure, the quantity will decrease; if supply increases by slightly more than the amount shown in the figure, the quantity will increase.

Increase in Demand and Decrease in Supply Figure 3.10(h) shows the case in which demand increases and supply decreases. Now, the price rises, and again the direction of the quantity change is uncertain.

REVIEW QUIZ

What is the effect on the price and quantity of MP3 players (such as the iPod) if
1   The price of a PC falls or the price of an MP3 download rises? (Draw the diagrams!)
2   More firms produce MP3 players or electronics workers' wages rise? (Draw the diagrams!)
3   Any two of the events in questions 1 and 2 occur together? (Draw the diagrams!)

You can work these questions in Study Plan 3.5 and get instant feedback.   MyEconLab

◆ To complete your study of demand and supply, take a look at *Reading Between the Lines* on pp. 74–75, which explains why the price of peanut butter increased in 2011. Try to get into the habit of using the demand and supply model to understand the movements in prices in your everyday life.

FIGURE 3.10   The Effects of All the Possible Changes in Demand and Supply

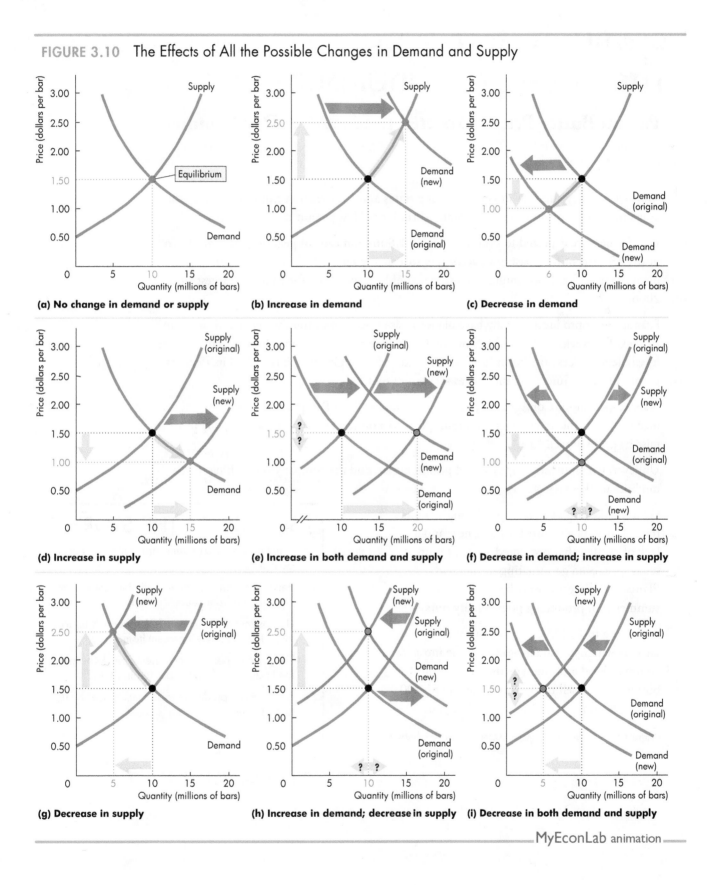

(a) **No change in demand or supply**

(b) **Increase in demand**

(c) **Decrease in demand**

(d) **Increase in supply**

(e) **Increase in both demand and supply**

(f) **Decrease in demand; increase in supply**

(g) **Decrease in supply**

(h) **Increase in demand; decrease in supply**

(i) **Decrease in both demand and supply**

Demand and Supply: The Price of Peanut Butter

Peanut Butter Prices Expected to Rise After Dry Summer

The Augusta Chronicle
October 12, 2011

Another hot, dry summer in key producing states and competition from more profitable crops including cotton have significantly shrunk the U.S. peanut crop this year.

U.S. farmers are expected to produce roughly 1.8 million tons of peanuts this year, down nearly 13 percent from last year, according to a survey released Wednesday by the Department of Agriculture. Assuming that estimate holds, it would be the smallest harvest since 2006.

Peanut butter producers already have plans to raise prices for peanut butter significantly in the next few weeks. ... The J.M. Smucker Co., which makes Jif peanut butter, plans to raise its wholesale prices 30 percent in November. Kraft Foods Co., which launched its Planters peanut butter in June, is raising prices 40 percent on Oct. 31.

A spokesperson for ConAgra Foods Inc., which makes Peter Pan peanut butter, was not immediately available to comment but multiple media outlets report that the company plans to raise its prices as well.

Unilever, which makes Skippy brand peanut butter, said the company is watching the commodities market very closely.

Georgia, the largest peanut-producing state in the country, saw record-breaking heat and a lack of rainfall that prevented some peanut seeds from even germinating in the field. Plants that did grow were baked in the hot summer sun, producing poor-quality nuts.

According to USDA estimates this week, farmers who had runner peanuts—the most common kind and the type used for peanut butter—could sell their crop for nearly $1,200 a ton, up from nearly $450 a ton last year.

ESSENCE OF THE STORY

- A hot and dry 2011 summer resulted in a poor peanut harvest.
- Because cotton was more profitable, some farmers switched from peanuts to cotton.
- U.S. peanut production in 2011 was 1.8 million tons, down nearly 13 percent from 2010.
- The price of peanuts increased from $450 per ton in 2010 to $1,200 per ton in 2011.
- Peanut butter producers raised their prices by up to 40 percent.

ECONOMIC ANALYSIS

- This news article reports events in two markets: the market for peanuts and the market for peanut butter.

- In the market for peanuts, a hot, dry summer decreased supply.

- Also, a rise in the price of cotton, a *substitute in production* for peanuts, led farmers to plant more cotton acres and fewer peanuts acres, so the supply of peanuts decreased for a second reason.

- The decrease in supply led to a large increase in price, a decrease in the quantity demanded, and a decrease in the equilibrium quantity of peanuts.

- Figure 1 illustrates the market for peanuts in 2010 and 2011.

- The demand curve for peanuts is D. In 2010, the supply curve was S_0. The equilibrium price was $450 per ton and 2 million tons of peanuts were produced.

- In 2011, supply decreased and the supply curve shifted leftward to S_1. The equilibrium price increased to $1,200 per ton and the equilibrium quantity decreased to 1.8 million tons. The quantity demanded decreased, shown by the movement along the demand curve D.

- Peanuts along with labor and capital are used to make peanut butter.

- So the rise in the price of peanuts increased the cost of producing peanut butter and decreased its supply.

- The decrease in the supply of peanut butter led to an increase in price, a decrease in the quantity demanded, and a decrease in the equilibrium quantity of peanut butter.

- Figure 2 illustrates the market for peanut butter in 2010 and 2011.

- The demand curve for peanut butter is D. In 2010, the supply curve was S_0. The equilibrium price was $2.00 per pound and 350 million pounds of peanut butter were produced.

- In 2011, supply decreased and the supply curve shifted leftward to S_1. The equilibrium price increased to $2.80 per pound and the equilibrium quantity decreased to 300 million pounds. The quantity of peanut butter demanded decreased, shown by the movement along the demand curve D.

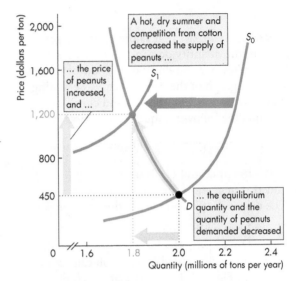

Figure 1 The Market for Peanuts

Figure 2 The Market for Peanut Butter

- Notice that the increase in the price of peanut butter, a 40 percent increase, was much smaller than the increase in the price of peanuts, an increase from $450 to $1,200 or a 167 percent increase. Can you explain why?

MATHEMATICAL NOTE

Demand, Supply, and Equilibrium

Demand Curve

The law of demand says that as the price of a good or service falls, the quantity demanded of that good or service increases. We can illustrate the law of demand by drawing a graph of the demand curve or writing down an equation. When the demand curve is a straight line, the following equation describes it:

$$P = a - bQ_D,$$

where P is the price and Q_D is the quantity demanded. The a and b are positive constants.

The demand equation tells us three things:

1. The price at which no one is willing to buy the good (Q_D is zero). That is, if the price is a, then the quantity demanded is zero. You can see the price a in Fig. 1. It is the price at which the demand curve hits the y-axis—what we call the demand curve's "y-intercept."

2. As the price falls, the quantity demanded increases. If Q_D is a positive number, then the price P must be less than a. As Q_D gets larger, the price P becomes smaller. That is, as the quantity increases, the maximum price that buyers are willing to pay for the last unit of the good falls.

3. The constant b tells us how fast the maximum price that someone is willing to pay for the good falls as the quantity increases. That is, the constant b tells us about the steepness of the demand curve. The equation tells us that the slope of the demand curve is $-b$.

Supply Curve

The law of supply says that as the price of a good or service rises, the quantity supplied of that good or service increases. We can illustrate the law of supply by drawing a graph of the supply curve or writing down an equation. When the supply curve is a straight line, the following equation describes it:

$$P = c + dQ_S,$$

where P is the price and Q_S is the quantity supplied. The c and d are positive constants.

The supply equation tells us three things:

1. The price at which sellers are not willing to supply the good (Q_S is zero). That is, if the price is c, then no one is willing to sell the good. You can see the price c in Fig. 2. It is the price at which the supply curve hits the y-axis—what we call the supply curve's "y-intercept."

2. As the price rises, the quantity supplied increases. If Q_S is a positive number, then the price P must be greater than c. As Q_S increases, the price P becomes larger. That is, as the quantity increases, the minimum price that sellers are willing to accept for the last unit rises.

3. The constant d tells us how fast the minimum price at which someone is willing to sell the good rises as the quantity increases. That is, the constant d tells us about the steepness of the supply curve. The equation tells us that the slope of the supply curve is d.

Figure 1 Demand Curve

Figure 2 Supply Curve

Market Equilibrium

Demand and supply determine market equilibrium. Figure 3 shows the equilibrium price (P^*) and equilibrium quantity (Q^*) at the intersection of the demand curve and the supply curve.

We can use the equations to find the equilibrium price and equilibrium quantity. The price of a good adjusts until the quantity demanded Q_D equals the quantity supplied Q_S. So at the equilibrium price (P^*) and equilibrium quantity (Q^*),

$$Q_D = Q_S = Q^*.$$

To find the equilibrium price and equilibrium quantity, substitute Q^* for Q_D in the demand equation and Q^* for Q_S in the supply equation. Then the price is the equilibrium price (P^*), which gives

$$P^* = a - bQ^*$$
$$P^* = c + dQ^*.$$

Notice that

$$a - bQ^* = c + dQ^*.$$

Now solve for Q^*:

$$a - c = bQ^* + dQ^*$$
$$a - c = (b + d)Q^*$$
$$Q^* = \frac{a - c}{b + d}.$$

To find the equilibrium price, (P^*), substitute for Q^* in either the demand equation or the supply equation.

Using the demand equation, we have

$$P^* = a - b\left(\frac{a - c}{b + d}\right)$$
$$P^* = \frac{a(b + d) - b(a - c)}{b + d}$$
$$P^* = \frac{ad + bc}{b + d}.$$

Alternatively, using the supply equation, we have

$$P^* = c + d\left(\frac{a - c}{b + d}\right)$$
$$P^* = \frac{c(b + d) + d(a - c)}{b + d}$$
$$P^* = \frac{ad + bc}{b + d}.$$

An Example

The demand for ice-cream cones is

$$P = 800 - 2Q_D.$$

The supply of ice-cream cones is

$$P = 200 + 1Q_S.$$

The price of a cone is expressed in cents, and the quantities are expressed in cones per day.

To find the equilibrium price (P^*) and equilibrium quantity (Q^*), substitute Q^* for Q_D and Q_S and P^* for P. That is,

$$P^* = 800 - 2Q^*$$
$$P^* = 200 + 1Q^*$$

Now solve for Q^*:

$$800 - 2Q^* = 200 + 1Q^*$$
$$600 = 3Q^*$$
$$Q^* = 200.$$

And

$$P^* = 800 - 2(200)$$
$$= 400.$$

The equilibrium price is $4 a cone, and the equilibrium quantity is 200 cones per day.

Figure 3 Market Equilibrium

◆ **SUMMARY**

Key Points

Markets and Prices (p. 56)

- A competitive market is one that has so many buyers and sellers that no single buyer or seller can influence the price.
- Opportunity cost is a relative price.
- Demand and supply determine relative prices.

Working Problem 1 will give you a better understanding of markets and prices.

Demand (pp. 57–61)

- Demand is the relationship between the quantity demanded of a good and its price when all other influences on buying plans remain the same.
- The higher the price of a good, other things remaining the same, the smaller is the quantity demanded—the law of demand.
- Demand depends on the prices of related goods (substitutes and complements), expected future prices, income, expected future income and credit, the population, and preferences.

Working Problems 2 to 5 will give you a better understanding of demand.

Supply (pp. 62–65)

- Supply is the relationship between the quantity supplied of a good and its price when all other influences on selling plans remain the same.
- The higher the price of a good, other things remaining the same, the greater is the quantity supplied—the law of supply.

- Supply depends on the prices of factors of production used to produce a good, the prices of related goods produced, expected future prices, the number of suppliers, technology, and the state of nature.

Working Problems 6 to 9 will give you a better understanding of supply.

Market Equilibrium (pp. 66–67)

- At the equilibrium price, the quantity demanded equals the quantity supplied.
- At any price above the equilibrium price, there is a surplus and the price falls.
- At any price below the equilibrium price, there is a shortage and the price rises.

Working Problems 10 and 11 will give you a better understanding of market equilibrium.

Predicting Changes in Price and Quantity (pp. 68–73)

- An increase in demand brings a rise in the price and an increase in the quantity supplied. A decrease in demand brings a fall in the price and a decrease in the quantity supplied.
- An increase in supply brings a fall in the price and an increase in the quantity demanded. A decrease in supply brings a rise in the price and a decrease in the quantity demanded.
- An increase in demand and an increase in supply bring an increased quantity but an uncertain price change. An increase in demand and a decrease in supply bring a higher price but an uncertain change in quantity.

Working Problems 12 and 13 will give you a better understanding of predicting changes in price and quantity.

Key Terms

Change in demand, 58
Change in supply, 63
Change in the quantity demanded, 61
Change in the quantity supplied, 64
Competitive market, 56
Complement, 59
Demand, 57

Demand curve, 58
Equilibrium price, 66
Equilibrium quantity, 66
Inferior good, 60
Law of demand, 57
Law of supply, 62
Money price, 56
Normal good, 60

Quantity demanded, 57
Quantity supplied, 62
Relative price, 56
Substitute, 59
Supply, 62
Supply curve, 62

STUDY PLAN PROBLEMS AND APPLICATIONS

MyEconLab   You can work Problems 1 to 17 in MyEconLab Chapter 3 Study Plan and get instant feedback.

Markets and Prices (Study Plan 3.1)

1. William Gregg owned a mill in South Carolina. In December 1862, he placed a notice in the *Edgehill Advertiser* announcing his willingness to exchange cloth for food and other items. Here is an extract:

   1 yard of cloth for 1 pound of bacon
   2 yards of cloth for 1 pound of butter
   4 yards of cloth for 1 pound of wool
   8 yards of cloth for 1 bushel of salt

   a. What is the relative price of butter in terms of wool?

   b. If the money price of bacon was 20¢ a pound, what do you predict was the money price of butter?

   c. If the money price of bacon was 20¢ a pound and the money price of salt was $2.00 a bushel, do you think anyone would accept Mr. Gregg's offer of cloth for salt?

Demand (Study Plan 3.2)

2. The price of food increased during the past year.

   a. Explain why the law of demand applies to food just as it does to all other goods and services.

   b. Explain how the substitution effect influences food purchases and provide some examples of substitutions that people might make when the price of food rises and other things remain the same.

   c. Explain how the income effect influences food purchases and provide some examples of the income effect that might occur when the price of food rises and other things remain the same.

3. Place the following goods and services into pairs of likely substitutes and pairs of likely complements. (You may use an item in more than one pair.) The goods and services are

   coal, oil, natural gas, wheat, corn, rye, pasta, pizza, sausage, skateboard, roller blades, video game, laptop, iPod, cell phone, text message, email, phone call, voice mail

4. During 2010, the average income in China increased by 10 percent. Compared to 2009,

how do you expect the following would change:

   a. The demand for beef. Explain your answer.

   b. The demand for rice. Explain your answer.

5. In January 2010, the price of gasoline was $2.70 a gallon. By spring 2010, the price had increased to $3.00 a gallon. Assume that there were no changes in average income, population, or any other influence on buying plans. Explain how the rise in the price of gasoline would affect

   a. The demand for gasoline.

   b. The quantity of gasoline demanded.

Supply (Study Plan 3.3)

6. In 2008, the price of corn increased by 35 percent and some cotton farmers in Texas stopped growing cotton and started to grow corn.

   a. Does this fact illustrate the law of demand or the law of supply? Explain your answer.

   b. Why would a cotton farmer grow corn?

Use the following information to work Problems 7 to 9.

Dairies make low-fat milk from full-cream milk. In the process of making low-fat milk, the dairies produce cream, which is made into ice cream. In the market for low-fat milk, the following events occur one at a time:

   (i)   The wage rate of dairy workers rises.

   (ii)   The price of cream rises.

   (iii) The price of low-fat milk rises.

   (iv)   With the period of low rainfall extending, dairies raise their expected price of low-fat milk next year.

   (v)   With advice from health-care experts, dairy farmers decide to switch from producing full-cream milk to growing vegetables.

   (vi)   A new technology lowers the cost of producing ice cream.

7. Explain the effect of each event on the supply of low-fat milk.

8. Use a graph to illustrate the effect of each event.

9. Does any event (or events) illustrate the law of supply?

Market Equilibrium (Study Plan 3.4)

10. "As more people buy computers, the demand for Internet service increases and the price of Internet service decreases. The fall in the price of Internet service decreases the supply of Internet service." Explain what is wrong with this statement.

11. The demand and supply schedules for gum are

Price (cents per pack)	Quantity demanded (millions of packs a week)	Quantity supplied (millions of packs a week)
20	180	60
40	140	100
60	100	140
80	60	180
100	20	220

a. Draw a graph of the market for gum and mark in the equilibrium price and quantity.

b. Suppose that the price of gum is 70¢ a pack. Describe the situation in the gum market and explain how the price adjusts.

c. Suppose that the price of gum is 30¢ a pack. Describe the situation in the gum market and explain how the price adjusts.

Predicting Changes in Price and Quantity

(Study Plan 3.5)

12. The following events occur one at a time:
    (i)   The price of crude oil rises.
    (ii) The price of a car rises.
    (iii) All speed limits on highways are abolished.
    (iv) Robots cut car production costs.

    Which of these events will increase or decrease (state which occurs)

    a. The demand for gasoline?
    b. The supply of gasoline?
    c. The quantity of gasoline demanded?
    d. The quantity of gasoline supplied?

13. In Problem 11, a fire destroys some factories that produce gum and the quantity of gum supplied decreases by 40 million packs a week at each price.

    a. Explain what happens in the market for gum and draw a graph to illustrate the changes.

    b. If at the time the fire occurs there is an increase in the teenage population, which increases the quantity of gum demanded by 40 million packs a week at each price, what are the new equilibrium price and quantity of gum? Illustrate these changes on your graph.

14. **Indian Weddings Boost Gold Price Hopes**

    Indian weddings traditionally take place between late September and December. The predilection for jewelery at this time usually gives a big boost to gold sales, and the record shows the price of gold has generally risen during this period.

    Source: *Financial News*, September 9, 2011

    a. Describe the changes in demand and supply in the market for gold in India during the wedding season.

    b. Given that the wedding season is a predictable event, how might expectations influence the market for gold in India?

15. **Pump Prices on Pace to Top 2009 High by Weekend**

    The cost of filling up the car is rising as the crude oil price soars and pump prices may exceed the peak price of 2009.

    Source: *USA Today*, January 7, 2010

    a. Does demand for or the supply of gasoline or both change when the price of oil soars?

    b. Use a demand-supply graph to illustrate what happens to the equilibrium price of gasoline and the equilibrium quantity of gasoline bought when the price of oil soars.

Economics in the News (Study Plan 3.N)

16. **American to Cut Flights, Charge for Luggage**

    American Airlines announced that it will charge passengers $15 for their first piece of checked luggage and cut domestic flights as it grapples with record-high fuel prices.

    Source: *Boston Herald*, May 22, 2008

    a. According to the news clip, what is the influence on the supply of American Airlines flights?

    b. Explain how supply changes.

17. **Frigid Florida Winter is Bad News for Tomato Lovers**

    An unusually cold January in Florida destroyed entire fields of tomatoes. Florida's growers are shipping only a quarter of their usual 5 million pounds a week. The price has risen from $6.50 for a 25-pound box a year ago to $30 now.

    Source: *USA Today*, March 3, 2010

    a. Make a graph to illustrate the market for tomatoes in January 2009 and January 2010.

    b. On the graph, show how the events in the news clip influence the market for tomatoes.

    c. Why is the news "bad for tomato lovers"?

ADDITIONAL PROBLEMS AND APPLICATIONS

MyEconLab   You can work these problems in MyEconLab if assigned by your instructor.

Markets and Prices

18. What features of the world market for crude oil make it a competitive market?

19. The money price of a textbook is $90 and the money price of the Wii game *Super Mario Galaxy* is $45.

   a. What is the opportunity cost of a textbook in terms of the Wii game?

   b. What is the relative price of the Wii game in terms of textbooks?

Demand

20. The price of gasoline has increased during the past year.

   a. Explain why the law of demand applies to gasoline just as it does to all other goods and services.

   b. Explain how the substitution effect influences gasoline purchases and provide some examples of substitutions that people might make when the price of gasoline rises and other things remain the same.

   c. Explain how the income effect influences gasoline purchases and provide some examples of the income effects that might occur when the price of gasoline rises and other things remain the same.

21. Think about the demand for the three game consoles: Xbox, PS3, and Wii. Explain the effect of the following events on the demand for Xbox games and the quantity of Xbox games demanded, other things remaining the same.

   a. The price of an Xbox falls.

   b. The prices of a PS3 and a Wii fall.

   c. The number of people writing and producing Xbox games increases.

   d. Consumers' incomes increase.

   e. Programmers who write code for Xbox games become more costly to hire.

   f. The expected future price of an Xbox game falls.

   g. A new game console that is a close substitute for Xbox comes onto the market.

Supply

22. Classify the following pairs of goods and services as substitutes in production, complements in production, or neither.

   a. Bottled water and health club memberships

   b. French fries and baked potatoes

   c. Leather purses and leather shoes

   d. Hybrids and SUVs

   e. Diet coke and regular coke

23. As the prices of homes fell across the United States in 2008, the number of homes offered for sale decreased.

   a. Does this fact illustrate the law of demand or the law of supply? Explain your answer.

   b. Why would home owners decide not to sell?

24. **G.M. Cuts Production for Quarter**

   General Motors cut its fourth-quarter production schedule by 10 percent because Ford Motor, Chrysler, and Toyota sales declined in August.

   Source: *The New York Times*, September 5, 2007

   Explain whether this news clip illustrates a change in the supply of cars or a change in the quantity supplied of cars.

Market Equilibrium

Use the following figure to work Problems 25 and 26.

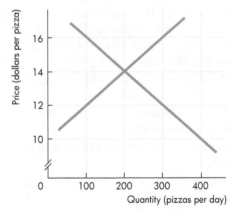

25. a. Label the curves. Which curve shows the willingness to pay for a pizza?

   b. If the price of a pizza is $16, is there a shortage or a surplus and does the price rise or fall?

c. Sellers want to receive the highest possible price, so why would they be willing to accept less than $16 a pizza?

26. a. If the price of a pizza is $12, is there a shortage or a surplus and does the price rise or fall?

b. Buyers want to pay the lowest possible price, so why would they be willing to pay more than $12 for a pizza?

27. The demand and supply schedules for potato chips are

Price (cents per bag)	Quantity demanded	Quantity supplied
	(millions of bags per week)	
50	160	130
60	150	140
70	140	150
80	130	160
90	120	170
100	110	180

a. Draw a graph of the potato chip market and mark in the equilibrium price and quantity.

b. If the price is 60¢ a bag, is there a shortage or a surplus, and how does the price adjust?

Predicting Changes in Price and Quantity

28. In Problem 27, a new dip increases the quantity of potato chips that people want to buy by 30 million bags per week at each price.

a. Does the demand for chips change? Does the supply of chips change? Describe the change.

b. How do the equilibrium price and equilibrium quantity of chips change?

29. In Problem 27, if a virus destroys potato crops and the quantity of potato chips produced decreases by 40 million bags a week at each price, how does the supply of chips change?

30. If the virus in Problem 29 hits just as the new dip in Problem 28 comes onto the market, how do the equilibrium price and equilibrium quantity of chips change?

31. **Strawberry Prices Drop as Late Harvest Hits Market**

Shoppers bought strawberries in March for $1.25 a pound rather than the $3.49 a pound they paid last year. With the price so low, some growers plowed over their strawberry plants to make way for spring melons; others froze their harvests and sold them to juice and jam makers.

Source: *USA Today*, April 5, 2010

a. Explain how the market for strawberries would have changed if growers had not plowed in their plants but offered locals "you pick for free."

b. Describe the changes in demand and supply in the market for strawberry jam.

32. **"Popcorn Movie" Experience Gets Pricier**

Cinemas are raising the price of popcorn. Demand for field corn, which is used for animal feed, corn syrup, and ethanol, has increased and its price has exploded. That's caused some farmers to shift from growing popcorn to easier-to-grow field corn.

Source: *USA Today*, May 24, 2008

Explain and illustrate graphically the events described in the news clip in the market for

a. Popcorn

b. Movie tickets

33. **Watch Out for Rising Dry-Cleaning Bills**

In the past year, the price of dry-cleaning solvent doubled. More than 4,000 dry cleaners across the United States disappeared as budget-conscious consumers cut back. This year the price of hangers used by dry cleaners is expected to double.

Source: CNN Money, June 4, 2012

a. Explain the effect of rising solvent prices on the market for dry cleaning.

b. Explain the effect of consumers becoming more budget conscious along with the rising price of solvent on the price of dry cleaning.

c. If the price of hangers does rise this year, do you expect additional dry cleaners to disappear? Explain why or why not.

Economics in the News

34. After you have studied *Reading Between the Lines* on pp. 74–75, answer the following questions.

a. What happened to the price of peanut butter in 2011?

b. What substitutions do you expect might have been made to decrease the quantity of peanut butter demanded?

c. What is the main complement of peanut butter and what do you predict happened in its market in 2011?

d. What is one of the main substitutes in production for peanuts and what do you predict happened in its market in 2011?

e. Do you predict that the higher prices of peanuts and peanut butter will persist or will they return to normal after one year?

f. Why did the percentage rise in the price of peanuts exceed the percentage rise in the price of peanut butter?

4

ELASTICITY

After studying this chapter,
you will be able to:

◆ Define, calculate, and explain the factors that
influence the price elasticity of demand

◆ Define, calculate, and explain the factors that
influence the income elasticity of demand and the
cross elasticity of demand

◆ Define, calculate, and explain the factors that
influence the elasticity of supply

In the winter of 2010, a Florida frost destroyed the
state's tomato crop, driving the price to almost five
times its normal level. Why did the price rise so
much?

To answer this and similar questions, we use the
neat tool that you study in this chapter: elasticity.

At the end of the chapter, in *Reading Between the
Lines*, we use the concept of elasticity to explain what
was happening in the Florida tomatoes market during
the winter of 2010. But we begin by explaining
elasticity in a familiar setting: the market for pizza.

◆ Price Elasticity of Demand

You know that when supply decreases, the equilibrium price rises and the equilibrium quantity decreases. But does the price rise by a large amount and the quantity decrease by a little? Or does the price barely rise and the quantity decrease by a large amount?

The answer depends on the responsiveness of the quantity demanded of a good to a change in its price. If the quantity demanded is not very responsive to a change in the price, the price rises a lot and the equilibrium quantity doesn't change much. If the quantity demanded *is* very responsive to a change in the price, the price barely rises and the equilibrium quantity changes a lot.

You might think about the responsiveness of the quantity demanded of a good to a change in its price in terms of the slope of the demand curve. If the demand curve is steep, the quantity demanded of the good isn't very responsive to a change in the price. If the demand curve is almost flat, the quantity demanded *is* very responsive to a change in the price.

But the slope of a demand curve depends on the units in which we measure the price and the quantity—we can make the curve steep or almost flat just by changing the units in which we measure the price and the quantity. Also we often want to compare the demand for different goods and services and quantities of these goods are measured in unrelated units. For example, a pizza producer might want to compare the demand for pizza with the demand for soft drinks. Which quantity demanded is more responsive to a price change? This question can't be answered by comparing the slopes of two demand curves. The units of measurement of pizza and soft drinks are unrelated. But the question *can* be answered with a measure of responsiveness that is *independent* of units of measurement. Elasticity is such a measure.

The **price elasticity of demand** is a units-free measure of the responsiveness of the quantity demanded of a good to a change in its price when all other influences on buying plans remain the same.

Calculating Price Elasticity of Demand

We calculate the *price elasticity of demand* by using the formula:

$$\text{Price elasticity of demand} = \frac{\text{Percentage change in quantity damanded}}{\text{Percentage change in price}}.$$

To calculate the price elasticity of demand for pizza, we need to know the quantity demanded of pizza at two different prices, when all other influences on buying plans remain the same.

Figure 4.1 zooms in on a section of the demand curve for pizza and shows how the quantity demanded responds to a small change in price. Initially, the price is $20.50 a pizza and 9 pizzas an hour are demanded—the original point. The price then falls to $19.50 a pizza, and the quantity demanded increases to 11 pizzas an hour—the new point. When the price falls by $1 a pizza, the quantity demanded increases by 2 pizzas an hour.

To calculate the price elasticity of demand, we express the change in price as a percentage of the *average price* and the change in the quantity demanded as a percentage of the *average quantity*. By using the average price and average quantity, we calculate the elasticity at a point on the demand curve midway between the original point and the new point.

The original price is $20.50 and the new price is $19.50, so the price change is $1 and the average price is $20 a pizza. Call the percentage change in the price $\%\Delta P$, then

$$\%\Delta P = \Delta P/P_{ave} \times 100 = (\$1/\$20) \times 100 = 5\%.$$

The original quantity demanded is 9 pizzas and the new quantity demanded is 11 pizzas, so the quantity change is 2 pizzas and the average quantity demanded is 10 pizzas. Call the percentage change in the quantity demanded $\%\Delta Q$, then

$$\%\Delta Q = \Delta Q/Q_{ave} \times 100 = (2/10) \times 100 = 20\%.$$

The price elasticity of demand equals the percentage change in the quantity demanded (20 percent) divided by the percentage change in price (5 percent) and is 4. That is,

$$\text{Price elasticity of demand} = \frac{\%\Delta Q}{\%\Delta P}$$

$$= \frac{20\%}{5\%} = 4.$$

Average Price and Quantity Notice that we use the *average* price and *average* quantity. We do this because it gives the most precise measurement of elasticity—at the *midpoint* between the original price and the new price. If the price falls from $20.50 to $19.50, the $1 price change is 4.9 percent of $20.50. The 2 pizza change in quantity is 22.2 percent of 9 pizzas, the original quantity. So if we use

FIGURE 4.1   Calculating the Elasticity of Demand

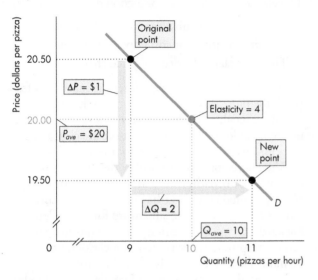

The elasticity of demand is calculated by using the formula:*

$$\text{Price elasticity of demand} = \frac{\text{Percentage change in quantity demanded}}{\text{Percentage change in price}}$$

$$= \frac{\%\Delta Q}{\%\Delta P}$$

$$= \frac{\Delta Q/Q_{ave}}{\Delta P/P_{ave}}$$

$$= \frac{2/10}{1/20} = 4.$$

This calculation measures the elasticity at an average price of $20 a pizza and an average quantity of 10 pizzas an hour.

* In the formula, the Greek letter delta (Δ) stands for "change in" and %Δ stands for "percentage change in."

───────── MyEconLab animation ─────────

these numbers, the price elasticity of demand is 22.2 divided by 4.9, which equals 4.5. But if the price rises from $19.50 to $20.50, the $1 price change is 5.1 percent of $19.50. The 2 pizza change in quantity is 18.2 percent of 11 pizzas, the original quantity. So if we use these numbers, the price elasticity of demand is 18.2 divided by 5.1, which equals 3.6.

By using percentages of the *average* price and *average* quantity, we get the *same value* for the elasticity regardless of whether the price falls from $20.50 to $19.50 or rises from $19.50 to $20.50.

Percentages and Proportions Elasticity is the ratio of two percentage changes, so when we divide one percentage change by another, the 100s cancel. A percentage change is a *proportionate* change multiplied by 100. The proportionate change in price is $\Delta P/P_{ave}$, and the proportionate change in quantity demanded is $\Delta Q/Q_{ave}$. So if we divide $\Delta Q/Q_{ave}$ by $\Delta P/P_{ave}$ we get the same answer as we get by using percentage changes.

A Units-Free Measure Now that you've calculated a price elasticity of demand, you can see why it is a *units-free measure*. Elasticity is a units-free measure because the percentage change in each variable is independent of the units in which the variable is measured. The ratio of the two percentages is a number without units.

Minus Sign and Elasticity When the price of a good *rises*, the quantity demanded *decreases*. Because a *positive* change in price brings a *negative* change in the quantity demanded, the price elasticity of demand is a negative number. But it is the magnitude, or *absolute value*, of the price elasticity of demand that tells us how responsive the quantity demanded is. So to compare price elasticities of demand, we use the *magnitude* of the elasticity and ignore the minus sign.

Inelastic and Elastic Demand

If the quantity demanded remains constant when the price changes, then the price elasticity of demand is zero and the good is said to have a **perfectly inelastic demand**. One good that has a very low price elasticity of demand (perhaps zero over some price range) is insulin. Insulin is of such importance to some diabetics that if the price rises or falls, they do not change the quantity they buy.

If the percentage change in the quantity demanded equals the percentage change in the price, then the price elasticity equals 1 and the good is said to have a **unit elastic demand**.

Between perfectly inelastic demand and unit elastic demand is a general case in which *the percentage change in the quantity demanded is less than the percentage change in the price*. In this case, the price elasticity of demand is between zero and 1 and the good is said to have an **inelastic demand**. Food and shelter are examples of goods with inelastic demand.

If the quantity demanded changes by an infinitely large percentage in response to a tiny price change, then the price elasticity of demand is infinity and the good is said to have a **perfectly elastic demand**. An example of a good that has a very high elasticity of demand (almost infinite) is a soft drink from two campus machines located side by side. If the two machines offer the same soft drinks for the same price, some people buy from one machine and some from the other. But if one machine's price is higher than the other's, by even a small amount, no one buys from the machine with the higher price. Drinks from the two machines are perfect substitutes. The demand for a good that has a perfect substitute is perfectly elastic.

Between unit elastic demand and perfectly elastic demand is another general case in which *the percentage change in the quantity demanded exceeds the percentage change in price*. In this case, the price elasticity of demand is greater than 1 and the good is said to have an **elastic demand**. Automobiles and furniture are examples of goods that have elastic demand.

Figure 4.2 shows three demand curves that cover the entire range of possible elasticities of demand that you've just reviewed. In Fig. 4.2(a), the quantity demanded is constant regardless of the price, so this demand is perfectly inelastic. In Fig. 4.2(b), the percentage change in the quantity demanded equals the percentage change in price, so this demand is unit elastic. In Fig. 4.2(c), the price is constant regardless of the quantity demanded, so this figure illustrates a perfectly elastic demand.

You now know the distinction between elastic and inelastic demand. But what determines whether the demand for a good is elastic or inelastic?

The Factors that Influence the Elasticity of Demand

The elasticity of demand for a good depends on

- The closeness of substitutes
- The proportion of income spent on the good
- The time elapsed since the price change

Closeness of Substitutes The closer the substitutes for a good, the more elastic is the demand for it. Oil as fuel or raw material for chemicals has no close substitutes so the demand for oil is inelastic. Plastics are close substitutes for metals, so the demand for metals is elastic.

The degree of substitutability depends on how narrowly (or broadly) we define a good. For example, a personal computer has no close substitutes, but a Dell PC is a close substitute for a Hewlett-Packard PC. So the elasticity of demand for personal computers is lower than the elasticity of demand for a Dell or a Hewlett-Packard.

In everyday language we call goods such as food and shelter *necessities* and goods such as exotic vacations *luxuries*. A necessity has poor substitutes, so it generally has an inelastic demand. A luxury usually has many substitutes, one of which is not buying it. So a luxury generally has an elastic demand.

Proportion of Income Spent on the Good Other things remaining the same, the greater the proportion of income spent on a good, the more elastic (or less inelastic) is the demand for it.

FIGURE 4.2   Inelastic and Elastic Demand

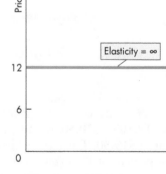

(a) Perfectly inelastic demand   **(b) Unit elastic demand**   **(c) Perfectly elastic demand**

Each demand illustrated here has a constant elasticity. The demand curve in part (a) illustrates the demand for a good that has a zero elasticity of demand. The demand curve in part (b) illustrates the demand for a good with a unit elasticity of demand. And the demand curve in part (c) illustrates the demand for a good with an infinite elasticity of demand.

MyEconLab animation

Think about your own elasticity of demand for chewing gum and housing. If the price of gum rises, you consume almost as much as before. Your demand for gum is inelastic. If apartment rents rise, you look for someone to share with. Your demand for housing is not as inelastic as your demand for gum. Why the difference? Housing takes a big chunk of your budget, and gum takes little. You barely notice the higher price of gum, while the higher rent puts your budget under severe strain.

Longer · elastic

Time Elapsed Since Price Change The longer the time that has elapsed since a price change, the more elastic is demand. When the price of oil increased by 400 percent during the 1970s, people barely changed the quantity of oil and gasoline they bought. But gradually, as more efficient auto and airplane engines were developed, the quantity bought decreased. The demand for oil became more elastic as more time elapsed following the huge price hike.

Elasticity Along a Linear Demand Curve

Elasticity of demand is not the same as slope. And a good way to see this fact is by studying a demand curve that has a constant slope but a varying elasticity.

The demand curve in Fig. 4.3 is linear, which means that it has a constant slope. Along this demand curve, a $5 rise in the price brings a decrease of 10 pizzas an hour.

But the price elasticity of demand is not constant along this demand curve. To see why, let's calculate some elasticities.

At the midpoint of the demand curve, the price is $12.50 and the quantity is 25 pizzas per hour. If the price rises from $10 to $15 a pizza the quantity demanded decreases from 30 to 20 pizzas an hour and the average price and average quantity are at the midpoint of the demand curve. So

$$\text{Price elasticity of demand} = \frac{10/25}{5/12.50}$$
$$= 1.$$

That is, at the midpoint of a linear demand curve, the price elasticity of demand is 1.

At prices *above* the midpoint, the price elasticity of demand is greater than 1: Demand is elastic. To see that demand is elastic, let's calculate the elasticity when the price rises from $15 to $25 a pizza. You can see that quantity demanded decreases from 20 to zero pizzas an hour. The average price is $20 a pizza, and

FIGURE 4.3   Elasticity Along a Linear Demand Curve

On a linear demand curve, demand is unit elastic at the midpoint (elasticity is 1), elastic above the midpoint, and inelastic below the midpoint.

———— MyEconLab animation ————

the average quantity is 10 pizzas. Putting these numbers into the elasticity formula,

$$\text{Price elasticity of demand} = \frac{\Delta Q/Q_{ave}}{\Delta P/P_{ave}}$$
$$= \frac{20/10}{10/20}$$
$$= 4.$$

That is, the price elasticity of demand at an average price of $20 a pizza is 4.

At prices *below* the midpoint, the price elasticity of demand is less than 1: Demand is inelastic. For example, if the price rises from zero to $10 a pizza, the quantity demanded decreases from 50 to 30 pizzas an hour. The average price is now $5 and the average quantity is 40 pizzas an hour. So

$$\text{Price elasticity of demand} = \frac{20/40}{10/5}$$
$$= 1/4.$$

That is, the price elasticity of demand at an average price of $5 a pizza is 1/4.

Total Revenue and Elasticity

The **total revenue** from the sale of a good equals the price of the good multiplied by the quantity sold. When a price changes, total revenue also changes. But a cut in the price does not always decrease total revenue. The change in total revenue depends on the elasticity of demand in the following way:

- If demand is elastic, a 1 percent price cut increases the quantity sold by more than 1 percent and total revenue increases.
- If demand is inelastic, a 1 percent price cut increases the quantity sold by less than 1 percent and total revenue decreases.
- If demand is unit elastic, a 1 percent price cut increases the quantity sold by 1 percent and total revenue does not change.

In Fig. 4.4(a), over the price range from $25 to $12.50, demand is elastic. Over the price range from $12.50 to zero, demand is inelastic. At a price of $12.50, demand is unit elastic.

Figure 4.4(b) shows total revenue. At a price of $25, the quantity sold is zero, so total revenue is zero. At a price of zero, the quantity demanded is 50 pizzas an hour and total revenue is again zero. A price cut in the elastic range brings an increase in total revenue—the percentage increase in the quantity demanded is greater than the percentage decrease in price. A price cut in the inelastic range brings a decrease in total revenue—the percentage increase in the quantity demanded is less than the percentage decrease in price. At unit elasticity, total revenue is at a maximum.

Figure 4.4 shows how we can use this relationship between elasticity and total revenue to estimate elasticity using the total revenue test. The **total revenue test** is a method of estimating the price elasticity of demand by observing the change in total revenue that results from a change in the price, when all other influences on the quantity sold remain the same.

- If a price cut increases total revenue, demand is elastic.
- If a price cut decreases total revenue, demand is inelastic.
- If a price cut leaves total revenue unchanged, demand is unit elastic.

FIGURE 4.4 Elasticity and Total Revenue

(a) Demand

(b) Total revenue

When demand is elastic, in the price range from $25 to $12.50, a decrease in price (part a) brings an increase in total revenue (part b). When demand is inelastic, in the price range from $12.50 to zero, a decrease in price (part a) brings a decrease in total revenue (part b). When demand is unit elastic, at a price of $12.50 (part a), total revenue is at a maximum (part b).

MyEconLab animation

Economics in Action
Elastic and Inelastic Demand

The real-world price elasticities of demand in the table range from 1.52 for metals, the item with the most elastic demand in the table, to 0.05 for oil, the item with the most inelastic demand in the table. The demand for food is also inelastic.

Oil and food, which have poor substitutes and inelastic demand, might be classified as necessities. Furniture and motor vehicles, which have good substitutes and elastic demand, might be classified as luxuries.

Price Elasticities of Demand

Good or Service	Elasticity
Elastic Demand	
Metals	1.52
Electrical engineering products	1.39
Mechanical engineering products	1.30
Furniture	1.26
Motor vehicles	1.14
Instrument engineering products	1.10
Transportation services	1.03
Inelastic Demand	
Gas, electricity, and water	0.92
Chemicals	0.89
Clothing	0.64
Banking and insurance services	0.56
Housing services	0.55
Agricultural and fish products	0.42
Books, magazines, and newspapers	0.34
Food	0.12
Cigarettes	0.11
Soft drinks	0.05
Oil	0.05

Sources of data: Ahsan Mansur and John Whalley, "Numerical Specification of Applied General Equilibrium Models: Estimation, Calibration, and Data," in *Applied General Equilibrium Analysis,* eds. Herbert E. Scarf and John B. Shoven (New York: Cambridge University Press, 1984), 109, and Henri Theil, Ching-Fan Chung, and James L. Seale, Jr., *Advances in Econometrics, Supplement I, 1989, International Evidence on Consumption Patterns* (Greenwich, Conn.: JAI Press Inc., 1989), Emilio Pagoulatos and Robert Sorensen, "What Determines the Elasticity of Industry Demand," *International Journal of Industrial Organization,* 1986, and Geoffrey Heal, Columbia University, Web site.

Price Elasticities of Demand for Food

The price elasticity of demand for food in the United States is estimated to be 0.12. This elasticity is an average over all types of food. The demand for most food items is inelastic, but there is a wide range of elasticities as the figure below shows for a range of fruits, vegetables, and meats.

The demand for grapes and beef is elastic. The demand for oranges is unit elastic. These food items, especially grapes and beef, have many good substitutes. Florida winter tomatoes have closer substitutes than tomatoes in general, so the demand for the Florida winter variety is more elastic (less inelastic) than the demand for tomatoes.

Carrots and cabbage, on which we spend a very small proportion of income, have an almost zero elastic demand.

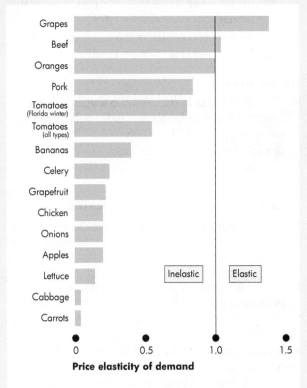

Price Elasticities of Demand for Food

Sources of data: Kuo S. Huang, *U.S. demand for food: A complete system of price and income effects* U.S. Dept. of Agriculture, Economic Research Service, Washington, DC, 1985, J. Scott Shonkwiler and Robert D. Emerson, "Imports and the Supply of Winter Tomatoes: An Application of Rational Expectations", *American Journal of Agricultural Economics,* Vol. 64, No. 4 (Nov., 1982), pp. 634–641 and Kuo S. Huang, "A Further Look at Flexibilities and Elasticities", *American Journal of Agricultural Economics,* Vol. 76, No. 2 (May, 1994), pp. 313–317.

◆ ECONOMICS IN THE NEWS

The Elasticity of Demand for Peanut Butter

Peanut Butter Prices to Rise 30 to 40 Percent
Scott Karns, president and CEO of Karns Foods, said "People are still going to need it for their family. It's still an extremely economical item." Patty Nolan, who is on a fixed income, said "I love peanut butter so I'm using a little less so I don't go through it."

Source: *The Patriot-News*, November 2, 2011

THE DATA

	Quantity (millions of tons per year)	Price (dollars per pound)
2011	350	2.00
2012	300	2.80

THE QUESTIONS

- Does the news clip imply that the demand for peanut butter is elastic or inelastic?
- If the data are two points on the demand curve for peanut butter, what is the price elasticity of demand?

THE ANSWERS

- The two remarks in the news clip suggest that the quantity of peanut butter demanded will decrease when the price rises, but not by much. The demand for peanut butter is inelastic.

- The data table says the price of peanut butter increased by $0.80 with an average price of $2.40, so the price increased by 33.3 percent. The quantity demanded decreased by 50 million tons with an average quantity of 325 million tons, so the quantity demanded decreased by 15.4 percent. The price elasticity of demand is 15.4 percent divided by 33.3 percent, which equals 0.46.

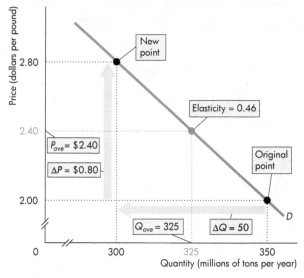

Calculating the Price Elasticity of Demand for Peanut Butter

Your Expenditure and Your Elasticity

When the price of a good changes, the change in your expenditure on the good depends on *your* elasticity of demand.

- If your demand for the good is elastic, a 1 percent price cut increases the quantity you buy by more than 1 percent and your expenditure on the item increases.
- If your demand for the good is inelastic, a 1 percent price cut increases the quantity you buy by less than 1 percent and your expenditure on the item decreases.
- If your demand for the good is unit elastic, a 1 percent price cut increases the quantity you buy by 1 percent and your expenditure on the item does not change.

So if you spend more on an item when its price falls, your demand for that item is elastic; if you spend the same amount, your demand is unit elastic; and if you spend less, your demand is inelastic.

◆ REVIEW QUIZ

1 Why do we need a units-free measure of the responsiveness of the quantity demanded of a good or service to a change in its price?
2 Define the price elasticity of demand and show how it is calculated.
3 What makes the demand for some goods elastic and the demand for other goods inelastic?
4 Why is the demand for a luxury generally more elastic (or less inelastic) than the demand for a necessity?
5 What is the total revenue test?

You can work these questions in Study Plan 4.1 and get instant feedback.   MyEconLab

You've now completed your study of the *price* elasticity of demand. Two other elasticity concepts tell us about the effects of other influences on demand. Let's look at these other elasticities of demand.

◆ More Elasticities of Demand

Suppose the economy is expanding and people are enjoying rising incomes. You know that a change in income changes demand. So this increased prosperity brings an increase in the demand for most types of goods and services. By how much will a rise in income increase the demand for pizza? This question is answered by the income elasticity of demand.

Income Elasticity of Demand

The **income elasticity of demand** is a measure of the responsiveness of the demand for a good or service to a change in income, other things remaining the same. It tells us by how much a demand curve shifts at a given price.

The income elasticity of demand is calculated by using the formula:

$$\text{Income elasticity of demand} = \frac{\text{Percentage change in quantity demanded}}{\text{Percentage change in income}}.$$

Income elasticities of demand can be positive or negative and they fall into three interesting ranges:

- Positive and greater than 1 (*normal* good, income elastic)
- Positive and less than 1 (*normal* good, income inelastic)
- Negative (*inferior* good)

Income Elastic Demand Suppose that the price of pizza is constant and 9 pizzas an hour are bought. Then incomes rise from $975 to $1,025 a week. No other influence on buying plans changes and the quantity of pizzas sold increases to 11 an hour.

The change in the quantity demanded is +2 pizzas. The average quantity is 10 pizzas, so the quantity demanded increases by 20 percent. The change in income is +$50 and the average income is $1,000, so incomes increase by 5 percent. The income elasticity of demand for pizza is

$$\frac{20\%}{5\%} = 4.$$

The demand for pizza is income elastic. The percentage increase in the quantity of pizza demanded exceeds the percentage increase in income.

Economics in Action
Necessities and Luxuries

The table shows estimates of some real-world income elasticities of demand. The demand for a necessity such as food or clothing is income inelastic, while the demand for a luxury such as transportation, which includes airline and foreign travel, is income elastic.

But what is a necessity and what is a luxury depends on the level of income. For people with a low income, food and clothing can be luxuries. So the level of income has a big effect on income elasticities of demand. The figure shows this effect on the income elasticity of demand for food in 10 countries. In countries with low incomes, such as Tanzania and India, the income elasticity of demand for food is high. In countries with high incomes, such as the United States, the income elasticity of

Some Real-World Income Elasticities of Demand

Income Elastic Demand

Airline travel	5.82
Movies	3.41
Foreign travel	3.08
Electricity	1.94
Restaurant meals	1.61
Local buses and trains	1.38
Haircuts	1.36
Automobiles	1.07

Income Inelastic Demand

Tobacco	0.86
Alcoholic drinks	0.62
Furniture	0.53
Clothing	0.51
Newspapers and magazines	0.38
Telephone	0.32
Food	0.14

Sources of data: H.S. Houthakker and Lester D. Taylor, *Consumer Demand in the United States* (Cambridge, Mass.: Harvard University Press, 1970), and Henri Theil, Ching-Fan Chung, and James L. Seale, Jr., *Advances in Econometrics, Supplement 1, 1989, International Evidence on Consumption Patterns* (Greenwich, Conn.: JAI Press, Inc., 1989).

demand for food is low. That is, as income increases, the income elasticity of demand for food decreases. Low-income consumers spend a larger percentage of any increase in income on food than do high-income consumers.

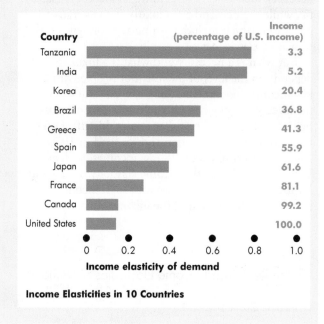

Income Elasticities in 10 Countries

Income Inelastic Demand If the income elasticity of demand is positive but less than 1, demand is income inelastic. The percentage increase in the quantity demanded is positive but less than the percentage increase in income.

Whether demand is income elastic or income inelastic has an important implication for the percentage of income spent on a good. If the demand for a good is *income elastic,* the percentage of income spent on that good *increases* as income increases. And if the demand for a good is *income inelastic,* the percentage of income spent on that good *decreases* as income increases.

Inferior Goods If the income elasticity of demand is negative, the good is an *inferior* good. The quantity demanded of an inferior good and the amount spent on it *decrease* when income increases. Goods in this category include small motorcycles, potatoes, and rice. Low-income consumers buy these goods and spend a large percentage of their incomes on them.

Cross Elasticity of Demand

The burger shop next to your pizzeria has just raised the prices of its burgers. You know that pizzas and burgers are substitutes. You also know that when the price of a substitute for pizza *rises,* the demand for pizza *increases.* But how big is the influence of the price of burgers on the demand for pizza?

You know, too, that pizza and soft drinks are complements. And you know that if the price of a complement of pizza *rises,* the demand for pizza *decreases.* So you wonder, by how much will a rise in the price of a soft drink decrease the demand for your pizza?

To answer this question, you need to know about the cross elasticity of demand for pizza. Let's examine this elasticity measure.

We measure the influence of a change in the price of a substitute or complement by using the concept of the cross elasticity of demand. The **cross elasticity of demand** is a measure of the responsiveness of the demand for a good to a change in the price of a substitute or complement, other things remaining the same.

We calculate the *cross elasticity of demand* by using the formula:

$$\text{Cross elasticity of demand} = \frac{\text{Percentage change in quantity demanded}}{\text{Percentage change in price of a substitute or complement}}.$$

The cross elasticity of demand can be positive or negative. If the cross elasticity of demand is *positive,* demand and the price of the other good change in the *same* direction, so the two goods are *substitutes.* If the cross elasticity of demand is *negative,* demand and the price of the other good change in *opposite* directions, so the two goods are *complements.*

Substitutes Suppose that the price of pizza is constant and people buy 9 pizzas an hour. Then the price of a burger rises from $1.50 to $2.50. No other influence on buying plans changes and the quantity of pizzas bought increases to 11 an hour.

The change in the quantity demanded at the current price is +2 pizzas—the new quantity, 11 pizzas, minus the original quantity, 9 pizzas. The average quantity is 10 pizzas. So the quantity of pizzas demanded increases by 20 percent. That is,

$$\Delta Q/Q_{ave} \times 100 = (+2/10) \times 100 = +20\%.$$

The change in the price of a burger, a substitute for pizza, is +$1—the new price, $2.50, minus the original price, $1.50. The average price is $2 a burger. So the price of a burger rises by 50 percent. That is,

$$\Delta P/P_{ave} \times 100 = (+\$1/\$2) \times 100 = +50\%.$$

So the cross elasticity of demand for pizza with respect to the price of a burger is

$$\frac{+20\%}{+50\%} = 0.4.$$

Figure 4.5 illustrates the cross elasticity of demand. Because pizza and burgers are substitutes, when the price of a burger rises, the demand for pizza increases. The demand curve for pizza shifts rightward from D_0 to D_1. Because a *rise* in the price of a burger brings an *increase* in the demand for pizza, the cross elasticity of demand for pizza with respect to the price of a burger is *positive*. Both the price and the quantity change in the same direction.

Complements   Now suppose that the price of pizza is constant and 11 pizzas an hour are bought. Then the price of a soft drink rises from $1.50 to $2.50. No other influence on buying plans changes and the quantity of pizzas bought falls to 9 an hour.

FIGURE 4.5   Cross Elasticity of Demand

A burger is a *substitute* for pizza. When the price of a burger rises, the demand for pizza increases and the demand curve for pizza shifts rightward from D_0 to D_1. The cross elasticity of demand is *positive*.

A soft drink is a *complement* of pizza. When the price of a soft drink rises, the demand for pizza decreases and the demand curve for pizza shifts leftward from D_0 to D_2. The cross elasticity of demand is *negative*.

MyEconLab animation

ECONOMICS IN THE NEWS

More Peanut Butter Demand Elasticities

Peanut Butter Related Markets
Professor Timothy Mathews teaches economics at Kennesaw State University, Georgia, the nation's number one peanut producing state. The data table below shows his guesses about some demand elasticities for peanut butter.
Source: Timothy Mathews

THE DATA

Income elasticity	−0.31
Cross elasticity peanut butter and grape jelly	−0.27
Cross elasticity peanut butter and American cheese	+0.18

THE QUESTIONS

 What do the data provided tell us about the demand for peanut butter? Is it a normal good?

- Is grape jelly a substitute for or a complement of peanut butter? Is American cheese a substitute for or a complement of peanut butter?

THE ANSWERS

- The income elasticity of demand for peanut butter is *negative*, which means that peanut butter is an *inferior good*. People buy less peanut butter as income rises.

- The cross elasticity of demand of peanut butter with respect to the price of grape jelly is *negative*, which means that peanut butter and grape jelly are *complements*.

- The cross elasticity of demand of peanut butter with respect to the price of American cheese is *positive*, which means that peanut butter and American cheese are *substitutes*.

The change in the quantity demanded is the opposite of what we've just calculated: The quantity of pizzas demanded decreases by 20 percent (−20%).

The change in the price of a soft drink, a rise of $1 from $1.50 to $2.50, is the same as the change in the price of a burger that we've just calculated. That is, the price rises by 50 percent (+50%).

So the cross elasticity of demand for pizza with respect to the price of a soft drink is

$$\frac{-20\%}{+50\%} = -0.4.$$

Because pizza and soft drinks are complements, when the price of a soft drink rises, the demand for pizza decreases.

In Fig. 4.5, when the price of soft drinks rises the demand curve for pizza shifts leftward from D_0 to D_2. Because a *rise* in the price of a soft drink brings a *decrease* in the demand for pizza, the cross elasticity of demand for pizza with respect to the price of a soft drink is *negative*. The price and quantity change in *opposite* directions.

The magnitude of the cross elasticity of demand determines how far the demand curve shifts. The larger the cross elasticity (absolute value), the greater is the change in demand and the larger is the shift in the demand curve.

If two items are close substitutes, such as two brands of spring water, the cross elasticity is large. If two items are close complements, such as movies and popcorn, the cross elasticity is large.

If two items are somewhat unrelated to each other, such as newspapers and orange juice, the cross elasticity is small—perhaps even zero.

REVIEW QUIZ

1 What does the income elasticity of demand measure?
2 What does the sign (positive/negative) of the income elasticity tell us about a good?
3 What does the cross elasticity of demand measure?
4 What does the sign (positive/negative) of the cross elasticity of demand tell us about the relationship between two goods?

You can work these questions in Study Plan 4.2 and get instant feedback.   MyEconLab

◆ Elasticity of Supply

You know that when demand increases, the equilibrium price rises and the equilibrium quantity increases. But does the price rise by a large amount and the quantity increase by a little? Or does the price barely rise and the quantity increase by a large amount?

The answer depends on the responsiveness of the quantity supplied to a change in the price. If the quantity supplied is not very responsive to price, then an increase in demand brings a large rise in the price and a small increase in the equilibrium quantity. If the quantity supplied is highly responsive to price, then an increase in demand brings a small rise in the price and a large increase in the equilibrium quantity.

The problems that arise from using the slope of the supply curve to indicate responsiveness are the same as those we considered when discussing the responsiveness of the quantity demanded, so we use a units-free measure—the elasticity of supply.

Calculating the Elasticity of Supply

The **elasticity of supply** measures the responsiveness of the quantity supplied to a change in the price of a good when all other influences on selling plans remain the same. It is calculated by using the formula:

$$\text{Elasticity of supply} = \frac{\text{Percentage change in quantity supplied}}{\text{Percentage change in price}}.$$

We use the same method that you learned when you studied the elasticity of demand. (Refer back to p. 85 to check this method.)

Elastic and Inelastic Supply If the elasticity of supply is greater than 1, we say that supply is elastic and if the elasticity of supply is less than 1, we say that supply is inelastic.

Suppose that when the price rises from $20 to $21, the quantity supplied increases from 10 to 20 pizzas per hour. The price rise is $1 and the average price is $20.50, so the price rises by 4.9 percent of the average price. The quantity increases from 10 to 20 pizzas an hour, so the increase is 10 pizzas, the average quantity is 15 pizzas, and the quantity increases by 67 percent. The elasticity of supply is equal to 67 percent divided by 4.9 percent, which equals 13.67. Because the elasticity of supply exceeds 1 (in this case by a lot), supply is elastic.

In contrast, suppose that when the price rises from $20 to $30, the quantity of pizza supplied increases from 10 to 13 per hour. The price rise is $10 and the average price is $25, so the price rises by 40 percent of the average price. The quantity increases from 10 to 13 pizzas an hour, so the increase is 3 pizzas, the average quantity is 11.5 pizzas an hour, and the quantity increases by 26 percent. The elasticity of supply is equal to 26 percent divided by 40 percent, which equals 0.65. Now, because the elasticity of supply is less than 1, supply is inelastic.

Figure 4.6 shows the range of elasticities of supply. If the quantity supplied is fixed regardless of the price, the supply curve is vertical and the elasticity of supply is zero. Supply is perfectly inelastic. This case is shown in Fig. 4.6(a). A special intermediate case occurs when the percentage change in price equals the percentage change in quantity. Supply is then unit elastic. This case is shown in Fig. 4.6(b). No matter how steep the supply curve is, if it is linear and passes through the origin, supply is unit elastic. If there is a price at which sellers are willing to offer any quantity for sale, the supply curve is horizontal and the elasticity of supply is infinite. Supply is perfectly elastic. This case is shown in Fig. 4.6(c).

The Factors That Influence the Elasticity of Supply

The elasticity of supply of a good depends on

- Resource substitution possibilities
- Time frame for the supply decision

Resource Substitution Possibilities Some goods and services can be produced only by using unique or rare productive resources. These items have a low, perhaps even a zero, elasticity of supply. Other goods and services can be produced by using commonly available resources that could be allocated to a wide variety of alternative tasks. Such items have a high elasticity of supply.

A Van Gogh painting is an example of a good with a vertical supply curve and a zero elasticity of supply. At the other extreme, wheat can be grown on land that is almost equally good for growing corn, so it is just as easy to grow wheat as corn. The opportunity cost of wheat in terms of forgone corn is almost constant. As a result, the supply curve of wheat is almost horizontal and its elasticity of supply is very large. Similarly, when a good is produced in many different countries (for example, sugar and beef), the supply of the good is highly elastic.

The supply of most goods and services lies between these two extremes. The quantity produced

---

FIGURE 4.6 Inelastic and Elastic Supply

(a) Perfectly inelastic supply

(b) Unit elastic supply

(c) Perfectly elastic supply

Each supply illustrated here has a constant elasticity. The supply curve in part (a) illustrates the supply of a good that has a zero elasticity of supply. Each supply curve in part (b) illustrates the supply of a good with a unit elasticity of supply. All linear supply curves that pass through the origin illustrate supplies that are unit elastic. The supply curve in part (c) illustrates the supply of a good with an infinite elasticity of supply.

can be increased but only by incurring a higher cost. If a higher price is offered, the quantity supplied increases. Such goods and services have an elasticity of supply between zero and infinity.

Time Frame for the Supply Decision To study the influence of the amount of time elapsed since a price change, we distinguish three time frames of supply:

- Momentary supply
- Short-run supply
- Long-run supply

Momentary Supply When the price of a good changes, the immediate response of the quantity supplied is determined by the *momentary supply* of that good.

Some goods, such as fruits and vegetables, have a perfectly inelastic momentary supply—a vertical supply curve. The quantities supplied depend on crop-planting decisions made earlier. In the case of oranges, for example, planting decisions have to be made many years in advance of the crop being available. Momentary supply is perfectly inelastic because, on a given day, no matter what the price of oranges, producers cannot change their output. They have picked, packed, and shipped their crop to market, and the quantity available for that day is fixed.

In contrast, some goods have a perfectly elastic momentary supply. Long-distance phone calls are an example. When many people simultaneously make a call, there is a big surge in the demand for telephone cables, computer switching, and satellite time. The quantity supplied increases, but the price remains constant. Long-distance carriers monitor fluctuations in demand and reroute calls to ensure that the quantity supplied equals the quantity demanded without changing the price.

Short-Run Supply The response of the quantity supplied to a price change when only *some* of the possible adjustments to production can be made is determined by *short-run supply*. Most goods have an inelastic short-run supply. To increase output in the short run, firms must work their labor force overtime and perhaps hire additional workers. To decrease their output in the short run, firms either lay off workers or reduce their hours of work. With the passage of time, firms can make more adjustments, perhaps training additional workers or buying additional tools and other equipment.

For the orange grower, if the price of oranges falls, some pickers can be laid off and oranges left on the trees to rot. Or if the price of oranges rises, the grower can use more fertilizer and improved irrigation to increase the yields of their existing trees.

But an orange grower can't change the number of trees producing oranges in the short run.

Long-Run Supply The response of the quantity supplied to a price change after *all* the technologically possible ways of adjusting supply have been exploited is determined by *long-run supply*. For most goods and services, long-run supply is elastic and perhaps perfectly elastic.

For the orange grower, the long run is the time it takes new tree plantings to grow to full maturity—about 15 years. In some cases, the long-run adjustment occurs only after a completely new production plant has been built and workers have been trained to operate it—typically a process that might take several years.

REVIEW QUIZ

1 Why do we need a units-free measure of the responsiveness of the quantity supplied of a good or service to a change in its price?
2 Define the elasticity of supply and show how it is calculated.
3 What are the main influences on the elasticity of supply that make the supply of some goods elastic and the supply of other goods inelastic?
4 Provide examples of goods or services whose elasticities of supply are (a) zero, (b) greater than zero but less than infinity, and (c) infinity.
5 How does the time frame over which a supply decision is made influence the elasticity of supply? Explain your answer.

You can work these questions in Study Plan 4.3 and get instant feedback.   MyEconLab

◆ You have now learned about the elasticities of demand and supply. Table 4.1 summarizes all the elasticities that you've met in this chapter. In the next chapter, we study the efficiency of competitive markets. But first study *Reading Between the Lines* on pp. 98–99, which puts the elasticity of demand to work and looks at the market for winter tomatoes.

TABLE 4.1 A Compact Glossary of Elasticities

Price Elasticities of Demand

A relationship is described as	When its magnitude is	Which means that
Perfectly elastic	Infinity	The smallest possible increase in price causes an infinitely large decrease in the quantity demanded*
Elastic	Less than infinity	The percentage decrease in the quantity demanded exceeds the percentage increase in price
Unit elastic	1	The percentage decrease in the quantity demanded equals the percentage increase in price
Inelastic	Less than 1 but greater than zero	The percentage decrease in the quantity demanded is less than the percentage increase in price
Perfectly inelastic	Zero	The quantity demanded is the same at all prices

Cross Elasticities of Demand

A relationship is described as	When its value is	Which means that
Close substitutes	Large	The smallest possible increase in the price of one good causes an infinitely large increase in the quantity* demanded of the other good
Substitutes	Positive	If the price of one good increases, the quantity demanded of the other good also increases
Unrelated goods	Zero	If the price of one good increases, the quantity demanded of the other good remains the same
Complements	Negative	If the price of one good increases, the quantity demanded of the other good decreases

Income Elasticities of Demand

A relationship is described as	When its value is	Which means that
Income elastic (normal good)	Greater than 1	The percentage increase in the quantity demanded is greater than the percentage increase in income*
Income inelastic (normal good)	Less than 1 but greater than zero	The percentage increase in the quantity demanded is greater than zero but less than the percentage increase in income
Negative (inferior good)	Less than zero	When income increases, quantity demanded decreases

Elasticities of Supply

A relationship is described as	When its magnitude is	Which means that
Perfectly elastic	Infinity	The smallest possible increase in price causes an infinitely large increase in the quantity supplied*
Elastic	Less than infinity but greater than 1	The percentage increase in the quantity supplied exceeds the percentage increase in the price
Unit elastic	1	The percentage increase in the quantity supplied equals the percentage increase in the price
Inelastic	Greater than zero but less than 1	The percentage increase in the quantity supplied is less than the percentage increase in the price
Perfectly inelastic	Zero	The quantity supplied is the same at all prices

*In each description, the directions of change may be reversed. For example, in this case, the smallest possible *decrease* in price causes an infinitely large *increase* in the quantity demanded.

The Elasticities of Demand and Supply for Tomatoes

Frigid Florida Winter Is Bad News for Tomato Lovers

USA Today
March 5, 2010

ST. PETERSBURG, Fla.—A frigid Florida winter is taking its toll on your sandwich. The Sunshine State is the main U.S. source for fresh winter tomatoes, and its growers lost some 70 percent of their crop during January's prolonged cold snap. . . .

The average wholesale price for a 25-pound box of tomatoes is now $30, up from $6.50 a year ago. Florida's growers would normally ship about 25 million pounds of tomatoes a week; right now, they're shipping less than a quarter of that, according to Reggie Brown of the Florida Tomato Grower's Exchange, a tomato farmer cooperative in Maitland. . . .

And because high demand has driven up domestic prices, many wholesalers are buying from Mexico instead.

"We're obviously losing market share to Mexico, and there's always a price to pay to get the customer to get back into the Florida market," Brown said.

Florida is the only place where tomatoes are grown on a large scale in the United States during winter. California doesn't grow them until later in the year, and much of that state's crop is used for processed foods, such as ketchup, sauce, and juice. Other states grow tomatoes in greenhouses year-round, but Florida's winter tomato crop is by far the largest. . . .

Some Wendy's restaurants posted signs saying tomatoes would only be provided upon request because of limited availability. . . .

ESSENCE OF THE STORY

- Florida is the main U.S. source for fresh winter tomatoes.

- California tomatoes come to market later in the year and are mainly used for ketchup, sauce, and juice.

- Other states grow tomatoes in greenhouses year-round.

- In January 2010, a prolonged cold snap wiped out 70 percent of the Florida crop.

- The average wholesale price for a 25-pound box of tomatoes rose from $6.50 in 2009 to $30 in 2010.

- The quantity of tomatoes shipped decreased from a normal 25 million pounds per week to less than a quarter of that quantity.

- The "high demand has driven up prices" and wholesalers are buying from Mexico.

- Some restaurants provided tomatoes only on request.

ECONOMIC ANALYSIS

- Using the information provided in this news article supplemented with an independent estimate of the price elasticity of demand, we can find the demand and supply curves in the market for winter tomatoes shown in Fig. 1.

- According to J. Scott Shonkwiler and Robert D. Emerson, two agricultural economists at the University of Florida, the price elasticity of demand for winter tomatoes is 0.8.

- A 1 percent rise in the price of these tomatoes brings a 0.8 percent decrease in the quantity demanded, other things remaining the same.

- According to the news article, in a normal period, the price of Florida winter tomatoes is $6.50 a box (25 pounds) and growers normally ship 25 million pounds a week.

- With the information just stated, we can determine the demand for winter tomatoes. It is the curve *D* in Figs. 1 and 2. This demand curve passes through the point that shows that 25 million pounds are demanded at a price of $6.50 a box. The elasticity of demand for winter tomatoes is 0.8.

- Figure 2 shows the calculation that confirms the price elasticity of demand is 0.8. When the price rises from $6.50 to $30 a box, as it did in 2010, the quantity demanded decreases from 25 million to 8 million pounds. Use the numbers and the midpoint formula to confirm that the elasticity of demand is 0.8.

- The news article says that Florida growers (the main producers of winter tomatoes) shipped less than a quarter of their normal 25 million pounds a week. So assume that they shipped 6 million pounds a week.

- Other growers (using greenhouses or in Mexico) make up the difference between what the Florida growers supply and the quantity demanded.

- The supply curve in 2010, S_1, must pass through the equilibrium point at that time of 8 million pounds and $30 a box. It also passes through the point 6 million pounds and $6.50 a box because that is the quantity that Florida growers would ship even if the price remained at $6.50 a box.

- Figure 3 zooms in on the supply curve S_1. We can calculate the elasticity of supply by using the numbers in Fig. 3 and the midpoint formula. The elasticity of supply is 0.22, which means that the supply of winter tomatoes is inelastic.

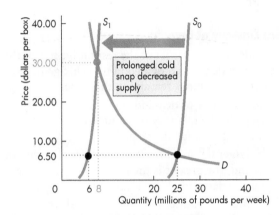

Figure 1 The Market for Winter Tomatoes

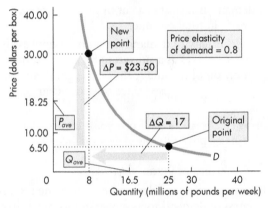

Figure 2 Price Elasticity of Demand for Winter Tomatoes

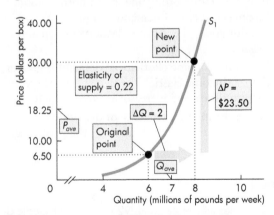

Figure 3 Price Elasticity of Supply of Winter Tomatoes

SUMMARY

Key Points

Price Elasticity of Demand (pp. 84–90)

- Elasticity is a measure of the responsiveness of the quantity demanded of a good to a change in its price, other things remaining the same.
- Price elasticity of demand equals the percentage change in the quantity demanded divided by the percentage change in the price.
- The larger the magnitude of the price elasticity of demand, the greater is the responsiveness of the quantity demanded to a given price change.
- If demand is elastic, a cut in price leads to an increase in total revenue. If demand is unit elastic, a cut in price leaves total revenue unchanged. And if demand is inelastic, a cut in price leads to a decrease in total revenue.
- Price elasticity of demand depends on how easily one good serves as a substitute for another, the proportion of income spent on the good, and the length of time elapsed since the price change.

Working Problems 1 to 8 will give you a better understanding of the price elasticity of demand.

More Elasticities of Demand (pp. 91–94)

- Income elasticity of demand measures the responsiveness of demand to a change in income, other things remaining the same. For a normal good, the income elasticity of demand is positive. For an inferior good, the income elasticity of demand is negative.
- When the income elasticity of demand is greater than 1 (income elastic), the percentage of income spent on the good increases as income increases.
- When the income elasticity of demand is less than 1 (income inelastic and inferior), the percentage of income spent on the good decreases as income increases.
- Cross elasticity of demand measures the responsiveness of the demand for one good to a change in the price of a substitute or a complement, other things remaining the same.
- The cross elasticity of demand with respect to the price of a substitute is positive. The cross elasticity of demand with respect to the price of a complement is negative.

Working Problems 9 to 16 will give you a better understanding of cross and income elasticities of demand.

Elasticity of Supply (pp. 94–96)

- Elasticity of supply measures the responsiveness of the quantity supplied of a good to a change in its price, other things remaining the same.
- The elasticity of supply is usually positive and ranges between zero (vertical supply curve) and infinity (horizontal supply curve).
- Supply decisions have three time frames: momentary, short run, and long run.
- Momentary supply refers to the response of the quantity supplied to a price change at the instant that the price changes.
- Short-run supply refers to the response of the quantity supplied to a price change after some of the technologically feasible adjustments in production have been made.
- Long-run supply refers to the response of the quantity supplied to a price change when all the technologically feasible adjustments in production have been made.

Working Problems 17 and 18 will give you a better understanding of the elasticity of supply.

Key Terms

Cross elasticity of demand, 92	Inelastic demand, 85	Total revenue, 88
Elastic demand, 86	Perfectly elastic demand, 85	Total revenue test, 88
Elasticity of supply, 94	Perfectly inelastic demand, 85	Unit elastic demand, 85
Income elasticity of demand, 91	Price elasticity of demand, 84	

STUDY PLAN PROBLEMS AND APPLICATIONS

MyEconLab   You can work Problems 1 to 18 in MyEconLab Chapter 4 Study Plan and get instant feedback.

Price Elasticity of Demand (Study Plan 4.1)

1. Rain spoils the strawberry crop, the price rises from $4 to $6 a box, and the quantity demanded decreases from 1,000 to 600 boxes a week.

   a. Calculate the price elasticity of demand over this price range. *E = 0.8*

   b. Describe the demand for strawberries. *inelastic*

2. If the quantity of dental services demanded increases by 10 percent when the price of dental services falls by 10 percent, is the demand for dental services inelastic, elastic, or unit elastic?

3. The demand schedule for hotel rooms is

Price (dollars per night)	Quantity demanded (millions of rooms per night)
200	100
250	80
400	50
500	40
800	25

   a. What happens to total revenue when the price falls from $400 to $250 a night and from $250 to $200 a night?

   b. Is the demand for hotel rooms elastic, inelastic, or unit elastic?

4. The figure shows the demand for pens.

   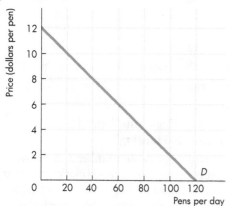

   Calculate the elasticity of demand when the price rises from $4 to $6 a pen. Over what price range is the demand for pens elastic?

5. In 2003, when music downloading first took off, Universal Music slashed the average price of a CD from $21 to $15. The company expected the price cut to boost the quantity of CDs sold by 30 percent, other things remaining the same.

   a. What was Universal Music's estimate of the price elasticity of demand for CDs?

   b. If you were making the pricing decision at Universal Music, what would be your pricing decision? Explain your decision.

6. The demand for illegal drugs is inelastic. Much of the expenditure on illegal drugs comes from crime. Assuming these statements to be correct,

   a. How will a successful campaign that decreases the supply of drugs influence the price of illegal drugs and the amount spent on them?

   b. What will happen to the amount of crime?

   c. What is the most effective way of decreasing the quantity of illegal drugs bought and decreasing the amount of drug-related crime?

7. **The Grip of Gas**

   U.S. drivers are ranked as the least sensitive to changes in the price of gasoline. For example, if the price rose from $3 to $4 per gallon and stayed there for a year U.S. purchases of gasoline would fall only about 5 percent.

   Source: *Slate*, September 27, 2005

   a. Calculate the price elasticity of demand for gasoline. Is the demand for gasoline elastic, unit elastic, or inelastic?

   b. Explain how the price rise from $3 to $4 a gallon changes the total revenue from gasoline sales.

8. **Spam Sales Rise as Food Costs Soar**

   Sales of Spam are rising as consumers realize that Spam and other lower-cost foods can be substituted for costlier cuts of meat as a way of controlling their already stretched food budgets.

   Source: *AOL Money & Finance*, May 28, 2008

   a. Is Spam a normal good or an inferior good? Explain. *inferior.*

   b. Would the income elasticity of demand for Spam be negative or positive? Explain. *negative.*

More Elasticities of Demand (Study Plan 4.2)

9. When Judy's income increased from $130 to $170 a week, she increased her demand for concert tickets by 15 percent and decreased her demand for bus rides by 10 percent. Calculate Judy's income elasticity of demand for (a) concert tickets and (b) bus rides.

10. If a 12 percent rise in the price of orange juice decreases the quantity of orange juice demanded by 22 percent and increases the quantity of apple juice demanded by 14 percent, calculate the
    a. Price elasticity of demand for orange juice.
    b. Cross elasticity of demand for apple juice with respect to the price of orange juice.

11. If a 5 percent rise in the price of sushi increases the quantity of soy sauce demanded by 2 percent and decreases the quantity of sushi demanded by 1 percent, calculate the
    a. Price elasticity of demand for sushi.
    b. Cross elasticity of demand for soy sauce with respect to the price of sushi.

12. **Swelling Textbook Costs Have College Students Saying "Pass"**

    Textbook prices have doubled and risen faster than average prices for the past two decades. Sixty percent of students do not buy textbooks. Some students hunt for used copies and sell them back at the end of the semester; some buy online, which is often cheaper than the campus store; some use the library copy and wait till it's free; some share the book with a classmate.

    Source: *Washington Post*, January 23, 2006

    Explain what this news clip implies about
    a. The price elasticity of demand for college textbooks.
    b. The income elasticity of demand for college textbooks.
    c. The cross elasticity of demand for college textbooks from the campus bookstore with respect to the online price of a textbook.

    Use the following information to work Problems 13 to 15.

    As Gas Costs Soar, Buyers Flock to Small Cars
    Faced with high gas prices, Americans are substituting smaller cars for SUVs. In April 2008, Toyota Yaris sales increased 46 percent and Ford Focus sales increased 32 percent from a year earlier. SUV sales decreased 25 percent in 2008 and Chevrolet Tahoe sales fell 35 percent. Full-size pickup sales decreased 15 percent in 2008 and Ford F-Series pickup sales decreased by 27 percent in April 2008. The effect of a downsized vehicle fleet on fuel consumption is unknown. In California in January 2008, gasoline consumption was 4 percent lower and the price of gasoline 30 percent higher than in January 2007.

    Source: *The New York Times*, May 2, 2009

13. Calculate the price elasticity of demand for gasoline in California. 4/30 = 0.13
14. Calculate the cross elasticity of demand for
    a. Toyota Yaris with respect to the price of gasoline. 46/30 = 1.53
    b. Ford Focus with respect to the price of gasoline. 32/30 = 1.06
15. Calculate the cross elasticity of demand for
    a. Chevrolet Tahoe with respect to the price of gasoline. 35/30 = 1.17
    b. A full-size pickup with respect to the price of gasoline. 0.5

16. **Home Depot Earnings Hammered**

    As gas and food prices increased and home prices slumped, people had less extra income to spend on home improvements. And the improvements that they made were on small inexpensive types of repairs and not major big-ticket items.

    Source: CNN, May 20, 2008

    a. What does this news clip imply about the income elasticity of demand for big-ticket home-improvement items?
    b. Would the income elasticity of demand be greater or less than 1? Explain.

Elasticity of Supply (Study Plan 4.3)

17. The table sets out the supply schedule of jeans.

Price (dollars per pair)	Quantity supplied (millions of pairs per year)
120	24
125	28
130	32
135	36

    Calculate the elasticity of supply when
    a. The price rises from $125 to $135 a pair.
    b. The average price is $125 a pair.

18. **Study Ranks Honolulu Third Highest for "Unaffordable Housing"**

    A study ranks Honolulu number 3 in the world for the most unaffordable housing market in urban locations, behind Los Angeles and San Diego and is deemed "severely unaffordable." With significant constraints on the supply of land for residential development, housing inflation has resulted.

    Source: *Hawaii Reporter*, September 11, 2007

    a. Would the supply of housing in Honolulu be elastic or inelastic?
    b. Explain how the elasticity of supply plays an important role in influencing how rapidly housing prices in Honolulu rise.

ADDITIONAL PROBLEMS AND APPLICATIONS

MyEconLab   You can work these problems in MyEconLab if assigned by your instructor.

Price Elasticity of Demand

19. With higher fuel costs, airlines raised their average fare from 75¢ to $1.25 per passenger mile and the number of passenger miles decreased from 2.5 million a day to 1.5 million a day.
    a. What is the price elasticity of demand for air travel over this price range?
    b. Describe the demand for air travel.

20. The figure shows the demand for DVD rentals.

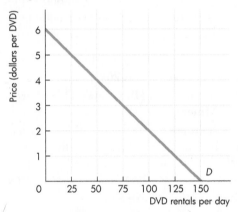

a. Calculate the elasticity of demand when the price of a DVD rental rises from $3 to $5.
b. At what price is the elasticity of demand for DVD rentals equal to 1?

Use the following table to work Problems 21 to 23.
The demand schedule for computer chips is

Price (dollars per chip)	Quantity demanded (millions of chips per year)
200	50
250	45
300	40
350	35
400	30

21. a. What happens to total revenue if the price falls from $400 to $350 a chip and from $350 to $300 a chip?
    b. At what price is total revenue at a maximum?

22. At an average price of $350, is the demand for chips elastic, inelastic, or unit elastic? Use the total revenue test to answer this question.

23. At $250 a chip, is the demand for chips elastic or inelastic? Use the total revenue test to answer this question.

24. Your price elasticity of demand for bananas is 4. If the price of bananas rises by 5 percent, what is
    a. The percentage change in the quantity of bananas you buy?
    b. The change in your expenditure on bananas?

25. **As Gasoline Prices Soar, Americans Slowly Adapt**
    As gas prices rose in March 2008, Americans drove 11 billion fewer miles than in March 2007. Realizing that prices are not going down, Americans are adapting to higher energy costs. Americans spend 3.7 percent of their disposable income on transportation fuels. How much we spend on gasoline depends on the choices we make: what car we drive, where we live, how much time we spend driving, and where we choose to go. For many people, higher energy costs mean fewer restaurant meals, deferred weekend outings with the kids, less air travel, and more time closer to home.
    Source: *International Herald Tribune*, May 23, 2008
    a. List and explain the elasticities of demand that are implicitly referred to in the news clip.
    b. Why, according to the news clip, is the demand for gasoline inelastic?

More Elasticities of Demand

Use this information to work Problems 26 and 27.
Economy Forces Many to Shorten Summer Vacation Plans
This year Americans are taking fewer exotic holidays by air and instead are visiting local scenic places by car. The global financial crisis has encouraged many Americans to cut their holiday budgets.
    Source: *USA Today*, May 22, 2009

26. Given the prices of the two holidays, is the income elasticity of demand for exotic holidays positive or negative? Are exotic holidays a normal good or an inferior good? Are local holidays a normal good or an inferior good?

27. Are exotic holidays and local holidays substitutes? Explain your answer.

28. When Alex's income was $3,000, he bought 4 bagels and 12 donuts a month. Now his income is $5,000 and he buys 8 bagels and 6 donuts a month.

Calculate Alex's income elasticity of demand for

a. Bagels.

b. Donuts.

29. **Wal-Mart's Recession-Time Pet Project**

During the recession, Wal-Mart moved its pet food and supplies to in front of its other fast-growing business, baby products. Retail experts point out that kids and pets tend to be fairly recession-resistant businesses—even in a recession, dogs will be fed and kids will get their toys.

Source: *CNN*, May 13, 2008

a. What does this news clip imply about the income elasticity of demand for pet food and baby products?

b. Would the income elasticity of demand be greater or less than 1? Explain.

30. If a 5 percent fall in the price of chocolate sauce increases the quantity of chocolate sauce demanded by 10 percent and increases the quantity of ice cream demanded by 15 percent, calculate the

a. Price elasticity of demand for chocolate sauce.

b. Cross elasticity of demand for ice cream with respect to the price of chocolate sauce.

31. **Netflix to Offer Online Movie Viewing**

Online movie rental service Netflix has introduced a new feature to allow customers to watch movies and television series on their personal computers. Netflix competes with video rental retailer Blockbuster, which added an online rental service to the in-store rental service.

Source: *CNN*, January 16, 2007

a. How will online movie viewing influence the price elasticity of demand for in-store movie rentals?

b. Would the cross elasticity of demand for on-line movies and in-store movie rentals be negative or positive? Explain.

c. Would the cross elasticity of demand for on-line movies with respect to high-speed Internet service be negative or positive? Explain.

32. **To Love, Honor, and Save Money**

In a survey of caterers and event planners, nearly half of them said that they were seeing declines in wedding spending in response to the economic slowdown; 12% even reported wedding cancellations because of financial concerns.

Source: *Time*, June 2, 2008

a. Based upon this news clip, are wedding events a normal good or inferior good? Explain.

normal.

b. Are wedding events more a necessity or a luxury? Would the income elasticity of demand be greater than 1, less than 1, or equal to 1? Explain.

Elasticity of Supply

33. The supply schedule of long-distance phone calls is

Price (cents per minute)	Quantity supplied (millions of minutes per day)
10	200
20	400
30	600
40	800

Calculate the elasticity of supply when

a. The price falls from 40¢ to 30¢ a minute.

b. The average price is 20¢ a minute.

34. **Weak Coal Prices Hit China's Third-Largest Coal Miner**

The chairman of Yanzhou Coal Mining reported that the recession had decreased the demand for coal, with its sales falling by 11.9 percent to 7.92 million tons from 8.99 million tons a year earlier, despite a 10.6 percent cut in the price.

Source: *Dow Jones*, April 27, 2009

Calculate the price elasticity of supply of coal. Is the supply of coal elastic or inelastic?

Economics in the News

35. After you have studied *Reading Between the Lines* on pp. 98–99, answer the following questions.

a. Which demand is more price elastic and why: tomatoes in general or Florida winter tomatoes?

b. When cold weather destroyed the Florida crop and more tomatoes came from Mexico and greenhouses, what happened to the supply of tomatoes and the quantity of tomatoes supplied?

c. The news article says the "high demand has driven up prices" and "wholesalers are buying from Mexico." What does this statement mean? Did demand increase? Did it decrease? Is the news article correct?

d. Reggie Brown says "We're obviously losing market share to Mexico, and there's always a price to pay to get the customer to get back into the Florida market." What does he mean and what does that imply about the elasticity of demand for Florida tomatoes when the price rises and when the price falls?

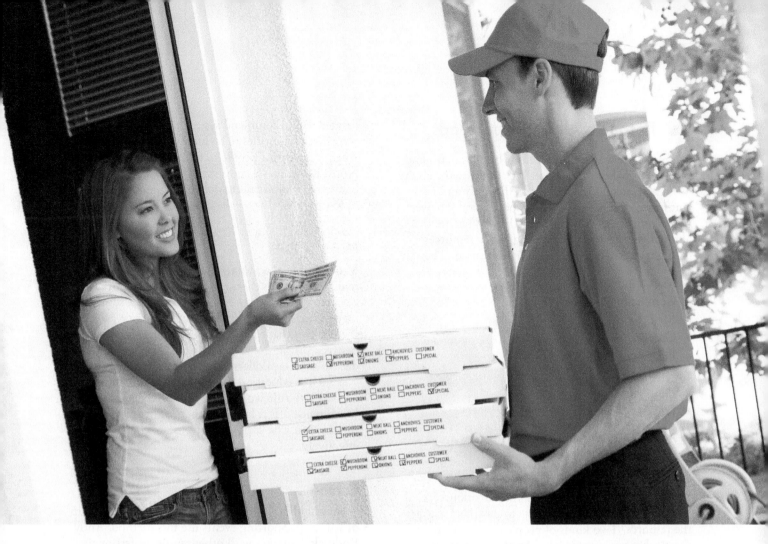

5

EFFICIENCY AND EQUITY

After studying this chapter, you will be able to:

◆ Describe the alternative methods of allocating scarce resources

◆ Explain the connection between demand and marginal benefit and define consumer surplus; and explain the connection between supply and marginal cost and define producer surplus

◆ Explain the conditions under which markets are efficient and inefficient

◆ Explain the main ideas about fairness and evaluate claims that markets result in unfair outcomes

When you order a pizza, your *self-interested* choice influences how resources are used. A market coordinates your choice with the self-interested choices of a pizza cook and a delivery person to fill your order. Do markets allocate resources between pizza and everything else efficiently?

Markets generate huge income inequality: *You* can afford to buy a pizza but it might be an unaffordable luxury for a very poor person. Is this situation fair?

You're now going to learn how economists approach these questions. At the end of the chapter, in *Reading Between the Lines*, you will apply what you've learned to see how congestion pricing could end the rush-hour crawl and make our road use efficient.

◆ Resource Allocation Methods

Resources are scarce, so they must be allocated somehow. The goal of this chapter is to evaluate the ability of markets to allocate resources efficiently and fairly. But to see whether the market does a good job, we must compare it with its alternatives. What are the alternative methods of allocating scarce resources?

Eight alternative methods might be used. They are

- Market price
- Command
- Majority rule
- Contest
- First-come, first-served
- Lottery
- Personal characteristics
- Force

Let's briefly examine each method.

Market Price

When a market price allocates a scarce resource, the people who are willing and able to pay that price get the resource. Two kinds of people decide not to pay the market price: those who can afford to pay but choose not to buy and those who are too poor and simply can't afford to buy.

For many goods and services, distinguishing between those who choose not to buy and those who can't afford to buy doesn't matter. But for a few items, it does matter. For example, poor people can't afford to pay school fees and doctors' fees. Because poor people can't afford items that most people consider to be essential, these items are usually allocated by one of the other methods.

Command

A **command system** allocates resources by the order (command) of someone in authority. In the U.S. economy, the command system is used extensively inside firms and government departments. For example, if you have a job, most likely someone tells you what to do. Your labor is allocated to specific tasks by a command.

A command system works well in organizations in which the lines of authority and responsibility are clear and it is easy to monitor the activities being per-formed. But a command system works badly when the range of activities to be monitored is large and when it is easy for people to fool those in authority. North Korea uses a command system and it works so badly that it even fails to deliver an adequate supply of food.

Majority Rule

Majority rule allocates resources in the way that a majority of voters choose. Societies use majority rule to elect representative governments that make some of the biggest decisions. For example, majority rule decides the tax rates that end up allocating scarce resources between private use and public use. And majority rule decides how tax dollars are allocated among competing uses such as education and health care.

Majority rule works well when the decisions being made affect large numbers of people and self-interest must be suppressed to use resources most effectively.

Contest

A contest allocates resources to a winner (or a group of winners). Sporting events use this method. Andy Roddick competes with other tennis professionals, and the winner gets the biggest payoff. But contests are more general than those in a sports arena, though we don't normally call them contests. For example, Bill Gates won a contest to provide the world's personal computer operating system.

Contests do a good job when the efforts of the "players" are hard to monitor and reward directly. When a manager offers everyone in the company the opportunity to win a big prize, people are motivated to work hard and try to become the winner. Only a few people end up with a big prize, but many people work harder in the process of trying to win. The total output produced by the workers is much greater than it would be without the contest.

First-Come, First-Served

A first-come, first-served method allocates resources to those who are first in line. Many casual restaurants won't accept reservations. They use first-come, first-served to allocate their scarce tables. Highway space is allocated in this way too: The first to arrive at the on-ramp gets the road space. If too many vehicles enter the highway, the speed slows and people wait in line for some space to become available.

First-come, first-served works best when, as in the above examples, a scarce resource can serve just one user at a time in a sequence. By serving the user who arrives first, this method minimizes the time spent waiting for the resource to become free.

Lottery

Lotteries allocate resources to those who pick the winning number, draw the lucky cards, or come up lucky on some other gaming system. State lotteries and casinos reallocate millions of dollars worth of goods and services every year.

But lotteries are more widespread than jackpots and roulette wheels in casinos. They are used to allocate landing slots to airlines at some airports, places in the New York and Boston marathons, and have been used to allocate fishing rights and the electromagnetic spectrum used by cell phones.

Lotteries work best when there is no effective way to distinguish among potential users of a scarce resource.

Personal Characteristics

When resources are allocated on the basis of personal characteristics, people with the "right" characteristics get the resources. Some of the resources that matter most to you are allocated in this way. For example, you will choose a marriage partner on the basis of personal characteristics. But this method can also be used in unacceptable ways. Allocating the best jobs to white, Anglo-Saxon males and discriminating against visible minorities and women is an example.

Force

Force plays a crucial role, for both good and ill, in allocating scarce resources. Let's start with the ill.

War, the use of military force by one nation against another, has played an enormous role historically in allocating resources. The economic supremacy of European settlers in the Americas and Australia owes much to the use of this method.

Theft, the taking of the property of others without their consent, also plays a large role. Both large-scale organized crime and small-scale petty crime collectively allocate billions of dollars worth of resources annually.

But force plays a crucial positive role in allocating resources. It provides the state with an effective method of transferring wealth from the rich to the poor, and it provides the legal framework in which voluntary exchange in markets takes place.

A legal system is the foundation on which our market economy functions. Without courts to enforce contracts, it would not be possible to do business. But the courts could not enforce contracts without the ability to apply force if necessary. The state provides the ultimate force that enables the courts to do their work.

More broadly, the force of the state is essential to uphold the principle of the rule of law. This principle is the bedrock of civilized economic (and social and political) life. With the rule of law upheld, people can go about their daily economic lives with the assurance that their property will be protected—that they can sue for violations against their property (and be sued if they violate the property of others).

Free from the burden of protecting their property and confident in the knowledge that those with whom they trade will honor their agreements, people can get on with focusing on the activity in which they have a comparative advantage and trading for mutual gain.

REVIEW QUIZ

1 Why do we need methods of allocating scarce resources?
2 Describe the alternative methods of allocating scarce resources.
3 Provide an example of each allocation method that illustrates when it works well.
4 Provide an example of each allocation method that illustrates when it works badly.

You can work these questions in Study Plan 5.1 and get instant feedback.   MyEconLab

In the next sections, we're going to see how a market can achieve an efficient use of resources, examine the obstacles to efficiency, and see how sometimes an alternative method might improve on the market. After looking at efficiency, we'll turn our attention to the more difficult issue of fairness.

Benefit, Cost, and Surplus

Resources are allocated efficiently and in the *social interest* when they are used in the ways that people value most highly. You saw in Chapter 2 that this outcome occurs when the quantities produced are at the point on the *PPF* at which marginal benefit equals marginal cost (see pp. 35–37). We're now going to see whether competitive markets produce the efficient quantities.

We begin on the demand side of a market.

Demand, Willingness to Pay, and Value

In everyday life, we talk about "getting value for money." When we use this expression, we are distinguishing between *value* and *price*. Value is what we get, and price is what we pay.

The value of one more unit of a good or service is its marginal benefit. We measure marginal benefit by the maximum price that is willingly paid for another unit of the good or service. But willingness to pay determines demand. *A demand curve is a marginal benefit curve.*

In Fig. 5.1(a), Lisa is willing to pay $1 for the 30th slice of pizza and $1 is her marginal benefit from that slice. In Fig. 5.1(b), Nick is willing to pay $1 for the 10th slice of pizza and $1 is his marginal benefit from that slice. But at what quantity is the market willing to pay $1 for the marginal slice? The answer is provided by the *market demand curve*.

Individual Demand and Market Demand

The relationship between the price of a good and the quantity demanded by one person is called *individual demand*. And the relationship between the price of a good and the quantity demanded by all buyers is called *market demand*.

> The market demand curve is the horizontal sum of the individual demand curves and is formed by adding the quantities demanded by all the individuals at each price.

Figure 5.1(c) illustrates the market demand for pizza if Lisa and Nick are the only people in the market. Lisa's demand curve in part (a) and Nick's demand curve in part (b) sum horizontally to the market demand curve in part (c).

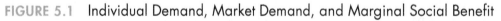

FIGURE 5.1   Individual Demand, Market Demand, and Marginal Social Benefit

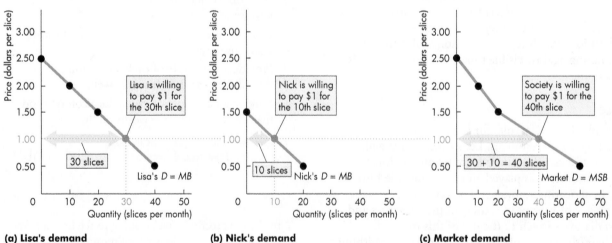

(a) Lisa's demand   **(b) Nick's demand**   **(c) Market demand**

At a price of $1 a slice, the quantity demanded by Lisa is 30 slices and the quantity demanded by Nick is 10 slices, so the quantity demanded by the market is 40 slices. Lisa's demand curve in part (a) and Nick's demand curve in part (b) sum horizontally to the market demand curve in part (c). The market demand curve is the marginal social benefit (*MSB*) curve.

At a price of $1 a slice, Lisa demands 30 slices and Nick demands 10 slices, so the market quantity demanded at $1 a slice is 40 slices.

For Lisa and Nick, their demand curves are their marginal benefit curves. For society, the market demand curve is the marginal benefit curve. We call the marginal benefit to the entire society *marginal social benefit*. So the market demand curve is also the *marginal social benefit* (*MSB*) *curve.*

Consumer Surplus

We don't always have to pay as much as we are willing to pay. We get a bargain. When people buy something for less than it is worth to them, they receive a consumer surplus. **Consumer surplus** is the excess of the benefit received from a good over the amount paid for it. We can calculate consumer surplus as the marginal benefit (or value) of a good minus its price, summed over the quantity bought.

Figure 5.2(a) shows Lisa's consumer surplus from pizza when the price is $1 a slice. At this price, she buys 30 slices a month because the 30th slice is worth exactly $1 to her. But Lisa is willing to pay $2 for the 10th slice, so her marginal benefit from this slice is

$1 more than she pays for it—she receives a surplus of $1 on the 10th slice.

Lisa's consumer surplus is the sum of the surpluses on *all of the slices she buys.* This sum is the area of the green triangle—the area below the demand curve and above the market price line. The area of this triangle is equal to its base (30 slices) multiplied by its height ($1.50) divided by 2, which is $22.50. The area of the blue rectangle in Fig. 5.2(a) shows what Lisa pays for 30 slices of pizza.

Figure 5.2(b) shows Nick's consumer surplus, and part (c) shows the consumer surplus for the market. The consumer surplus for the market is the sum of the consumer surpluses of Lisa and Nick.

All goods and services have decreasing marginal benefit, so people receive more benefit from their consumption than the amount they pay.

Supply and Marginal Cost

Your next task is to see how market supply reflects marginal cost. The connection between supply and cost closely parallels the related ideas about demand and benefit that you've just studied. Firms are in business to make a profit. To do so, they must sell

FIGURE 5.2   Demand and Consumer Surplus

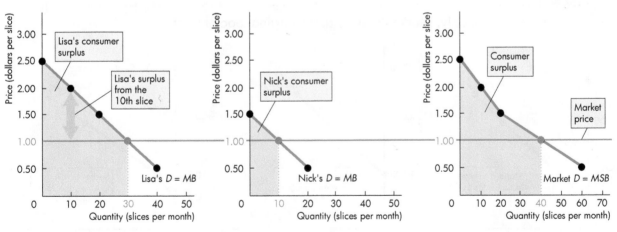

(a) Lisa's consumer surplus   **(b) Nick's consumer surplus**   **(c) Market consumer surplus**

Lisa is willing to pay $2 for her 10th slice of pizza in part (a). At a market price of $1 a slice, Lisa receives a surplus of $1 on the 10th slice. The green triangle shows her consumer surplus on the 30 slices she buys at $1 a slice. The

green triangle in part (b) shows Nick's consumer surplus on the 10 slices that he buys at $1 a slice. The green area in part (c) shows the consumer surplus for the market. The blue rectangles show the amounts spent on pizza.

their output for a price that exceeds the cost of production. Let's investigate the relationship between cost and price.

Supply, Cost, and Minimum Supply-Price

Firms make a profit when they receive more from the sale of a good or service than the cost of producing it. Just as consumers distinguish between value and price, so producers distinguish between *cost* and *price*. Cost is what a firm gives up when it produces a good or service and price is what a firm receives when it sells the good or service.

The cost of producing one more unit of a good or service is its marginal cost. Marginal cost is the minimum price that producers must receive to induce them to offer one more unit of a good or service for sale. But the minimum supply-price determines supply. *A supply curve is a marginal cost curve.*

In Fig. 5.3(a), Maria is willing to produce the 100th pizza for $15, her marginal cost of that pizza. In Fig. 5.3(b), Max is willing to produce the 50th pizza for $15, his marginal cost.

What quantity is this market willing to produce for $15 a pizza? The answer is provided by the *market supply curve*.

Individual Supply and Market Supply

The relationship between the price of a good and the quantity supplied by one producer is called *individual supply*. And the relationship between the price of a good and the quantity supplied by all producers is called *market supply*.

> The market supply curve is the horizontal sum of the individual supply curves and is formed by adding the quantities supplied by all the producers at each price.

Figure 5.3(c) illustrates the market supply of pizzas if Maria and Max are the only producers. Maria's supply curve in part (a) and Max's supply curve in part (b) sum horizontally to the market supply curve in part (c).

At a price of $15 a pizza, Maria supplies 100 pizzas and Max supplies 50 pizzas, so the quantity supplied by the market at $15 a pizza is 150 pizzas.

For Maria and Max, their supply curves are their marginal cost curves. For society, the market supply curve is its marginal cost curve. We call the society's marginal cost *marginal social cost*. So the market supply curve is also the *marginal social cost (MSC) curve*.

FIGURE 5.3   Individual Supply, Market Supply, and Marginal Social Cost

(a) Maria's supply   **(b) Max's supply**   **(c) Market supply**

At a price of $15 a pizza, the quantity supplied by Maria is 100 pizzas and the quantity supplied by Max is 50 pizzas, so the quantity supplied by the market is 150 pizzas. Maria's

supply curve in part (a) and Max's supply curve in part (b) sum horizontally to the market supply curve in part (c). The market supply curve is the marginal social cost (*MSC*) curve.

Producer Surplus

When price exceeds marginal cost, the firm receives a producer surplus. **Producer surplus** is the excess of the amount received from the sale of a good or service over the cost of producing it. We calculate producer surplus as the price received minus the marginal cost (or minimum supply-price), summed over the quantity sold.

Figure 5.4(a) shows Maria's producer surplus from pizza when the price is $15 a pizza. At this price, she sells 100 pizzas a month because the 100th pizza costs her $15 to produce. But Maria is willing to produce the 50th pizza for her marginal cost, which is $10, so she receives a surplus of $5 on this pizza.

Maria's producer surplus is the sum of the surpluses on the pizzas she sells. This sum is the area of the blue triangle—the area below the market price and above the supply curve. The area of this triangle is equal to its base (100) multiplied by its height ($10) divided by 2, which is $500.

The red area below the supply curve in Fig. 5.4(a) shows what it costs Maria to produce 100 pizzas.

The area of the blue triangle in Fig. 5.4(b) shows Max's producer surplus and the blue area in Fig. 5.4(c) shows the producer surplus for the market.

The producer surplus for the market is the sum of the producer surpluses of Maria and Max.

Consumer surplus and producer surplus can be used to measure the efficiency of a market. Let's see how we can use these concepts to study the efficiency of a competitive market.

▶ REVIEW QUIZ

1 What is the relationship between the marginal benefit, value, and demand?
2 What is the relationship between individual demand and market demand?
3 What is consumer surplus? How is it measured?
4 What is the relationship between the marginal cost, minimum supply-price, and supply?
5 What is the relationship between individual supply and market supply?
6 What is producer surplus? How is it measured?

You can work these questions in Study Plan 5.2 and get instant feedback.   MyEconLab

---

FIGURE 5.4   Supply and Producer Surplus

(a) Maria's producer surplus   **(b) Max's producer surplus**   **(c) Market producer surplus**

Maria is willing to produce the 50th pizza for $10 in part (a). At a market price of $15 a pizza, Maria gets a surplus of $5 on the 50th pizza. The blue triangle shows her producer surplus on the 100 she sells at $15 each.

The blue triangle in part (b) shows Max's producer surplus on the 50 pizzas that he sells at $15 each. The blue area in part (c) shows producer surplus for the market. The red areas show the cost of producing the pizzas sold.

Is the Competitive Market Efficient?

Figure 5.5(a) shows the market for pizza. The market forces that you studied in Chapter 3 (pp. 66–67) pull the pizza market to its equilibrium price of $15 a pizza and equilibrium quantity of 10,000 pizzas a day. Buyers enjoy a consumer surplus (green area) and sellers enjoy a producer surplus (blue area), but is this competitive equilibrium efficient?

Efficiency of Competitive Equilibrium

You've seen that the market demand curve for a good or service tells us the marginal social benefit from it. You've also seen that the market supply curve of a good or service tells us the marginal social cost of producing it.

Equilibrium in a competitive market occurs when the quantity demanded equals the quantity supplied at the intersection of the demand curve and the supply curve. At this intersection point, marginal social benefit on the demand curve equals marginal social cost on the supply curve. This equality is the condition for allocative efficiency. So in equilibrium, a competitive market achieves allocative efficiency.

Figure 5.5 illustrates the efficiency of competitive equilibrium. The demand curve and the supply curve intersect in part (a) and marginal social benefit equals marginal social cost in part (b).

If production is less than 10,000 pizzas a day, the marginal pizza is valued more highly than it costs to produce. If production exceeds 10,000 pizzas a day, the marginal pizza costs more to produce than the value that consumers place on it. Only when 10,000 pizzas a day are produced is the marginal pizza worth exactly what it costs.

The competitive market pushes the quantity of pizzas produced to its efficient level of 10,000 a day. If production is less than 10,000 pizzas a day, a shortage raises the price, which increases production. If production exceeds 10,000 pizzas a day, a surplus of pizzas lowers the price, which decreases production. So a competitive pizza market is efficient.

Figure 5.5(a) also shows the consumer surplus and producer surplus. The sum of consumer surplus and producer surplus is called **total surplus**. When the efficient quantity is produced, total surplus is maximized. Buyers and sellers acting in their self-interest end up promoting the social interest.

FIGURE 5.5   An Efficient Market for Pizza

(a) Equilibrium and surpluses

(b) Efficiency

Competitive equilibrium in part (a) occurs when the quantity demanded equals the quantity supplied. Resources are used efficiently in part (b) when marginal social benefit, *MSB*, equals marginal social cost, *MSC*. Total surplus, which is the sum of consumer surplus (the green triangle) and producer surplus (the blue triangle) is maximized.

The efficient quantity in part (b) is the same as the equilibrium quantity in part (a). The competitive pizza market produces the efficient quantity of pizzas.

MyEconLab animation

Economics in Action
Seeing the Invisible Hand

Adam Smith said that each participant in a competitive market is "led by *an invisible hand* to promote an end [the efficient use of resources] which was no part of his intention" (see p. 8). Smith believed that the invisible hand sends resources to the uses in which they have the highest value.

You can't *see* an invisible hand, but you can imagine one, and you can see its consequences in the cartoon and in today's world.

Umbrella for Sale The cold drinks vendor has cold drinks and shade and he has a marginal cost and a minimum supply-price of each. The reader on the park bench has a marginal benefit and willingness to pay for each. The reader's marginal benefit from shade exceeds the vendor's marginal cost; but the vendor's marginal cost of a cold drink exceeds the reader's marginal benefit. They trade the umbrella. The vendor gets a producer surplus from selling the shade for more than its marginal cost, and the reader gets a consumer surplus from buying the shade for less than its marginal benefit. Both are better off and the umbrella has moved to its highest-valued use.

The Invisible Hand at Work Today The market economy relentlessly performs the activity illustrated in the cartoon to achieve an efficient allocation of resources.

Suppose that a Florida frost cuts the supply of tomatoes. With fewer tomatoes available, the marginal social benefit increases. A shortage of tomatoes raises their price, so the market allocates the quantity available to the people who value them most highly.

If a new technology cuts the cost of producing a smart phone, the supply of smart phones increases and the price of a smart phone falls. The lower price

encourages an increase in the quantity demanded of this now less-costly tool. The marginal social benefit from a smart phone is brought to equality with its lower marginal social cost.

Market Failure

Markets do not always achieve an efficient outcome. We call a situation in which a market delivers an inefficient outcome one of **market failure**. Market failure can occur because too little of an item is produced (underproduction) or too much is produced (overproduction). We'll describe these two market failure outcomes and then see why they arise.

Underproduction In Fig. 5.6(a), the quantity of pizzas produced is 5,000 a day. At this quantity, consumers are willing to pay $20 for a pizza that costs only $10 to produce. By producing only 5,000 pizzas a day, total surplus is smaller than its maximum possible level. The quantity produced is inefficient—there is underproduction.

We measure the scale of inefficiency by **deadweight loss**, which is the decrease in total surplus that results

FIGURE 5.6 Underproduction and Overproduction

(a) Underproduction

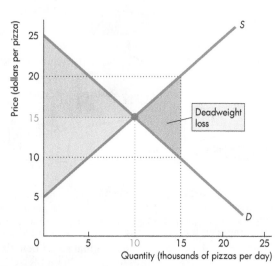

(b) Overproduction

If 5,000 pizzas a day are produced, in part (a), total surplus (the sum of the green and blue areas) is smaller than its maximum by the amount of the deadweight loss (the gray triangle). At all quantities below 10,000 pizzas a day, the benefit from one more pizza exceeds its cost.

If 15,000 pizzas a day are produced, in part (b), total surplus is also smaller than its maximum by the amount of the deadweight loss. At all quantities in excess of 10,000 pizzas a day, the cost of one more pizza exceeds its benefit.

———— MyEconLab animation ————

from an inefficient level of production. The gray triangle in Fig. 5.6(a) shows the deadweight loss.

Overproduction In Fig. 5.6(b), the quantity of pizzas produced is 15,000 a day. At this quantity, consumers are willing to pay only $10 for a pizza that costs $20 to produce. By producing the 15,000th pizza, $10 of resources are wasted. Again, the gray triangle shows the deadweight loss, which reduces the total surplus to less than its maximum.

Inefficient production creates a deadweight loss that is borne by the entire society: It is a social loss.

Sources of Market Failure

Obstacles to efficiency that bring market failure and create deadweight losses are

- Price and quantity regulations
- Taxes and subsidies
- Externalities
- Public goods and common resources
- Monopoly
- High transactions costs

Price and Quantity Regulations *Price regulations* that put a cap on the rent a landlord is permitted to charge and laws that require employers to pay a minimum wage sometimes block the price adjustments that balance the quantity demanded and the quantity supplied and lead to underproduction. *Quantity regulations* that limit the amount that a farm is permitted to produce also lead to underproduction.

Taxes and Subsidies *Taxes* increase the prices paid by buyers and lower the prices received by sellers. So taxes decrease the quantity produced and lead to underproduction. *Subsidies*, which are payments by the government to producers, decrease the prices paid by buyers and increase the prices received by sellers. So subsidies increase the quantity produced and lead to overproduction.

Externalities An *externality* is a cost or a benefit that affects someone other than the seller or the buyer. An *external cost* arises when an electric utility burns coal and emits carbon dioxide. The utility doesn't consider the cost of climate change when it decides how much power to produce. The result is overproduction. An *external benefit* arises when an apartment owner installs a smoke detector and decreases her neighbor's fire risk. She doesn't consider the benefit to her neighbor when she decides how many detectors to install. The result is underproduction.

Public Goods and Common Resources

A *public good* is a good or service that is consumed simultaneously by everyone even if they don't pay for it. National defense is an example. Competitive markets would underproduce national defense because it is in each person's interest to free ride on everyone else and avoid paying for her or his share of such a good.

A *common resource* is owned by no one but is available to be used by everyone. Atlantic salmon is an example. It is in everyone's self-interest to ignore the costs they impose on others when they decide how much of a common resource to use. The result is that the resource is overused.

Monopoly

A *monopoly* is a firm that is the sole provider of a good or service. Local water supply and cable television are supplied by firms that are monopolies. The monopoly's self-interest is to maximize its profit. Because the monopoly has no competitors, it can set the price to achieve its self-interested goal. To achieve its goal, a monopoly produces too little and charges too high a price. It leads to underproduction.

High Transactions Costs

When you go to Starbucks, you pay for more than the coffee. You pay your share of the cost of the barrista's time, the espresso maker, and the decor. When you buy your first apartment, you will pay for more than the apartment. You will buy the services of an agent and a lawyer. Economists call the costs of the services that enable a market to bring buyers and sellers together **transactions costs**.

It is costly to operate *any* market so to use market price to allocate resources, it must be worth bearing the transactions costs. Some markets are too costly to operate. For example, it is too costly to operate a market in time slots on a local tennis court. Instead of a market, the court uses first-come, first-served: You hang around until the court becomes vacant and "pay" with your waiting time. When transactions costs are high, the market might underproduce.

You now know the conditions under which resource allocation is efficient. You've seen how a competitive market can be efficient, and you've seen some obstacles to efficiency. Can alternative allocation methods improve on the market?

Alternatives to the Market

When a market is inefficient, can one of the alternative nonmarket methods that we described at the beginning of this chapter do a better job? Sometimes it can.

Often, majority rule might be used in an attempt to improve the allocation of resources. But majority rule has its own shortcomings. A group that pursues the self-interest of its members can become the majority. For example, a price or quantity regulation that creates inefficiency is almost always the result of a self-interested group becoming the majority and imposing costs on the minority. Also, with majority rule, votes must be translated into actions by bureaucrats who have their own agendas based on their self-interest.

Managers in firms issue commands and avoid the transactions costs that they would incur if they went to a market every time they needed a job done.

First-come, first-served works best in some situations. Think about the scene at a busy ATM. Instead of waiting in line people might trade places at a "market" price. But someone would need to ensure that trades were honored. At a busy ATM, first-come, first-served is the most efficient arrangement.

There is no one efficient mechanism that allocates all resources efficiently. But markets, when supplemented by other mechanisms such as majority rule, command systems, and first-come, first-served, do an amazingly good job.

▶ REVIEW QUIZ

1 Do competitive markets use resources efficiently? Explain why or why not.
2 What is deadweight loss and under what conditions does it occur?
3 What are the obstacles to achieving an efficient allocation of resources in the market economy?

You can work these questions in Study Plan 5.3 and get instant feedback.   MyEconLab

Is an efficient allocation of resources also a fair allocation? Does the competitive market provide people with fair incomes for their work? Do people always pay a fair price for the things they buy? Don't we need the government to step into some competitive markets to prevent the price from rising too high or falling too low? Let's now study these questions.

◆ Is the Competitive Market Fair?

When a natural disaster strikes, such as a severe winter storm or a hurricane, the prices of many essential items jump. The reason prices jump is that the demand and willingness to pay for these items has increased, but the supply has not changed. So the higher prices achieve an efficient allocation of scarce resources. News reports of these price hikes almost never talk about efficiency. Instead, they talk about equity or fairness. The claim that is often made is that it is unfair for profit-seeking dealers to cheat the victims of natural disaster.

Similarly, when low-skilled people work for a wage that is below what most would regard as a "living wage," the media and politicians talk of employers taking unfair advantage of their workers.

How do we decide whether something is fair or unfair? You know when you *think* something is unfair, but how do you *know?* What are the *principles* of fairness?

Philosophers have tried for centuries to answer this question. Economists have offered their answers too. But before we look at the proposed answers, you should know that there is no universally agreed upon answer.

Economists agree about efficiency. That is, they agree that it makes sense to make the economic pie as large as possible and to produce it at the lowest possible cost. But they do not agree about equity. That is, they do not agree about what are fair shares of the economic pie for all the people who make it. The reason is that ideas about fairness are not exclusively economic ideas. They touch on politics, ethics, and religion. Nevertheless, economists have thought about these issues and have a contribution to make. Let's examine the views of economists on this topic.

To think about fairness, think of economic life as a game—a serious game. All ideas about fairness can be divided into two broad groups. They are

- It's not fair if the *result* isn't fair.
- It's not fair if the *rules* aren't fair.

It's Not Fair If the *Result* Isn't Fair

The earliest efforts to establish a principle of fairness were based on the view that the result is what matters. The general idea was that it is unfair if people's incomes are too unequal. For example, it is unfair

that a bank president earns millions of dollars a year while a bank teller earns only thousands of dollars. It is unfair that a store owner makes a larger profit and her customers pay higher prices in the aftermath of a winter storm.

During the nineteenth century, economists thought they had made an incredible discovery: Efficiency requires equality of incomes. To make the economic pie as large as possible, it must be cut into equal pieces, one for each person. This idea turns out to be wrong. But there is a lesson in the reason that it is wrong, so this idea is worth a closer look.

Utilitarianism The nineteenth-century idea that only equality brings efficiency is called *utilitarianism*. **Utilitarianism** is a principle that states that we should strive to achieve "the greatest happiness for the greatest number." The people who developed this idea were known as utilitarians. They included the most eminent thinkers, such as Jeremy Bentham and John Stuart Mill.

Utilitarians argued that to achieve "the greatest happiness for the greatest number," income must be transferred from the rich to the poor up to the point of complete equality—to the point at which there are no rich and no poor.

They reasoned in the following way: First, everyone has the same basic wants and a similar capacity to enjoy life. Second, the greater a person's income, the smaller is the marginal benefit of a dollar. The millionth dollar spent by a rich person brings a smaller marginal benefit to that person than the marginal benefit that the thousandth dollar spent brings to a poorer person. So by transferring a dollar from the millionaire to the poorer person, more is gained than is lost. The two people added together are better off.

Figure 5.7 illustrates this utilitarian idea. Tom and Jerry have the same marginal benefit curve, *MB*. (Marginal benefit is measured on the same scale of 1 to 3 for both Tom and Jerry.) Tom is at point *A*. He earns $5,000 a year, and his marginal benefit from a dollar is 3 units. Jerry is at point *B*. He earns $45,000 a year, and his marginal benefit from a dollar is 1 unit. If a dollar is transferred from Jerry to Tom, Jerry loses 1 unit of marginal benefit and Tom gains 3 units. So together, Tom and Jerry are better off—they are sharing the economic pie more efficiently. If a second dollar is transferred, the same thing happens: Tom gains more than Jerry loses. And the same is true for every dollar transferred until they both reach point *C*. At point *C*, Tom and Jerry have $25,000

FIGURE 5.7 Utilitarian Fairness

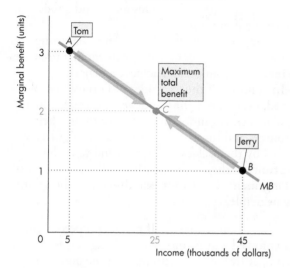

Tom earns $5,000 and has 3 units of marginal benefit at point A. Jerry earns $45,000 and has 1 unit of marginal benefit at point B. If income is transferred from Jerry to Tom, Jerry's loss is less than Tom's gain. Only when each of them has $25,000 and 2 units of marginal benefit (at point C) can the sum of their total benefit increase no further.

MyEconLab animation

each and a marginal benefit of 2 units. Now they are sharing the economic pie in the most efficient way. It brings the greatest happiness to Tom and Jerry.

The Big Tradeoff One big problem with the utilitarian ideal of complete equality is that it ignores the costs of making income transfers. Recognizing the costs of making income transfers leads to what is called the **big tradeoff**, which is a tradeoff between efficiency and fairness.

The big tradeoff is based on the following facts. Income can be transferred from people with high incomes to people with low incomes only by taxing the high incomes. Taxing people's income from employment makes them work less. It results in the quantity of labor being less than the efficient quantity. Taxing people's income from capital makes them save less. It results in the quantity of capital being less than the efficient quantity. With smaller quantities of both labor and capital, the quantity of goods and services produced is less than the efficient quantity. The economic pie shrinks.

The tradeoff is between the size of the economic pie and the degree of equality with which it is shared. The greater the amount of income redistribution through income taxes, the greater is the inefficiency—the smaller is the economic pie.

There is a second source of inefficiency. A dollar taken from a rich person does not end up as a dollar in the hands of a poorer person. Some of the dollar is spent on administration of the tax and transfer system. The cost of tax-collecting agencies, such as the Internal Revenue Service (IRS), and welfare-administering agencies, such as the Centers for Medicare and Medicaid, must be paid with some of the taxes collected. Also, taxpayers hire accountants, auditors, and lawyers to help them ensure that they pay the correct amount of taxes. These activities use skilled labor and capital resources that could otherwise be used to produce goods and services that people value.

When all these costs are taken into account, taking a dollar from a rich person does not give a dollar to a poor person. It is possible that with high taxes, people with low incomes might end up being worse off. Suppose, for example, that highly taxed entrepreneurs decide to work less hard and shut down some of their businesses. Low-income workers get fired and must seek other, perhaps even lower-paid, work.

Today, because of the big tradeoff, no one says that fairness requires complete equality of incomes.

Make the Poorest as Well Off as Possible A new solution to the big-tradeoff problem was proposed by philosopher John Rawls in a classic book entitled *A Theory of Justice*, published in 1971. Rawls says that, taking all the costs of income transfers into account, the fair distribution of the economic pie is the one that makes the poorest person as well off as possible. The incomes of rich people should be taxed, and after paying the costs of administering the tax and transfer system, what is left should be transferred to the poor. But the taxes must not be so high that they make the economic pie shrink to the point at which the poorest person ends up with a smaller piece. A bigger share of a smaller pie can be less than a smaller share of a bigger pie. The goal is to make the piece enjoyed by the poorest person as big as possible. Most likely, this piece will not be an equal share.

The "fair results" idea requires a change in the results after the game is over. Some economists say that these changes are themselves unfair and propose a different way of thinking about fairness.

It's Not Fair If the *Rules* Aren't Fair

The idea that it's not fair if the rules aren't fair is based on a fundamental principle that seems to be hardwired into the human brain: the symmetry principle. The **symmetry principle** is the requirement that people in similar situations be treated similarly. It is the moral principle that lies at the center of all the big religions and that says, in some form or other, "Behave toward other people in the way you expect them to behave toward you."

different religions.

In economic life, this principle translates into *equality of opportunity*. But equality of opportunity to do what? This question is answered by the philosopher Robert Nozick in a book entitled *Anarchy, State, and Utopia*, published in 1974.

Nozick argues that the idea of fairness as an outcome or result cannot work and that fairness must be based on the fairness of the rules. He suggests that fairness obeys two rules:

1. The state must enforce laws that establish and protect private property.
2. Private property may be transferred from one person to another only by voluntary exchange.

The first rule says that everything that is valuable must be owned by individuals and that the state must ensure that theft is prevented. The second rule says that the only legitimate way a person can acquire property is to buy it in exchange for something else that the person owns. If these rules, which are the only fair rules, are followed, then the result is fair. It doesn't matter how unequally the economic pie is shared, provided that the pie is made by people, each one of whom voluntarily provides services in exchange for the share of the pie offered in compensation.

These rules satisfy the symmetry principle. If these rules are not followed, the symmetry principle is broken. You can see these facts by imagining a world in which the laws are not followed.

First, suppose that some resources or goods are not owned. They are common property. Then everyone is free to participate in a grab to use them. The strongest will prevail. But when the strongest prevails, the strongest effectively *owns* the resources or goods in question and prevents others from enjoying them.

Second, suppose that we do not insist on voluntary exchange for transferring ownership of resources from one person to another. The alternative is *involuntary* transfer. In simple language, the alternative is theft.

Both of these situations violate the symmetry principle. Only the strong acquire what they want. The weak end up with only the resources and goods that the strong don't want.

In a majority-rule political system, the strong are those in the majority or those with enough resources to influence opinion and achieve a majority.

In contrast, if the two rules of fairness are followed, everyone, strong and weak, is treated in a similar way. All individuals are free to use their resources and human skills to create things that are valued by themselves and others and to exchange the fruits of their efforts with all others. This set of arrangements is the only one that obeys the symmetry principle.

Fair Rules and Efficiency   If private property rights are enforced and if voluntary exchange takes place in a competitive market with none of the obstacles described above (p. 115), resources will be allocated efficiently.

According to the Nozick fair rules view, no matter how unequal is the resulting distribution of income and wealth, it will be fair.

It would be better if everyone were as well off as those with the highest incomes, but scarcity prevents that outcome and the best attainable outcome is the efficient one.

Case Study: A Generator Shortage in a Natural Disaster

Hurricane Katrina shut down electricity supplies over a wide area and increased the demand for portable generators. What is the fair way to allocate the available generators?

If the market price is used, the outcome is efficient. Sellers *and buyers* are better off and no one is worse off. But people who own generators make a larger profit and the generators go to those who want them most and can afford them. Is that fair?

On the Nozick rules view, the outcome is fair. On the fair outcome view, the outcome might be considered unfair. But what are the alternatives? They are command, majority rule, contest, first-come-first-served, lottery, personal characteristics, and force. Except by chance, none of these methods delivers an allocation of generators that is either fair or efficient. It is unfair in the rules view because the distribution involves involuntary transfers of resources among citizens. It is unfair in the results view because the poorest don't end up being made as well off as possible.

◆ AT ISSUE

Price Gouging

Price gouging is the practice of offering an essential item for sale following a natural disaster at a price much higher price than its normal price.

In the aftermath of Hurricane Katrina, John Shepperson bought 19 generators and rented a U-Haul truck to transport them from his Kentucky home to a town in Mississippi that had lost its electricity supply. He offered the generators to eager buyers at twice the price he had paid for them. But before Mr. Shepperson had made a sale, the Mississippi police confiscated the generators and put him in jail for four days for price gouging.

In Favor of a Law Against Price Gouging

Supporters of laws against price gouging say:

- It unfairly exploits vulnerable needy buyers.
- It unfairly rewards unscrupulous sellers.
- In situations of extraordinary shortage, prices should be regulated to prevent these abuses and scarce resources should be allocated by one of the non-market mechanisms such as majority vote or equal shares for all.

Should the price that this seller of generators may charge be regulated?

The Economist's Response

Economists say that preventing a voluntary market transaction leads to inefficiency—it makes some people worse off without making anyone better off.

- In the figure below, when the demand for generators increases from D_0 to D_1, the equilibrium price rises from $200 to $600.
- Calling the price rise "gouging" and blocking it with a law prevents additional units from being made available and creates a deadweight loss.

The Effects of a Price-Gouging Law

▶ REVIEW QUIZ

1 What are the two big approaches to thinking about fairness?
2 What is the utilitarian idea of fairness and what is wrong with it?
3 Explain the big tradeoff. What idea of fairness has been developed to deal with it?
4 What is the idea of fairness based on fair rules?

You can work these questions in Study Plan 5.4 and get instant feedback. **MyEconLab**

◆ You've now studied efficiency and equity (fairness), the two biggest issues that run through the whole of economics. *Reading Between the Lines* on pp. 120–121 looks at an example of an efficiency in our economy today. At many points throughout this book—and in your life—you will return to and use the ideas you've learned in this chapter. We start to apply these ideas in the next chapter where we study some sources of *in*efficiency and *un*fairness.

Making Traffic Flow Efficiently

Rail No Cure-All for Metro Atlanta's Traffic Congestion

The Atlanta Journal-Constitution
September 6, 2011

… On its face, the problem seems simple. If a person who commutes alone by car takes the train instead, then that's one less car on the road. … Multiple experts told PolitiFact Georgia that even if thousands of drivers take the train rather than a major road, congestion on that road doesn't end.

It might drop initially, but travelers soon notice the better traffic. Commuters who once avoided the road return. Others take additional trips, or start using it during peak traffic times. People who car pooled start commuting alone.

Eventually, congestion returns, said Anthony Downs, a Brookings Institution fellow who has studied traffic congestion for decades. He thinks congestion is extremely hard to avoid, and likely will grow worse. Brookings is a liberal-leaning think tank. …

A 2009 University of Toronto study that analyzed interstate highway and vehicle travel data across the United States found there is little evidence that additional public transit reduces traffic. Other researchers have come to similar conclusions.

But there's another important side to the traffic conundrum … : Decades of research shows that additional highway lanes don't end gridlock, either. As with rail, drivers fill up the new lanes. Once again, they're stuck in traffic.

… In the end, though, the bulk of the experts we interviewed agreed that the one tested way to cut down on gridlock is "congestion pricing." That's when drivers pay a surcharge to use roads during peak traffic hours. Cities such as London and Singapore have used the strategy and eased downtown traffic.

ESSENCE OF THE STORY

- There is little evidence that additional public transit or additional freeway lanes reduces road congestion.

- If one car user takes the train, so there is one less car on the road, traffic flows faster and others are encouraged to switch from train to car, so eventually congestion returns.

- Additional drivers fill up new highway lanes and again, congestion returns.

- The one tested way to reduce congestion is congestion pricing—paying to use roads during peak traffic hours.

- London and Singapore use this method to keep traffic moving.

ECONOMIC ANALYSIS

- The Texas Transportation Institute says that in 2010 on 10 stretches of Atlanta's most congested corridors, 2 million person hours and 6.6 million gallons of gasoline were wasted at a cost of $302 million; and on the nation's 328 most congested corridors, 78 million person hours and 284 million gallons of gasoline were wasted at a cost of $12.6 billion.

- When one additional vehicle enters an uncongested road, it imposes no costs on other road users. But when one additional vehicle enters a congested road, the traffic slows and time and gasoline costs increase for all road users.

- The figures show the marginal social cost curve (MSC) for a road that can carry 15,000 vehicles per hour with no congestion. Up to 15,000 vehicles per hour, $MSC = 0$. Above 15,000 vehicles per hour congestion occurs and MSC increases as more vehicles enter the road.

- During the night and at off-peak parts of the day, the marginal social benefit (MSB) and demand for road space is low and there is no congestion.

- Figure 1 illustrates off-peak road use. The demand and marginal benefit curve is $D_o = MSB_o$; the marginal cost curve is MSC; and the equilibrium and efficient outcome occurs at a zero price for road use.

- Figure 2 illustrates road use at a peak congestion time. The demand and marginal benefit curve is $D_p = MSB_p$ and with a zero price for road use, 40,000 vehicles per

hour enter the road. There is a deadweight loss (of time and gasoline) shown by the gray triangle.

- Imposing a congestion charge of $2 per mile brings an equilibrium at 25,000 vehicles per hour, which is the efficient quantity. In this situation, total surplus, the sum of consumer surplus (green) *plus* producer surplus (blue), is maximized.

- Singapore has the world's most sophisticated congestion pricing with the price displayed on gantries (see photo), and the price rises as congestion increases and falls as congestion eases.

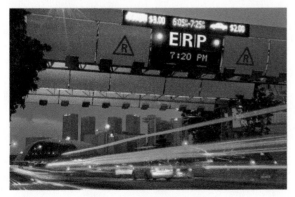

Traffic grinds to a halt on a U.S. freeway, but electronic Road Pricing (ERP) keeps vehicles moving in Singapore.

Figure 1 Off-Peak Road Use

Figure 2 Peak Road Use

121

SUMMARY

Key Points

Resource Allocation Methods (pp. 106–107)

- Because resources are scarce, some mechanism must allocate them.
- The alternative allocation methods are market price; command; majority rule; contest; first-come, first-served; lottery; personal characteristics; and force.

Working Study Plan Problems 1 and 2 will give you a better understanding of resource allocation methods.

Benefit, Cost, and Surplus (pp. 108–111)

- The maximum price willingly paid is marginal benefit, so a demand curve is also a marginal benefit curve.
- The market demand curve is the horizontal sum of the individual demand curves and is the marginal social benefit curve.
- Value is what people are *willing to* pay; price is what people *must* pay.
- Consumer surplus is the excess of the benefit received from a good or service over the amount paid for it.
- The minimum supply-price is marginal cost, so a supply curve is also a marginal cost curve.
- The market supply curve is the horizontal sum of the individual supply curves and is the marginal social cost curve.
- Cost is what producers pay; price is what producers receive.

- Producer surplus is the excess of the amount received from the sale of a good or service over the cost of producing it.

Working Study Plan Problems 3 to 10 will give you a better understanding of benefit, cost, and surplus.

Is the Competitive Market Efficient? (pp. 112–115)

- In a competitive equilibrium, marginal social benefit equals marginal social cost and resource allocation is efficient.
- Buyers and sellers acting in their self-interest end up promoting the social interest.
- Total surplus, consumer surplus plus producer surplus, is maximized.
- Producing less than or more than the efficient quantity creates deadweight loss.
- Price and quantity regulations; taxes and subsidies; externalities; public goods and common resources; monopoly; and high transactions costs can lead to market failure.

Working Study Plan Problems 11 to 13 will give you a better understanding of the efficiency of competitive markets.

Is the Competitive Market Fair? (pp. 116–119)

- Ideas about fairness can be divided into two groups: fair *results* and fair *rules*.
- Fair-results ideas require income transfers from the rich to the poor.
- Fair-rules ideas require property rights and voluntary exchange.

Working Study Plan Problems 14 and 15 will give you a better understanding of the fairness of competitive markets.

Key Terms

MyEconLab   You can work Problems 1 to 17 in MyEconLab Chapter 5 Study Plan and get instant feedback.

Resource Allocation Methods (Study Plan 5.1)

Use the following information to work Problems 1 and 2.

At Chez Panisse, the restaurant in Berkeley that is credited with having created California cuisine, reservations are essential. At Mandarin Dynasty, a restaurant near the University of California San Diego, reservations are recommended. At Eli Cannon's, a restaurant in Middletown, Connecticut, reservations are not accepted.

1. a. Describe the method of allocating scarce table resources at these three restaurants.

   b. Why do you think restaurants have different reservations policies?

2. Why do you think restaurants don't use the market price to allocate their tables?

Benefit, Cost, and Surplus (Study Plan 5.2)

Use the following table to work Problems 3 to 5.

The table gives the demand schedules for train travel for the only buyers in the market, Ann, Beth, and Cy.

Price (dollars per mile)	Quantity demanded (miles)		
	Ann	Beth	Cy
3	30	25	20
4	25	20	15
5	20	15	10
6	15	10	5
7	10	5	0
8	5	0	0
9	0	0	0

3. a. Construct the market demand schedule.

   b. What is the maximum price that each traveler, Ann, Beth, and Cy, is willing to pay to travel 20 miles? Why?

4. a. What is the marginal social benefit when the total distance travelled is 60 miles?

   b. When the three people travel a total of 60 miles, how many miles does each travel and what is the marginal private benefit of each traveler?

5. a. What is each traveler's consumer surplus when the price is $4 a mile?

b. What is the market consumer surplus when the price is $4 a mile?

Use the following table to work Problems 6 to 8.

The table gives the supply schedules of hot air balloon rides for the only sellers in the market, Xavier, Yasmin, and Zack.

Price (dollars per ride)	Quantity supplied (rides per week)		
	Xavier	Yasmin	Zack
100	30	25	20
90	25	20	15
80	20	15	10
70	15	10	5
60	10	5	0
50	5	0	0
40	0	0	0

6. a. Construct the market supply schedule.

   b. What are the minimum prices that Xavier, Yasmin, and Zack are willing to accept to supply 20 rides? Why?

7. a. What is the marginal social cost when the total number of rides is 30?

   b. What is the marginal cost for each supplier when the total number of rides is 30 and how many rides does each of the firms supply?

8. When the price is $70 a ride, what is each firm's producer surplus? What is the market producer surplus?

Use the following news clip to work Problems 9 and 10.

eBay Saves Billions for Bidders

If you think you would save money by bidding on eBay auctions, you would likely be right. Two Maryland researchers calculated the difference between the actual purchase price paid for auction items and the top price bidders stated they were willing to pay. They found that the difference averaged at least $4 per auction.

Source: *InformationWeek*, January 28, 2008

9. What method is used to allocate goods on eBay? How does the allocation method used by eBay auctions influence consumer surplus?

10. a. Can an eBay auction give the seller a surplus?
    b. On a graph show the consumer surplus and producer surplus from an eBay auction.

Is the Competitive Market Efficient? (Study Plan 5.3)

11. The figure illustrates the competitive market for cell phones.

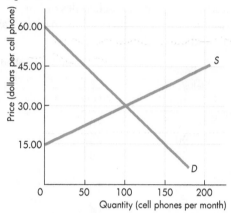

a. What are the equilibrium price and equilibrium quantity of cell phones?
b. Shade in and label the consumer surplus at the competitive equilibrium.
c. Shade in and label the producer surplus at the competitive equilibrium.
d. Calculate total surplus at the competitive equilibrium.
e. Is the competitive market for cell phones efficient?

12. The table gives the demand and supply schedules for sunscreen.

Price	Quantity demanded	Quantity supplied
(dollars per bottle)	(bottles per day)	
0	400	0
5	300	100
10	200	200
15	100	300
20	0	400

Sunscreen factories are required to limit production to 100 bottles a day.

a. What is the maximum price that consumers are willing to pay for the 100th bottle?
b. What is the minimum price that producers are willing to accept for the 100th bottle?
c. Describe the situation in this market.

13. Explain why each restaurant in Problem 1 might be using an efficient allocation method.

Is the Competitive Market Fair? (Study Plan 5.4)

14. Explain why the allocation method used by each restaurant in Problem 1 is fair or not fair.

15. In Problem 12, how can the 100 bottles available be allocated to beach-goers? Which possible methods would be fair and which would be unfair?

Economics in the News (Study Plan 5.N)

16. **The World's Largest Tulip and Flower Market**
    Every day 20 million tulips, roses, and other cut flowers are auctioned at the Dutch market called *The Bloemenveiling*. Each day 55,000 Dutch auctions take place, matching buyers and sellers.
    Source: Tulip-Bulbs.com

    A Dutch auction is one in which the auctioneer starts by announcing the highest price. If no one offers to buy the flowers, the auctioneer lowers the price until a buyer is found.
    a. What method is used to allocate flowers at the Bloemenveiling?
    b. How does a Dutch flower auction influence consumer surplus and producer surplus?
    c. Are the flower auctions at the Bloemenveiling efficient?

17. **Wii Sells Out Across Japan**
    After a two-month TV-ad blitz for Wii in Japan, demand was expected to exceed supply. Yodobashi Camera was selling Wii games on a first-come, first-served basis. Eager customers showed up early and those who tried to join the line after 6 or 7 a.m. were turned away—many rushed off to the smaller stores that were holding raffles to decide who got a Wii.
    Source: *Gamespot News*, December 1, 2006
    a. Why was the quantity demanded of Wii expected to exceed the quantity supplied?
    b. Did Nintendo produce the efficient quantity of Wii? Explain.
    c. Can you think of reasons why Nintendo might want to underproduce and leave the market with fewer Wii than people want to buy?
    d. What are the two methods of resource allocation described in the news clip? Is either method of allocating Wii efficient?
    e. What do you think some of the people who managed to buy a Wii did with it?
    f. Explain which is the fairer method of allocating the Wii: the market price or the two methods described in the news clip.

ADDITIONAL PROBLEMS AND APPLICATIONS

MyEconLab You can work these problems in MyEconLab if assigned by your instructor.

Resource Allocation Methods

18. At McDonald's, no reservations are accepted; at Puck's at St. Louis Art Museum, reservations are accepted; at the Bissell Mansion restaurant, reservations are essential. Describe the method of allocating table resources in these three restaurants. Why do you think restaurants have different reservations policies?

Benefit, Cost, and Surplus

Use the following table to work Problems 19 to 22. The table gives the supply schedules for jet-ski rides by the only suppliers: Rick, Sam, and Tom.

Price	Quantity supplied (rides per day)		
(dollars per ride)	Rick	Sam	Tom
10.00	0	0	0
12.50	5	0	0
15.00	10	5	0
17.50	15	10	5
20.00	20	15	10

19. What is each owner's minimum supply-price of 10 rides a day?

20. Which owner has the largest producer surplus when the price of a ride is $17.50? Explain.

21. What is the marginal social cost of 45 rides a day?

22. Construct the market supply schedule of jet-ski rides.

23. The table gives the demand and supply schedules for sandwiches.

Price	Quantity demanded	Quantity supplied
(dollars per sandwich)	(sandwiches per hour)	
0	300	0
1	250	50
2	200	100
3	150	150
4	100	200
5	50	250
6	0	300

a. What is the maximum price that consumers are willing to pay for the 200th sandwich?

b. What is the minimum price that producers are willing to accept for the 200th sandwich?

c. If 200 sandwiches a day are available, what is the total surplus?

24. "Two Buck Chuck" Wine Cult

"Two Buck Chuck" is a cheap, good wine. After a year flooding the West Coast market, it is still being sold by the case to wine lovers. An over-abundance of grapes has made the wine cheap to bottle—about 5 million cases so far.

Source: *CBS*, June 2, 2003

How has "Two Buck Chuck" influenced the consumer surplus from wine, the producer surplus for its producer, and the producer surplus for the producers of other wines?

Is the Competitive Market Efficient?

25. Use the data in the table in Problem 23.

a. If the sandwich market is efficient, what is the consumer surplus, what is the producer surplus, and what is the total surplus?

b. If the demand for sandwiches increases and sandwich makers produce the efficient quantity, what happens to producer surplus and deadweight loss?

Use the following news clip to work Problems 26 to 28.

The Right Price for Digital Music

Apple's $1.29-for-the-latest-songs model isn't perfect and isn't it too much to pay for music that appeals to just a few people? What we need is a system that will be profitable but fair to music lovers. The solution: Price song downloads according to demand. The more people who download a particular song, the higher will be the price of that song; the fewer people who buy a particular song, the lower will be the price of that song. That is a free-market solution—the market would determine the price.

Source: *Slate*, December 5, 2005

Assume that the marginal social cost of downloading a song from the iTunes Store is zero. (This assumption means that the cost of operating the iTunes Store doesn't change if people download more songs.)

26. a. Draw a graph of the market for downloadable music with a price of $1.29 for all the latest songs. On your graph, show consumer surplus and producer surplus.

b. With a price of $1.29 for all the latest songs, is the market efficient or inefficient? If it is inefficient, show the deadweight loss on your graph.

27. If the pricing scheme described in the news clip were adopted, how would consumer surplus, producer surplus, and the deadweight loss change?

28. a. If the pricing scheme described in the news clip were adopted, would the market be efficient or inefficient? Explain.

    b. Is the pricing scheme described in the news clip a "free-market solution"? Explain.

29. Only 1 percent of the world supply of water is fit for human consumption. Some places have more water than they can use; some could use much more than they have. The 1 percent available would be sufficient if only it were in the right place.

    a. What is the major problem in achieving an efficient use of the world's water?

    b. If there were a global market in water, like there is in oil, how do you think the market would be organized?

    c. Would a free world market in water achieve an efficient use of the world's water resources? Explain why or why not.

Is the Competitive Market Fair?

30. Use the information in Problem 28. Would a free world market in water achieve a fair use of the world's water resources? Explain why or why not and be clear about the concept of fairness that you are using.

31. The winner of the men's and women's tennis singles at the U.S. Open is paid twice as much as the runner-up, but it takes two players to have a singles final. Is the compensation arrangement fair?

32. **The Scandal of Phone Call Price Gouging by Prisons**

    In most states, the phone company guarantees the prison a commission of a percentage on every call. The average commission is 42% of the cost of the call, but in some states it is 60%. So 60% of what families pay to receive a collect call from their imprisoned relative has nothing to do with the cost of the phone service. Also, the phone company that offers the highest commission is often the company to get the prison contract.

    Source: *The Guardian*, May 23, 2012

    a. Who is practicing price gouging: the prison, the phone company, or both? Explain.

    b. Evaluate the "fairness" of the prison's commission.

Economics in the News

33. After you have studied *Reading Between the Lines* on pp. 120–121, answer the following questions.

    a. What is the method used to allocate highway space in the United States and what is the method used in Singapore?

    b. Who benefits from the U.S. method of highway resource allocation? Explain your answer using the ideas of marginal social benefit, marginal social cost, consumer surplus, and producer surplus.

    c. Who benefits from the Singaporean method of highway resource allocation? Explain your answer using the ideas of marginal social benefit, marginal social cost, consumer surplus, and producer surplus.

    d. If road use were rationed by limiting drivers with even-date birthdays to drive only on even days (and odd-date birthdays to drive only on odd days), would highway use be more efficietn? Explain your answer.

34. **Fight over Water Rates; Escondido Farmers Say Increase Would Put Them Out of Business**

    Agricultural users of water pay less than residential and business users. Since 1993, water rates have increased by more than 90 percent for residential customers and by only 50 percent for agricultural users.

    Source: *The San Diego Union-Tribune*, June 14, 2006

    a. Do you think that the allocation of water between agricultural and residential users is likely to be efficient? Explain your answer.

    b. If agricultural users paid a higher price, would the allocation of resources be more efficient?

    c. If agricultural users paid a higher price, what would happen to consumer surplus and producer surplus from water?

    d. Is the difference in price paid by agricultural and residential users fair?

6

GOVERNMENT ACTIONS IN MARKETS

◆

After studying this chapter, you will be able to:

◆ Explain how a rent ceiling creates a housing shortage

◆ Explain how a minimum wage law creates unemployment

◆ Explain the effects of a tax

◆ Explain the effects of production quotas and subsidies

◆ Explain how markets for illegal goods work

Can governments cap rents to help low-income renters live in affordable housing and raise incomes of low-paid workers with a minimum wage law? Who *really* pays the sales tax: buyers or sellers? Do subsidies to farmers and production limits help to make markets efficient? How do markets work in the "underground economy" where people trade illegal goods? These are the questions you study in this chapter. In *Reading Between the Lines* at the end of the chapter, we apply what you have learned and examine the effects of the New York minimum wage in the Buffalo–Niagara region labor market.

A Housing Market with a Rent Ceiling

We spend more of our income on housing than on any other good or service, so it isn't surprising that rents can be a political issue. When rents are high, or when they jump by a large amount, renters might lobby the government for limits on rents.

A government regulation that makes it illegal to charge a price higher than a specified level is called a **price ceiling** or **price cap**.

The effects of a price ceiling on a market depend crucially on whether the ceiling is imposed at a level that is above or below the equilibrium price.

A price ceiling set *above the equilibrium price* has no effect. The reason is that the price ceiling does not constrain the market forces. The force of the law and the market forces are not in conflict. But a price ceiling *below the equilibrium price* has powerful effects on a market. The reason is that the price ceiling attempts to prevent the price from regulating the quantities demanded and supplied. The force of the law and the market forces are in conflict.

When a price ceiling is applied to a housing market, it is called a **rent ceiling**. A rent ceiling set below the equilibrium rent creates *inefficient*.

- A housing shortage
- Increased search activity
- A black market

A Housing Shortage

At the equilibrium price, the quantity demanded equals the quantity supplied. In a housing market, when the rent is at the equilibrium level, the quantity of housing supplied equals the quantity of housing demanded and there is neither a shortage nor a surplus of housing.

But at a rent set below the equilibrium rent, the quantity of housing demanded exceeds the quantity of housing supplied—there is a shortage. So if a rent ceiling is set below the equilibrium rent, there will be a shortage of housing.

When there is a shortage, the quantity available is the quantity supplied, and somehow this quantity must be allocated among the frustrated demanders. One way in which this allocation occurs is through increased search activity.

Increased Search Activity

The time spent looking for someone with whom to do business is called **search activity**. We spend some time in search activity almost every time we make a purchase. When you're shopping for the latest hot new cell phone, and you know four stores that stock it, how do you find which store has the best deal? You spend a few minutes on the Internet, checking out the various prices. In some markets, such as the housing market, people spend a lot of time checking the alternatives available before making a choice.

When a price is regulated and there is a shortage, search activity increases. In the case of a rent-controlled housing market, frustrated would-be renters scan the newspapers, not only for housing ads but also for death notices! Any information about newly available housing is useful, and apartment seekers race to be first on the scene when news of a possible supplier breaks.

The *opportunity cost* of a good is equal not only to its price but also to the value of the search time spent finding the good. So the opportunity cost of housing is equal to the rent (a regulated price) plus the time and other resources spent searching for the restricted quantity available. Search activity is costly. It uses time and other resources, such as phone calls, automobiles, and gasoline that could have been used in other productive ways.

A rent ceiling controls only the rent portion of the cost of housing. The cost of increased search activity might end up making the full cost of housing *higher* than it would be without a rent ceiling.

A Black Market

A rent ceiling also encourages illegal trading in a **black market**, an illegal market in which the equilibrium price exceeds the price ceiling. Black markets occur in rent-controlled housing and many other markets. For example, scalpers run black markets in tickets for big sporting events and rock concerts.

When a rent ceiling is in force, frustrated renters and landlords constantly seek ways of increasing rents. One common way is for a new tenant to pay a high price for worthless fittings, such as charging $2,000 for threadbare drapes. Another is for the tenant to pay an exorbitant price for new locks and keys—called "key money."

The level of a black market rent depends on how tightly the rent ceiling is enforced. With loose enforcement, the black market rent is close to the unregulated rent. But with strict enforcement, the black market rent is equal to the maximum price that a renter is willing to pay.

Figure 6.1 illustrates the effects of a rent ceiling. The demand curve for housing is *D* and the supply curve is *S*. A rent ceiling is imposed at $800 a month. Rents that exceed $800 a month are in the gray-shaded illegal region in the figure. You can see that the equilibrium rent, where the demand and supply curves intersect, is in the illegal region.

At a rent of $800 a month, the quantity of housing supplied is 60,000 units and the quantity demanded is 100,000 units. So with a rent of $800 a month, there is a shortage of 40,000 units of housing.

To rent the 60,000th unit, someone is willing to pay $1,200 a month. They might pay this amount by incurring search costs that bring the total cost of housing to $1,200 a month, or they might pay a black market price of $1,200 a month. Either way, they end up incurring a cost that exceeds what the equilibrium rent would be in an unregulated market.

Inefficiency of a Rent Ceiling   *unfair*

A rent ceiling set below the equilibrium rent results in an inefficient underproduction of housing services. The *marginal social benefit* of housing exceeds its *marginal social cost* and a deadweight loss shrinks the producer surplus and consumer surplus (Chapter 5, pp. 112–114).

Figure 6.2 shows this inefficiency. The rent ceiling ($800 per month) is below the equilibrium rent ($1,000 per month) and the quantity of housing supplied (60,000 units) is less than the efficient quantity (80,000 units).

Because the quantity of housing supplied (the quantity available) is less than the efficient quantity, there is a deadweight loss, shown by the gray triangle. Producer surplus shrinks to the blue triangle and consumer surplus shrinks to the green triangle. The red rectangle represents the potential loss from increased search activity. This loss is borne by consumers and the full loss from the rent ceiling is the sum of the deadweight loss and the increased cost of search.

FIGURE 6.1   A Rent Ceiling

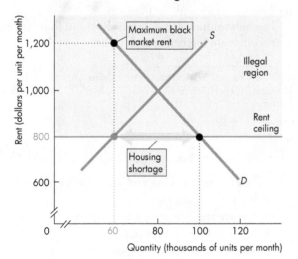

A rent above the rent ceiling of $800 a month is illegal (in the gray-shaded illegal region). At a rent of $800 a month, the quantity of housing supplied is 60,000 units. Frustrated renters spend time searching for housing and they make deals with landlords in a black market. Someone is willing to pay $1,200 a month for the 60,000th unit.

— MyEconLab animation —

FIGURE 6.2   The Inefficiency of a Rent Ceiling

Without a rent ceiling, the market produces an efficient 80,000 units of housing at a rent of $1,000 a month. A rent ceiling of $800 a month decreases the quantity of housing supplied to 60,000 units. Producer surplus and consumer surplus shrink and a deadweight loss arises. The red rectangle represents the cost of resources used in increased search activity. The full loss from the rent ceiling equals the sum of the red rectangle and gray triangle.

— MyEconLab animation —

Are Rent Ceilings Fair?

Rent ceilings might be inefficient, but don't they achieve a fairer allocation of scarce housing? Let's explore this question.

Chapter 5 (pp. 116–118) reviews two key ideas about fairness. According to the *fair rules* view, anything that blocks voluntary exchange is unfair, so rent ceilings are unfair. But according to the *fair result* view, a fair outcome is one that benefits the less well off. So according to this view, the fairest outcome is the one that allocates scarce housing to the poorest. To see whether rent ceilings help to achieve a fairer outcome in this sense, we need to consider how the market allocates scarce housing resources in the face of a rent ceiling.

Blocking rent adjustments doesn't eliminate scarcity. Rather, because it decreases the quantity of housing available, it creates an even bigger challenge for the housing market. Somehow, the market must ration a smaller quantity of housing and allocate that housing among the people who demand it.

When the rent is not permitted to allocate scarce housing, what other mechanisms are available, and are *they* fair? Some possible mechanisms are

- A lottery
- First-come, first-served
- Discrimination

A lottery allocates housing to those who are lucky, not to those who are poor. First-come, first-served (a method used to allocate housing in England after World War II) allocates housing to those who have the greatest foresight and who get their names on a list first, not to the poorest. Discrimination allocates scarce housing based on the views and self-interest of the owner of the housing. In the case of public housing, what counts is the self-interest of the bureaucracy that administers the allocation.

In principle, self-interested owners and bureaucrats could allocate housing to satisfy some criterion of fairness, but they are not likely to do so. Discrimination based on friendship, family ties, and criteria such as race, ethnicity, or sex is more likely to enter the equation. We might make such discrimination illegal, but we cannot prevent it from occurring.

It is hard, then, to make a case for rent ceilings on the basis of fairness. When rent adjustments are blocked, other methods of allocating scarce housing resources operate that do not produce a fair outcome.

Economics in Action
Rent Control Winners: The Rich and Famous

New York, San Francisco, London, and Paris, four of the world's great cities, have rent ceilings in some part of their housing markets. Boston had rent ceilings for many years but abolished them in 1997. Many other U.S. cities do not have, and have never had, rent ceilings. Among them are Atlanta, Baltimore, Chicago, Dallas, Philadelphia, Phoenix, and Seattle.

To see the effects of rent ceilings in practice we can compare the housing markets in cities with ceilings with those without ceilings. We learn two main lessons from such a comparison.

First, rent ceilings definitely create a housing shortage. Second, they do lower the rents for some but raise them for others.

A survey* conducted in 1997 showed that the rents of housing units *actually available for rent* were 2.5 times the average of all rents in New York but equal to the average rent in Philadelphia. The winners from rent ceilings are the families that have lived in a city for a long time. In New York, these families include some rich and famous ones. The voting power of the winners keeps the rent ceilings in place. Mobile newcomers are the losers in a city with rent ceilings.

The bottom line is that, in principle and in practice, rent ceilings are inefficient and unfair.

———————————————
* William Tucker, "How Rent Control Drives Out Affordable Housing," Cato Policy Analysis No. 274, May 21, 1997, Cato Institute.

REVIEW QUIZ

1 What is a rent ceiling and what are its effects if it is set above the equilibrium rent?
2 What are the effects of a rent ceiling that is set below the equilibrium rent?
3 How are scarce housing resources allocated when a rent ceiling is in place?
4 Why does a rent ceiling create an inefficient and unfair outcome in the housing market?

You can work these questions in Study Plan 6.1 and get instant feedback.   MyEconLab

You now know how a price ceiling (rent ceiling) works. Next, we'll learn about the effects of a price floor by studying a minimum wage in a labor market.

◆ A Labor Market with a Minimum Wage

For each one of us, the labor market is the market that influences the jobs we get and the wages we earn. Firms decide how much labor to demand, and the lower the wage rate, the greater is the quantity of labor demanded. Households decide how much labor to supply, and the higher the wage rate, the greater is the quantity of labor supplied. The wage rate adjusts to make the quantity of labor demanded equal to the quantity supplied.

When wage rates are low, or when they fail to keep up with rising prices, labor unions might turn to governments and lobby for a higher wage rate.

A government regulation that makes it illegal to charge a price lower than a specified level is called a **price floor**.

The effects of a price floor on a market depend crucially on whether the floor is imposed at a level that is above or below the equilibrium price.

A price floor set *below the equilibrium price* has no effect. The reason is that the price floor does not constrain the market forces. The force of the law and the market forces are not in conflict. But a price floor *above the equilibrium price* has powerful effects on a market. The reason is that the price floor attempts to prevent the price from regulating the quantities demanded and supplied. The force of the law and the market forces are in conflict.

When a price floor is applied to a labor market, it is called a **minimum wage**. A minimum wage imposed at a level that is above the equilibrium wage creates unemployment. Let's look at the effects of a minimum wage.

Minimum Wage Brings Unemployment

At the equilibrium price, the quantity demanded equals the quantity supplied. In a labor market, when the wage rate is at the equilibrium level, the quantity of labor supplied equals the quantity of labor demanded: There is neither a shortage of labor nor a surplus of labor.

But at a wage rate above the equilibrium wage, the quantity of labor supplied exceeds the quantity of labor demanded—there is a surplus of labor. So when a minimum wage is set above the equilibrium wage, there is a surplus of labor. The demand for labor determines the level of employment, and the surplus of labor is unemployed.

FIGURE 6.3   Minimum Wage and Unemployment

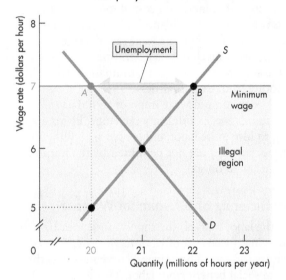

The minimum wage rate is set at $7 an hour. Any wage rate below $7 an hour is illegal (in the gray-shaded illegal region). At the minimum wage of $7 an hour, 20 million hours are hired but 22 million hours are available. Unemployment—*AB*—of 2 million hours a year is created. With only 20 million hours demanded, someone is willing to supply the 20 millionth hour for $5.

———— MyEconLab animation ————

Figure 6.3 illustrates the effect of the minimum wage on unemployment. The demand for labor curve is *D* and the supply of labor curve is *S*. The horizontal red line shows the minimum wage set at $7 an hour. A wage rate below this level is illegal, in the gray-shaded illegal region of the figure. At the minimum wage rate, 20 million hours of labor are demanded (point *A*) and 22 million hours of labor are supplied (point *B*), so 2 million hours of available labor are unemployed.

With only 20 million hours demanded, someone is willing to supply that 20 millionth hour for $5. Frustrated unemployed workers spend time and other resources searching for hard-to-find jobs.

Is the Minimum Wage Fair?

The minimum wage is unfair on both views of fairness: It delivers an unfair *result* and imposes an unfair *rule*.

The *result* is unfair because only those people who have jobs and keep them benefit from the minimum wage. The unemployed end up worse off than they would be with no minimum wage. Some of those who search for jobs and find them end up worse off because of the increased cost of job search they incur. Also those who search and find jobs aren't always the least well off. When the wage rate doesn't allocate labor, other mechanisms determine who finds a job. One such mechanism is discrimination, which is yet another source of unfairness.

The minimum wage imposes an unfair *rule* because it blocks voluntary exchange. Firms are willing to hire more labor and people are willing to work more, but they are not permitted by the minimum wage law to do so.

Inefficiency of a Minimum Wage

In the labor market, the supply curve measures the marginal social cost of labor to workers. This cost is leisure forgone. The demand curve measures the marginal social benefit from labor. This benefit is the value of the goods and services produced. An unregu-

lated labor market allocates the economy's scarce labor resources to the jobs in which they are valued most highly. The market is efficient.

The minimum wage frustrates the market mechanism and results in unemployment and increased job search. At the quantity of labor employed, the marginal social benefit of labor exceeds its marginal social cost and a deadweight loss shrinks the firms' surplus and the workers' surplus.

Figure 6.4 shows this inefficiency. The minimum wage ($7 an hour) is above the equilibrium wage ($6 an hour) and the quantity of labor demanded and employed (20 million hours) is less than the efficient quantity (21 million hours).

Because the quantity of labor employed is less than the efficient quantity, there is a deadweight loss, shown by the gray triangle. The firms' surplus shrinks to the blue triangle and the workers' surplus shrinks to the green triangle. The red rectangle shows the potential loss from increased job search, which is borne by workers. The full loss from the minimum wage is the sum of the deadweight loss and the increased cost of job search.

◆ AT **ISSUE**

Does the Minimum Wage Cause Unemployment?

In the United States, the federal government's Fair Labor Standards Act sets the minimum wage, which has fluctuated between 35 percent and 50 percent of the average wage, and in 2012 it was $7.25 an hour. Most states have minimum wages that exceed the federal minimum.

Does the minimum wage result in unemployment, and if so, how much unemployment does it create?

No, It Doesn't	Yes, It Does
David Card of the University of California at Berkeley and Alan Krueger of Princeton University and who is President Obama's chief economic adviser say:	Most economists are skeptical about Card and Krueger's conclusion.

No, It Doesn't

David Card of the University of California at Berkeley and Alan Krueger of Princeton University and who is President Obama's chief economic adviser say:

- An increase in the minimum wage *increases teenage employment* and *decreases unemployment.*
- Their study of minimum wages in California, New Jersey, and Texas found that the employment rate of low-income workers increased following an increase in the minimum wage.
- A higher wage *increases* employment by making workers more conscientious and productive as well as less likely to quit, which lowers unproductive labor turnover.
- A higher wage rate makes managers seek ways to increase labor productivity.

Yes, It Does

Most economists are skeptical about Card and Krueger's conclusion.

- The consensus view is that a 10 percent rise in the minimum wage *decreases teenage employment* by between 1 and 3 percent.
- Firms freely pay wage rates above the equilibrium wage to encourage more productive work habits.
- Daniel Hamermesh of the University of Texas at Austin says that firms anticipate the rise and cut employment *before* the minimum wage goes up.
- Finis Welch of Texas A&M University and Kevin Murphy of the University of Chicago say the employment effects that Card and Krueger found are caused by regional differences in economic growth and not by a rise in the minimum wage.

FIGURE 6.4   The Inefficiency of a Minimum Wage

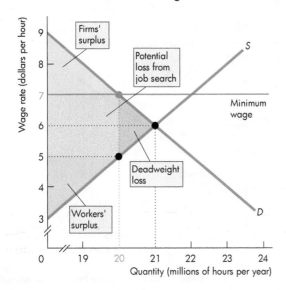

A minimum wage decreases employment. Firms' surplus (blue area) and workers' surplus (green area) shrink and a deadweight loss (gray area) arises. Job search increases and the red area shows the loss from this activity.

MyEconLab animation

REVIEW QUIZ

1 What is a minimum wage and what are its effects if it is set above the equilibrium wage?
2 What are the effects of a minimum wage set below the equilibrium wage?
3 Explain how scarce jobs are allocated when a minimum wage is in place.
4 Explain why a minimum wage creates an inefficient allocation of labor resources.
5 Explain why a minimum wage is unfair.

You can work these questions in Study Plan 6.2 and get instant feedback.   MyEconLab

Next we're going to study a more widespread government action in markets: taxes. We'll see how taxes change prices and quantities. You will discover the surprising fact that while the government can impose a tax, it can't decide who will pay the tax! You will also see that a tax creates a deadweight loss.

Taxes

Everything you earn and almost everything you buy is taxed. Income taxes and Social Security taxes are deducted from your earnings and sales taxes are added to the bill when you buy something. Employers also pay a Social Security tax for their workers, and producers of tobacco products, alcoholic drinks, and gasoline pay a tax every time they sell something.

Who *really* pays these taxes? Because the income tax and Social Security tax are deducted from your pay, and the sales tax is added to the prices that you pay, isn't it obvious that *you* pay these taxes? And isn't it equally obvious that your employer pays the employer's contribution to the Social Security tax and that tobacco producers pay the tax on cigarettes?

You're going to discover that it isn't obvious who *really* pays a tax and that lawmakers don't make that decision. We begin with a definition of tax incidence.

Tax Incidence

Tax incidence is the division of the burden of a tax between buyers and sellers. When the government imposes a tax on the sale of a good,* the price paid by buyers might rise by the full amount of the tax, by a lesser amount, or not at all. If the price paid by buyers rises by the full amount of the tax, then the burden of the tax falls entirely on buyers—the buyers pay the tax. If the price paid by buyers rises by a lesser amount than the tax, then the burden of the tax falls partly on buyers and partly on sellers. And if the price paid by buyers doesn't change at all, then the burden of the tax falls entirely on sellers.

Tax incidence does not depend on the tax law. The law might impose a tax on sellers or on buyers, but the outcome is the same in either case. To see why, let's look at the tax on cigarettes in New York City.

A Tax on Sellers

On July 1, 2002, Mayor Bloomberg put a tax of $1.50 a pack on cigarettes sold in New York City. To work out the effects of this tax on the sellers of cigarettes, we begin by examining the effects on demand and supply in the market for cigarettes.

---

*These propositions also apply to services and factors of production (land, labor, and capital).

In Fig. 6.5, the demand curve is *D*, and the supply curve is *S*. With no tax, the equilibrium price is $3 per pack and 350 million packs a year are bought and sold.

A tax on sellers is like an increase in cost, so it decreases supply. To determine the position of the new supply curve, we add the tax to the minimum price that sellers are willing to accept for each quantity sold. You can see that without the tax, sellers are willing to offer 350 million packs a year for $3 a pack. So with a $1.50 tax, they will offer 350 million packs a year only if the price is $4.50 a pack. The supply curve shifts to the red curve labeled *S + tax on sellers*.

Equilibrium occurs where the new supply curve intersects the demand curve at 325 million packs a year. The price paid by buyers rises by $1 to $4 a pack. And the price received by sellers falls by 50¢ to $2.50 a pack. So buyers pay $1 of the tax and sellers pay the other 50¢.

A Tax on Buyers

Suppose that instead of taxing sellers, New York City taxes cigarette buyers $1.50 a pack.

A tax on buyers lowers the amount they are willing to pay sellers, so it decreases demand and shifts the demand curve leftward. To determine the position of this new demand curve, we subtract the tax from the maximum price that buyers are willing to pay for each quantity bought. You can see, in Fig. 6.6, that without the tax, buyers are willing to buy 350 million packs a year for $3 a pack. So with a $1.50 tax, they are willing to buy 350 million packs a year only if the price including the tax is $3 a pack, which means that they're willing to pay sellers only $1.50 a pack. The demand curve shifts to become the red curve labeled *D – tax on buyers*.

Equilibrium occurs where the new demand curve intersects the supply curve at a quantity of 325 million packs a year. The price received by sellers is $2.50 a pack, and the price paid by buyers is $4.

Equivalence of Tax on Buyers and Sellers

You can see that the tax on buyers in Fig. 6.6 has the same effects as the tax on sellers in Fig. 6.5. In both cases, the equilibrium quantity decreases to 325 million packs a year, the price paid by buyers rises to $4 a pack, and the price received by sellers falls to $2.50 a pack. Buyers pay $1 of the $1.50 tax, and sellers pay the other 50¢ of the tax.

FIGURE 6.5   A Tax on Sellers

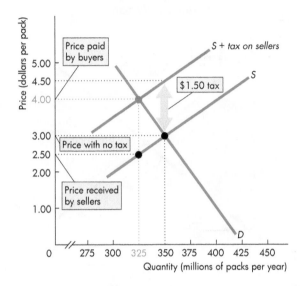

With no tax, 350 million packs a year are bought and sold at $3 a pack. A tax on sellers of $1.50 a pack shifts the supply curve from *S* to *S + tax on sellers*. The equilibrium quantity decreases to 325 million packs a year, the price paid by buyers rises to $4 a pack, and the price received by sellers falls to $2.50 a pack. The tax raises the price paid by buyers by less than the tax and lowers the price received by sellers, so buyers and sellers share the burden of the tax.

—— MyEconLab animation ——

Can We Share the Burden Equally? Suppose that Mayor Bloomberg wants the burden of the cigarette tax to fall equally on buyers and sellers and declares that a 75¢ tax be imposed on each. Is the burden of the tax then shared equally?

You can see that it is not. The tax is still $1.50 a pack. You've seen that the tax has the same effect regardless of whether it is imposed on sellers or buyers. So imposing half the tax on sellers and half on buyers is like an average of the two cases you've just examined. (Draw the demand-supply graph and work out what happens in this case. The demand curve shifts downward by 75¢ and the supply curve shifts upward by 75¢. The new equilibrium quantity is still 325 million packs a year. Buyers pay $4 a pack, of which 75¢ is tax. Sellers receive $3.25 from buyers, but pay a 75¢ tax, so sellers net $2.50 a pack.)

When a transaction is taxed, there are two prices: the price paid by buyers, which includes the tax; and the price received by sellers, which excludes the tax.

FIGURE 6.6   A Tax on Buyers

With no tax, 350 million packs a year are bought and sold at $3 a pack. A tax on buyers of $1.50 a pack shifts the demand curve from D to D – tax on buyers. The equilibrium quantity decreases to 325 million packs a year, the price paid by buyers rises to $4 a pack, and the price received by sellers falls to $2.50 a pack. The tax raises the price paid by buyers by less than the tax and lowers the price received by sellers, so buyers and sellers share the burden of the tax.

—— MyEconLab animation ——

Buyers respond to the price that *includes* the tax and sellers respond to the price that *excludes* the tax.

A tax is like a wedge between the price buyers pay and the price sellers receive. The size of the wedge determines the effects of the tax, not the side of the market on which the government imposes the tax.

The Social Security Tax The Social Security tax is an example of a tax that Congress imposes equally on both buyers and sellers. But the principles you've just learned apply to this tax too. The market for labor, not Congress, decides how the burden of the Social Security tax is divided between firms and workers.

In the New York City cigarette tax example, buyers bear twice the burden of the tax borne by sellers. In special cases, either buyers or sellers bear the entire burden. The division of the burden of a tax between buyers and sellers depends on the elasticities of demand and supply, as you will now see.

Tax Incidence and Elasticity of Demand

The division of the tax between buyers and sellers depends in part on the elasticity of demand. There are two extreme cases:

- Perfectly inelastic demand—buyers pay.
- Perfectly elastic demand—sellers pay.

Perfectly Inelastic Demand Figure 6.7 shows the market for insulin, a vital daily medication for those with diabetes. Demand is perfectly inelastic at 100,000 doses a day, regardless of the price, as shown by the vertical demand curve D. That is, a diabetic would sacrifice all other goods and services rather than not consume the insulin dose that provides good health. The supply curve of insulin is S. With no tax, the price is $2 a dose and the quantity is 100,000 doses a day.

If insulin is taxed at 20¢ a dose, we must add the tax to the minimum price at which drug companies are willing to sell insulin. The result is the new supply curve S + tax. The price rises to $2.20 a dose, but the quantity does not change. Buyers pay the entire tax of 20¢ a dose.

FIGURE 6.7   Tax with Perfectly Inelastic Demand

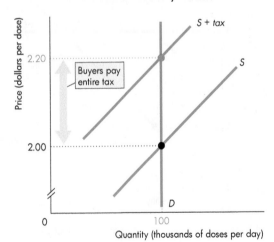

In this market for insulin, demand is perfectly inelastic. With no tax, the price is $2 a dose and the quantity is 100,000 doses a day. A tax of 20¢ a dose shifts the supply curve to S + tax. The price rises to $2.20 a dose, but the quantity bought does not change. Buyers pay the entire tax.

—— MyEconLab animation ——

Perfectly Elastic Demand Figure 6.8 shows the market for pink marker pens. Demand is perfectly elastic at $1 a pen, as shown by the horizontal demand curve *D*. If pink pens are less expensive than the other colors, everyone uses pink. If pink pens are more expensive than other colors, no one uses pink. The supply curve is *S*. With no tax, the price of a pink pen is $1 and the quantity is 4,000 pens a week.

Suppose that the government imposes a tax of 10¢ a pen on pink marker pens but not on other colors. The new supply curve is *S* + *tax*. The price remains at $1 a pen, and the quantity decreases to 1,000 pink pens a week. The 10¢ tax leaves the price paid by buyers unchanged but lowers the amount received by sellers by the full amount of the tax. Sellers pay the entire tax of 10¢ a pink pen.

We've seen that when demand is perfectly inelastic, buyers pay the entire tax and when demand is perfectly elastic, sellers pay the entire tax. In the usual case, demand is neither perfectly inelastic nor perfectly elastic and the tax is split between buyers and sellers. But the division depends on the elasticity of demand: The more inelastic the demand, the larger is the amount of the tax paid by buyers.

Tax Incidence and Elasticity of Supply

The division of the tax between buyers and sellers also depends, in part, on the elasticity of supply. Again, there are two extreme cases:

- Perfectly inelastic supply—sellers pay.
- Perfectly elastic supply—buyers pay.

Perfectly Inelastic Supply Figure 6.9(a) shows the market for water from a mineral spring that flows at a constant rate that can't be controlled. Supply is perfectly inelastic at 100,000 bottles a week, as shown by the supply curve *S*. The demand curve for the water from this spring is *D*. With no tax, the price is 50¢ a bottle and the quantity is 100,000 bottles.

Suppose this spring water is taxed at 5¢ a bottle. The supply curve does not change because the spring owners still produce 100,000 bottles a week, even though the price they receive falls. But buyers are willing to buy the 100,000 bottles only if the price is 50¢ a bottle, so the price remains at 50¢ a bottle. The tax reduces the price received by sellers to 45¢ a bottle, and sellers pay the entire tax.

Perfectly Elastic Supply Figure 6.9(b) shows the market for sand from which computer-chip makers extract silicon. Supply of this sand is perfectly elastic at a price of 10¢ a pound, as shown by the supply curve *S*. The demand curve for sand is *D*. With no tax, the price is 10¢ a pound and 5,000 pounds a week are bought.

If this sand is taxed at 1¢ a pound, we must add the tax to the minimum supply-price. Sellers are now willing to offer any quantity at 11¢ a pound along the curve *S* + *tax*. A new equilibrium is determined where the new supply curve intersects the demand curve: at a price of 11¢ a pound and a quantity of 3,000 pounds a week. The tax has increased the price buyers pay by the full amount of the tax—1¢ a pound—and has decreased the quantity sold. Buyers pay the entire tax.

We've seen that when supply is perfectly inelastic, sellers pay the entire tax, and when supply is perfectly elastic, buyers pay the entire tax. In the usual case, supply is neither perfectly inelastic nor perfectly elastic and the tax is split between buyers and sellers. But how the tax is split depends on the elasticity of supply: The more elastic the supply, the larger is the amount of the tax paid by buyers.

FIGURE 6.8   Tax with Perfectly Elastic Demand

In this market for pink pens, demand is perfectly elastic. With no tax, the price of a pen is $1 and the quantity is 4,000 pens a week. A tax of 10¢ a pink pen shifts the supply curve to *S* + *tax*. The price remains at $1 a pen, and the quantity of pink pens sold decreases to 1,000 a week. Sellers pay the entire tax.

——— MyEconLab animation ———

FIGURE 6.9   Tax and the Elasticity of Supply

(a) Perfectly inelastic supply

(b) Perfectly elastic supply

Part (a) shows the market for water from a mineral spring. Supply is perfectly inelastic. With no tax, the price is 50¢ a bottle. With a tax of 5¢ a bottle, the price remains at 50¢ a bottle. The number of bottles bought remains the same, but the price received by sellers decreases to 45¢ a bottle. Sellers pay the entire tax.

Part (b) shows the market for sand. Supply is perfectly elastic. With no tax, the price is 10¢ a pound. A tax of 1¢ a pound increases the minimum supply-price to 11¢ a pound. The supply curve shifts to $S + tax$. The price increases to 11¢ a pound. Buyers pay the entire tax.

—— MyEconLab animation ——

Taxes and Efficiency

A tax drives a wedge between the buying price and the selling price and results in inefficient underproduction. The price buyers pay is also the buyers' willingness to pay, which measures *marginal social benefit*. The price sellers receive is also the sellers' minimum supply-price, which equals *marginal social cost*.

A tax makes marginal social benefit exceed marginal social cost, shrinks the producer surplus and consumer surplus, and creates a deadweight loss.

Figure 6.10 shows the inefficiency of a tax on MP3 players. The demand curve, *D*, shows marginal social benefit, and the supply curve, *S*, shows marginal social cost. Without a tax, the market produces the efficient quantity (5,000 players a week).

With a tax, the sellers' minimum supply-price rises by the amount of the tax and the supply curve shifts to $S + tax$. This supply curve does *not* show marginal social cost. The tax component isn't a *social* cost of

FIGURE 6.10   Taxes and Efficiency

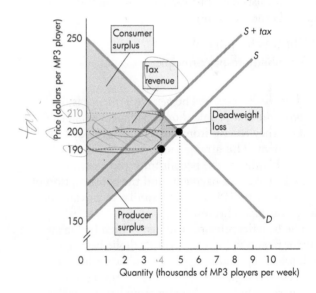

With no tax, 5,000 players a week are produced. With a $20 tax, the buyers' price rises to $210, the sellers' price falls to $190, and the quantity decreases to 4,000 players a week. Consumer surplus shrinks to the green area, and the producer surplus shrinks to the blue area. Part of the loss of consumer surplus and producer surplus goes to the government as tax revenue (the purple area) and part becomes a deadweight loss (the gray area).

—— MyEconLab animation ——

production. It is a transfer of resources to the government. At the new equilibrium quantity (4,000 players a week), both consumer surplus and producer surplus shrink. Part of each surplus goes to the government in tax revenue—the purple area; part becomes a deadweight loss—the gray area.

Only in the extreme cases of perfectly inelastic demand and perfectly inelastic supply does a tax not change the quantity bought and sold so that no deadweight loss arises.

Taxes and Fairness

We've examined the incidence and the efficiency of taxes. But when political leaders debate tax issues, it is fairness, not incidence and efficiency, that gets the most attention. Democrats complain that Republican tax cuts are unfair because they give the benefits of lower taxes to the rich. Republicans counter that it is fair that the rich get most of the tax cuts because they pay most of the taxes. No easy answers are available to the questions about the fairness of taxes.

Economists have proposed two conflicting principles of fairness to apply to a tax system:

- The benefits principle
- The ability-to-pay principle

The Benefits Principle The *benefits principle* is the proposition that people should pay taxes equal to the benefits they receive from the services provided by government. This arrangement is fair because it means that those who benefit most pay the most taxes. It makes tax payments and the consumption of government-provided services similar to private consumption expenditures.

The benefits principle can justify high fuel taxes to pay for freeways, high taxes on alcoholic beverages and tobacco products to pay for public health-care services, and high rates of income tax on high incomes to pay for the benefits from law and order and from living in a secure environment, from which the rich might benefit more than the poor.

The Ability-to-Pay Principle The *ability-to-pay principle* is the proposition that people should pay taxes according to how easily they can bear the burden of the tax. A rich person can more easily bear the burden than a poor person can, so the ability-to-pay principle can reinforce the benefits principle to justify high rates of income tax on high incomes.

Economics in Action
Workers and Consumers Pay the Most Tax

Because the elasticity of the supply of labor is low and the elasticity of demand for labor is high, workers pay most of the personal income taxes and most of the Social Security taxes. Because the elasticities of demand for alcohol, tobacco, and gasoline are low and the elasticities of supply are high, the burden of these taxes (excise taxes) falls more heavily on buyers than on sellers.

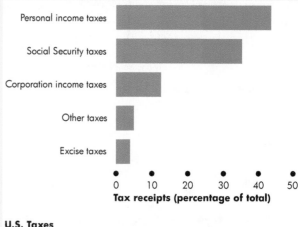

U.S. Taxes

Source of data: Budget of the United States Government, Fiscal Year 2012, Historical Tables, Table 2.2.

REVIEW QUIZ

1 How does the elasticity of demand influence the incidence of a tax, the tax revenue, and the deadweight loss?
2 How does the elasticity of supply influence the incidence of a tax, the quantity bought, the tax revenue, and the deadweight loss?
3 Why is a tax inefficient?
4 When would a tax be efficient?
5 What are the two principles of fairness that are applied to tax systems?

You can work these questions in Study Plan 6.3 and get instant feedback.   MyEconLab

Your next task is to study production quotas and subsidies, tools that are used to influence the markets for farm products.

Production Quotas and Subsidies

An early or late frost, a hot dry summer, and a wet spring present just a few of the challenges that fill the lives of farmers with uncertainty and sometimes with economic hardship. Fluctuations in the weather bring fluctuations in farm output and prices and sometimes leave farmers with low incomes. To help farmers avoid low prices and low incomes, governments intervene in the markets for farm products.

Price floors that work a bit like the minimum wage that you've already studied might be used. But as you've seen, this type of government action creates a surplus and is inefficient. These same conclusions apply to the effects of a price floor for farm products.

Governments often use two other methods of intervention in the markets for farm products:

- Production quotas
- Subsidies

Production Quotas

In the markets for sugarbeets, tobacco leaf, and cotton (among others), governments have, from time to time, imposed production quotas. A **production quota** is an upper limit to the quantity of a good that may be produced in a specified period. To discover the effects of a production quota, let's look at what a quota does to the market for sugarbeets.

Suppose that the growers of sugarbeets want to limit total production to get a higher price. They persuade the government to introduce a production quota on sugarbeets.

The effect of the production quota depends on whether it is set below or above the equilibrium quantity. If the government introduced a production quota above the equilibrium quantity, nothing would change because sugarbeet growers would already be producing less than the quota. But a production quota set *below the equilibrium quantity* has big effects, which are

- A decrease in supply
- A rise in price
- A decrease in marginal cost
- Inefficient underproduction
- An incentive to cheat and overproduce

Figure 6.11 illustrates these effects.

FIGURE 6.11   The Effects of a Production Quota

With no quota, growers produce 60 million tons a year and the price is $30 a ton. A production quota of 40 million tons a year restricts total production to that amount. The quantity produced decreases to 40 million tons a year, the price rises to $50 a ton, and the farmers' marginal cost falls to $20 a ton. Because marginal social cost (on the supply curve) is less than marginal social benefit (on the demand curve), a deadweight loss arises from the underproduction.

MyEconLab animation

A Decrease in Supply   A production quota on sugarbeets decreases the supply of sugarbeets. Each grower is assigned a production limit that is less than the amount that would be produced—and supplied—without the quota. The total of the growers' limits equals the quota, and any production in excess of the quota is illegal.

The quantity supplied becomes the amount permitted by the production quota, and this quantity is fixed. The supply of sugarbeets becomes perfectly inelastic at the quantity permitted under the quota.

In Fig. 6.11, with no quota, growers would produce 60 million tons of sugarbeets a year—the market equilibrium quantity. With a production quota set at 40 million tons a year, the gray-shaded area shows the illegal region. As in the case of price ceilings and price floors, market forces and political forces are in conflict in this illegal region.

The vertical red line labeled "Quota" becomes the supply curve of sugarbeets at prices above $20 a ton.

A Rise in Price The production quota raises the price of sugarbeets. When the government sets a production quota, it leaves market forces free to determine the price. Because the quota decreases the supply of sugarbeets, it raises the price. In Fig. 6.11, with no quota, the price is $30 a ton. With a quota of 40 million tons, the price rises to $50 a ton.

A Decrease in Marginal Cost The production quota lowers the marginal cost of growing sugarbeets. Marginal cost decreases because growers produce less and stop using the resources with the highest marginal cost. Sugarbeet growers slide down their supply (and marginal cost) curves. In Fig. 6.11, marginal cost decreases to $20 a ton.

Inefficiency The production quota results in inefficient underproduction. Marginal social benefit at the quantity produced is equal to the market price, which has increased. Marginal social cost at the quantity produced has decreased and is less than the market price. So marginal social benefit exceeds marginal social cost and a deadweight loss arises.

An Incentive to Cheat and Overproduce The production quota creates an incentive for growers to cheat and produce more than their individual production limit. With the quota, the price exceeds marginal cost, so the grower can get a larger profit by producing one more unit. Of course, if all growers produce more than their assigned limit, the production quota becomes ineffective, and the price falls to the equilibrium (no quota) price.

To make the production quota effective, growers must set up a monitoring system to ensure that no one cheats and overproduces. But it is costly to set up and operate a monitoring system and it is difficult to detect and punish producers who violate their quotas.

Because of the difficulty of operating a quota, producers often lobby governments to establish a quota and provide the monitoring and punishment systems that make it work.

Subsidies

In the United States, the producers of peanuts, sugarbeets, milk, wheat, and many other farm products receive subsidies. A **subsidy** is a payment made by the government to a producer. A large and controversial Farm Bill passed by Congress in 2008 renewed and extended a wide range of subsidies.

The effects of a subsidy are similar to the effects of a tax but they go in the opposite directions. These effects are

- An increase in supply
- A fall in price and increase in quantity produced
- An increase in marginal cost
- Payments by government to farmers
- Inefficient overproduction

Figure 6.12 illustrates the effects of a subsidy to peanut farmers.

An Increase in Supply In Fig. 6.12, with no subsidy, the demand curve *D* and the supply curve *S* determine the price of peanuts at $40 a ton and the quantity of peanuts at 40 million tons a year.

Suppose that the government introduces a subsidy of $20 a ton to peanut farmers. A subsidy is like a negative tax. A tax is equivalent to an increase in cost, so a subsidy is equivalent to a decrease in cost. The subsidy brings an increase in supply.

To determine the position of the new supply curve, we subtract the subsidy from the farmers' minimum supply-price. In Fig. 6.12, with no subsidy, farmers are willing to offer 40 million tons a year at a price of $40 a ton. With a subsidy of $20 a ton, they will offer 40 million tons a year if the price is as low as $20 a ton. The supply curve shifts to the red curve labeled *S – subsidy*.

A Fall in Price and Increase in Quantity Produced The subsidy lowers the price of peanuts and increases the quantity produced. In Fig. 6.12, equilibrium occurs where the new supply curve intersects the demand curve at a price of $30 a ton and a quantity of 60 million tons a year.

An Increase in Marginal Cost The subsidy lowers the price paid by consumers but increases the marginal cost of producing peanuts. Marginal cost increases because farmers grow more peanuts, which means that they must begin to use some resources that are less ideal for growing peanuts. Peanut farmers slide up their supply (and marginal cost) curves. In Fig. 6.12, marginal cost increases to $50 a ton.

Payments by Government to Farmers The government pays a subsidy to peanut farmers on each ton of peanuts produced. In this example, farmers increase production to 60 million tons a year and receive a

FIGURE 6.12 The Effects of a Subsidy

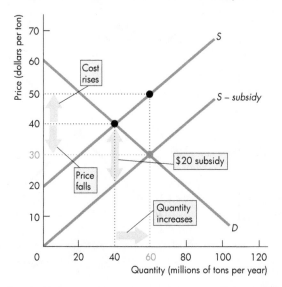

With no subsidy, farmers produce 40 million tons a year at $40 a ton. A subsidy of $20 a ton shifts the supply curve rightward to S – subsidy. The equilibrium quantity increases to 60 million tons a year, the price falls to $30 a ton, and the price plus the subsidy received by farmers rises to $50 a ton. In the new equilibrium, marginal social cost (on the supply curve) exceeds marginal social benefit (on the demand curve) and the subsidy results in inefficient overproduction.

————— MyEconLab animation —————

subsidy of $20 a ton. So peanut farmers receive payments from the government that total $1,200 million a year.

Inefficient Overproduction The subsidy results in inefficient overproduction. At the quantity produced with the subsidy, marginal social benefit is equal to the market price, which has fallen. Marginal social cost has increased and it exceeds the market price. Because marginal social cost exceeds marginal social benefit, the increased production brings inefficiency.

Subsidies spill over to the rest of the world. Because a subsidy lowers the domestic market price, subsidized farmers will offer some of their output for sale on the world market. The increase in supply on the world market lowers the price in the rest of the world. Faced with lower prices, farmers in other countries decrease production and receive smaller revenues.

Economics in Action
Rich High-Cost Farmers the Winners

Farm subsidies are a major obstacle to achieving an efficient use of resources in the global markets for farm products and are a source of tension between the United States, Europe, and developing nations.

The United States and the European Union are the world's two largest and richest economies. They also pay their farmers the biggest subsidies, which create inefficient overproduction of food in these rich economies.

At the same time, U.S. and European subsidies make it more difficult for farmers in the developing nations of Africa, Asia, and Central and South America to compete in global food markets. Farmers in these countries can often produce at a lower opportunity cost than the U.S. and European farmers.

Two rich countries, Australia and New Zealand, have stopped subsidizing farmers. The result has been an improvement in the efficiency of farming in these countries. New Zealand is so efficient at producing lamb and dairy products that it has been called the Saudi Arabia of milk (an analogy with Saudi Arabia's huge oil reserve and production.)

International opposition to U.S. and European farm subsidies is strong. Opposition to farm subsidies inside the United States and Europe is growing, but it isn't as strong as the pro-farm lobby, so don't expect an early end to these subsidies.

◆ REVIEW QUIZ

1 Summarize the effects of a production quota on the market price and the quantity produced.
2 Explain why a production quota is inefficient.
3 Explain why a voluntary production quota is difficult to operate.
4 Summarize the effects of a subsidy on the market price and the quantity produced.
5 Explain why a subsidy is inefficient.

You can work these questions in Study Plan 6.4 and get instant feedback.   MyEconLab

Governments intervene in some markets by making it illegal to trade in a good. Let's now see how these markets work.

◆ Markets for Illegal Goods

The markets for many goods and services are regulated, and buying and selling some goods is illegal. The best-known examples of such goods are drugs, such as marijuana, cocaine, ecstasy, and heroin.

Despite the fact that these drugs are illegal, trade in them is a multibillion-dollar business. This trade can be understood by using the same economic model and principles that explain trade in legal goods. To study the market for illegal goods, we're first going to examine the prices and quantities that would prevail if these goods were not illegal. Next, we'll see how prohibition works. Then we'll see how a tax might be used to limit the consumption of these goods.

A Free Market for a Drug

Figure 6.13 shows the market for a drug. The demand curve, D, shows that, other things remaining the same, the lower the price of the drug, the larger is the quantity of the drug demanded. The supply curve, S, shows that, other things remaining the same, the lower the price of the drug, the smaller is the quantity supplied. If the drug were not illegal, the quantity bought and sold would be Q_C and the price would be P_C.

A Market for an Illegal Drug

When a good is illegal, the cost of trading in the good increases. By how much the cost increases and who bears the cost depend on the penalties for violating the law and the degree to which the law is enforced. The larger the penalties and the better the policing, the higher are the costs. Penalties might be imposed on sellers, buyers, or both.

Penalties on Sellers Drug dealers in the United States face large penalties if their activities are detected. For example, a marijuana dealer could pay a $200,000 fine and serve a 15-year prison term. A heroin dealer could pay a $500,000 fine and serve a 20-year prison term. These penalties are part of the cost of supplying illegal drugs, and they bring a decrease in supply—a leftward shift in the supply curve. To determine the new supply curve, we add the cost of breaking the law to the minimum price that drug dealers are willing to accept. In Fig. 6.13, the cost of breaking the law by selling drugs (*CBL*) is added to the minimum price that

FIGURE 6.13   A Market for an Illegal Good

The demand curve for drugs is D, and the supply curve is S. If drugs are not illegal, the quantity bought and sold is Q_C at a price of P_C—point E. If selling drugs is illegal, the cost of breaking the law by selling drugs (*CBL*) is added to the minimum supply-price and supply decreases to $S + CBL$. The market moves to point F. If buying drugs is illegal, the cost of breaking the law is subtracted from the maximum price that buyers are willing to pay, and demand decreases to $D - CBL$. The market moves to point G. With both buying and selling illegal, the supply curve and the demand curve shift and the market moves to point H. The market price remains at P_C, but the market price plus the penalty for buying rises—point J—and the market price minus the penalty for selling falls—point K.

MyEconLab animation

dealers will accept and the supply curve shifts leftward to $S + CBL$. If penalties were imposed only on sellers, the market equilibrium would move from point E to point F.

Penalties on Buyers In the United States, it is illegal to *possess* drugs such as marijuana, cocaine, ecstasy, and heroin. Possession of marijuana can bring a prison term of 1 year, and possession of heroin can bring a prison term of 2 years. Penalties fall on buyers, and the cost of breaking the law must be subtracted from the value of the good to determine the maximum price buyers are willing to pay for the drugs. Demand decreases, and the demand curve shifts leftward. In Fig. 6.13, the demand curve shifts to $D - CBL$. If penalties were imposed only on buyers, the market equilibrium would move from point E to point G.

Penalties on Both Sellers and Buyers

If penalties are imposed on both sellers *and* buyers, both supply and demand decrease and both the supply curve and the demand curve shift. In Fig. 6.13, the costs of breaking the law are the same for both buyers and sellers, so both curves shift leftward by the same amount. The market equilibrium moves to point H. The market price remains at the competitive market price P_C, but the quantity bought decreases to Q_P. Buyers pay P_C plus the cost of breaking the law, which equals P_B. Sellers receive P_C minus the cost of breaking the law, which equals P_S.

The larger the penalties and the greater the degree of law enforcement, the larger is the decrease in demand and/or supply. If the penalties are heavier on sellers, the supply curve shifts farther than the demand curve and the market price rises above P_C. If the penalties are heavier on buyers, the demand curve shifts farther than the supply curve and the market price falls below P_C. In the United States, the penalties on sellers are larger than those on buyers, so the quantity of drugs traded decreases and the market price increases compared with a free market.

With high enough penalties and effective law enforcement, it is possible to decrease demand and/or supply to the point at which the quantity bought is zero. But in reality, such an outcome is unusual. It does not happen in the United States in the case of illegal drugs. The key reason is the high cost of law enforcement and insufficient resources for the police to achieve effective enforcement. Because of this situation, some people suggest that drugs (and other illegal goods) should be legalized and sold openly but also taxed at a high rate in the same way that legal drugs such as alcohol are taxed. How would such an arrangement work?

Legalizing and Taxing Drugs

From your study of the effects of taxes, it is easy to see that the quantity bought of a drug could be decreased if the drug was legalized and taxed. Imposing a sufficiently high tax could decrease the supply, raise the price, and achieve the same decrease in the quantity bought as does a prohibition on drugs. The government would collect a large tax revenue.

Illegal Trading to Evade the Tax

It is likely that an extremely high tax rate would be needed to cut the quantity of drugs bought to the level prevailing with a prohibition. It is also likely that many drug dealers and consumers would try to cover up their activities to evade the tax. If they did act in this way, they would face the cost of breaking the law—the tax law. If the penalty for tax law violation is as severe and as effectively policed as drug-dealing laws, the analysis we've already conducted applies also to this case. The quantity of drugs bought would depend on the penalties for law breaking and on the way in which the penalties are assigned to buyers and sellers. *tax: law enforcement education.*

Taxes Versus Prohibition: Some Pros and Cons

Which is more effective: prohibition or taxes? In favor of taxes and against prohibition is the fact that the tax revenue can be used to make law enforcement more effective. It can also be used to run a more effective education campaign against illegal drug use. In favor of prohibition and against taxes is the fact that prohibition sends a signal that might influence preferences, decreasing the demand for illegal drugs. Also, some people intensely dislike the idea of the government profiting from trade in harmful substances.

<hr/>

REVIEW QUIZ

1 How does the imposition of a penalty for selling an illegal drug influence demand, supply, price, and the quantity of the drug consumed?

2 How does the imposition of a penalty for possessing an illegal drug influence demand, supply, price, and the quantity of the drug consumed?

3 How does the imposition of a penalty for selling *or* possessing an illegal drug influence demand, supply, price, and the quantity of the drug consumed?

4 Is there any case for legalizing drugs?

You can work these questions in Study Plan 6.5 and get instant feedback.   MyEconLab

<hr/>

◆ You now know how to use the demand and supply model to predict prices, to study government actions in markets, and to study the sources and costs of inefficiency. In *Reading Between the Lines* on pp. 144–145, you will see how to apply what you've learned by looking at the effects of the minimum wage in the Buffalo–Niagara region labor market.

Push to Raise the Minimum Wage

Push Is On for Higher Minimum Wage

Buffalo News
February 5, 2012

Remember those signs you'd see when you walked into Mighty Taco and other stores a few years ago—before the recession hit—offering entry-level jobs that paid a few dimes more than minimum wage?

You don't see many of those signs these days. Then again, the job market is a lot different, too.

Back in the day, when unemployment in the Buffalo–Niagara region was under 5 percent, businesses that rely on minimum wage workers regularly had to sweeten the pot a little to find both the quantity—and quality—of employees they needed to fill their entry-level jobs.

Now, with the economy still moving in fits and starts, local unemployment is just under 8 percent and there are almost 17,000 more people without jobs in the Buffalo–Niagara region than there were five years ago. . . .

It's a matter of supply and demand. Before the recession, even minimum wage workers had a little leverage. Now, when it comes to pay, employers are in more of a position to tell new hires to take it or leave it.

It's against that backdrop that Assembly Speaker Sheldon Silver, D-Manhattan, is proposing to boost the state's minimum wage by $1.25 an hour, or 17 percent, to $8.50 an hour beginning next year. He also wants the minimum wage, which last increased in 2009, to be adjusted each year, beginning in 2014, to keep pace with inflation. . . .

Would a higher minimum wage break the bank of employers? No. But it might make them cut back, either by hiring fewer part-time workers or giving them fewer hours.

And that's the problem with raising the minimum wage right now, when market forces are keeping a lid on wages across the board and jobs are in short supply.

ESSENCE OF THE STORY

- Before the recession (in 2007) when the unemployment rate was less than 5 percent, firms paid above the minimum wage to fill entry-level jobs.

- In 2012, with an unemployment rate close to 8 percent, employers can hire workers at the minimum wage.

- Sheldon Silver wants to increase the New York State minimum wage by $1.25 an hour to $8.50 an hour and then to adjust it each year to keep pace with inflation.

- A higher minimum wage might make employers hire fewer workers or hire a worker for fewer hours.

ECONOMIC ANALYSIS

- The news article describes the labor market in New York State in two periods with different outcomes and different consequences of the state's minimum wage law.

- On January 1, 2007, the New York minimum wage rate was increased from $6.75 to $7.15 an hour.

- In 2007, the U.S. economy was booming and the unemployment rate in New York was less than 5 percent, a level at which it is easy for workers to find jobs and hard for employers to fill job vacancies.

- When the minimum wage rate was set at $7.15 an hour, it had no effect on employers because they already found it necessary to pay a higher wage to attract the quantity of labor demanded.

- Figure 1 illustrates the Buffalo–Niagara region labor market in 2007.

- The supply of labor curve is S, the demand for labor curve is D_{07}, and the equilibrium wage rate is $7.25 an hour.

- With the equilibrium wage rate greater than the minimum wage rate, the quantity of labor demanded equals the quantity of labor supplied and the minimum wage rate has no effect on the market outcome.

- In 2008 and with effects lasting into 2012, the U.S. economy was hit by a global financial crisis and slump in production and jobs.

- The demand for labor decreased and the equilibrium wage rate fell.

- During this period, in July 2009, the New York state minimum wage rate increased to $7.25 an hour.

- With a *fall* in the equilibrium wage rate and a *rise* in the minimum wage rate, the quantity of labor supplied exceeded the quantity of labor demanded and unemployment increased.

- The news article says that 17,000 more people were without jobs in the Buffalo–Niagara region in 2012 than five years earlier.

- Figure 2 illustrates the Buffalo–Niagara region labor market in 2012.

- The supply of labor curve is S, but the demand for labor curve is now D_{12}. The equilibrium wage rate is $6.75 per hour (an assumption).

- With the equilibrium wage rate less than the minimum wage rate, the quantity of labor demanded is less than the quantity of labor supplied and the minimum wage rate brings an increase in unemployment.

Figure 1 The Buffalo–Niagara Labor Market in 2007

Figure 2 The Buffalo–Niagara Labor Market in 2012

SUMMARY

Key Points

A Housing Market with a Rent Ceiling (pp. 128–130)

- A rent ceiling that is set above the equilibrium rent has no effect.
- A rent ceiling that is set below the equilibrium rent creates a housing shortage, increased search activity, and a black market.
- A rent ceiling that is set below the equilibrium rent is inefficient and unfair.

Working Problems 1 to 6 will give you a better understanding of a housing market with a rent ceiling.

A Labor Market with a Minimum Wage (pp. 131–133)

- A minimum wage set below the equilibrium wage rate has no effect.
- A minimum wage set above the equilibrium wage rate creates unemployment and increases the amount of time people spend searching for a job.
- A minimum wage set above the equilibrium wage rate is inefficient, unfair, and hits low-skilled young people hardest.

Working Problems 7 to 12 will give you a better understanding of a labor market with a minimum wage.

Taxes (pp. 133–138)

- A tax raises the price paid by buyers, but usually by less than the tax.
- The elasticity of demand and the elasticity of supply determine the share of a tax paid by buyers and sellers.

- The less elastic the demand or the more elastic the supply, the larger is the share of the tax paid by buyers.
- If demand is perfectly elastic or supply is perfectly inelastic, sellers pay the entire tax. And if demand is perfectly inelastic or supply is perfectly elastic, buyers pay the entire tax.

Working Problems 13 to 15 will give you a better understanding of taxes.

Production Quotas and Subsidies (pp. 139–141)

- A production quota leads to inefficient underproduction, which raises the price.
- A subsidy is like a negative tax. It lowers the price, increases the cost of production, and leads to inefficient overproduction.

Working Problems 16 and 17 will give you a better understanding of production quotas and subsidies.

Markets for Illegal Goods (pp. 142–143)

- Penalties on sellers increase the cost of selling the good and decrease the supply of the good.
- Penalties on buyers decrease their willingness to pay and decrease the demand for the good.
- Penalties on buyers and sellers decrease the quantity of the good, raise the price buyers pay, and lower the price sellers receive.
- Legalizing and taxing can achieve the same outcome as penalties on buyers and sellers.

Working Problem 18 will give you a better understanding of markets for illegal goods.

Key Terms

Black market, 128
Minimum wage, 131
Price cap, 128
Price ceiling, 128

Price floor, 131
Production quota, 139
Rent ceiling, 128
Search activity, 128

Subsidy, 140
Tax incidence, 133

STUDY PLAN PROBLEMS AND APPLICATIONS

MyEconLab   You can work Problems 1 to 18 in MyEconLab Chapter 6 Study Plan and get instant feedback.

A Housing Market with a Rent Ceiling (Study Plan 6.1)

Use the following graph of the market for rental housing in Townsville to work Problems 1 and 2.

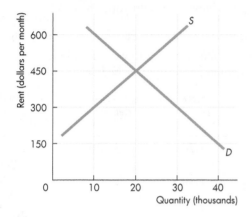

1. a. What are the equilibrium rent and equilibrium quantity of rental housing?

   b. If a rent ceiling is set at $600 a month, what is the quantity of housing rented and what is the shortage of housing?

2. If a rent ceiling is set at $300 a month, what is the quantity of housing rented, the shortage of housing, and the maximum price that someone is willing to pay for the last unit of housing available?

Use the following news clip to work Problems 3 to 6.

Capping Gasoline Prices

As gasoline prices rise, many people are calling for price caps, but price caps generate a distorted reflection of reality, which leads buyers and suppliers to act in ways inconsistent with the price cap. By masking reality, price caps only make matters worse.

Source: *Pittsburgh Tribune-Review*,
September 12, 2005

Suppose that a price ceiling is set below the equilibrium price of gasoline.

3. How does the price cap influence the quantity of gasoline supplied and the quantity demanded?

4. How does the price cap influence

   a. The quantity of gasoline sold and the shortage or surplus of gasoline?

   b. The maximum price that someone is willing to pay for the last gallon of gasoline available on a black market?

5. Draw a graph to illustrate the effects of a price ceiling set below the equilibrium price in the market for gasoline.

6. Explain the various ways in which a price ceiling on gasoline that is set below the equilibrium price would make buyers and sellers of gasoline better off or worse off. What would happen to total surplus and deadweight loss in this market?

A Labor Market with a Minimum Wage

(Study Plan 6.2)

Use the following data to work Problems 7 to 9.
The table gives the demand and supply schedules of teenage labor.

Wage rate (dollars per hour)	Quantity demanded	Quantity supplied
	(hours per month)	
4	3,000	1,000
5	2,500	1,500
6	2,000	2,000
7	1,500	2,500
8	1,000	3,000

7. Calculate the equilibrium wage rate, the number of hours worked, and the quantity of unemployment.

8. If a minimum wage for teenagers is set at $5 an hour, how many hours do they work and how many hours of teenage labor are unemployed?

9. If a minimum wage for teenagers is set at $7 an hour,

   a. How many hours do teenagers work and how many hours are unemployed?

   b. Demand for teenage labor increases by 500 hours a month. What is the wage rate paid to teenagers and how many hours of teenage labor are unemployed?

Use the following news clip to work Problems 10 to 12.

India Steps Up Pressure for Minimum Wage for Its Workers in the Gulf

Oil-rich countries in the [Persian] Gulf, already confronted by strong labor protests, are facing renewed pressure from India to pay minimum wages for unskilled workers. With five million immigrant workers in the region, India is trying to win better conditions for their citizens.

Source: *International Herald Tribune*,
March 27, 2008

Suppose that the Gulf countries paid a minimum wage above the equilibrium wage to Indian workers.

10. How would the market for labor be affected in the Gulf countries? Draw a supply and demand graph to illustrate your answer.

11. How would the market for labor be affected in India? Draw a supply and demand graph to illustrate your answer. [Be careful: the minimum wage is in the Gulf countries, not in India.]

12. Would migrant Indian workers be better off or worse off or unaffected by this minimum wage?

Taxes (Study Plan 6.3)

13. The table gives the demand and supply schedules for chocolate brownies.

Price (cents per brownie)	Quantity demanded	Quantity supplied
	(millions per day)	
50	5	3
60	4	4
70	3	5
80	2	6
90	1	7

a. If brownies are not taxed, what is the price of a brownie and how many are bought?

b. If sellers are taxed 20¢ a brownie, what is the price? How many are sold? Who pays the tax?

c. If buyers are taxed 20¢ a brownie, what is the price? How many are bought? Who pays the tax?

14. **Will Cuts on China's Luxury Goods Tax Prevent Chinese from Buying Abroad?**

Last year Chinese tourists bought almost two-thirds of luxury goods sold in Europe. If you look at China's luxury goods tax, it is easy to see why shopping overseas is so popular. According to the Chinese Ministry of Commerce, prices for luxury goods in China are 45% higher than in Hong Kong, 51% higher than the United States, and 72% higher than France.

Source: PRLog, March 21, 2012

a. Explain why it is "easy to see why shopping overseas is so popular" with wealthy Chinese shoppers.

b. Who pays most of the Chinese luxury tax: sellers or buyers? Explain your answer.

c. Explain how a cut in China's luxury tax rate will change the quantity of luxury goods purchased in China.

15. **How to Take a Gas Holiday**

High fuel prices will probably keep Americans closer to home this summer, despite the gas-tax "holiday" that would shave 18¢ off every gallon.

Source: *Time*, May 19, 2008

Would the price of gasoline that consumers pay fall by 18¢ a gallon? How would consumer surplus change? Explain your answers.

Production Quotas and Subsidies (Study Plan 6.4)

Use the following data to work Problems 16 and 17. The demand and supply schedules for rice are

Price (dollars per box)	Quantity demanded	Quantity supplied
	(boxes per week)	
1.20	3,000	1,500
1.30	2,750	2,000
1.40	2,500	2,500
1.50	2,250	3,000
1.60	2,000	3,500

16. Calculate the price, the marginal cost of rice, and the quantity produced if the government sets a production quota of 2,000 boxes a week.

17. Calculate the price, the marginal cost of rice, and the quantity produced if the government introduces a subsidy of $0.30 a box.

Markets for Illegal Goods (Study Plan 6.5)

18. The figure illustrates the market for a banned substance.

Calculate the market price and the quantity consumed if a penalty of $20 a unit is imposed on

a. Sellers only.

b. Buyers only.

c. Both sellers and buyers.

ADDITIONAL PROBLEMS AND APPLICATIONS

MyEconLab   You can work these problems in MyEconLab if assigned by your instructor.

A Housing Market with a Rent Ceiling

Use this news clip to work Problems 19 and 20.

Despite Protests, Rent Board Sets 7.25% Increase

New York's Rent Guidelines Board voted for a rent increase of up to 7.25 percent over the next two years on rent-stabilized apartments. A survey reported that last year costs for the owners of rent-stabilized buildings rose by 7.8 percent. In addition there is growing concern about the ability of the middle class to afford to live in New York City.

Source: *The New York Times*, June 28, 2006

19. a. If rents for rent-stabilized apartments do not increase, how do you think the market for rental units in New York City will develop?

    b. Are rent ceilings in New York City helpful to the middle class? Why or why not?

20. a. Explain the effect of the increase in the rent ceiling on the quantity of rent-stabilized apartments.

    b. Why is rent stabilization a source of conflict between renters and owners of apartments?

A Labor Market with a Minimum Wage

Use the following news clip to work Problems 21 and 22.

Malaysia Passes Its First Minimum Wage Law

About 3.2 million low-income workers across Malaysia are expected to benefit from the country's first minimum wage, which the government says will transform Malaysia into a high-income nation. Employer groups argue that paying the minimum wage, which is not based on productivity or performance would raise their costs and reduce business profits.

Source: *The New York Times*, May 1, 2012

21. On a graph of the market for low-skilled labor, show the effect of the minimum wage on the quantity of labor employed.

22. Explain the effects of the minimum wage on the workers' surplus, the firms' surplus, and the efficiency of the market for low-skilled workers.

Taxes

23. Use the news clip in Problem 21.

    a. If the Malaysian government cut the tax on business profits, would it offset the effect of the minimum wage on employment? Explain.

    b. Would a cut in the Social Security tax that small businesses pay offset the effect of the higher minimum wage on employment? Explain.

24. The demand and supply schedules for tulips are

Price (dollars per bunch)	Quantity demanded	Quantity supplied
	(bunches per week)	
10	100	40
12	90	60
14	80	80
16	70	100
18	60	120

    a. If tulips are not taxed, what is the price and how many bunches are bought?

    b. If tulips are taxed $6 a bunch, what are the price and quantity bought? Who pays the tax?

25. **Cigarette Taxes, Black Markets, and Crime: Lessons from New York's 50-Year Losing Battle**

    New York City has the highest cigarette taxes in the country. During the four months following the recent tax hike, sales of taxed cigarettes in the city fell by more than 50 percent as consumers turned to the city's bustling black market. The thriving illegal market for cigarettes has diverted billions of dollars from legitimate businesses and governments to criminals.

    Source: Cato Institute, February 6, 2003

    a. How has the market for cigarettes in New York City responded to the high cigarette taxes?

    b. How does the emergence of a black market impact the elasticity of demand in a legal market?

    c. Why might an increase in the tax rate actually cause a decrease in the tax revenue?

Production Quotas and Subsidies

Use the following news clip to work Problems 26 to 28.

Crop Prices Erode Farm Subsidy Program

High corn and soybean prices mean farmers are making the most money in their lives. The reason: Grain prices are far too high to trigger payouts under the U.S. primary farm-subsidy program's "price support" formula. The market has done what Congress couldn't do and that is "slash farm subsidies."

Source: *The Wall Street Journal*, July 25, 2011

26. a. Why are U.S. soybean farmers subsidized?

b. Explain how a subsidy paid to soybean farmers affects the price of soybean and the marginal cost of producing it.

27. Show in a graph how a subsidy paid to soybean farmers affects the consumer surplus and the producer surplus from soybean. Does the subsidy make the soybean market more efficient or less efficient? Explain.

28. In the market for corn with a price support, explain why the corn price has risen and ended up being too high to "trigger payouts."

Markets for Illegal Goods

29. The table gives the demand and supply schedules for an illegal drug.

Price (dollars per unit)	Quantity demanded	Quantity supplied
	(units per day)	
50	500	300
60	400	400
70	300	500
80	200	600
90	100	700

a. If there are no penalties on buying or selling the drug, what is the price and how many units are consumed?

b. If the penalty on sellers is $20 a unit, what are the price and quantity consumed?

c. If the penalty on buyers is $20 a unit, what are the price and quantity consumed?

Economics in the News

30. After you have studied *Reading Between the Lines* on pp. 144–145, answer the following questions.

a. Suppose the New York minimum wage rate had been raised to $7.25 an hour in 2007 and the demand for and supply of labor were as shown in Fig. 1 on p. 145. Describe the situation in the Buffalo–Niagara region labor market.

b. How does Assembly Speaker Sheldon Silver want to change the New York minimum wage law?

c. How would Mr. Silver's proposal change the minimum wage in 2013 and 2014 and how would you expect the labor market to be influenced by the changes you've described?

d. Draw a graph of the Buffalo–Niagara region labor market in 2014 to illustrate your answer to part (c).

31. **Hollywood: Organized Crime Hits the Movies**
The Mexican army seized 1,180 disc burners and 3.14 million copies of movies and TV shows from 23 warehouses in a move to fight piracy that costs Hollywood about $590 million a year.
Source: Bloomberg *Businessweek*, April 7, 2011

Assume that the marginal cost of producing a DVD (legal or illegal) is a constant $3 and that legal DVDs bear an additional marginal cost of $5 each in royalty payments to film studios.

a. Draw a graph of the market for counterfeit DVDs, assuming that there are no effective penalties on either buyers or sellers for breaking the law.

b. How do the events reported in the news clip change the market outcome? Show the effects in your graph.

c. With no penalty on buyers, if a penalty for breaking the law is imposed on sellers at more than $5 a disc, how does the market work and what is the equilibrium price?

d. With no penalty on sellers, if a penalty for breaking the law is imposed on buyers at more than $5 a disc, how does the market work and what is the equilibrium price?

e. What is the marginal benefit of an illegal DVD in the situations described in parts (c) and (d)?

f. In light of your answer to part (e), why does law enforcement usually focus on sellers rather than buyers?

32. **Drivers Feel the Pinch as Diesel Hits $4 a Gallon**
"The high price of gasoline is hurting our economy," said Mark Kirsch, a trucker, who organized a rally in Washington. "It's hurting middle-class people."
Source: *The Washington Post*, April 29, 2008
Explain to truck drivers why a cap on the price of gasoline would hurt middle-class people more than the high price of gasoline hurts.

33. On December 31, 1776, Rhode Island established wage controls to limit wages to 70¢ a day for carpenters and 42¢ a day for tailors.

a. Are these wage controls a price ceiling or a price floor? Why might they have been introduced?

b. If these wage controls are effective, would you expect to see a surplus or a shortage of carpenters and tailors?

The Amazing Market

PART TWO

The chapters that you've just studied explain how markets work. The market is an amazing instrument. It enables people who have never met and who know nothing about each other to interact and do business. It also enables us to allocate our scarce resources to the uses that we value most highly. Markets can be very simple or highly organized. Markets are ancient and they are modern.

A simple and ancient market is one that the American historian Daniel J. Boorstin describes in *The Discoverers* (p. 161). In the late fourteenth century,

> *The Muslim caravans that went southward from Morocco across the Atlas Mountains arrived after twenty days at the shores of the Senegal River. There the Moroccan traders laid out separate piles of salt, of beads from Ceutan coral, and cheap manufactured goods. Then they retreated out of sight. The local tribesmen, who lived in the strip mines where they dug their gold, came to the shore and put a heap of gold beside each pile of Moroccan goods. Then they, in turn, went out of view, leaving the Moroccan traders either to take the gold offered for a particular pile or to reduce the pile of their merchandise to suit the offered price in gold. Once again the Moroccan traders withdrew, and the process went on. By this system of commercial etiquette, the Moroccans collected their gold.*

Organized and modern markets are auctions on e-Bay and U.S. government auction of the airwaves that cell phone companies use. Susan Athey, whom you will meet on the following page, is a world-renowned expert on the design of auctions.

Everything and anything that can be exchanged is traded in markets to the benefit of both buyers and sellers.

Alfred Marshall *(1842–1924) grew up in an England that was being transformed by the railroad and by the expansion of manufacturing. Mary Paley was one of Marshall's students at Cambridge, and when Alfred and Mary married, in 1877, celibacy rules barred Alfred from continuing to teach at Cambridge. By 1884, with more liberal rules, the Marshalls returned to Cambridge, where Alfred became Professor of Political Economy.*

Many economists had a hand in refining the demand and supply model, but the first thorough and complete statement of the model as we know it today was set out by Alfred Marshall, with the help of Mary Paley Marshall. Published in 1890, this monumental treatise, The Principles of Economics, *became the textbook on economics on both sides of the Atlantic for almost half a century.*

"The forces to be dealt with are . . . so numerous, that it is best to take a few at a time. . . . Thus we begin by isolating the primary relations of supply, demand, and price."

ALFRED MARSHALL
The Principles of Economics

151

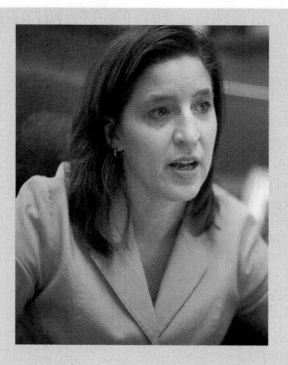

SUSAN ATHEY is Professor of Economics at Harvard University. Born in 1970, she completed high school in three years, wrapped up three majors—in economics, mathematics, and computer science—at Duke University at 20, completed her Ph.D. at Stanford University at 24, and was voted tenure at MIT and Stanford at 29. After teaching at MIT for six years and Stanford for five years, she moved to Harvard in 2006. Among her many honors and awards, the most prestigious is the John Bates Clark Medal given to the best economist under 40. She is the first woman to receive this award.

Professor Athey's research is broad both in scope and style. A government that wants to auction natural resources will turn to her fundamental discoveries (and possibly consult with her) before deciding how to organize the auction. An economist who wants to test a theory using a large data set will use her work on statistics and econometrics.

Michael Parkin talked with Susan Athey about her research, what economists have learned about designing markets, and her advice to students.

Professor Athey, what sparked your interest in economics?

I was studying mathematics and computer science, but I felt that the subjects were not as relevant as I would like. I discovered economics through a research project with a professor who was working on auctions. I had a summer job working for a firm that sold computers to the government through auctions. Eventually my professor, Bob Marshall, wrote two articles on the topic and testified before Congress to help reform the system for government procurement of computers. That really inspired me and showed me the power of economic ideas to change the world and to make things work more efficiently.

What is the connection between an auction and the supply and demand model?

The basic laws of supply and demand can be seen in evidence in an auction market like eBay. The more sellers that are selling similar products, the lower the prices they can expect to achieve. Similarly the more buyers there are demanding those objects, the higher the prices the sellers can achieve.

An important thing for an auction marketplace is to attract a good balance of buyers and sellers so that both the buyers and the sellers find it more profitable to transact in that marketplace rather than using some other mechanism. From a seller's perspective, the more bidders there are on the platform, the greater the demand and the higher the prices. And from the buyer's perspective, the more sellers there are on the platform, the greater the supply and the lower the prices.

> The basic laws of supply and demand can be seen in evidence in an auction market like eBay.

Can we think of an auction as a mechanism for finding the equilibrium price and quantity?

Exactly. We can think of the whole collection of auctions on eBay as being a mechanism to discover a market clearing price, and individual items might sell a little higher or a little lower but over all we believe that the prices on eBay auctions will represent equilibrium prices.

*Read the full interview with Susan Athey in MyEconLab.

7

UTILITY AND DEMAND

After studying this chapter, you will be able to:

◆ Explain the limits to consumption and describe preferences using the concept of utility

◆ Explain the marginal utility theory of consumer choice

◆ Use marginal utility theory to predict the effects of changes in prices and incomes and to explain the paradox of value

◆ Describe some new ways of explaining consumer choices

You want Adele's album *21*. Will you buy a CD for $9.99, or will you download it for $10.99? What determines our choices about how we buy recorded music?

You know that diamonds are expensive and water is cheap. Doesn't that seem odd? Why do we place a higher value on useless diamonds than on essential-to-life water?

The theory of consumer choice that you're going to study in this chapter answers questions like the ones we've just posed. *Reading Between the Lines* at the end of the chapter applies what you learn to a debate about whether sugary drinks should be banned or taxed to discourage their consumption.

◆ Consumption Choices

The choices that you make as a buyer of goods and services—your consumption choices—are influenced by many factors. We can summarize them under two broad headings:

■ Consumption possibilities
■ Preferences

Consumption Possibilities

Your consumption possibilities are all the things that you can afford to buy. You can afford many different combinations of goods and services, but they are all limited by your income and by the prices that you must pay. For example, you might decide to spend a big part of your income on a gym membership and personal trainer and little on movies and music, or you might spend lots on movies and music and use the free gym at school.

The easiest way to describe consumption possibilities is to consider a model consumer who buys only two items. That's what we'll now do. We'll study the consumption possibilities of Lisa, who buys only movies and soda.

A Consumer's Budget Line Consumption possibilities are limited by income and by the prices of movies and soda. When Lisa spends all her income, she reaches the limits to her consumption possibilities. We describe this limit with a **budget line**, which marks the boundary between those combinations of goods and services that a household can afford to buy and those that it cannot afford.

Figure 7.1 illustrates Lisa's consumption possibilities of movies and soda and her budget line. Lisa has an income of $40 a month, the price of a movie is $8, and the price of soda is $4 a case. Rows A through F in the table show six possible ways of allocating $40 to these two goods. For example, in row A Lisa buys 10 cases of soda and sees no movies; in row F she sees 5 movies and buys no soda; and in row C she sees 2 movies and buys 6 cases of soda.

Points A through F in the graph illustrate the possibilities presented in the table, and the line passing through these points is Lisa's budget line.

The budget line constrains choices: It marks the boundary between what is affordable and unafford-able. Lisa can afford all the points on the budget line and inside it. Points outside the line are unaffordable.

FIGURE 7.1   Lisa's Budget Line

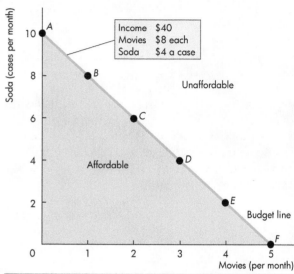

| Possibility | Movies | | Soda | |
	Quantity	Expenditure (dollars)	Cases	Expenditure (dollars)
A	0	0	10	40
B	1	8	8	32
C	**2**	**16**	**6**	**24**
D	3	24	4	16
E	4	32	2	8
F	5	40	0	0

The graph and the table show six possible ways in which Lisa can allocate $40 to movies and soda. In row C and at point C, she sees 2 movies and buys 6 cases of soda. The line AF is Lisa's budget line and is a boundary between what she can afford and what she cannot afford. Her choices must lie along the line AF or inside the orange area.

MyEconLab animation

Changes in Consumption Possibilities Consumption possibilities change when income or prices change. A rise in income shifts the budget line outward but leaves its slope unchanged. A change in a price changes the slope of the line. Our goal is to predict the effects of such changes on consumption choices. To do so, we must determine the choice a consumer makes. The budget line shows what is possible; prefer-ences determine which possibility is chosen. We'll now describe a consumer's preferences.

Preferences

Lisa's income and the prices that she faces limit her consumption choices, but she still has lots of choice. The choice that she makes depends on her **preferences**—a description of her likes and dislikes.

You saw one way that economists use to describe preferences in Chapter 2 (p. 36), the concept of *marginal benefit* and the *marginal benefit curve*. But you also saw in Chapter 5 (p. 108) that a marginal benefit curve is also a demand curve. The goal of a theory of consumer choice is to derive the demand curve from a deeper account of how consumers make their buying plans. That is, we want to *explain what determines demand and marginal benefit.*

To achieve this goal, we need a deeper way of describing preferences. One approach to this problem uses the idea of utility, and defines **utility** as the benefit or satisfaction that a person gets from the consumption of goods and services. We distinguish two utility concepts:

- Total utility
- Marginal utility

Total Utility The total benefit that a person gets from the consumption of all the different goods and services is called **total utility**. Total utility depends on the level of consumption—more consumption generally gives more total utility.

To illustrate the concept of total utility, think about Lisa's choices. We tell Lisa that we want to measure her utility from movies and soda. We can use any scale that we wish to measure her total utility and we give her two starting points: (1) We will call the total utility from no movies and no soda zero utility; and (2) We will call the total utility she gets from seeing 1 movie a month 50 units.

We then ask Lisa to tell us, using the same scale, how much she would like 2 movies, and more, up to 10 movies a month. We also ask her to tell us, on the same scale, how much she would like 1 case of soda a month, 2 cases, and more, up to 10 cases a month.

In Table 7.1, the columns headed "Total utility" show Lisa's answers. Looking at those numbers, you can say a lot about how much Lisa likes soda and movies. She says that 1 case of soda gives her 75 units of utility—50 percent more than the utility that she gets from seeing 1 movie. You can also see that her total utility from soda climbs more slowly than her total utility from movies. This difference turns on the second utility concept: *marginal utility.*

TABLE 7.1 Lisa's Utility from Movies and Soda

Movies			Soda		
Quantity (per month)	Total utility	Marginal utility	Cases (per month)	Total utility	Marginal utility
0	0		0	0	
		 50			 75
1	50		1	75	
		 40			 48
2	90		2	123	
		 32			 36
3	122		3	159	
		 28			 24
4	150		4	183	
		 26			 22
5	176		5	205	
		 24			 20
6	200		6	225	
		 22			 13
7	222		7	238	
		 20			 10
8	242		8	248	
		 17			 7
9	259		9	255	
		 16			 5
10	275		10	260	

Marginal Utility We define **marginal utility** as the *change* in total utility that results from a one-unit increase in the quantity of a good consumed.

In Table 7.1, the columns headed "Marginal utility" show Lisa's marginal utility from movies and soda. You can see that if Lisa increases the soda she buys from 1 to 2 cases a month, her total utility from soda increases from 75 units to 123 units. For Lisa, the marginal utility from the second case each month is 48 units (123 − 75).

The marginal utility numbers appear midway between the quantities of soda because it is the *change* in the quantity she buys from 1 to 2 cases that produces the marginal utility of 48 units.

Marginal utility is *positive,* but it *diminishes* as the quantity of a good consumed increases.

Positive Marginal Utility All the things that people enjoy and want more of have a positive marginal utility. Some objects and activities can generate negative marginal utility—and lower total utility. Two examples are hard labor and polluted air. But all the goods and services that people value and that we are thinking about here have positive marginal utility: Total utility increases as the quantity consumed increases.

Diminishing Marginal Utility As Lisa sees more movies, her total utility from movies increases but her marginal utility from movies decreases. Similarly, as she

FIGURE 7.2   Total Utility and Marginal Utility

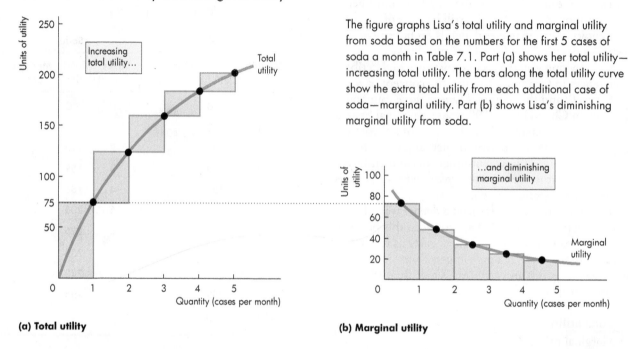

The figure graphs Lisa's total utility and marginal utility from soda based on the numbers for the first 5 cases of soda a month in Table 7.1. Part (a) shows her total utility—increasing total utility. The bars along the total utility curve show the extra total utility from each additional case of soda—marginal utility. Part (b) shows Lisa's diminishing marginal utility from soda.

(a) Total utility

(b) Marginal utility

MyEconLab animation

consumes more soda, her total utility from soda increases but her marginal utility from soda decreases.

The tendency for marginal utility to decrease as the consumption of a good increases is so general and universal that we give it the status of a *principle*—the principle of **diminishing marginal utility**.

You can see Lisa's diminishing marginal utility by calculating a few numbers. Her marginal utility from soda decreases from 75 units from the first case to 48 units from the second case and to 36 units from the third. Her marginal utility from movies decreases from 50 units for the first movie to 40 units for the second and 32 units for the third. Lisa's marginal utility diminishes as she buys more of each good.

Your Diminishing Marginal Utility You've been studying all day and into the evening, and you've been too busy finishing an assignment to shop for soda. A friend drops by with a can of soda. The utility you get from that soda is the marginal utility from your first soda of the day—from *one* can. On another day you've been on a soda binge. You've been working on an assignment, but you've guzzled 10 cans of soda while doing so, and are now totally wired. You are happy enough to have one more can, but the thrill that you get from it is not very large. It is the marginal utility from the *eleventh* can in a day.

Graphing Lisa's Utility Schedules   Figure 7.2(a) illustrates Lisa's total utility from soda. The more soda Lisa consumes in a month, the more total utility she gets. Her total utility curve slopes upward.

Figure 7.2(b) illustrates Lisa's marginal utility from soda. It is a graph of the marginal utility numbers in Table 7.1. This graph shows Lisa's diminishing marginal utility from soda. Her marginal utility curve slopes downward as she consumes more soda.

We've described Lisa's consumption possibilities and preferences. Your next task is to see how Lisa chooses what to consume.

REVIEW QUIZ

1 Explain how a consumer's income and the prices of goods limit consumption possibilities.
2 What is utility and how do we use the concept of utility to describe a consumer's preferences?
3 What is the distinction between total utility and marginal utility?
4 What is the key assumption about marginal utility?

You can work these questions in Study Plan 7.1 and get instant feedback.   *MyEconLab*

◆ Utility-Maximizing Choice

Consumers want to get the most utility possible from their limited resources. They make the choice that maximizes utility. To discover this choice, we combine the constraint imposed by the budget and the consumer's preferences and find the point on the budget line that gives the consumer the maximum attainable utility. Let's find Lisa's utility-maximizing choice.

A Spreadsheet Solution

Lisa's most direct way of finding the quantities of movies and soda that maximize her utility is to make a table in a spreadsheet with the information and calculations shown in Table 7.2. Let's see what that table tells us.

Find the Just-Affordable Combinations Table 7.2 shows the combinations of movies and soda that Lisa can afford and that exhaust her $40 income. For example, in row A, Lisa buys only soda and at $4 a case she can buy 10 cases. In row B, Lisa sees 1 movie and buys 8 cases of soda. She spends $8 on the movie. At $4 a case, she spends $32 on soda and can buy 8 cases. The combination in row B just exhausts her $40. The combinations shown in the table are the same as those plotted on her budget line in Fig. 7.1.

We noted that the budget line shows that Lisa can also afford any combination *inside* the budget line. The quantities in those combinations would be smaller than the ones shown in Table 7.2 and they do not exhaust her $40. But smaller quantities don't maximize her utility. Why? The marginal utilities of movies and soda are positive, so the more of each that Lisa buys, the more total utility she gets.

Find the Total Utility for Each Just-Affordable Combination Table 7.2 shows the total utility that Lisa gets from the just-affordable quantities of movies and soda. The second and third columns show the numbers for movies and fourth and fifth columns show those for soda. The center column adds the total utility from movies to the total utility from soda. This number, the total utility from movies *and* soda, is what Lisa wants to maximize.

In row A of the table, Lisa sees no movies and buys 10 cases of soda. She gets no utility from movies and 260 units of utility from soda. Her total utility from movies and soda (the center column) is 260 units.

TABLE 7.2   Lisa's Utility-Maximizing Choice

	Movies $8		Total utility from movies and soda	Soda $4	
	Quantity (per month)	Total utility		Total utility	Cases (per month)
A	0	0	260	260	10
B	1	50	298	248	8
C	2	90	315	225	6
D	3	122	305	183	4
E	4	150	273	123	2
F	5	176	176	0	0

In row C of the table, Lisa sees 2 movies and buys 6 cases of soda. She gets 90 units of utility from movies and 225 units of utility from soda. Her total utility from movies and soda is 315 units. This combination of movies and soda maximizes Lisa's total utility. That is, given the prices of movies and soda, Lisa's best choice when she has $40 to spend is to see 2 movies and buy 6 cases of soda.

If Lisa sees 1 movie, she can buy 8 cases of soda, but she gets only 298 units of total utility—17 units less than the maximum attainable. If she sees 3 movies, she can buy only 4 cases of soda. She gets 305 units of total utility—10 units less than the maximum attainable.

Consumer Equilibrium We've just described Lisa's consumer equilibrium. A **consumer equilibrium** is a situation in which a consumer has allocated all of his or her available income in the way that maximizes his or her total utility, given the prices of goods and services. Lisa's consumer equilibrium is 2 movies and 6 cases of soda.

To find Lisa's consumer equilibrium, we did something that an economist might do but that a consumer is not likely to do: We measured her total utility from all the affordable combinations of movies and soda and then, by inspection of the numbers, selected the combination that gives the highest total utility. There is a more natural way of finding a consumer's equilibrium—a way that uses the idea that choices are made at the margin, as you first met in Chapter 1. Let's look at this approach.

Choosing at the Margin

When you go shopping you don't do utility calculations. But you do decide how to allocate your budget, and you do so in a way that you think is best for you. If you could make yourself better off by spending a few more dollars on an extra unit of one item and the same number of dollars less on something else, you would make that change. So, when you've allocated your budget in the best possible way, you can't make yourself better off by spending more on one item and less on others.

Marginal Utility per Dollar Economists interpret your best possible choice by using the idea of marginal utility per dollar. *Marginal utility* is the increase in total utility that results from consuming *one more unit* of a good. **Marginal utility per dollar** is the *marginal utility* from a good that results from spending *one more dollar* on it.

The distinction between these two marginal concepts is clearest for a good that is infinitely divisible, such as gasoline. You can buy gasoline by the smallest fraction of a gallon and literally choose to spend one more or one less dollar at the pump. The increase in total utility that results from spending one more dollar at the pump is the marginal utility per dollar from gasoline. When you buy a movie ticket or a case of soda, you must spend your dollars in bigger lumps. To buy our marginal movie ticket or case of soda, you must spend the price of one unit and your total utility increases by the marginal utility from that item. So to calculate the marginal utility per dollar for movies (or soda), we must divide marginal utility from the good by its price.

Call the marginal utility from movies MU_M and the price of a movie P_M. Then the *marginal utility per dollar from movies* is

$$MU_M/P_M.$$

Call the marginal utility from soda MU_S and the price of a case of soda P_S. Then the *marginal utility per dollar from soda* is

$$MU_S/P_S.$$

By comparing the marginal utility per dollar from all the goods that a person buys, we can determine whether the budget has been allocated in the way that maximizes total utility.

Let's see how we use the marginal utility per dollar to define a utility-maximizing rule.

Utility-Maximizing Rule A consumer's total utility is maximized by following the rule:

- Spend all the available income
- Equalize the marginal utility per dollar for all goods

Spend All the Available Income Because more consumption brings more utility, only those choices that exhaust income can maximize utility. For Lisa, combinations of movies and soda that leave her with money to spend don't give her as much total utility as those that exhaust her $40 per month income.

Equalize the Marginal Utility per Dollar The basic idea behind this rule is to move dollars from good *A* to good *B* if doing so increases the utility from good *A* by more than it decreases the utility from good *B*. Such a utility-increasing move is possible if the marginal utility per dollar from good *A* exceeds that from good *B*.

But buying more of good *A* decreases its marginal utility. And buying less of good *B* increases its marginal utility. So by moving dollars from good *A* to good *B*, total utility rises, but the gap between the marginal utilities per dollar gets smaller.

As long as the gap exists—as long as the marginal utility per dollar from good *A* exceeds that from good *B*—total utility can be increased by spending more on *A* and less on *B*. But when enough dollars have been moved from *B* to *A* to make the two marginal utilities per dollar equal, total utility cannot be increased further. Total utility is maximized.

Lisa's Marginal Calculation Let's apply the basic idea to Lisa. To calculate Lisa's marginal utility per dollar, we divide her marginal utility numbers for each quantity of each good by the price of the good. The table in Fig. 7.3 shows these calculations for Lisa, and the graph illustrates the situation on Lisa's budget line. The rows of the table are three of her affordable combinations of movies and soda.

Too Much Soda and Too Few Movies In row *B*, Lisa sees 1 movie a month and consumes 8 cases of soda a month. Her marginal utility from seeing 1 movie a month is 50 units. Because the price of a movie is $8, Lisa's marginal utility per dollar from movies is 50 units divided by $8, or 6.25 units of utility per dollar.

Lisa's marginal utility from soda when she consumes 8 cases of soda a month is 10 units. Because the price of soda is $4 a case, Lisa's marginal utility per dollar from soda is 10 units divided by $4, or 2.50 units of utility per dollar.

When Lisa sees 1 movie and consumes 8 cases of soda a month, her marginal utility per dollar from soda is *less than* her marginal utility per dollar from movies. That is,

$$MU_S/P_S < MU_M/P_M.$$

If Lisa spent an extra dollar on movies and a dollar less on soda, her total utility would increase. She would get 6.25 units from the extra dollar spent on movies and lose 2.50 units from the dollar less spent on soda. Her total utility would increase by 3.75 units (6.25 − 2.50).

Too Little Soda and Too Many Movies In row *D*, Lisa sees 3 movies a month and consumes 4 cases of soda. Her marginal utility from seeing the third movie a month is 32 units. At a price of $8 a movie, Lisa's marginal utility per dollar from movies is 32 units divided by $8, or 4 units of utility per dollar.

Lisa's marginal utility from soda when she buys 4 cases a month is 24 units. At a price of $4 a case, Lisa's marginal utility per dollar from soda is 24 units divided by $4, or 6 units of utility per dollar.

When Lisa sees 3 movies and consumes 4 cases of soda a month, her marginal utility from soda *exceeds* her marginal utility from movies. That is,

$$MU_S/P_S > MU_M/P_M.$$

If Lisa spent an extra dollar on soda and a dollar less on movies, her total utility would increase. She would get 6 units from the extra dollar spent on soda and she would lose 4 units from the dollar less spent on movies. Her total utility would increase by 2 units (6 − 4).

Utility-Maximizing Movies and Soda In Fig. 7.3, if Lisa moves from row *B* to row *C*, she increases the movies she sees from 1 to 2 a month and decreases the soda she consumes from 8 to 6 cases a month. Her marginal utility per dollar from movies falls to 5 and her marginal utility per dollar from soda rises to 5.

Similarly, if Lisa moves from row *D* to row *C*, she decreases the movies she sees from 3 to 2 a month and increases the soda she consumes from 4 to 6 cases a month. Her marginal utility per dollar from movies rises to 5 and her marginal utility per dollar from soda falls to 5.

When Lisa sees 2 movies and consumes 6 cases of soda a month, her marginal utility per dollar from soda *equals* her marginal utility per dollar from

FIGURE 7.3   Equalizing Marginal Utilities per Dollar

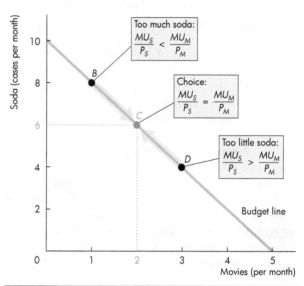

	Movies ($8 each)			Soda ($4 per case)		
	Quantity	Marginal utility	Marginal utility per dollar	Cases	Marginal utility	Marginal utility per dollar
B	1	50	6.25	8	10	2.50
C	2	40	5.00	6	20	5.00
D	3	32	4.00	4	24	6.00

The graph shows Lisa's budget line and identifies three points on it. The rows of the table describe these points.

At point *B* (row *B*), with 1 movie and 8 cases of soda, Lisa's marginal utility per dollar from soda is less than that from movies: Buy less soda and see more movies.

At point *D* (row *D*), with 3 movies and 4 cases of soda, Lisa's marginal utility per dollar from soda is greater than that from movies: Buy more soda and see fewer movies.

At point *C* (row *C*), with 2 movies and 6 cases of soda, Lisa's marginal utility per dollar from soda is equal to that from movies: Lisa's utility is maximized.

―――― MyEconLab animation ―――

movies. That is,

$$MU_S/P_S = MU_M/P_M.$$

Lisa can't move from this allocation of her budget without making herself worse off.

The Power of Marginal Analysis

The method we've just used to find Lisa's utility-maximizing choice of movies and soda is an example of the power of marginal analysis. Lisa doesn't need a computer and a spreadsheet program to maximize utility. She can achieve this goal by comparing the marginal gain from having more of one good with the marginal loss from having less of another good.

The rule that she follows is simple: If the marginal utility per dollar from movies exceeds the marginal utility per dollar from soda, see more movies and buy less soda; if the marginal utility per dollar from soda exceeds the marginal utility per dollar from movies, buy more soda and see fewer movies.

More generally, if the marginal gain from an action exceeds the marginal loss, take the action. You will meet this principle time and again in your study of economics, and you will find yourself using it when you make your own economic choices, especially when you must make big decisions.

Revealing Preferences

When we introduced the idea of utility, we arbitrarily chose 50 units as Lisa's total utility from 1 movie, and we pretended that we asked Lisa to tell us how many units of utility she got from different quantities of soda and movies.

You're now about to discover that we don't need to ask Lisa to tell us her preferences. We can figure them out for ourselves by observing what she buys at various prices.

Also, the units in which we measure Lisa's preferences don't matter. Any arbitrary units will work. In this respect, utility is like temperature. Predictions about the freezing point of water don't depend on the temperature scale; and predictions about a household's consumption choice don't depend on the units of utility.

Lisa's Preferences   In maximizing total utility by making the marginal utility per dollar equal for all goods, the units in which utility is measured do not matter.

You've seen that when Lisa maximizes her total utility, her marginal utility per dollar from soda, MU_S/P_S, equals her marginal utility per dollar from movies, MU_M/P_M. That is,

$$MU_S/P_S = MU_M/P_M.$$

Multiply both sides of this equation by the price of soda, P_S, to obtain

$$MU_S = MU_M \times (P_S/P_M).$$

This equation says that the marginal utility from soda, MU_S, is equal to the marginal utility from movies, MU_M, multiplied by the ratio of the price of soda, P_S, to the price of a movie, P_M.

The ratio P_S/P_M is the relative price of soda in terms of movies: It is the number of movies that must be forgone to get 1 case of soda. It is also the opportunity cost of soda. (See Chapter 2, p. 33 and Chapter 3, p. 56.)

For Lisa, when $P_M = \$8$ and $P_S = \$4$ we observe that in a month she goes to the movies twice and buys 6 cases of soda. So we know that her MU_S from 6 cases of soda equals her MU_M from 2 movies multiplied by $\$4/\$8$ or 0.5. That is, for Lisa, the marginal utility from 6 cases of soda equals one-half of the marginal utility from 2 movies.

If we observe the choices that Lisa makes at more prices, we can find more rows in her utility schedule. By her choices, Lisa reveals her preferences.

Units of Utility Don't Matter   Lisa's marginal utility from 2 movies is a half of her marginal utility from 6 cases of soda. So if the marginal utility from the second movie is 40 units, then the marginal utility from the sixth case of soda is 20 units. But if we call the marginal utility from the second movie 50 units, then the marginal utility from the sixth case of soda is 25 units. The units of utility are arbitrary.

▶ REVIEW QUIZ

1 Why does a consumer spend the entire budget?
2 What is the marginal utility per dollar and how is it calculated?
3 What two conditions are met when a consumer is maximizing utility?
4 Explain why equalizing the marginal utility per dollar for all goods maximizes utility.

You can work these questions in Study Plan 7.2 and get instant feedback.   MyEconLab

You now understand the marginal utility theory of consumer choices. Your next task is to see what the theory predicts.

Predictions of Marginal Utility Theory

We're now going to use marginal utility theory to make some predictions. You will see that marginal utility theory predicts the law of demand. The theory also predicts that a fall in the price of a substitute of a good decreases the demand for the good and that for a normal good, a rise in income increases demand. All these effects, which in Chapter 3 we simply assumed, are predictions of marginal utility theory.

To derive these predictions, we will study the effects of three events:

- A fall in the price of a movie
- A rise in the price of soda
- A rise in income

A Fall in the Price of a Movie

With the price of a movie at $8 and the price of soda at $4, Lisa is maximizing utility by seeing 2 movies and buying 6 cases of soda each month. Then, with no change in her $40 income and no change in the price of soda, the price of a movie falls from $8 to $4. How does Lisa change her buying plans?

Finding the New Quantities of Movies and Soda
You can find the effect of a fall in the price of a movie on the quantities of movies and soda that Lisa buys in a three-step calculation.

1. Determine the just-affordable combinations of movies and soda at the new prices.
2. Calculate the new marginal utilities per dollar from the good whose price has changed.
3. Determine the quantities of movies and soda that make their marginal utilities per dollar equal.

Affordable Combinations The lower price of a movie means that Lisa can afford more movies or more soda. Table 7.3 shows her new affordable combinations. In row *A*, if she continues to see 2 movies a month, she can now afford 8 cases of soda and in row *B*, if she continues to buy 6 cases of soda, she can now afford 4 movies. Lisa can afford any of the combinations shown in the rows of Table 7.3.

The next step is to find her new marginal utilities per dollar from movies.

New Marginal Utilities per Dollar from Movies A person's preferences don't change just because a price has changed. With no change in her preferences, Lisa's marginal utilities in Table 7.3 are the same as those in Table 7.1. But because the price of a movie has changed, the marginal utility *per dollar* from movies changes. In fact, with a halving of the price of a movie from $8 to $4, the marginal utility per dollar from movies has doubled.

The numbers in Table 7.3 show Lisa's new marginal utility per dollar from movies for each quantity of movies. The table also shows Lisa's marginal utility per dollar from soda for each quantity.

Equalizing the Marginal Utilities per Dollar You can see that if Lisa continues to see 2 movies a month and buy 6 cases of soda, her marginal utility per dollar from movies (row *A*) is 10 units and her marginal utility per dollar from soda (row *B*) is 5 units. Lisa is buying too much soda and too few movies. If she spends a dollar more on movies and a dollar less on soda, her total utility increases by 5 units (10 − 5).

If Lisa continues to buy 6 cases of soda and increases the number of movies to 4 (row *B*), her

---

TABLE 7.3 How a Change in the Price of Movies Affects Lisa's Choices

	Movies ($4 each)			Soda ($4 per case)		
	Quantity	Marginal utility	Marginal utility per dollar	Cases	Marginal utility	Marginal utility per dollar
	0	0		10	5	1.25
	1	50	12.50	9	7	1.75
A	2	40	**10.00**	8	10	2.50
	3	32	8.00	7	13	3.25
B	4	28	7.00	**6**	20	**5.00**
	5	26	6.50	5	22	5.50
C	6	24	6.00	4	24	6.00
	7	22	5.50	3	36	9.00
	8	20	5.00	2	48	12.00
	9	17	4.25	1	75	18.75
	10	16	4.00	0	0	

marginal utility per dollar from movies falls to 7 units, but her marginal utility per dollar from soda is 5 units. Lisa is still buying too much soda and seeing too few movies. If she spends a dollar more on movies and a dollar less on soda, her total utility increases by 2 units (7 – 5).

But if Lisa sees 6 movies and buys 4 cases of soda a month (row C), her marginal utility per dollar from movies (6 units) equals her marginal utility per dollar from soda and she is maximizing utility. If Lisa moves from this allocation of her budget in either direction, her total utility decreases.

Lisa's increased purchases of movies results from a substitution effect—she substitutes the now lower-priced movies for soda—and an income effect—she can afford more movies.

A Change in the Quantity Demanded Lisa's increase in the quantity of movies that she sees is a change in the quantity demanded. It is the change in the quantity of movies that she plans to see each month when the price of a movie changes and all other influences on buying plans remain the same. We illustrate a change in the quantity demanded by a movement along a demand curve.

Figure 7.4(a) shows Lisa's demand curve for movies. When the price of a movie is $8, Lisa sees 2 movies a month. When the price of a movie falls to $4, she sees 6 movies a month. Lisa moves downward along her demand curve for movies.

The demand curve traces the quantities that maximize utility at each price, with all other influences remaining the same. You can also see that utility-maximizing choices generate a downward-sloping demand curve. Utility maximization with diminishing marginal utility implies the law of demand.

A Change in Demand The decrease in the quantity of soda that Lisa buys is the change in the quantity of soda that she plans to buy at a given price of soda when the price of a movie changes. It is a change in her demand for soda. We illustrate a change in demand by a shift of a demand curve.

Figure 7.4(b) shows Lisa's demand curve for soda. The price of soda is fixed at $4 a case. When the price of a movie is $8, Lisa buys 6 cases of soda on demand curve D_0. When the price of a movie falls to $4, Lisa buys 4 cases of soda on demand curve D_1. The fall in the price of a movie decreases Lisa's demand for soda. Her demand curve for soda shifts leftward. For Lisa, soda and movies are substitutes.

FIGURE 7.4   A Fall in the Price of a Movie

(a) Demand for movies

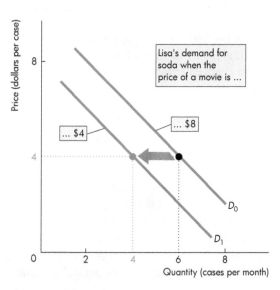

(b) Demand for soda

When the price of a movie falls and the price of soda remains the same, the quantity of movies demanded by Lisa increases, and in part (a), Lisa moves along her demand curve for movies. Also, when the price of a movie falls, Lisa's demand for soda decreases, and in part (b), her demand curve for soda shifts leftward. For Lisa, soda and movies are substitutes.

MyEconLab animation

A Rise in the Price of Soda

Now suppose that with the price of a movie at $4, the price of soda rises from $4 to $8 a case. How does this price change influence Lisa's buying plans? We find the answer by repeating the three-step calculation with the new price of soda.

Table 7.4 shows Lisa's new affordable combinations. In row *A*, if she continues to buy 4 cases of soda a month she can afford to see only 2 movies; and in row *B*, if she continues to see 6 movies a month, she can afford only 2 cases of soda.

Table 7.4 show Lisa's marginal utility per dollar from soda for each quantity of soda when the price is $8 a case. The table also shows Lisa's marginal utility per dollar from movies for each quantity.

If Lisa continues to buy 4 cases of soda (row *A*), her marginal utility per dollar from soda is 3. But she must cut the movies she sees to 2, which increases her marginal utility per dollar from movies to 10. Lisa is buying too much soda and too few movies. If she spends a dollar less on soda and a dollar more on movies, her utility increases by 7 units (10 – 3) .

But if Lisa sees 6 movies a month and cuts her soda to 2 cases (row *B*), her marginal utility per dollar from movies (6 units) equals her marginal utility per dollar from soda. She is maximizing utility.

Lisa's decreased purchases of soda results from an income effect—she can afford fewer cases and she buys fewer cases. But she continues to buy the same quantity of movies.

Lisa's Demand for Soda Now that we've calculated the effect of a change in the price of soda on Lisa's buying plans when income and the price of movies remain the same, we have found two points on her demand curve for soda: When the price of soda is $4 a case, Lisa buys 4 cases a month; and when the price of soda is $8 a case, she buys 2 cases a month.

Figure 7.5 shows these points on Lisa's demand curve for soda. It also shows the change in the quantity of soda demanded when the price of soda rises and all other influences on Lisa's buying plans remain the same.

In this example, Lisa continues to buy the same quantity of movies, but this outcome does not always occur. It is a consequence of Lisa's preferences. With different marginal utilities, she might have decreased or increased the quantity of movies that she sees when the price of soda changes.

You've seen that marginal utility theory predicts the law of demand—the way in which the quantity demanded of a good changes when its price changes. Next, we'll see how marginal utility theory predicts the effect of a change in income on demand.

TABLE 7.4   How a Change in the Price of Soda Affects Lisa's Choices

	Movies ($4 each)			Soda ($8 per case)		
	Quantity	Marginal utility	Marginal utility per dollar	Cases	Marginal utility	Marginal utility per dollar
	0	0		5	22	2.75
A	2	40	10.00	**4**	24	**3.00**
	4	28	7.00	3	36	4.50
B	6	24	6.00	2	48	6.00
	8	20	5.00	1	75	9.38
	10	16	4.00	0	0	

FIGURE 7.5   A Rise in the Price of Soda

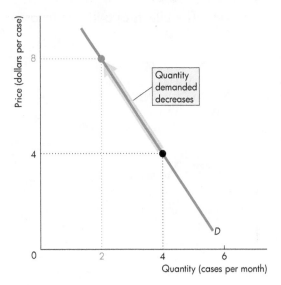

When the price of soda rises and the price of a movie and Lisa's income remain the same, the quantity of soda demanded by Lisa decreases. Lisa moves along her demand curve for soda.

A Rise in Income

Suppose that Lisa's income increases from $40 to $56 a month and that the price of a movie is $4 and the price of soda is $4 a case. With these prices and with an income of $40 a month, Lisa sees 6 movies and buys 4 cases of soda a month (Table 7.3). How does the increase in Lisa's income from $40 to $56 change her buying plans?

Table 7.5 shows the calculations needed to answer this question. If Lisa continues to see 6 movies a month, she can now afford to buy 8 cases of soda (row A); if she continues to buy 4 cases of soda, she can now afford to see 10 movies (row C).

In row A, Lisa's marginal utility per dollar from movies is greater than her marginal utility per dollar from soda. She is buying too much soda and too few movies. In row C, Lisa's marginal utility per dollar from movies is less than her marginal utility per dollar from soda. She is buying too little soda and too many movies. But in row B, when Lisa sees 8 movies a month and buys 6 cases of soda, her marginal utility per dollar from movies equals that from soda. She is maximizing utility.

Figure 7.6 shows the effects of the rise in Lisa's income on her demand curves for movies and soda. The price of each good is $4. When Lisa's income

TABLE 7.5 Lisa's Choices with an Income of $56 a Month

	Movies ($4 each)			Soda ($4 per case)		
	Quantity	Marginal utility	Marginal utility per dollar	Cases	Marginal utility	Marginal utility per dollar
	4	28	7.00	10	5	1.25
	5	26	6.50	9	7	1.75
A	6	24	**6.00**	8	10	2.50
	7	22	5.50	7	13	3.25
B	8	20	5.00	6	20	5.00
	9	17	4.25	5	22	5.50
C	10	16	4.00	**4**	24	**6.00**

rises to $56 a month, she sees 2 more movies and buys 2 more cases of soda. Her demand curves for both movies and soda shift rightward—her demand for both movies and soda increases. With a larger income, the consumer always buys more of a *normal* good. For Lisa, movies and soda are normal goods.

FIGURE 7.6 The Effects of a Rise in Income

(a) Demand for movies

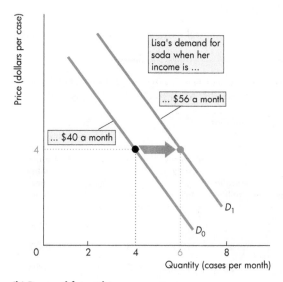

(b) Demand for soda

When Lisa's income increases, her demand for movies and her demand for soda increase. Lisa's demand curves for

movies, in part (a), and for soda, in part (b), shift rightward. For Lisa, movies and soda are normal goods.

The Paradox of Value

The price of water is low and the price of a diamond is high, but water is essential to life while diamonds are used mostly for decoration. How can valuable water be so cheap while a relatively useless diamond is so expensive? This so-called *paradox of value* has puzzled philosophers for centuries. Not until the theory of marginal utility had been developed could anyone give a satisfactory answer.

The Paradox Resolved The paradox is resolved by distinguishing between *total* utility and *marginal* utility. The total utility that we get from water is enormous. But remember, the more we consume of something, the smaller is its marginal utility.

We use so much water that its marginal utility—the benefit we get from one more glass of water or another 30 seconds in the shower—diminishes to a small value.

Diamonds, on the other hand, have a small total utility relative to water, but because we buy few diamonds, they have a high marginal utility.

When a household has maximized its total utility, it has allocated its income in the way that makes the marginal utility per dollar equal for all goods. That is, the marginal utility from a good divided by the price of the good is equal for all goods.

This equality of marginal utilities per dollar holds true for diamonds and water: Diamonds have a high price and a high marginal utility. Water has a low price and a low marginal utility. When the high marginal utility from diamonds is divided by the high price of a diamond, the result is a number that equals the low marginal utility from water divided by the low price of water. The marginal utility per dollar is the same for diamonds and water.

Value and Consumer Surplus Another way to think about the paradox of value and illustrate how it is resolved uses *consumer surplus*. Figure 7.7 explains the paradox of value by using this idea. The supply of water in part (a) is perfectly elastic at price P_W, so the quantity of water consumed is Q_W and the large green area shows the consumer surplus from water. The supply of diamonds in part (b) is perfectly inelastic at the quantity Q_D, so the price of a diamond is P_D and the small green area shows the consumer surplus from diamonds. Water is cheap, but brings a large consumer surplus; diamonds are expensive, but bring a small consumer surplus.

FIGURE 7.7   The Paradox of Value

(a) Water

(b) Diamonds

Part (a) shows the demand for and supply of water. Supply is perfectly elastic at the price P_W. At this price, the quantity of water consumed is Q_W and the large green triangle shows consumer surplus. Part (b) shows the demand for and supply of diamonds. Supply is perfectly inelastic at the quantity Q_D. At this quantity, the price of a diamond is P_D and the small green triangle shows consumer surplus. Water is valuable—has a large consumer surplus—but cheap. Diamonds are less valuable than water—have a smaller consumer surplus—but are expensive.

—— MyEconLab animation ——

Temperature: An Analogy

Utility is similar to temperature—both are abstract concepts. You can't *observe* temperature. You can observe water turning to steam if it is hot enough or turning to ice if it is cold enough. You can also construct an instrument—a thermometer—that can help you to predict when such changes will occur. We call the scale on the thermometer *temperature* and we call the units of temperature *degrees*. But like the units of utility, these degree units are arbitrary. We can use Celsius units or Fahrenheit units or some other units.

The concept of utility helps us to make predictions about consumption choices in much the same way that the concept of temperature helps us to make predictions about physical phenomena.

Admittedly, marginal utility theory does not enable us to predict how buying plans change with the same precision that a thermometer enables us to predict when water will turn to ice or steam. But the theory provides important insights into buying plans and has some powerful implications. It helps us to understand why people buy more of a good or service when its price falls and why people buy more of most goods when their incomes increase. It also resolves the paradox of value.

We're going to end this chapter by looking at some new ways of studying individual economic choices and consumer behavior.

REVIEW QUIZ

1   When the price of a good falls and the prices of other goods and a consumer's income remain the same, explain what happens to the consumption of the good whose price has fallen and to the consumption of other goods.

2   Elaborate on your answer to the previous question by using demand curves. For which good does demand change and for which good does the quantity demanded change?

3   If a consumer's income increases and if all goods are normal goods, explain how the quantity bought of each good changes.

4   What is the paradox of value and how is the paradox resolved?

5   What are the similarities between utility and temperature?

You can work these questions in Study Plan 7.3 and get instant feedback.   MyEconLab

Economics in Action
Maximizing Utility from Recorded Music

In 2011, Americans spent $7 billion on recorded music, down from more than $14 billion in 1999. But the combined quantity of discs and downloads bought increased from 1.2 billion in 1999 to 1.8 billion in 2011 and the average price of a unit of recorded music fell from $12.60 to $3.89.

The average price fell because the mix of formats bought changed dramatically. In 1999, we bought 940 million CDs; in 2011, we bought only 241 million CDs and downloaded almost 1.5 billion music files. Figure 1 shows the longer history of the changing formats of recorded music.

The music that we buy isn't just one good—it is several goods. Singles and albums are different goods; downloads and discs are different goods; and downloads to a computer and downloads to a cell phone are different goods. There are five major categories and the table shows the quantities of each that we bought in 2011 (excluding DVDs and cassettes).

Format	Singles	Albums
	(millions in 2011)	
Disc	2	241
Download	1,306	105
Mobile	116	–

Source of data: Recording Industry Association of America.

Most people buy all their music in digital form, but many still buy physical CDs and some people buy both downloads and CDs.

We get utility from the singles and albums that we buy, and the more songs and albums we have, the more utility we get. But our marginal utility from songs and albums decreases as the quantity that we own increases.

We also get utility from convenience. A song that we can buy with a mouse click and play with the spin of a wheel is more convenient both to buy and to use than a song on a CD. The convenience of songs downloaded over the Internet means that, song for song, we get more utility from a song downloaded than we get from a song on a physical CD.

But most albums are still played at home on a CD player. So for most people, a physical CD is a more convenient medium for delivering an album. Album for album, people on average get more utility from a CD than from a download.

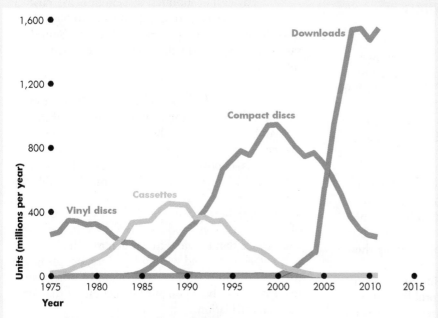

Figure 1 Changing Formats of Recorded Music

Sources of data: U.S. Census Bureau, *The 2012 Statistical Abstract*, Table 1140; and the Recording Industry Association of America.

In the 1970s, recorded music came on vinyl discs. Cassettes gradually replaced vinyl, then compact discs (CDs) gradually replaced cassettes, and today, digital files downloaded to computers and mobile devices are replacing physical CDs.

When we decide how many singles and albums to download and how many to buy on CD, we compare the marginal utility per dollar from each type of music in each format. We make the marginal utility per dollar from each type of music in each format equal, as the equations below show.

The market for single downloads has created an enormous consumer surplus. In 2011, 1,306 million singles were downloaded at an average price of $1.14. In the same year, 2 million singles were bought on a disc (either a CD or vinyl) at an average price of $4.76 a disc. If we assume that $4.76 is the most that anyone would pay for a single download (probably an underestimate), the demand curve for single downloads is that shown in Fig. 2.

With the average price of a single download at $1.14, consumer surplus (the area of the green triangle in Fig. 2) is $2.4 billion.

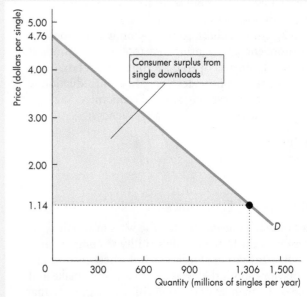

Figure 2 The Demand for Single Downloads

$$\frac{MU_{single\ downloads}}{P_{single\ downloads}} = \frac{MU_{album\ downloads}}{P_{album\ downloads}} = \frac{MU_{physical\ singles}}{P_{physical\ singles}} = \frac{MU_{physical\ albums}}{P_{physical\ albums}} = \frac{MU_{mobile}}{P_{mobile}}$$

$$\frac{MU_{single\ downloads}}{\$1.14} = \frac{MU_{album\ downloads}}{\$10.99} = \frac{MU_{physical\ singles}}{\$4.76} = \frac{MU_{physical\ albums}}{\$9.99} = \frac{MU_{mobile}}{\$2.39}$$

◆ New Ways of Explaining Consumer Choices

When William Stanley Jevons developed marginal utility theory in the 1860s, he would have loved to look inside people's brains and "see" their utility. But he believed that the human brain was the ultimate black box that could never be observed directly. For Jevons, and for most economists today, the purpose of marginal utility theory is to explain our *actions*, not what goes on inside our brains.

Economics has developed over the past 150 years with little help from and paying little attention to advances being made in psychology. Both economics and psychology seek to explain human behavior, but they have developed different ways of attacking the challenge.

A few researchers *have* paid attention to the potential payoff from exploring economic problems by using the tools of psychology. These researchers, some economists and some psychologists, think that marginal utility theory is based on a view of how people make choices that attributes too much to reason and rationality. They propose an alternative approach based on the methods of psychology.

Other researchers, some economists and some neuroscientists, are using new tools to look inside the human brain and open up Jevons' "black box."

This section provides a very brief introduction to these new and exciting areas of economics. We'll explore the two related research agendas:

- Behavioral economics
- Neuroeconomics

Behavioral Economics

Behavioral economics studies the ways in which limits on the human brain's ability to compute and implement rational decisions influences economic behavior—both the decisions that people make and the consequences of those decisions for the way markets work.

Behavioral economics starts with observed behavior. It looks for anomalies—choices that do not seem to be rational. It then tries to account for the anomalies by using ideas developed by psychologists that emphasize features of the human brain that limit rational choice.

In behavioral economics, instead of being rational utility maximizers, people are assumed to have three impediments that prevent rational choice: bounded rationality, bounded willpower, and bounded self-interest.

Bounded Rationality Bounded rationality is rationality that is limited by the computing power of the human brain. We can't always work out the rational choice.

For Lisa, choosing between movies and soda, it seems unlikely that she would have much trouble figuring out what to buy. But toss Lisa some uncertainty and the task becomes harder. She's read the reviews of "Ironman 2" on Fandango, but does she really want to see that movie? How much marginal utility will it give her? Faced with uncertainty, people might use rules of thumb, listen to the views of others, and make decisions based on gut instinct rather than on rational calculation.

Bounded Willpower Bounded willpower is the less-than-perfect willpower that prevents us from making a decision that we know, at the time of implementing the decision, we will later regret.

Lisa might be feeling particularly thirsty when she passes a soda vending machine. Under Lisa's rational utility-maximizing plan, she buys her soda at the discount store, where she gets it for the lowest possible price. Lisa has already bought her soda for this month, but it is at home. Spending $1 on a can now means giving up a movie later this month.

Lisa's rational choice is to ignore the temporary thirst and stick to her plan. But she might not possess the willpower to do so—sometimes she will and sometimes she won't.

Bounded Self-Interest Bounded self-interest is the limited self-interest that results in sometimes suppressing our own interests to help others.

A hurricane hits the Florida coast and Lisa, feeling sorry for the victims, donates $10 to a fund-raiser. She now has only $30 to spend on movies and soda this month. The quantities that she buys are not, according to her utility schedule, the ones that maximize her utility.

The main applications of behavioral economics are in two areas: finance, where uncertainty is a key factor in decision making, and savings, where the future is a key factor. But one behavior observed by behavioral economists is more general and might affect your choices. It is called the endowment effect.

The Endowment Effect The endowment effect is the tendency for people to value something more highly simply because they own it. If you have allocated your income to maximize utility, then the price you would be willing to accept to give up something that you own (for example, your coffee mug) should be the same as the price you are willing to pay for an identical one.

In experiments, students seem to display the endowment effect: The price they are willing to pay for a coffee mug that is identical to the one they own is less than the price they would be willing to accept to give up the coffee mug that they own. Behavioral economists say that this behavior contradicts marginal utility theory.

Neuroeconomics

Neuroeconomics is the study of the activity of the human brain when a person makes an economic decision. The discipline uses the observational tools and ideas of neuroscience to obtain a better understanding of economic decisions.

Neuroeconomics is an experimental discipline. In an experiment, a person makes an economic decision and the electrical or chemical activity of the person's brain is observed and recorded using the same type of equipment that neurosurgeons use to diagnose brain disorders.

The observations provide information about which regions of the brain are active at different points in the process of making an economic decision.

Observations show that some economic decisions generate activity in the area of the brain (called the prefrontal cortex) where we store memories, analyze data, and anticipate the consequences of our actions. If people make rational utility-maximizing decisions, it is in this region of the brain that the decision occurs.

But observations also show that some economic decisions generate activity in the region of the brain (called the hippocampus) where we store memories of anxiety and fear. Decisions that are influenced by activity in this part of the brain might not be rational and be driven by fear or panic.

Neuroeconomists are also able to observe the amount of a brain hormone (called dopamine), the quantity of which increases in response to pleasurable events and decreases in response to disappointing events. These observations might one day enable neuroeconomists to actually measure utility and shine a bright light inside what was once believed to be the ultimate black box.

Controversy

The new ways of studying consumer choice that we've briefly described here are being used more widely to study business decisions and decisions in financial markets, and this type of research is surely going to become more popular.

But behavioral economics and neuroeconomics generate controversy. Most economists hold the view of Jevons that the goal of economics is to explain the decisions that we observe people making and not to explain what goes on inside people's heads.

Most economists would prefer to probe apparent anomalies more deeply and figure out why they are not anomalies after all.

Economists also point to the power of marginal utility theory and its ability to explain consumer choice and demand as well as resolve the paradox of value.

REVIEW QUIZ

1 Define behavioral economics.
2 What are the three limitations on human rationality that behavioral economics emphasizes?
3 Define neuroeconomics.
4 What do behavioral economics and neuroeconomics seek to achieve?

You can work these questions in Study Plan 7.4 and get instant feedback.   MyEconLab

◆ You have now completed your study of the marginal utility theory and some new ideas about how people make economic choices. You can see marginal utility theory in action once again in *Reading Between the Lines* on pp. 170–171, where it is used to compare the effects of a tax on or a ban on big cups of sugary soft drinks.

Influencing Consumer Choice for Sugary Drinks

Drinks Groups Sue Over NY "Supersize" Ban

Financial Times
October 13, 2012

The U.S. beverage industry is taking the administration of Michael Bloomberg, New York mayor, to court over its decision to ban sales of "supersized" sugary drinks.

Trade groups led by the American Beverage Association filed a lawsuit late on Friday in New York state court attempting to block the rule, which is set to be imposed next spring.

Last month, New York's board of health voted to approve a proposal made by Mr. Bloomberg in May that would prohibit restaurants, theaters, and stadiums from selling sugary drinks in portions bigger than 16fl oz. ...

The lawsuit comes as the soda industry is locked in an increasingly contentious battle with regulators over labeling and taxation of their products. Industry groups are currently fighting soda tax proposals in two California cities and have successfully pushed back several other similar efforts. ...

Marc La Vorgna, a spokesman for Mr. Bloomberg, called the lawsuit baseless and suggested that the drinks industry would fail to stop the ban.

"For 100 years, major public health decisions—the posting of calorie counts, the ban of transfats, the sanitation of the sewage system, the fluoridation of the water system, and much more—have been left to a board of health professionals and it has benefited the health of New Yorkers," he said. "The mayor's plan to limit the size of sugary beverages—the leading contributor to the obesity epidemic—has spurred a long overdue national dialogue on obesity."

Copyright The Financial Times Limited 2012.

ESSENCE OF THE STORY

- New York City mayor Michael Bloomberg has banned the sale of sweetened drinks larger than 16 ounces at many venues.

- Two cities in California are considering placing a tax on sugar-sweetened beverages.

- Trade groups that sell these drinks are seeking court orders to block the ban and taxes.

- A spokesman for mayor Bloomberg says sugary drinks are the leading contributor to obesity and the ban is a public health measure like the sanitation system.

ECONOMIC ANALYSIS

■ Concerned that people are choosing to consume more sugary soda than is healthy, New York mayor Michael Bloomberg wants to ban large serves and the City of Richmond, CA, is considering a 1-penny-per-ounce tax.

■ Consumers choose to buy the quantity of sugary drinks that maximizes utility.

■ To do so, they make the marginal utility per dollar for all other goods and services equal to the marginal utility per dollar for sugary drinks. That is:

$$\frac{MU_O}{P_O} = \frac{MU_S}{P_S}.$$

■ Because of the way in which drinks are sold, there isn't a single price. The table shows some prices in St. Louis in June 2012.

Prices of Sugary Drinks

Size (ounces)	At the movies	At a 7-Eleven
20	4.00	1.09
32	4.50	1.29
44	5.00	1.49
52	5.50	1.69
104	[free refill]	

■ These prices tell us that people who buy their drinks in big cups pay a lower price per ounce.

■ Because a person who buys a 52-ounce cup gets a free refill, the price of the marginal ounce for that person is zero. With a price of zero, the buyer drinks the quantity at which marginal utility is also zero.

■ The suggestions for decreasing the consumption of sugary drinks are ways of raising the price.

■ A tax raises the price because the tax is added to the price received by the seller. A ban on large cups raises the price because the price per ounce is higher for small cups than for large cups. Both have a similar outcome.

■ Faced with a higher price of sugary drinks, a consumer maximizes utility by consuming a smaller quantity of sugary drinks.

■ The reason is that consumer equilibrium becomes

$$\frac{MU_O}{P_O} = \frac{MU_S}{(P_S + tax)}.$$

■ When a tax is imposed, the price doesn't rise by the entire amount of the tax, but generally $P_S + tax$ is greater than the price before that tax was imposed.

■ Because $P_S + tax$ is greater than P_S, MU_S must rise to restore the equality of the marginal utilities per dollar. But to increase MU_S, the quantity of sugary drinks consumed must decrease.

■ Figure 1 illustrates and makes clear why consumption of sugary drinks decreases.

■ Suppose that with no tax, the budget line is BL_0 and to make the marginal utilities per dollar equal, the consumer buys 60 ounces of drinks and 100 units of other goods and services per day.

■ A tax raises the price to $P_S + tax$ and the budget line becomes steeper as BL_1.

■ If the consumer continues to drink 60 ounces per day, the quantity of other items bought must fall to 50 units a day. MU_O rises and

$$\frac{MU_O}{P_O} > \frac{MU_S}{(P_S + tax)}.$$

■ To restore maximum utility, the consumer buys a smaller quantity of sugary drinks, which increases MU_S, and a greater quantity of other goods, which decreases MU_O. A movement up along the budget line BL_1 shows these changes in quantities consumed.

■ The consumer substitutes other goods and services for sugary drinks until

$$\frac{MU_O}{P_O} = \frac{MU_S}{(P_S + tax)}.$$

■ At this point, the consumer is again maximizing utility.

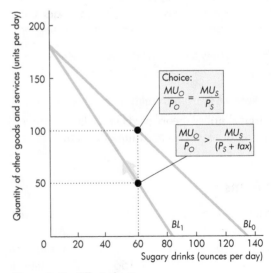

Figure 1 The Effect of a Tax

171

SUMMARY

Key Points

Consumption Choices (pp. 154–156)

- A household's consumption choices are determined by its consumption possibilities and preferences.
- A budget line defines a household's consumption possibilities.
- A household's preferences can be described by a utility schedule that lists the total utility and marginal utility derived from various quantities of goods and services consumed.
- The principle of diminishing marginal utility is that the marginal utility from a good or service decreases as consumption of the good or service increases.

Working Problems 1 to 5 will give you a better understanding of consumption choices.

Utility-Maximizing Choice (pp. 157–160)

- A consumer's objective is to maximize total utility.
- Total utility is maximized when all the available income is spent and when the marginal utility per dollar from all goods is equal.
- If the marginal utility per dollar for good *A* exceeds that for good *B*, total utility increases if the quantity purchased of good *A* increases and the quantity purchased of good *B* decreases.

Working Problems 6 to 11 will give you a better understanding of a consumer's utility-maximizing choice.

Predictions of Marginal Utility Theory (pp. 161–167)

- Marginal utility theory predicts the law of demand. That is, other things remaining the same, the higher the price of a good, the smaller is the quantity demanded of that good.
- Marginal utility theory also predicts that, other things remaining the same, an increase in the consumer's income increases the demand for a normal good.
- Marginal utility theory resolves the paradox of value.
- Total value is *total* utility or consumer surplus. But price is related to *marginal* utility.
- Water, which we consume in large amounts, has a high total utility and a large consumer surplus, but the price of water is low and the marginal utility from water is low.
- Diamonds, which we buy in small quantities, have a low total utility and a small consumer surplus, but the price of a diamond is high and the marginal utility from diamonds is high.

Working Problems 12 to 21 will give you a better understanding of the predictions of marginal utility theory.

New Ways of Explaining Consumer Choices (pp. 168–169)

- Behavioral economics studies limits on the ability of the human brain to compute and implement rational decisions.
- Bounded rationality, bounded willpower, and bounded self-interest are believed to explain some choices.
- Neuroeconomics uses the ideas and tools of neuroscience to study the effects of economic events and choices inside the human brain.

Working Problems 22 and 23 will give you a better understanding of the new ways of explaining consumer choices.

Key Terms

Behavioral economics, 168
Budget line, 154
Consumer equilibrium, 157
Diminishing marginal utility, 156

Marginal utility, 155
Marginal utility per dollar, 158
Neuroeconomics, 169
Preferences, 155

Total utility, 155
Utility, 155

STUDY PLAN PROBLEMS AND APPLICATIONS

MyEconLab   You can work Problems 1 to 23 in MyEconLab Chapter 7 Study Plan and get instant feedback.

Consumption Choices (Study Plan 7.1)

Jerry has $12 a week to spend on yogurt and magazines. The price of yogurt is $2, and the price of a magazine is $4.

1. List the combinations of yogurt and magazines that Jerry can afford. Draw a graph of Jerry's budget line with the quantity of magazines plotted on the *x*-axis.

2. Describe how Jerry's consumption possibilities change if, other things remaining the same, (i) the price of a magazine falls and (ii) Jerry's income increases.

Use the following data to work Problems 3 to 9.

Max enjoys windsurfing and snorkeling. Max has $35 a day to spend, and he can spend as much time as he likes on his leisure pursuits. The price of renting equipment for windsurfing is $10 an hour and for snorkeling is $5 an hour. The table shows the total utility Max gets from each activity.

Hours per day	Total utility from windsurfing	Total utility from snorkeling
1	120	40
2	220	76
3	300	106
4	360	128
5	396	140
6	412	150
7	422	158

3. Calculate Max's marginal utility from windsurfing at each number of hours per day. Does Max's marginal utility from windsurfing obey the principle of diminishing marginal utility?

4. Calculate Max's marginal utility from snorkeling at each number of hours per day. Does Max's marginal utility from snorkeling obey the principle of diminishing marginal utility?

5. Which does Max enjoy more: his 6th hour of windsurfing or his 6th hour of snorkeling?

Utility-Maximizing Choice (Study Plan 7.2)

6. Make a table that shows the various combinations of hours spent windsurfing and snorkeling that Max can afford.

7. In your table in Problem 6, add two columns and list Max's marginal utility per dollar from windsurfing and from snorkeling.

8. a. How many hours does Max windsurf and how many hours does he snorkel to maximize his utility?
   b. If Max spent a dollar more on windsurfing and a dollar less on snorkeling than in part (a), by how much would his total utility change?
   c. If Max spent a dollar less on windsurfing and a dollar more on snorkeling than in part (a), by how much would his total utility change?

9. Explain why, if Max equalized the marginal utility per hour from windsurfing and from snorkeling, he would *not* maximize his utility.

10. **Schools Get a Lesson in Lunch Line Economics**

    Sharp rises in the cost of milk, grain, and fresh fruits and vegetables are hitting cafeterias across the country, forcing cash-strapped schools to raise prices or serve more economical dishes. For example, Fairfax schools serve oranges —14¢ each—instead of grapes, which are 25¢ a serving.

    Source: *The Washington Post*, April 14, 2008

    Assume that a Fairfax school has a $14 daily fruit budget.

    a. How many oranges a day can the school afford to serve if it serves no grapes? How many servings of grapes can the school afford each day if it serves no oranges?
    b. If the school provides 50 oranges a day and maximizes utility, how many servings of grapes does it provide? If the marginal utility from an orange is 14 units, what is the marginal utility from a serving of grapes?

11. **Can Money Buy Happiness?**

    Whoever said money can't buy happiness isn't spending it right. There must be some connection, but once your basic human needs are met, does more money buy more happiness? An increase in income from $20,000 a year to $50,000 makes you twice as likely to be happy, but the payoff from more than $90,000 is slight.

    Source: CNN, July 18, 2006

a. What does the fundamental assumption of marginal utility theory suggest about the connection between money and happiness?

b. Explain why this news clip is consistent with marginal utility theory.

Predictions of Marginal Utility Theory

(Study Plan 7.3)

Use the data in Problem 3 to work Problems 12 to 16.

12. Max is offered a special deal: The price of renting windsurfing equipment is cut to $5 an hour. How many hours does Max spend windsurfing and how many hours does he spend snorkeling?

13. Draw Max's demand curve for rented windsurfing equipment. Over the price range from $5 to $10 an hour, is Max's demand for windsurfing equipment elastic or inelastic?

14. How does Max's demand for snorkeling equipment change when the price of windsurfing equipment falls? What is Max's cross elasticity of demand for snorkeling with respect to the price of windsurfing? Are windsurfing and snorkeling substitutes or complements for Max?

15. If Max's income increases from $35 to $55 a day, how does his demand for rented windsurfing equipment change? Is windsurfing a normal good or an inferior good for Max? Explain.

16. If Max's income increases from $35 to $55 a day, how does his demand for rented snorkeling equipment change? Is snorkeling a normal good or an inferior good for Max? Explain.

Use the following news clip to work Problems 17 and 18.

Compared to Other Liquids, Gasoline is Cheap

In 2008, when gasoline hit $4 a gallon, motorists complained, but they didn't complain about $1.59 for a 20-oz Gatorade and $18 for 16 mL of HP ink.

Source: *The New York Times*, May 27, 2008

The prices per gallon are $10.17 for Gatorade and $4,294.58 for printer ink.

17. a. What does marginal utility theory predict about the marginal utility per dollar from gasoline, Gatorade, and printer ink?

b. What do the prices per gallon tell you about the marginal utility from a gallon of gasoline, Gatorade, and printer ink?

18. a. What do the prices per unit reported in the news clip tell you about the marginal utility from a gallon of gasoline, a 20-oz bottle of Gatorade, and a cartridge of printer ink?

b. How can the paradox of value be used to explain why the fluids listed in the news clip might be less valuable than gasoline, yet far more expensive?

Use the following news clip to work Problems 19 to 21.

Exclusive Status: It's in the Bag; $52,500 Purses. 24 Worldwide. 1 in Washington.

Forget your Coach purse. Put away your Kate Spade. Even Hermes's famous Birkin bag seems positively discount. The Louis Vuitton Tribute Patchwork is this summer's ultimate status bag, ringing in at $52,500, and the company is offering only five for sale in North America and 24 worldwide.

Source: *The Washington Post*, August 21, 2007

19. Use marginal utility theory to explain the facts reported in the news clip.

20. If Louis Vuitton offered 500 Tribute Patchwork bags in North America and 2,400 worldwide, what do you predict would happen to the price that buyers would be willing to pay and what would happen to the consumer surplus?

21. If the Tribute Patchwork bag is copied and thousands are sold illegally, what do you predict would happen to the price that buyers would be willing to pay for a genuine bag and what would happen to the consumer surplus?

New Ways of Explaining Consumer Choices

(Study Plan 7.4)

Use the following news clip to work Problems 22 and 23.

Eating Away the Innings in Baseball's Cheap Seats

Baseball and gluttony, two of America's favorite pastimes, are merging and taking hold at Major League Baseball stadiums: all-you-can-eat seats. Some fans try to "set personal records" during their first game in the section, but by their second or third time in such seats they eat normally, just as they would at a game.

Source: *USA Today*, March 6, 2008

22. a. What conflict might exist between utility-maximization and setting "personal records" for eating?

b. What does the fact that fans eat less at subsequent games indicate about the marginal utility from ballpark food as the quantity consumed increases?

23. a. How can setting personal records for eating be reconciled with marginal utility theory?

b. Which ideas of behavioral economics are consistent with the information in the news clip?

ADDITIONAL PROBLEMS AND APPLICATIONS

MyEconLab   You can work these problems in MyEconLab if assigned by your instructor.

Consumption Choices

24. Tim buys 2 pizzas and sees 1 movie a week when he has $16 to spend, a movie ticket is $8, and a pizza is $4. Draw Tim's budget line. If the price of a movie ticket falls to $4, describe how Tim's consumption possibilities change.

25. Cindy has $70 a month to spend, and she can spend as much time as she likes playing golf and tennis. The price of an hour of golf is $10, and the price of an hour of tennis is $5. The table shows Cindy's marginal utility from each sport.

Hours per month	Marginal utility from golf	Marginal utility from tennis
1	80	40
2	60	36
3	40	30
4	30	10
5	20	5
6	10	2
7	6	1

Make a table that shows Cindy's affordable combinations of hours playing golf and tennis. If Cindy increases her expenditure to $100, describe how her consumption possibilities change.

Utility-Maximizing Choice

Use the information in Problem 25 to work Problems 26 and 27.

26. a. When Cindy has $70 to spend on golf and tennis, how many hours of golf and how many hours of tennis does she play to maximize her utility?
    b. Compared to part (a), if Cindy spent a dollar more on golf and a dollar less on tennis, by how much would her total utility change?
    c. Compared to part (a), if Cindy spent a dollar less on golf and a dollar more on tennis, by how much would her total utility change?

27. Explain why, if Cindy equalized the marginal utility per hour of golf and tennis, she would *not* maximize her utility.

Predictions of Marginal Utility Theory

28. Use the information in Problem 25. Cindy's tennis club raises its price of an hour of tennis to $10. The price of golf remains at $10 an hour and Cindy continues to spend $70 on tennis and golf.
    a. List the combinations of hours spent playing golf and tennis that Cindy can now afford.
    b. Along with the combinations in part (a), list Cindy's marginal utility per dollar from golf and from tennis.
    c. How many hours does Cindy now spend playing golf and how many hours does she spend playing tennis?

Use the information in Problems 25, 26, and 28 to work Problems 29 to 32.

29. Use your answers to Problems 26a and 28 to draw Cindy's demand curve for tennis. Over the price range of $5 to $10 an hour of tennis, is Cindy's demand for tennis elastic or inelastic?

30. Use your answers to Problems 26a and 28 to explain how Cindy's demand for golf changed when the price of an hour of tennis increased. What is Cindy's cross elasticity of demand for golf with respect to the price of tennis? Are tennis and golf substitutes or complements for Cindy?

31. Cindy loses her math tutoring job and the amount she has to spend on golf and tennis falls to $35 a month. How does Cindy's demand for golf change? For Cindy, is golf a normal good or an inferior good? Is tennis a normal good or an inferior good?

32. Cindy takes a Club Med vacation, the cost of which includes unlimited sports activities. With no extra charge for golf and tennis, Cindy allocates a total of 4 hours a day to these activities.
    a. How many hours does Cindy play golf and how many hours does she play tennis?
    b. What is Cindy's marginal utility from golf and from tennis?
    c. Why does Cindy equalize the marginal utilities rather than the marginal utility per dollar from golf and from tennis?

33. **Blu-Ray Format Expected to Dominate, but When?**

    Blu-ray stomped HD DVD to become the standard format for high-definition movie discs, but when will it claim victory over the old DVD? Buyers of $2,000, 40-inch TVs are the ones that will lead the charge. Everyone else will follow when the price falls. Blu-ray machine prices are now starting to drop and Wal-Mart Stores Inc. began stocking a $298 Magnavox model. That's cheaper than most alternatives, but a hefty price hike from a typical $50 DVD player.

    Source: *CNN*, June 2, 2008

    a. What does marginal utility theory predict about the marginal utility from a Magnavox Blu-ray machine compared to the marginal utility from a typical DVD player?

    b. What will have to happen to the marginal utility from a Blu-ray machine before it is able to "claim victory over the old DVD"?

34. Ben spends $50 a year on 2 bunches of flowers and $50 a year on 10,000 gallons of tap water. Ben is maximizing utility and his marginal utility from water is 0.5 unit per gallon.

    a. Are flowers or water more valuable to Ben?

    b. Explain how Ben's expenditure on flowers and water illustrates the paradox of value.

New Ways of Explaining Consumer Choices

Use the following news clip to work Problems 35 to 37.

Putting a Price on Human Life

Researchers at Stanford and the University of Pennsylvania estimated that a healthy human life is worth about $129,000. Using Medicare records on treatment costs for kidney dialysis as a benchmark, the authors tried to pinpoint the threshold beyond which ensuring another "quality" year of life was no longer financially worthwhile. The study comes amid debate over whether Medicare should start rationing health care on the basis of cost effectiveness.

Source: *Time*, June 9, 2008

35. Why might Medicare ration health care according to treatment that is "financially worthwhile" as opposed to providing as much treatment as is needed by a patient, regardless of costs?

36. What conflict might exist between a person's valuation of his or her own life and the rest of society's valuation of that person's life?

37. How does the potential conflict between self-interest and the social interest complicate setting a financial threshold for Medicare treatments?

Economics in the News

38. After you have studied *Reading Between the Lines* (pp. 170–171), answer the following questions.

    a. If big cups of sugary drinks are banned at restaurants, theaters, and stadiums:

       (i)   How will the price of an ounce of sugary drink change?

       (ii) How will consumers respond to the change in price?

    b. If a tax is imposed on sugary drinks, how does

       (i)   The marginal utility of a sugary drink change?

       (ii) The consumer surplus in the market for sugary drinks change?

39. **Five Signs You Have Too Much Money**

    When a bottle of water costs $38, it's hard not to agree that bottled water is a fool's drink. The drink of choice among image-conscious status seekers and high-end tee-totalers in L.A. is Bling H2O. It's not the water that accounts for the cost of the $38, but the "limited edition" bottle decked out in Swarovski crystals.

    Source: *CNN*, January 17, 2006

    a. Assuming that the price of a bottle of Bling H2O is $38 in all the major U.S. cities, what might its popularity in Los Angeles reveal about consumers' incomes or preferences in Los Angeles relative to other U.S. cities?

    b. Why might the marginal utility from a bottle of Bling H2O decrease more rapidly than the marginal utility from ordinary bottled water?

40. **How to Buy Happiness. Cheap**

    On any day, the rich tend to be a bit happier than the poor, but increases in average living standards don't seem to make people happier. The average American's income is up 80% since 1972, but the percentage describing themselves as "very happy" (roughly a third) hasn't changed. As living standards increase, most of us respond by raising our own standards: Things that once seemed luxuries now are necessities and we work harder to buy stuff that satisfies us less and less.

    Source: *CNN*, October 1, 2004

    According to the news clip,

    a. How do widespread increases in living standards influence total utility?

    b. How do total utility and marginal utility from consumption change over time?

Making the Most of Life

The powerful forces of demand and supply shape the fortunes of families, businesses, nations, and empires in the same unrelenting way that the tides and winds shape rocks and coastlines. You saw in Chapters 3 through 6 how these forces raise and lower prices, increase and decrease quantities bought and sold, cause revenues to fluctuate, and send resources to their most valuable uses.

These powerful forces begin quietly and privately with the choices that each one of us makes. Chapter 7 probes these individual choices, offering two alternative approaches to explaining both consumption plans and the allocation of time. These explanations of consumption plans can also explain "non-economic" choices, such as whether to marry and how many children to have. In a sense, there are no non-economic choices. If there is scarcity, there must be choice, and economics studies all choices.

The earliest economists (Adam Smith and his contemporaries) did not have a very deep understanding of households' choices. It was not until the nineteenth century that progress was made in this area when Jeremy Bentham (below) introduced the concept of utility and applied it to the study of human choices. Today, Steven Levitt, whom you will meet on the following page, is one of the most influential students of human behavior.

Jeremy Bentham *(1748–1832), who lived in London, was the son and grandson of lawyers and was himself trained as a barrister. But Bentham rejected the opportunity to maintain the family tradition and, instead, spent his life as a writer, activist, and Member of Parliament in the pursuit of rational laws that would bring the greatest happiness to the greatest number of people.*

Bentham, whose embalmed body is preserved to this day in a glass cabinet in the University of London, was the first person to use the concept of utility to explain human choices. But in Bentham's day, the distinction between explaining and prescribing was not a sharp one, and Bentham was ready to use his ideas to tell people how they ought to behave. He was one of the first to propose pensions for the retired, guaranteed employment, minimum wages, and social benefits such as free education and free medical care.

"... It is the greatest happiness of the greatest number that is the measure of right and wrong."

JEREMY BENTHAM
Fragment on Government

> I think of economics as being primarily about a way of looking at the world and a set of tools for thinking clearly.

STEVEN D. LEVITT is William B. Ogden Distinguished Service Professor of Economics at the University of Chicago. Born in Minneapolis, he was an undergraduate at Harvard and a graduate student at MIT. Among his many honors, he was recently awarded the John Bates Clark Medal, given to the best economist under 40.

Professor Levitt has studied an astonishingly wide range of human choices and their outcomes. He has examined the effects of policing on crime, shown that real estate agents get a higher price when they sell their own homes than when they sell other people's, devised a test to detect cheating teachers, and studied the choices of drug dealers and gang members. Much of this research has been popularized in Freakonomics (Steven D. Levitt and Stephen J. Dubner, HarperCollins, 2005). What unifies this apparently diverse body of research is the use of natural experiments. Professor Levitt has an incredible ability to find just the right set of events and the data the events have generated to enable him to isolate the effect he's looking for.

Michael Parkin talked with Steven Levitt about his work and what economists have discovered about how people respond to incentives.

Why did you become an economist?

As a freshman in college, I took introductory economics. All the ideas made perfect sense to me—it was the way I naturally thought. My friends were befuddled. I thought, "This is the field for me!"

The idea of rational choice made at the margin lies at the heart of economics. Would you say that your work generally supports that idea or challenges it? Can you provide some examples?

I don't like the word "rational" in this context. I think economists model agents as being rational just for convenience. What really matters is whether people respond to incentives. My work very much supports the idea that humans in all types of circumstances respond strongly to incentives. I've seen it with drug dealers, auto thieves, sumo wrestlers, real estate agents, and elementary school teachers, just to name a few examples.

Drug dealers, for instance, want to make money, but they also want to avoid being arrested or even killed. In the data we have on drug sellers, we see that when the drug trade is more lucrative, dealers are willing to take greater risks of arrest to carve out a share of the market.... Sumo wrestlers, on the other hand, care mostly about their official ranking. Sometimes matches occur where one wrestler has more to lose or gain than the other wrestler. We find that sumo wrestlers make corrupt deals to make sure the wrestler who wins is the one who needs to win.

Why is an economist interested in crime and cheating?

I think of economics as being primarily about a way of looking at the world and a set of tools for thinking clearly. The topics you apply these tools to are unlimited. That is why I think economics has been so powerful. If you understand economics and use the tools wisely, you will be a better business person, doctor, public servant, parent.

*Read the full interview with Steven Levitt in MyEconLab.

8

ORGANIZING PRODUCTION

After studying this chapter, you will be able to:

- ◆ Explain the economic problem that all firms face
- ◆ Distinguish between technological efficiency and economic efficiency
- ◆ Define and explain the principal–agent problem
- ◆ Distinguish among different types of markets
- ◆ Explain why markets coordinate some economic activities and why firms coordinate others

In the fall of 1990, a British scientist named Tim Berners-Lee invented the World Wide Web, a remarkable idea that paved the way for the creation of thousands of profitable businesses such as Facebook, Twitter, Apple, and Google.

How do firms make their business decisions?

That's the question you study in this chapter. In *Reading Between the Lines* at the end of the chapter, we'll apply some of what you've learned and look at some of the choices made by Facebook and Google in an Internet advertising game.

179

[handwritten: TC=R-C.]

The Firm and Its Economic Problem

The 20 million firms in the United States differ in size and in the scope of what they do, but they all perform the same basic economic functions. Each **firm** is an institution that hires factors of production and organizes those factors to produce and sell goods and services. Our goal is to predict firms' behavior. To do so, we need to know a firm's goal and the constraints it faces. We start with the goal.

The Firm's Goal

When economists ask entrepreneurs what they are trying to achieve, they get many different answers. Some talk about making a high-quality product, others about business growth, others about market share, others about the job satisfaction of their workforce, and an increasing number today talk about social and environmental responsibility. All of these goals are pursued by firms, but they are not the fundamental goal: They are the means to that goal.

A firm's goal is to maximize profit. A firm that does not seek to maximize profit is either eliminated or taken over by a firm that does seek that goal.

What is the profit that a firm seeks to maximize? To answer this question, we'll look at Campus Sweaters, Inc., a small producer of knitted sweaters owned and operated by Cindy.

Accounting Profit

[handwritten: 400-80-20 -120-5 -5 =170]

In 2012, Campus Sweaters received $400,000 for the sweaters it sold and paid out $80,000 for wool, $20,000 for utilities, $120,000 for wages, $5,000 for the lease of a computer, and $5,000 in interest on a bank loan. These expenses total $230,000, so the firm had a cash surplus of $170,000.

To measure the profit of Campus Sweaters, Cindy's accountant subtracted $20,000 for the depreciation of buildings and knitting machines from the $170,000 cash surplus. *Depreciation* is the fall in the value of a firm's capital. To calculate depreciation, accountants use Internal Revenue Service rules based on standards established by the Financial Accounting Standards Board. Using these rules, Cindy's accountant calculated that Campus Sweaters made a profit of $150,000 in 2012.

Economic Accounting

[handwritten: total cost = opportunity cost of production.]

Accountants measure a firm's profit to ensure that the firm pays the correct amount of income tax and to show its investors how their funds are being used.

Economists measure a firm's profit to enable them to predict the firm's decisions, and the goal of these decisions is to maximize *economic profit*. **Economic profit** is equal to total revenue minus total cost, with total cost measured as the *opportunity cost of production*.

A Firm's Opportunity Cost of Production

The *opportunity cost* of any action is the highest-valued alternative forgone. The *opportunity cost of production* is the value of the best alternative use of the resources that a firm uses in production.

A firm's opportunity cost of production is the value of real alternatives forgone. We express opportunity cost in money units so that we can compare and add up the value of the alternatives forgone.

A firm's opportunity cost of production is the sum of the cost of using resources

- Bought in the market
- Owned by the firm
- Supplied by the firm's owner

Resources Bought in the Market A firm incurs an opportunity cost when it buys resources in the market. The amount spent on these resources is an opportunity cost of production because the firm could have bought different resources to produce some other good or service. For Campus Sweaters, the resources bought in the market are wool, utilities, labor, a leased computer, and a bank loan. The $230,000 spent on these items in 2012 could have been spent on something else, so it is an opportunity cost of producing sweaters.

Resources Owned by the Firm A firm incurs an opportunity cost when it uses its own capital. The cost of using capital owned by the firm is an opportunity cost of production because the firm could sell the capital that it owns and rent capital from another firm. When a firm uses its own capital, it implicitly rents it from itself. In this case, the firm's opportunity cost of using the capital it owns is called the **implicit rental rate** of capital. The implicit rental rate of capital has two components: economic depreciation and forgone interest.

Economic Depreciation Accountants measure *depreciation*, the fall in the value of a firm's capital, using formulas that are unrelated to the change in the market value of capital. **Economic depreciation** is the fall in the *market value* of a firm's capital over a given period. It equals the market price of the capital at the beginning of the period minus the market price of the capital at the end of the period.

Suppose that Campus Sweaters could have sold its buildings and knitting machines on January 1, 2012, for $400,000 and that it can sell the same capital on December 31, 2012, for $375,000. The firm's economic depreciation during 2012 is $25,000 ($400,000 – $375,000). This forgone $25,000 is an opportunity cost of production.

Forgone Interest The funds used to buy capital could have been used for some other purpose, and in their next best use, they would have earned interest. This forgone interest is an opportunity cost of production.

Suppose that Campus Sweaters used $300,000 of its own funds to buy capital. If the firm invested its $300,000 in bonds instead of a knitting factory (and rented the capital it needs to produce sweaters), it would have earned $15,000 a year in interest. This forgone interest is an opportunity cost of production.

Resources Supplied by the Firm's Owner A firm's owner might supply *both* entrepreneurship and labor.

Entrepreneurship The factor of production that organizes a firm and makes its decisions might be supplied by the firm's owner or by a hired entrepreneur. The return to entrepreneurship is profit, and the profit that an entrepreneur earns *on average* is called **normal profit**. Normal profit is the cost of entrepreneurship and is an opportunity cost of production.

If Cindy supplies entrepreneurial services herself, and if the normal profit she can earn on these services is $45,000 a year, this amount is an opportunity cost of production at Campus Sweaters.

Owner's Labor Services *In addition* to supplying entrepreneurship, the owner of a firm might supply labor but not take a wage. The opportunity cost of the owner's labor is the wage income forgone by not taking the best alternative job.

If Cindy supplies labor to Campus Sweaters, and if the wage she can earn on this labor at another firm is $55,000 a year, this amount of wages forgone is an opportunity cost of production at Campus Sweaters.

Economic Accounting: A Summary

Table 8.1 summarizes the economic accounting. Campus Sweaters' total revenue is $400,000; its opportunity cost of production is $370,000; and its economic profit is $30,000.

Cindy's personal income is the $30,000 of economic profit plus the $100,000 that she earns by supplying resources to Campus Sweaters.

Decisions

To achieve the objective of maximum economic profit, a firm must make five decisions:

1. What to produce and in what quantities
2. How to produce
3. How to organize and compensate its managers and workers
4. How to market and price its products
5. What to produce itself and buy from others

In all these decisions, a firm's actions are limited by the constraints that it faces. Your next task is to learn about these constraints.

TABLE 8.1   Economic Accounting

Item		Amount
Total Revenue		**$400,000**
Cost of Resources Bought in Market		
Wool	$80,000	
Utilities	20,000	
Wages	120,000	
Computer lease	5,000	
Bank interest	5,000	$230,000
Cost of Resources Owned by Firm		
Economic depreciation	$25,000	
Forgone interest	15,000	$40,000
Cost of Resources Supplied by Owner		
Cindy's normal profit	$45,000	
Cindy's forgone wages	55,000	$100,000
Opportunity Cost of Production		**$370,000**
Economic Profit		**$30,000**

The Firm's Constraints

Three features of a firm's environment limit the maximum economic profit it can make. They are

- Technology constraints
- Information constraints
- Market constraints

Technology Constraints Economists define technology broadly. A **technology** is any method of producing a good or service. Technology includes the detailed designs of machines and the layout of the workplace. It includes the organization of the firm. For example, the shopping mall is one technology for producing retail services. It is a different technology from the catalog store, which in turn is different from the downtown store.

It might seem surprising that a firm's profit is limited by technology because it seems that technological advances are constantly increasing profit opportunities. Almost every day, we learn about some new technological advance that amazes us. With computers that speak and recognize our own speech and cars that can find the address we need in a city we've never visited, we can accomplish more than ever.

Technology advances over time. But at each point in time, to produce more output and gain more revenue, a firm must hire more resources and incur greater costs. The increase in profit that a firm can achieve is limited by the technology available. For example, by using its current plant and workforce, Ford can produce some maximum number of cars per day. To produce more cars per day, Ford must hire more resources, which increases its costs and limits the increase in profit that it can make by selling the additional cars.

Information Constraints We never possess all the information we would like to have to make decisions. We lack information about both the future and the present. For example, suppose you plan to buy a new computer. When should you buy it? The answer depends on how the price is going to change in the future. Where should you buy it? The answer depends on the prices at hundreds of different computer stores. To get the best deal, you must compare the quality and prices in every store. But the opportunity cost of this comparison exceeds the cost of the computer!

A firm is constrained by limited information about the quality and efforts of its workforce, the current and future buying plans of its customers, and the plans of its competitors. Workers might make too little effort, customers might switch to competing suppliers, and a competitor might enter the market and take some of the firm's business.

To address these problems, firms create incentives to boost workers' efforts even when no one is monitoring them; conduct market research to lower uncertainty about customers' buying plans, and "spy" on each other to anticipate competitive challenges. But these efforts don't eliminate incomplete information and uncertainty, which limit the economic profit that a firm can make.

Market Constraints The quantity each firm can sell and the price it can obtain are constrained by its customers' willingness to pay and by the prices and marketing efforts of other firms. Similarly, the resources that a firm can buy and the prices it must pay for them are limited by the willingness of people to work for and invest in the firm. Firms spend billions of dollars a year marketing and selling their products. Some of the most creative minds strive to find the right message that will produce a knockout television advertisement. Market constraints and the expenditures firms make to overcome them limit the profit a firm can make.

REVIEW QUIZ

1 What is a firm's fundamental goal and what happens if the firm doesn't pursue this goal?
2 Why do accountants and economists calculate a firm's cost and profit in different ways?
3 What are the items that make opportunity cost differ from the accountant's measure of cost?
4 Why is normal profit an opportunity cost?
5 What are the constraints that a firm faces? How does each constraint limit the firm's profit?

You can work these questions in Study
Plan 8.1 and get instant feedback.   MyEconLab

In the rest of this chapter and in Chapters 9 through 11, we study the choices that firms make. You're going to learn how we can predict a firm's decisions as those that maximize profit given the constraints the firm faces. We begin by taking a closer look at a firm's technology constraints.

◆ Technological and Economic Efficiency

Microsoft employs a large workforce, and most Microsoft workers possess a large amount of human capital. But the firm uses a small amount of physical capital. In contrast, a coal-mining company employs a huge amount of mining equipment (physical capital) and almost no labor. Why? The answer lies in the concept of efficiency. There are two concepts of production efficiency: technological efficiency and economic efficiency. **Technological efficiency** occurs when the firm produces a given output by using the least amount of inputs. **Economic efficiency** occurs when the firm produces a given output at the least cost. Let's explore the two concepts of efficiency by studying an example.

Suppose that there are four alternative techniques for making TVs:

A. *Robot production.* One person monitors the entire computer-driven process.
B. *Production line.* Workers specialize in a small part of the job as the emerging TV passes them on a production line.
C. *Hand-tool production.* A single worker uses a few hand tools to make a TV.
D. *Bench production.* Workers specialize in a small part of the job but walk from bench to bench to perform their tasks.

Table 8.2 sets out the amounts of labor and capital required by each of these four methods to make 10 TVs a day.

Which of these alternative methods are technologically efficient?

Technological Efficiency

Recall that *technological efficiency* occurs when the firm produces a given output by using the least amount of inputs. Look at the numbers in the table and notice that method A uses the most capital and the least labor. Method C uses the most labor and the least capital. Method B and method D lie between the two extremes. They use less capital and more labor than method A and less labor but more capital than method C.

Compare methods B and D. Method D requires 100 workers and 10 units of capital to produce 10

TABLE 8.2   Four Ways of Making 10 TVs a Day

	Method	Quantities of inputs	
		Labor	Capital
A	Robot production	1	1,000
B	Production line	10	10
C	Hand-tool production	1,000	1
D	Bench production	100	10

TVs. Those same 10 TVs can be produced by method B with 10 workers and the same 10 units of capital. Because method D uses the same amount of capital and more labor than method B, method D is not technologically efficient.

Are any of the other methods not technologically efficient? The answer is no. Each of the other methods is technologically efficient. Method A uses more capital but less labor than method B, and method C uses more labor but less capital than method B.

Which of the methods are economically efficient?

Economic Efficiency

Recall that *economic efficiency* occurs when the firm produces a given output at the least cost.

Method D, which is technologically inefficient, is also economically inefficient. It uses the same amount of capital as method B but 10 times as much labor, so it costs more. A technologically inefficient method is never economically efficient.

One of the three technologically efficient methods is economically efficient. The other two are economically inefficient. But which method is economically efficient depends on factor prices.

In Table 8.3(a), the wage rate is $75 per day and the rental rate of capital is $250 per day. By studying Table 8.3(a), you can see that method B has the lowest cost and is the economically efficient method.

In Table 8.3(b), the wage rate is $150 a day and the rental rate of capital is $1 a day. Looking at Table 8.3(b), you can see that method A has the lowest cost and is the economically efficient method. In this case, capital is so cheap relative to labor that the

TABLE 8.3   The Costs of Different Ways of Making 10 TVs a Day

(a) Wage rate $75 per day; Capital rental rate $250 per day

Method	Inputs Labor	Inputs Capital	Labor cost ($75 per day)		Capital cost ($250 per day)		Total cost
A	1	1,000	$75	+	$250,000	=	$250,075
B	10	10	750	+	2,500	=	3,250
C	1,000	1	75,000	+	250	=	75,250

(b) Wage rate $150 per day; Capital rental rate $1 per day

Method	Inputs Labor	Inputs Capital	Labor cost ($150 per day)		Capital cost ($1 per day)		Total cost
A	1	1,000	$150	+	$1,000	=	$1,150
B	10	10	1,500	+	10	=	1,510
C	1,000	1	150,000	+	1	=	150,001

(c) Wage rate $1 per day; Capital rental rate $1,000 per day

Method	Inputs Labor	Inputs Capital	Labor cost ($1 per day)		Capital cost ($1,000 per day)		Total cost
A	1	1,000	$1	+	$1,000,000	=	$1,000,001
B	10	10	10	+	10,000	=	10,010
C	1,000	1	1,000	+	1,000	=	2,000

method that uses the most capital is the economically efficient method.

In Table 8.3(c), the wage rate is $1 a day and the rental rate of capital is $1,000 a day. You can see that method C has the lowest cost and is the economically efficient method. In this case, labor is so cheap relative to capital that the method that uses the most labor is the economically efficient method.

Economic efficiency depends on the relative costs of resources. The economically efficient method is the one that uses a smaller amount of the more expensive resource and a larger amount of the less expensive resource.

A firm that is not economically efficient does not maximize profit. Natural selection favors efficient firms and inefficient firms disappear. Inefficient firms go out of business or are taken over by firms that produce at lower costs.

1 Is a firm technologically efficient if it uses the latest technology? Why or why not?

2 Is a firm economically inefficient if it can cut its costs by producing less? Why or why not?

3 Explain the key distinction between technological efficiency and economic efficiency.

4 Why do some firms use large amounts of capital and small amounts of labor while others use small amounts of capital and large amounts of labor?

You can work these questions in Study Plan 8.2 and get instant feedback.   MyEconLab

Next we study the information constraints that firms face and the wide array of organization structures these constraints generate.

◢ Information and Organization

Each firm organizes the production of goods and services using a combination of two systems:

- Command systems
- Incentive systems

Command Systems

A **command system** is a method of organizing production that uses a managerial hierarchy. Commands pass downward through the hierarchy, and information passes upward.

The military uses the purest form of command system. A commander-in-chief makes the big decisions about strategic goals. Beneath this highest level, generals organize their military resources. Beneath the generals, successively lower ranks organize smaller and smaller units but pay attention to ever-increasing degrees of detail. At the bottom of the hierarchy are the people who operate weapons systems.

Command systems in firms are not as rigid as those in the military, but they share some similar features. A chief executive officer (CEO) sits at the top of a firm's command system. Senior executives specialize in managing production, marketing, finance, and personnel. Beneath these senior managers are the people who supervise the day-to-day operations of the business and beneath them, the people who operate the firm's machines and who make and sell the firm's products.

Managers try to be well informed, but they almost always have incomplete information about what is happening in the divisions for which they are responsible. For this reason, firms also use incentive systems.

Incentive Systems

An **incentive system** is a method of organizing production that uses a market-like mechanism inside the firm. Instead of issuing commands, senior managers create compensation schemes to induce workers to perform in ways that maximize the firm's profit.

Incentive systems operate at all levels in a firm. The compensation plan of a CEO might include a share in the firm's profit, factory floor workers sometimes receive compensation based on the quantity they produce, and salespeople, who spend most of their working time alone, are induced to work hard by being paid a small salary and a large performance-related bonus.

The Principal–Agent Problem

The **principal–agent problem** is the problem of devising compensation rules that induce an *agent* to act in the best interest of a *principal*. For example, the stockholders of Texaco are *principals,* and the firm's managers are *agents*. The stockholders (the principals) must induce the managers (agents) to act in the stockholders' best interest. Similarly, Mark Zuckerberg (a principal) must induce the designers who are working on the next generation Facebook (agents) to work efficiently.

Agents, whether they are managers or workers, pursue their own goals and often impose costs on a principal. For example, the goal of stockholders of Citicorp (principals) is to maximize the firm's profit—its true profit, not some fictitious paper profit. But the firm's profit depends on the actions of its managers (agents), and they have their own goals. Perhaps a bank manager takes a customer to a ball game on the pretense that she is building customer loyalty, when in fact she is simply enjoying on-the-job leisure. This same manager is also a principal, and her tellers are agents. The manager wants the tellers to work hard and attract new customers so that she can meet her operating targets. But the workers slack off and take on-the-job leisure.

Coping with the Principal–Agent Problem

A principal must create incentives that induce each agent to work in the interests of the principal. Three ways of coping with the principal–agent problem are

- Ownership
- Incentive pay
- Long-term contracts

Ownership By assigning ownership (or part-ownership) of a business to managers or workers, it is sometimes possible to induce a job performance that increases a firm's profits. Part-ownership is quite common for senior managers but less common for workers. When United Airlines was running into problems a few years ago, it made most of its employees owners of the company.

Incentive Pay Incentive pay—pay related to performance—is very common. Incentives are based on a variety of performance criteria such as profits, production, or sales targets. Promoting an employee for good performance is another example of the use of incentive pay.

Long-Term Contracts Long-term contracts tie the long-term fortunes of managers and workers (agents) to the success of the principal(s)—the owner(s) of the firm. For example, a multiyear employment contract for a CEO encourages that person to take a long-term view and devise strategies that achieve maximum profit over a sustained period.

These three ways of coping with the principal–agent problem give rise to different types of business organization.

Types of Business Organization

The three main types of business organization are

- Proprietorship
- Partnership
- Corporation

Proprietorship A *proprietorship* is a firm with a single owner—a proprietor—who has unlimited liability. *Unlimited liability* is the legal responsibility for all the

---

 ECONOMICS IN THE NEWS

Principals and Agents Get It Wrong

JPMorgan Pay May Be Clawed Back

In May 2012, JPMorgan Chase announced that traders in London had incurred losses of $2 billion. CEO Jamie Dimon said the losses arose from a "flawed, complex, poorly reviewed, poorly executed, and poorly monitored" trading strategy. JPMorgan Chase's stock price fell on the news. One top executive took early retirement. JPMorgan executives and traders are compensated by results with bonus payments in cash and stock options. Dimon said "It's likely that there will be clawbacks" of compensation.

Sources: *AP, Bloomberg,* and *Reuters,* May/June, 2012

THE QUESTIONS

- Who are the principals and who are the agents?
- How did JPMorgan try to cope with its principal–agent problem?
- How, on the occasion reported here, how did JPMorgan get it wrong?
- What role did JPMorgan's share price play?

THE ANSWERS

- The JPMorgan stockholders are principals and Jamie Dimon is their agent.
- Jamie Dimon, as CEO, is a principal and the top executives are agents.
- JPMorgan top executives are principals, and the traders who incurred the losses are agents.
- JPMorgan tried to cope with the principal–agent problem by compensating agents with performance bonuses, profit shares through stock options, and with the possibility of clawbacks for poor performance.
- We don't know the details but based on what

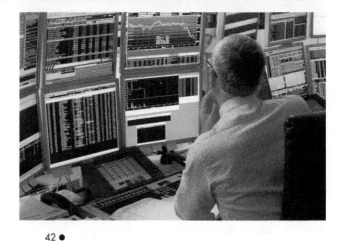

Figure 1 JPMorgan Share Price

Jamie Dimon said, it seems that the specific trading activities that incurred a $2 billion loss were complex and not properly understood either by the traders (the agents at the end of the line) or the managers who designed the trading activities.

- The fall in JPMorgan's stock price not only lowered the wealth of stockholders but also lowered the compensation of Jamie Dimon and the other executives compensated with stock options.

debts of a firm up to an amount equal to the entire personal wealth of the owner. Farmers, computer programmers, and artists are often proprietorships.

The proprietor makes management decisions, receives the firm's profits, and is responsible for its losses. Profits from a proprietorship are taxed at the same rate as other sources of the proprietor's personal income.

Partnership A *partnership* is a firm with two or more owners who have unlimited liability. Partners must agree on an appropriate management structure and on how to divide the firm's profits among themselves. The profits of a partnership are taxed as the personal income of the owners, but each partner is legally liable for all the debts of the partnership (limited only by the wealth of that individual partner). Liability for the full debts of the partnership is called *joint unlimited liability*. Most law firms are partnerships.

Corporation A *corporation* is a firm owned by one or more limited liability stockholders. *Limited liability* means that the owners have legal liability only for the value of their initial investment. This limi-

tation of liability means that if the corporation becomes bankrupt, its owners do not use their personal wealth to pay the corporation's debts.

Corporations' profits are taxed independently of stockholders' incomes. Stockholders pay a capital gains tax on the profit they earn when they sell a stock for a higher price than they paid for it. Corporate stocks generate capital gains when a corporation retains some of its profit and reinvests it in profitable activities. So retained earnings are taxed twice because the capital gains they generate are taxed. Dividend payments are also taxed but at a lower rate than other sources of income.

Pros and Cons of Different Types of Firms

The different types of business organization arise from firms trying to cope with the principal–agent problem. Each type has advantages in particular situations and because of its special advantages, each type continues to exist. Each type of business organization also has disadvantages.

Table 8.4 summarizes these and other pros and cons of the different types of firms.

TABLE 8.4   The Pros and Cons of Different Types of Firms

Type of Firm	Pros	Cons
Proprietorship	▪ Easy to set up ▪ Simple decision making ▪ Profits taxed only once as owner's income	▪ Bad decisions not checked; no need for consensus ▪ Owner's entire wealth at risk ▪ Firm dies with owner ▪ Cost of capital and labor is high relative to that of a corporation
Partnership	▪ Easy to set up ▪ Diversified decision making ▪ Can survive withdrawal of partner ▪ Profits taxed only once as owners' incomes	▪ Achieving consensus may be slow and expensive ▪ Owners' entire wealth at risk ▪ Withdrawal of partner may create capital shortage ▪ Cost of capital and labor is high relative to that of a corporation
Corporation	▪ Owners have limited liability ▪ Large-scale, low-cost capital available ▪ Professional management not restricted by ability of owners ▪ Perpetual life ▪ Long-term labor contracts cut labor costs	▪ Complex management structure can make decisions slow and expensive ▪ Retained profits taxed twice: as company profit and as stockholders' capital gains

Economics in Action

Types of Firms in the Economy

Three types of firms operate in the United States: proprietorships, partnerships, and corporations. Which type of firm dominates? Which produces most of the output of the U.S. economy?

Proprietorships Most Common Three quarters of the firms in the United States are proprietorships and they are mainly small businesses. Almost one fifth of the firms are corporations, and only a twentieth are partnerships (see Fig. 1).

Corporations Produce Most Corporations generate almost 90 percent of business revenue. Revenue is a measure of the value of production, so corporations produce most of the output in the U.S. economy.

Variety Across Industries In agriculture, forestry, and fishing, proprietorships generate about 40 percent of the total revenue. Proprietorships also generate a significant percentage of the revenue in services, construction, and retail trade. Partnerships account for a small percentage of revenue in all sectors and feature most in agriculture, forestry, and fishing, services, and mining. Corporations dominate all sectors and have the manufacturing industries almost to themselves.

Why do corporations dominate the business scene? Why do the other types of businesses survive? And why are proprietorships and partnerships more prominent in some sectors? The answers lie in the pros and cons of the different types of business organization. Corporations dominate where a large amount of capital is used; proprietorships dominate where flexibility in decision making is critical.

Figure 1   Number of Firms and Total Revenue

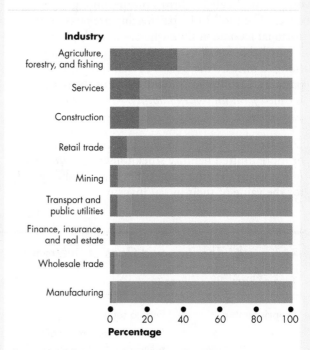

Figure 2   Total Revenue in Various Industries

Source of data: U.S. Bureau of the Census, *Statistical Abstract of the United States,* 2001.

REVIEW QUIZ

1 Explain the distinction between a command system and an incentive system.
2 What is the principal–agent problem? What are three ways in which firms try to cope with it?
3 What are the three types of firms? Explain the major advantages and disadvantages of each.

You can work these questions in Study Plan 8.3 and get instant feedback.   MyEconLab

You've now seen how technology constraints and information constraints influence the way firms operate. You've seen why some firms operate with a large amount of labor and human capital and a small amount of physical capital. You've also seen how firms use a mixture of command and incentive systems and employ different types of business organization to cope with the principal–agent problem.

Your next task is to look at the variety of market situations in which firms operate and classify the different market environments in which firms do business.

Markets and the Competitive Environment

The markets in which firms operate vary a great deal. Some are highly competitive, and profits in these markets are hard to come by. Some appear to be almost free from competition, and firms in these markets earn large profits. Some markets are dominated by fierce advertising campaigns in which each firm seeks to persuade buyers that it has the best products. And some markets display the character of a strategic game.

Economists identify four market types:

1. Perfect competition
2. Monopolistic competition
3. Oligopoly
4. Monopoly

Perfect competition arises when there are many firms, each selling an identical product, many buyers, and no restrictions on the entry of new firms into the industry. The many firms and buyers are all well informed about the prices of the products of each firm in the industry. The worldwide markets for wheat, corn, rice, and other grain crops are examples of perfect competition.

Monopolistic competition is a market structure in which a large number of firms compete by making similar but slightly different products. Making a product slightly different from the product of a competing firm is called **product differentiation**. Product differentiation gives a firm in monopolistic competition an element of market power. The firm is the sole producer of the particular version of the good in question. For example, in the market for pizzas, hundreds of firms make their own version of the perfect pizza. Each of these firms is the sole producer of a particular brand. Differentiated products are not necessarily different products. What matters is that consumers perceive them to be different. For example, different brands of potato chips and ketchup might be almost identical but be perceived by consumers to be different.

Oligopoly is a market structure in which a small number of firms compete. Computer software, airplane manufacture, and international air transportation are examples of oligopolistic industries. Oligopolies might produce almost identical products, such as the colas produced by Coke and Pepsi. Or they might produce differentiated products such as Boeing and Airbus aircraft.

Monopoly arises when there is one firm, which produces a good or service that has no close substitutes and in which the firm is protected by a barrier preventing the entry of new firms. In some places, the phone, gas, electricity, cable television, and water suppliers are local monopolies—monopolies restricted to a given location. Microsoft Corporation, the software developer that created Windows, the operating system for the personal computer, is an example of a global monopoly.

Perfect competition is the most extreme form of competition. Monopoly is the most extreme absence of competition. The other two market types fall between these extremes.

Many factors must be taken into account to determine which market structure describes a particular real-world market. One of these factors is the extent to which a small number of firms dominates the market. To measure this feature of markets, economists use indexes called measures of concentration. Let's look at these measures.

Measures of Concentration

Economists use two measures of concentration:

- The four-firm concentration ratio
- The Herfindahl-Hirschman Index

The Four-Firm Concentration Ratio   The **four-firm concentration ratio** is the percentage of the value of sales accounted for by the four largest firms in an industry. The range of the concentration ratio is from almost zero for perfect competition to 100 percent for monopoly. This ratio is the main measure used to assess market structure.

Table 8.5 shows two calculations of the four-firm concentration ratio: one for tire makers and one for printers. In this example, 14 firms produce tires. The largest four have 80 percent of the sales, so the four-firm concentration ratio is 80 percent. In the printing industry, with 1,004 firms, the largest four firms have only 0.5 percent of the sales, so the four-firm concentration ratio is 0.5 percent.

A low concentration ratio indicates a high degree of competition, and a high concentration ratio indicates an absence of competition. A monopoly has a concentration ratio of 100 percent—the largest (and only) firm has 100 percent of the sales. A four-firm concentration ratio that exceeds 60 percent is regarded as an indication of a market that is highly concentrated and dominated by a few firms in an oligopoly. A ratio of less than 60 percent is regarded as an indication of a competitive market.

The Herfindahl-Hirschman Index   The **Herfindahl-Hirschman Index**—also called the HHI—is the square of the percentage market share of each firm summed over the largest 50 firms (or summed over all the firms if there are fewer than 50) in a market. For example, if there are four firms in a market and the market shares of the firms are 50 percent, 25 percent, 15 percent, and 10 percent, the Herfindahl-Hirschman Index is

$$HHI = 50^2 + 25^2 + 15^2 + 10^2 = 3,450.$$

TABLE 8.5   Calculating the Four-Firm Concentration Ratio

Tire makers		Printers	
Firm	**Sales** (millions of dollars)	**Firm**	**Sales** (millions of dollars)
Top, Inc.	200	Fran's	2.5
ABC, Inc.	250	Ned's	2.0
Big, Inc.	150	Tom's	1.8
XYZ, Inc.	100	Jill's	1.7
Largest 4 firms	700	Largest 4 firms	8.0
Other 10 firms	175	Other 1,000 firms	1,592.0
Industry	875	Industry	1,600.0

Four-firm concentration ratios:

Tire makers: $\dfrac{700}{875} \times 100 = 80$ percent

Printers: $\dfrac{8}{1,600} \times 100 = 0.5$ percent

Economics in Action

Concentration in the U.S. Economy

The U.S. Department of Commerce calculates and publishes data showing concentration ratios and the HHI for each industry in the United States. The bars in the figure show the four-firm concentration ratio and the number at the end of each bar is the HHI.

Chewing gum is one of the most concentrated industries. William Wrigley Jr. Company of Chicago employs 16,000 people and sells $5 billion worth of gum a year. It does have some competitors, but they have a very small market share.

Household laundry equipment, light bulbs, breakfast cereal, and motor vehicles are highly concentrated industries. They are oligopolies.

Pet food, cookies and crackers, computers, and soft drinks are moderately concentrated industries. They are examples of monopolistic competition.

Ice cream, milk, clothing, concrete blocks and bricks, and commercial printing have low concentration measures and are highly competitive industries.

Concentration measures are useful indicators of the degree of competition in a market, but they must be supplemented by other information to determine the structure of the market.

Newspapers and automobiles are examples of how the concentration measures give a misleading reading of the degree of competition. Most newspapers are local. They serve a single city or even a smaller area. So despite the low concentration measure, newspapers are concentrated in their own local areas. Automobiles are traded internationally and foreign cars are freely imported into the United States. Despite the high U.S. concentration measure, the automobile industry is competitive.

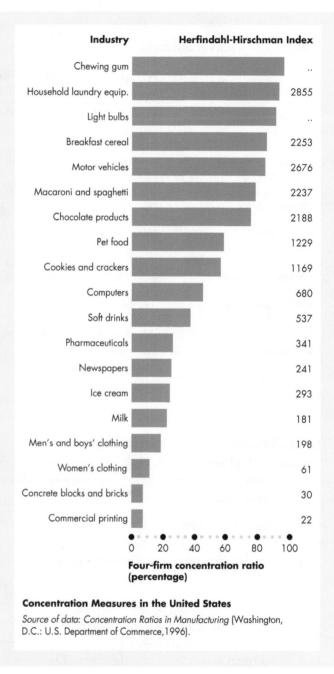

Concentration Measures in the United States

Source of data: Concentration Ratios in Manufacturing (Washington, D.C.: U.S. Department of Commerce, 1996).

In perfect competition, the HHI is small. For example, if each of the largest 50 firms in an industry has a market share of 0.1 percent, then the HHI is $0.1^2 \times 50 = 0.5$. In a monopoly, the HHI is 10,000. The firm has 100 percent of the market: $100^2 = 10,000$.

The HHI became a popular measure of the degree of competition during the 1980s, when the Justice Department used it to classify markets. A market in which the HHI is less than 1,000 is regarded as being competitive. A market in which the HHI lies between 1,000 and 1,800 is regarded as being moderately competitive. But a market in which the HHI exceeds 1,800 is regarded as being uncompetitive. The Justice Department scrutinizes any merger of firms in a market in which the HHI exceeds 1,000 and is likely to challenge a merger if the HHI exceeds 1,800.

TABLE 8.6   Market Structure

Characteristics	Perfect competition	Monopolistic competition	Oligopoly	Monopoly
Number of firms in industry	Many	Many	Few	One
Product	Identical	Differentiated	Either identical or differentiated	No close substitutes
Barriers to entry	None	None	Moderate	High
Firm's control over price	None	Some	Considerable	Considerable or regulated
Concentration ratio	0	Low	High	100
HHI (approx. ranges)	Less than 100	101 to 1,800	More than 1,800	10,000
Examples	Wheat, corn	Food, clothing	Computer chips	Local water supply

Limitations of a Concentration Measure

The three main limitations of using only concentration measures as determinants of market structure are their failure to take proper account of

- The geographical scope of the market
- Barriers to entry and firm turnover
- The correspondence between a market and an industry

Geographical Scope of Market Concentration measures take a national view of the market. Many goods are sold in a *national* market, but some are sold in a *regional* market and some in a *global* one. The concentration measures for newspapers are low, indicating competition, but in most cities the newspaper industry is highly concentrated. The concentration measures for automobiles are high, indicating little competition, but the biggest three U.S. car makers compete with foreign car makers in a highly competitive global market.

Barriers to Entry and Firm Turnover Some markets are highly concentrated but entry is easy and the turnover of firms is large. For example, small towns have few restaurants, but no restrictions hinder a new restaurant from opening and many attempt to do so.

Also, a market with only a few firms might be competitive because of *potential entry*. The few firms in a market face competition from the many potential firms that will enter the market if economic profit opportunities arise.

Market and Industry Correspondence To calculate concentration ratios, the Department of Commerce classifies each firm as being in a particular industry. But markets do not always correspond closely to industries for three reasons.

First, markets are often narrower than industries. For example, the pharmaceutical industry, which has a low concentration ratio, operates in many separate markets for individual products—for example, measles vaccine and AIDS-fighting drugs. These drugs do not compete with each other, so this industry, which looks competitive, includes firms that are monopolies (or near monopolies) in markets for individual drugs.

Second, most firms make several products. For example, Westinghouse makes electrical equipment and, among other things, gas-fired incinerators and plywood. So this one firm operates in at least three separate markets, but the Department of Commerce classifies Westinghouse as being in the electrical goods and equipment industry. The fact that Westinghouse competes with other producers of plywood does not

Economics in Action
A Competitive Environment

How competitive are markets in the United States? Do most U.S. firms operate in competitive markets, in monopolistic competition, in oligopoly, or in monopoly markets?

The data needed to answer these questions are hard to get. The last attempt to answer the questions, in a study by William G. Shepherd, an economics professor at the University of Massachusetts at Amherst, covered the years from 1939 to 1980. The figure shows what he discovered.

In 1980, three quarters of the value of goods and services bought and sold in the United States was traded in markets that are essentially competitive—markets that have almost perfect competition or monopolistic competition. Monopoly and the dominance of a single firm accounted for about 5 percent of sales. Oligopoly, which is found mainly in manufacturing, accounted for about 18 percent of sales.

Over the period studied, the U.S. economy became increasingly competitive. The percentage of output sold by firms operating in competitive markets (blue bars) has expanded most, and has shrunk most in oligopoly markets (red bars).

The Market Structure of the U.S. Economy

Source of data: William G. Shepherd, "Causes of Increased Competition in the U.S. Economy, 1939–1980," *Review of Economics and Statistics*, Vol 64, No 4 (November, 1982), pp. 613–626. © 1982 by the President and Fellows of Harvard College. Reprinted with permission.

But also during the past decades, the U.S. economy has become much more exposed to competition from the rest of the world. The data used by William G. Shepherd don't capture this international competition, so the data probably understate the degree of true competition in the U.S. economy.

show up in the concentration numbers for the plywood market.

Third, firms switch from one market to another depending on profit opportunities. For example, Motorola, which today produces cellular telephones and other communications products, has diversified from being a TV and computer chip maker. Motorola no longer produces TVs. Publishers of newspapers, magazines, and textbooks are today rapidly diversifying into Internet and multimedia products. These switches among markets show that there is much scope for entering and exiting a market, and so measures of concentration have limited usefulness.

Despite their limitations, concentration measures do provide a basis for determining the degree of competition in a market when they are combined with information about the geographical scope of the market, barriers to entry, and the extent to which large, multiproduct firms straddle a variety of markets.

REVIEW QUIZ

1 What are the four market types? Explain the distinguishing characteristics of each.
2 What are the two measures of concentration? Explain how each measure is calculated.
3 Under what conditions do the measures of concentration give a good indication of the degree of competition in a market?
4 Is the U.S. economy competitive? Is it becoming more competitive or less competitive?

You can work these questions in Study Plan 8.4 and get instant feedback.   MyEconLab

You now know the variety of market types and how we identify them. Our final question in this chapter is: What determines the things that firms decide to buy from other firms rather than produce for themselves?

◆ Produce or Outsource? Firms and Markets

To produce a good or service, even a simple one such as a shirt, factors of production must be hired and their activities coordinated. To produce a good as complicated as an iPhone, an enormous range of specialist factors of production must be coordinated.

Factors of production can be coordinated either by firms or markets. We'll describe these two ways of organizing production and then see why firms play a crucial role in achieving an efficient use of resources.

Firm Coordination

Firms hire labor, capital, and land, and by using a mixture of command systems and incentive systems (see p. 185) organize and coordinate their activities to produce goods and services.

Firm coordination occurs when you take your car to the garage for an oil change, brake check, and service. The garage owner hires a mechanic and tools and coordinates all the activities that get your car serviced. Firms also coordinate the production of cornflakes, golf clubs, and a host of other items.

Market Coordination

Markets coordinate production by adjusting prices and making the decisions of buyers and sellers of factors of production and components consistent.

Market coordination occurs to produce a rock concert. A promoter books a stadium, rents some stage equipment, hires some audio and video recording engineers and technicians, engages some rock groups, a superstar, a publicity agent, and a ticket agent. The promoter sells tickets to thousands of rock fans, audio rights to a recording company, and video and broadcasting rights to a television network. All these transactions take place in markets that coordinate the buying and selling of this huge variety of factors of production.

Outsourcing, buying parts or products from other firms, is another example of market coordination. Dell outsources the production of all the components of its computers. Automakers outsource the production of windshields, windows, transmission systems, engines, tires, and many other auto parts. Apple outsources the entire production of iPods, iPads, and iPhones.

Why Firms?

What determines whether a firm or a market coordinates a particular set of activities? How does a firm decide whether to buy an item from another firm or manufacture it itself? The answer is cost. Taking account of the opportunity cost of time as well as the costs of the other inputs, a firm uses the method that costs least. In other words, it uses the economically efficient method.

If a task can be performed at a lower cost by markets than by a firm, markets will do the job, and any attempt to set up a firm to replace such market activity will be doomed to failure.

Firms coordinate economic activity when a task can be performed more efficiently by a firm than by markets. In such a situation, it is profitable to set up a firm. Firms are often more efficient than markets as coordinators of economic activity because they can achieve

- Lower transactions costs
- Economies of scale
- Economies of scope
- Economies of team production

Transactions Costs Firms eliminate transactions costs. **Transactions costs** are the costs that arise from finding someone with whom to do business, of reaching an agreement about the price and other aspects of the exchange, and of ensuring that the terms of the agreement are fulfilled. Market transactions require buyers and sellers to get together and to negotiate the terms and conditions of their trading. Sometimes, lawyers have to be hired to draw up contracts. A broken contract leads to still more expense. A firm can lower such transactions costs by reducing the number of individual transactions undertaken.

Imagine getting your car fixed using market coordination. You hire a mechanic to diagnose the problems and make a list of the parts and tools needed to fix them. You buy the parts from several dealers, rent the tools from ABC Rentals, hire an auto mechanic, return the tools, and pay your bills. You can avoid all these transactions and the time they cost you by letting your local garage fix the car.

Economies of Scale When the cost of producing a unit of a good falls as its output rate increases, **economies of scale** exist. An automaker experiences economies of scale because as the scale of production increases, the firm can use cost-saving equipment and

Economics in Action

Apple Doesn't Make the iPhone!

Apple designed the iPhone and markets it, but Apple doesn't manufacture it. Why? Apple wants to produce the iPhone at the lowest possible cost. Apple achieves its goal by assigning the production task to more than 30 firms, some of which are listed in the table opposite. These 30 firms produce the components in Asia, Europe, and North America and then the components are assembled in its sleek, iconic case by Foxconn and Quanta in Taiwan.

Most electronic products—TVs, DVD players, iPods and iPads, and personal computers—are produced in a similar way to the iPhone with a combination of firm and market coordination. Hundreds of little-known firms compete fiercely to get their components into well-known consumer products.

Altus Technology	Taiwan
Balda	Germany
Broadcom	United States
Cambridge Silicon Radio	UK
Catcher	Taiwan
Cyntec	Taiwan
Delta Electronics	Taiwan
Epson	Japan
Foxconn	Taiwan
Infineon Technologies	Germany
Intel	United States
Largan Precision	Taiwan
Lite-On	Taiwan
Marvell	United States
Micron	United States
National Semiconductor	United States
Novatek	Taiwan
Primax	Taiwan
Quanta	Taiwan
Samsung	Korea
Sanyo	Japan
Sharp	Japan
Taiwan Semiconductor	Taiwan
TMD	Japan

highly specialized labor. An automaker that produces only a few cars a year must use hand-tool methods that are costly. Economies of scale arise from specialization and the division of labor that can be reaped more effectively by firm coordination rather than market coordination.

Economies of Scope A firm experiences **economies of scope** when it uses specialized (and often expensive) resources to produce a *range of goods and services*. For example, Toshiba uses its designers and specialized equipment to make the hard drive for the iPod. But it makes many different types of hard drives and other related products. As a result, Toshiba produces the iPod hard drive at a lower cost than a firm making only the iPod hard drive could achieve.

Economies of Team Production A production process in which the individuals in a group specialize in mutually supportive tasks is *team production*. Sports provide the best examples of team activity. In baseball, some team members specialize in pitching and others in fielding. In basketball, some team members specialize in defense and some in offense. The production of goods and services offers many examples of team activity. For example, production lines in a TV manufacturing plant work most efficiently when individual activity is organized in teams, each worker specializing in a few tasks. You can also think of an entire firm as being a team. The team has buyers of raw materials and other inputs, production workers, and salespeople. Each individual member of the team

specializes, but the value of the output of the team and the profit that it earns depend on the coordinated activities of all the team's members.

Because firms can economize on transactions costs, reap economies of scale and economies of scope, and organize efficient team production, it is firms rather than markets that coordinate most of our economic activity.

REVIEW QUIZ

1 What are the two ways in which economic activity can be coordinated?

2 What determines whether a firm or markets coordinate production?

3 What are the main reasons why firms can often coordinate production at a lower cost than markets can?

You can work these questions in Study Plan 8.5 and get instant feedback.   MyEconLab

◆ *Reading Between the Lines* on pp. 196–197 explores the market for Internet advertising. In the next four chapters, we continue to study firms and their decisions. In Chapter 9, we learn about the relationships between cost and output at different output levels. These relationships are common to all types of firms in all types of markets. We then turn to problems that are specific to firms in different types of markets.

Battling for Markets in Internet Advertising

Facebook Rolls Out Real-Time Ad Platform

Financial Times
September 13, 2102

Some of the world's largest advertising companies have signed up to Facebook's new real-time advertising platform, in a move that the social network hopes will bolster its revenue streams.

On Thursday, Facebook officially launched the platform, called Facebook Ad Exchange, or FBX, following months of testing. The system allows marketers to bid in real-time to buy ad impressions on the social networking site, and deliver their ads to users based on their immediate web-browsing habits, or linked to current events, such as sports results.

"Real-time marketing is getting to be a really important component of digital advertising," said Rebecca Lieb, an analyst with the Altimeter Group. "We'll see a lot of event-triggered marketing in the upcoming election cycle."

The ads use information gathered from computer browsing histories to target individual Facebook users, and the ad prices fluctuate as in auction-style bidding system. So a user who looks at shoes on a retail site could then see an ad for the same brand when clicking back to Facebook.

The capacity will help Facebook compete more directly with advertising rivals Google and Yahoo, which have long provided real-time bidding to advertisers. ...

Within one tenth of a second, the system notifies when an ad space is available, evaluates 2,000 data points to determine the most relevant ad, calculates a price and prompts the ad to appear.

The global real-time bidding sector is estimated to be worth some $3bn-$4bn, but industry observers expect this to reach as much as $20bn by 2015. ...

ESSENCE OF THE STORY

- Facebook is under pressure to generate advertising revenue.

- Real-time bidding is widely used for Internet advertising and its market share is growing rapidly.

- Facebook and Google are getting better at capturing user activity.

- A new Facebook system will target ads at the user's current interests.

- Advertisers will bid to get their ads in front of the right users.

ECONOMIC ANALYSIS

- Like all firms, Facebook and Google aim to maximize profit.

- Facebook provides social networking services and Google provides search services, a variety of other services, and with Google+ is offering a social networking service.

- Facebook and Google face constraints imposed by the market and technology.

- People who use social networks demand their services, and at the latest count Facebook and another 198 firms supply social networking services.

- People looking for information demand Internet search services, and Google and more than another 100 firms supply Internet search services.

- The equilibrium price of social networking services and of Internet search services is zero, and the equilibrium quantity of each is the quantity demanded at a zero price.

- Social network and Internet search providers enjoy economies of scope: They produce advertising services as well as their other service.

- Unlike social networking and search, Internet advertising is a big revenue and profit generator.

- Because the providers of social networking and search know a lot about their users, they can offer advertisers access to potential customers and charge a high price for this precision.

- Google has been enormously successful at delivering advertising based on a user's search activity, and its revenue has grown from almost zero in 2001 to $38 billion in 2011 (see Fig. 1). Google's profit in 2011 was almost $12 billion (see Fig. 2).

- Facebook is still learning how to tap its advertising potential and the news article describes its plans in 2012 to develop real-time bidding for advertising based on a user's browsing.

- Facebook's revenue is beginning to grow, but by 2011 it had reached only $4 billion (see Fig. 1).

- Providing a social networking service or search service doesn't guarantee success in generating advertising revenue and profit.

- Yahoo! is an example of a firm that hasn't performed as well as its owners would wish.

- As Google and Facebook have seen explosive growth in users and revenues, Yahoo! has struggled.

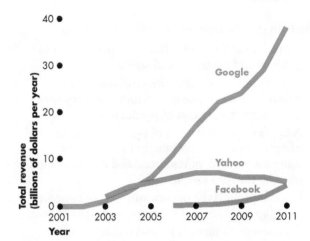

Figure 1 Total Revenue Comparison

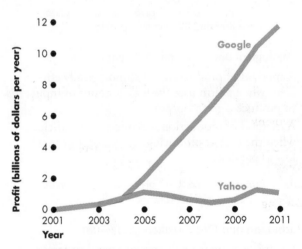

Figure 2 Profit Comparison

- Figure 1 shows that Yahoo's revenue peaked in 2008 and has been falling while Google's has soared and Facebook's has grown to almost equal that of Yahoo!.

- Figure 2 shows that Yahoo's profit has been flat while Google's has soared. (We don't know how much profit Facebook has made.)

- The data shown in Figs. 1 and 2 suggest that so far, Internet search is a more effective tool for generating revenue and profit than social networking. Perhaps Facebook's new revenue model will change that.

- The data also suggest that Facebook's and Google's expansion is tightening the market constraint that Yahoo! faces.

197

SUMMARY

Key Points

The Firm and Its Economic Problem (pp. 180–182)

- Firms hire and organize factors of production to produce and sell goods and services.
- A firm's goal is to maximize economic profit, which is total revenue minus total cost measured as the opportunity cost of production.
- A firm's opportunity cost of production is the sum of the cost of resources bought in the market, using the firm's own resources, and resources supplied by the firm's owner.
- Normal profit is the opportunity cost of entrepreneurship and is part of the firm's opportunity cost.
- Technology, information, and markets limit the economic profit that a firm can make.

Working Problems 1 and 2 will give you a better understanding of the firm and its economic problem.

Technological and Economic Efficiency (pp. 183–184)

- A method of production is technologically efficient when a firm uses the least amount of inputs to produce a given output.
- A method of production is economically efficient when the cost of producing a given output is as low as possible.

Working Problems 3 and 4 will give you a better understanding of technological and economic efficiency.

Information and Organization (pp. 185–188)

- Firms use a combination of command systems and incentive systems to organize production.
- Faced with incomplete information and uncertainty, firms induce managers and workers to perform in ways that are consistent with the firms' goals.
- Proprietorships, partnerships, and corporations use ownership, incentive pay, and long-term contracts to cope with the principal–agent problem.

Working Problems 5 to 8 will give you a better understanding of information and organization.

Markets and the Competitive Environment (pp. 179–193)

- In perfect competition, many sellers offer an identical product to many buyers and entry is free.
- In monopolistic competition, many sellers offer slightly different products to many buyers and entry is free.
- In oligopoly, a small number of sellers compete and barriers to entry limit the number of firms.
- In monopoly, one firm produces an item that has no close substitutes and the firm is protected by a barrier to entry that prevents the entry of competitors.

Working Problems 9 and 10 will give you a better understanding of markets and the competitive environment.

Produce or Outsource? Firms and Markets (pp. 194–195)

- Firms coordinate economic activities when they can perform a task more efficiently—at lower cost—than markets can.
- Firms economize on transactions costs and achieve the benefits of economies of scale, economies of scope, and economies of team production.

Working Problems 11 and 12 will give you a better understanding of firms and markets.

Key Terms

Command system, 185
Economic depreciation, 181
Economic efficiency, 183
Economic profit, 180
Economies of scale, 194
Economies of scope, 195
Firm, 180

Four-firm concentration ratio, 190
Herfindahl-Hirschman Index, 190
Implicit rental rate, 180
Incentive system, 185
Monopolistic competition, 189
Monopoly, 189
Normal profit, 181

Oligopoly, 189
Perfect competition, 189
Principal–agent problem, 185
Product differentiation, 189
Technological efficiency, 183
Technology, 182
Transactions costs, 194

STUDY PLAN PROBLEMS AND APPLICATIONS

MyEconLab   You can work Problems 1 to 13 in MyEconLab Chapter 8 Study Plan and get instant feedback.

The Firm and Its Economic Problem (Study Plan 8.1)

1. One year ago, Jack and Jill set up a vinegar-bottling firm (called JJVB). Use the following information to calculate JJVB's opportunity cost of production during its first year of operation:
   - Jack and Jill put $50,000 of their own money into the firm.
   - They bought equipment for $30,000.
   - They hired one employee to help them for an annual wage of $20,000.
   - Jack gave up his previous job, at which he earned $30,000, and spent all his time working for JJVB.
   - Jill kept her old job, which paid $30 an hour, but gave up 10 hours of leisure each week (for 50 weeks) to work for JJVB.
   - JJVB bought $10,000 of goods and services from other firms.
   - The market value of the equipment at the end of the year was $28,000.
   - Jack and Jill have a $100,000 home loan on which they pay interest of 6 percent a year.

2. Joe, who has no skills, no job experience, and no alternative employment, runs a shoeshine stand at the airport. Operators of other shoeshine stands earn $10,000 a year. Joe pays rent to the airport of $2,000 a year, and his total revenue from shining shoes is $15,000 a year. Joe spent $1,000 on a chair, polish, and brushes, using his credit card to buy them. The interest on a credit card balance is 20 percent a year. At the end of the year, Joe was offered $500 for his business and all its equipment. Calculate Joe's opportunity cost of production and his economic profit.

Technological and Economic Efficiency (Study Plan 8.2)

3. Alternative ways of laundering 100 shirts are

Method	Labor (hours)	Capital (machines)
A	1	10
B	5	8
C	20	4
D	50	1

   a. Which methods are technologically efficient?
   b. Which method is economically efficient if the

hourly wage rate and the implicit rental rate of capital are as follows:
   (i)   Wage rate $1, rental rate $100?
   (ii) Wage rate $5, rental rate $50?
   (iii) Wage rate $50, rental rate $5?

4. **John Deere's Farm Team**
   Deere opened up the Pune [India] center in 2001. Deere's move was unexpected: Deere is known for its heavy-duty farm equipment and big construction gear whereas many of India's 300 million farmers still use oxen-pulled plows.
   Source: *Fortune*, April 14, 2008

   a. Why do many Indian farmers still use oxen-pulled plows? Are they efficient or inefficient? Explain.
   b. How might making John Deere farm equipment available to Indian farmers change the technology constraint they face?

Information and Organization (Study Plan 8.3)

5. **Here It Is. Now, You Design It!**
   The idea is that the most successful companies no longer invent new products and services on their own. They create them along with their customers, and they do it in a way that produces a unique experience for each customer. The important corollary is that no company owns enough resources—or can possibly own enough—to furnish unique experiences for each customer, so companies must organize a constantly shifting global web of suppliers and partners to do the job.
   Source: *Fortune*, May 26, 2008

   a. Describe this method of organizing and coordinating production: Does it use a command system or incentive system?
   b. How does this method of organizing and coordinating production help firms achieve lower costs?

6. **Rewarding Failure**
   Over the past 25 years CEO pay has risen faster than corporate profits, economic growth, or average wages. A more sensible alternative to the current compensation system would require CEOs to own a lot of company stock. If the stock is given to the boss, his salary and bonus should be docked to reflect its value. As for bonuses, they

should be based on improving a company's cash earnings relative to its cost of capital, not to manipulated measures like earnings per share. Bonuses should not be capped but be unavailable to the CEO for some period of years.

Source: *Fortune*, April 28, 2008

a. What is the economic problem that CEO compensation schemes are designed to solve?

b. How do the proposed changes to CEO compensation outlined in the news clip address the problem you described in part (a)?

Use the following news clip to work Problems 7 and 8.

Steps to Creating a Super Startup

Starting a business is a complicated and risky task. Just two-thirds of new small businesses survive at least two years, and only 44 percent survive at least four years. Most entrepreneurs start their businesses by dipping into their savings, borrowing from the family, and using the founder's credit cards. Getting a bank loan is tough unless you have assets—and that often means using your home as collateral.

Source: CNN, October 18, 2007

7. When starting a business, what are the risks identified in the news clip that are associated with a proprietorship?

8. How might (i) a partnership and (ii) a corporation help to overcome the risks identified in the news clip?

Markets and the Competitive Environment

(Study Plan 8.4)

9. Sales of the firms in the tattoo industry are

Firm	Sales (dollars per year)
Bright Spots	450
Freckles	325
Love Galore	250
Native Birds	200
Other 15 firms	800

Calculate the four-firm concentration ratio. What is the structure of the tattoo industry?

10. **GameStop Racks Up the Points**

No retailer has more cachet among gamers than GameStop. For now, only Wal-Mart has a larger market share—21.3% last year. GameStop's share was 21.1% last year, and may well overtake Wal-Mart this year. But if new women gamers prefer shopping at Target to GameStop, Wal-Mart and Target might erode GameStop's market share.

Source: *Fortune*, June 9, 2008

a. According to the news clip, what is the structure of the U.S. retail video-game market?

b. Estimate a range for the four-firm concentration ratio and the HHI for the game market in the United States based on the information provided in this news clip.

Produce or Outsource? Firms and Markets

(Study Plan 8.5)

11. American automakers buy auto parts from independent suppliers rather than produce the parts themselves. In the 1980s, Chrysler got about 70 percent of its auto parts from independent suppliers, while Ford got about 60 percent and General Motors got 25 percent. A decade earlier, the proportions were 50 percent at Chrysler, 5 percent at Ford, and 20 percent at General Motors.

Source: The Cato Institute Policy Analysis, 1987

a. Why did American automakers decide to outsource most of their parts production?

b. Explain why independent producers of auto parts are more efficient than the automakers.

12. Federal Express enters into contracts with independent truck operators who offer FedEx service and who are rewarded by the volume of packages they carry. Why doesn't FedEx buy more trucks and hire more drivers? What incentive problems might arise from this arrangement?

Economics in the News (Study Plan 8.N)

13. Lego, the Danish toymaker, incurred economic losses in 2003 and 2004 as it faced competition from low-cost copiers of its products and a fall in demand. In 2004, to restore profits, Lego fired 3,500 of its 8,000 workers; closed factories in Switzerland and the United States; opened factories in Eastern Europe and Mexico; and introduced performance-based pay for its managers. Lego returned to profit in 2005.

Based on **Picking Up the Pieces**, *The Economist*, October 28, 2006

a. Describe the problems that Lego faced in 2003 and 2004, using the concepts of the three types of constraints that all firms face.

b. Which of the actions that Lego took to restore profits addressed an inefficiency? How did Lego seek to achieve economic efficiency?

c. Which of Lego's actions addressed an information and organization problem? How did Lego change the way in which it coped with the principal–agent problem?

d. In what type of market does Lego operate?

MyEconLab You can work these problems in MyEconLab if assigned by your instructor.

The Firm and Its Economic Problem

Use the following information to work Problems 14 and 15.

Lee is a computer programmer who earned $35,000 in 2011. But on January 1, 2012, Lee opened a body board manufacturing business. At the end of the first year of operation, he submitted the following information to his accountant:

- He stopped renting out his cottage for $3,500 a year and used it as his factory. The market value of the cottage increased from $70,000 to $71,000.
- He spent $50,000 on materials, phone, etc.
- He leased machines for $10,000 a year.
- He paid $15,000 in wages.
- He used $10,000 from his savings account, which earns 5 percent a year interest.
- He borrowed $40,000 at 10 percent a year.
- He sold $160,000 worth of body boards.
- Normal profit is $25,000 a year.

14. Calculate Lee's opportunity cost of production and his economic profit.

15. Lee's accountant recorded the depreciation on his cottage during 2012 as $7,000. According to the accountant, what profit did Lee make?

16. In 2011, Toni taught music and earned $20,000. She also earned $4,000 by renting out her basement. On January 1, 2012, she quit teaching, stopped renting out her basement, and began to use it as the office for her new Web site design business. She took $2,000 from her savings account to buy a computer. During 2012, she paid $1,500 for the lease of a Web server and $1,750 for high-speed Internet service. She received a total revenue from Web site designing of $45,000 and earned interest at 5 percent a year on her savings account balance. Normal profit is $55,000 a year. At the end of 2012, Toni could have sold her computer for $500. Calculate Toni's opportunity cost of production and her economic profit in 2012.

17. **The Colvin Interview: Chrysler**

The key driver of profitability will be that the focus of the company isn't on profitability. Our focus is on the customer. If we can find a way to give customers what they want better than anybody else, then what can stop us?

Source: *Fortune*, April 14, 2008

a. In spite of what Chrysler's vice chairman and co-president claims, why is Chrysler's focus actually on profitability?

b. What would happen to Chrysler if it didn't focus on maximizing profit, but instead focused its production and pricing decisions to "give customers what they want"?

18. **Must Watches**

Stocks too volatile? Bonds too boring? Then try an alternative investment—one you can wear on your wrist. ... [The] typical return on a watch over five to ten years is roughly 10%. [One could] do better in an index fund, but ... what other investment is so wearable?

Source: *Fortune*, April 14, 2008

a. What is the cost of buying a watch?

b. What is the opportunity cost of owning a watch?

c. Does owning a watch create an economic profit opportunity?

Technological and Economic Efficiency

Use the following information to work Problems 19 and 20.

Four methods of completing a tax return and the time taken by each method are: with a PC, 1 hour; with a pocket calculator, 12 hours; with a pocket calculator and paper and pencil, 12 hours; and with a pencil and paper, 16 hours. The PC and its software cost $1,000, the pocket calculator costs $10, and the pencil and paper cost $1.

19. Which, if any, of the methods is technologically efficient?

20. Which method is economically efficient if the wage rate is

(i) $5 an hour?

(ii) $50 an hour?

(iii) $500 an hour?

21. **A Medical Sensation**

Hospitals are buying da Vinci surgical robots. Surgeons, sitting comfortably at a da Vinci console, can use various robotic attachments to perform even the most complex procedures.

Source: *Fortune*, April 28, 2008

a. Assume that performing a surgery with a surgical robot requires fewer surgeons and nurses.

Is using the surgical robot technologically efficient?

b. What additional information would you need to be able to say that switching to surgical robots is economically efficient for a hospital?

Information and Organization

22. Wal-Mart has more than 3,700 stores, more than one million employees, and total revenues of close to a quarter of a trillion dollars in the United States alone. Sarah Frey-Talley runs the family-owned Frey Farms in Illinois and supplies Wal-Mart with pumpkins and other fresh produce.

a. How does Wal-Mart coordinate its activities? Is it likely to use mainly a command system or also to use incentive systems? Explain.

b. How do you think Sarah Frey-Talley coordinates the activities of Frey Farms? Is she likely to use mainly a command system or also to use incentive systems? Explain.

c. Describe, compare, and contrast the principal–agent problems faced by Wal-Mart and Frey Farms. How might these firms cope with their principal–agent problems?

23. **Where Does Google Go Next?**

Google gives its engineers one day a week to work on whatever project they want. A couple of colleagues did what many of the young geniuses do at Google: They came up with a cool idea. At Google, you often end up with a laissez-faire mess instead of resource allocation.

Source: *Fortune*, May 26, 2008

a. Describe Google's method of organizing production with their software engineers.

b. What are the potential gains and opportunity costs associated with this method?

Markets and the Competitive Environment

24. Market shares of chocolate makers are

Firm	Market share (percent)
Truffles, Inc.	25
Magic, Inc.	20
Mayfair, Inc.	15
All Natural, Inc.	15
Gold, Inc.	15
Bond, Inc.	10

Calculate the Herfindahl-Hirschman Index. What is the structure of the chocolate industry?

Produce or Outsource? Firms and Markets

Use the following information to work Problems 25 to 27.

Two leading design firms, Astro Studios of San Francisco and Hers Experimental Design Laboratory, Inc. of Osaka, Japan, worked with Microsoft to design the Xbox 360 video game console. IBM, ATI, and SiS designed the Xbox 360's hardware. Three firms—Flextronics, Wistron, and Celestica—manufacture the Xbox 360 at their plants in China and Taiwan.

25. Describe the roles of market coordination and coordination by firms in the design, manufacture, and marketing of the Xbox 360.

26. a. Why do you think Microsoft works with a large number of other firms, rather than performing all the required tasks itself?

b. What are the roles of transactions costs, economies of scale, economies of scope, and economies of team production in the design, manufacture, and marketing of the Xbox?

27. Why do you think the Xbox is designed in the United States and Japan but built in China?

Economics in the News

28. After you have studied *Reading Between the Lines* on pp. 196–197, answer the following questions.

a. What products do Facebook and Google sell?

b. In what types of markets do Facebook and Google compete?

c. How do social networks and Internet search providers generate revenue?

d. What is special about social networking sites that make them attractive to advertisers?

e. What is special about Internet search providers that make them attractive to advertisers?

f. What technological changes might increase the profitability of social networks compared to Internet search providers?

29. **Long Reviled, Merit Pay Gains Among Teachers**

School districts in many states experiment with plans that compensate teachers partly based on classroom performance, rather than their years on the job and coursework completed. Working with mentors to improve their instruction and getting bonuses for raising student achievement encourages efforts to raise teaching quality.

Source: *The New York Times*, June 18, 2007

How does "merit pay" attempt to cope with the principal–agent problem in public education?

9

OUTPUT AND COSTS

After studying this chapter, you will be able to:

◆ Distinguish between the short run and the long run

◆ Explain and illustrate a firm's short-run product curves

◆ Explain and derive a firm's short-run cost curves

◆ Explain and derive a firm's long-run average cost curve

What do McDonald's and Campus Sweaters, a small (fictional) producer of knitwear that we'll study in this chapter, have in common? They must decide how much to produce, how many people to employ, and how much and what type of capital equipment to use. How do firms make these decisions?

We are going to answer these questions in this chapter and apply what we learn to the real-world costs of a grocery store checkout line. In *Reading Between the Lines*, we'll look at how recent decisions made by McDonald's in Ohio affect its production costs.

◆ Decision Time Frames

People who operate firms make many decisions, and all of their decisions are aimed at achieving one over-riding goal: maximum attainable profit. But not all decisions are equally critical. Some decisions are big ones. Once made, they are costly (or impossible) to reverse. If such a decision turns out to be incorrect, it might lead to the failure of the firm. Other decisions are small. They are easily changed. If one of these decisions turns out to be incorrect, the firm can change its actions and survive.

The biggest decision that an entrepreneur makes is in what industry to establish a firm. For most entre-preneurs, their background knowledge and interests drive this decision. But the decision also depends on profit prospects—on the expectation that total rev-enue will exceed total cost.

Cindy has decided to set up Campus Sweaters. She has also decided the most effective method of organiz-ing the firm. But she has not decided the quantity to produce, the factors of production to hire, or the price to charge for sweaters.

Decisions about the quantity to produce and the price to charge depend on the type of market in which the firm operates. Perfect competition, monopolistic competition, oligopoly, and monopoly all confront the firm with *different* problems. Decisions about *how* to produce a given output do not depend on the type of market in which the firm operates. *All* types of firms in *all* types of markets make similar decisions about how to produce.

The actions that a firm can take to influence the relationship between output and cost depend on how soon the firm wants to act. A firm that plans to change its output rate tomorrow has fewer options than one that plans to change its output rate six months or six years in the future.

To study the relationship between a firm's output decision and its costs, we distinguish between two decision time frames:

- The short run
- The long run

The Short Run

The **short run** is a time frame in which the quantity of at least one factor of production is fixed. For most firms, capital, land, and entrepreneurship are fixed fac-tors of production and labor is the variable factor of production. We call the fixed factors of production the firm's *plant*: In the short run, a firm's plant is fixed.

For Campus Sweaters, the fixed plant is its factory building and its knitting machines. For an electric power utility, the fixed plant is its buildings, genera-tors, computers, and control systems.

To increase output in the short run, a firm must increase the quantity of a variable factor of production, which is usually labor. So to produce more output, Campus Sweaters must hire more labor and operate its knitting machines for more hours a day. Similarly, an electric power utility must hire more labor and operate its generators for more hours a day.

Short-run decisions are easily reversed. The firm can increase or decrease its output in the short run by increasing or decreasing the amount of labor it hires.

The Long Run

The **long run** is a time frame in which the quantities of *all* factors of production can be varied. That is, the long run is a period in which the firm can change its *plant*.

To increase output in the long run, a firm can change its plant as well as the quantity of labor it hires. Campus Sweaters can decide whether to install more knitting machines, use a new type of machine, reorgan-ize its management, or hire more labor. Long-run deci-sions are *not* easily reversed. Once a plant decision is made, the firm usually must live with it for some time. To emphasize this fact, we call the past expendi-ture on a plant that has no resale value a **sunk cost**. A sunk cost is irrelevant to the firm's current decisions. The only costs that influence its current decisions are the short-run cost of changing its labor inputs and the long-run cost of changing its plant.

REVIEW QUIZ

1 Distinguish between the short run and the long run.
2 Why is a sunk cost irrelevant to a firm's current decisions?

You can work these questions in Study
Plan 9.1 and get instant feedback.   MyEconLab

We're going to study costs in the short run and the long run. We begin with the short run and describe a firm's technology constraint.

Short-Run Technology Constraint

To increase output in the short run, a firm must increase the quantity of labor employed. We describe the relationship between output and the quantity of labor employed by using three related concepts:

1. Total product
2. Marginal product
3. Average product

These product concepts can be illustrated either by product schedules or by product curves. Let's look first at the product schedules.

Product Schedules

Table 9.1 shows some data that describe Campus Sweaters' total product, marginal product, and average product. The numbers tell us how the quantity of sweaters produced increases as Campus Sweaters employs more workers. The numbers also tell us about the productivity of the labor that Campus Sweaters employs.

Focus first on the columns headed "Labor" and "Total product." **Total product** is the maximum output that a given quantity of labor can produce. You can see from the numbers in these columns that as Campus Sweaters employs more labor, total product increases. For example, when 1 worker is employed, total product is 4 sweaters a day, and when 2 workers are employed, total product is 10 sweaters a day. Each increase in employment increases total product.

The **marginal product** of labor is the increase in total product that results from a one-unit increase in the quantity of labor employed, with all other inputs remaining the same. For example, in Table 9.1, when Campus Sweaters increases employment from 2 to 3 workers and does not change its capital, the marginal product of the third worker is 3 sweaters—total product increases from 10 to 13 sweaters.

Average product tells how productive workers are on average. The **average product** of labor is equal to total product divided by the quantity of labor employed. For example, in Table 9.1, the average product of 3 workers is 4.33 sweaters per worker—13 sweaters a day divided by 3 workers.

If you look closely at the numbers in Table 9.1, you can see some patterns. As Campus Sweaters hires more labor, marginal product increases initially, and

TABLE 9.1 Total Product, Marginal Product, and Average Product

	Labor (workers per day)	Total product (sweaters per day)	Marginal product (sweaters per additional worker)	Average product (sweaters per worker)
A	0	0		
			4	
B	1	4		4.00
			6	
C	2	10		5.00
			3	
D	3	13		4.33
			2	
E	4	15		3.75
			1	
F	5	16		3.20

Total product is the total amount produced. Marginal product is the change in total product that results from a one-unit increase in labor. For example, when labor increases from 2 to 3 workers a day (row C to row D), total product increases from 10 to 13 sweaters a day. The marginal product of going from 2 to 3 workers is 3 sweaters. Average product is total product divided by the quantity of labor employed. For example, the average product of 3 workers is 4.33 sweaters per worker (13 sweaters a day divided by 3 workers).

then begins to decrease. For example, marginal product increases from 4 sweaters a day for the first worker to 6 sweaters a day for the second worker and then decreases to 3 sweaters a day for the third worker. Average product also increases at first and then decreases. You can see the relationships between the quantity of labor hired and the three product concepts more clearly by looking at the product curves.

Product Curves

The product curves are graphs of the relationships between employment and the three product concepts you've just studied. They show how total product, marginal product, and average product change as employment changes. They also show the relationships among the three concepts. Let's look at the product curves.

Total Product Curve

Figure 9.1 shows Campus Sweaters' total product curve, *TP*, which is a graph of the total product schedule. Points *A* through *F* correspond to rows *A* through *F* in Table 9.1. To graph the entire total product curve, we vary labor by hours rather than whole days.

Notice the shape of the total product curve. As employment increases from zero to 1 worker a day, the curve becomes steeper. Then, as employment increases to 3, 4, and 5 workers a day, the curve becomes less steep.

The total product curve is similar to the *production possibilities frontier* (explained in Chapter 2). It separates the attainable output levels from those that are unattainable. All the points that lie above the curve are unattainable. Points that lie below the curve, in the orange area, are attainable, but they are inefficient—they use more labor than is necessary to produce a given output. Only the points *on* the total product curve are technologically efficient.

FIGURE 9.1   Total Product Curve

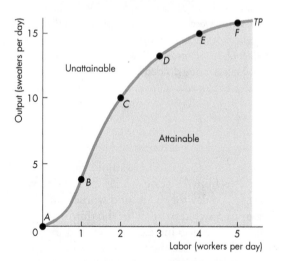

The total product curve, *TP*, is based on the data in Table 9.1. The total product curve shows how the quantity of sweaters produced changes as the quantity of labor employed changes. For example, 2 workers can produce 10 sweaters a day (point *C*). Points *A* through *F* on the curve correspond to the rows of Table 9.1. The total product curve separates attainable outputs from unattainable outputs. Points below the *TP* curve are inefficient.

MyEconLab animation

Marginal Product Curve

Figure 9.2 shows Campus Sweaters' marginal product of labor. Part (a) reproduces the total product curve from Fig. 9.1 and part (b) shows the marginal product curve, *MP*.

In part (a), the orange bars illustrate the marginal product of labor. The height of a bar measures marginal product. Marginal product is also measured by the slope of the total product curve. Recall that the slope of a curve is the change in the value of the variable measured on the *y*-axis—output—divided by the change in the variable measured on the *x*-axis—labor—as we move along the curve. A one-unit increase in labor, from 2 to 3 workers, increases output from 10 to 13 sweaters, so the slope from point *C* to point *D* is 3 sweaters per additional worker, the same as the marginal product we've just calculated.

Again varying the amount of labor in the smallest units possible, we can draw the marginal product curve shown in Fig. 9.2(b). The *height* of this curve measures the *slope* of the total product curve at a point. Part (a) shows that an increase in employment from 2 to 3 workers increases output from 10 to 13 sweaters (an increase of 3). The increase in output of 3 sweaters appears on the *y*-axis of part (b) as the marginal product of going from 2 to 3 workers. We plot that marginal product at the midpoint between 2 and 3 workers. Notice that the marginal product shown in Fig. 9.2(b) reaches a peak at 1.5 workers, and at that point, marginal product is 6 sweaters per additional worker. The peak occurs at 1.5 workers because the total product curve is steepest when employment increases from 1 worker to 2 workers.

The total product and marginal product curves differ across firms and types of goods. GM's product curves are different from those of PennPower, whose curves in turn are different from those of Campus Sweaters. But the shapes of the product curves are similar because almost every production process has two features:

- Increasing marginal returns initially
- Diminishing marginal returns eventually

Increasing Marginal Returns Increasing marginal returns occur when the marginal product of an additional worker exceeds the marginal product of the previous worker. Increasing marginal returns arise from increased specialization and division of labor in the production process.

FIGURE 9.2   Total Product and Marginal Product

(a) Total product

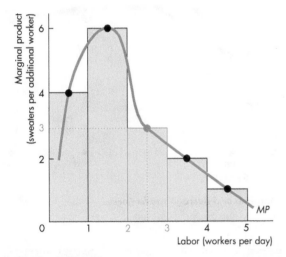

(b) Marginal product

Marginal product is illustrated by the orange bars. For example, when labor increases from 2 to 3 workers a day, marginal product is the orange bar whose height is 3 sweaters. (Marginal product is shown midway between the quantities of labor to emphasize that marginal product results from *changing* the quantity of labor.) The steeper the slope of the total product curve (*TP*) in part (a), the larger is marginal product (*MP*) in part (b). Marginal product increases to a maximum (in this example when 1.5 workers a day are employed) and then declines—diminishing marginal product.

———— MyEconLab animation ————

For example, if Campus Sweaters employs one worker, that person must learn all the aspects of sweater production: running the knitting machines, fixing breakdowns, packaging and mailing sweaters, buying and checking the type and color of the wool. All these tasks must be performed by that one person.

If Campus Sweaters hires a second person, the two workers can specialize in different parts of the production process and can produce more than twice as much as one worker. The marginal product of the second worker is greater than the marginal product of the first worker. Marginal returns are increasing.

Diminishing Marginal Returns Most production processes experience increasing marginal returns initially, but all production processes eventually reach a point of *diminishing* marginal returns. **Diminishing marginal returns** occur when the marginal product of an additional worker is less than the marginal product of the previous worker.

Diminishing marginal returns arise from the fact that more and more workers are using the same capital and working in the same space. As more workers are added, there is less and less for the additional workers to do that is productive. For example, if Campus Sweaters hires a third worker, output increases but not by as much as it did when it hired the second worker. In this case, after two workers are hired, all the gains from specialization and the division of labor have been exhausted. By hiring a third worker, the factory produces more sweaters, but the equipment is being operated closer to its limits. There are even times when the third worker has nothing to do because the machines are running without the need for further attention. Hiring more and more workers continues to increase output but by successively smaller amounts. Marginal returns are diminishing. This phenomenon is such a pervasive one that it is called a "law"—the law of diminishing returns. The **law of diminishing returns** states that

> As a firm uses more of a variable factor of production with a given quantity of the fixed factor of production, the marginal product of the variable factor eventually diminishes.

You are going to return to the law of diminishing returns when we study a firm's costs, but before we do that, let's look at the average product of labor and the average product curve.

Average Product Curve

Figure 9.3 illustrates Campus Sweaters' average product of labor and shows the relationship between average product and marginal product. Points *B* through *F* on the average product curve *AP* correspond to those same rows in Table 9.1. Average product increases from 1 to 2 workers (its maximum value at point *C*) but then decreases as yet more workers are employed. Notice also that average product is largest when average product and marginal product are equal. That is, the marginal product curve cuts the average product curve at the point of maximum average product. For the number of workers at which marginal product exceeds average product, average product is *increasing*. For the number of workers at which marginal product is less than average product, average product is *decreasing*.

The relationship between the average product and marginal product is a general feature of the relationship between the average and marginal values of any variable—even your grades.

FIGURE 9.3 Average Product

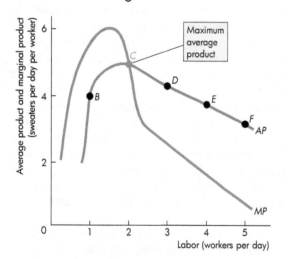

The figure shows the average product of labor and the connection between average product and marginal product. With 1 worker, marginal product exceeds average product, so average product is increasing. With 2 workers, marginal product equals average product, so average product is at its maximum. With more than 2 workers, marginal product is less than average product, so average product is decreasing.

MyEconLab animation

Economics in Action

How to Pull Up Your Average

Do you want to pull up your average grade? Then make sure that your grade this semester is better than your current average! This semester is your marginal semester. If your marginal grade exceeds your average grade (like the second semester in the figure), your average will rise. If your marginal grade equals your average grade (like the third semester in the figure), your average won't change. If your marginal grade is below your average grade (like the fourth semester in the figure), your average will fall.

The relationship between your marginal and average grades is exactly the same as that between marginal product and average product.

Marginal and Average Grade Curves

Campus Sweaters' product curves influence its costs, as you are now going to see.

Short-Run Cost

To produce more output in the short run, a firm must employ more labor, which means that it must increase its costs. We describe the relationship between output and cost by using three cost concepts:

- Total cost
- Marginal cost
- Average cost

Total Cost

A firm's **total cost** (TC) is the cost of *all* the factors of production it uses. We separate total cost into total *fixed* cost and total *variable* cost.

Total fixed cost (TFC) is the cost of the firm's fixed factors. For Campus Sweaters, total fixed cost includes the cost of renting knitting machines and *normal profit*, which is the opportunity cost of Cindy's entrepreneurship (see Chapter 8, p. 181). The quantities of fixed factors don't change as output changes, so total fixed cost is the same at all outputs.

Total variable cost (TVC) is the cost of the firm's variable factors. For Campus Sweaters, labor is the variable factor, so this component of cost is its wage bill. Total variable cost changes as output changes.

Total cost is the sum of total fixed cost and total variable cost. That is,

$$TC = TFC + TVC.$$

The table in Fig. 9.4 shows total costs. Campus Sweaters rents one knitting machine for $25 a day, so its TFC is $25. To produce sweaters, the firm hires labor, which costs $25 a day. TVC is the number of workers multiplied by $25. For example, to produce 13 sweaters a day, in row D, the firm hires 3 workers and TVC is $75. TC is the sum of TFC and TVC, so to produce 13 sweaters a day, TC is $100. Check the calculations in the other rows of the table.

Figure 9.4 shows Campus Sweaters' total cost curves, which graph total cost against output. The green TFC curve is horizontal because total fixed cost ($25 a day) does not change when output changes. The purple TVC curve and the blue TC curve both slope upward because to increase output, more labor must be employed, which increases total variable cost. Total fixed cost equals the vertical distance between the TVC and TC curves.

Let's now look at a firm's marginal cost.

FIGURE 9.4   Total Cost Curves

$TC = TFC + TVC$

	Labor (workers per day)	Output (sweaters per day)	Total fixed cost (TFC)	Total variable cost (TVC)	Total cost (TC)
			(dollars per day)		
A	0	0	25	0	25
B	1	4	25	25	50
C	2	10	25	50	75
D	**3**	**13**	**25**	**75**	**100**
E	4	15	25	100	125
F	5	16	25	1	50

Campus Sweaters rents a knitting machine for $25 a day, so this cost is the firm's total fixed cost. The firm hires workers at a wage rate of $25 a day, and this cost is its total variable cost. For example, in row D, Campus Sweaters employs 3 workers and its total variable cost is $3 \times \$25$, which equals $75. Total cost is the sum of total fixed cost and total variable cost. For example, when Campus Sweaters employs 3 workers, total cost is $100—total fixed cost of $25 plus total variable cost of $75.

The graph shows Campus Sweaters' total cost curves. Total fixed cost is constant—the TFC curve is a horizontal line. Total variable cost increases as output increases, so the TVC curve and the TC curve increase as output increases. The vertical distance between the TC curve and the TVC curve equals total fixed cost, as illustrated by the two arrows.

—— MyEconLab animation ——

Marginal Cost

Figure 9.4 shows that total variable cost and total cost increase at a decreasing rate at small outputs but eventually, as output increases, total variable cost and total cost increase at an increasing rate. To understand this pattern in the change in total cost as output increases, we need to use the concept of *marginal cost*.

A firm's **marginal cost** is the increase in total cost that results from a one-unit increase in output. We calculate marginal cost as the increase in total cost divided by the increase in output. The table in Fig. 9.5 shows this calculation. When, for example, output increases from 10 sweaters to 13 sweaters, total cost increases from $75 to $100. The change in output is 3 sweaters, and the change in total cost is $25. The marginal cost of one of those 3 sweaters is ($25 ÷ 3), which equals $8.33.

Figure 9.5 graphs the marginal cost data in the table as the red marginal cost curve, *MC*. This curve is U-shaped because when Campus Sweaters hires a second worker, marginal cost decreases, but when it hires a third, a fourth, and a fifth worker, marginal cost successively increases.

At small outputs, marginal cost decreases as output increases because of greater specialization and the division of labor. But as output increases further, marginal cost eventually increases because of the *law of diminishing returns*. The law of diminishing returns means that the output produced by each additional worker is successively smaller. To produce an additional unit of output, ever more workers are required, and the cost of producing the additional unit of output—marginal cost—must eventually increase.

Marginal cost tells us how total cost changes as output increases. The final cost concept tells us what it costs, on average, to produce a unit of output. Let's now look at Campus Sweaters' average costs.

Average Cost

Three average costs of production are

1. Average fixed cost
2. Average variable cost
3. Average total cost

Average fixed cost (*AFC*) is total fixed cost per unit of output. **Average variable cost** (*AVC*) is total variable cost per unit of output. **Average total cost** (*ATC*) is total cost per unit of output. The average cost con-

cepts are calculated from the total cost concepts as follows:

$$TC = TFC + TVC.$$

Divide each total cost term by the quantity produced, Q, to get

$$\frac{TC}{Q} = \frac{TFC}{Q} + \frac{TVC}{Q},$$

or

$$ATC = AFC + AVC.$$

The table in Fig. 9.5 shows the calculation of average total cost. For example, in row *C*, output is 10 sweaters. Average fixed cost is ($25 ÷ 10), which equals $2.50, average variable cost is ($50 ÷ 10), which equals $5.00, and average total cost is ($75 ÷ 10), which equals $7.50. Note that average total cost is equal to average fixed cost ($2.50) plus average variable cost ($5.00).

Figure 9.5 shows the average cost curves. The green average fixed cost curve (*AFC*) slopes downward. As output increases, the same constant total fixed cost is spread over a larger output. The blue average total cost curve (*ATC*) and the purple average variable cost curve (*AVC*) are U-shaped. The vertical distance between the average total cost and average variable cost curves is equal to average fixed cost—as indicated by the two arrows. That distance shrinks as output increases because average fixed cost declines with increasing output.

Marginal Cost and Average Cost

The marginal cost curve (*MC*) intersects the average variable cost curve and the average total cost curve *at their minimum points*. When marginal cost is less than average cost, average cost is decreasing, and when marginal cost exceeds average cost, average cost is increasing. This relationship holds for both the *ATC* curve and the *AVC* curve. It is another example of the relationship you saw in Fig. 9.3 for average product and marginal product and in your average and marginal grades.

Why the Average Total Cost Curve Is U-Shaped

Average total cost is the sum of average fixed cost and average variable cost, so the shape of the *ATC* curve

FIGURE 9.5   Marginal Cost and Average Costs

Marginal cost is calculated as the change in total cost divided by the change in output. When output increases from 4 to 10 sweaters, an increase of 6 sweaters, total cost increases by $25. Marginal cost is $25 ÷ 6, which is $4.17.

Each average cost concept is calculated by dividing the related total cost by output. When 10 sweaters are produced, AFC is $2.50 ($25 ÷ 10), AVC is $5 ($50 ÷ 10), and ATC is $7.50 ($75 ÷ 10).

The graph shows that the MC curve is U-shaped and intersects the AVC curve and the ATC curve at their minimum points. The average fixed cost curve (AFC) is downward sloping. The ATC curve and AVC curve are U-shaped. The vertical distance between the ATC curve and the AVC curve is equal to average fixed cost, as illustrated by the two arrows.

	Labor (workers per day)	Output (sweaters per day)	Total fixed cost (TFC)	Total variable cost (TVC)	Total cost (TC)	Marginal cost (MC) (dollars per additional sweater)	Average fixed cost (AFC)	Average variable cost (AVC)	Average total cost (ATC)
			(dollars per day)				(dollars per sweater)		
A	0	0	25	0	25		—	—	—
						. . . . 6.25			
B	1	4	25	25	50		6.25	6.25	12.50
						. . . . 4.17			
C	2	10	25	50	75		2.50	5.00	7.50
						. . . . 8.33			
D	3	13	25	75	100		1.92	5.77	7.69
						. . . . . . .12.50			
E	4	15	25	100	125		1.67	6.67	8.33
						. . . . . . .25.00			
F	5	16	25	125	150		1.56	7.81	9.38

MyEconLab animation

combines the shapes of the *AFC* and *AVC* curves. The U shape of the *ATC* curve arises from the influence of two opposing forces:

1. Spreading total fixed cost over a larger output
2. Eventually diminishing returns

When output increases, the firm spreads its total fixed cost over a larger output and so its average fixed cost decreases—its *AFC* curve slopes downward.

Diminishing returns means that as output increases, ever-larger amounts of labor are needed to produce an additional unit of output. So as output increases, average variable cost decreases initially but eventually increases, and the *AVC* curve slopes upward. The *AVC* curve is U-shaped.

The shape of the *ATC* curve combines these two effects. Initially, as output increases, both average fixed cost and average variable cost decrease, so average total cost decreases. The *ATC* curve slopes downward.

But as output increases further and diminishing returns set in, average variable cost starts to increase. With average fixed cost decreasing more quickly than average variable cost is increasing, the *ATC* curve continues to slope downward. Eventually, average variable cost starts to increase more quickly than average fixed cost decreases, so average total cost starts to increase. The *ATC* curve slopes upward.

Cost Curves and Product Curves

The technology that a firm uses determines its costs. A firm's cost curves come directly from its product curves. You've used this link in the tables in which we have calculated total cost from the total product schedule and information about the prices of the factors of production. We're now going to get a clearer view of the link between the product curves and the cost curves. We'll look first at the link between total cost and total product and then at the links between the average and marginal product and cost curves.

Total Product and Total Variable Cost Figure 9.6 shows the links between the firm's total product curve, *TP*, and its total *variable* cost curve, *TVC*. The graph is a bit unusual in two ways. First, it measures two variables on the *x*-axis—labor and variable cost. Second, it graphs the *TVC* curve but with variable cost on the *x*-axis and output on the *y*-axis. The graph can show labor and cost on the *x*-axis because variable cost is proportional to labor. One worker costs $25 a day. Graphing output against labor gives the *TP* curve and graphing variable cost against output gives the *TVC* curve.

FIGURE 9.6   Total Product and Total Variable Cost

Output plotted against labor is the *TP* curve. Output plotted against the cost of labor is the *TVC* curve.

The figure shows the total product curve, *TP*, as a graph of output (sweaters per day) plotted against labor (workers per day). It also shows the total variable cost curve, *TVC*, as a graph of total variable cost (dollars per day) against output. The only difference between the *TVC* curve here and that in Fig. 9.4 is that we've switched the *x*-axis and *y*-axis.

MyEconLab animation

 ECONOMICS IN THE NEWS

Checkout Cost Curves

Welcome to More Self-Checkouts
Self-checkout is expanding. One estimate is that it will grow by 84 percent over the next five years. And new technologies will enable customers armed with smart phones to use apps that scan and pay for items in the aisles.

Source: MSNBC.com, July 22, 2011

DATA AND ASSUMPTIONS

A grocery store paid $20,000 to install 5 worker-operated checkout lines. With a life of 9 years and operating for 10 hours a day, these machines have an *implicit rental rate* of $1.00 an hour. Checkout clerks can be hired for $10 an hour. The total product schedule (checkouts per hour) for this store is:

Checkout clerks	1	2	3	4	5
Checkouts per hour	12	22	30	36	40

Another grocery store has converted to all self-checkout. It paid $100,000 to install a 5-line self-operated system. With a 5-year life and operating for 10 hours a day, the system has an *implicit rental rate* of $7.00 an hour. It hires checkout assistants to help customers at $10 an hour—the same wage as paid to checkout clerks. The total product schedule for this store is:

Checkout assistants	1	1	1	2
Checkouts per hour	12	22	30	36

That is, one checkout assistant can help shoppers check out up to a rate of 30 an hour and a second assistant can boost output to 36 an hour. (Shoppers using self-checkout aren't as quick as clerks, so the fastest rate at which this store can check out customers is 36 an hour.)

THE PROBLEM

- Which checkout system has the lower average total cost (*ATC*)? Which system has the lower marginal cost (*MC*)? Sketch the *ATC* and *MC* curves for the two systems.

THE SOLUTION

- Start with the worker-operated checkout system. Fixed cost is $1.00 per hour and variable cost is $10.00 per clerk. So the total cost schedule is:

Checkout clerks	1	2	3	4	5
Checkouts per hour	12	22	30	36	40
Total cost (*TC*) per hour	11	21	31	41	51

- Calculate *MC* as the change in *TC* divided by the change in output (change in number of checkouts) and calculate *ATC* as *TC* divided by output to get:

Checkouts per hour	12	22	30	36	40
Marginal cost (*MC*)	0.83	1.00	1.25	1.67	2.50
Average total cost (*ATC*)	0.92	0.95	1.03	1.14	1.28

- Figure 1 graphs the *MC* and *ATC* values at each output rate.

Figure 1   Operator Checkout

Figure 2   Self-Checkout

- Now do similar calculations for the self-checkout system. Fixed cost is $7.00 per hour and variable cost is $10.00 per clerk hour. So the total cost schedule is:

Checkout assistants	1	1	1	2
Checkouts per hour	12	22	30	36
Total cost (*TC*) per hour	17	17	17	27

- Calculate *MC* and *ATC* in the same way as before to get

Checkouts per hour	12	22	30	36
Marginal cost (*MC*)	0.83	0	0	1.67
Average total cost (*ATC*)	1.42	0.77	0.57	0.75

- Figure 2 graphs the *MC* and *ATC* values at each output rate.

- Figure 3 compares the *ATC* of the two systems. You can see that the self-checkout system has higher *ATC* at low output rates and lower *ATC* at higher output rates. The reason is that self-checkout has a higher fixed cost and lower variable cost than the worker-operated system.

Figure 3   ATC Compared

Average and Marginal Product and Cost Figure 9.7 shows the links between the firm's average and marginal product curves and its average and marginal cost curves. The upper graph shows the average product curve, *AP,* and the marginal product curve, *MP*—like those in Fig. 9.3. The lower graph shows the average variable cost curve, *AVC,* and the marginal cost curve, *MC*—like those in Fig. 9.5.

As labor increases up to 1.5 workers a day (upper graph), output increases to 6.5 sweaters a day (lower graph). Marginal product and average product rise and marginal cost and average variable cost fall. At the point of maximum marginal product, marginal cost is at a minimum.

As labor increases from 1.5 workers to 2 workers a day, (upper graph) output increases from 6.5 sweaters to 10 sweaters a day (lower graph). Marginal product falls and marginal cost rises, but average product continues to rise and average variable cost continues to fall. At the point of maximum average product, average variable cost is at a minimum. As labor increases further, output increases. Average product diminishes and average variable cost increases.

Shifts in the Cost Curves

The position of a firm's short-run cost curves depends on two factors:

- Technology
- Prices of factors of production

Technology A technological change that increases productivity increases the marginal product and average product of labor. With a better technology, the same factors of production can produce more output, so the technological advance lowers the costs of production and shifts the cost curves downward.

For example, advances in robot production techniques have increased productivity in the automobile industry. As a result, the product curves of Chrysler, Ford, and GM have shifted upward and their cost curves have shifted downward. But the relationships between their product curves and cost curves have not changed. The curves are still linked in the way shown in Figs. 9.6 and 9.7.

Often, as in the case of robots producing cars, a technological advance results in a firm using more capital, a fixed factor, and less labor, a variable factor.

FIGURE 9.7 Average and Marginal Product Curves and Cost Curves

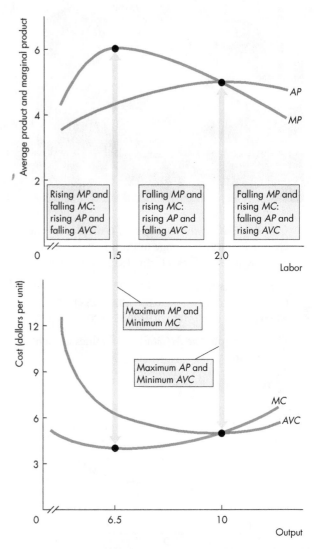

A firm's *MP* curve is linked to its *MC* curve. If, as the firm increases its labor from 0 to 1.5 workers a day, the firm's marginal product rises, its marginal cost falls. If marginal product is at a maximum, marginal cost is at a minimum. If, as the firm hires more labor, its marginal product diminishes, its marginal cost rises.

A firm's *AP* curve is linked to its *AVC* curve. If, as the firm increases its labor to 2 workers a day, its average product rises, its average variable cost falls. If average product is at a maximum, average variable cost is at a minimum. If, as the firm hires more labor, its average product diminishes, its average variable cost rises.

MyEconLab animation

TABLE 9.2   A Compact Glossary of Costs

Term	Symbol	Definition	Equation
Fixed cost		Cost that is independent of the output level; cost of a fixed factor of production	
Variable cost		Cost that varies with the output level; cost of a variable factor of production	
Total fixed cost	TFC	Cost of the fixed factors of production	
Total variable cost	TVC	Cost of the variable factors of production	
Total cost	TC	Cost of all factors of production	$TC = TFC + TVC$
Output (total product)	TP	Total quantity produced (output Q)	
Marginal cost	MC	Change in total cost resulting from a one-unit increase in total product	$MC = \Delta TC \div \Delta Q$
Average fixed cost	AFC	Total fixed cost per unit of output	$AFC = TFC \div Q$
Average variable cost	AVC	Total variable cost per unit of output	$AVC = TVC \div Q$
Average total cost	ATC	Total cost per unit of output	$ATC = AFC + AVC$

Another example is the use of ATMs by banks to dispense cash. ATMs, which are fixed capital, have replaced tellers, which are variable labor. Such a technological change decreases total cost but increases fixed costs and decreases variable cost. This change in the mix of fixed cost and variable cost means that at small outputs, average total cost might increase, while at large outputs, average total cost decreases.

Prices of Factors of Production   An increase in the price of a factor of production increases the firm's costs and shifts its cost curves. How the curves shift depends on which factor price changes.

An increase in rent or some other component of *fixed* cost shifts the *TFC* and *AFC* curves upward and shifts the *TC* curve upward but leaves the *AVC* and *TVC* curves and the *MC* curve unchanged. For example, if the interest expense paid by a trucking company increases, the fixed cost of transportation services increases.

An increase in wages, gasoline, or another component of *variable* cost shifts the *TVC* and *AVC* curves upward and shifts the *MC* curve upward but leaves the *AFC* and *TFC* curves unchanged. For example, if

truck drivers' wages or the price of gasoline increases, the variable cost and marginal cost of transportation services increase.

You've now completed your study of short-run costs. All the concepts that you've met are summarized in a compact glossary in Table 9.2.

REVIEW QUIZ

1   What relationships do a firm's short-run cost curves show?
2   How does marginal cost change as output increases (a) initially and (b) eventually?
3   What does the law of diminishing returns imply for the shape of the marginal cost curve?
4   What is the shape of the *AFC* curve and why does it have this shape?
5   What are the shapes of the *AVC* curve and the *ATC* curve and why do they have these shapes?

You can work these questions in Study Plan 9.3 and get instant feedback.   MyEconLab

▶ Long-Run Cost

We are now going to study the firm's long-run costs. In the long run, a firm can vary both the quantity of labor and the quantity of capital, so in the long run, all the firm's costs are variable.

The behavior of long-run cost depends on the firm's *production function*, which is the relationship between the maximum output attainable and the quantities of both labor and capital.

The Production Function

Table 9.3 shows Campus Sweaters' production function. The table lists total product schedules for four different quantities of capital. The quantity of capital identifies the plant size. The numbers for plant 1 are for a factory with 1 knitting machine—the case we've just studied. The other three plants have 2, 3, and 4 machines. If Campus Sweaters uses plant 2 with 2 knitting machines, the various amounts of labor can produce the outputs shown in the second column of the table. The other two columns show the outputs of yet larger quantities of capital. Each column of the table could be graphed as a total product curve for each plant.

Diminishing Returns Diminishing returns occur with each of the four plant sizes as the quantity of labor increases. You can check that fact by calculating the marginal product of labor in each of the plants with 2, 3, and 4 machines. With each plant size, as the firm increases the quantity of labor employed, the marginal product of labor (eventually) diminishes.

Diminishing Marginal Product of Capital Diminishing returns also occur with each quantity of labor as the quantity of capital increases. You can check that fact by calculating the marginal product of capital at a given quantity of labor. The *marginal product of capital* is the change in total product divided by the change in capital when the quantity of labor is constant—equivalently, the change in output resulting from a one-unit increase in the quantity of capital. For example, if Campus Sweaters has 3 workers and increases its capital from 1 machine to 2 machines, output increases from 13 to 18 sweaters a day. The marginal product of the second machine is 5 sweaters a day. If Campus Sweaters continues to employ 3 workers

TABLE 9.3   The Production Function

Labor (workers per day)	Output (sweaters per day)			
	Plant 1	Plant 2	Plant 3	Plant 4
1	4	10	13	15
2	10	15	18	20
3	13	18	22	24
4	15	20	24	26
5	16	21	25	27
Knitting machines (number)	1	2	3	4

The table shows the total product data for four quantities of capital (plant sizes). The greater the plant size, the larger is the output produced by any given quantity of labor. For a given plant size, the marginal product of labor diminishes as more labor is employed. For a given quantity of labor, the marginal product of capital diminishes as the quantity of capital used increases.

and increases the number of machines from 2 to 3, output increases from 18 to 22 sweaters a day. The marginal product of the third machine is 4 sweaters a day, down from 5 sweaters a day for the second machine.

Let's now see what the production function implies for long-run costs.

Short-Run Cost and Long-Run Cost

As before, Campus Sweaters can hire workers for $25 a day and rent knitting machines for $25 a day. Using these factor prices and the data in Table 9.3, we can calculate the average total cost and graph the ATC curves for factories with 1, 2, 3, and 4 knitting machines. We've already studied the costs of a factory with 1 machine in Figs. 9.4 and 9.5. In Fig. 9.8, the average total cost curve for that case is ATC_1. Figure 9.8 also shows the average total cost curve for a factory with 2 machines, ATC_2, with 3 machines, ATC_3, and with 4 machines, ATC_4.

You can see, in Fig. 9.8, that the plant size has a big effect on the firm's average total cost.

FIGURE 9.8   Short-Run Costs of Four Different Plants

The figure shows short-run average total cost curves for four different quantities of capital at Campus Sweaters. The firm can produce 13 sweaters a day with 1 knitting machine on ATC_1 or with 3 knitting machines on ATC_3 for an average cost of $7.69 a sweater. The firm can produce 13 sweaters a day by using 2 machines on ATC_2 for $6.80 a sweater or by using 4 machines on ATC_4 for $9.50 a sweater.

If the firm produces 13 sweaters a day, the least-cost method of production, *the long-run method*, is with 2 machines on ATC_2.

In Fig. 9.8, two things stand out:

1. Each short-run *ATC* curve is U-shaped.
2. For each short-run *ATC* curve, the larger the plant, the greater is the output at which average total cost is at a minimum.

Each short-run *ATC* curve is U-shaped because, as the quantity of labor increases, its marginal product initially increases and then diminishes. This pattern in the marginal product of labor, which we examined in some detail for the plant with 1 knitting machine on pp. 210–211, occurs at all plant sizes.

The minimum average total cost for a larger plant occurs at a greater output than it does for a smaller plant because the larger plant has a higher total fixed cost and therefore, for any given output, a higher average fixed cost.

Which short-run *ATC* curve a firm operates on depends on the plant it has. In the long run, the firm can choose its plant and the plant it chooses is the one that enables it to produce its planned output at the lowest average total cost.

To see why, suppose that Campus Sweaters plans to produce 13 sweaters a day. In Fig. 9.8, with 1 machine, the average total cost curve is ATC_1 and the

average total cost of 13 sweaters a day is $7.69 a sweater. With 2 machines, on ATC_2, average total cost is $6.80 a sweater. With 3 machines, on ATC_3, average total cost is $7.69 a sweater, the same as with 1 machine. Finally, with 4 machines, on ATC_4, average total cost is $9.50 a sweater.

The economically efficient plant for producing a given output is the one that has the lowest average total cost. For Campus Sweaters, the economically efficient plant to use to produce 13 sweaters a day is the one with 2 machines.

In the long run, Cindy chooses the plant that minimizes average total cost. When a firm is producing a given output at the least possible cost, it is operating on its *long-run average cost curve*.

The **long-run average cost curve** is the relationship between the lowest attainable average total cost and output when the firm can change both the plant it uses and the quantity of labor it employs.

The long-run average cost curve is a planning curve. It tells the firm the plant and the quantity of labor to use at each output to minimize average cost. Once the firm chooses a plant, the firm operates on the short-run cost curves that apply to that plant.

The Long-Run Average Cost Curve

Figure 9.9 shows how a long-run average cost curve is derived. The long-run average cost curve *LRAC* consists of pieces of the four short-run *ATC* curves. For outputs up to 10 sweaters a day, average total cost is the lowest on ATC_1. For outputs between 10 and 18 sweaters a day, average total cost is the lowest on ATC_2. For outputs between 18 and 24 sweaters a day, average total cost is the lowest on ATC_3. And for outputs in excess of 24 sweaters a day, average total cost is the lowest on ATC_4. The piece of each *ATC* curve with the lowest average total cost is highlighted in dark blue in Fig. 9.9. This dark blue scallop-shaped curve made up of the pieces of the four *ATC* curves is the *LRAC* curve.

Economies and Diseconomies of Scale

Economies of scale are features of a firm's technology that make average total cost *fall* as output increases. When economies of scale are present, the *LRAC* curve slopes downward. In Fig. 9.9, Campus Sweaters has economies of scale for outputs up to 15 sweaters a day.

Greater specialization of both labor and capital is the main source of economies of scale. For example, if

GM produces 100 cars a week, each worker must perform many different tasks and the capital must be general-purpose machines and tools. But if GM produces 10,000 cars a week, each worker specializes in a small number of tasks, uses task-specific tools, and becomes highly proficient.

Diseconomies of scale are features of a firm's technology that make average total cost *rise* as output increases. When diseconomies of scale are present, the *LRAC* curve slopes upward. In Fig. 9.9, Campus Sweaters experiences diseconomies of scale at outputs greater than 15 sweaters a day.

The challenge of managing a large enterprise is the main source of diseconomies of scale.

Constant returns to scale are features of a firm's technology that keep average total cost constant as output increases. When constant returns to scale are present, the *LRAC* curve is horizontal.

Economies of Scale at Campus Sweaters The economies of scale and diseconomies of scale at Campus Sweaters arise from the firm's production function in Table 9.3. With 1 machine and 1 worker, the firm produces 4 sweaters a day. With 2 machines and 2 workers, total cost doubles but out-

FIGURE 9.9   Long-Run Average Cost Curve

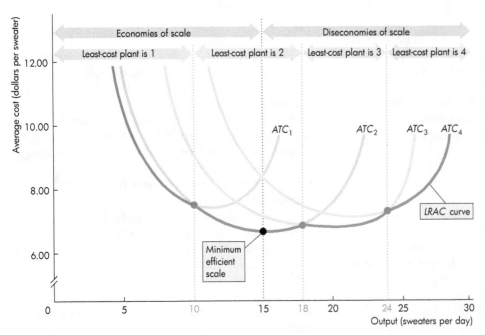

The long-run average cost curve traces the lowest attainable *ATC* when both labor and capital change. The green arrows highlight the output range over which each plant achieves the lowest *ATC*. Within each range, to change the quantity produced, the firm changes the quantity of labor it employs.

Along the *LRAC* curve, economies of scale occur if average cost falls as output increases; diseconomies of scale occur if average cost rises as output increases. Minimum efficient scale is the output at which average cost is lowest, 15 sweaters a day.

Economics in Action

Produce More to Cut Cost

Why do GM, Ford, and the other automakers have expensive equipment lying around that isn't fully used? You can answer this question with what you've learned in this chapter.

The basic answer is that auto production enjoys economies of scale. A larger output rate brings a lower long-run average cost—the firm's *LRAC* curve slopes downward.

An auto producer's average total cost curves look like those in the figure. To produce 20 vehicles an hour, the firm installs the plant with the short-run average total cost curve ATC_1. The average cost of producing a vehicle is \$20,000.

Producing 20 vehicles an hour doesn't use the plant at its lowest possible average total cost. If the firm could sell enough cars for it to produce 40 vehicles an hour, the firm could use its current plant and produce at an average cost of \$15,000 a vehicle.

But if the firm planned to produce 40 vehicles an hour, it would not stick with its current plant. The firm would install a bigger plant with the short-run average total cost curve ATC_2, and produce 40 vehicles an hour for \$10,000 a car.

Automobile Plant Average Cost Curves

---

put more than doubles to 15 sweaters a day, so average cost decreases and Campus Sweaters experiences economies of scale. With 4 machines and 4 workers, total cost doubles again but output less than doubles to 26 sweaters a day, so average cost increases and the firm experiences diseconomies of scale.

Minimum Efficient Scale A firm's **minimum efficient scale** is the *smallest* output at which long-run average cost reaches its lowest level. At Campus Sweaters, the minimum efficient scale is 15 sweaters a day.

The minimum efficient scale plays a role in determining market structure. In a market in which the minimum efficient scale is small relative to market demand, the market has room for many firms, and the market is competitive. In a market in which the minimum efficient scale is large relative to market demand, only a small number of firms, and possibly only one firm, can make a profit and the market is either an oligopoly or monopoly. We will return to this idea in the next three chapters.

REVIEW QUIZ

1 What does a firm's production function show and how is it related to a total product curve?
2 Does the law of diminishing returns apply to capital as well as labor? Explain why or why not.
3 What does a firm's *LRAC* curve show? How is it related to the firm's short-run *ATC* curves?
4 What are economies of scale and diseconomies of scale? How do they arise? What do they imply for the shape of the *LRAC* curve?
5 What is a firm's minimum efficient scale?

You can work these questions in Study Plan 9.4 and get instant feedback.   MyEconLab

◆ *Reading Between the Lines* on pp. 220–221 applies what you've learned about a firm's cost curves. It looks at McDonald's cost curves and explains how increasing plant size can lower average total cost.

Expanding Capacity at McDonald's

McDonald's Rebuilds 12 Restaurants

Dayton Daily News
June 19, 2012

… Construction began last week of a new McDonald's restaurant … in Dayton, bringing to 12 the number of McDonald's restaurants across the Miami Valley scheduled for either a total rebuild or extensive renovations in 2012. …

"We are increasing the capacity to serve more customers more often," said Phil Saken, communications manager for the Ohio region of McDonald's—and that often requires more employees. …

McDonald's and its franchise owners have been aggressively rebuilding or improving their Miami Valley locations for several years in projects that modernize the restaurants' kitchens, service areas and dining rooms, and at most locations, create two drive-through lanes to accommodate more customers during peak times. The rebuilt restaurants usually require hiring additional crew members to accommodate the increased capacity. …

The Troy McDonald's at 1560 W. Main St., which closed March 31, was razed and rebuilt … employed 80 to 85 people when it closed, but will reopen with about 95 employees. …

The McDonald's locations that were built decades ago become inefficient in utilities, service, and operations, Herzog said. "We want to make these stores modern and attractive for customers," he said.

The new Keowee Street restaurant's seating capacity will grow by only a handful to 65, in part because Herzog said about 75 percent of his stores' sales are either drive-through or carry-out.

Employment at the Keowee location will grow slightly: "We've got about 60 to 65 employees now, and we'll probably go to 70 to 80 when we move into the new site," Herzog said.

ESSENCE OF THE STORY

- In 2012, McDonald's rebuilt or extensively renovated 12 restaurants in the Miami Valley, Ohio.

- The goal was to increase capacity to serve more customers.

- Capacity was increased by modernizing the kitchens, service areas, and dining rooms and by creating two drive-through lanes.

- In addition to increasing plant size, McDonald's planned to hire more workers—up from 80–85 to 95 employees in Troy and up from 60–65 to 70–80 at Keowee.

ECONOMIC ANALYSIS

- McDonald's is increasing its output in the Miami Valley.

- A firm can increase output with its existing plant by hiring more labor, or it can increase its plant size, or it can both increase its plant size and hire more labor.

- The decision turns on comparing costs and McDonald's has figured that it minimizes cost by increasing its plant size and hiring more labor.

- We don't know McDonald's actual costs (and they vary from one restaurant to another) but we can gain insight into the firm's decision with an example.

- The table shows an assumed total product schedule for a McDonald's restaurant. It also shows total cost (TC), marginal cost (MC), and average total cost, (ATC).

	Labor (workers per day)	Output (meals per day)	Total cost (TC) (dollars per day)	Marginal cost (MC)	Average total cost (ATC)
				(dollars per meal)	
A	0	0	1,000		—
				. . . . . 2.00	
B	10	400	1,800		4.50
				. . . . . 1.33	
C	20	1,000	2,600		2.60
				. . . . . 2.67	
D	30	1,300	3,400		2.62
				. . . . . 4.00	
E	40	1,500	4,200		2.80
				. . . . . 8.00	
F	50	1,600	5,000		3.13

- Figure 1 graphs the marginal cost and average total cost curves.

- If McDonald's wants to increase production above 1,000 meals per day, marginal cost rises sharply and pulls upward the firm's average total cost.

- But if McDonald's replaces an old restaurant with a new one that has a greater capacity (a modern kitchen, expanded service area, more dining space, and two drive-through lanes), a given quantity of labor can produce a greater output.

- With a bigger capacity, fixed cost increases, so at low output levels, average total cost also increases. But at higher output levels average total cost decreases.

- Figure 2 shows McDonald's original ATC curve, ATC_0, and the new ATC curve for the new, larger, more modern restaurant, ATC_1.

- Increasing output in the larger plant avoids the sharply rising marginal cost and average total cost of the old restaurant.

- In this example, McDonald's can now hire more labor to operate the larger restaurant and average total cost falls as output increases above 1,000 meals per day.

- Figure 2 also shows McDonald's long-run average cost curve (LRAC).

- If the firm wants to expand output yet further and avoid the rising costs along ATC_1, it can build an even bigger restaurant and move along its long-run average cost curve.

Figure 1 McDonald's Short-Run Cost Curves

Figure 2 McDonald's Long-Run Cost Curves

221

222   CHAPTER 9 Output and Costs

SUMMARY

Key Points

Decision Time Frames (p. 204)

- In the short run, the quantity of at least one factor of production is fixed and the quantities of the other factors of production can be varied.
- In the long run, the quantities of all factors of production can be varied.

Working Problems 1 and 2 will give you a better understanding of a firm's decision time frames.

Short-Run Technology Constraint (pp. 205–208)

- A total product curve shows the quantity a firm can produce with a given quantity of capital and different quantities of labor.
- Initially, the marginal product of labor increases as the quantity of labor increases, because of increased specialization and the division of labor.
- Eventually, marginal product diminishes because an increasing quantity of labor must share a fixed quantity of capital—the law of diminishing returns.
- Initially, average product increases as the quantity of labor increases, but eventually average product diminishes.

Working Problems 3 to 8 will give you a better understanding of a firm's short-run technology constraint.

Short-Run Cost (pp. 209–215)

- As output increases, total fixed cost is constant, and total variable cost and total cost increase.
- As output increases, average fixed cost decreases and average variable cost, average total cost, and marginal cost decrease at low outputs and increase at high outputs. These cost curves are U-shaped.

Working Problems 9 to 14 will give you a better understanding of a firm's short-run cost.

Long-Run Cost (pp. 216–219)

- A firm has a set of short-run cost curves for each different plant. For each output, the firm has one least-cost plant. The larger the output, the larger is the plant that will minimize average total cost.
- The long-run average cost curve traces out the lowest attainable average total cost at each output when both capital and labor inputs can be varied.
- With economies of scale, the long-run average cost curve slopes downward. With diseconomies of scale, the long-run average cost curve slopes upward.

Working Problems 15 to 20 will give you a better understanding of a firm's long-run cost.

Key Terms

Average fixed cost, 210
Average product, 205
Average total cost, 210
Average variable cost, 210
Constant returns to scale, 218
Diminishing marginal returns, 207
Diseconomies of scale, 218

Economies of scale, 218
Law of diminishing returns, 207
Long run, 204
Long-run average cost curve, 217
Marginal cost, 210
Marginal product, 205
Minimum efficient scale, 219

Short run, 204
Sunk cost, 204
Total cost, 209
Total fixed cost, 209
Total product, 205
Total variable cost, 209

MyEconLab   You can work Problems 1 to 21 in MyEconLab Chapter 9 Study Plan and get instant feedback.

Decision Time Frames (Study Plan 9.1)

1. Which of the following news items involves a short-run decision and which involves a long-run decision? Explain.
   January 31, 2008: Starbucks will open 75 more stores abroad than originally predicted, for a total of 975.
   February 25, 2008: For three hours on Tuesday, Starbucks will shut down every single one of its 7,100 stores so that baristas can receive a refresher course.
   June 2, 2008: Starbucks replaces baristas with vending machines.
   July 18, 2008: Starbucks is closing 616 stores by the end of March.

2. **Maryland Farmers Turn from Tobacco to Flowers**
   Maryland tobacco farmers will be subsidized if they switch from growing tobacco to growing crops such as flowers and organic vegetables.
   Source: *The New York Times*, February 25, 2001
   a. How does offering farmers a payment to exit tobacco growing influence the opportunity cost of growing tobacco?
   b. What is the opportunity cost of using the equipment owned by a tobacco farmer?

Short-Run Technology Constraint (Study Plan 9.2)

Use the following table to work Problems 3 to 7. The table sets out Sue's Surfboards' total product schedule.

Labor (workers per week)	Output (surfboards per week)
1	30
2	70
3	120
4	160
5	190
6	210
7	220

3. Draw the total product curve.
4. Calculate the average product of labor and draw the average product curve.
5. Calculate the marginal product of labor and draw the marginal product curve.

6. a. Over what output range does Sue's Surfboards enjoy the benefits of increased specialization and division of labor?
   b. Over what output range does the firm experience diminishing marginal product of labor?
   c. Over what output range does the firm experience an increasing average product of labor but a diminishing marginal product of labor?

7. Explain how it is possible for a firm to experience simultaneously an increasing *average* product but a diminishing *marginal* product.

8. **Business Boot Camp**
   At a footwear company called Caboots, sales rose from $160,000 in 2000 to $2.3 million in 2006, but in 2007 sales dipped to $1.5 million. Joey and Priscilla Sanchez, who run Caboots, blame the decline partly on a flood that damaged the firm's office and sapped morale.
   Source: CNN, April 23, 2008
   If the Sanchezes are correct in their assumptions and the prices of footwear didn't change
   a. Explain the effect of the flood on the total product curve and marginal product curve at Caboots.
   b. Draw a graph to show the effect of the flood on the total product curve and marginal product curve at Caboots.

Short-Run Cost (Study Plan 9.3)

Use the following data to work Problems 9 to 13.
Sue's Surfboards, in Problem 3, hires workers at $500 a week and its total fixed cost is $1,000 a week.

9. Calculate total cost, total variable cost, and total fixed cost of each output in the table. Plot these points and sketch the short-run total cost curves passing through them.
10. Calculate average total cost, average fixed cost, average variable cost, and marginal cost of each output in the table. Plot these points and sketch the short-run average and marginal cost curves passing through them.
11. Illustrate the connection between Sue's *AP, MP, AVC*, and *MC* curves in graphs like those in Fig. 9.7.

12. Sue's Surfboards rents a factory building. If the rent is increased by $200 a week and other things remain the same, how do Sue's Surfboards' short-run average cost curves and marginal cost curve change?

13. Workers at Sue's Surfboards negotiate a wage increase of $100 a week for each worker. If other things remain the same, explain how Sue's Surfboards' short-run average cost curves and marginal cost curve change.

14. **Grain Prices Go the Way of the Oil Price**

Every morning millions of Americans confront the latest trend in commodities markets at their kitchen table. Rising prices for crops have begun to drive up the cost of breakfast.

Source: *The Economist*, July 21, 2007

Explain how the rising price of crops affects the average total cost and marginal cost of producing breakfast cereals.

Long-Run Cost (Study Plan 9.4)

Use the table in Problem 3 and the following information to work Problems 15 and 16.

Sue's Surfboards buys a second plant and the output produced by each worker increases by 50 percent. The total fixed cost of operating each plant is $1,000 a week. Each worker is paid $500 a week.

15. Calculate the average total cost of producing 180 and 240 surfboards a week when Sue's Surfboards operates two plants. Graph these points and sketch the *ATC* curve.

16. a. To produce 180 surfboards a week, is it efficient to operate one or two plants?

    b. To produce 160 surfboards a week, is it efficient for Sue's to operate one or two plants?

Use the following table to work Problems 17 to 20. The table shows the production function of Jackie's Canoe Rides.

Labor (workers per day)	Output (rides per day)			
	Plant 1	Plant 2	Plant 3	Plant 4
10	20	40	55	65
20	40	60	75	85
30	65	75	90	100
40	75	85	100	110
Canoes	10	20	30	40

Jackie's pays $100 a day for each canoe it rents and $50 a day for each canoe operator it hires.

17. Graph the *ATC* curves for Plant 1 and Plant 2. Explain why these *ATC* curves differ.

18. Graph the *ATC* curves for Plant 3 and Plant 4. Explain why these *ATC* curves differ.

19. a. On Jackie's *LRAC* curve, what is the average cost of producing 40, 75, and 85 rides a week?

    b. What is Jackie's minimum efficient scale?

20. a. Explain how Jackie's uses its *LRAC* curve to decide how many canoes to rent.

    b. Does Jackie's production function feature economies of scale or diseconomies of scale?

Economics in the News (Study Plan 9.N)

21. **Airlines Seek Out New Ways to Save on Fuel as Costs Soar**

The financial pain of higher fuel prices is particularly acute for airlines because it is their single biggest expense. Airlines pump about 7,000 gallons into a Boeing 737 and about 60,000 gallons into the bigger 747 jet. Each generation of aircraft is more efficient: An Airbus A330 long-range jet uses 38 percent less fuel than the DC-10 it replaced, while the Airbus A319 medium-range jet is 27 percent more efficient than the DC-9 it replaced.

Source: *The New York Times*, June 11, 2008

a. Is the price of fuel a fixed cost or a variable cost for an airline?

b. Explain how an increase in the price of fuel changes an airline's total costs, average costs, and marginal cost.

c. Draw a graph to show the effects of an increase in the price of fuel on an airline's *TFC*, *TVC*, *AFC*, *AVC*, and *MC* curves.

d. Explain how a technological advance that makes an airplane engine more fuel efficient changes an airline's total product, marginal product, and average product.

e. Draw a graph to illustrate the effects of a more fuel-efficient aircraft on an airline's *TP*, *MP*, and *AP* curves.

f. Explain how a technological advance that makes an airplane engine more fuel efficient changes an airline's average variable cost, marginal cost, and average total cost.

g. Draw a graph to illustrate how a technological advance that makes an airplane engine more fuel efficient changes an airline's *AVC*, *MC*, and *ATC* curves.

ADDITIONAL PROBLEMS AND APPLICATIONS

MyEconLab   You can work these problems in MyEconLab if assigned by your instructor.

Decision Time Frames

22. A Bakery on the Rise

Some 500 customers a day line up to buy Avalon's breads, scones, muffins, and coffee. Staffing and management are worries. Avalon now employs 35 and plans to hire 15 more. Its payroll will climb by 30 percent to 40 percent. The new CEO has executed an ambitious agenda that includes the move to a larger space, which will increase the rent from $3,500 to $10,000 a month.

Source: CNN, March 24, 2008

a. Which of Avalon's decisions described in the news clip is a short-run decision and which is a long-run decision?

b. Why is Avalon's long-run decision riskier than its short-run decision?

23. The Sunk-Cost Fallacy

You have good tickets to a basketball game an hour's drive away. There's a blizzard raging outside, and the game is being televised. You can sit warm and safe at home and watch it on TV, or you can bundle up, dig out your car, and go to the game. What do you do?

Source: *Slate*, September 9, 2005

a. What type of cost is your expenditure on tickets?

b. Why is the cost of the ticket irrelevant to your current decision about whether to stay at home or go to the game?

Short-Run Technology Constraint

24. Terri runs a rose farm. One worker produces 1,000 roses a week; hiring a second worker doubles her total product; hiring a third worker doubles her output again; hiring a fourth worker increased her total product but by only 1,000 roses. Construct Terri's marginal product and average product schedules. Over what range of workers do marginal returns increase?

Short-Run Cost

25. Use the events described in the news clip in Problem 22. By how much will Avalon's short-run decision increase its total variable cost? By how much will Avalon's long-run decision increase its monthly total fixed cost? Sketch Avalon's short-run *ATC* curve before and after the events described in the news clip.

26. Bill's Bakery has a fire and Bill loses some of his cost data. The bits of paper that he recovers after the fire provide the information in the following table (all the cost numbers are dollars).

TP	AFC	AVC	ATC	MC
10	120	100	220	
				80
20	*A*	*B*	150	
				90
30	40	90	130	
				130
40	30	*C*	*D*	
				E
50	24	108	132	

Bill asks you to come to his rescue and provide the missing data in the five spaces identified as *A, B, C, D*, and *E*.

Use the following table to work Problems 27 and 28. ProPainters hires students at $250 a week to paint houses. It leases equipment at $500 a week. The table sets out its total product schedule.

Labor (students)	Output (houses painted per week)
1	2
2	5
3	9
4	12
5	14
6	15

27. If ProPainters paints 12 houses a week, calculate its total cost, average total cost, and marginal cost. At what output is average total cost a minimum?

28. Explain why the gap between ProPainters' total cost and total variable cost is the same no matter how many houses are painted.

29. A Pepsi, a Business Decision

PepsiCo has done a deal with 300 small Mexican farmers close to their two factories to buy corn at a guaranteed price. PepsiCo saves transportation costs and the use of local farms assures it access to the type of corn best suited to its products and processes. "That gives us great leverage because corn prices don't fluctuate so much, but transportation costs do," said Pedro Padierna, president of PepsiCo in Mexico.

Source: *The New York Times*, February 21, 2011

a. How do fluctuations in the price of corn and in transportation costs influence PepsiCo's short-run cost curves?

b. How does the deal with the farmers to avoid fluctuations in costs benefit PepsiCo?

Long-Run Cost

Use the table in Problem 28 and the following information to work Problems 30 and 31.

If ProPainters doubles the number of students it hires and doubles the amount of equipment it leases, it experiences diseconomies of scale.

30. Explain how the *ATC* curve with one unit of equipment differs from that when ProPainters uses double the amount of equipment.

31. Explain what might be the source of the diseconomies of scale that ProPainters experiences.

Use the following information to work Problems 32 and 33.

The table shows the production function of Bonnie's Balloon Rides. Bonnie's pays $500 a day for each balloon it rents and $25 a day for each balloon operator it hires.

Labor (workers per day)	Output (rides per day)			
	Plant 1	Plant 2	Plant 3	Plant 4
10	6	10	13	15
20	10	15	18	20
30	13	18	22	24
40	15	20	24	26
50	16	21	25	27
Balloons (number)	1	2	3	4

32. Graph the *ATC* curves for Plant 1 and Plant 2. Explain why these *ATC* curves differ.

33. Graph the *ATC* curves for Plant 3 and Plant 4 Explain why these *ATC* curves differ.

34. a. On Bonnie's *LRAC* curve, what is the average cost of producing 18 rides and 15 rides a day?

b. Explain how Bonnie's uses its long-run average cost curve to decide how many balloons to rent.

Use the following news clip to work Problems 35 and 36.

Gap Will Focus on Smaller Scale Stores

Gap has too many stores that are 12,500 square feet.

The target store size is 6,000 square feet to 10,000 square feet, so Gap plans to combine previously separate concept stores. Some Gap body, adult, maternity, baby and kids stores will be combined in one store.

Source: CNN, June 10, 2008

35. Thinking of a Gap store as a production plant, explain why Gap is making a decision to reduce the size of its stores. Is Gap's decision a long-run decision or a short-run decision?

36. How might combining Gap's concept stores into one store help better take advantage of economies of scale?

Economics in the News

37. After you have studied *Reading Between the Lines* on pp. 220–221, answer the following questions.

a. Explain the distinction between the short run and the long run and identify when McDonald's would want to make each type of change.

b. Given the cost differences between the old and new restaurants described on p. 221, why would it ever be efficient to stick with an old restaurant?

c. Explain economies of scale. Does McDonald's reap economies of scale in the example on p. 221?

d. Draw a graph to illustrate McDonald's cost curves if it builds an even larger restaurant than the one whose costs are shown in Fig. 2 on p. 221.

38. **Starbucks Unit Brews Up Self-Serve Espresso Bars**

Coinstar has installed automated, self-serve espresso kiosks in grocery stores. Kiosks cost just under $40,000 each and Coinstar provides maintenance. The self-serve kiosk removes the labor costs of having a barista serve Starbucks' coffee, and store personnel refill the machine.

Source: MSNBC, June 1, 2008

a. What is Coinstar's total fixed cost of operating one self-serve kiosk? What are its variable costs of providing coffee at a self-serve kiosk?

b. Assume that a coffee machine operated by a barista costs less than $40,000. Explain how the fixed costs, variable costs, and total costs of barista-served and self-served coffee differ.

c. Sketch the marginal cost and average cost curves implied by your answer to part (b).

10

PERFECT COMPETITION

After studying this chapter, you will be able to:

◆ Define perfect competition

◆ Explain how a firm makes its output decision

◆ Explain how price and output are determined in perfect competition

◆ Explain why firms enter and leave a market

◆ Predict the effects of technological change in a competitive market

◆ Explain why perfect competition is efficient

A million "apps" have been created for smartphones and tablets. Most of these apps are the work of individuals in intense competition with each other. No single app writer can influence the price of an app, but each can and must decide how much to work and how many apps to produce.

In this chapter, we study producers who, like small app developers, are in intense competition—in *perfect competition.*

At the end of the chapter, in *Reading Between the Lines,* we apply the perfect competition model to the highly competitive market in apps.

◢ What Is Perfect Competition?

The firms that you study in this chapter face the force of raw competition. We call this extreme form of competition perfect competition. **Perfect competition** is a market in which

- Many firms sell identical products to many buyers.
- There are no restrictions on entry into the market.
- Established firms have no advantage over new ones.
- Sellers and buyers are well informed about prices.

Farming, fishing, wood pulping and paper milling, the manufacture of paper cups and shopping bags, grocery and fresh flower retailing, photo finishing, lawn services, plumbing, painting, dry cleaning, and laundry services are all examples of highly competitive industries.

How Perfect Competition Arises

Perfect competition arises if the minimum efficient scale of a single producer is small relative to the market demand for the good or service. In this situation, there is room in the market for many firms. A firm's *minimum efficient scale* is the smallest output at which long-run average cost reaches its lowest level. (See Chapter 9, p. 219.)

In perfect competition, each firm produces a good that has no unique characteristics, so consumers don't care which firm's good they buy.

Price Takers

Firms in perfect competition are price takers. A **price taker** is a firm that cannot influence the market price because its production is an insignificant part of the total market.

Imagine that you are a wheat farmer in Kansas. You have a thousand acres planted—which sounds like a lot. But compared to the millions of acres in Colorado, Oklahoma, Texas, Nebraska, and the Dakotas, as well as the millions more in Canada, Argentina, Australia, and Ukraine, your thousand acres are a drop in the ocean. Nothing makes your wheat any better than any other farmer's, and all the buyers of wheat know the price at which they can do business.

If the market price of wheat is $4 a bushel, then that is the highest price you can get for your wheat. Ask for $4.10 and no one will buy from you. Offer it for $3.90 and you'll be sold out in a flash and have given away 10¢ a bushel. You take the market price.

Economic Profit and Revenue

A firm's goal is to maximize *economic profit*, which is equal to total revenue minus total cost. Total cost is the *opportunity cost* of production, which includes *normal profit*. (See Chapter 8, p. 181.)

A firm's **total revenue** equals the price of its output multiplied by the number of units of output sold (price × quantity). **Marginal revenue** is the change in total revenue that results from a one-unit increase in the quantity sold. Marginal revenue is calculated by dividing the change in total revenue by the change in the quantity sold.

Figure 10.1 illustrates these revenue concepts. In part (a), the market demand curve, *D*, and market supply curve, *S*, determine the market price. The market price is $25 a sweater. Campus Sweaters is just one of many producers of sweaters, so the best it can do is to sell its sweaters for $25 each.

Total Revenue Total revenue is equal to the price multiplied by the quantity sold. In the table in Fig. 10.1, if Campus Sweaters sells 9 sweaters, its total revenue is $225 (9 × $25).

Figure 10.1(b) shows the firm's total revenue curve (*TR*), which graphs the relationship between total revenue and the quantity sold. At point *A* on the *TR* curve, the firm sells 9 sweaters and has a total revenue of $225. Because each additional sweater sold brings in a constant amount—$25—the total revenue curve is an upward-sloping straight line.

Marginal Revenue Marginal revenue is the change in total revenue that results from a one-unit increase in quantity sold. In the table in Fig. 10.1, when the quantity sold increases from 8 to 9 sweaters, total revenue increases from $200 to $225, so marginal revenue is $25 a sweater.

Because the firm in perfect competition is a price taker, the change in total revenue that results from a one-unit increase in the quantity sold equals the market price. *In perfect competition, the firm's marginal revenue equals the market price.* Figure 10.1(c) shows the firm's marginal revenue curve (*MR*) as the horizontal line at the market price.

Demand for the Firm's Product The firm can sell any quantity it chooses at the market price. So the demand curve for the firm's product is a horizontal line at the market price, the same as the firm's marginal revenue curve.

FIGURE 10.1   Demand, Price, and Revenue in Perfect Competition

(a) Sweater market

(b) Campus Sweaters' total revenue

(c) Campus Sweaters' marginal revenue

Quantity sold (Q) (sweaters per day)	Price (P) (dollars per sweater)	Total revenue (TR = P × Q) (dollars)	Marginal revenue (MR = ΔTR/ΔQ) (dollars per additional sweater)
8	25	200	
			 25
9	25	225	
			 25
10	25	250	

In part (a), market demand and market supply determine the market price (and quantity). Part (b) shows the firm's total revenue curve (*TR*). Point *A* corresponds to the second row of the table—Campus Sweaters sells 9 sweaters at $25 a sweater, so total revenue is $225. Part (c) shows the firm's marginal revenue curve (*MR*). This curve is also the demand curve for the firm's sweaters. The demand for sweaters from Campus Sweaters is perfectly elastic at the market price of $25 a sweater.

MyEconLab animation

A horizontal demand curve illustrates a perfectly elastic demand, so the demand for the firm's product is perfectly elastic. A sweater from Campus Sweaters is a *perfect substitute* for a sweater from any other factory. But the *market* demand for sweaters is *not* perfectly elastic: Its elasticity depends on the substitutability of sweaters for other goods and services.

The Firm's Decisions

The goal of the competitive firm is to maximize economic profit, given the constraints it faces. To achieve its goal, a firm must decide

1. How to produce at minimum cost
2. What quantity to produce
3. Whether to enter or exit a market

You've already seen how a firm makes the first decision. It does so by operating with the plant that minimizes long-run average cost—by being on its long-run average cost curve. We'll now see how the firm makes the other two decisions. We start by looking at the firm's output decision.

REVIEW QUIZ

1 Why is a firm in perfect competition a price taker?
2 In perfect competition, what is the relationship between the demand for the firm's output and the market demand?
3 In perfect competition, why is a firm's marginal revenue curve also the demand curve for the firm's output?
4 What decisions must a firm make to maximize profit?

You can work these questions in Study Plan 10.1 and get instant feedback.   *MyEconLab*

The Firm's Output Decision

A firm's cost curves (total cost, average cost, and marginal cost) describe the relationship between its output and costs (see pp. 209–215). And a firm's revenue curves (total revenue and marginal revenue) describe the relationship between its output and revenue (pp. 228–229). From the firm's cost curves and revenue curves, we can find the output that maximizes the firm's economic profit.

Figure 10.2 shows how to do this for Campus Sweaters. The table lists the firm's total revenue and total cost at different outputs, and part (a) of the figure shows the firm's total revenue curve, *TR*, and total cost curve, *TC*. These curves are graphs of numbers in the first three columns of the table.

Economic profit equals total revenue minus total cost. The fourth column of the table in Fig. 10.2 shows the economic profit made by Campus Sweaters, and part (b) of the figure graphs these numbers as its economic profit curve, *EP*.

Campus Sweaters maximizes its economic profit by producing 9 sweaters a day: Total revenue is $225, total cost is $183, and economic profit is $42. No other output rate achieves a larger profit.

At outputs of less than 4 sweaters and more than 12 sweaters a day, Campus Sweaters would incur an economic loss. At either 4 or 12 sweaters a day, Campus Sweaters would make zero economic profit, called a *break-even point*.

FIGURE 10.2   Total Revenue, Total Cost, and Economic Profit

(a) Revenue and cost

(b) Economic profit and loss

Quantity (Q) (sweaters per day)	Total revenue (TR) (dollars)	Total cost (TC) (dollars)	Economic profit (TR − TC) (dollars)
0	0	22	−22
1	25	45	−20
2	50	66	−16
3	75	85	−10
4	100	100	0
5	125	114	11
6	150	126	24
7	175	141	34
8	200	160	40
9	225	183	42
10	250	210	40
11	275	245	30
12	300	300	0
13	325	360	−35

The table lists Campus Sweaters' total revenue, total cost, and economic profit. Part (a) graphs the total revenue and total cost curves and part (b) graphs economic profit.

Campus Sweaters makes maximum economic profit, $42 a day ($225 − $183), when it produces 9 sweaters a day. At outputs of 4 sweaters and 12 sweaters a day, Campus Sweaters makes zero economic profit—these are break-even points. At outputs less than 4 sweaters and greater than 12 sweaters a day, Campus Sweaters incurs an economic loss.

Marginal Analysis and the Supply Decision

Another way to find the profit-maximizing output is to use marginal analysis, which compares marginal revenue, *MR*, with marginal cost, *MC*. As output increases, the firm's marginal revenue is constant but its marginal cost eventually increases.

If marginal revenue exceeds marginal cost (*MR* > *MC*), then the revenue from selling one more unit exceeds the cost of producing it and an increase in output increases economic profit. If marginal revenue is less than marginal cost (*MR* < *MC*), then the revenue from selling one more unit is less than the cost of producing that unit and a *decrease* in output *increases* economic profit. If marginal revenue equals marginal cost (*MR* = *MC*), then the revenue from selling one more unit equals the cost incurred to produce that unit. Economic profit is maximized and either an increase or a decrease in output decreases economic profit.

Figure 10.3 illustrates these propositions. If Campus Sweaters increases its output from 8 sweaters to 9 sweaters a day, marginal revenue ($25) exceeds marginal cost ($23), so by producing the 9th sweater economic profit increases by $2 from $40 to $42 a day. The blue area in the figure shows the increase in economic profit when the firm increases production from 8 to 9 sweaters per day.

If Campus Sweaters increases its output from 9 sweaters to 10 sweaters a day, marginal revenue ($25) is less than marginal cost ($27), so by producing the 10th sweater, economic profit decreases. The last column of the table shows that economic profit decreases from $42 to $40 a day. The red area in the figure shows the economic loss that arises from increasing production from 9 to 10 sweaters a day.

Campus Sweaters maximizes economic profit by producing 9 sweaters a day, the quantity at which marginal revenue equals marginal cost.

A firm's profit-maximizing output is its quantity supplied at the market price. The quantity supplied at a price of $25 a sweater is 9 sweaters a day. If the price were higher than $25 a sweater, the firm would increase production. If the price were lower than $25 a sweater, the firm would decrease production. These profit-maximizing responses to different market prices are the foundation of the law of supply:

> Other things remaining the same, the higher the market price of a good, the greater is the quantity supplied of that good.

FIGURE 10.3   Profit-Maximizing Output

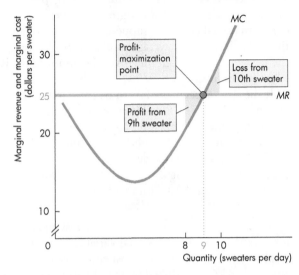

Quantity (Q) (sweaters per day)	Total revenue (TR) (dollars)	Marginal revenue (MR) (dollars per additional sweater)	Total cost (TC) (dollars)	Marginal cost (MC) (dollars per additional sweater)	Economic profit (TR − TC) (dollars)
7	175		141		34
		 25		 19	
8	200		160		40
		 25		 23	
9	225		183		42
		 25		 27	
10	250		210		40
		 25		 35	
11	275		245		30

The firm maximizes profit by producing the output at which marginal revenue equals marginal cost and marginal cost is increasing. The table and figure show that marginal cost equals marginal revenue and economic profit is maximized when Campus Sweaters produces 9 sweaters a day. The table shows that if Campus Sweaters increases output from 8 to 9 sweaters, marginal cost is $23, which is less than the marginal revenue of $25. If output increases from 9 to 10 sweaters, marginal cost is $27, which exceeds the marginal revenue of $25. If marginal revenue exceeds marginal cost, an increase in output increases economic profit. If marginal revenue is less than marginal cost, an increase in output decreases economic profit. If marginal revenue equals marginal cost, economic profit is maximized.

MyEconLab animation

Temporary Shutdown Decision

You've seen that a firm maximizes profit by producing the quantity at which marginal revenue (price) equals marginal cost. But suppose that at this quantity, price is less than average total cost. In this case, the firm incurs an economic loss. Maximum profit is a loss (a minimum loss). What does the firm do?

If the firm expects the loss to be permanent, it goes out of business. But if it expects the loss to be temporary, the firm must decide whether to shut down temporarily and produce no output, or to keep producing. To make this decision, the firm compares the loss from shutting down with the loss from producing and takes the action that minimizes its loss.

Loss Comparisons A firm's economic loss equals total fixed cost, *TFC*, plus total variable cost minus total revenue. Total variable cost equals average variable cost, *AVC*, multiplied by the quantity produced, *Q*, and total revenue equals price, *P*, multiplied by the quantity *Q*. So

$$\text{Economic loss} = TFC + (AVC - P) \times Q.$$

If the firm shuts down, it produces no output ($Q = 0$). The firm has no variable costs and no revenue but it must pay its fixed costs, so its economic loss equals total fixed cost.

If the firm produces, then in addition to its fixed costs, it incurs variable costs. But it also receives revenue. Its economic loss equals total fixed cost—the loss when shut down—plus total variable cost minus total revenue. If total variable cost exceeds total revenue, this loss exceeds total fixed cost and the firm shuts down. Equivalently, if average variable cost *exceeds* price, this loss exceeds total fixed cost and the firm *shuts down.*

The Shutdown Point A firm's **shutdown point** is the price and quantity at which it is indifferent between producing and shutting down. The shutdown point occurs at the price and the quantity at which average variable cost is a minimum. At the shutdown point, the firm is minimizing its loss and its loss equals total fixed cost. If the price falls below minimum average variable cost, the firm shuts down temporarily and continues to incur a loss equal to total fixed cost. At prices above minimum average variable cost but below average total cost, the firm produces the loss-minimizing output and incurs a loss, but a loss that is less than total fixed cost.

Figure 10.4 illustrates the firm's shutdown decision and the shutdown point that we've just described for Campus Sweaters.

The firm's average variable cost curve is *AVC* and the marginal cost curve is *MC*. Average variable cost has a minimum of $17 a sweater when output is 7 sweaters a day. The *MC* curve intersects the *AVC* curve at its minimum. (We explained this relationship in Chapter 9; see pp. 210–211.)

The figure shows the marginal revenue curve *MR* when the price is $17 a sweater, a price equal to minimum average variable cost. Marginal revenue equals marginal cost at 7 sweaters a day, so this quantity maximizes economic profit (minimizes economic loss). The *ATC* curve shows that the firm's average total cost of producing 7 sweaters a day is $20.14 a sweater. The firm incurs a loss equal to $3.14 a sweater on 7 sweaters a day, so its loss is $22 a day. The table in Fig. 10.3 shows that Campus Sweaters' loss equals its total fixed cost.

FIGURE 10.4   The Shutdown Decision

The shutdown point is at minimum average variable cost. At a price below minimum average variable cost, the firm shuts down and produces no output. At a price equal to minimum average variable cost, the firm is indifferent between shutting down and producing no output or producing the output at minimum average variable cost. Either way, the firm minimizes its economic loss and incurs a loss equal to total fixed cost.

MyEconLab animation

The Firm's Supply Curve

A perfectly competitive firm's supply curve shows how its profit-maximizing output varies as the market price varies, other things remaining the same. The supply curve is derived from the firm's marginal cost curve and average variable cost curves. Figure 10.5 illustrates the derivation of the supply curve.

When the price *exceeds* minimum average variable cost (more than $17), the firm maximizes profit by producing the output at which marginal cost equals price. If the price rises, the firm increases its output—it moves up along its marginal cost curve.

When the price is *less than* minimum average variable cost (less than $17 a sweater), the firm maximizes profit by temporarily shutting down and producing no output. The firm produces zero output at all prices below minimum average variable cost.

When the price *equals* minimum average variable cost, the firm maximizes profit *either* by temporarily shutting down and producing no output *or* by producing the output at which average variable cost is a minimum—the shutdown point, *T*. The firm never produces a quantity between zero and the quantity at the shutdown point *T* (a quantity greater than zero and less than 7 sweaters a day).

The firm's supply curve in Fig. 10.5(b) runs along the *y*-axis from a price of zero to a price equal to minimum average variable cost, jumps to point *T*, and then, as the price rises above minimum average variable cost, follows the marginal cost curve.

◆ REVIEW QUIZ

1 Why does a firm in perfect competition produce the quantity at which marginal cost equals price?
2 What is the lowest price at which a firm produces an output? Explain why.
3 What is the relationship between a firm's supply curve, its marginal cost curve, and its average variable cost curve?

You can work these questions in Study Plan 10.2 and get instant feedback.   MyEconLab

So far, we've studied a single firm in isolation. We've seen that the firm's profit-maximizing decision depends on the market price, which it takes as given. How is the market price determined? Let's find out.

FIGURE 10.5   A Firm's Supply Curve

(a) Marginal cost and average variable cost

(b) Campus Sweaters' short-run supply curve

Part (a) shows the firm's profit-maximizing output at various market prices. At $25 a sweater, it produces 9 sweaters, and at $17 a sweater, it produces 7 sweaters. At all prices below $17 a sweater, Campus Sweaters produces nothing. Its shutdown point is *T*. Part (b) shows the firm's supply curve—the quantity of sweaters it produces at each price. Its supply curve is made up of the marginal cost curve at all prices above minimum average variable cost and the vertical axis at all prices below minimum average variable cost.

—— MyEconLab animation ——

Output, Price, and Profit in the Short Run

To determine the price and quantity in a perfectly competitive market, we need to know how market demand and market supply interact. We start by studying a perfectly competitive market in the short run. The short run is a situation in which the number of firms is fixed.

Market Supply in the Short Run

The **short-run market supply curve** shows the quantity supplied by all the firms in the market at each price when each firm's plant and the number of firms remain the same.

You've seen how an individual firm's supply curve is determined. The market supply curve is derived from the individual supply curves. The quantity supplied by the market at a given price is the sum of the quantities supplied by all the firms in the market at that price.

Figure 10.6 shows the supply curve for the competitive sweater market. In this example, the market consists of 1,000 firms exactly like Campus Sweaters. At each price, the quantity supplied by the market is 1,000 times the quantity supplied by a single firm.

The table in Fig. 10.6 shows the firm's and the market's supply schedules and how the market supply curve is constructed. At prices below $17 a sweater, every firm in the market shuts down; the quantity supplied by the market is zero. At $17 a sweater, each firm is indifferent between shutting down and producing nothing or operating and producing 7 sweaters a day. Some firms will shut down, and others will supply 7 sweaters a day. The quantity supplied by each firm is *either* 0 or 7 sweaters, and the quantity supplied by the market is *between* 0 (all firms shut down) and 7,000 (all firms produce 7 sweaters a day each).

The market supply curve is a graph of the market supply schedules and the points on the supply curve *A* through *D* represent the rows of the table.

To construct the market supply curve, we sum the quantities supplied by all the firms at each price. Each of the 1,000 firms in the market has a supply schedule like Campus Sweaters. At prices below $17 a sweater, the market supply curve runs along the *y*-axis. At $17 a sweater, the market supply curve is horizontal—supply is perfectly elastic. As the price

FIGURE 10.6   Short-Run Market Supply Curve

	Price (dollars per sweater)	Quantity supplied by Campus Sweaters (sweaters per day)	Quantity supplied by market (sweaters per day)
A	17	0 or 7	0 to 7,000
B	20	8	8,000
C	25	9	9,000
D	31	10	10,000

The market supply schedule is the sum of the supply schedules of all the individual firms. A market that consists of 1,000 identical firms has a supply schedule similar to that of one firm, but the quantity supplied by the market is 1,000 times as large as that of the one firm (see the table). The market supply curve is S_M. Points *A*, *B*, *C*, and *D* correspond to the rows of the table. At the shutdown price of $17 a sweater, each firm produces either 0 or 7 sweaters a day and the quantity supplied by the market is between 0 and 7,000 sweaters a day. The market supply is perfectly elastic at the shutdown price.

—— MyEconLab animation ——

rises above $17 a sweater, each firm increases its quantity supplied and the quantity supplied by the market increases by 1,000 times that of one firm.

Short-Run Equilibrium

Market demand and short-run market supply determine the market price and market output. Figure 10.7(a) shows a short-run equilibrium. The short-run supply curve, S, is the same as S_M in Fig. 10.6. If the market demand curve is D_1, the market price is $20 a sweater. Each firm takes this price as given and produces its profit-maximizing output, which is 8 sweaters a day. Because the market has 1,000 identical firms, the market output is 8,000 sweaters a day.

A Change in Demand

Changes in demand bring changes to short-run market equilibrium. Figure 10.7(b) shows these changes.

If demand increases and the demand curve shifts rightward to D_2, the market price rises to $25 a sweater. At this price, each firm maximizes profit by increasing its output to 9 sweaters a day. The market output increases to 9,000 sweaters a day.

If demand decreases and the demand curve shifts leftward to D_3, the market price falls to $17. At this price, each firm maximizes profit by decreasing its output. If each firm produces 7 sweaters a day, the market output decreases to 7,000 sweaters a day.

If the demand curve shifts farther leftward than D_3, the market price remains at $17 a sweater because the market supply curve is horizontal at that price. Some firms continue to produce 7 sweaters a day, and others temporarily shut down. Firms are indifferent between these two activities, and whichever they choose, they incur an economic loss equal to total fixed cost. The number of firms continuing to produce is just enough to satisfy the market demand at a price of $17 a sweater.

Profits and Losses in the Short Run

In short-run equilibrium, although the firm produces the profit-maximizing output, it does not necessarily end up making an economic profit. It might do so, but it might alternatively break even or incur an economic loss. Economic profit (or loss) per sweater is price, P, minus average total cost, ATC. So economic profit (or loss) is $(P - ATC) \times Q$. If price

---

FIGURE 10.7   Short-Run Equilibrium

(a) Equilibrium

(b) Change in equilibrium

In part (a), the market supply curve is S and the market demand curve is D_1. The market price is $20 a sweater. At this price, each firm produces 8 sweaters a day and the market produces 8,000 sweaters a day.

In part (b), if the market demand increases to D_2, the

price rises to $25 a sweater. Each firm produces 9 sweaters a day and market output is 9,000 sweaters. If market demand decreases to D_3, the price falls to $17 a sweater and each firm decreases its output. If each firm produces 7 sweaters a day, the market output is 7,000 sweaters a day.

MyEconLab animation

equals average total cost, a firm breaks even—the entrepreneur makes normal profit. If price exceeds average total cost, a firm makes an economic profit. If price is less than average total cost, a firm incurs an economic loss. Figure 10.8 shows these three possible short-run profit outcomes for Campus Sweaters. These outcomes correspond to the three different levels of market demand that we've just examined.

Three Possible Short-Run Outcomes

Figure 10.8(a) corresponds to the situation in Fig. 10.7(a) where the market demand is D_1. The equilibrium price of a sweater is $20 and the firm produces 8 sweaters a day. Average total cost is $20 a sweater. Price equals average total cost (*ATC*), so the firm breaks even (makes zero economic profit).

Figure 10.8(b) corresponds to the situation in Fig. 10.7(b) where the market demand is D_2. The equilibrium price of a sweater is $25 and the firm produces 9 sweaters a day. Here, price exceeds average total cost, so the firm makes an economic profit. Its economic profit is $42 a day, which equals $4.67 per sweater ($25.00 − $20.33) multiplied by 9, the

profit-maximizing number of sweaters produced. The blue rectangle shows this economic profit. The height of that rectangle is profit per sweater, $4.67, and the length is the quantity of sweaters produced, 9 a day. So the area of the rectangle is economic profit of $42 a day.

Figure 10.8(c) corresponds to the situation in Fig. 10.7(b) where the market demand is D_3. The equilibrium price of a sweater is $17. Here, the price is less than average total cost, so the firm incurs an economic loss. Price and marginal revenue are $17 a sweater, and the profit-maximizing (in this case, loss-minimizing) output is 7 sweaters a day. Total revenue is $119 a day (7 × $17). Average total cost is $20.14 a sweater, so the economic loss is $3.14 per sweater ($20.14 − $17.00). This loss per sweater multiplied by the number of sweaters is $22. The red rectangle shows this economic loss. The height of that rectangle is economic loss per sweater, $3.14, and the length is the quantity of sweaters produced, 7 a day. So the area of the rectangle is the firm's economic loss of $22 a day. If the price dips below $17 a sweater, the firm temporarily shuts down and incurs an economic loss equal to total fixed cost.

FIGURE 10.8   Three Short-Run Outcomes for the Firm

(a) Break even

(b) Economic profit

(c) Economic loss

In the short run, the firm might break even (make zero economic profit), make an economic profit, or incur an economic loss. In part (a), the price equals minimum average total cost. At the profit-maximizing output, the firm breaks even and makes zero economic profit. In part (b), the market price is $25 a sweater. At the profit-maximizing output,

the price exceeds average total cost and the firm makes an economic profit equal to the area of the blue rectangle. In part (c), the market price is $17 a sweater. At the profit-maximizing output, the price is below minimum average total cost and the firm incurs an economic loss equal to the area of the red rectangle.

MyEconLab animation

Economics in Action
Production Cutback and Temporary Shutdown

The high price of gasoline and anxiety about unemployment and future incomes brought a decrease in the demand for luxury goods including high-end motorcycles such as Harley-Davidsons.

Harley-Davidson's profit-maximizing response to the decrease in demand was to cut production and lay off workers. Some of the production cuts and layoffs were temporary and some were permanent.

Harley-Davidson's bike production plant in York County, Pennsylvania, was temporarily shut down in the summer of 2008 because total revenue was insufficient to cover total variable cost.

The firm also permanently cut its workforce by 300 people. This permanent cut was like that at Campus Sweaters when the market demand for sweaters decreased from D_1 to D_3 in Fig. 10.7(b).

REVIEW QUIZ

1 How do we derive the short-run market supply curve in perfect competition?

2 In perfect competition, when market demand increases, explain how the price of the good and the output and profit of each firm changes in the short run.

3 In perfect competition, when market demand decreases, explain how the price of the good and the output and profit of each firm changes in the short run.

You can work these questions in Study Plan 10.3 and get instant feedback.   MyEconLab

Output, Price, and Profit in the Long Run

In short-run equilibrium, a firm might make an economic profit, incur an economic loss, or break even. Although each of these three situations is a short-run equilibrium, only one of them is a long-run equilibrium. The reason is that in the long run, firms can enter or exit the market.

Entry and Exit

Entry occurs in a market when new firms come into the market and the number of firms increases. Exit occurs when existing firms leave a market and the number of firms decreases.

Firms respond to economic profit and economic loss by either entering or exiting a market. New firms enter a market in which existing firms are making an economic profit. Firms exit a market in which they are incurring an economic loss. Temporary economic profit and temporary economic loss don't trigger entry and exit. It's the prospect of persistent economic profit or loss that triggers entry and exit.

Entry and exit change the market supply, which influences the market price, the quantity produced by each firm, and its economic profit (or loss).

If firms enter a market, supply increases and the market supply curve shifts rightward. The increase in supply lowers the market price and eventually eliminates economic profit. When economic profit reaches zero, entry stops.

If firms exit a market, supply decreases and the market supply curve shifts leftward. The market price rises and economic loss decreases. Eventually, economic loss is eliminated and exit stops.

To summarize:

- New firms enter a market in which existing firms are making an economic profit.
- As new firms enter a market, the market price falls and the economic profit of each firm decreases.
- Firms exit a market in which they are incurring an economic loss.
- As firms leave a market, the market price rises and the economic loss incurred by the remaining firms decreases.
- Entry and exit stop when firms make zero economic profit.

A Closer Look at Entry

The sweater market has 800 firms with cost curves like those in Fig. 10.9(a). The market demand curve is D, the market supply curve is S_1, and the price is $25 a sweater in Fig. 10.9(b). Each firm produces 9 sweaters a day and makes an economic profit.

This economic profit is a signal for new firms to enter the market. As entry takes place, supply increases and the market supply curve shifts rightward toward S^*. As supply increases with no change in demand, the market price gradually falls from $25 to $20 a sweater. At this lower price, each firm makes zero economic profit and entry stops.

Entry results in an increase in market output, but each firm's output *decreases*. Because the price falls, each firm moves down its supply curve and produces less. Because the number of firms increases, the market produces more.

A Closer Look at Exit

The sweater market has 1,200 firms with cost curves like those in Fig. 10.9(a). The market demand curve is D, the market supply curve is S_2, and the price is $17 a sweater in Fig. 10.9(b). Each firm produces 7 sweaters a day and incurs an economic loss.

This economic loss is a signal for firms to exit the market. As exit takes place, supply decreases and the market supply curve shifts leftward toward S^*. As supply decreases with no change in demand, the market price gradually rises from $17 to $20 a sweater. At this higher price, losses are eliminated, each firm makes zero economic profit, and exit stops.

Exit results in a decrease in market output, but each firm's output *increases*. Because the price rises, each firm moves up its supply curve and produces more. Because the number of firms decreases, the market produces less.

FIGURE 10.9   Entry, Exit, and Long-Run Equilibrium

(a) Campus Sweaters

(b) The sweater market

Each firm has cost curves like those of Campus Sweaters in part (a). The market demand curve is D in part (b).

When the market supply curve in part (b) is S_1, the price is $25 a sweater. In part (a), each firm produces 9 sweaters a day and makes an economic profit. Profit triggers the entry of new firms and as new firms enter, the market supply curve shifts rightward, from S_1 toward S^*. The price falls from $25 to $20 a sweater, and the quantity produced increases from 7,200 to 8,000 sweaters. Each firm decreases its output to 8

sweaters a day and its economic profit falls to zero.

When the market supply curve is S_2, the price is $17 a sweater. In part (a), each firm produces 7 sweaters a day and incurs an economic loss. Loss triggers exit and as firms exit, the market supply curve shifts leftward, from S_2 toward S^*. The price rises from $17 to $20 a sweater, and the quantity produced decreases from 8,400 to 8,000 sweaters. Each firm increases its output from 7 to 8 sweaters a day and its economic profit rises to zero.

MyEconLab animation

Economics in Action

Entry and Exit

An example of entry and falling prices occurred during the 1980s and 1990s in the personal computer market. When IBM introduced its first PC in 1981, IBM had little competition. The price was $7,000 (about $16,850 in today's money) and IBM made a large economic profit selling the new machine.

Observing IBM's huge success, new firms such as Gateway, NEC, Dell, and a host of others entered the market with machines that were technologically identical to IBM's. In fact, they were so similar that they came to be called "clones." The massive wave of entry into the personal computer market increased the market supply and lowered the price. The economic profit for all firms decreased.

Today, a $400 computer is vastly more powerful than its 1981 ancestor that cost 42 times as much.

The same PC market that saw entry during the 1980s and 1990s has seen some exit more recently. In 2001, IBM, the firm that first launched the PC, announced that it was exiting the market. The intense competition from Gateway, NEC, Dell, and others that entered the market following IBM's lead has lowered the price and eliminated the economic profit. So IBM now concentrates on servers and other parts of the computer market.

IBM exited the PC market because it was incurring economic losses. Its exit decreased market supply and made it possible for the remaining firms in the market to make zero economic profit.

International Harvester, a manufacturer of farm equipment, provides another example of exit. For decades, people associated the name "International Harvester" with tractors, combines, and other farm machines. But International Harvester wasn't the only maker of farm equipment. The market became intensely competitive, and the firm began to incur economic losses. Now the firm has a new name, Navistar International, and it doesn't make tractors any more. After years of economic losses and shrinking revenues, it got out of the farm-machine business in 1985 and started to make trucks.

International Harvester exited because it was incurring an economic loss. Its exit decreased supply and made it possible for the remaining firms in the market to break even.

Long-Run Equilibrium

You've now seen how economic profit induces entry, which in turn eliminates the profit. You've also seen how economic loss induces exit, which in turn eliminates the loss.

When economic profit and economic loss have been eliminated and entry and exit have stopped, a competitive market is in *long-run equilibrium.*

You've seen how a competitive market adjusts toward its long-run equilibrium. But a competitive market is rarely *in* a state of long-run equilibrium. Instead, it is constantly and restlessly evolving toward long-run equilibrium. The reason is that the market is constantly bombarded with events that change the constraints that firms face.

Markets are constantly adjusting to keep up with changes in tastes, which change demand, and changes in technology, which change costs.

In the next sections, we're going to see how a competitive market reacts to changing tastes and technology and how the market guides resources to their highest-valued use.

◀ REVIEW QUIZ

1. What triggers entry in a competitive market? Describe the process that ends further entry.
2. What triggers exit in a competitive market? Describe the process that ends further exit.

You can work these questions in Study Plan 10.4 and get instant feedback.   MyEconLab

◆ Changes in Demand and Supply as Technology Advances

The arrival of high-speed Internet service increased the demand for personal computers and the demand for music and movie downloads. At the same time, the arrival of these technologies decreased the demand for the retail services of record stores.

What happens in a competitive market when the demand for its product changes? The perfect competition model can answer this questions.

An Increase in Demand

Producers of computer components are in long-run equilibrium making zero economic profit when the arrival of the high-speed Internet brings an increase in the demand for computers and the components from which they are built. The equilibrium price of a component rises and producers make economic profits. New firms start to enter the market. Supply

increases and the price stops rising and then begins to fall. Eventually, enough firms have entered for the supply and the increased demand to be in balance at a price that enables the firms in the market to return to zero economic profit—long-run equilibrium.

Figure 10.10 illustrates. In the market in part (a), demand is D_0, supply is S_0, price is P_0 and market output is Q_0. At the firm in part (b), profit is maximized with marginal revenue, MR_0, equal to marginal cost, MC, at output q_0. Economic profit is zero.

Market demand increases and the demand curve shifts rightward to D_1, in Fig. 10.10(a). The price rises to P_1, and the quantity supplied increases from Q_0 to Q_1 as the market moves up along its short-run supply curve S_0. In Fig. 10.10(b), the firm maximizes profit by producing q_1, where marginal revenue MR_1 equals MC. The market is now in short-run equilibrium in which each firm makes an economic profit.

The economic profit brings entry and short-run supply increases—the market supply curve starts to shift rightward. The increase in supply lowers the

---

FIGURE 10.10   An Increase in Demand

(a) Market

(b) Firm

A market starts out in long-run competitive equilibrium. Part (a) shows the market demand curve D_0, the market supply curve S_0, the market price P_0, and the equilibrium quantity Q_0. Each firm sells its output at the price P_0, so its marginal revenue curve is MR_0 in part (b). Each firm produces q_0 and makes zero economic profit.

Market demand increases from D_0 to D_1 in part (a) and the market price rises to P_1. Each firm maximizes profit by increasing its output to q_1 in part (b), and the market output

increases to Q_1 in part (a). Firms now make economic profits. New firms enter the market, and as they do so, the market supply curve gradually shifts rightward, from S_0 toward S_1. This shift gradually lowers the market price from P_1 back to P_0. While the price is above P_0, firms make economic profits, so new firms keep entering the market. Once the price has returned to P_0, each firm makes zero economic profit and there is no incentive for firms to enter. Each firm produces q_0, and the market output is Q_2.

price and firms decrease output—move down along their marginal cost or supply curve in Fig. 10.10(b).

Eventually, entry shifts the supply curve to S_1 in Fig. 10.10(a). The market price has returned to its original level, P_0. At this price, each firm produces q_0, the same as the quantity produced before the increase in demand. Market output is Q_2 in a long-run equilibrium.

The difference between the initial long-run equilibrium and the new long-run equilibrium is the number of firms in the market. An increase in demand has increased the number of firms. In the

process of moving from the initial equilibrium to the new one, each firm makes an economic profit.

A Decrease in Demand

A *decrease* in demand triggers a similar response to the one you've just studied but in the opposite direction. A decrease in demand brings a lower price, economic losses, and exit. Exit decreases supply, which raises the price to its original level and economic profit returns to zero in a new long-run equilibrium. *Economics in the News* below looks at an example.

◆ ECONOMICS IN THE NEWS

Record Stores Exit

Iconic Central Texas Record Store Set to Close
Bobby Barnard opened Sundance Records & Tapes in San Marcos in 1977. But the customers stopped coming, so in 2012 this oldest continually operating music store in Central Texas closed its doors.

Source: Associated Press, March 28, 2012

THE PROBLEM

Provide a graphical analysis to explain why Sundance exited the market and the effects of exit on the market for record store services.

THE SOLUTION

■ With demand D_0 and supply S_0, Q_0 customers are served at a price P_0 in part (a) of Fig. 1.

■ With marginal revenue MR_0 and marginal cost MC, a record store serves q_0 customers in long-run equilibrium in part (b) of Fig. 1.

■ Demand decreases to D_1, the price falls to P_1, and marginal revenue falls to MR_1. Customers decrease to q_1 (and Q_1) and stores incur economic losses.

■ Faced with economic loss, Sundance and other stores exit and the market supply decreases to S_1.

■ The decrease in supply raises the price and firms remaining return to zero economic profit.

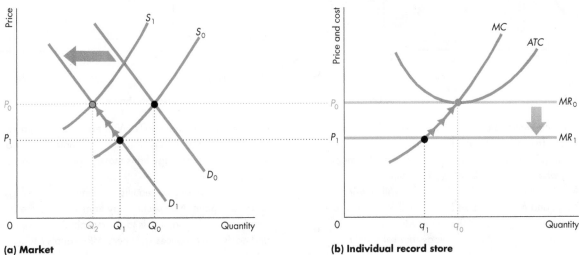

(a) Market

(b) Individual record store

Figure 1 The Market for Record Store Services

Technological Advances Change Supply

We've studied the effects of technological change on demand and to isolate those effects we've kept the individual firm's cost curves unchanged. But new technologies also lower production costs. We now study those effects of advancing technology.

Starting from a long-run equilibrium, when a new technology becomes available that lowers production costs, the first firms to use it make economic profit. But as more firms begin to use the new technology, market supply increases and the price falls. At first, new-technology firms continue to make positive economic profits, so more enter. But firms that continue to use the old technology incur economic losses. Why? Initially they were making zero economic profit and now with the lower price they incur economic losses. So old-technology firms exit.

Eventually, all the old-technology firms have exited and enough new-technology firms have entered to increase the market supply to a level that lowers the price to equal the minimum average total cost using the new technology. In this situation, all the firms, all of which are now new-technology firms, are making zero economic profit.

Figure 10.11 illustrates the process that we've just described. Part (a) shows the market demand and supply curves and market equilibrium. Part (b) shows the cost and revenue curves for a firm using the original old technology. Initially these are the only firms. Part (c) shows the cost and revenue curves for a firm using a new technology after it becomes available.

In part (a), the demand curve is D and initially the supply curve is S_0, so the price is P_0 and the equilibrium quantity is Q_0.

In part (b), marginal revenue is MR_0 and each firm produces q_0 where MR_0 equals MC_{Old}. Economic profit is zero and firms are producing at minimum average total cost on the curve ATC_{Old}.

When a new technology becomes available, average total cost and marginal cost of production fall, and firms that use the new technology produce with the average total cost curve ATC_{New} and marginal cost curve MC_{New} in part (c).

When one firm adopts the new technology, it is too small to influence supply, so the price remains at P_0 and the firm makes an economic profit. But economic profit brings entry of new-technology firms. Market supply increases and the price falls.

FIGURE 10.11   A Technological Advance Lowers Production Costs

(a) Market

(b) Old-technology firm

(c) New-technology firm

In part (a), the demand curve is D and initially the supply curve is S_0. The price is P_0 and the equilibrium quantity is Q_0. In part (b), marginal revenue is MR_0 and each firm produces q_0 where MR_0 equals MC_{Old}. Economic profit is zero.

A new technology becomes available with lower costs of ATC_{New} and MC_{New} in part (c). A firm that uses this technology produces q_0 where MR_0 equals MC_{New}.

As more firms use this technology, market supply increases and the price falls. With price below P_0 and above P_1, old-technology firms incur economic losses and exit and new-technology firms make economic profits and new firms enter the market.

In the new long-run equilibrium, the old-technology firms have gone. New-technology firms increase the market supply to S_1. The price falls to P_1, marginal revenue is MR_1, and each firm produces q_1 where MR_1 equals MC_{New}.

ECONOMICS IN THE NEWS

The Falling Cost of Sequencing DNA

Company Announces Low-Cost DNA Decoding Machine

Life Technologies Corp. announced it has developed a $149,000 machine that can decode a person's DNA in a day, at a long-sought price goal of $1,000, making a person's genome useful for medical care.

Source: *USA Today*, January 11, 2012

SOME DATA

The graph shows how the cost of sequencing a person's entire genome has fallen. Life Technologies (in the news clip) is one of around 40 firms competing to develop a machine that can lower that cost from the current $5,000 to $1,000 or less. Many dozens of firms operate DNA sequencing machines and sell their services in a competitive market.

THE QUESTIONS

- What are the competitive markets in the news clip?
- Are any of these markets in long-run equilibrium?
- Are any firms in these markets likely to be making an economic profit?
- Are any of the firms in these markets likely to be incurring an economic loss?
- Are these markets likely to be experiencing entry, exit, or both? If both, which is likely to be greater?
- Who gains from the advances in DNA sequencing technology in the short run and in the long run: producers, consumers, or both?

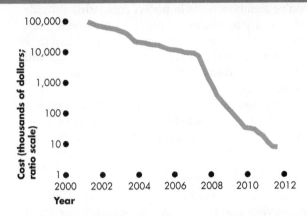

Figure 1 Cost per Genome

Source of data: National Human Genome Research Institute.

THE ANSWERS

- The markets are for DNA sequencing machines and for DNA sequencing services.
- With massive ongoing technological change, neither market is likely to be in long-run equilibrium.
- Firms using the latest technology are likely to be making economic profit.
- Firms using the older technology are likely to be incurring economic loss.
- New-technology firms are entering and old-technology firms are exiting, but with falling prices, there is more entry than exit.
- In the short run, firms gain from higher profit and consumers gain from the lower price. In the long run, economic profit will be zero but consumers will continue to gain from the low price.

With price below P_0, old-technology firms incur an economic loss and exit. With price above P_1, new-technology firms make an economic profit and enter. When a new long-run equilibrium is achieved, the old-technology firms have gone. The number of new-technology firms that have entered have shifted the supply curve to S_1. The price is P_1, marginal revenue is MR_1, and each firm in Fig. 10.11(c) produces q_1 using the new technology where MR_1 equals MC_{New}.

Technological change brings only temporary gains to producers. But the lower prices and better products that technological advances bring are permanent gains for consumers.

 ## REVIEW QUIZ

Describe what happens to output, price, and economic profit in the short run and in the long run in a competitive market following:

1 An increase in demand.
2 A decrease in demand.
3 The adoption of a new technology that lowers production costs.

You can work these questions in Study Plan 10.5 and get instant feedback.   MyEconLab

Competition and Efficiency

You've seen how firms in perfect competition decide the quantity to produce in the short run and in the long run. You've also seen how these individual decisions determine the market supply that interacts with market demand to determine the equilibrium price and quantity.

We're now going to use what you've learned to gain a deeper understanding of why competition achieves an efficient allocation of resources.

Efficient Use of Resources

Resource use is efficient when we produce the goods and services that people value most highly (see Chapter 2, pp. 35–37, and Chapter 5, p. 108). If it is possible to make someone better off without anyone else becoming worse off, resources are *not* being used efficiently. For example, suppose we produce a computer that no one wants and no one will ever use and, at the same time, some people are clamoring for more video games. If we produce fewer computers and reallocate the unused resources to produce more video games, some people will be better off and no one will be worse off. So the initial resource allocation was inefficient.

We can test whether resources are allocated efficiently by comparing marginal social benefit and marginal social cost. In the computer and video games example, the marginal social benefit of a video game exceeds its marginal social cost; the marginal social cost of a computer exceeds its marginal social benefit. So by producing fewer computers and more video games, we move resources toward a higher-valued use.

Choices, Equilibrium, and Efficiency

We can use what you have learned about the decisions of consumers and firms and equilibrium in a competitive market to describe an efficient use of resources.

Choices Consumers allocate their budgets to get the most value possible out of them. We derive a consumer's demand curve by finding how the best budget allocation changes as the price of a good changes. So consumers get the most value out of their resources at all points along their demand curves. If the people who consume a good or service are the only ones who benefit from it, then the market demand curve measures the benefit to the entire society and is the marginal social benefit curve.

Competitive firms produce the quantity that maximizes profit. We derive the firm's supply curve by finding the profit-maximizing quantity at each price. So firms get the most value out of their resources at all points along their supply curves. If the firms that produce a good or service bear all the costs of producing it, then the market supply curve measures the marginal cost to the entire society and the market supply curve is the marginal social cost curve.

Equilibrium and Efficiency Resources are used efficiently when marginal social benefit equals marginal social cost. Competitive equilibrium achieves this efficient outcome because, with no externalities, price equals marginal social benefit for consumers, and price equals marginal social cost for producers.

The gains from trade are the sum of consumer surplus and producer surplus. The gains from trade for consumers are measured by *consumer surplus*, which is the area below the demand curve and above the price paid. (See Chapter 5, p. 109.) The gains from trade for producers are measured by *producer surplus*, which is the area above the supply curve and below the price received. (See Chapter 5, p. 111.) The total gains from trade equals *total surplus*—the sum of consumer surplus and producer surplus. When the market for a good or service is in equilibrium, the gains from trade are maximized.

Efficiency in the Sweater Market Figure 10.12 illustrates the efficiency of perfect competition in the sweater market. Part (a) shows the market, and part (b) shows Campus Sweaters.

In part (a), consumers get the most value from their budgets at all points on the market demand curve, $D = MSB$. Producers get the most value from their resources at all points on the market supply curve, $S = MSC$. At the equilibrium quantity and price, marginal social benefit equals marginal social cost, and resources are allocated efficiently. Consumer surplus is the green area, producer surplus is the blue area, and *total surplus* (the sum of producer surplus and consumer surplus) is maximized.

In part (b), at the equilibrium price Campus Sweaters (and every other firm) makes zero economic profit and each firm has the plant that enables it to produce at the lowest possible average total cost.

FIGURE 10.12   Efficiency of Perfect Competition

(a) The sweater market

(b) Campus Sweaters

In part (a), market demand, *D*, and market supply, *S*, determine the equilibrium price and quantity. Consumers have made the best available choices on the demand curve, and firms are producing at least cost on the supply curve.

Marginal social benefit, *MSB*, equals marginal social cost, *MSC*, so resources are used efficiently. In part (b) Campus Sweaters produces at the lowest possible long-run average total cost and makes zero economic profit.

MyEconLab animation

Consumers are as well off as possible because the good cannot be produced at a lower cost and the price equals that least possible cost.

When firms in perfect competition are away from long-run equilibrium, either entry or exit moves the market toward the situation depicted in Fig. 10.12. During this process, the market is efficient because marginal social benefit equals marginal social cost. But it is only in long-run equilibrium that economic profit is driven to zero and consumers pay the lowest feasible price.

◆ You've now completed your study of perfect competition. *Reading Between the Lines* on pp. 246–247 gives you an opportunity to use what you have learned to understand the market for smartphone and tablet computer "apps."

Although many markets approximate the model of perfect competition, many do not. In Chapter 11, we study markets at the opposite extreme of market

REVIEW QUIZ

1 State the conditions that must be met for resources to be allocated efficiently.
2 Describe the choices that consumers make and explain why consumers are efficient on the market demand curve.
3 Describe the choices that producers make and explain why producers are efficient on the market supply curve.
4 Explain why resources are used efficiently in a competitive market.

You can work these questions in Study Plan 10.6 and get instant feedback.   MyEconLab

power: monopoly. When you have completed this study, you'll have a tool kit that will enable you to understand the variety of real-world markets.

Perfect Competition in iPhone "Apps"

Because of the iPhone, There Is an App for That

GigaOM

June 29, 2012

... The iPhone only offered web apps when it debuted in 2007. But the powerful hardware and unique user interface lit a fire of demand among developers for a software development kit. Apple obliged a year later and also introduced the App Store, kicking off the modern mobile app era. That market is now worth $8.5 billion and is expected to grow to $46 billion in 2016.

As we celebrate the five-year anniversary of the iPhone's launch on Friday, the true impact of the device can't be measured without talking about the era of mobile apps it spawned, creating success stories like Instagram, Angry Birds, Foursquare, and many others. Suddenly, "apps" became an easy way of understanding software, opening up opportunities to thousands of eager developers who could sell directly to a fast growing base of users. And that has in turn changed the way people compute, weaning them off of PCs to smaller devices: first smartphones, and now tablets. ...

Apple's App Store now boasts 650,000 apps, including 225,000 for the iPad. Apple users have downloaded 30 billion apps from the App Store, generating $5 billion in revenue for developers after Apple's 30 percent cut. To be sure, there were mobile apps prior to the iPhone, but they were either found on third-party app stores or they were controlled by carriers, which chose which apps got to appear on phones sold for their networks.

ESSENCE OF THE STORY

- The iPhone has created opportunities for thousands of "apps" developers who can sell directly to a fast growing base of users.

- The mobile app market had total revenue of $8.5 billion in 2012 and is expected to grow to $46 billion in 2016.

- Apple's App Store offers 650,000 "apps," including 225,000 for the iPad.

- Apple users have downloaded 30 billion "apps" from the App Store, generating $5 billion in revenue for developers after Apple's 30 percent cut.

ECONOMIC ANALYSIS

- The iPhone, iPad, and Android smartphones and tablet computers have created a large demand for apps.

- Although apps are not like corn or sweaters and come in thousands of varieties, the market for apps is highly competitive and we can use the perfect competition model to explain what is happening in that market.

- In 2007, the market for apps didn't exist. There was no supply and almost no demand.

- The market began to operate in 2008, when the first app developers got to work using a software development kit made available by Apple.

- During 2009 through 2012, the number of iPhones and Android smartphones increased dramatically. By 2012, 218 million iPhones and 400 million Android phones had been sold.

- The increase in the number of devices in use increased the demand for apps.

- Thousands of developers, most of them individuals, saw a profit opportunity and got to work creating apps. Their entry into the market increased the supply of apps.

- But the demand for apps kept growing and despite the entry of more developers, profit opportunities remained.

- Figure 1 illustrates the market for apps. In 2011, the demand for apps was D_0 and the supply was S_0. The equilibrium price was P_0 and the quantity was Q_0.

- Figure 2 illustrates the cost and revenue curves of an individual app developer. With marginal revenue MR and marginal cost MC, the developer maximizes profit by producing an app that sells q_0 units. Average total cost of an app (on the ATC curve) is less than the price, so the developer makes an economic profit.

- Economic profit brings entry, so in Fig. 1, supply increases in 2012 to S_1. But the demand for apps also keeps increasing and in 2012 the demand curve is D_1.

- The equilibrium quantity increases to Q_1, and this quantity is produced by an increased number of developers—each producing q_0 units and each continuing to make an economic profit.

- The developer's cost curves in Fig. 2 are unchanged, but as development tools improve, development costs will fall and the cost curves will shift downward, which will further increase supply.

- At some future date, market supply will increase by enough to eliminate economic profit and the market for apps will be in long-run equilibrium. That date is unknown but likely to be a long way off.

Figure 1 The Market for Apps

Figure 2 An Individual App Developer

247

SUMMARY

Key Points

What Is Perfect Competition? (pp. 228–229)

- In perfect competition, many firms sell identical products to many buyers; there are no restrictions on entry; sellers and buyers are well informed about prices.
- A perfectly competitive firm is a price taker.
- A perfectly competitive firm's marginal revenue always equals the market price.

Working Problems 1 to 3 will give you a better understanding of perfect competition.

The Firm's Output Decision (pp. 230–233)

- The firm produces the output at which marginal revenue (price) equals marginal cost.
- In short-run equilibrium, a firm can make an economic profit, incur an economic loss, or break even.
- If price is less than minimum average variable cost, the firm temporarily shuts down.
- At prices below minimum average variable cost, a firm's supply curve runs along the y-axis; at prices above minimum average variable cost, a firm's supply curve is its marginal cost curve.

Working Problems 4 to 7 will give you a better understanding of a firm's output decision.

Output, Price, and Profit in the Short Run (pp. 234–237)

- The market supply curve shows the sum of the quantities supplied by each firm at each price.
- Market demand and market supply determine price.
- A firm might make a positive economic profit, a zero economic profit, or incur an economic loss.

Working Problems 8 and 9 will give you a better understanding of output, price, and profit in the short run.

Output, Price, and Profit in the Long Run (pp. 237–239)

- Economic profit induces entry and economic loss induces exit.
- Entry increases supply and lowers price and profit. Exit decreases supply and raises price and profit.
- In long-run equilibrium, economic profit is zero. There is no entry or exit.

Working Problems 10 and 11 will give you a better understanding of output, price, and profit in the long run.

Changes in Demand and Supply as Technology Advances (pp. 240–243)

- A permanent increase in demand leads to a larger market output and a larger number of firms. A permanent decrease in demand leads to a smaller market output and a smaller number of firms.
- New technologies lower the cost of production, increase supply, and in the long run lower the price and increase the quantity.

Working Problems 12 to 16 will give you a better understanding of changes in demand and supply as technology advances.

Competition and Efficiency (pp. 244–245)

- Resources are used efficiently when we produce goods and services in the quantities that people value most highly.
- Perfect competition achieves an efficient allocation. In long-run equilibrium, consumers pay the lowest possible price and marginal social benefit equals marginal social cost.

Working Problems 17 and 18 will give you a better understanding of competition and efficiency.

Key Terms

Marginal revenue, 228
Perfect competition, 228

Price taker, 228
Short-run market supply curve, 234

Shutdown point, 232
Total revenue, 228

STUDY PLAN PROBLEMS AND APPLICATIONS

MyEconLab   You can work Problems 1 to 18 in MyEconLab Chapter 10 Study Plan and get instant feedback.

What Is Perfect Competition? (Study Plan 10.1)

Use the following information to work Problems 1 to 3.

Lin's makes fortune cookies that are identical to those made by dozens of other firms, and there is free entry in the fortune cookie market. Buyers and sellers are well informed about prices.

1. In what type of market does Lin's operate? What determines the price of fortune cookies and what determines Lin's marginal revenue from fortune cookies?

2. a. If fortune cookies sell for $10 a box and Lin's offers its cookies for sale at $10.50 a box, how many boxes does it sell?

   b. If fortune cookies sell for $10 a box and Lin's offers its cookies for sale at $9.50 a box, how many boxes does it sell?

3. What is the elasticity of demand for Lin's fortune cookies and how does it differ from the elasticity of the market demand for fortune cookies?

The Firm's Output Decision (Study Plan 10.2)

Use the following table to work Problems 4 to 6. Pat's Pizza Kitchen is a price taker. Its costs are

Output (pizzas per hour)	Total cost (dollars per hour)
0	10
1	21
2	30
3	41
4	54
5	69

4. Calculate Pat's profit-maximizing output and economic profit if the market price is
   (i) $14 a pizza.
   (ii) $12 a pizza.
   (iii) $10 a pizza.

5. What is Pat's shutdown point and what is Pat's economic profit if it shuts down temporarily?

6. Derive Pat's supply curve.

7. The market for paper is perfectly competitive and there are 1,000 firms that produce paper. The table sets out the market demand schedule for paper.

Price (dollars per box)	Quantity demanded (thousands of boxes per week)
3.65	500
5.20	450
6.80	400
8.40	350
10.00	300
11.60	250
13.20	200

Each producer of paper has the following costs when it uses its least-cost plant:

Output (boxes per week)	Marginal cost (dollars per additional box)	Average variable cost	Average total cost
		(dollars per box)	
200	6.40	7.80	12.80
250	7.00	7.00	11.00
300	7.65	7.10	10.43
350	8.40	7.20	10.06
400	10.00	7.50	10.00
450	12.40	8.00	10.22
500	20.70	9.00	11.00

   a. What is the market price of paper?
   b. What is the market's output?
   c. What is the output produced by each firm?
   d. What is the economic profit made or economic loss incurred by each firm?

Output, Price, and Profit in the Short Run

(Study Plan 10.3)

8. In Problem 7, as more and more computer users read documents online rather than print them, the market demand for paper decreases and in the short run the demand schedule becomes

Price (dollars per box)	Quantity demanded (thousands of boxes per week)
2.95	500
4.13	450
5.30	400
6.48	350
7.65	300
8.83	250
10.00	200
11.18	150

If each firm producing paper has the costs set out in Problem 7, what is the market price and the economic profit or loss of each firm in the short run?

9. **Fuel Prices Could Squeeze Cheap Flights**

Airlines are having difficulty keeping prices low, especially as fuel prices keep rising. Airlines have raised fares to make up for the fuel costs. American Airlines increased its fuel surcharge by $20 a round-trip, which Delta, United Airlines, and Continental matched.

Source: *CNN*, June 12, 2008

a. Explain how an increase in fuel prices might cause an airline to change its output (number of flights) in the short run.

b. Draw a graph to show the increase in fuel prices on an airline's output in the short run.

c. Explain why an airline might incur an economic loss in the short run as fuel prices rise.

Output, Price, and Profit in the Long Run

(Study Plan 10.4)

10. The pizza market is perfectly competitive, and all pizza producers have the same costs as Pat's Pizza Kitchen in Problem 4.

a. At what price will some firms exit the pizza market in the long run?

b. At what price will firms enter the pizza market in the long run?

11. In Problem 7, in the long run,

a. Do firms have an incentive to enter or exit the paper market?

b. If firms do enter or exit the market, explain how the economic profit or loss of the remaining paper producers will change.

c. What is the long-run equilibrium market price and the quantity of paper produced? What is the number of firms in the market?

Changes in Demand and Supply as Technology Advances (Study Plan 10.5)

12. If in the long run, the market demand for paper remains the same as in Problem 8, what is the long-run equilibrium price of paper, the market output, and the economic profit or loss of each firm?

13. Explain and illustrate graphically how the growing world population is influencing the world market for wheat and a representative individual wheat farmer.

14. Explain and illustrate graphically how the market for vacation air travel has been affected by the introduction of low-cost budget airlines.

Use the following news clip to work Problems 15 and 16.

Coors Brewing Expanding Plant

Coors Brewing Co. of Golden will expand its Virginia packaging plant at a cost of $24 million. The addition will accommodate a new production line, which will bottle beer faster. Coors Brewing employs 470 people at its Virginia plant. The expanded packaging line will add another eight jobs.

Source: *Denver Business Journal*, January 6, 2006

15. a. How will Coors' expansion change its marginal cost curve and short-run supply curve?

b. What does this expansion decision imply about the point on Coors' *LRAC* curve at which the firm was before the expansion?

16. a. If other breweries follow the lead of Coors, what will happen to the market price of beer?

b. How will the adjustment that you have described in part (a) influence the economic profit of Coors and other beer producers?

Competition and Efficiency (Study Plan 10.6)

17. In a perfectly competitive market in long-run equilibrium, can consumer surplus be increased? Can producer surplus be increased? Can a consumer become better off by making a substitution away from this market?

18. **Never Pay Retail Again**

Not only has scouring the Web for the best possible price become standard protocol before buying a big-ticket item, but more consumers are employing creative strategies for scoring hot deals. Comparison shopping, haggling and swapping discount codes are all becoming mainstream marks of savvy shoppers. Online shoppers can check a comparison service like Price Grabber before making a purchase.

Source: *CNN*, May 30, 2008

a. Explain the effect of the Internet on the degree of competition in the market.

b. Explain how the Internet influences market efficiency.

ADDITIONAL PROBLEMS AND APPLICATIONS

MyEconLab   You can work these problems in MyEconLab if assigned by your instructor.

What Is Perfect Competition?

Use the following news clip to work Problems 19 to 21.

Money in the Tank

Two gas stations stand on opposite sides of the road: Rutter's Farm Store and Sheetz gas station. Rutter's doesn't even have to look across the highway to know when Sheetz changes its price for a gallon of gas. When Sheetz raises the price, Rutter's pumps are busy. When Sheetz lowers prices, there's not a car in sight. Both gas stations survive but each has no control over the price.

Source: *The Mining Journal*, May 24, 2008

19. In what type of market do these gas stations operate? What determines the price of gasoline and the marginal revenue from gasoline?

20. Describe the elasticity of demand that each of these gas stations faces.

21. Why does each of these gas stations have so little control over the price of the gasoline it sells?

The Firm's Output Decision

22. The figure shows the costs of Quick Copy, one of many copy shops near campus.

If the market price of copying is 10¢ a page, calculate Quick Copy's

a. Profit-maximizing output.

b. Economic profit.

23. The market for smoothies is perfectly competitive. The following table sets out the market demand schedule.

Price (dollars per smoothie)	Quantity demanded (smoothies per hour)
1.90	1,000
2.00	950
2.20	800
2.91	700
4.25	550
5.25	400
5.50	300

Each of the 100 producers of smoothies has the following costs when it uses its least-cost plant:

Output (smoothies per hour)	Marginal cost (dollars per additional smoothie)	Average variable cost	Average total cost
		(dollars per smoothie)	
3	2.50	4.00	7.33
4	2.20	3.53	6.03
5	1.90	3.24	5.24
6	2.00	3.00	4.67
7	2.91	2.91	4.34
8	4.25	3.00	4.25
9	8.00	3.33	4.44

a. What is the market price of a smoothie?

b. What is the market quantity of smoothies?

c. How many smoothies does each firm sell?

d. What is the economic profit made or economic loss incurred by each firm?

24. **Cadillac Plant Shuts Down Temporarily, Future Uncertain**

Delta Truss in Cadillac [Michigan] is shutting down and temporarily discontinuing truss production. Workers fear this temporary shutdown will become permanent, but the firm announced that it anticipates that production will resume when the spring business begins.

Source: *9&10 News*, February 18, 2008

a. Explain how the shutdown decision will affect Delta Truss' *TFC*, *TVC*, and *TC*.

b. Under what conditions would this shutdown decision maximize Delta Truss' economic profit (or minimize its loss)?

c. Under what conditions will Delta Truss start producing again?

Output, Price, and Profit in the Short Run

25. **Big Drops in Prices for Crops Make It Tough Down on the Farm**

    Grain prices have fallen roughly 50 percent from earlier this year. With better-than-expected crop yields, world grain production this year will rise 5 percent from 2007 to a record high.

    Source: *USA Today*, October 23, 2008

    Why did grain prices fall in 2008? Draw a graph to show that short-run effect on an individual farmer's economic profit.

Output, Price, and Profit in the Long Run

26. In Problem 23, do firms enter or exit the market in the long run? What is the market price and the equilibrium quantity in the long run?

27. In Problem 24, under what conditions will Delta Truss exit the market?

28. **Exxon Mobil Selling All Its Retail Gas Stations**

    Exxon Mobil is not alone among Big Oil exiting the retail gas business, a market where profits have gotten tougher as crude oil prices have risen. Gas station owners say they're struggling to turn a profit because while wholesale gasoline prices have risen sharply, they've been unable to raise pump prices fast enough to keep pace.

    Source: *Houston Chronicle*, June 12, 2008

    a. Is Exxon Mobil making a shutdown or exit decision in the retail gasoline market?

    b. Under what conditions will this decision maximize Exxon Mobil's economic profit?

    c. How might Exxon Mobil's decision affect the economic profit of other gasoline retailers?

Changes in Demand and Supply as Technology Advances

29. **Another DVD Format, but It's Cheaper**

    New Medium Enterprises claims that its new system, HD VMD, is equal to Blu-ray's but at $199 it's cheaper than the $300 Blu-ray player. The Blu-ray Disc Association says New Medium will fail because it believes that Blu-ray technology will always be more expensive. But mass production will cut the cost of a Blu-ray player to $90.

    Source: *The New York Times*, March 10, 2008

    a. Explain how technological change in Blu-ray production might support the prediction of lower prices in the long run. Illustrate your explanation with a graph.

    b. Even if Blu-ray prices do drop to $90 in the long run, why might the HD VMD still end up being less expensive at that time?

Competition and Efficiency

30. In a perfectly competitive market, each firm maximizes its profit by choosing only the quantity to produce. Regardless of whether the firm makes an economic profit or incurs an economic loss, the short-run equilibrium is efficient. Is the statement true? Explain why or why not.

Economics in the News

31. After you have studied *Reading Between the Lines* on pp. 246–247, answer the following questions.

    a. What are the features of the market for apps that make it competitive?

    b. Does the information provided in the news article suggest that the app market is in long-run equilibrium? Explain why or why not.

    c. How would an advance in development technology that lowered a developer's costs change the market supply and the developer's marginal revenue, marginal cost, average total cost, and economic profit?

    d. Illustrate your answer to part (c) with an appropriate graphical analysis.

32. **Cell Phone Sales Hit 1 Billion Mark**

    More than 1.15 billion mobile phones were sold worldwide in 2007, a 16 percent increase in a year. Emerging markets, especially China and India, provided much of the growth as many people bought their first phone. Carolina Milanesi, research director for mobile devices at Gartner, reported that in mature markets, such as Japan and Western Europe, consumers' appetite for feature-laden phones was met with new models packed with TV tuners, global positioning satellite functions, touch screens, and cameras.

    Source: *CNET News*, February 27, 2008

    a. Explain the effects of the increase in global demand for cell phones on the market for cell phones and on an individual cell-phone producer in the short run.

    b. Draw a graph to illustrate your explanation in part (a).

    c. Explain the long-run effects of the increase in global demand for cell phones on the market for cell phones.

11

MONOPOLY

After studying this chapter, you will be able to:

- Explain how monopoly arises
- Explain how a single-price monopoly determines its output and price
- Compare the performance and efficiency of single-price monopoly and competition
- Explain how price discrimination increases profit
- Explain how monopoly regulation influences output, price, economic profit, and efficiency

Google and Microsoft are big players in the markets for Web search and advertising and for computer operating systems, markets that are obviously not perfectly competitive.

In this chapter, we study markets dominated by one big firm. We call such a market *monopoly*. We study the performance and the efficiency of monopoly and compare it with perfect competition.

In *Reading Between the Lines* at the end of the chapter, we look at the remarkable success of Google and ask whether Google is serving the social interest or violating the U.S. antitrust law.

◆ Monopoly and How It Arises

A **monopoly** is a market with a single firm that produces a good or service with no close substitutes and that is protected by a barrier that prevents other firms from entering that market.

How Monopoly Arises

Monopoly arises for two key reasons:

- No close substitutes
- Barrier to entry

No Close Substitutes If a good has a close substitute, even though only one firm produces it, that firm effectively faces competition from the producers of the substitute. A monopoly sells a good or service that has no good substitutes. Tap water and bottled water are close substitutes for drinking, but tap water has no effective substitutes for showering or washing a car and a local public utility that supplies tap water is a monopoly.

Barrier to Entry A constraint that protects a firm from potential competitors is called a **barrier to entry**. The three types of barrier to entry are

- Natural
- Ownership
- Legal

Natural Barrier to Entry A natural barrier to entry creates a **natural monopoly**: a market in which economies of scale enable one firm to supply the entire market at the lowest possible cost. The firms that deliver gas, water, and electricity to our homes are examples of natural monopoly.

Figure 11.1 illustrates a natural monopoly. The market demand curve for electric power is *D*, and the long-run average cost curve is *LRAC*. Economies of scale prevail over the entire length of the *LRAC* curve. At a price of 5 cents per kilowatt-hour, the quantity demanded is 4 million kilowatt-hours and one firm can produce that quantity at a cost of 5 cents per kilowatt-hour. If two firms shared the market equally, it would cost each of them 10 cents per kilowatt-hour to produce a total of 4 million kilowatt-hours.

Ownership Barrier to Entry An ownership barrier to entry occurs if one firm owns a significant portion of a key resource. An example of this type of monopoly occurred during the last century when De Beers con-

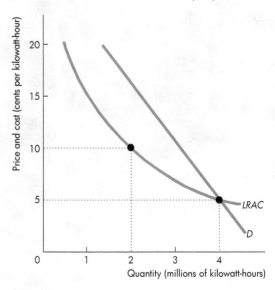

FIGURE 11.1   Natural Monopoly

The market demand curve for electric power is *D*, and the long-run average cost curve is *LRAC*. Economies of scale exist over the entire *LRAC* curve. One firm can distribute 4 million kilowatt-hours at a cost of 5 cents a kilowatt-hour. This same total output costs 10 cents a kilowatt-hour with two firms. One firm can meet the market demand at a lower cost than two or more firms can. The market is a natural monopoly.

MyEconLab animation

trolled up to 90 percent of the world's supply of diamonds. (Today, its share is only 65 percent.)

Legal Barrier to Entry A legal barrier to entry creates a **legal monopoly**: a market in which competition and entry are restricted by the granting of a public franchise, government license, patent, or copyright.

A *public franchise* is an exclusive right granted to a firm to supply a good or service. An example is the U.S. Postal Service, which has the exclusive right to carry first-class mail. A *government license* controls entry into particular occupations, professions, and industries. Examples of this type of barrier to entry occur in medicine, law, dentistry, schoolteaching, architecture, and many other professional services. Licensing does not always create a monopoly, but it does restrict competition.

A *patent* is an exclusive right granted to the inventor of a product or service. A *copyright* is an exclusive right granted to the author or composer of a literary, musical, dramatic, or artistic work. Patents and copyrights are valid for a limited time period that varies from country to country. In the United States, a patent is valid for 20 years. Patents encourage the *invention* of new products and production methods. They also stimulate *innovation*—the use of new inventions—by encouraging inventors to publicize their discoveries and offer them for use under license. Patents have stimulated innovations in areas as diverse as soybean seeds, pharmaceuticals, memory chips, and video games.

Economics in Action
Information-Age Monopolies

Information-age technologies have created four big natural monopolies—firms with large plant costs but almost zero marginal cost, so they experience economies of scale.

These firms are: Microsoft, with 92 percent of personal computers using a version of Windows and 54 percent using Internet Explorer for Web browsing; Google, which performs 83 percent of Internet searches; Facebook, with 64 percent of the social media market; and eBay, with 62 percent of the Internet auction market.

These same information-age technologies have also destroyed monopolies. FedEx, UPS, the fax machine, and e-mail have weakened the monopoly of the U.S. Postal Service; and the satellite dish has weakened cable television monopolies.

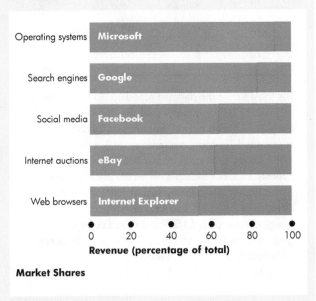

Market Shares

Monopoly *Price-Setting* Strategies

A major difference between monopoly and competition is that a monopoly sets its own price. In doing so, the monopoly faces a market constraint: To sell a larger quantity, the monopoly must set a lower price. There are two monopoly situations that create two pricing strategies:

- Single price
- Price discrimination

Single Price A **single-price monopoly** is a firm that must sell each unit of its output for the same price to all its customers. De Beers sells diamonds (of a given size and quality) for the same price to all its customers. If it tried to sell at a low price to some customers and at a higher price to others, only the low-price customers would buy from De Beers. Others would buy from De Beers' low-price customers. De Beers is a *single-price* monopoly.

Price Discrimination When a firm practices **price discrimination**, it sells different units of a good or service for different prices. Many firms price discriminate. Microsoft sells its Windows and Office software at different prices to different buyers. Computer manufacturers who install the software on new machines, students and teachers, governments, and businesses all pay different prices. Pizza producers offer a second pizza for a lower price than the first one. These are examples of *price discrimination*.

When a firm price discriminates, it looks as though it is doing its customers a favor. In fact, it is charging the highest possible price for each unit sold and making the largest possible profit.

▶ REVIEW QUIZ

1 How does monopoly arise?
2 How does a natural monopoly differ from a legal monopoly?
3 Distinguish between a price-discriminating monopoly and a single-price monopoly.

You can work these questions in Study Plan 11.1 and get instant feedback.   MyEconLab

We start with a single-price monopoly and see how it makes its decisions about the quantity to produce and the price to charge to maximize its profit.

A Single-Price Monopoly's Output and Price Decision

To understand how a single-price monopoly makes its output and price decision, we must first study the link between price and marginal revenue.

Price and Marginal Revenue

Because in a monopoly there is only one firm, the demand curve facing the firm is the market demand curve. Let's look at Bobbie's Barbershop, the sole supplier of haircuts in Cairo, Nebraska. The table in Fig. 11.2 shows the market demand schedule. At a price of $20, Bobbie sells no haircuts. The lower the price, the more haircuts per hour she can sell. For example, at $12, consumers demand 4 haircuts per hour (row *E*).

Total revenue (*TR*) is the price (*P*) multiplied by the quantity sold (*Q*). For example, in row *D*, Bobbie sells 3 haircuts at $14 each, so total revenue is $42. *Marginal revenue* (*MR*) is the change in total revenue (ΔTR) resulting from a one-unit increase in the quantity sold. For example, if the price falls from $16 (row *C*) to $14 (row *D*), the quantity sold increases from 2 to 3 haircuts. Total revenue increases from $32 to $42, so the change in total revenue is $10. Because the quantity sold increases by 1 haircut, marginal revenue equals the change in total revenue and is $10. Marginal revenue is placed between the two rows to emphasize that marginal revenue relates to the *change* in the quantity sold.

Figure 11.2 shows the market demand curve and marginal revenue curve (*MR*) and also illustrates the calculation we've just made. Notice that at each level of output, marginal revenue is less than price—the marginal revenue curve lies below the demand curve. Why is marginal revenue *less* than price? It is because when the price is lowered to sell one more unit, two opposing forces affect total revenue. The lower price results in a revenue loss, and the increased quantity sold results in a revenue gain. For example, at a price of $16, Bobbie sells 2 haircuts (point *C*). If she lowers the price to $14, she sells 3 haircuts and has a revenue gain of $14 on the third haircut. But she now receives only $14 on the first two haircuts—$2 less than before. As a result, she loses $4 of revenue on the first 2 haircuts. To calculate marginal revenue, she must deduct this amount from the revenue gain of $14. So her marginal revenue is $10, which is less than the price.

FIGURE 11.2   Demand and Marginal Revenue

	Price (P) (dollars per haircut)	Quantity demanded (Q) (haircuts per hour)	Total revenue (TR = P × Q) (dollars)	Marginal revenue (MR = ΔTR/ΔQ) (dollars per haircut)
A	20	0	0	
				18
B	18	1	18	
				14
C	**16**	**2**	**32**	
				10
D	**14**	**3**	**42**	
				6
E	12	4	48	
				2
F	10	5	50	

The table shows the demand schedule. Total revenue (*TR*) is price multiplied by quantity sold. For example, in row *C*, the price is $16 a haircut, Bobbie sells 2 haircuts, and total revenue is $32. Marginal revenue (*MR*) is the change in total revenue that results from a one-unit increase in the quantity sold. For example, when the price falls from $16 to $14 a haircut, the quantity sold increases from 2 to 3, an increase of 1 haircut, and total revenue increases by $10. Marginal revenue is $10. The demand curve and the marginal revenue curve, *MR*, are based on the numbers in the table and illustrate the calculation of marginal revenue when the price falls from $16 to $14 a haircut.

MyEconLab animation

Marginal Revenue and Elasticity

A single-price monopoly's marginal revenue is related to the *elasticity of demand* for its good. The demand for a good can be *elastic* (the elasticity is greater than 1), *inelastic* (the elasticity is less than 1), or *unit elastic* (the elasticity is equal to 1). Demand is *elastic* if a 1 percent fall in the price brings a greater than 1 percent increase in the quantity demanded. Demand is *inelastic* if a 1 percent fall in the price brings a less than 1 percent increase in the quantity demanded. Demand is *unit elastic* if a 1 percent fall in the price brings a 1 percent increase in the quantity demanded. (See Chapter 4, pp. 84–86.)

If demand is elastic, a fall in the price brings an increase in total revenue—the revenue gain from the increase in quantity sold outweighs the revenue loss from the lower price—and marginal revenue is *positive*. If demand is inelastic, a fall in the price brings a decrease in total revenue—the revenue gain from the increase in quantity sold is outweighed by the revenue loss from the lower price—and marginal revenue is *negative*. If demand is unit elastic, total revenue does not change—the revenue gain from the increase in the quantity sold offsets the revenue loss from the lower price—and marginal revenue is *zero*. (See Chapter 4, p. 88.)

Figure 11.3 illustrates the relationship between marginal revenue, total revenue, and elasticity. As the price gradually falls from $20 to $10 a haircut, the quantity demanded increases from 0 to 5 haircuts an hour. Over this output range, marginal revenue is positive in part (a), total revenue increases in part (b), and the demand for haircuts is elastic. As the price falls from $10 to $0 a haircut, the quantity of haircuts demanded increases from 5 to 10 an hour. Over this output range, marginal revenue is negative in part (a), total revenue decreases in part (b), and the demand for haircuts is inelastic. When the price is $10 a haircut, marginal revenue is zero in part (a), total revenue is at a maximum in part (b), and the demand for haircuts is unit elastic.

In Monopoly, Demand Is Always Elastic The relationship between marginal revenue and elasticity of demand that you've just discovered implies that a profit-maximizing monopoly never produces an output in the inelastic range of the market demand curve. If it did so, it could charge a higher price, produce a smaller quantity, and increase its profit. Let's now look at a monopoly's price and output decision.

FIGURE 11.3   Marginal Revenue and Elasticity

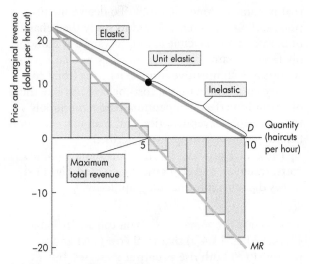

(a) Demand and marginal revenue curves

(b) Total revenue curve

In part (a), the demand curve is *D* and the marginal revenue curve is *MR*. In part (b), the total revenue curve is *TR*. Over the range 0 to 5 haircuts an hour, a price cut increases total revenue, so marginal revenue is positive—as shown by the blue bars. Demand is elastic. Over the range 5 to 10 haircuts an hour, a price cut decreases total revenue, so marginal revenue is negative—as shown by the red bars. Demand is inelastic. At 5 haircuts an hour, total revenue is maximized and marginal revenue is zero. Demand is unit elastic.

——————— MyEconLab animation ———————

Price and Output Decision

A monopoly sets its price and output at the levels that maximize economic profit. To determine this price and output level, we need to study the behavior of both cost and revenue as output varies. A monopoly faces the same types of technology and cost constraints as a competitive firm, so its costs (total cost, average cost, and marginal cost) behave just like those of a firm in perfect competition. And a monopoly's revenues (total revenue, price, and marginal revenue) behave in the way we've just described.

Table 11.1 provides information about Bobbie's costs, revenues, and economic profit, and Fig. 11.4 shows the same information graphically.

Maximizing Economic Profit You can see in Table 11.1 and Fig. 11.4(a) that total cost (*TC*) and total revenue (*TR*) both rise as output increases, but *TC* rises at an increasing rate and *TR* rises at a decreasing rate. Economic profit, which equals *TR* minus *TC*, increases at small output levels, reaches a maximum, and then decreases. The maximum profit ($12) occurs when Bobbie sells 3 haircuts for $14 each. If she sells 2 haircuts for $16 each or 4 haircuts for $12 each, her economic profit will be only $8.

Marginal Revenue Equals Marginal Cost You can see Bobbie's marginal revenue (*MR*) and marginal cost (*MC*) in Table 11.1 and Fig. 11.4(b).

When Bobbie increases output from 2 to 3 haircuts, *MR* is $10 and *MC* is $6. *MR* exceeds *MC* by $4 and Bobbie's profit increases by that amount. If Bobbie increases output yet further, from 3 to 4 haircuts, *MR* is $6 and *MC* is $10. In this case, *MC* exceeds *MR* by $4, so profit decreases by that amount. When *MR* exceeds *MC*, profit increases if output increases. When *MC* exceeds *MR*, profit increases if output *decreases*. When *MC* equals *MR*, profit is maximized.

Figure 11.4(b) shows the maximum profit as price (on the demand curve *D*) minus average total cost (on the *ATC* curve) multiplied by the quantity produced—the blue rectangle.

Maximum Price the Market Will Bear Unlike a firm in perfect competition, a monopoly influences the price of what it sells. But a monopoly doesn't set the price at the maximum *possible* price. At the maximum possible price, the firm would be able to sell only one unit of output, which in general is less than the profit-maximizing quantity. Rather, a monopoly produces the profit-maximizing quantity and sells that quantity for the highest price it can get.

TABLE 11.1 A Monopoly's Output and Price Decision

Price (P) (dollars per haircut)	Quantity demanded (Q) (haircuts per hour)	Total revenue (TR = P × Q) (dollars)	Marginal revenue (MR = ΔTR/ΔQ) (dollars per haircut)	Total cost (TC) (dollars)	Marginal cost (MC = ΔTC/ΔQ) (dollars per haircut)	Profit (TR − TC) (dollars)
20	0	0		20		−20
			18		1	
18	1	18		21		−3
			14		3	
16	2	32		24		+8
			10		6	
14	3	42		30		+12
			6		10	
12	4	48		40		+8
			2		15	
10	5	50		55		−5

This table gives the information needed to find the profit-maximizing output and price. Total revenue (*TR*) equals price multiplied by the quantity sold. Profit equals total revenue minus total cost (*TC*). Profit is maximized when 3 haircuts are sold at a price of $14 each. Total revenue is $42, total cost is $30, and economic profit is $12 ($42 − $30).

FIGURE 11.4   A Monopoly's Output and Price

(a) Total revenue and total cost curves

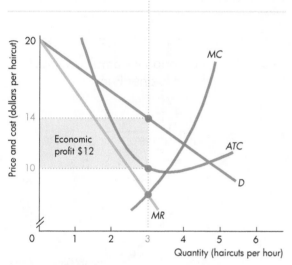

(b) Demand and marginal revenue and cost curves

In part (a), economic profit is the vertical distance equal to total revenue (*TR*) minus total cost (*TC*) and it is maximized at 3 haircuts an hour.

In part (b), economic profit is maximized when marginal cost (*MC*) equals marginal revenue (*MR*). The profit-maximizing output is 3 haircuts an hour. The price is determined by the demand curve (*D*) and is $14 a haircut. The average total cost of a haircut is $10, so economic profit, the blue rectangle, is $12—the profit per haircut ($4) multiplied by 3 haircuts.

—— MyEconLab animation ——

All firms maximize profit by producing the output at which marginal revenue equals marginal cost. For a competitive firm, price equals marginal revenue, so price also equals marginal cost. For a monopoly, price exceeds marginal revenue, so price also exceeds marginal cost.

A monopoly charges a price that exceeds marginal cost, but does it always make an economic profit? In Fig. 11.4(b), Bobbie produces 3 haircuts an hour. Her average total cost is $10 (on the *ATC* curve) and her price is $14 (on the *D* curve), so her profit per haircut is $4 ($14 minus $10). Bobbie's economic profit is shown by the area of the blue rectangle, which equals the profit per haircut ($4) multiplied by the number of haircuts (3), for a total of $12.

If firms in a perfectly competitive market make a positive economic profit, new firms enter. That does *not* happen in monopoly. Barriers to entry prevent new firms from entering the market, so a monopoly can make a positive economic profit and might continue to do so indefinitely. Sometimes that economic profit is large, as in the international diamond business.

Bobbie makes a positive economic profit. But suppose that Bobbie's landlord increases the rent on her salon. If Bobbie pays an additional $12 an hour for rent, her fixed cost increases by $12 an hour. Her marginal cost and marginal revenue don't change, so her profit-maximizing output remains at 3 haircuts an hour. Her profit decreases by $12 an hour to zero. If Bobbie's salon rent increases by more than $12 an hour, she incurs an economic loss. If this situation were permanent, Bobbie would go out of business.

REVIEW QUIZ

1 What is the relationship between marginal cost and marginal revenue when a single-price monopoly maximizes profit?

2 How does a single-price monopoly determine the price it will charge its customers?

3 What is the relationship between price, marginal revenue, and marginal cost when a single-price monopoly is maximizing profit?

4 Why can a monopoly make a positive economic profit even in the long run?

You can work these questions in Study Plan 11.2 and get instant feedback.   MyEconLab

◆ Single-Price Monopoly and Competition Compared

Imagine a market that is made up of many small firms operating in perfect competition. Then imagine that a single firm buys out all these small firms and creates a monopoly.

What will happen in this market? Will the price rise or fall? Will the quantity produced increase or decrease? Will economic profit increase or decrease? Will either the original competitive situation or the new monopoly situation be efficient?

These are the questions we're now going to answer. First, we look at the effects of monopoly on the price and quantity produced. Then we turn to the questions about efficiency.

Comparing Price and Output

Figure 11.5 shows the market we'll study. The market demand curve is D. The demand curve is the same regardless of how the industry is organized. But the supply side and the equilibrium are different in monopoly and competition. First, let's look at the case of perfect competition.

Perfect Competition Initially, with many small perfectly competitive firms in the market, the market supply curve is S. This supply curve is obtained by summing the supply curves of all the individual firms in the market.

In perfect competition, equilibrium occurs where the supply curve and the demand curve intersect. The price is P_C, and the quantity produced by the industry is Q_C. Each firm takes the price P_C and maximizes its profit by producing the output at which its own marginal cost equals the price. Because each firm is a small part of the total industry, there is no incentive for any firm to try to manipulate the price by varying its output.

Monopoly Now suppose that this industry is taken over by a single firm. Consumers do not change, so the market demand curve remains the same as in the case of perfect competition. But now the monopoly recognizes this demand curve as a constraint on the price at which it can sell its output. The monopoly's marginal revenue curve is MR.

The monopoly maximizes profit by producing the quantity at which marginal revenue equals marginal cost. To find the monopoly's marginal cost curve, first

recall that in perfect competition, the market supply curve is the sum of the supply curves of the firms in the industry. Also recall that each firm's supply curve is its marginal cost curve (see Chapter 10, p. 233). So when the market is taken over by a single firm, the competitive market's supply curve becomes the monopoly's marginal cost curve. To remind you of this fact, the supply curve is also labeled MC.

The output at which marginal revenue equals marginal cost is Q_M. This output is smaller than the competitive output Q_C. And the monopoly charges the price P_M, which is higher than P_C. We have established that

> Compared to a perfectly competitive market, a single-price monopoly produces a smaller output and charges a higher price.

We've seen how the output and price of a monopoly compare with those in a competitive market. Let's now compare the efficiency of the two types of market.

FIGURE 11.5 Monopoly's Smaller Output and Higher Price

A competitive market produces the quantity Q_C at price P_C. A single-price monopoly produces the quantity Q_M at which marginal revenue equals marginal cost and sells that quantity for the price P_M. Compared to perfect competition, a single-price monopoly produces a smaller output and charges a higher price.

——— MyEconLab animation ———

Efficiency Comparison

Perfect competition (with no externalities) is efficient. Figure 11.6(a) illustrates the efficiency of perfect competition and serves as a benchmark against which to measure the inefficiency of monopoly. Along the demand and marginal social benefit curve ($D = MSB$), consumers are efficient. Along the supply curve and marginal social cost curve ($S = MSC$), producers are efficient. In competitive equilibrium, the price is P_C, the quantity is Q_C, and marginal social benefit equals marginal social cost.

Consumer surplus is the green triangle under the demand curve and above the equilibrium price (see Chapter 5, p. 109). *Producer surplus* is the blue area above the supply curve and below the equilibrium price (see Chapter 5, p. 111). Total surplus (consumer surplus and producer surplus) is maximized.

Also, in long-run competitive equilibrium, entry and exit ensure that each firm produces its output at the minimum possible long-run average cost.

To summarize: At the competitive equilibrium, marginal social benefit equals marginal social cost; total surplus is maximized; firms produce at the lowest possible long-run average cost; and resource use is efficient.

Figure 11.6(b) illustrates the inefficiency of monopoly and the sources of that inefficiency. A monopoly produces Q_M and sells its output for P_M. The smaller output and higher price drive a wedge between marginal social benefit and marginal social cost and create a *deadweight loss*. The gray triangle shows the deadweight loss and its magnitude is a measure of the inefficiency of monopoly.

Consumer surplus shrinks for two reasons. First, consumers lose by having to pay more for the good. This loss to consumers is a gain for monopoly and increases the producer surplus. Second, consumers lose by getting less of the good, and this loss is part of the deadweight loss.

Although the monopoly gains from a higher price, it loses some producer surplus because it produces a smaller output. That loss is another part of the deadweight loss.

A monopoly produces a smaller output than perfect competition and faces no competition, so it does not produce at the lowest possible long-run average cost. As a result, monopoly damages the consumer interest in three ways: A monopoly produces less, increases the cost of production, and raises the price by more than the increased cost of production.

FIGURE 11.6   Inefficiency of Monopoly

(a) Perfect competition

(b) Monopoly

In perfect competition in part (a), output is Q_C and the price is P_C. Marginal social benefit (*MSB*) equals marginal social cost (*MSC*); total surplus, the sum of consumer surplus (the green triangle) and producer surplus (the blue area), is maximized; and in the long run, firms produce at the lowest possible average cost. Monopoly in part (b) produces Q_M and raises the price to P_M. Consumer surplus shrinks, the monopoly gains, and a deadweight loss (the gray triangle) arises.

—— MyEconLab animation ——

Redistribution of Surpluses

You've seen that monopoly is inefficient because marginal social benefit exceeds marginal social cost and there is deadweight loss—a social loss. But monopoly also brings a *redistribution* of surpluses.

Some of the lost consumer surplus goes to the monopoly. In Fig. 11.6, the monopoly takes the difference between the higher price, P_M, and the competitive price, P_C, on the quantity sold, Q_M. So the monopoly takes that part of the consumer surplus. This portion of the loss of consumer surplus is not a loss to society. It is redistribution from consumers to the monopoly producer.

Rent Seeking

You've seen that monopoly creates a deadweight loss and is inefficient. But the social cost of monopoly can exceed the deadweight loss because of an activity called rent seeking. Any surplus—consumer surplus, producer surplus, or economic profit—is called **economic rent**. The pursuit of wealth by capturing economic rent is called **rent seeking**.

You've seen that a monopoly makes its economic profit by diverting part of consumer surplus to itself—by converting consumer surplus into economic profit. So the pursuit of economic profit by a monopoly is rent seeking. It is the attempt to capture consumer surplus.

Rent seekers pursue their goals in two main ways. They might

- Buy a monopoly
- Create a monopoly

Buy a Monopoly To rent seek by buying a monopoly, a person searches for a monopoly that is for sale at a lower price than the monopoly's economic profit. Trading of taxicab licenses is an example of this type of rent seeking. In some cities, taxicabs are regulated. The city restricts both the fares and the number of taxis that can operate so that operating a taxi results in economic profit. A person who wants to operate a taxi must buy a license from someone who already has one. People rationally devote time and effort to seeking out profitable monopoly businesses to buy. In the process, they use up scarce resources that could otherwise have been used to produce goods and services. The value of this lost production is part of the social cost of monopoly. The amount paid for a monopoly is not a social cost because the payment is just a transfer of an existing producer surplus from the buyer to the seller.

Create a Monopoly Rent seeking by creating a monopoly is mainly a political activity. It takes the form of lobbying and trying to influence the political process. Such influence might be sought by making campaign contributions in exchange for legislative support or by indirectly seeking to influence political outcomes through publicity in the media or more direct contacts with politicians and bureaucrats. An example of a monopoly created in this way is the government-imposed restrictions on the quantities of textiles that may be imported into the United States. Another is a regulation that limits the number of oranges that may be sold in the United States. These are regulations that restrict output and increase price.

This type of rent seeking is a costly activity that uses up scarce resources. Taken together, firms spend billions of dollars lobbying Congress, state legislators, and local officials in the pursuit of licenses and laws that create barriers to entry and establish a monopoly.

Rent-Seeking Equilibrium

Barriers to entry create monopoly. But there is no barrier to entry into rent seeking. Rent seeking is like perfect competition. If an economic profit is available, a new rent seeker will try to get some of it. And competition among rent seekers pushes up the price that must be paid for a monopoly, to the point at which the rent seeker makes zero economic profit by operating the monopoly. For example, competition for the right to operate a taxi in New York City leads to a price of more than $100,000 for a taxi license, which is sufficiently high to eliminate the economic profit made by a taxi operator.

Figure 11.7 shows a rent-seeking equilibrium. The cost of rent seeking is a fixed cost that must be added to a monopoly's other costs. Rent seeking and rent-seeking costs increase to the point at which no economic profit is made. The average total cost curve, which includes the fixed cost of rent seeking, shifts upward until it just touches the demand curve. Economic profit is zero. It has been lost in rent seeking.

Consumer surplus is unaffected, but the deadweight loss from monopoly is larger. The deadweight loss now includes the original deadweight loss triangle plus the lost producer surplus, shown by the enlarged gray area in Fig. 11.7.

FIGURE 11.7   Rent-Seeking Equilibrium

With competitive rent seeking, a single-price monopoly uses all its economic profit to maintain its monopoly. The firm's rent-seeking costs are fixed costs. They add to total fixed cost and to average total cost. The *ATC* curve shifts upward until, at the profit-maximizing price, the firm breaks even.

MyEconLab animation

REVIEW QUIZ

1   Why does a single-price monopoly produce a smaller output and charge more than the price that would prevail if the market were perfectly competitive?
2   How does a monopoly transfer consumer surplus to itself?
3   Why is a single-price monopoly inefficient?
4   What is rent seeking and how does it influence the inefficiency of monopoly?

You can work these questions in Study Plan 11.3 and get instant feedback.   *MyEconLab*

So far, we've considered only a single-price monopoly. But many monopolies do not operate with a single price. Instead, they price discriminate. Let's now see how a price-discriminating monopoly works.

◆ Price Discrimination

You encounter *price discrimination*—selling a good or service at a number of different prices—when you travel, go to the movies, get your hair cut, visit an art museum or theme park, or buy pizza. These are all examples of firms with market power, setting the prices of an identical good or service at different levels for different customers.

Not all price *differences* are price *discrimination*: they reflect differences in production costs. For example, real-time meters for electricity enable power utilities to charge a different price at peak-load times than during the night. But it costs more per kilowatt-hour to generate electricity at peak-load times so this price difference reflects production cost differences and is not price discrimination.

At first sight, price discrimination appears to be inconsistent with profit maximization. Why would a movie theater allow children to see movies at a discount? Why would a hairdresser charge students and senior citizens less? Aren't these firms losing profit by being nice to their customers? The answer, as you are about to discover, is that price discrimination is profitable: It increases economic profit.

But to be able to price discriminate, the firm must sell a product that cannot be resold; and it must be possible to identify and separate different buyer types.

Two Ways of Price Discriminating

Firms price discriminate in two broad ways. They discriminate:

- Among groups of buyers
- Among units of a good

Discriminating Among Groups of Buyers People differ in the value they place on a good—their marginal benefit and willingness to pay. Some of these differences are correlated with features such as age, employment status, and other easily distinguished characteristics. When such a correlation is present, firms can profit by price discriminating among the different groups of buyers.

For example, salespeople and other business travelers know that a face-to-face sales meeting with a customer might bring a large and profitable order. So for these travelers, the marginal benefit from a trip is large and the price that such a traveler is willing to pay for a trip is high. In contrast, for a leisure traveler, any of several different trips and even no trip at all are options. So for leisure travelers, the marginal benefit of a trip is small and the price that such a traveler is willing to pay for a trip is low. Because the price that business travelers are willing to pay exceeds what leisure travelers are willing to pay, it is possible for an airline to price discriminate between these two groups and increase its profit. We'll return to this example of price discrimination below.

Discriminating Among Units of a Good Everyone experiences diminishing marginal benefit so if all the units of the good are sold for a single price, buyers end up with a consumer surplus equal to the value they get from each unit minus the price paid for it.

A firm that price discriminates by charging a buyer one price for a single item and a lower price for a second or third item can capture some of the consumer surplus. Buy one pizza and get a second one for a lower price is an example of this type of price discrimination.

Increasing Profit and Producer Surplus

By getting buyers to pay a price as close as possible to their maximum willingness to pay, a monopoly captures the consumer surplus and converts it into producer surplus. And more producer surplus means more economic profit.

To see why more producer surplus means more economic profit, recall some definitions. With total revenue TR and total cost TC,

$$\text{Economic profit} = TR - TC.$$

Producer surplus is total revenue minus the area under the marginal cost curve. But the area under the marginal cost curve is total *variable* cost, TVC. So producer surplus equals total revenue minus TVC, or

$$\text{Producer surplus} = TR - TVC.$$

You can see that the difference between economic profit and producer surplus is the same as the difference between TC and TVC. But TC minus TVC equals total *fixed* cost, TFC. So

$$\text{Economic profit} = \text{Producer surplus} - TFC.$$

For a given level of total fixed cost, anything that increases producer surplus also increases economic profit.

Let's now see how price discrimination works by looking at a price-discriminating airline.

A Price-Discriminating Airline

Inter-City Airlines has a monopoly on passenger flights between two cities. Figure 11.8 shows the market demand curve, D, for travel on this route. It also shows Inter-City Airline's marginal revenue curve, MR, and marginal cost curve, MC. Inter-City's marginal cost is a constant $40 per trip. (It is easier to see how price discrimination works for a firm with constant marginal cost.)

Single-Price Profit Maximization As a single-price monopoly, Inter-City maximizes profit by producing the quantity of trips at which MR equals MC, which is 8,000 trips a week, and charging $120 a trip. With a marginal cost of $40 a trip, producer surplus is $80 a trip, and Inter-City's producer surplus is $640,000 a week, shown by the area of the blue rectangle. Inter-City's customers enjoy a consumer surplus shown by the area of the green triangle.

FIGURE 11.8   A Single Price of Air Travel

Inter-City Airlines has a monopoly on an air route with a market demand curve D. Inter-City's marginal cost, MC, is $40 per trip. As a single-price monopoly, Inter-City's marginal revenue curve is MR. Profit is maximized by selling 8,000 trips a week at $120 a trip. Producer surplus is $640,000 a week—the blue rectangle—and Inter-City's customers enjoy a consumer surplus—the green triangle.

MyEconLab animation

Discrimination Between Two Types of Travelers

Inter-City surveys its customers and discovers that they are all business travelers. It also surveys people who are *not* its customers and discovers that they are mainly people who travel for leisure. These people travel by bus or car, but would travel by air at a low fare. Inter-City would like to attract some of these travelers and knows that to do so, it must offer a fare below the current $120 a trip. How can it do that?

Inter-City digs more deeply into its survey results and discovers that its current customers always plan their travel less than two weeks before departure. In contrast, the people who travel by bus or car know their travel plans at least two weeks ahead of time.

Inter-City sees that it can use what it has discovered about its current and potential new customers to separate the two types of travelers into two markets: one market for business travel and another for leisure travel.

Figure 11.9 shows Inter-City's two markets. Part (a), the market for business travel, is the same as Fig. 11.8. Part (b) shows the market for leisure travel. No leisure traveler is willing to pay the business fare of $120 a trip, so at that price, the quantity demanded in part (b) is zero. The demand curve D_L is the demand for travel on this route after satisfying the demand of business travelers. Inter-City's marginal cost remains at $40 a trip, so its marginal revenue curve is MR_L. Inter-City maximizes profit by setting the leisure fare at $80 a trip and attracting 4,000 leisure travelers a week. Inter-City's producer surplus increases by $160,000 a week—the area of the blue rectangle in Fig. 11.9(b) and leisure travelers enjoy a consumer surplus—the area of the green triangle.

Inter-City announces its new fare schedule: no restrictions, $120 and 14-day advance purchase, $80. Inter-City increases its passenger count by 50 percent and increases its producer surplus by $160,000.

FIGURE 11.9 Price Discrimination

(a) Business travel

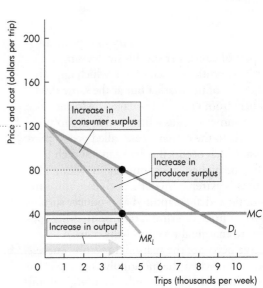

(b) Leisure travel

Inter-City separates its market into two types of travel: business travel with no restrictions in part (a) and leisure travel that requires a 14-day advance purchase in part (b). For business travel, the profit-maximizing price is $120 a trip with 8,000 trips a week. For leisure travel, the profit-maximizing price is $80 a trip with 4,000 trips a week.

Inter-City continues to make the same producer surplus on business travel as it did with a single price and business travelers continue to enjoy the same consumer surplus. But in part (b), Inter-City sells 4,000 trips to leisure travelers, which increases its producer surplus—the blue rectangle—and increases consumer surplus—the green triangle.

MyEconLab animation

Discrimination Among Several Types of Travelers
Pleased with the success of its price discrimination between business and leisure travelers, Inter-City sees that it might be able to profit even more by dividing its customers into a larger number of types. So it does another customer survey, which reveals that some business travelers are willing to pay $160 for a fully-refundable, unrestricted ticket while others are willing to pay only $120 for a nonrefundable ticket. So applying the same principles as it used to discriminate between business and leisure travelers, Inter-City now discriminates between business travelers who want a refundable ticket and those who want a nonrefundable ticket.

Another survey of leisure travelers reveals that they fall into two goups: those who are able to plan 14 days ahead and others who can plan 21 days ahead. So Inter-City discriminates between these two groups with two fares: an $80 and a $60 fare.

By offering travelers four different fares, the airline increases its producer surplus and increases its economic profit. But why only four fares? Why not keep looking for ever more traveler types and offer even more fares?

Perfect Price Discrimination Firms try to capture an ever larger part of consumer surplus by devising a host of special conditions, each one of which appeals to a tiny segment of the market but at the same time excludes others from taking advantage of a lower price. The more consumer surplus a firm is able to capture, the closer it gets to the extreme case called **perfect price discrimination**, which occurs if a firm can sell each unit of output for the highest price someone is willing to pay for it. In this extreme (hypothetical) case consumer surplus is eliminated and captured as producer surplus.

With perfect price discrimination, something special happens to marginal revenue—the market demand curve becomes the marginal revenue curve. The reason is that when the monopoly cuts the price to sell a larger quantity, it sells only the marginal unit at the lower price. All the other units continue to be sold for the highest price that each buyer is willing to pay. So for the perfect price discriminator, marginal revenue *equals* price and the market demand curve becomes the monopoly's marginal revenue curve.

With marginal revenue equal to price, Inter-City can obtain even greater producer surplus by increasing output up to the point at which price (and marginal revenue) equals marginal cost.

So Inter-City seeks new travelers who will not pay as much as $60 a trip but who will pay more than $40, its marginal cost. Inter-City offers a variety of vacation specials at different low fares that appeal only to new travelers. Existing customers continue to pay the higher fares and some, with further perks and frills that have no effect on cost, are induced to pay fares going all the way up to $200 a trip.

With all these special conditions and fares, Inter-City increases its output to the quantity demanded at marginal cost, extracts the entire consumer surplus on that quantity, and maximizes economic profit.

Figure 11.10 shows the outcome with perfect price discrimination and compares it with the single-price monopoly outcome. The range of business-class fares extract the entire consumer surplus from this group. The new leisure-class fares going down to $40 a trip attract an additional 8,000 travelers and take the entire consumer surplus of leisure travelers. Inter-City makes the maximum possible economic profit.

FIGURE 11.10   Perfect Price Discrimination

Dozens of fares discriminate among many different types of business travelers, and many new low fares with restrictions appeal to leisure travelers. With perfect price discrimination, the market demand curve becomes Inter-City's marginal revenue curve. Producer surplus is maximized when the lowest fare equals marginal cost. Inter-City sells 16,000 trips and makes the maximum possible economic profit.

*Would it bother you to hear how
little I paid for this flight?*

From William Hamilton, "Voodoo Economics," © 1992 by
The Chronicle Publishing Company, p. 3.
Reprinted with permission of Chronicle Books.

Efficiency and Rent Seeking with Price Discrimination

With perfect price discrimination, output increases to the point at which price equals marginal cost. This output is identical to that of perfect competition. Perfect price discrimination pushes consumer surplus to zero but increases the monopoly's producer surplus to equal the total surplus in perfect competition. With perfect price discrimination, no deadweight loss is created, so perfect price discrimination achieves efficiency.

> The more perfectly the monopoly can price discriminate, the closer its output is to the competitive output and the more efficient is the outcome.

But the outcomes of perfect competition and perfect price discrimination differ. First, the distribution of the total surplus is not the same. In perfect competition, total surplus is shared by consumers and producers, while with perfect price discrimination, the monopoly takes it all. Second, because the monopoly takes all the total surplus, rent seeking is profitable.

People use resources in pursuit of economic rent, and the bigger the rents, the more resources are used in pursuing them. With free entry into rent seeking, the long-run equilibrium outcome is that rent seekers use up the entire producer surplus.

Real-world airlines are as creative as Inter-City Airlines, as you can see in the cartoon! Disney Corporation is creative too in extracting consumer surplus, as Economics in Action shows.

We next study some key monopoly policy issues.

Economics in Action
Attempting Perfect Price Discrimination

If you want to spend a day at Disney World in Orlando, it will cost you $94.79. You can spend a second consecutive day for an extra $92.65. A third day will cost you $70.29. But for a fourth day, you'll pay only $14.91 and for a fifth day, $12.78. For more days all the way up to 10, you'll pay only $10.65 a day. The Disney Corporation hopes that it has read your willingness to pay correctly and not left you with too much consumer surplus.

Disney's Ticket Prices

ECONOMICS IN THE NEWS

Microsoft Monopoly

Microsoft Windows 8 to Go on Sale in October

Microsoft announced that its Windows 8 operating system will be released in October 2012, three years after Windows 7 went public. Windows 8 will be available in 109 languages across 231 markets worldwide.

Source: AFP, July 9, 2012

SOME DATA

Microsoft Windows 7 Versions and U.S. Prices

Version	Price
Full from Microsoft	299.99
Upgrade from Microsoft	199.99
Full from Amazon	136.48
Full from Mission Softs (OEM)	77.50
Student from Microsoft	64.95

Microsoft sold 240 million Windows 7 licenses per year and at different prices in different national markets.

THE QUESTIONS

- Is Microsoft a monopoly?
- Is Microsoft a natural monopoly or a legal monopoly?
- Does Microsoft price discriminate or do the different prices of Windows reflect cost differences?
- Sketch a demand curve for Windows, Microsoft's marginal cost curve, and the distribution of the total surplus between consumers and Microsoft.

THE ANSWERS

- Microsoft controls 92 percent of the market for computer operating systems, and almost 100 percent of the non-Apple market, which makes it an effective monopoly.
- Microsoft is a natural monopoly. It has large fixed costs and almost zero marginal cost, so its long-run average cost curve (*LRAC*) slopes downward and economies of scale are achieved when the *LRAC* curve intersects the demand curve.
- Microsoft sells Windows for a number of different prices to different market segments and the marginal cost of a Windows license is the same for all market segments, so Microsoft is a price-discriminating monopoly.

- The figure illustrates the demand curve, *D*, and marginal cost curve, *MC*, for Windows licenses.
- Using the U.S. prices in the data table, the figure shows how Microsoft converts consumer surplus into producer surplus by price discriminating.
- Because Microsoft also price discriminates among its different national markets, it gains even more producer surplus than the figure illustrates.

Microsoft Grabs Consumer Surplus

Windows 8 will have many more foreign language versions than Windows 7 and greater scope for price discrimination.

Monopoly Regulation

Natural monopoly presents a dilemma. With economies of scale, it produces at the lowest possible cost. But with market power, it has an incentive to raise the price above the competitive price and produce too little—to operate in the self-interest of the monopolist and not in the social interest.

Regulation—rules administered by a government agency to influence prices, quantities, entry, and other aspects of economic activity in a firm or industry—is a possible solution to this dilemma.

To implement regulation, the government establishes agencies to oversee and enforce the rules. For example, the Surface Transportation Board regulates prices on interstate railroads, some trucking and bus lines, and water and oil pipelines. By the 1970s, almost a quarter of the nation's output was produced by regulated industries (far more than just natural monopolies) and a process of deregulation began.

Deregulation is the process of removing regulation of prices, quantities, entry, and other aspects of economic activity in a firm or industry. During the past 30 years, deregulation has occurred in domestic air transportation, telephone service, interstate trucking, and banking and financial services. Cable TV was deregulated in 1984, re-regulated in 1992, and deregulated again in 1996.

Regulation is a possible solution to the dilemma presented by natural monopoly but not a guaranteed solution. There are two theories about how regulation actually works: the *social interest theory* and the *capture theory*.

The **social interest theory** is that the political and regulatory process relentlessly seeks out inefficiency and introduces regulation that eliminates deadweight loss and allocates resources efficiently.

The **capture theory** is that regulation serves the self-interest of the producer, who captures the regulator and maximizes economic profit. Regulation that benefits the producer but creates a deadweight loss gets adopted because the producer's gain is large and visible while each individual consumer's loss is small and invisible. No individual consumer has an incentive to oppose the regulation but the producer has a big incentive to lobby for it.

We're going to examine efficient regulation that serves the social interest and see why it is not a simple matter to design and implement such regulation.

Efficient Regulation of a Natural Monopoly

A cable TV company is a *natural monopoly*—it can supply the entire market at a lower price than two or more competing firms can. Cox Communications, based in Atlanta, provides cable TV to households in 20 states. The firm has invested heavily in satellite receiving dishes, cables, and control equipment and so has large fixed costs. These fixed costs are part of the firm's average total cost. Its average total cost decreases as the number of households served increases because the fixed cost is spread over a larger number of households.

Unregulated, Cox produces the quantity that maximizes profit. Like all single-price monopolies, the profit-maximizing quantity is less than the efficient quantity, and underproduction results in a deadweight loss.

How can Cox be regulated to produce the efficient quantity of cable TV service? The answer is by being regulated to set its price equal to marginal cost, known as the **marginal cost pricing rule**. The quantity demanded at a price equal to marginal cost is the efficient quantity—the quantity at which marginal benefit equals marginal cost.

Figure 11.11 illustrates the marginal cost pricing rule. The demand curve for cable TV is *D*. Cox's marginal cost curve is *MC*. That marginal cost curve is (assumed to be) horizontal at $10 per household per month—that is, the cost of providing each additional household with a month of cable programming is $10. The efficient outcome occurs if the price is regulated at $10 per household per month with 10 million households served.

But there is a problem: At the efficient output, average total cost exceeds marginal cost, so a firm that uses marginal cost pricing incurs an economic loss. A cable TV company that is required to use a marginal cost pricing rule will not stay in business for long. How can the firm cover its costs and, at the same time, obey a marginal cost pricing rule?

There are two possible ways of enabling the firm to cover its costs: price discrimination and a two-part price (called a *two-part tariff*).

For example, Verizon offers plans at a fixed monthly price that give access to the cell-phone network and unlimited free calls. The price of a call (zero) equals Verizon's marginal cost of a call. Similarly, a cable TV operator can charge a one-time connection fee that covers its fixed cost and then charge a monthly fee equal to marginal cost.

FIGURE 11.11   Regulating a Natural Monopoly

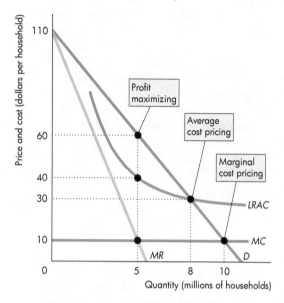

A natural monopoly cable TV supplier faces the demand curve *D*. The firm's marginal cost is constant at $10 per household per month, as shown by the curve labeled *MC*. The long-run average cost curve is *LRAC*.

Unregulated, as a profit-maximizer, the firm serves 5 million households at a price of $60 a month. An efficient marginal cost pricing rule sets the price at $10 a month. The monopoly serves 10 million households and incurs an economic loss. A second-best average cost pricing rule sets the price at $30 a month. The monopoly serves 8 million households and earns zero economic profit.

———————————— MyEconLab animation ————————————

Second-Best Regulation of a Natural Monopoly

A natural monopoly cannot always be regulated to achieve an efficient outcome. Two possible ways of enabling a regulated monopoly to avoid an economic loss are

- Average cost pricing
- Government subsidy

Average Cost Pricing The **average cost pricing rule** sets price equal to average total cost. With this rule the firm produces the quantity at which the average

total cost curve cuts the demand curve. This rule results in the firm making zero economic profit—breaking even. But because for a natural monopoly average total cost exceeds marginal cost, the quantity produced is less than the efficient quantity and a deadweight loss arises.

Figure 11.11 illustrates the average cost pricing rule. The price is $30 a month and 8 million households get cable TV.

Government Subsidy A government subsidy is a direct payment to the firm equal to its economic loss. To pay a subsidy, the government must raise the revenue by taxing some other activity. You saw in Chapter 6 that taxes themselves generate deadweight loss.

And the Second-Best Is … Which is the better option, average cost pricing or marginal cost pricing with a government subsidy? The answer depends on the relative magnitudes of the two deadweight losses. Average cost pricing generates a deadweight loss in the market served by the natural monopoly. A subsidy generates deadweight losses in the markets for the items that are taxed to pay for the subsidy. The smaller deadweight loss is the second-best solution to regulating a natural monopoly. Making this calculation in practice is too difficult and average cost pricing is generally preferred to a subsidy.

Implementing average cost pricing presents the regulator with a challenge because it is not possible to be sure what a firm's costs are. So regulators use one of two practical rules:

- Rate of return regulation
- Price cap regulation

Rate of Return Regulation Under **rate of return regulation**, a firm must justify its price by showing that its return on capital doesn't exceed a specified target rate. This type of regulation can end up serving the self-interest of the firm rather than the social interest. The firm's managers have an incentive to inflate costs by spending on items such as private jets, free baseball tickets (disguised as public relations expenses), and lavish entertainment. Managers also have an incentive to use more capital than the efficient amount. The rate of return on capital is regulated but not the total return on capital, and the greater the amount of capital, the greater is the total return.

Price Cap Regulation For the reason that we've just examined, rate of return regulation is increasingly being replaced by price cap regulation. A **price cap regulation** is a price ceiling—a rule that specifies the highest price the firm is permitted to set. This type of regulation gives a firm an incentive to operate efficiently and keep costs under control. Price cap regulation has become common for the electricity and telecommunications industries and is replacing rate of return regulation.

To see how a price cap works, let's suppose that the cable TV operator is subject to this type of regulation. Figure 11.12 shows that without regulation, the firm maximizes profit by serving 5 million households and charging a price of $60 a month. If a price cap is set at $30 a month, the firm is permitted to sell any quantity it chooses at that price or at a lower price. At 5 million households, the firm now incurs an economic loss. It can decrease the loss by increasing output to 8 million households. To increase output above 8 million households, the firm would have to lower the price and again it would incur a loss. So the profit-maximizing quantity is 8 million households—the same as with average cost pricing.

Notice that a price cap lowers the price and increases output. This outcome is in sharp contrast to the effect of a price ceiling in a competitive market that you studied in Chapter 6 (pp. 128–130). The reason is that in a monopoly, the unregulated equilibrium output is less than the competitive equilibrium output, and the price cap regulation replicates the conditions of a competitive market.

In Fig. 11.12, the price cap delivers average cost pricing. In practice, the regulator might set the cap too high. For this reason, price cap regulation is often combined with *earnings sharing regulation*—a regulation that requires firms to make refunds to customers when profits rise above a target level.

FIGURE 11.12   Price Cap Regulation

A natural monopoly cable TV supplier faces the demand curve *D*. The firm's marginal cost is constant at $10 per household per month, as shown by the curve labeled *MC*. The long-run average cost curve is *LRAC*.

Unregulated, the firm serves 5 million households at a price of $60 a month. A price cap sets the maximum price at $30 a month. The firm has an incentive to minimize cost and serve the quantity of households that demand service at the price cap. The price cap regulation lowers the price and increases the quantity.

—— MyEconLab animation ——

1   What is the pricing rule that achieves an efficient outcome for a regulated monopoly? What is the problem with this rule?

2   What is the average cost pricing rule? Why is it not an efficient way of regulating monopoly?

3   What is a price cap? Why might it be a more effective way of regulating monopoly than rate of return regulation?

4   Compare the consumer surplus, producer surplus, and deadweight loss that arise from average cost pricing with those that arise from profit-maximization pricing and marginal cost pricing.

You can work these questions in Study Plan 11.5 and get instant feedback.   MyEconLab

---

◆ You've now completed your study of monopoly. *Reading Between the Lines* on pp. 272–273 looks at Google's dominant position in the market for Internet search advertising.

Is Google Misusing Monopoly Power?

Data Show Google Abuses Search Role, Group Contends

http://www.sfgate.com
June 3, 2010

Consumer Watchdog continues to push its case that Google Inc.'s behavior necessitates antitrust scrutiny, releasing a report Wednesday that alleges that the company is abusing its dominance in online search to direct users to its own services.

The study, which will be sent to U.S. and European antitrust regulators, cites online traffic data that the Santa Monica group claims shows the Mountain View Internet giant seized large portions of market share in areas like online maps, video and comparison shopping after its search engine began highlighting links to its products in results.

Google called the report's methodology and premise flawed and said its practices are designed to benefit users.

"Our goal is to give users the info they're seeking as quickly as possible," a spokesman said in a statement. "Sometimes that means showing a map, a streaming audio link, or an answer to a question at the top of the page if we think that's what users want. We strive to deliver what we think is the most relevant result from a variety of content types, and if we're not giving users the information they want then other sources of information are always one click away."

Google doubled its market share in online video to nearly 80 percent since 2007, the year in which the company began returning high or prominent links to videos from its YouTube subsidiary in search results, according to the report by Consumer Watchdog's Inside Google project.

. . .

ESSENCE OF THE STORY

- Consumer Watchdog says that Google should be scrutinized by U.S. and European antitrust regulators because it is abusing its dominant position in online search by directing users to its own services.

- The claim is that Google has grown a large market share in online maps, video, and comparison shopping because its search engine highlights links to these products in search results.

- Google says its goal is to give users the information they are seeking, in the format required, as quickly as possible.

- Google's market share in online video has doubled to nearly 80 percent since 2007, when it began returning links to YouTube videos.

ECONOMIC ANALYSIS

- Google began selling advertisements associated with search keywords in 2000.

- Google sells keywords based on a combination of willingness-to-pay and the number of clicks an advertisement receives, with bids starting at 5 cents per click.

- Google has steadily improved its search engine and refined and simplified its interface with both searchers and advertisers to make searches more powerful and advertising more effective.

- Figure 1 shows Google's extraordinary success in terms of its revenue, cost, and profit.

- Google could have provided a basic search engine with none of the features of today's Google.

- If Google had followed this strategy, people seeking information would have used other search engines and advertisers would have been willing to pay low prices for Google ads.

- Google would have faced the market described in Fig. 2 and earned a small economic profit.

- Instead, Google improved its search and the effectiveness of advertising. The demand for Google ads increased.

- By selling keywords to the highest bidder, Google is able to achieve perfect price discrimination.

- Figure 3 shows the consequences of Google's successful strategy. With perfect price discrimination, Google's producer surplus is maximized. Google produces the efficient quantity of search and advertising by accepting ads as long as price exceeds marginal cost.

- Google does not appear to be acting against the social interest: There is no antitrust case to answer.

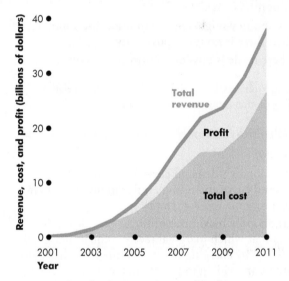

Figure 1 Google's Revenue, Cost, and Profit

Figure 2 Basic Search Engine

Figure 3 Google with AdWords and Other Features

273

SUMMARY

Key Points

Monopoly and How It Arises (pp. 254–255)

- A monopoly is a market with a single supplier of a good or service that has no close substitutes and in which barriers to entry prevent competition.
- Barriers to entry may be legal (public franchise, license, patent, or copyright), ownership (one firm controls a resource), or natural (created by economies of scale).
- A monopoly might be able to price discriminate when there is no resale possibility.
- Where resale is possible, a firm charges one price.

Working Problems 1 to 4 will give you a better understanding of monopoly and how it arises.

A Single-Price Monopoly's Output and Price Decision (pp. 256–259)

- A monopoly's demand curve is the market demand curve and a single-price monopoly's marginal revenue is less than price.
- A monopoly maximizes profit by producing the output at which marginal revenue equals marginal cost and by charging the maximum price that consumers are willing to pay for that output.

Working Problems 5 to 9 will give you a better understanding of a single-price monopoly's output and price decision.

Single-Price Monopoly and Competition Compared (pp. 260–263)

- A single-price monopoly charges a higher price and produces a smaller quantity than a perfectly competitive market.
- A single-price monopoly restricts output and creates a deadweight loss.

- The total loss that arises from monopoly equals the deadweight loss plus the cost of the resources devoted to rent seeking.

Working Problems 10 to 12 will give you a better understanding of the comparison of single-price monopoly and perfect competition.

Price Discrimination (pp. 263–268)

- Price discrimination converts consumer surplus into economic profit.
- Perfect price discrimination extracts the entire consumer surplus; each unit is sold for the maximum price that each consumer is willing to pay; the quantity produced is the efficient quantity.
- Rent seeking with perfect price discrimination might eliminate the entire consumer surplus and producer surplus.

Working Problems 13 to 16 will give you a better understanding of price discrimination.

Monopoly Regulation (pp. 269–271)

- Monopoly regulation might serve the social interest or the interest of the monopoly (the monopoly captures the regulator).
- Price equal to marginal cost achieves efficiency but results in economic loss.
- Price equal to average cost enables the firm to cover its cost but is inefficient.
- Rate of return regulation creates incentives for inefficient production and inflated cost.
- Price cap regulation with earnings sharing regulation can achieve a more efficient outcome than rate of return regulation.

Working Problems 17 to 19 will give you a better understanding of monopoly regulation.

Key Terms

Average cost pricing rule, 270
Barrier to entry, 254
Capture theory, 269
Deregulation, 269
Economic rent, 262
Legal monopoly, 254

Marginal cost pricing rule, 269
Monopoly, 254
Natural monopoly, 254
Perfect price discrimination, 266
Price cap regulation, 271
Price discrimination, 255

Rate of return regulation, 270
Regulation, 269
Rent seeking, 262
Single-price monopoly, 255
Social interest theory, 269

STUDY PLAN PROBLEMS AND APPLICATIONS

MyEconLab   You can work problems 1 to 19 in MyEconLab Chapter 11 Study Plan and get instant feedback.

Monopoly and How It Arises (Study Plan 11.1)

Use the following information to work Problems 1 to 3.
The United States Postal Service has a monopoly on non-urgent First Class Mail and the exclusive right to put mail in private mailboxes. Pfizer Inc. makes LIPITOR, a prescription drug that lowers cholesterol. Cox Communications is the sole provider of cable television service in some parts of San Diego.

1. a. What are the substitutes, if any, for the goods and services described above?
    b. What are the barriers to entry, if any, that protect these three firms from competition?

2. Which of these three firms, if any, is a natural monopoly? Explain your answer and draw a graph to illustrate it.

3. a. Which of these three firms, if any, is a legal monopoly? Explain your answer.
    b. Which of these three firms are most likely to be able to profit from price discrimination and which are most likely to sell their good or service for a single price?

4. **Barbie's Revenge: Brawl over Doll Is Heading to Trial**

    Four years ago, Mattel Inc. exhorted its executives to help save Barbie from a new doll clique called the Bratz. With its market share dropping at a "chilling rate," Barbie needed to be more "aggressive, revolutionary, and ruthless." Mattel has gone to court and is trying to seize ownership of the Bratz line, which Mattel accuses of stealing the idea for the pouty-lipped dolls with the big heads.

    Source: *The Wall Street Journal*, May 23, 2008

    a. Before Bratz entered the market, what type of monopoly did Mattel Inc. possess in the market for "the pouty-lipped dolls with the big heads"?
    b. What is the barrier to entry that Mattel might argue should protect it from competition in the market for Barbie dolls?
    c. Explain how the entry of Bratz dolls might be expected to change the demand for Barbie dolls.

A Single-Price Monopoly's Output and Price Decision (Study Plan 11.2)

Use the following table to work Problems 5 to 9.
Minnie's Mineral Springs, a single-price monopoly, faces the market demand schedule:

Price (dollars per bottle)	Quantity demanded (bottles per hour)
10	0
8	1
6	2
4	3
2	4
0	5

5. a. Calculate Minnie's total revenue schedule.
    b. Calculate its marginal revenue schedule.

6. a. Draw a graph of the market demand curve and Minnie's marginal revenue curve.
    b. Why is Minnie's marginal revenue less than the price?

7. a. At what price is Minnie's total revenue maximized?
    b. Over what range of prices is the demand for water from Minnie's Mineral Springs elastic?

8. Why will Minnie not produce a quantity at which the market demand for water is inelastic?

9. Minnie's Mineral Springs faces the market demand schedule in Problem 5 and has the following total cost schedule:

Quantity produced (bottles per hour)	Total cost (dollars)
0	1
1	3
2	7
3	13
4	21
5	31

a. Calculate Minnie's profit-maximizing output and price.
b. Calculate the economic profit.

Single-Price Monopoly and Competition Compared
(Study Plan 11.3)

Use the following news clip to work Problems 10 to 12.

Zoloft Faces Patent Expiration

Pfizer's antidepressant Zoloft, with $3.3 billion in 2005 sales, loses patent protection on June 30. When a brand name drug loses its patent, both the price of the drug and the dollar value of its sales each tend to drop 80 percent over the next year, as competition opens to a host of generic drugmakers. The real winners are the patients and the insurers, who pay much lower prices. The Food and Drug Administration insists that generics work identically to brand-names.

Source: *CNN*, June 15, 2006

10. a. Assume that Pfizer has a monopoly in the antidepressant market and that Pfizer cannot price discriminate. Use a graph to illustrate the market price and quantity of Zoloft sold.

b. On your graph, identify consumer surplus, producer surplus, and deadweight loss.

11. How might you justify protecting Pfizer from competition with a legal barrier to entry?

12. a. Explain how the market for an antidepressant drug changes when a patent expires.

b. Draw a graph to illustrate how the expiration of the Zoloft patent will change the price and quantity in the market for antidepressants.

c. Explain how consumer surplus, producer surplus, and deadweight loss change with the expiration of the Zoloft patent.

Price Discrimination (Study Plan 11.4)

Use the following news clip to work Problems 13 and 14.

The Saturday-Night Stay Requirement Is on Its Final Approach

The Saturday-night stay—the requirement that airlines instituted to ensure that business travelers pay an outrageous airfare if he or she wants to go home for the weekend—has gone the way of the dodo bird. Experts agree that low-fare carriers, such as Southwest, are the primary reason major airlines are adopting more consumer-friendly fare structures, which include the elimination of the Saturday-night stay, the introduction of one-way and walk-up fares, and the general restructuring of fares.

Source: *Los Angeles Times*, August 15, 2004

13. Explain why the opportunity for price discrimination exists for air travel. How does an airline profit from price discrimination?

14. Describe the change in price discrimination in the market for air travel when discount airlines entered the market and explain the effect of discount airlines on the price and the quantity of air travel.

Use the following information to work Problems 15 and 16.

La Bella Pizza can produce a pizza for a marginal cost of $2. Its standard price is $15 a pizza. It offers a second pizza for $5. It also distributes coupons that give a $5 rebate on a standard-priced pizza.

15. How can La Bella Pizza make a larger economic profit with this range of prices than it could if it sold every pizza for $15? Use a graph to illustrate your answer.

16. How might La Bella Pizza make even more economic profit? Would La Bella Pizza then be more efficient than it would be if it charged $15 for each pizza?

Monopoly Regulation (Study Plan 11.5)

Use the following information to work Problems 17 to 19.

The figure shows a situation similar to that of Calypso U.S. Pipeline, a firm that operates a natural gas distribution system in the United States. Calypso is a natural monopoly that cannot price discriminate.

What quantity will Calypso produce, what price will it charge, what is the total surplus, and what is the deadweight loss if Calypso is

17. An unregulated profit-maximizing firm?

18. Regulated to make zero economic profit?

19. Regulated to be efficient?

ADDITIONAL PROBLEMS AND APPLICATIONS

MyEconLab   You can work these problems in MyEconLab if assigned by your instructor.

Monopoly and How It Arises

Use the following list, which gives some information about seven firms, to answer Problems 20 and 21.

- Coca-Cola cuts its price below that of Pepsi-Cola in an attempt to increase its market share.
- A single firm, protected by a barrier to entry, produces a personal service that has no close substitutes.
- A barrier to entry exists, but the good has some close substitutes.
- A firm offers discounts to students and seniors.
- A firm can sell any quantity it chooses at the going price.
- The government issues Nike an exclusive license to produce golf balls.
- A firm experiences economies of scale even when it produces the quantity that meets the entire market demand.

20. In which of the seven cases might monopoly arise?
21. Which of the seven cases are natural monopolies and which are legal monopolies? Which can price discriminate, which cannot, and why?

A Single-Price Monopoly's Output and Price Decision

Use the following information to work Problems 22 to 26.

Hot Air Balloon Rides is a single-price monopoly. Columns 1 and 2 of the table set out the market demand schedule and columns 2 and 3 set out the total cost schedule:

Price (dollars per ride)	Quantity demanded (rides per month)	Total cost (dollars per month)
220	0	80
200	1	160
180	2	260
160	3	380
140	4	520
120	5	680

22. Construct Hot Air's total revenue and marginal revenue schedules.
23. Draw a graph of the market demand curve and Hot Air's marginal revenue curve.
24. Find Hot Air's profit-maximizing output and price and calculate the firm's economic profit.

25. If the government imposes a tax on Hot Air's profit, how do its output and price change?
26. If instead of taxing Hot Air's profit, the government imposes a sales tax on balloon rides of $30 a ride, what are the new profit-maximizing quantity, price, and economic profit?
27. The figure illustrates the situation facing the publisher of the only newspaper containing local news in an isolated community.

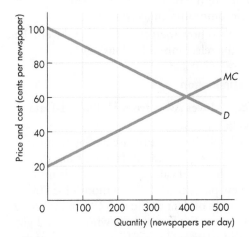

a. On the graph, mark the profit-maximizing quantity and price and the publisher's total revenue per day.
b. At the price charged, is the demand for this newspaper elastic or inelastic? Why?

Single-Price Monopoly and Competition Compared

28. Show on the graph in Problem 27 the consumer surplus from newspapers and the deadweight loss created by the monopoly. Explain why this market might encourage rent seeking.
29. If the newspaper market in Problem 27 were perfectly competitive, what would be the quantity, price, consumer surplus, and producer surplus? Mark each on the graph.
30. **Telecoms Look to Grow by Acquisition**
Multibillion-dollar telecommunications mergers show how global cellular powerhouses are scouting for growth in emerging economies while consolidating in their own, crowded backyards. France Télécom offered to buy TeliaSonera, a Swedish-Finnish telecommunications operator, but

within hours, TeliaSonera rejected the offer as too low. Analysts said higher bids—either from France Télécom or others—could persuade TeliaSonera to accept a deal. In the United States, Verizon Wireless agreed to buy Alltel for $28.1 billion—a deal that would make the company the biggest mobile phone operator in the United States. A combination of France Télécom and TeliaSonera would create the world's fourth-largest mobile operator, smaller only than China Mobile, Vodafone, and Telefónica of Spain.

Source: *International Herald Tribune*, June 5, 2008

a. Explain the rent-seeking behavior of global telecommunications companies.

b. Explain how mergers may affect the efficiency of the telecommunications market.

Price Discrimination

31. **AT&T Moves Away from Unlimited-Data Pricing**

AT&T said it will eliminate its $30 unlimited data plan as the crush of data use from the iPhone has hurt call quality. AT&T is introducing new plans costing $15 a month for 200 megabytes of data traffic or $25 a month for 2 gigabytes. AT&T says those who exceed 2 gigabytes of usage will pay $10 a month for each additional gigabyte. AT&T hopes that these plans will attract more customers.

Source: *The Wall Street Journal*, June 2, 2010

a. Explain why AT&T's new plans might be price discrimination.

b. Draw a graph to illustrate the original plan and the new plans.

Monopoly Regulation

32. **iSurrender**

In 2008, getting your hands the new iPhone meant signing a two-year AT&T contract. Some markets, because of the costs of being a player, tend toward either a single firm or a small number of firms. Everyone hoped the wireless market would be different. A telephone monopoly has been the norm for most of American telecommunication history, except for what may turn out to have been a brief experimental period from 1984 through 2012 or so. It may be that telephone monopolies in America are a national tradition.

Source: *Slate*, June 10, 2008

a. How did AT&T, the exclusive provider of wireless service for the iPhone in 2008, influence the wireless telecommunication market?

b. Explain why the wireless market might "tend toward either a single firm or a small number of firms." Why might this justify allowing a regulated monopoly to exist in this market?

Economics in the News

33. After you have studied *Reading Between the Lines* on pp. 272–273, answer the following questions.

a. Why does Consumer Watchdog say that Google needs to be investigated? Do you agree? Explain why or why not.

b. Explain why it would be inefficient to regulate Google to make it charge the same price per keyword click to all advertisers.

c. Explain why selling keywords to the highest bidder can lead to an efficient allocation of advertising resources.

34. **F.C.C. Planning Rules to Open Cable Market**

The Federal Communications Commission (F.C.C.) is setting new regulations to open the cable television market to independent programmers and rival video services. The new rules will make it easier for small independent programmers to lease access to cable channels and the size of the nation's largest cable companies will be capped at 30 percent of the market.

Source: *The New York Times*, November 10, 2007

a. What barriers to entry exist in the cable television market?

b. Are high cable prices evidence of monopoly power?

c. Draw a graph to illustrate the effects of the F.C.C.'s new regulations on the price, quantity, total surplus, and deadweight loss.

35. **Antitrust Inquiry Launched into Intel**

Intel, the world's largest chipmaker, holds 80 percent of the microprocessor market. Advanced Micro Devices complains that Intel stifles competition, but Intel says that the 42.4 percent fall in prices between 2000 and 2007 shows that this industry is fiercely competitive.

Source: *The Washington Post*, June 7, 2008

a. Is Intel a monopoly in the chip market?

b. Evaluate the argument made by Intel that the fall in prices "shows that this industry is fiercely competitive."

CHAPTER 2

Externalities, Environmental Policy, and Public Goods

Chapter Outline and **Learning Objectives**

Can Economic Policy Help Protect the Environment?

Most scientists believe that burning fossil fuels generates carbon dioxide and other greenhouse gases that can increase global warming and cause potentially costly changes in climate. Should the government act to reduce greenhouse gases? If so, what policy would be best? In 2013, Duke University conducted a public opinion poll that found that about two-thirds of those surveyed believed that the government should regulate greenhouse gases. A large majority believed that the government should attempt to directly control the emission of greenhouse gases by, for instance, requiring that new cars have better gas mileage.

According to a poll conducted by the business school at the University of Chicago, most economists agreed that government policy should attempt to reduce greenhouse gases but they disagreed with the public about which government policies would be best. When the federal government orders firms to use particular methods to reduce pollution—for example, by requiring that automobile companies produce cars with better gas mileage—the government is using *command-and-control policies*. Many economists argue that a more efficient way to reduce pollution is through *market-based policies* that rely on economic incentives rather than on administrative rules.

A carbon tax is an example of a market-based policy. If the government taxes oil, coal, and other carbon-based fuels that generate carbon dioxide when burned, households and firms would have an economic incentive to reduce their use of those fuels. Government policies to reduce pollution, including the carbon tax, have been controversial, however. Some businesses oppose the carbon tax because they believe it will raise their costs of production. For example, the National Corn Growers Association stated that if a carbon tax were enacted, "every corn grower in the country will experience increased costs of production." Similarly, a spokesman for the American Fuel & Petrochemical Manufacturers argued against a carbon tax because "energy consumption can't simply be quit nor can it be reduced without considerable costs to consumers and especially to the nation's most vulnerable populations." Other businesses view the carbon tax favorably, particularly in comparison with command-and-control policies that they see as more costly and less effective. The Pacific Gas and Electric Company, a utility based in California, has praised "the flexibility and power of market incentives to promote a cleaner environment and more sustainable economy."

As we will see in this chapter, economic analysis has an important role to play in the debate over environmental policies.

Sources: "Americans Want Climate Rules but Not Taxes," UPI, February 7, 2013; Jonathan Marshall, "California's Cap-and-Trade Program: In Good Company," *Currents: News and Perspectives from Pacific Gas and Electric Company*, November 20, 2012; "NCDA Says Cap and Trade Will Hurt Corn Growers," www.agwired.com, January 20, 2010; Paoloa Sapienza and Luigi Zingales, "Economic Experts vs. Average Americans," University of Chicago, Booth School of Business, Working Paper 13-11; and Charles Drevna, "Energy Experts Blog," www.energy.nationaljournal.com, November 19, 2012.

Economics in Your Life

What's the "Best" Level of Pollution?

Policymakers debate alternative approaches for achieving the goal of reducing carbon dioxide emissions. But how do we know the "best" level of carbon emissions? If carbon dioxide emissions hurt the environment, should the government take action to eliminate them completely? As you read this chapter, try to answer these questions. You can check your answers against those we provide on **page 305** at the end of this chapter.

P
ollution is a part of economic life. Consumers create air pollution by burning gasoline to power their cars and natural gas to heat their homes. Firms create air pollution when they produce electricity, pesticides, or plastics, among other products. Utilities produce sulfur dioxide when they burn coal to generate electricity. Sulfur dioxide contributes to acid rain, which can damage trees, crops, and buildings. The burning of fossil fuels generates carbon dioxide and other greenhouse gases that can increase global warming.

Pollution is just one example of an *externality*. An **externality** is a benefit or cost that affects someone who is not directly involved in the production or consumption of a good or service. In the case of air pollution, there is a *negative externality* because, for example, people with asthma may bear a cost even though they were not involved in the buying or selling of the electricity that caused the pollution. *Positive externalities* are also possible. For instance, medical research can provide a positive externality because people who are not directly involved in producing it or paying for it can benefit. A competitive market usually does a good job of producing the economically efficient amount of a good or service. This result may not hold, though, if there is an externality in the market. When there is a negative externality, the market may produce a quantity of the good that is greater than the efficient amount. When there is a positive externality, the market may produce a quantity that is less than the efficient amount. Government interventions in the economy—such as price floors on agricultural products or price ceilings on rents—can reduce economic efficiency. But, when there are externalities, government intervention may actually increase economic efficiency and enhance the well-being of society. The way in which government intervenes is important, however. Economists can help policymakers ensure that government programs are as efficient as possible.

In this chapter, we explore how best to deal with the problem of pollution and other externalities. We also look at *public goods*, which may not be produced at all unless the government produces them.

Externality A benefit or cost that affects someone who is not directly involved in the production or consumption of a good or service.

12.1 LEARNING OBJECTIVE

Identify examples of positive and negative externalities and use graphs to show how externalities affect economic efficiency.

Externalities and Economic Efficiency

When you consume a Big Mac, only you benefit, but when you consume a college education, other people also benefit. College-educated people are less likely to commit crimes, and by being better-informed voters, they are more likely to contribute to better government policies. So, although you capture most of the benefits of your college education, you do not capture all of them.

When you buy a Big Mac, the price you pay covers all of McDonald's costs of producing the Big Mac. When you buy electricity from a utility that burns coal and generates acid rain, the price you pay does not cover the cost of the damage caused by the acid rain.

So, there is a *positive externality* in the production of college educations because people who do not pay for them will nonetheless benefit from them. There is a *negative externality* in the generation of electricity because, for example, people with homes on a lake from which fish and wildlife have disappeared because of acid rain have incurred a cost, even though they might not have bought their electricity from the polluting utility.

The Effect of Externalities

Externalities interfere with the *economic efficiency* of a market equilibrium. A competitive market achieves economic efficiency by maximizing the sum of consumer surplus and producer surplus. *But that result holds only if there are no externalities in production or consumption.* An externality causes a difference between the *private cost* of production and the *social cost*, or the *private benefit* from consumption and the *social benefit*. The **private cost** is the cost borne by the producer of a good or service. The

Private cost The cost borne by the producer of a good or service.

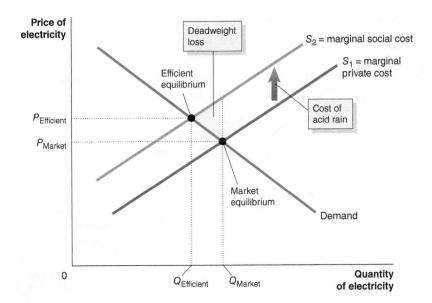

MyEconLab Animation

Figure 12.1

The Effect of Pollution on Economic Efficiency

Because utilities do not bear the cost of acid rain, they produce electricity beyond the economically efficient level. Supply curve S_1 represents just the marginal private cost that the utility has to pay. Supply curve S_2 represents the marginal social cost, which includes the costs to those affected by acid rain. If the supply curve were S_2 rather than S_1, market equilibrium would occur at price $P_{Efficient}$ and quantity $Q_{Efficient}$, the economically efficient level of output. But, when the supply curve is S_1, the market equilibrium occurs at price P_{Market} and quantity Q_{Market} where there is a deadweight loss equal to the area of the yellow triangle. Because of the deadweight loss, this equilibrium is not efficient.

social cost is the total cost of producing a good or service, and it is equal to the private cost plus any external cost, such as the cost of pollution. Unless there is an externality, the private cost and the social cost are equal. The **private benefit** is the benefit received by the consumer of a good or service. The **social benefit** is the total benefit from consuming a good or service, and it is equal to the private benefit plus any external benefit, such as the benefit to others resulting from your college education. Unless there is an externality, the private benefit and the social benefit are equal.

Social cost The total cost of producing a good or service, including both the private cost and any external cost.

Private benefit The benefit received by the consumer of a good or service.

Social benefit The total benefit from consuming a good or service, including both the private benefit and any external benefit.

How a Negative Externality in Production Reduces Economic Efficiency

Consider how a negative externality in production reduces economic efficiency. Typically, economists assume that the producer of a good or service must bear all the costs of production. We now know that this observation is not always true. In the production of electricity, private costs are borne by the utility, but some external costs of pollution are borne by people who are not customers of the utility. The social cost of producing electricity is the sum of the private cost plus the external cost. Figure 12.1 shows the effect on the market for electricity of a negative externality in production.

S_1 is the market supply curve and represents only the private costs that utilities have to bear in generating electricity. Firms will supply an additional unit of a good or service only if they receive a price equal to the additional cost of producing that unit, so a supply curve represents the *marginal cost* of producing a good or service. If utilities also had to bear the cost of pollution, the supply curve would be S_2, which represents the true marginal social cost of generating electricity. The equilibrium with price $P_{Efficient}$ and quantity $Q_{Efficient}$ is efficient. The equilibrium with price P_{Market} and quantity Q_{Market} is not efficient.

To see why, remember that an equilibrium is economically efficient if economic surplus—which is the sum of consumer surplus plus producer surplus—is at a maximum. When economic surplus is at a maximum, the net benefit to society from the production of the good or service is at a maximum. With an equilibrium quantity of $Q_{Efficient}$, economic surplus is at a maximum, and the equilibrium is efficient. But, with an equilibrium quantity of Q_{Market}, economic surplus is reduced by the deadweight loss, shown in Figure 12.1 by the yellow triangle, and the equilibrium is not efficient. The deadweight loss occurs because the supply curve is above the demand curve for the production of the units of electricity between $Q_{Efficient}$ and Q_{Market}. That is, the additional cost—including the external cost—of producing these units is greater than the marginal benefit to consumers, as represented by the demand curve. In other words, because of the cost of the pollution, economic efficiency would be improved if less electricity were produced.

Figure 12.2

The Effect of a Positive Externality on Economic Efficiency

People who do not consume college educations can still benefit from them. As a result, the marginal social benefit from a college education is greater than the marginal private benefit to college students. Because only the marginal private benefit is represented in the market demand curve D_1, the quantity of college educations produced, Q_{Market}, is too low. If the market demand curve were D_2 instead of D_1, the level of college educations produced would be $Q_{Efficient}$, which is the efficient level. At the market equilibrium of Q_{Market}, there is a deadweight loss equal to the area of the yellow triangle.

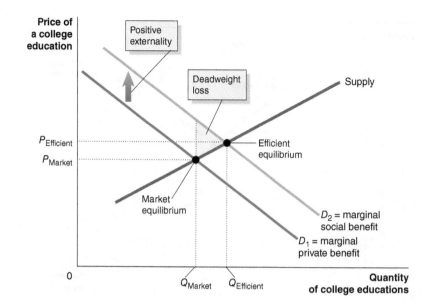

We can conclude the following: *When there is a negative externality in producing a good or service, too much of the good or service will be produced at market equilibrium.*

How a Positive Externality in Consumption Reduces Economic Efficiency

We have seen that a negative externality interferes with achieving economic efficiency. The same holds true for a positive externality. In earlier chapters, we assumed that the demand curve represents all the benefits that come from consuming a good. But a college education generates benefits that are not captured by the student receiving the education and so are not included in the market demand curve for college educations. Figure 12.2 shows the effect of a positive externality in consumption on the market for college educations.

If students receiving a college education could capture all its benefits, the demand curve would be D_2, which represents the marginal social benefits. The actual demand curve is D_1, however, which represents only the marginal private benefits received by students. The efficient equilibrium would come at price $P_{Efficient}$ and quantity $Q_{Efficient}$. At this equilibrium, economic surplus is maximized. The market equilibrium, at price P_{Market} and quantity Q_{Market}, will not be efficient because the demand curve is above the supply curve for production of the units between Q_{Market} and $Q_{Efficient}$. That is, the marginal benefit—including the external benefit—for producing these units is greater than the marginal cost. As a result, there is a deadweight loss equal to the area of the yellow triangle. Because of the positive externality, economic efficiency would be improved if more college educations were produced.

We can conclude the following: *When there is a positive externality in consuming a good or service, too little of the good or service will be produced at market equilibrium.*

MyEconLab Concept Check

Externalities and Market Failure

We have seen that because of externalities, the efficient level of output may not occur in either the market for electricity or the market for college educations. These are examples of **market failure**: situations in which the market fails to produce the efficient level of output. Later, we will discuss possible solutions to problems of externalities. But, first, we need to consider why externalities occur.

MyEconLab Concept Check

Market failure A situation in which the market fails to produce the efficient level of output.

What Causes Externalities?

Governments need to guarantee *property rights* in order for a market system to function well. **Property rights** refer to the rights individuals or businesses have to the exclusive use of their property, including the right to buy or sell it. Property can be tangible or physical, such as a store or factory. Property can also be intangible, such as the right to an idea. Most of the time, the governments of the United States and other

Property rights The rights individuals or businesses have to the exclusive use of their property, including the right to buy or sell it.

high-income countries do a good job of enforcing property rights, but in certain situations, property rights do not exist or cannot be legally enforced.

Consider the following situation: Lee owns land that includes a lake. A paper company wants to lease some of Lee's land to build a paper mill. The paper mill will discharge pollutants into Lee's lake. Because Lee owns the lake, he can charge the paper company the cost of cleaning up the pollutants. The result is that the cost of the pollution is a private cost to the paper company and is included in the price of the paper it sells. There is no externality, the efficient level of paper is produced, and there is no market failure.

Now suppose that the paper company again builds its paper mill on privately owned land but discharges its pollutants into a lake that is owned by the state government rather than by an individual. In the absence of any government regulations, the company can discharge pollutants into the lake without having to pay a fee. The cost of the pollution will be external to the company because it doesn't have to pay the cost of cleaning it up. The paper mill will produce a quantity of paper that is greater than the economically efficient level, and a market failure will occur. Or, suppose that Lee owns the lake, but the pollution is caused by acid rain generated by an electric utility hundreds of miles away. The law does not allow Lee to charge the electric utility for the damage caused by the acid rain. Even though someone is damaging Lee's property, he cannot enforce his property rights in this situation. Once again, there is an externality, and the market failure will result in too much electricity being produced.

If you buy a house, the government will protect your right to exclusive use of that house. No one else can use the house without your permission. Because of your property rights in the house, your private benefit from the house and the social benefit are the same. When you buy a college education, however, other people are able to benefit from it. You have no property right that will enable you to prevent them from benefiting or to charge them for the benefits they receive. As a result, there is a positive externality, and the market failure will result in too few college educations being supplied.

We can conclude the following: *Externalities and market failures result from incomplete property rights or from the difficulty of enforcing property rights in certain situations.*

MyEconLab Concept Check

MyEconLab Study Plan

Private Solutions to Externalities: The Coase Theorem

12.2 LEARNING OBJECTIVE

Discuss the Coase theorem and explain how private bargaining can lead to economic efficiency in a market with an externality.

As noted at the beginning of this chapter, government intervention may actually increase economic efficiency and enhance the well-being of society when externalities are present. It is also possible, however, for people to find private solutions to the problem of externalities.

Can the market cure market failure? In an influential article written in 1960, Ronald Coase of the University of Chicago, winner of the 1991 Nobel Prize in Economics, argued that under some circumstances, private solutions to the problem of externalities will occur. To understand Coase's argument, it is important to recognize that completely eliminating an externality usually is not economically efficient. Consider pollution, for example. There is, in fact, an *economically efficient level of pollution reduction*. At first, this seems paradoxical. Pollution is bad, and you might think the efficient amount of a bad thing is zero. But it isn't zero.

The Economically Efficient Level of Pollution Reduction

The important idea that the optimal decision is to continue any activity up to the point where the marginal benefit equals the marginal cost. This idea applies to reducing pollution just as much as it does to other activities. Sulfur dioxide emissions contribute to smog and acid rain. As sulfur dioxide emissions—or any other type of pollution—decline, society benefits: Fewer trees die, fewer buildings are damaged, and fewer people suffer breathing problems. But, a key point is that the additional benefit—that is, the *marginal benefit*—received from eliminating another ton of sulfur dioxide declines as sulfur dioxide emissions are reduced. To see why, consider what happens if utilities generate electricity without attempting to reduce sulfur dioxide emissions. In this situation, many smoggy days will occur in the cities of the Midwest and Northeast. Even healthy people may experience breathing problems. As sulfur dioxide emissions are reduced, the number of smoggy days will fall, and healthy people will no longer experience breathing problems. Eventually, if sulfur dioxide emissions fall to low levels, people with asthma will no longer be affected. Further reductions in sulfur dioxide emissions will have little additional benefit. The same will be true of the other benefits from reducing sulfur dioxide emissions: As the reductions increase, the additional benefits from fewer buildings and trees being damaged and lakes polluted will decline.

Making the Connection
MyEconLab Video

The Clean Air Act: How a Government Policy Reduced Infant Mortality

The following bar graphs show that the United States has made tremendous progress in reducing air pollution since Congress passed the Clean Air Act in 1970: Total emissions of the six main air pollutants have fallen dramatically. Over the same period, real U.S. gross domestic product (GDP)—which measures the value, corrected for inflation, of all the final goods and services produced in the country—more than tripled, energy consumption increased by half, and the number of miles traveled by all vehicles doubled.

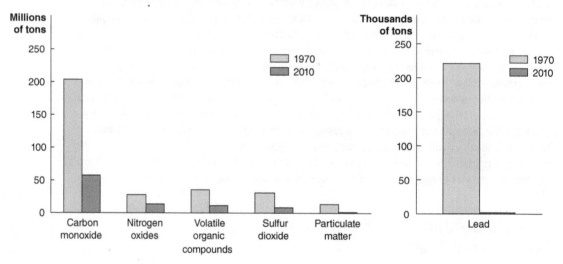

Source: U.S. Environmental Protection Agency, "Air Quality Trends," www.epa.gov/airtrends/aqtrends.html.

As we have seen, when levels of pollution are high, the marginal benefit of reducing pollution is also high. We would expect, then, that the benefit of reducing air pollution in 1970 was much higher than the benefit from a proportional reduction in air pollution would be today, when the level of pollution is much lower. Kenneth Y. Chay of Brown University and Michael Greenstone of MIT have shown that the benefits from the reductions in air pollution that occurred in the period immediately after passage of the Clean Air Act were indeed high. They argue that the exposure of pregnant women to high levels of air pollution can be damaging to their unborn children, possibly by reducing lung functioning. This damage would increase the chance that the infant would die in the first weeks after being born. In the two years following passage of the Clean Air Act, there was a sharp reduction in air pollution and also in infant mortality. The decline in infant mortality was mainly due to a reduction in deaths within one month of birth. Of course, other factors may also have been responsible for the decline in infant mortality, but Chay and Greenstone use statistical analysis to isolate the effect of the decline in air pollution. They conclude that: "1,300 fewer infants died in 1972 than would have in the absence of the Clean Air Act."

Source: Kenneth Y. Chay and Michael Greenstone, "Air Quality, Infant Mortality, and the Clean Air Act of 1970," National Bureau of Economic Research Working Paper 10053, October 2003.

MyEconLab Study Plan   **Your Turn:** Test your understanding by doing related problem 2.8 on pages 308–309 at the end of this chapter.

What about the marginal cost to electric utilities of reducing pollution? To reduce sulfur dioxide emissions, utilities have to switch from burning high-sulfur coal to burning more costly fuel, or they have to install pollution control devices, such as scrubbers. As the level of pollution falls, further reductions become increasingly costly. Reducing emissions or other types of pollution to very low levels can require complex and expensive new technologies. For example, Arthur Fraas, formerly of the federal Office of Management and Budget, and Vincent Munley, of Lehigh University, have shown that the marginal cost of removing 97 percent of pollutants from municipal wastewater is more than twice as high as the marginal cost of removing 95 percent.

The *net benefit* to society from reducing pollution is equal to the difference between the benefit of reducing pollution and the cost. To maximize the net benefit to society, sulfur dioxide emissions—or any other type of pollution—should be reduced up to the point where the marginal benefit from another ton of reduction is equal to the marginal cost. Figure 12.3 illustrates this point.

In Figure 12.3, we measure *reductions* in sulfur dioxide emissions on the horizontal axis. We measure the marginal benefit and marginal cost in dollars from eliminating another ton of sulfur dioxide emissions on the vertical axis. As reductions in pollution increase, the marginal benefit declines and the marginal cost increases. The economically efficient amount of pollution reduction occurs where the marginal benefit equals the marginal cost. The figure shows that, in this case, the economically efficient reduction of sulfur dioxide emissions is 8.5 million tons per year. In a program begun in 1990, this is the amount of reduction Congress decided should occur by 2010. At that level of emission reduction, the marginal benefit and the marginal cost of the last ton of sulfur dioxide emissions eliminated are both $200 per ton. Suppose instead that the emissions target was only 7.0 million tons. The figure shows that, at that level of reduction, the last ton of reduction has added $250 to the benefits received by society, but it has added only $175 to the costs of utilities. There has been a net benefit to society from this ton of pollution reduction of $75. In fact, the figure shows a net benefit to society from pollution reduction for every ton from 7.0 million to 8.5 million. Only when sulfur dioxide

MyEconLab Animation

Figure 12.3

The Marginal Benefit from Pollution Reduction Should Equal the Marginal Cost

If the reduction of sulfur dioxide emissions is at 7.0 million tons per year, the marginal benefit of $250 per ton is greater than the marginal cost of $175 per ton. Further reductions in emissions will increase the net benefit to society. If the reduction of sulfur dioxide emissions is at 10.0 million tons, the marginal cost of $225 per ton is greater than the marginal benefit of $150 per ton. An increase in sulfur dioxide emissions will increase the net benefit to society. Only when the reduction is at 8.5 million tons is the marginal benefit equal to the marginal cost. This level is the economically efficient level of pollution reduction.

emissions are reduced by 8.5 million tons per year will marginal benefit fall enough and marginal cost rise enough that the two are equal.

Now suppose Congress had set the target for sulfur dioxide emissions reduction at 10 million tons per year. Figure 12.3 shows that the marginal benefit at that level of reduction has fallen to only $150 per ton and the marginal cost has risen to $225 per ton. The last ton of reduction has actually *reduced* the net benefit to society by $75 per ton. In fact, every ton of reduction beyond 8.5 million reduces the net benefit to society.

To summarize: If the marginal benefit of reducing sulfur dioxide emissions is greater than the marginal cost, further reductions will make society better off. But if the marginal cost of reducing sulfur dioxide emissions is greater than the marginal benefit, further reductions will actually make society worse off.   MyEconLab Concept Check

The Basis for Private Solutions to Externalities

In arguing that private solutions to the problem of externalities were possible, Ronald Coase emphasized that when more than the optimal level of pollution is occurring, the benefits from reducing the pollution to the optimal level are greater than the costs. Figure 12.4 illustrates this point.

The marginal benefit curve shows the additional benefit from each reduction in a ton of sulfur dioxide emissions. The area under the marginal benefit curve between the two emission levels is the *total* benefit received from reducing emissions from one level to another. For instance, in Figure 12.4, the total benefit from increasing the reduction in sulfur dioxide emissions from 7.0 million tons to 8.5 million tons is the sum of the areas of *A* and *B*. The marginal cost curve shows the additional cost from each reduction in a ton of emissions. The *total* cost of reducing emissions from one level to another is the

Figure 12.4

The Benefits of Reducing Pollution to the Optimal Level Are Greater than the Costs

Increasing the reduction in sulfur dioxide emissions from 7.0 million tons to 8.5 million tons results in total benefits equal to the sum of the areas of *A* and *B* under the marginal benefit curve. The total cost of this decrease in pollution is equal to the area of *B* under the marginal cost curve. The total benefits are greater than the total costs by an amount equal to the area of *A*. Because the total benefits from reducing pollution are greater than the total costs, it is possible for those receiving the benefits to arrive at a private agreement with polluters to pay them to reduce pollution.

Total cost of increasing the reduction of sulfur dioxide emissions from 7.0 million tons to 8.5 million tons = *B*

Total benefit from increasing the reduction of sulfur dioxide emissions from 7.0 million tons to 8.5 million tons = *A* + *B*

Net benefit to society from increasing the reduction of sulfur dioxide emissions from 7.0 million tons to 8.5 million tons = *A*

Don't Let This Happen to You

Remember That It's the *Net* Benefit That Counts

Why would we not want to *completely* eliminate anything unpleasant? As long as any person suffers any unpleasant consequences from air pollution, the marginal benefit of reducing air pollution will be positive. Therefore, removing every particle of air pollution will result in the largest *total* benefit to society. But removing every particle of air pollution is not optimal for the same reason that it is not optimal to remove every particle of dirt or dust from a room when cleaning it. The cost of cleaning your room is not just the price of the cleaning products but also the opportunity cost of your time. The more time you devote to cleaning your room, the less time you have for other activities. As

you devote more and more additional hours to cleaning your room, the alternative activities you have to give up are likely to increase in value, raising the opportunity cost of cleaning: Cleaning instead of watching television may not be too costly, but cleaning instead of eating any meals or getting any sleep is very costly. Optimally, you should eliminate dirt in your room up to the point where the marginal benefit of the last dirt removed equals the marginal cost of removing it. Society should take the same approach to air pollution. The result is the largest *net* benefit to society.

MyEconLab Study Plan

Your Turn: Test your understanding by doing related problem 2.9 on page 309 at the end of this chapter.

---

area under the marginal cost curve between the two emission levels. The total cost from increasing the reduction in emissions from 7.0 million tons to 8.5 million tons is the area of *B*. The net benefit from reducing emissions is the difference between the total cost and the total benefit, which is equal to the area of *A*.

In Figure 12.4, the benefits from further reductions in sulfur dioxide emissions are much greater than the costs. We reviewed the formula for calculating the area of a triangle, which is ½ × Base × Height, and the formula for the area of a rectangle, which is Base × Height. Using these formulas, we can calculate the value of the total benefits from the reduction in emissions and the value of the total costs. The value of the benefits (*A* + *B*) is $375 million. The value of the costs (*B*) is $255 million. If the people who would benefit from a reduction in pollution could get together, they could offer to pay the electric utilities $255 million to reduce the pollution to the optimal level. After making the payment, they would still be left with a net benefit of $120 million. In other words, a private agreement to reduce pollution to the optimal level is possible, without any government intervention.   MyEconLab Concept Check

---

Making the Connection
MyEconLab Video

The Fable of the Bees

Apple trees must be pollinated by bees to bear fruit. Bees need the nectar from apple trees (or other plants) to produce honey. In an important article published in the early 1950s, the British economist James Meade, winner of the 1977 Nobel Prize in Economics, argued that there were positive externalities in both apple growing and beekeeping. The more apple trees growers planted, the more honey would be produced in the hives of local beekeepers. And the more hives beekeepers kept, the larger the apple crops in neighboring apple orchards. Meade assumed that apple growers were not compensating beekeepers for the pollination services they were providing for apple crops and that beekeepers were not compensating apple growers for the use of their nectar in honey making. Therefore, he concluded that unless the government intervened, the market would not supply enough apple trees and beehives.

Steven Cheung of the University of Washington showed, however, that government intervention was not necessary because beekeepers and apple growers had long since arrived at private agreements. In fact, in Washington State, farmers with fruit orchards had been renting beehives to pollinate their trees since at least as early as 1917. According to Cheung, "Pollination contracts usually include stipulations regarding the number

Some apple growers and beekeepers make private arrangements to arrive at an economically efficient outcome.

and strength of the [bee] colonies, the rental fee per hive, the time of delivery and removal of hives, the protection of bees from pesticide sprays, and the strategic placing of hives."

Today, honeybees pollinate more than $14 billion worth of crops annually, from blueberries in Maine to almonds in California. Increasing demand for almonds has expanded the crop in California until it now stretches for 300 miles, across 800,000 acres, producing 80 percent of the country's almonds. Currently, about 1.6 million beehives are required to pollinate the California almond crop. Beehives are shipped into the state in February and March to pollinate the almond trees, and then they are shipped to Oregon and Washington to pollinate the cherry, pear, and apple orchards during April and May.

A mysterious disease that began wiping out beehives beginning in 2005 was still reducing the bee population in 2013. But private agreements between beekeepers and farmers continued to play an important role in U.S. agriculture.

Sources: James E. Meade, "External Economies and Diseconomies in a Competitive Situation," *Economic Journal*, Vol. 62, March 1952, pp. 54–67; Steven N. S. Cheung, "The Fable of the Bees: An Economic Investigation," *Journal of Law and Economics*, Vol. 16, No. 1, April 1973, pp. 11–33; and Michael Wines, "Mystery Malady Kills More Bees, Heightening Worry on Farms," *New York Times*, March 18, 2013.

MyEconLab Study Plan | **Your Turn:** Test your understanding by doing related problem 2.11 on page 309 at the end of this chapter.

Do Property Rights Matter?

In discussing the bargaining between the electric utilities and the people suffering the effects of the utilities' pollution, we assumed that the electric utilities were not legally liable for the damage they were causing. In other words, the victims of pollution could not legally enforce the right of their property not to be damaged, so they would have to pay the utilities to reduce the pollution. But would it make any difference if the utilities were legally liable for the damages? Surprisingly, as Coase was the first to point out, it does not matter for the amount of pollution reduction. The only difference would be that now the electric utilities would have to pay the victims of pollution for the right to pollute rather than the victims having to pay the utilities to reduce pollution. Because the marginal benefits and marginal costs of pollution reduction would not change, the bargaining should still result in the efficient level of pollution reduction—in this case, 8.5 million tons.

In the absence of the utilities being legally liable, the victims of pollution have an incentive to pay the utilities to reduce pollution up to the point where the marginal benefit of the last ton of reduction is equal to the marginal cost. If the utilities are legally liable, they have an incentive to pay the victims of pollution to allow them to pollute up to the same point.

MyEconLab Concept Check

The Problem of Transactions Costs

Transactions costs The costs in time and other resources that parties incur in the process of agreeing to and carrying out an exchange of goods or services.

Unfortunately, there are frequently practical difficulties that interfere with a private solution to the problem of externalities. In cases of pollution, for example, there are often both many polluters and many people suffering from the negative effects of pollution. Negotiating an agreement between the people suffering from pollution and the firms causing the pollution often fails because of the *transactions costs* involved. **Transactions costs** are the costs in time and other resources that parties incur in the process of agreeing to and carrying out an exchange of goods or services. In this case, the transactions costs would include the time and other costs of negotiating an agreement, drawing up a binding contract, and monitoring the agreement. Unfortunately, when many people are involved, the transactions costs are often higher than the net benefits from reducing the externality. In that case, the cost of transacting ends up exceeding the gain from the transaction, and a private solution to an externality problem is not feasible.

MyEconLab Concept Check

The Coase Theorem

Coase's argument that private solutions to the problem of externalities are possible is summed up in the **Coase theorem**: *If transactions costs are low, private bargaining will result in an efficient solution to the problem of externalities.* We have seen the basis for the Coase theorem in the preceding example of pollution by electric utilities: Because the benefits from reducing an externality are often greater than the costs, private bargaining can lead to an efficient outcome. But we have also seen that this outcome will occur only if transactions costs are low, and in the case of pollution, they usually are not. In general, private bargaining is most likely to reach an efficient outcome if the number of parties bargaining is small.

In practice, we must add a couple of other qualifications to the Coase theorem. In addition to low transactions costs, private solutions to the problem of externalities will occur only if all parties to the agreement have full information about the costs and benefits associated with the externality, and all parties must be willing to accept a reasonable agreement. For example, if those suffering from the effects of pollution do not have information on the costs of reducing pollution, it is unlikely that the parties can reach an agreement. Unreasonable demands can also hinder an agreement. For instance, in the example of pollution by electric utilities, we saw that the total benefit of reducing sulfur dioxide emissions was $375 million. Even if transactions costs are very low, if the utilities insist on being paid more than $375 million to reduce emissions, no agreement will be reached because the amount paid exceeds the value of the reduction to those suffering from the emissions. MyEconLab Concept Check

Coase theorem The argument of economist Ronald Coase that if transactions costs are low, private bargaining will result in an efficient solution to the problem of externalities.

Government Policies to Deal with Externalities

When private solutions to externalities are not feasible, how should the government intervene? British economist A. C. Pigou of Cambridge University was the first to analyze market failure systematically. Pigou argued that to deal with a negative externality in production, the government should impose a tax equal to the cost of the externality. The effect of such a tax is shown in Figure 12.5, which reproduces the negative externality from acid rain shown in Figure 12.1 on page 283.

By imposing a tax on the production of electricity equal to the cost of acid rain, the government will cause electric utilities to *internalize* the externality. As a consequence, the cost of the acid rain will become a private cost borne by the utilities, and the supply

MyEconLab Study Plan

12.3 LEARNING OBJECTIVE

Analyze government policies to achieve economic efficiency in a market with an externality.

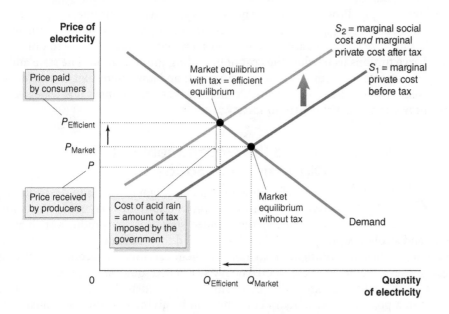

MyEconLab Animation

Figure 12.5

When There Is a Negative Externality, a Tax Can Lead to the Efficient Level of Output

Because utilities do not bear the cost of acid rain, they produce electricity beyond the economically efficient level. If the government imposes a tax equal to the cost of acid rain, the utilities will internalize the externality. As a consequence, the supply curve will shift up, from S_1 to S_2. The market equilibrium quantity changes from Q_{Market}, where an inefficiently high level of electricity is produced, to $Q_{Efficient}$, the economically efficient equilibrium quantity. The price of electricity will rise from P_{Market}—which does not include the cost of acid rain—to $P_{Efficient}$—which does include the cost. Consumers pay the price $P_{Efficient}$, while producers receive the price P, which is equal to $P_{Efficient}$ minus the amount of the tax.

Figure 12.6

When There Is a Positive Externality, a Subsidy Can Bring about the Efficient Level of Output

People who do not consume college educations can benefit from them. As a result, the social benefit from a college education is greater than the private benefit to college students. If the government pays a subsidy equal to the external benefit, students will internalize the externality. The subsidy will cause the demand curve to shift up, from D_1 to D_2. As a result, the market equilibrium quantity will shift from Q_{Market}, where an inefficiently low level of college educations is supplied, to $Q_{\text{Efficient}}$, the economically efficient equilibrium quantity. Producers receive the price $P_{\text{Efficient}}$, while consumers pay the price P, which is equal to $P_{\text{Efficient}}$ minus the amount of the subsidy.

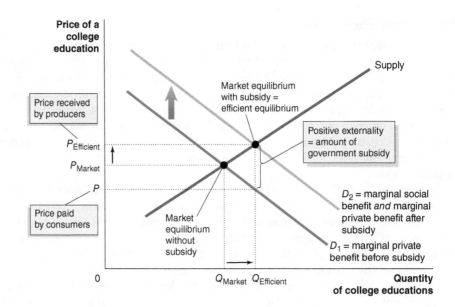

curve for electricity will shift from S_1 to S_2. The result will be a decrease in the equilibrium output of electricity from Q_{Market} to the efficient level, $Q_{\text{Efficient}}$. The price consumers pay for electricity will rise from P_{Market} —which does not include the cost of acid rain—to $P_{\text{Efficient}}$—which does include the cost. Producers will receive a price P, which is equal to $P_{\text{Efficient}}$ minus the amount of the tax.

Pigou also reasoned that the government can deal with a positive externality in consumption by giving consumers a subsidy, or payment, equal to the value of the externality. The effect of the subsidy is shown in Figure 12.6, which reproduces the positive externality from college education shown in Figure 12.2 on page 284.

By paying college students a subsidy equal to the external benefit from a college education, the government will cause students to *internalize* the externality. That is, the external benefit from a college education will become a private benefit received by college students, and the demand curve for college educations will shift from D_1 to D_2. The equilibrium number of college educations supplied will increase from Q_{Market} to the efficient level, $Q_{\text{Efficient}}$. Producers receive the price $P_{\text{Efficient}}$, while consumers pay the price P, which is equal to $P_{\text{Efficient}}$ minus the amount of the subsidy. In fact, the government does heavily subsidize college educations. All states have government-operated universities that charge tuitions well below the cost of providing the education. The state and federal governments also provide students with grants and low-interest loans that subsidize college educations. The economic justification for these programs is that college educations provide an external benefit to society.

Making the Connection

MyEconLab Video

Should the Government Tax Cigarettes and Soda?

Generally, governments use Pigovian taxes to deal with negative externalities in *production*. Governments also impose taxes—sometimes called *sin taxes*—on products such as cigarettes and alcohol. Some policymakers have argued that these products generate negative externalities in *consumption*, so a tax on them can increase economic efficiency. Recently, several cities have considered taxing sweetened soda, on the grounds that these sodas cause a negative externality by raising medical costs. Just as governments can deal with a positive externality in consumption by giving consumers a subsidy, they can deal with a negative externality by imposing a tax.

The effect of a tax on soda is shown in the following figure. By imposing a tax on soda, the government will cause consumers to internalize the externality. That is, the external cost to drinking soda will become a private cost paid by consumers. Because consumers now have to pay a tax on soda, at every quantity they are willing to pay less than they would have without the tax, so the demand curve for soda will shift down by the amount of the tax, from D_1 to D_2. The equilibrium quantity of sodas consumed will decrease from Q_{Market} to the efficient level, $Q_{Efficient}$.

But do people actually cause a negative externality by smoking and drinking sweetened sodas? It might seem that they don't because consumers of cigarettes and sodas bear the costs of any health problems they experience. In fact, though, the higher medical expenses from treating the complications of cigarette smoking or obesity are not paid entirely by the smokers or soda drinkers. A smoker who receives health insurance through his employer may increase the costs of that insurance, which all the workers at the firm will pay. Similarly, taxpayers partly pay for the health care of someone who is over age 65 and is enrolled in the federal government's Medicare program. The costs of medical care that smokers or soda drinkers do not pay themselves represent a negative externality.

There is a complication to this conclusion, however: Smokers and people who are obese tend to die early. This tragic outcome means that smokers and the obese may have been paying taxes to help pay for Social Security and Medicare benefits that they will never receive. They may also have made payments into company and public employee pension plans and purchased long-term care insurance, but they may not have lived long enough to receive many pension payments or to have spent time in a nursing home. So, there are offsetting effects: While alive, smokers and obese people may impose costs on others who bear the expense of their higher medical costs, but because they are likely to die early, they provide a financial gain to recipients of Social Security, Medicare, company and public employee pension plans, and purchasers of long-term care insurance.

W. Kip Viscusi of Vanderbilt University has studied the case of tobacco smoking and concluded that the external costs and benefits roughly offset each other, meaning that there doesn't appear to be a significant negative externality from smoking. Studies of obesity have arrived at somewhat conflicting results: A study of obesity in the Netherlands found that the cost savings from premature death offset the additional lifetime medical costs of obese people. But another study on U.S. data found that obesity did lead to a net increase in lifetime medical costs, even taking into account the shorter average life spans of obese people.

There may also be costs to smoking and obesity beyond additional medical costs. Smokers may inflict costs on others because of secondhand smoke or because smoking during pregnancy can lead to low birth weights and other health problems for babies. Airlines have noted that they spend more on fuel costs because of the increasing weight of passengers.

In the end, economists and policymakers continue to debate whether the government should use taxes to deal with negative externalities in consumption.

Sources: David Leonhardt, "Obama Likes Some Sin Taxes More Than Others," *New York Times*, April 10, 2013; W. Kip Viscusi, "Cigarette Taxation and the Social Consequences of Smoking," in James Poterba, ed., *Tax Policy and the Economy*, Vol. 9, Cambridge: MIT Press, 1995; Pieter H. M. van Baal, et al., "Lifetime Medical Costs of Obesity: Prevention No Cure for Increasing Health Expenditure," *PLoS Medicine*, Vol. 5, No. 2, February 2008, pp. 242–249; Pierre-Carl Michaud, "Understanding the Economic Consequences of Shifting Trends in Population Health," National Bureau of Economic Research Working Paper 15231, August 2009; and "Feds Say Obesity Epidemic Hurts Airlines by Increasing Fuel Costs," Associated Press, November 5, 2004.

MyEconLab Study Plan   **Your Turn:** Test your understanding by doing related problem 3.12 on page 310 at the end of this chapter.

Solved Problem 12.3

MyEconLab Interactive Animation

Dealing with the Externalities of Car Driving

When you drive a car, you generate several negative externalities: You cause some additional air pollution, you increase the chances that other drivers will have an accident, and you cause some additional congestion on roads, causing other drivers to waste time in traffic. Ian Parry of the International Monetary Fund and Kenneth Small of the University of California, Irvine, have estimated that these external costs amount to about $1.00 per gallon of gasoline. Taxes on gasoline are currently about $0.50 per gallon.

a. Draw a graph showing the gasoline market. Indicate the efficient equilibrium quantity and the market equilibrium quantity.

b. Given this information, if the federal government wanted to bring about the efficient level of gasoline production, how large a tax should the government impose on gasoline? Will the price consumers pay for gasoline rise by the full amount of the tax? Briefly explain using your graph from part (a).

Solving the Problem

Step 1: **Review the chapter material.** This problem is about the government using a tax to deal with a negative externality, so you may want to review the section "Government Policies to Deal with Externalities," which begins on page 291.

Step 2: **Answer part (a) by drawing a graph of the gasoline market.** In this case, the tax is levied on the consumption of gasoline rather than on its production, so your graph can show the demand curve representing marginal social benefit being below the demand curve showing marginal private benefit. (Of course, the government actually collects the tax from sellers rather than from consumers, but we get the same result whether the government imposes a tax on the buyers of a good or on the sellers.) Your graph should also show the market equilibrium quantity of gasoline, Q_{Market}, being greater than the efficient equilibrium quantity, $Q_{Efficient}$.

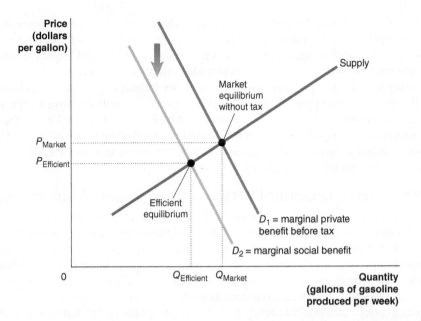

Step 3: **Answer part (b) by explaining the size of the necessary tax, indicating the tax on your graph from part (a), and explaining the effect of the tax on the equilibrium price.** If Parry and Small are correct that the external cost from consuming gasoline is $1.00 per gallon, then the tax per gallon should be raised from $0.50 to $1.00 per gallon. You should show the effect of the increase in the tax on your graph.

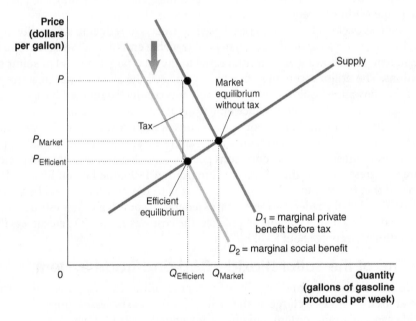

The graph shows that although the tax shifts down the demand curve for gasoline by $0.50 per gallon, the price consumers pay increases by less than $0.50. To see this, note that the price consumers pay rises from P_{Market} to P, which is smaller than the $0.50 per gallon tax, which equals the vertical distance between $P_{\text{Efficient}}$ and P.

Source: Ian W. H. Parry and Kenneth A. Small, "Does Britain or the United States Have the Right Gasoline Tax?" *American Economic Review*, Vol. 95, No. 4, September 2005, pp. 1276–1289.

Your Turn: For more practice, do related problems 3.9, 3.10, and 3.11 on page 310 at the end of this chapter.

MyEconLab Study Plan

Pigovian taxes and subsidies
Government taxes and subsidies intended to bring about an efficient level of output in the presence of externalities.

Command-and-control approach
A policy that involves the government imposing quantitative limits on the amount of pollution firms are allowed to emit or requiring firms to install specific pollution control devices.

Because Pigou was the first economist to propose using government taxes and subsidies to deal with externalities, they are sometimes referred to as **Pigovian taxes and subsidies**. Note that a Pigovian tax eliminates deadweight loss and improves economic efficiency, unlike most taxes, which are intended simply to raise revenue and can reduce consumer surplus and producer surplus and create a deadweight loss. In fact, one reason that economists support Pigovian taxes as a way to deal with negative externalities is that the government can use the revenues raised by Pigovian taxes to lower other taxes that reduce economic efficiency. For instance, the Canadian province of British Columbia has enacted a Pigovian tax on carbon dioxide emissions and uses the revenue raised to reduce personal income taxes.

Command-and-Control versus Market-Based Approaches

Although the federal government has sometimes used taxes and subsidies to deal with externalities, in dealing with pollution, it has traditionally used a *command-and-control approach*. A **command-and-control approach** to reducing pollution involves the government imposing quantitative limits on the amount of pollution firms are allowed to emit or requiring firms to install specific pollution control devices. For example, in the 1980s, the federal government required auto manufacturers such as Ford and General Motors to install catalytic converters to reduce auto emissions on all new automobiles.

Congress could have used direct pollution controls to deal with the problem of acid rain. To achieve its objective of a reduction of 8.5 million tons per year in sulfur dioxide emissions by 2010, Congress could have required every utility to reduce sulfur dioxide emissions by the same specified amount. However, this approach would not have been an economically efficient solution to the problem because utilities can have very different costs of reducing sulfur dioxide emissions. Some utilities that already used low-sulfur coal could reduce emissions further only at a high cost. Other utilities, particularly those in the Midwest, were able to reduce emissions at a lower cost.

Congress decided to use a market-based approach to reducing sulfur dioxide emissions by setting up a *cap-and-trade system* of tradable emission allowances. The federal government gave allowances to utilities equal to the total target amount of sulfur dioxide emissions. The utilities were then free to buy and sell the allowances. An active market where the allowances could be bought and sold was conducted on the Chicago Mercantile Exchange. Utilities that could reduce emissions at low cost did so and sold their allowances. Utilities that could only reduce emissions at high cost bought allowances. Using tradable emission allowances to reduce acid rain was a success in that it made it possible for utilities to meet Congress's emissions goal at a much lower cost than expected. Just before Congress enacted the allowances program in 1990, the Edison Electric Institute estimated that the cost to utilities of complying with the program would be $7.4 billion by 2010. By 1994, the federal government's General Accounting Office estimated that the cost would be less than $2 billion. In practice, the cost was almost 90 percent less than the initial estimate, or only about $870 *million*.   MyEconLab Concept Check

The End of the Sulfur Dioxide Cap-and-Trade System

The dollar value of the total benefits of reducing sulfur dioxide emissions turned out to be at least 25 times as large as the costs. Despite its successes, however, the sulfur dioxide cap-and-trade system had effectively ended by 2013. Over the years, research showed that the amount of illnesses caused by sulfur dioxide emissions was greater than had been thought. In response to these findings, President George W. Bush proposed legislation lowering the cap on sulfur dioxide emissions, but Congress did not pass the legislation. Court rulings kept the Environmental Protection Agency (EPA) from using regulations to set up a new trading system for sulfur dioxide allowances with a lower cap. As a result, the EPA reverted to the previous system of setting limits on sulfur dioxide emissions at the state or the individual power plant level.

Because nationwide trading of emission allowances was no longer possible, the allowances lost their value. Many economists continue to believe that market-based policies, such as the sulfur dioxide cap-and-trade system, are an efficient way to deal with the externalities of pollution. But in the end, any policy requires substantial political support to be enacted and maintained.   MyEconLab Concept Check

Are Tradable Emission Allowances Licenses to Pollute?

Tradable emission allowances also face a political problem because some environmentalists have criticized them for being "licenses to pollute." These environmentalists argue that just as the government does not issue licenses to rob banks or drive drunk, it should not issue licenses to pollute. But, this criticism ignores one of the central lessons of economics: Resources are scarce, and trade-offs exist. Resources that are spent on reducing one type of pollution are not available to reduce other types of pollution or for any other use. Because reducing acid rain using tradable emission allowances has cost utilities $870 million per year, rather than $7.4 billion, as originally estimated, society has saved more than $6.5 billion per year. MyEconLab Concept Check

Making the Connection MyEconLab Video	**Can a Carbon Tax Reduce Global Warming?** In the past 35 years, the global temperature has increased about 0.75 degree Fahrenheit (or 0.40 degree Centigrade) compared with the average for the period between 1951 and 1980. The following graph shows changes in temperature over the years since 1880.

Source: NASA, Goddard Institute for Space Studies, data.giss.nasa.gov/gistemp/tabledata_v3/GLB.Ts.txt.

Over the centuries, global temperatures have gone through many long periods of warming and cooling. Nevertheless, many scientists are convinced that the recent warming trend is not part of the natural fluctuations in temperature but is primarily caused by the burning of fossil fuels, such as coal, natural gas, and petroleum. Burning these fuels releases carbon dioxide, which accumulates in the atmosphere as a "greenhouse gas." Greenhouse gases cause some of the heat released from the earth to be reflected back, increasing temperatures. Annual carbon dioxide emissions have increased from about 50 million metric tons of carbon in 1850 to 1,600 million metric tons in 1950 and to nearly 9,500 million metric tons in 2011.

If greenhouse gases continue to accumulate in the atmosphere, according to some estimates global temperatures could increase by 3 degrees Fahrenheit or more during the next 100 years. Such an increase in temperature could lead to significant changes in climate, which might result in more hurricanes and other violent weather conditions, disrupt farming in many parts of the world, and lead to increases in sea levels, which could lead to flooding in coastal areas.

Although most economists and policymakers agree that emitting carbon dioxide results in a significant negative externality, there has been an extensive debate over which policies should be adopted. Part of the debate arises from disagreements over how rapidly global warming is likely to occur and what the economic cost will be. In addition, carbon dioxide emissions are a global problem; sharp reductions in carbon dioxide emissions only in the United States and Europe, for instance, would not be enough to stop global warming. But coordinating policy across countries has proven difficult. Finally, policymakers and economists debate the relative effectiveness of different policies.

Governments have used several approaches to reducing carbon dioxide emissions. In 2005, 24 countries in the European Union established a cap-and-trade system, similar to the one used successfully in the United States to reduce sulfur dioxide emissions. Under this program, each country issues emission allowances that can be freely traded among firms in different countries. In 2013, the system suffered a setback when the European Parliament voted against a plan to reduce the number of allowances available. Without a reduction in allowances, it was unclear how the system could be used to further reduce carbon dioxide emissions. In 2009, President Barack Obama proposed a cap-and-trade system for the United States to reduce carbon dioxide emissions to their 1990 level by 2020. However, Congress failed to approve the plan. California has introduced its own carbon dioxide cap-and-trade system, as have Australia, South Korea, and several provinces in China.

In 2013, members of Congress introduced a bill to reduce carbon dioxide emissions. Economists working at federal government agencies have estimated that the marginal social cost of carbon dioxide emissions is about $21 per ton. The Congressional Budget Office estimates that a Pigovian tax equal to that amount would reduce carbon dioxide emissions in the United States by about 8 percent over 10 years. The federal government would collect about $1.2 trillion in revenues from the tax over the same period. One government study indicates that 87 percent of a carbon tax would be borne by consumers in the form of higher prices for gasoline, electricity, natural gas, and other goods. For example, a $21 per ton carbon tax would increase the price of gasoline by about $0.18 to $0.20 per gallon. Because lower-income households spend a larger fraction of their incomes on gasoline than do higher income households, they would bear a proportionally larger share of the tax. Most proposals for a carbon tax include a way of refunding to lower-income households some part of their higher tax payments.

As of late 2013, it seemed doubtful that Congress would pass a carbon tax. The debate over policies toward global warming is likely to continue for many years.

Sources: "ETS, RIP?" *The Economist*, April 20, 2013; Congressional Budget Office, "Effects of a Carbon Tax on the Economy and the Environment," May 2013, www.cbo.gov/publication/44223; and Daniel F. Morris and Clayton Munnings, "Progressing to a Fair Carbon Tax," Resources for the Future, April 2013, www.rff.org/RFF/Documents/RFF-IB-13-03.pdf.

MyEconLab Study Plan

Your Turn: Test your understanding by doing related problem 3.16 on page 311 at the end of this chapter.

12.4 LEARNING OBJECTIVE

Explain how goods can be categorized on the basis of whether they are rival or excludable and use graphs to illustrate the efficient quantities of public goods and common resources.

Rivalry The situation that occurs when one person consuming a unit of a good means no one else can consume it.

Excludability The situation in which anyone who does not pay for a good cannot consume it.

Private good A good that is both rival and excludable.

Four Categories of Goods

We can explore further the question of when the market is likely to succeed in supplying the efficient quantity of a good by understanding that goods differ on the basis of whether their consumption is *rival* and *excludable*. **Rivalry** occurs when one person consuming a unit of a good means no one else can consume it. If you consume a Big Mac, for example, no one else can consume it. **Excludability** means that anyone who does not pay for a good cannot consume it. If you don't pay for a Big Mac, McDonald's can exclude you from consuming it. The consumption of a Big Mac is therefore rival and excludable. The consumption of some goods, however, can be either *nonrival* or *nonexcludable*. Nonrival means that one person's consumption does not interfere with another person's consumption. Nonexcludable means that it is impossible to exclude others from consuming the good, whether they have paid for it or not. Figure 12.7 shows four possible categories into which goods can fall.

We next consider each of the four categories:

1. A **private good** is both rival and excludable. Food, clothing, haircuts, and many other goods and services fall into this category. One person consuming a unit of these goods precludes other people from consuming that unit, and no one can consume these goods

	Excludable	Nonexcludable
Rival	**Private Goods** *Examples:* *Big Macs* *Running shoes*	**Common Resources** *Examples:* *Tuna in the ocean* *Public pasture land*
Nonrival	**Quasi-Public Goods** *Examples:* *Cable TV* *Toll road*	**Public Goods** *Examples:* *National defense* *Court system*

MyEconLab Animation

Figure 12.7

Four Categories of Goods

Goods and services can be divided into four categories on the basis of whether people can be excluded from consuming them and whether they are rival in consumption. A good or service is rival in consumption if one person consuming a unit of a good means that another person cannot consume that unit.

without buying them. Although we didn't state it explicitly, when we analyzed the demand and supply for goods and services in earlier chapters, we assumed that the goods and services were all private goods.

2. A **public good** is both nonrival and nonexcludable. Public goods are often, although not always, supplied by a government rather than private firms. The classic example of a public good is national defense. Your consuming national defense does not interfere with your neighbor consuming it, so consumption is nonrival. You also cannot be excluded from consuming it, whether you pay for it or not. No private firm would be willing to supply national defense because everyone can consume national defense whether they pay for it or not. The behavior of consumers in this situation is called **free riding** because individuals benefit from a good—in this case, the provision of national defense—without paying for it.

3. A *quasi-public good* is excludable but not rival. An example is cable television. People who do not pay for cable television do not receive it, but one person watching it doesn't affect other people watching it. The same is true of a toll road. Anyone who doesn't pay the toll doesn't get on the road, but one person using the road doesn't interfere with someone else using the road (unless so many people are using the road that it becomes congested). Goods that fall into this category are called *quasi-public goods*.

4. A **common resource** is rival but not excludable. Forest land in many poor countries is a common resource. If one person cuts down a tree, no one else can use the tree. But if no one has a property right to the forest, no one can be excluded from using it. As we will discuss in more detail later, people often overuse common resources.

Public good A good that is both nonrival and nonexcludable.

Free riding Benefiting from a good without paying for it.

Common resource A good that is rival but not excludable.

We discussed the demand and supply for private goods in earlier chapters. For the remainder of this chapter, we focus on the categories of public goods and common resources. To determine the optimal quantity of a public good, we have to modify our usual demand and supply analysis to take into account that a public good is both nonrival and nonexcludable.

The Demand for a Public Good

We can determine the market demand curve for a good or service by adding up the quantity of the good demanded by each consumer at each price. To keep things simple, let's consider the case of a market with only two consumers. Figure 12.8 shows that the market demand curve for hamburgers depends on the individual demand curves of Jill and Joe.

At a price of $4.00, Jill demands 2 hamburgers per week and Joe demands 4. Adding horizontally, the combination of a price of $4.00 per hamburger and a quantity demanded of 6 hamburgers will be a point on the market demand curve for hamburgers. Similarly, adding horizontally at a price of $1.50, we have a price of $1.50 and a quantity demanded of 11 as another point on the market demand curve. A consumer's demand curve for a good represents the marginal benefit the consumer receives from the good, so when we add together the consumers' demand curves, we have not only the market demand curve but also the marginal social benefit curve for this good, assuming that there is no externality in consumption.

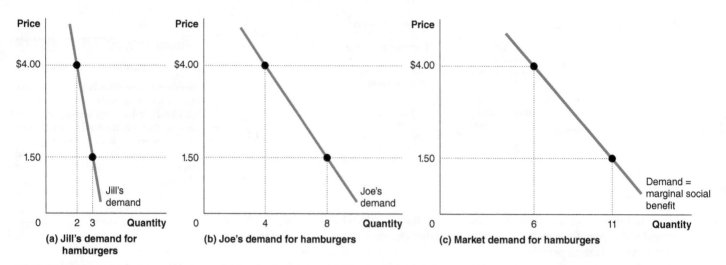

MyEconLab Animation

Figure 12.8 Constructing the Market Demand Curve for a Private Good

The market demand curve for private goods is determined by adding horizontally the quantity of the good demanded at each price by each consumer. For instance, in panel (a), Jill demands 2 hamburgers when the price is $4.00, and in panel (b), Joe demands 4 hamburgers when the price is $4.00. So, a quantity of 6 hamburgers and a price of $4.00 is a point on the market demand curve in panel (c).

How can we find the demand curve or marginal social benefit curve for a public good? Once again, for simplicity, assume that Jill and Joe are the only consumers. Unlike with a private good, where Jill and Joe can end up consuming different quantities, with a public good, they will consume *the same quantity*. Suppose that Jill owns a service station on an isolated rural road, and Joe owns a car dealership next door. These are the only two businesses around for miles. Both Jill and Joe are afraid that unless they hire a security guard at night, their businesses may be burgled. Like national defense, the services of a security guard are in this case a public good: Once hired, the guard will be able to protect both businesses, so the good is nonrival. It also will not be possible to exclude either business from being protected, so the good is nonexcludable.

To arrive at a demand curve for a public good, we don't add quantities at each price, as with a private good. Instead, we add the price each consumer is willing to pay for each quantity of the public good. This value represents the total dollar amount consumers as a group would be willing to pay for that quantity of the public good. In other words, to find the demand curve, or marginal social benefit curve, for a private good, we add the demand curves of individual consumers horizontally; for public goods, we add individual demand curves vertically. Figure 12.9 shows how the marginal social benefit curve for security guard services depends on the individual demand curves of Jill and Joe.

The figure shows that Jill is willing to pay $8 per hour for the guard to provide 10 hours of protection per night. Joe would suffer a greater loss from a burglary, so he is willing to pay $10 per hour for the same amount of protection. Adding the dollar amount that each is willing to pay gives us a price of $18 per hour and a quantity of 10 hours as a point on the marginal social benefit curve for security guard services. The figure also shows that because Jill is willing to spend $4 per hour for 15 hours of guard services and Joe is willing to pay $5, a price of $9 per hour and a quantity of 15 hours is another point on the marginal social benefit curve for security guard services. MyEconLab Concept Check

The Optimal Quantity of a Public Good

We know that to achieve economic efficiency, a good or service should be produced up to the point where the sum of consumer surplus and producer surplus is maximized, or, alternatively, where the marginal social cost equals the marginal social benefit. Therefore, the optimal quantity of security guard services—or any other public good—will

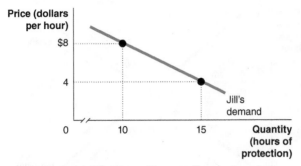

(a) Jill's demand for security guard services

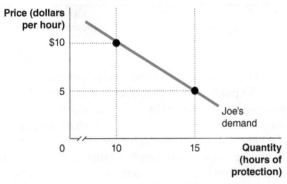

(b) Joe's demand for security guard services

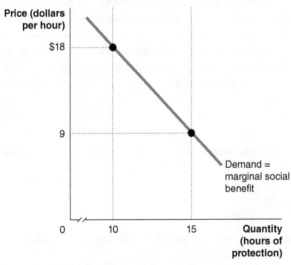

(c) Total demand for security guard services

MyEconLab Animation

Figure 12.9

Constructing the Demand Curve for a Public Good

To find the demand curve for a public good, we add up the price at which each consumer is willing to purchase each quantity of the good. In panel (a), Jill is willing to pay $8 per hour for a security guard to provide 10 hours of protection. In panel (b), Joe is willing to pay $10 for that level of protection. Therefore, in panel (c), the price of $18 per hour and the quantity of 10 hours will be a point on the demand curve for security guard services.

occur where the marginal social benefit curve intersects the supply curve. As with private goods, in the absence of an externality in production, the supply curve represents the marginal social cost of supplying the good. Figure 12.10 shows that the optimal quantity of security guard services supplied is 15 hours, at a price of $9 per hour.

Will the market provide the economically efficient quantity of security guard services? One difficulty is that the individual preferences of consumers, as shown by their demand curves, are not revealed in this market. This difficulty does not arise with private goods because consumers must reveal their preferences in order to purchase private goods. If the market price of Big Macs is $4.00, Joe either reveals that he is willing to pay that much by buying it or he does without it. In our example, neither Jill nor Joe can be excluded from consuming the services provided by a security guard once either hires one, and, therefore, neither has an incentive to reveal her or his preferences. In this

Figure 12.10

The Optimal Quantity of a Public Good

The optimal quantity of a public good is produced where the sum of consumer surplus and producer surplus is maximized, which occurs where the demand curve intersects the supply curve. In this case, the optimal quantity of security guard services is 15 hours, at a price of $9 per hour.

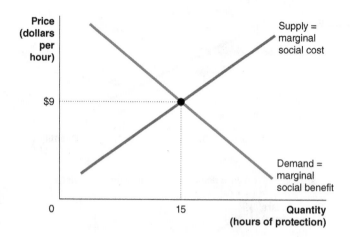

case, though, with only two consumers, it is likely that private bargaining will result in an efficient quantity of the public good. This outcome is not likely for a public good—such as national defense—that is supplied by the government to millions of consumers.

Governments sometimes use *cost–benefit analysis* to determine what quantity of a public good should be supplied. For example, before building a dam on a river, the federal government will attempt to weigh the costs against the benefits. The costs include the opportunity cost of other projects the government cannot carry out if it builds the dam. The benefits include improved flood control or new recreational opportunities on the lake formed by the dam. However, for many public goods, including national defense, the government does not use a formal cost–benefit analysis. Instead, the quantity of national defense supplied is determined by a political process involving Congress and the president. Even here, of course, Congress and the president realize that trade-offs are involved: The more resources used for national defense, the fewer resources available for other public or private goods.   MyEconLab Concept Check

Solved Problem 12.4

Determining the Optimal Level of Public Goods

Suppose, once again, that Jill and Joe run businesses that are next door to each other on an isolated road and both need a security guard. Their demand schedules for security guard services are as follows:

Joe			Jill	
Price (dollars per hour)	Quantity (hours of protection)		Price (dollars per hour)	Quantity (hours of protection)
$20	0		$20	1
18	1		18	2
16	2		16	3
14	3		14	4
12	4		12	5
10	5		10	6
8	6		8	7
6	7		6	8
4	8		4	9
2	9		2	10

The supply schedule for security guard services is as follows:

Price (dollars per hour)	Quantity (hours of protection)
$8	1
10	2
12	3
14	4
16	5
18	6
20	7
22	8
24	9

a. Draw a graph that shows the optimal level of security guard services. Be sure to label the curves on the graph.
b. Briefly explain why 8 hours of security guard protection is not an optimal quantity.

Solving the Problem

Step 1: **Review the chapter material.** This problem is about determining the optimal level of public goods, so you may want to review the section "The Optimal Quantity of a Public Good," which begins on page 300.

Step 2: **Begin by deriving the demand curve or marginal social benefit curve for security guard services.** To calculate the marginal social benefit of guard services, we need to add the prices that Jill and Joe are willing to pay at each quantity:

Demand or Marginal Social Benefit

Price (dollars per hour)	Quantity (hours of protection)
$38	1
34	2
30	3
26	4
22	5
18	6
14	7
10	8
6	9

Step 3: **Answer part (a) by plotting the demand (marginal social benefit) and supply (marginal social cost) curves.** The graph shows that the optimal level of security guard services is 6 hours.

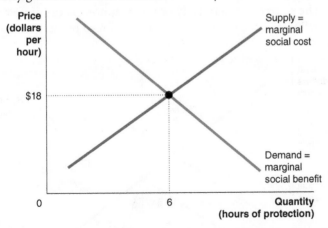

Step 4: **Answer part (b) by explaining why 8 hours of security guard protection is not an optimal quantity.** For each hour beyond 6, the supply curve is above the demand curve. Therefore, the marginal social benefit received will be less than the marginal social cost of supplying these hours. This results in a deadweight loss and a reduction in economic surplus.

Your Turn: For more practice, do related problem 4.4 on page 312 at the end of this chapter.   MyEconLab Study Plan

Common Resources

In England during the Middle Ages, each village had an area of pasture, known as the *commons*, on which any family in the village was allowed to graze its cows or sheep without charge. Of course, the grass one family's cow ate was not available for another family's cow, so consumption was rival. But every family in the village had the right to use the commons, so it was nonexcludable. Without some type of restraint on usage, the commons would be overgrazed. To see why, consider the economic incentives facing a family that was thinking of buying another cow and grazing it on the commons. The family would gain the benefits from increased milk production, but adding another cow to the commons would create a negative externality by reducing the amount of grass available for the cows of other families. Because this family—and the other families in the village—did not take this negative externality into account when deciding whether to add another cow to the commons, too many cows would be added. The grass on the commons would eventually be depleted, and no family's cow would get enough to eat.

Tragedy of the commons The tendency for a common resource to be overused.

The Tragedy of the Commons The tendency for a common resource to be overused is called the **tragedy of the commons**. The forests in many poor countries are a modern example. When a family chops down a tree in a public forest, it takes into account the benefits of gaining firewood or wood for building, but it does not take into account the costs of deforestation. Haiti, for example, was once heavily forested. Today, 80 percent of the country's forests have been cut down, primarily to be burned to create charcoal for heating and cooking. Because the mountains no longer have tree roots to hold the soil, heavy rains lead to devastating floods.

Figure 12.11 shows that with a common resource such as wood from a forest, the efficient level of use, $Q_{Efficient}$, is determined by the intersection of the demand curve, which represents the marginal social benefit received by consumers, and S_2, which represents the marginal social cost of cutting the wood. As in our discussion of negative externalities, the social cost is equal to the private cost of cutting the wood plus the external cost. In this case, the external cost represents the fact that the more wood each person cuts, the less wood there is available for others and the greater the deforestation, which increases the chances of floods. Because each individual tree cutter ignores the external cost, the equilibrium quantity of wood cut is Q_{Actual}, which is greater than the efficient quantity. At the actual equilibrium level of output, there is a deadweight loss, as shown in Figure 12.11 by the yellow triangle.

Is There a Way out of the Tragedy of the Commons? Notice that our discussion of the tragedy of the commons is very similar to our earlier discussion of negative externalities. The source of the tragedy of the commons is the same as the source of negative externalities: lack of clearly defined and enforced property rights. For instance,

MyEconLab Animation

Figure 12.11

Overuse of a Common Resource

For a common resource such as wood from a forest, the efficient level of use, $Q_{Efficient}$, is determined by the intersection of the demand curve, which represents the marginal benefit received by consumers, and S_2, which represents the marginal social cost of cutting the wood. Because each individual tree cutter ignores the external cost, the equilibrium quantity of wood cut is Q_{Actual}, which is greater than the efficient quantity. At the actual equilibrium level of output, there is a deadweight loss, as shown by the yellow triangle.

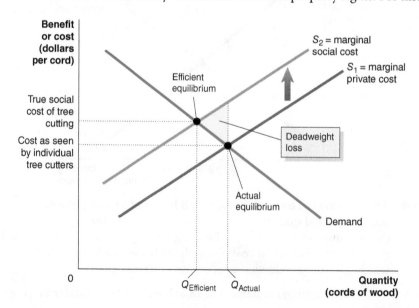

suppose that instead of being held as a collective resource, a piece of pastureland is owned by one person. That person will take into account the effect of adding another cow on the grass available to cows already using the pasture. As a result, the optimal number of cows will be placed on the pasture. Over the years, most of the commons lands in England were converted to private property. Most of the forestland in Haiti and other developing countries is actually the property of the government. The failure of the government to protect the forests against trespassers or convert them to private property is the key to their overuse.

In some situations, though, enforcing property rights is not feasible. An example is the oceans. Because no country owns the oceans beyond its own coastal waters, the fish and other resources of the ocean will remain a common resource. In situations in which enforcing property rights is not feasible, two types of solutions to the tragedy of the commons are possible. If the geographic area involved is limited and the number of people involved is small, access to the commons can be restricted through community norms and laws. If the geographic area or the number of people involved is large, legal restrictions on access to the commons are required. As an example of the first type of solution, the tragedy of the commons was avoided in the Middle Ages by traditional limits on the number of animals each family was allowed to put on the common pasture. Although these traditions were not formal laws, they were usually enforced adequately by social pressure.

With the second type of solution, the government imposes restrictions on access to the common resources. These restrictions can take several different forms, of which taxes, quotas, and tradable permits are the most common. By setting a tax equal to the external cost, governments can ensure that the efficient quantity of a resource is used. Quotas, or legal limits, on the quantity of the resource that can be taken during a given time period have been used in the United States to limit access to pools of oil that are beneath property owned by many different persons.   MyEconLab Concept Check   MyEconLab Study Plan

Continued from page 281

Economics in Your Life

What's the "Best" Level of Pollution?

At the beginning of this chapter, we asked you to think about what is the "best" level of carbon emissions. Conceptually, this is a straightforward question to answer: The efficient level of carbon emissions is the level for which the marginal benefit of reducing carbon emissions exactly equals the marginal cost of reducing carbon emissions. In practice, however, this question is very difficult to answer. For example, scientists disagree about how much carbon emissions are contributing to climate change and what the damage from climate change will be. In addition, the cost of reducing carbon emissions depends on the method of reduction used. As a result, neither the marginal cost curve nor the marginal benefit curve for reducing carbon emissions is known with certainty. This uncertainty makes it difficult for policymakers to determine the economically efficient level of carbon emissions and is the source of much of the current debate. In any case, economists agree that the total cost of *completely* eliminating carbon emissions is much greater than the total benefit.

Conclusion

Government interventions in the economy, such as imposing price ceilings and price floors, can reduce economic efficiency. But in this chapter, we have seen that the government plays an indispensable role in the economy when the absence of well-defined and enforceable property rights keeps the market from operating efficiently. For instance, because no one has a property right for clean air, in the absence of government intervention, firms will produce too great a quantity of products that generate air pollution. We have also seen that public goods are nonrival and nonexcludable and are, therefore, often supplied directly by the government.

Visit MyEconLab for a news article and analysis related to the concepts in this chapter.

Chapter Summary and Problems

Key Terms

12.1 | **Externalities and Economic Efficiency, pages 282–285**

LEARNING OBJECTIVE: Identify examples of positive and negative externalities and use graphs to show how externalities affect economic efficiency.

Summary

An **externality** is a benefit or cost to parties who are not involved in a transaction. Pollution and other externalities in production cause a difference between the **private cost** borne by the producer of a good or service and the **social cost**, which includes any external cost, such as the cost of pollution. An externality in consumption causes a difference between the **private benefit** received by the consumer and the **social benefit**, which includes any external benefit. If externalities exist in production or consumption, the market will not produce the optimal level of a good or service. This outcome is referred to as **market failure**. Externalities arise when property rights do not exist or cannot be legally enforced. **Property rights** are the rights individuals or businesses have to the exclusive use of their property, including the right to buy or sell it.

 MyEconLab Visit **www.myeconlab.com** to complete these exercises online and get instant feedback.

Review Questions

1.1 What is an externality? Give an example of a positive externality, and give an example of a negative externality.

1.2 When will the private cost of producing a good differ from the social cost? Give an example. When will the private benefit from consuming a good differ from the social benefit? Give an example.

1.3 What is economic efficiency? How do externalities affect the economic efficiency of a market equilibrium?

1.4 What is market failure? When is market failure likely to arise?

1.5 Briefly explain the relationship between property rights and the existence of externalities.

Problems and Applications

1.6 The chapter states that your consuming a Big Mac does not create an externality. But suppose you arrive at your favorite McDonald's at lunchtime and get in a long line to be served. By the time you reach the counter, there

are 10 people in line behind you. Because you decided to have a Big Mac for lunch—instead of, say, a pizza—each of those 10 people must wait in line an additional 2 minutes. Is it still correct to say that your consuming a Big Mac creates no externalities? Might there be a justification here for the government to intervene in the market for Big Macs? Briefly explain.

1.7 A neighbor's barking dog can be both a positive externality and a negative externality. Under what circumstances would the barking dog serve as a positive externality? Under what circumstances would the barking dog be a negative externality?

1.8 Yellowstone National Park is in bear country. The National Park Service, at its Yellowstone Web site, states the following about camping and hiking in bear country:

> Do not leave packs containing food unattended, even for a few minutes. Allowing a bear to obtain human food even once often results in the bear becoming aggressive about obtaining such food in the future. Aggressive bears present a threat to human safety and eventually must be destroyed or removed from the park. Please obey the law and do not allow bears or other wildlife to obtain human food.

What negative externality does obtaining human food pose for bears? What negative externality do bears obtaining human food pose for future campers and hikers?

Source: National Park Service, Yellowstone National Park, "Backcountry Camping and Hiking," June 7, 2013, www.nps.gov/yell/planyourvisit/backcountryhiking.htm.

1.9 Every year at the beginning of flu season, many people, including the elderly, get a flu shot to reduce their chances of contracting the flu. One result is that people who do *not* get a flu shot are less likely to contract the flu.

a. What type of externality (negative or positive) arises from getting a flu shot?

b. On the graph that follows, show the effects of this externality by drawing in and labelling any additional curves that are needed and by labeling the efficient quantity and the efficient price of flu shots. Label the area representing deadweight loss in this market.

1.10 John Cassidy, a writer for the *New Yorker* magazine, wrote a blog post arguing against New York City's having installed bike lanes. Cassidy complained that the bike lanes had eliminated traffic lanes on some streets as well as some on-street parking. A writer for the *Economist* magazine disputed Cassidy's argument with the following comment: "I hate to belabour the point, but driving, as it turns out, is associated with a number of negative externalities." What externalities are associated with driving? How do these externalities affect the debate over whether big cities should install more bike lanes?

Sources: John Cassidy, "Battle of the Bike Lanes," *New Yorker*, March 8, 2011; and "The World Is His Parking Spot," *Economist*, March 9, 2011.

1.11 In a study at a large state university, students were randomly assigned roommates. Researchers found that, on average, males assigned to roommates who reported drinking alcohol in the year before entering college had GPAs one-quarter point lower than those assigned to non-drinking roommates. For males who drank frequently before college, being assigned to a roommate who also drank frequently before college reduced their GPAs by two-thirds of a point. Draw a graph showing the price of alcohol and the quantity of alcohol consumption on college campuses. Include in the graph the demand for drinking and the private and social costs of drinking. Label any deadweight loss that arises in this market.

Source: Michael Kremer and Dan M. Levy, "Peer Effects and Alcohol Use among College Students," *Journal of Economic Perspectives*, Vol. 22, No. 3, Summer 2008, pp. 189–206.

1.12 Tom and Jacob are college students. Each of them will probably get married later and have two or three children. Each knows that if he studies more in college, he'll get a better job and earn more money. Earning more will enable them to spend more on their future families for things such as orthodontia, nice clothes, admission to expensive colleges, and travel. Tom thinks about the potential

benefits to his potential children when he decides how much studying to do. Jacob doesn't.
   a. What type of externality arises from studying?
   b. Draw a graph showing this externality, contrasting the responses of Tom and Jacob. Who studies more? Who acts more efficiently? Briefly explain.

1.13 Fracking, or hydraulic fracturing, has been used more frequently in recent years to drill for oil and natural gas that previously was too expensive to obtain. According to an article in the *New York Times*, "horizontal drilling has enabled engineers to inject millions of gallons of high-pressure water directly into layers of shale to create the fractures that release the gas. Chemicals added to the water dissolve minerals, kill bacteria that might plug up the well, and insert sand to prop open the fractures." Experts are divided about whether fracking results in significant pollution, but some people worry that chemicals used in fracking might lead to pollution of underground supplies of water used by households and farms.
   a. First, assume that fracking causes no significant pollution. Use a demand and supply graph to show the effect of fracking on the market for natural gas.
   b. Now assume that fracking does result in pollution. On your graph from part (a), show the effect of fracking. Be sure to carefully label all curves and all equilibrium points.
   c. In your graph in part (b), what has happened to the efficient level of output and the efficient price in the market for natural gas compared with the situation before fracking? Can you be certain that the efficient level of output and the efficient price have risen or fallen as a result of fracking? Briefly explain.

Source: Susan L. Brantley and Anna Meyendorff, "The Facts on Fracking," *New York Times*, March 13, 2013.

1.14 The following information regarding cable television is from the Federal Communications Commission Web site:

> In general, a cable television operator has the right to select the channels and services that are available on its cable system. With the exception of certain channels like local broadcast television channels which are required to be carried by federal law, the cable operator has broad discretion in choosing which channels will be available and how those channels will be packaged and marketed to subscribers.... With the exception of broadcast channels that elect "must carry" status and PEG channels, all other programming on the cable system is based on terms negotiated between the cable operator and the entity that owns the channel or programming service. Terms may include whether the channel or service will be offered in a package with other programming or whether the channel or service will be offered on a per-channel or pay-per-view basis....

Suppose you are a fan of *The Daily Show* with Jon Stewart and *The Colbert Report*, both on the Comedy

Central cable channel, but the only way you can get Comedy Central from your local cable provider is to subscribe to a package that includes 30 other channels. Is there an externality involved here? If so, is it an externality in production or consumption, and is it positive or negative? If there is an externality, discuss possible solutions.

Source: Consumer and Government Affairs Bureau, "Choosing Cable Channels," June 7, 2013, www.fcc.gov/cgb/consumerfacts /cablechannels.html.

1.15 In an article in the agriculture magazine *Choices*, Oregon State University economist JunJie Wu made the following observation about the conversion of farmland to urban development:

> Land use provides many economic and social benefits, but often comes at a substantial cost to the environment. Although most economic costs are figured into land use decisions, most environmental externalities

are not. These environmental "externalities" cause a divergence between private and social costs for some land uses, leading to an inefficient land allocation. For example, developers may not bear all the environmental and infrastructural costs generated by their projects. Such "market failures" provide a justification for private conservation efforts and public land use planning and regulation.

What does the author mean by *market failures* and *inefficient land allocation*? Explain why the author describes inefficient land allocation as a market failure. Illustrate your argument with a graph showing the market for land to be used for urban development.

Source: JunJie Wu, "Land Use Changes: Economic, Social, and Environmental Impacts," *Choices*, Vol. 23, No. 4, Fourth Quarter 2008, pp. 6–10.

12.2 Private Solutions to Externalities: The Coase Theorem, pages 285–291

LEARNING OBJECTIVE: Discuss the Coase theorem and explain how private bargaining can lead to economic efficiency in a market with an externality.

Summary

Externalities and market failures result from incomplete property rights or from the difficulty of enforcing property rights in certain situations. When an externality exists, and the efficient quantity of a good is not being produced, the total cost of reducing the externality is usually less than the total benefit. According to the **Coase theorem**, if **transactions costs** are low, private bargaining will result in an efficient solution to the problem of externalities.

 MyEconLab Visit **www.myeconlab.com** to complete these exercises online and get instant feedback.

Review Questions

2.1 What do economists mean by "an economically efficient level of pollution"?

2.2 What is the Coase theorem? Why do the parties involved in an externality have an incentive to reach an efficient solution?

2.3 What are transactions costs? When are we likely to see private solutions to the problem of externalities?

Problems and Applications

2.4 Is it ever possible for an *increase* in pollution to make society better off? Briefly explain, using a graph like Figure 12.3 on page 287.

2.5 If the marginal cost of reducing a certain type of pollution is zero, should all that type of pollution be eliminated? Briefly explain.

2.6 Discuss the factors that determine the marginal cost of reducing crime. Discuss the factors that determine the marginal benefit of reducing crime. Would it be economically efficient to reduce the amount of crime to zero? Briefly explain.

2.7 In discussing the reduction of air pollution in the developing world, Richard Fuller of the Blacksmith Institute, an environmental organization, observed, "It's the 90/10 rule. To do 90 percent of the work only costs 10 percent of the money. It's the last 10 percent of the cleanup that costs 90 percent of the money." Why should it be any more costly to clean up the last 10 percent of polluted air than to clean up the first 90 percent? What trade-offs would be involved in cleaning up the final 10 percent?

Source: Tiffany M. Luck, "The World's Dirtiest Cities," *Forbes*, February 28, 2008.

2.8 **[Related to the** Making the Connection **on page 286]** In the first years following the passage of the Clean Air Act in 1970, air pollution declined sharply, and there were important health benefits, including a decline in infant mortality. According to an article in the *Economist* magazine, however, recently some policymakers "worry that the EPA is constantly tightening restrictions on pollution, at ever higher cost to business but with diminishing returns in terms of public health."

a. Why might additional reductions in air pollution come at "ever higher cost"? What does the article mean that these reductions will result in "ever diminishing returns in terms of public health"?

b. How should the federal government decide whether further reductions in air pollution are needed?

Source: "Soaring Emissions," *Economist*, June 2, 2011.

2.9 **[Related to the** Don't Let This Happen to You **on page 289]** Briefly explain whether you agree or disagree with the following statement: "Sulfur dioxide emissions cause acid rain and breathing difficulties for people with respiratory problems. The total benefit to society is greatest if we completely eliminate sulfur dioxide emissions. Therefore, the economically efficient level of emissions is zero."

2.10 According to the Coase theorem, why would a steel plant that creates air pollution agree to curtail production (and, therefore, pollution) if it were not legally liable for the damage the pollution was causing? Must the property right to clean air be assigned to the victims of air pollution for the steel plant to agree to reduce pollution?

2.11 **[Related to the** Making the Connection **on page 289]** We know that owners of apple orchards and beehives are able to negotiate private agreements. Is it likely that as a result of these private agreements, the market supplies the efficient quantities of apple trees and beehives? Are there any real-world difficulties that might stand in the way of achieving this efficient outcome?

12.3 **Government Policies to Deal with Externalities, pages 291–298**

LEARNING OBJECTIVE: Analyze government policies to achieve economic efficiency in a market with an externality.

Summary

When private solutions to externalities are unworkable, the government sometimes intervenes. One way to deal with a negative externality in production is to impose a tax equal to the cost of the externality. The tax causes the producer of the good to internalize the externality. The government can deal with a positive externality in consumption by giving consumers a subsidy, or payment, equal to the value of the externality. Government taxes and subsidies intended to bring about an efficient level of output in the presence of externalities are called **Pigovian taxes and subsidies**. Although the federal government has sometimes used subsidies and taxes to deal with externalities, in dealing with pollution it has more often used a command-and-control approach. A **command-and-control approach** involves the government imposing quantitative limits on the amount of pollution allowed or requiring firms to install specific pollution control devices. Direct pollution controls of this type are not economically efficient, however. As a result, economists generally prefer reducing pollution by using market-based policies.

 Visit **www.myeconlab.com** to complete these exercises online and get instant feedback.

Review Questions

3.1 What is a Pigovian tax? At what level must a Pigovian tax be set to achieve efficiency?

3.2 What does it mean for a producer or consumer to internalize an externality? What would cause a producer or consumer to internalize an externality?

3.3 Why do most economists prefer tradable emission allowances to the command-and-control approach to pollution?

Problems and Applications

3.4 The author of a newspaper article remarks that many economists "support Pigovian taxes because, in some sense, we are already paying them." In what sense might consumers in a market be "paying" a Pigovian tax even if the government hasn't imposed an explicit tax?

Source: Adam Davidson, "Should We Tax People for Being Annoying?" *New York Times*, January 8, 2013.

3.5 The federal government's nutrition guidelines urge adults to eat at least five cups of fruits and vegetables each day. Does consuming fruits and vegetables have a positive externality? Should the government subsidize the consumption of fruits and vegetables? Briefly explain.

3.6 Many antibiotics that once were effective in eliminating infections no longer are because bacteria have evolved to become resistant to them. Some bacteria are now resistant to all but one or two existing antibiotics. Some policymakers have argued that pharmaceutical companies should receive subsidies for developing new antibiotics. A newspaper article states:

> While the notion of directly subsidizing drug companies may be politically unpopular in many quarters, proponents say it is necessary to bridge the gap between the high value that new antibiotics have for society and the low returns they provide to drug companies.

Is there a positive externality in the production of antibiotics? Should firms producing every good where there is a gap between the value of the good to society and the profit to the firms making the good receive subsidies? Briefly explain.

Source: Andrew Pollack, "Antibiotics Research Subsidies Weighed by U.S.," *New York Times*, November 5, 2010.

3.7 A newspaper article has the headline: "Should We Tax People for Being Annoying?"

  a. Do annoying people cause a negative externality? Should they be taxed? Do crying babies on a bus or plane cause a negative externality? Should the babies (or their parents) be taxed?

  b. Do people who plant flowers and otherwise have beautiful gardens visible from the street cause a positive externality? Should these people receive a government subsidy?

  c. Should every negative externality be taxed? Should every positive externality be subsidized? How might the government decide whether using Pigovian taxes and subsidies is appropriate?

  Source: Adam Davison, "Should We Tax People for Being Annoying?" *New York Times*, January 8, 2013.

3.8 Writing in the *New York Times*, Michael Lewis argued, "Good new technologies are a bit like good new roads: Their social benefits far exceed what any one person or company can get paid for creating them." Does this observation justify the government subsidizing the production of new technologies? If so, how might the government do this?

  Source: Michael Lewis, "In Defense of the Boom," *New York Times*, October 27, 2002.

3.9 **[Related to** Solved Problem 12.3 **on page 294]** Solved Problem 12.3 contains the statement: "Of course, the government actually collects the tax from sellers rather than from consumers, but we get the same result whether the government imposes a tax on the buyers of a good or on the sellers." Demonstrate that this statement is correct by solving the problem assuming that the increase in the tax on gasoline shifts the supply curve rather than the demand curve.

3.10 **[Related to** Solved Problem 12.3 **on page 294]** The fumes from dry cleaners can contribute to air pollution. Suppose the following graph illustrates the situation in the dry cleaning market.

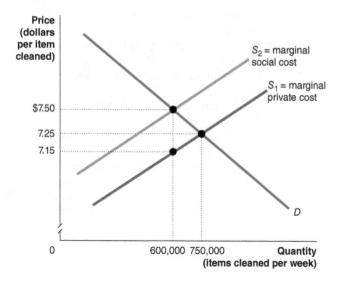

  a. Explain how a government can use a tax on dry cleaning to bring about the efficient level of production. What should the value of the tax be?

  b. How large is the deadweight loss (in dollars) from excessive dry cleaning, according to the figure?

3.11 **[Related to** Solved Problem 12.3 **on page 294]** Companies that produce toilet paper bleach the paper to make it white. Some paper plants discharge the bleach into rivers and lakes, causing substantial environmental damage. Suppose the following graph illustrates the situation in the toilet paper market.

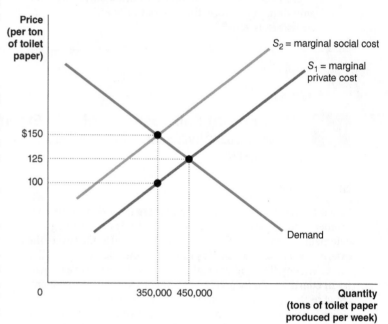

Explain how the federal government can use a tax on toilet paper to bring about the efficient level of production. What should be the value of the tax?

3.12 **[Related to the** Making the Connection **on page 292]** Eric Finklestein, an economist at Duke University, has argued that the external costs from being obese are larger than the external costs from smoking because "the mortality effect for obesity is much smaller than it is for smoking and the costs start much earlier in life."

  a. What does Finklestein mean by the "mortality effect"? Why would the mortality effect of obesity being smaller than the mortality effect of smoking result in obesity having a larger external cost?

  b. Tobacco taxes have been more politically popular than taxes on soda. Why might the general public be more willing to support cigarette taxes than soda taxes?

  Source: David Leonhardt, "Obama Likes Some Sin Taxes More Than Others," *New York Times*, April 10, 2013.

3.13 A few years ago, Governor Deval Patrick of Massachusetts proposed that criminals would have to pay a "safety fee" to the government. The size of the fee would be based on the seriousness of the crime (that is, the fee would be larger for more serious crimes).

a. Is there an economically efficient amount of crime? Briefly explain.

b. Briefly explain whether the "safety fee" is a Pigovian tax of the type discussed in this chapter.

Source: Michael Levenson, "Patrick Proposes New Fee on Criminals," *Boston Globe*, January 14, 2007.

3.14 The following graph illustrates the situation in the dry cleaning market assuming that the marginal social cost of the pollution *increases* as the quantity of items cleaned per week increases. The graph includes two demand curves: one for a smaller city, D_S, and the other for a larger city, D_L.

a. Explain why the marginal social cost curve has a different slope than the marginal private cost curve.

b. What tax per item cleaned will achieve economic efficiency in the smaller city? In the larger city? Explain why the efficient tax is different in the two cities.

3.15 **[Related to the** Chapter Opener **on page 281]** According to an article in the *New York Times*: "Top economists agree a tax on fuels and the carbon they spew into the atmosphere would be the cheapest way to combat climate change." Why would a carbon tax be a cheaper way to reduce carbon dioxide emissions than the command-and-control approach of ordering utilities to emit less carbon dioxide and automobile companies to produce more fuel-efficient cars?

Source: Eduardo Porter, "In Energy Taxes, Tools to Help Tackle Climate Change," *New York Times*, January 29, 2013.

3.16 **[Related to the** Making the Connection **on page 297]** According to a Congressional Budget Office report, the burden of a carbon tax would fall disproportionately on low-income households.

a. What does the report mean by the "burden" of the tax?

b. Why would the burden of a carbon tax fall disproportionately on low-income households? What actions might the government take to reduce the burden on these households?

Source: Congressional Budget Office, "Effects of a Carbon Tax on the Economy and the Environment," May 2013, p. 8.

 12.4

Four Categories of Goods, pages 298–305

LEARNING OBJECTIVE: Explain how goods can be categorized on the basis of whether they are rival or excludable and use graphs to illustrate the efficient quantities of public goods and common resources.

Summary

There are four categories of goods: private goods, public goods, quasi-public goods, and common resources. **Private goods** are both rival and excludable. **Rivalry** means that when one person consumes a unit of a good, no one else can consume that unit. **Excludability** means that anyone who does not pay for a good cannot consume it. **Public goods** are both nonrival and nonexcludable. Private firms are usually not willing to supply public goods because of free riding. **Free riding** involves benefiting from a good without paying for it. *Quasi-public goods* are excludable but not rival. **Common resources** are rival but not excludable. The **tragedy of the commons** refers to the tendency for a common resource to be overused. The tragedy of the commons results from a lack of clearly defined and enforced property rights. We find the market demand curve for a private good by adding the quantity of the good demanded by each consumer at each price. We find the demand curve for a public good by adding vertically the price each consumer would be willing to pay for each quantity of the good. The optimal quantity of a public good occurs where the demand curve intersects the curve representing the marginal cost of supplying the good.

MyEconLab   Visit **www.myeconlab.com** to complete these exercises online and get instant feedback.

Review Questions

4.1 Define *rivalry* and *excludability* and use these terms to discuss the four categories of goods.

4.2 What is free riding? How is free riding related to the tendency of a public good to create market failure?

4.3 What is the tragedy of the commons? How can it be avoided?

Problems and Applications

4.4 **[Related to** Solved Problem 12.4 **on page 302]** Suppose that Jill and Joe are the only two people in the small town of Andover. Andover has land available to build a park of no more than 9 acres. Jill and Joe's demand schedules for the park are as follows:

Joe

Price per Acre	Number of Acres
$10	0
9	1
8	2
7	3
6	4
5	5
4	6
3	7
2	8
1	9

Jill

Price per Acre	Number of Acres
$15	0
14	1
13	2
12	3
11	4
10	5
9	6
8	7
7	8
6	9

The supply curve is as follows:

Price per Acre	Number of Acres
$11	1
13	2
15	3
17	4
19	5
21	6
23	7
25	8
27	9

a. Draw a graph showing the optimal size of the park. Be sure to label the curves on the graph.

b. Briefly explain why a park of 2 acres is not optimal.

4.5 Commercial whaling has been described as a modern example of the tragedy of the commons. Briefly explain whether you agree.

4.6 Nancy Folbre, an economist at the University of Massachusetts, Amherst, argued, "We must take responsibility for governing the commons—not just the quaint old-fashioned village green, but things that cannot easily be privatized—[such as] clean air." Do you agree that clean air is like a common pasture in England in the Middle Ages? Briefly explain.

Source: Nancy Folbre, "Taking Responsibility for the Commons," *New York Times*, February 26, 2009.

4.7 The more frequently bacteria are exposed to antibiotics, the more quickly the bacteria will develop resistance to the antibiotics. An article from MayoClinic.com includes the following about antibiotic use:

> If antibiotics are used too often for things they can't treat—like colds, flu or other viral infections—not only are they of no benefit, they become less effective against the bacteria they're intended to treat.... Nearly all significant bacterial infections in the world are becoming resistant to commonly used antibiotics. When you misuse antibiotics, you help create resistant microorganisms that can cause new and hard-to-treat infections.

Briefly discuss in what sense antibiotics can be considered a common resource.

Source: Mayo Clinic Staff, "Antibiotics: Misuse Puts You and Others at Risk," www.MayoClinic.com, February 4, 2012.

4.8 Put each of these goods or services into one of the boxes in Figure 12.7 on page 299. That is, categorize them as private goods, public goods, quasi-public goods, or common resources.

a. A television broadcast of baseball's World Series
b. Home mail delivery
c. Education in a public school
d. Education in a private school
e. Hiking in a park surrounded by a fence
f. Hiking in a park not surrounded by a fence
g. An apple

4.9 Explain whether you agree with the following statement:

> Health care is obviously a public good. If one person becomes ill and doesn't receive treatment, that person may infect many other people. If many people become ill, then the output of the economy will be negatively affected. Therefore, health care is a public good that the government should supply.

4.10 Deer-hunting clubs in southeast Virginia impose a fine on anyone harvesting a buck with antlers below a certain size on land where those clubs have exclusive rights to hunt. The hunt clubs, however, do not impose a fine for harvesting a buck with small antlers on land where several clubs have the right to hunt. Why would the hunt clubs treat the harvesting of bucks on the two lands differently?

4.11 In the early 1800s, more than 60 million American bison (commonly known as the buffalo) roamed the Great Plains. By the late 1800s, the buffalo was nearly extinct. Considering the four categories of goods discussed in this chapter, why might it be that hunters nearly killed buffalo to extinction but not cattle?

4.12 William Easterly in *The White Man's Burden* shares the following account by New York University Professor Leonard Wantchekon of how Professor Wantchekon's village in Benin, Africa, managed the local fishing pond when he was growing up:

> To open the fishing season, elders performed ritual tests at Amlé, a lake fifteen kilometers from the village. If the fish were large enough, fishing was allowed for two or three days. If they were too small, all fishing was forbidden, and anyone who secretly fished the lake at this time was outcast, excluded from the formal and informal groups that formed the village's social structure. Those who committed this breach of trust were often shunned by the whole community; no one would speak to the offender, or even acknowledge his existence for a year or more.

What economic problem were the village elders trying to prevent? Do you think their solution was effective?

Source: William Easterly, *The White Man's Burden: Why the West's Efforts to Aid the Rest Have Done So Much Ill and So Little Good*, New York: Penguin Books, 2006, p. 94.

This next chapter is not discussed in this course but is provided because students find them useful for future courses and/or find it of interest.

PART SIX FACTOR MARKETS, INEQUALITY, AND UNCERTAINTY

13

MARKETS FOR FACTORS OF PRODUCTION

After studying this chapter,
you will be able to:

◆ Describe the anatomy of factor markets

◆ Explain how the value of marginal product determines the demand for a factor of production

◆ Explain how wage rates and employment are determined and how labor unions influence labor markets

◆ Explain how capital and land rental rates and natural resource prices are determined

Your college basketball coach earns much more than your economics professor. Why? What determines the wages that people earn? Wages are important, but finding a job is important too. Why are so many manufacturing jobs disappearing and what new jobs are being created?

In this chapter, we study labor markets as well as markets for capital and natural resources. *In Reading Between the Lines* at the end of the chapter we look at the effects of a labor union in the market for teachers.

315

The Anatomy of Factor Markets

The four factors of production are

- Labor
- Capital
- Land (natural resources)
- Entrepreneurship

Let's take a brief look at the anatomy of the markets in which these factors of production are traded.

Markets for Labor Services

Labor services are the physical and mental work effort that people supply to produce goods and services. A labor market is a collection of people and firms who trade labor services. The price of labor services is the wage rate.

Some labor services are traded day by day. These services are called *casual labor*. People who pick fruit and vegetables often just show up at a farm and take whatever work is available that day. But most labor services are traded on a job contract.

Most labor markets have many buyers and many sellers and are competitive. In these markets, supply and demand determine the wage rate and quantity of labor employed. Jobs expand when demand increases and jobs disappear when demand decreases.

In some labor markets, a labor union operates like a monopoly on the supply-side of the labor market. In this type of labor market, a bargaining process between the union and the employer determines the wage rate.

We'll study both competitive labor markets and labor unions in this chapter.

Markets for Capital Services

Capital consists of the tools, instruments, machines, buildings, and other constructions that have been produced in the past and that businesses now use to produce goods and services. These physical objects are themselves goods—capital goods. Capital goods are traded in goods markets, just as bottled water and toothpaste are. The price of a dump truck, a capital good, is determined by supply and demand in the market for dump trucks. This market is not a market for capital services.

A market for *capital services* is a *rental market*—a market in which the services of capital are hired.

An example of a market for capital services is the vehicle rental market in which Avis, Budget, Hertz,

U-Haul, and many other firms offer automobiles and trucks for hire. The price in a capital services market is a *rental rate*.

Most capital services are not traded in a market. Instead, a firm buys capital and uses it itself. The services of the capital that a firm owns and operates have an implicit price that arises from depreciation and interest costs (see Chapter 8, pp. 180–181). You can think of this price as the implicit rental rate of capital. Firms that buy capital and use it themselves are *implicitly* renting the capital to themselves.

Markets for Land Services and Natural Resources

Land consists of all the gifts of nature—natural resources. The market for land as a factor of production is the market for the *services of land*—the use of land. The price of the services of land is a rental rate.

Most natural resources, such as farm land, can be used repeatedly. But a few natural resources are non-renewable. **Nonrenewable natural resources** are resources that can be used only once. Examples are oil, natural gas, and coal. The prices of nonrenewable natural resources are determined in global *commodity markets* and are called *commodity prices*.

Entrepreneurship

Entrepreneurial services are not traded in markets. Entrepreneurs receive the profit or bear the loss that results from their business decisions.

REVIEW QUIZ

1 What are the factors of production and their prices?
2 What is the distinction between capital and the services of capital?
3 What is the distinction between the price of capital equipment and the rental rate of capital?

You can work these questions in Study Plan 13.1 and get instant feedback.   MyEconLab

The rest of this chapter explores the influences on the demand and supply of factors of production. We begin by studying the demand for a factor of production.

The Demand for a Factor of Production

The demand for a factor of production is a **derived demand**—it is derived from the demand for the goods and services that the labor produces. You've seen, in Chapters 8 through 11, how a firm determines its profit-maximizing output. The quantities of factors of production demanded are a consequence of the firm's output decision. A firm hires the quantities of factors of production that produce the firm's profit-maximizing output.

To decide the quantity of a factor of production to hire, a firm compares the cost of hiring an additional unit of the factor with its value to the firm. The cost of hiring an additional unit of a factor of production is the factor price. The value to the firm of hiring one more unit of a factor of production is called the factor's **value of marginal product**. We calculate the value of marginal product as the price of a unit of output multiplied by the marginal product of the factor of production.

To study the demand for a factor of production, we'll use labor as the example. But what you learn here about the demand for labor applies to the demand for all factors of production.

Value of Marginal Product

Table 13.1 shows you how to calculate the value of the marginal product of labor at Angelo's Bakery.

The first two columns show Angelo's total product schedule—the number of loaves per hour that each quantity of labor can produce. The third column shows the marginal product of labor—the change in total product that results from a one-unit increase in the quantity of labor employed. (See Chapter 9, pp. 205–208 for a refresher on product schedules.)

Angelo can sell bread at the going market price of $2 a loaf. Given this information, we can calculate the value of marginal product (fourth column). It equals price multiplied by marginal product. For example, the marginal product of hiring the second worker is 6 loaves. Each loaf sold brings in $2, so the value of the marginal product of the second worker is $12 (6 loaves at $2 each).

A Firm's Demand for Labor

The value of the marginal product of labor tells us what an additional worker is worth to a firm. It tells us the revenue that the firm earns by hiring one more worker. The wage rate tells us what an additional worker costs a firm.

The value of the marginal product of labor and the wage rate together determine the quantity of labor demanded by a firm. Because the value of marginal product decreases as the quantity of labor employed increases, there is a simple rule for maximizing profit: Hire the quantity of labor at which the value of marginal product equals the wage rate.

If the value of marginal product of labor exceeds the wage rate, a firm can increase its profit by hiring

---

TABLE 13.1   Value of Marginal Product at Angelo's Bakery

Quantity of labor (L) (workers)	Total product (TP) (loaves per hour)	Marginal product ($MP = \Delta TP / \Delta L$) (loaves per worker)	Value of marginal product ($VMP = MP \times P$) (dollars per worker)
A 0	0		
		7	14
B 1	7		
		6	**12**
C **2**	13		
		5	10
D 3	18		
		4	8
E 4	22		
		3	6
F 5	25		

The value of the marginal product of labor equals the price of the product multiplied by marginal product of labor. If Angelo's hires 2 workers, the marginal product of the second worker is 6 loaves (in the third column). The price of a loaf is $2, so the value of the marginal product of the second worker is $2 a loaf multiplied by 6 loaves, which is $12 (in fourth column).

one more worker. If the wage rate exceeds the value of marginal product of labor, a firm can increase its profit by firing one worker. But if the wage rate equals the value of the marginal product of labor, the firm cannot increase its profit by changing the number of workers it employs. The firm is making the maximum possible profit. So

> The quantity of labor demanded by a firm is the quantity at which the value of the marginal product of labor equals the wage rate.

A Firm's Demand for Labor Curve

A firm's demand for labor curve is derived from its value of marginal product curve. Figure 13.1 shows these two curves. Figure 13.1(a) shows the value of marginal product curve at Angelo's Bakery. The blue bars graph the numbers in Table 13.1. The curve labeled *VMP* is Angelo's value of marginal product curve.

If the wage rate falls and other things remain the same, a firm hires more workers. Figure 13.1(b) shows Angelo's demand for labor curve.

Suppose the wage rate is $10 an hour. You can see in Fig.13.1(a) that if Angelo hires 2 workers, the value of the marginal product of labor is $12 an hour. At a wage rate of $10 an hour, Angelo makes a profit of $2 an hour on the second worker. If Angelo hires a third worker, the value of the marginal product of that worker is $10 an hour. So on this third worker, Angelo breaks even.

If Angelo hired 4 workers, his profit would fall. The fourth worker generates a value of marginal product of only $8 an hour but costs $10 an hour, so Angelo does not hire the fourth worker. When the wage rate is $10 an hour, the quantity of labor demanded by Angelo is 3 workers.

Figure 13.1(b) shows Angelo's demand for labor curve, *D*. At $10 an hour, the quantity of labor demanded by Angelo is 3 workers. If the wage rate increased to $12 an hour, Angelo would decrease the quantity of labor demanded to 2 workers. If the wage rate decreased to $8 an hour, Angelo would increase the quantity of labor demanded to 4 workers.

A change in the wage rate brings a change in the quantity of labor demanded and a movement along the demand for labor curve.

A change in any other influence on a firm's labor-hiring plans changes the demand for labor and shifts the demand for labor curve.

FIGURE 13.1   The Demand for Labor at Angelo's Bakery

(a) Value of marginal product

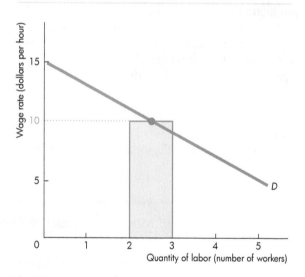

(b) Demand for labor

Angelo's Bakery can sell any quantity of bread at $2 a loaf. The blue bars in part (a) represent the firm's value of marginal product of labor (based on Table 13.1). The line labeled *VMP* is the firm's value of marginal product curve. Part (b) shows Angelo's demand for labor curve. Angelo hires the quantity of labor that makes the value of marginal product equal to the wage rate. The demand for labor curve slopes downward because the value of marginal product diminishes as the quantity of labor employed increases.

MyEconLab animation

Changes in a Firm's Demand for Labor

A firm's demand for labor depends on

- The price of the firm's output
- The prices of other factors of production
- Technology

The Price of the Firm's Output The higher the price of a firm's output, the greater is the firm's demand for labor. The price of output affects the demand for labor through its influence on the value of marginal product of labor. A higher price for the firm's output increases the value of the marginal product of labor. A change in the price of a firm's output leads to a shift in the firm's demand for labor curve. If the price of the firm's output increases, the demand for labor increases and the demand for labor curve shifts rightward.

For example, if the price of bread increased to $3 a loaf, the value of the marginal product of Angelo's fourth worker would increase from $8 an hour to $12 an hour. At a wage rate of $10 an hour, Angelo would now hire 4 workers instead of 3.

The Prices of Other Factors of Production If the price of using capital decreases relative to the wage rate, a firm substitutes capital for labor and increases the quantity of capital it uses. Usually, the demand for labor will decrease when the price of using capital falls. For example, if the price of a bread-making machine falls, Angelo might decide to install one machine and lay off a worker. But the demand for labor could increase if the lower price of capital led to a sufficiently large increase in the scale of production. For example, with cheaper machines available, Angelo might install a machine and hire more labor to operate it. This type of factor substitution occurs in the long run when the firm can change the size of its plant.

Technology New technologies decrease the demand for some types of labor and increase the demand for other types. For example, if a new automated bread-making machine becomes available, Angelo might install one of these machines and fire most of his workforce—a decrease in the demand for bakery workers. But the firms that manufacture and service automated bread-making machines hire more labor, so there is an increase in the demand for this type of labor. An event similar to this one occurred during the 1990s when the introduction of electronic telephone exchanges decreased the demand for telephone operators and increased the demand for computer programmers and electronics engineers.

Table 13.2 summarizes the influences on a firm's demand for labor.

TABLE 13.2   A Firm's Demand for Labor

The Law of Demand

(Movements along the demand curve for labor)

The quantity of labor demanded by a firm

Decreases if:	Increases if:
■ The wage rate increases	■ The wage rate decreases

Changes in Demand

(Shifts in the demand curve for labor)

A firm's demand for labor

Decreases if:	Increases if:
■ The price of the firm's output decreases	■ The price of the firm's output increases
■ The price of a substitute for labor falls	■ The price of a substitute for labor rises
■ The price of a complement of labor rises	■ The price of a complement of labor falls
■ A new technology or new capital decreases the marginal product of labor	■ A new technology or new capital increases the marginal product of labor

REVIEW QUIZ

1 What is the value of marginal product of labor?
2 What is the relationship between the value of marginal product of labor and the marginal product of labor?
3 How is the demand for labor derived from the value of marginal product of labor?
4 What are the influences on the demand for labor?

You can work these questions in Study Plan 13.2 and get instant feedback.   MyEconLab

◆ Labor Markets

Labor services are traded in many different labor markets. Examples are markets for bakery workers, van drivers, crane operators, computer support specialists, air traffic controllers, surgeons, and economists. Some of these markets, such as the market for bakery workers, are local. They operate in a given urban area. Some labor markets, such as the market for air traffic controllers, are national. Firms and workers search across the nation for the right match of worker and job. And some labor markets are global, such as the market for superstar hockey, basketball, and soccer players.

We'll look at a local market for bakery workers as an example. First, we'll look at a *competitive* labor market. Then, we'll see how monopoly elements can influence a labor market.

A Competitive Labor Market

A competitive labor market is one in which many firms demand labor and many households supply labor.

Market Demand for Labor Earlier in the chapter, you saw how an individual firm decides how much labor to hire. The market demand for labor is derived from the demand for labor by individual firms. We determine the market demand for labor by adding together the quantities of labor demanded by all the firms in the market at each wage rate. (The market demand for a good or service is derived in a similar way—see Chapter 5, pp. 108–109.)

Because each firm's demand for labor curve slopes downward, the market demand for labor curve also slopes downward.

The Market Supply of Labor The market supply of labor is derived from the supply of labor decisions made by individual households.

Individual's Labor Supply Decision People can allocate their time to two broad activities: labor supply and leisure. (Leisure is a catch-all term. It includes all activities other than supplying labor.) For most people, leisure is more fun than work so to induce them to work they must be offered a wage.

Think about the labor supply decision of Jill, one of the workers at Angelo's Bakery. Let's see how the wage rate influences the quantity of labor she is willing to supply.

Reservation Wage Rate Jill enjoys her leisure time, and she would be pleased if she didn't have to spend her time working at Angelo's Bakery. But Jill wants to earn an income, and as long as she can earn a wage rate of at least $5 an hour, she's willing to work. This wage is called her *reservation wage*. At any wage rate above her reservation wage, Jill supplies some labor.

The wage rate at Angelo's is $10 an hour, and at that wage rate, Jill chooses to work 30 hours a week. At a wage rate of $10 an hour, Jill regards this use of her time as the best available. Figure 13.2 illustrates.

Backward-Bending Labor Supply Curve If Jill were offered a wage rate between $5 and $10 an hour, she would want to work fewer hours. If she were offered a wage rate above $10 an hour, she would want to work more hours, but only up to a point. If Jill could

FIGURE 13.2   Jill's Labor Supply Curve

Jill's labor supply curve is S. Jill supplies no labor at wage rates below her reservation wage of $5 an hour. As the wage rate rises above $5 an hour, the quantity of labor that Jill supplies increases to a maximum of 40 hours a week at a wage rate of $25 an hour. As the wage rate rises above $25 an hour, Jill supplies a decreasing quantity of labor: her labor supply curve bends backward. The income effect on the demand for leisure dominates the substitution effect.

MyEconLab animation

earn $25 an hour, she would be willing to work 40 hours a week (and earn $1,000 a week). But at a wage rate above $25 an hour, with the goods and services that Jill can buy for $1,000, her priority would be a bit more leisure time. So if the wage rate increased above $25 an hour, Jill would cut back on her work hours and take more leisure. Jill's labor supply curve eventually bends backward.

Jill's labor supply decisions are influenced by a substitution effect and an income effect.

Substitution Effect At wage rates below $25 an hour, the higher the wage rate Jill is offered, the greater is the quantity of labor that she supplies. Jill's wage rate is her *opportunity cost of leisure*. If she quits work an hour early to catch a movie, the cost of that extra hour of leisure is the wage rate that Jill forgoes. The higher the wage rate, the less willing Jill is to forgo the income and take the extra leisure time. This tendency for a higher wage rate to induce Jill to work longer hours is a *substitution effect*.

Income Effect The higher Jill's wage rate, the higher is her income. A higher income, other things remaining the same, induces Jill to increase her demand for most goods and services. Leisure is one of those goods. Because an increase in income creates an increase in the demand for leisure, it also creates a decrease in the quantity of labor supplied.

Market Supply Curve The market supply curve shows the quantity of labor supplied by all households in a particular job market. It is found by adding together the quantities of labor supplied by all households to a given job market at each wage rate, so the greater the number of households (the greater is the working-age population), the greater is the market supply of labor.

Despite the fact that an individual's labor supply curve eventually bends backward, the market supply curve of labor slopes upward. The higher the wage rate for bakery workers, the greater is the quantity of bakery workers supplied in that labor market.

One reason why the market supply curve doesn't bend backward is that different households have different reservation wage rates and different wage rates at which their labor supply curves bend backward.

Also, along a supply curve in a particular job market, the wage rates available in other job markets remain the same. For example, along the supply curve of bakers, the wage rates of salespeople and all other types of labor are constant.

Let's now look at labor market equilibrium.

Competitive Labor Market Equilibrium Labor market equilibrium determines the wage rate and employment. In Fig. 13.3, the market demand curve for bakery workers is *D* and the market supply curve of bakery workers is *S*. The equilibrium wage rate is $10 an hour, and the equilibrium quantity is 300 bakery workers. If the wage rate exceeded $10 an hour, there would be a surplus of bakery workers. More people would be looking for jobs in bakeries than firms were willing to hire. In such a situation, the wage rate would fall as firms found it easy to hire people at a lower wage rate. If the wage rate were less than $10 an hour, there would be a shortage of bakery workers. Firms would not be able to fill all the positions they had available. In this situation, the wage rate would rise as firms found it necessary to offer higher wages to attract labor. Only at a wage rate of $10 an hour are there no forces operating to change the wage rate.

FIGURE 13.3   The Market for Bakery Workers

A competitive labor market coordinates firms' and households' plans. The market is in equilibrium—the quantity of labor demanded equals the quantity supplied at a wage rate of $10 an hour when 300 workers are employed. If the wage rate exceeds $10 an hour, the quantity supplied exceeds the quantity demanded and the wage rate will fall. If the wage rate is below $10 an hour, the quantity demanded exceeds the quantity supplied and the wage rate will rise.

MyEconLab animation

Economics in Action
Wage Rates in the United States

In 2011, the average wage rate in the United States was a bit less than $20 an hour. The figure shows the *average hourly wage rates* for twenty jobs selected from the more than 700 jobs for which the Bureau of Labor Statistics reports wage rate data.

You can see that a general internist, on average, earns 10 times as much per hour as a fast-food worker and more than twice as much as an economist. Remember that these numbers are averages. Some doctors earn much more and some earn less than the average general internist.

Many more occupations earn a wage rate below the national average than above it. Most of the occupations that earn more than the national average require a college degree and postgraduate training.

Earning differences are explained by differences in the value of the marginal product of the skills in the various occupations and in market power.

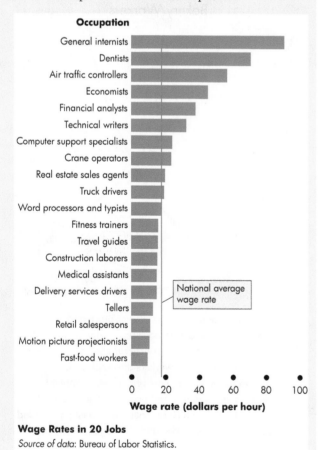

Wage Rates in 20 Jobs
Source of data: Bureau of Labor Statistics.

Differences and Trends in Wage Rates

You can use what you've learned about labor markets to explain some of the differences in wage rates across occupations and the trends in wage rates.

Wage rates are unequal, and *Economics in Action* on this page shows a sample of the inequality in wages in 2011. The differences in wage rates across occupations—including college professors and basketball coaches—are driven by differences in demand and supply in labor markets. The highest wage rates are earned in occupations where the value of marginal product is highest and where few people have the ability and training to perform the job.

Rising Wage Rates Wage rates increase over time and trend upward. The reason is that the value of marginal product of labor also increases over time. Technological change and the new types of capital that it brings make workers more productive. With greater labor productivity, the demand for labor increases, which increases the wage rate. Even jobs in which physical productivity doesn't increase experience increases in the *value* of marginal product. Child care is an example. A child-care worker can't care for an increasing number of children, but an increasing number of parents who earn high wages are willing to hire child-care workers. The *value* of marginal product of these workers increases, so the demand for their services increases, and so does their wage rate.

Increased Wage Inequality In recent years wage inequality has increased. High wage rates have increased more rapidly than the low ones, and some low wage rates have stagnated or even fallen. The reasons are complex and not fully understood, but the best explanation is that there is an interaction between technology and education.

The new information technologies of the 1990s and 2000s made well-educated, skilled workers more productive, so it raised their wage rates. For example, the computer created the jobs and increased the wage rates of computer programmers and electronic engineers.

These same technologies destroyed some low-skilled jobs. For example, the ATM took the jobs and lowered the wage rate of bank tellers, and automatic telephones took the jobs of telephone operators.

Another reason for increased inequality is that globalization has brought increased competition for low-skilled workers and at the same time opened global markets for high-skilled workers.

◆ ECONOMICS IN THE NEWS

College Major and Job Prospects

The Most Valuable College Major
Which college major is most likely to land you a well-paying job right out of school? Katie Bardaro, an economist at PayScale, a compensation research firm, says biomedical engineering is your best bet. The median salary starts at $53,800 and by mid-career reaches $84,700 and keeps rising. The median salary for all biomedical engineers in 2012 was $88,000.

Some other science and engineering jobs pay more but don't have as good an outlook for jobs growth. The Bureau of Labor Statistics projects that the number of jobs for biomedical engineers will increase from today's 20,000 to 32,000 in 2020—an increase of more than 60 percent. In contrast, the working-age population will increase by only 8 percent by 2020.

Sources: The Bureau of Labor Statistics and *Forbes*, May 15, 2012

THE QUESTIONS

- Why is the number of jobs for biomedical engineering graduates increasing?
- What determines the demand for biomedical engineers and why might it be increasing?
- What determines the supply of biomedical engineers and why might it be increasing?
- What determines whether the wage rate of biomedical engineers will rise?
- Provide a graphical illustration of the market for biomedical engineers in 2012 and 2020.

Biomedical engineers design and build replacement parts for the human body.

THE ANSWERS

- The number of jobs for biomedical engineers is growing because *both* demand for and supply of biomedical engineers are increasing.
- The demand for biomedical engineers is *derived* from the demand for biomedical products. The demand for replacement parts for the human body is increasing because technological advances are creating new and improved products.
- The supply of biomedical engineers is determined by the working-age population and the number of people who decide to major in the subject. The supply is increasing because the working-age population is increasing and good job prospects are attracting a larger percentage of people to study biomedical engineering.
- The wage rate of biomedical engineers will rise if the demand for their services increases faster than supply.
- The figure illustrates the market for biomedical engineers in 2012 and in 2020.
- Demand is expected to increase from D_{12} to D_{20}.
- Supply is expected to increase from S_{12} to S_{20}.
- The increase in demand is much greater than the increase in supply.
- The equilibrium quantity (the number of jobs) increases from 20,000 in 2012 to 32,000 in 2020.
- Because demand increases by more than supply, the equilibrium wage rate rises. (The 2020 wage rate is an assumption.)

The Market for Biomedical Engineers in 2012 and 2020

A Labor Market with a Union

A **labor union** is an organized group of workers that aims to increase the wage rate and influence other job conditions. Let's see what happens when a union enters a competitive labor market.

Influences on Labor Supply One way of raising the wage rate is to decrease the supply of labor. In some labor markets, a union can restrict supply by controlling entry into apprenticeship programs or by influencing job qualification standards. Markets for skilled workers, doctors, dentists, and lawyers are the easiest ones to control in this way.

If there is an abundant supply of nonunion labor, a union can't decrease supply. For example, in the market for farm labor in southern California, the flow of nonunion labor from Mexico makes it difficult for a union to control the supply.

On the demand side of the labor market, the union faces a tradeoff: The demand for labor curve slopes downward, so restricting supply to raise the wage rate costs jobs. For this reason, unions also try to influence the demand for union labor.

Influences on Labor Demand A union tries to increase the demand for the labor of its members in four main ways:

1. Increasing the value of marginal product of its members by organizing and sponsoring training schemes and apprenticeship programs, and by professional certification.

2. Lobbying for import restrictions and encouraging people to buy goods made by unionized workers.

3. Supporting minimum wage laws, which increase the cost of employing low-skilled labor and lead firms to substitute high-skilled union labor for low-skilled nonunion labor.

4. Lobbying for restrictive immigration laws to decrease the supply of foreign workers.

Labor Market Equilibrium with a Union Figure 13.4 illustrates what happens to the wage rate and employment when a union successfully enters a competitive labor market. With no union, the demand curve is D_C, the supply curve is S_C, the wage rate is $10 an hour, and 300 workers have jobs.

Now a union enters this labor market. First, look at what happens if the union has sufficient control over the supply of labor to be able to restrict supply

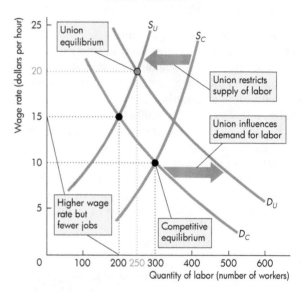

FIGURE 13.4   A Union Enters a Competitive Labor Market

In a competitive labor market, the demand curve is D_C and the supply curve is S_C. The wage rate is $10 an hour and 300 workers are employed. If a union decreases the supply of labor and the supply of labor curve shifts to S_U, the wage rate rises to $15 an hour and employment decreases to 200 workers. If the union can also increase the demand for labor and shift the demand for labor curve to D_U, the wage rate rises to $20 an hour and 250 workers are employed.

MyEconLab animation

below its competitive level—to S_U. If that is all the union is able to do, employment falls to 200 workers and the wage rate rises to $15 an hour.

Suppose now that the union is also able to increase the demand for labor to D_U. The union can get an even bigger increase in the wage rate and with a smaller fall in employment. By maintaining the restricted labor supply at S_U, the union increases the wage rate to $20 an hour and achieves an employment level of 250 workers.

Because a union restricts the supply of labor in the market in which it operates, the union's actions spill over into nonunion markets. Workers who can't get union jobs must look elsewhere for work. This action increases the supply of labor in nonunion markets and lowers the wage rate in those markets. This spillover effect further widens the gap between union and nonunion wages.

Monopsony in the Labor Market Not all labor markets in which unions operate are competitive. Rather, some are labor markets in which the employer possesses market power and the union enters to try to counteract that power.

A market in which there is a single buyer is called a **monopsony**. A monopsony labor market has one employer. In some parts of the country, managed health-care organizations are the major employer of health-care professionals. In some communities, Wal-Mart is the main employer of salespeople. These firms have monopsony power.

A monopsony acts on the buying side of a market in a similar way to a monopoly on the selling side. The firm maximizes profit by hiring the quantity of labor that makes the marginal cost of labor equal to the value of marginal product of labor and by paying the lowest wage rate at which it can attract this quantity of labor.

Figure 13.5 illustrates a monopsony labor market. Like all firms, a monopsony faces a downward-sloping value of marginal product curve, *VMP*, which is its demand for labor curve, *D*—the curve labeled *VMP* = *D* in the figure.

What is special about monopsony is the marginal cost of labor. For a firm in a competitive labor market, the marginal cost of labor is the wage rate. For a monopsony, the marginal cost of labor exceeds the wage rate. The reason is that being the only buyer in the market, the firm faces an upward-sloping supply of labor curve—the curve *S* in the figure.

To attract one more worker, the monopsony must offer a higher wage rate. But it must pay this higher wage rate to all its workers, so the marginal cost of a worker is the wage rate plus the increased wage bill that arises from paying all the workers the higher wage rate.

The supply curve is now the average cost of labor curve and the relationship between the supply curve and the marginal cost of labor curve, *MCL*, is similar to that between a monopoly's demand curve and marginal revenue curve (see p. 300). The relationship between the supply curve and the *MCL* curve is also similar to that between a firm's average cost curve and marginal cost curve (see pp. 214–215).

To find the profit-maximizing quantity of labor to hire, the monopsony sets the marginal cost of labor equal to the value of marginal product of labor. In Fig. 13.5, this outcome occurs when the firm employs 100 workers.

To hire 100 workers, the firm must pay $10 an hour (on the supply of labor curve). Each worker is paid $10 an hour, but the value of marginal product of labor is $20 an hour, so the firm makes an economic profit of $10 an hour on the marginal worker.

If the labor market in Fig. 13.5 were competitive, the equilibrium wage rate and employment would be determined by the demand and supply curves. The wage rate would be $15 an hour, and 150 workers would be employed. So compared with a competitive labor market, a monopsony pays a lower wage rate and employs fewer workers.

A Union and a Monopsony A union is like a monopoly. If the union (monopoly seller) faces a monopsony buyer, the situation is called **bilateral monopoly**. An example of bilateral monopoly is the Writers Guild of America that represents film, television, and radio

---

FIGURE 13.5   A Monopsony Labor Market

A monopsony is a market structure in which there is a single buyer. A monopsony in the labor market has a value of marginal product curve *VMP* and faces a labor supply curve *S*. The marginal cost of labor curve is *MCL*. Making the marginal cost of labor equal to the value of marginal product maximizes profit. The monopsony hires 100 hours of labor and pays the lowest wage rate for which that quantity of labor will work, which is $10 an hour.

MyEconLab animation

◆ AT **ISSUE**

Monopoly Power for Evil or Good?

The standard view of economists is that monopoly is bad. It prevents resources from being used efficiently, and on any criterion of fairness or equity, monopoly is unfair. It fails to serve the social interest.

We normally think of a monopoly as a big firm that gouges its customers. But a surprising monopoly (and monopsony) has attracted attention—the National Collegiate Athletic Association (NCAA).

Does the NCAA do a good job at efficiently allocating the talents of college athletes and providing those athletes with a fair return for their efforts?

The standard economist's view is that the NCAA doesn't serve the social interest. But there is a contrarian view.

Let's look at both sides of this argument.

The **Standard View**

Robert Barro expresses the standard economist view. While acknowledging that the NCAA has boosted the productivity of college sports programs, he says that the NCAA monopoly:

- Suppresses financial competition in college sports.

- Restricts scholarships and other payments to college athletes.

- Prevents college basketball players who come from poor families from accumulating wealth during a college career.

- Keeps poor students poor.

- Despite doing these bad things, the NCAA manages to convince most people that the bad guys are the colleges that violate NCAA rules by attempting to pay their athletes competitive wages.

The contenders for best monopoly in America include the Post Office, Microsoft, and the NCAA. And the winner is . . . the NCAA.

Robert Barro, "The Best Little Monopoly in America", *BusinessWeek*, December 9, 2002

A **Contrarian View**

Richard B. McKenzie of the University of California, Irvine, and Dwight R. Lee of the University of Georgia, in their book, *In Defense of Monopoly: How Market Power Fosters Creative Production*, (University of Michigan Press, 2008) say the NCAA:

- Helps its members to cooperate to everyone's benefit.

- Has enabled healthy growth of college athletics over the past 50 years.

- Has generated economic profits for member schools.

- Does not lower student athletes' wages.

- Has stimulated the demand for student athletes and increased their wages and employment opportunities.

- Permitting NCAA colleges to pay athletes competitive wages is misguided.

The Kentucky Wildcats celebrate their victory at the 2012 NCAA National Championship writers, and an employers' alliance that represents CBS, MGM, NBC, and other entertainment companies. Every three years, the Writers Guild and the employers' alliance negotiate a pay deal.

In bilateral monopoly, the outcome is determined by bargaining, which depends on the costs that each party can inflict on the other. The firm can shut down temporarily and lock out its workers, and the workers can shut down the firm by striking. Each party estimates the other's strength and what it will lose if it does not agree to the other's demands.

Usually, an agreement is reached without a strike or a lockout. The threat is usually enough to bring the bargaining parties to an agreement. When a strike or lockout does occur, it is because one party has misjudged the costs each party can inflict on the other. Such an event occurred in November 2007 when the writers and entertainment producers failed to agree on a compensation deal. A 100-day strike followed that ended up costing the entertainment industry an estimated $2 billion.

In the example in Fig. 13.5, if the union and employer are equally strong, and each party knows the strength of the other, they will agree to split the gap between $10 (the wage rate on the supply curve) and $20 (the wage rate on the demand curve) and agree to a wage rate of $15 an hour.

You've now seen that in a monopsony, a union can bargain for a higher wage rate without sacrificing jobs. A similar outcome can arise in a monopsony labor market when a minimum wage law is enforced. Let's look at the effect of a minimum wage.

Monopsony and the Minimum Wage In a competitive labor market, a minimum wage that exceeds the equilibrium wage decreases employment (see Chapter 6, pp. 131–132). In a monopsony labor market, a minimum wage can increase both the wage rate and employment. Let's see how.

Figure 13.6 shows a monopsony labor market without a union. The wage rate is $10 an hour and 100 workers are employed.

A minimum wage law is passed that requires employers to pay at least $15 an hour. The monopsony now faces a perfectly elastic supply of labor at $15 an hour up to 150 workers (along the minimum wage line). To hire more than 150 workers, a wage rate above $15 an hour must be paid (along the supply curve). Because the wage rate is $15 an hour up to 150 workers, so is the marginal cost of labor $15 an hour up to 150 workers. To maximize profit, the monopsony sets the marginal cost of labor equal to the value of marginal product of

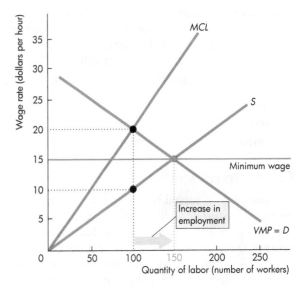

FIGURE 13.6   Minimum Wage Law in Monopsony

In a monopsony labor market, the wage rate is $10 an hour and 100 workers are hired. If a minimum wage law increases the wage rate to $15 an hour, the wage rate rises to this level and employment increases to 150 workers.

MyEconLab animation

labor (on the demand curve). That is, the monopsony hires 150 workers and pays $15 an hour. The minimum wage law has succeeded in raising the wage rate and increasing the number of workers employed.

REVIEW QUIZ

1 What determines the amount of labor that households plan to supply?

2 How are the wage rate and employment determined in a competitive labor market?

3 How do labor unions influence wage rates?

4 What is a monopsony and why is a monopsony able to pay a lower wage rate than a firm in a competitive labor market?

5 How is the wage rate determined when a union faces a monopsony?

6 What is the effect of a minimum wage law in a monopsony labor market?

You can work these questions in Study Plan 13.3 and get instant feedback.   MyEconLab

Capital and Natural Resource Markets

The markets for capital and land can be understood by using the same basic ideas that you've seen when studying a competitive labor market. But markets for nonrenewable natural resources are different. We'll now examine three groups of factor markets:

- Capital rental markets
- Land rental markets
- Nonrenewable natural resource markets

Capital Rental Markets

The demand for capital is derived from the *value of marginal product of capital*. Profit-maximizing firms hire the quantity of capital services that makes the value of marginal product of capital equal to the *rental rate of capital*. The *lower* the rental rate of capital, other things remaining the same, the *greater* is the quantity of capital demanded. The supply of capital responds in the opposite way to the rental rate. The *higher* the rental rate, other things remaining the same, the *greater* is the quantity of capital supplied. The equilibrium rental rate makes the quantity of capital demanded equal to the quantity of capital supplied.

Figure 13.7 illustrates the rental market for tower cranes—capital used to construct high-rise buildings. The value of marginal product and the demand curve is *VMP = D*. The supply curve is *S*. The equilibrium rental rate is $1,000 per day and 100 tower cranes are rented.

Rent-Versus-Buy Decision Some capital services are obtained in a rental market like the market for tower cranes. And like tower cranes, many of the world's large airlines rent their airplanes. But not all capital services are obtained in a rental market. Instead, firms buy the capital equipment that they use. You saw in Chapter 8 (pp. 180–181) that the cost of the services of the capital that a firm owns and operates itself is an implicit rental rate that arises from depreciation and interest costs. Firms that buy capital *implicitly* rent the capital to themselves.

The decision to obtain capital services in a rental market rather than buy capital and rent it implicitly is made to minimize cost. The firm compares the cost of explicitly renting the capital and the cost of buying and implicitly renting it. This decision is the same as

FIGURE 13.7   A Rental Market for Capital

The value of marginal product of tower cranes, *VMP*, determines the demand, *D*, for tower crane rentals. With the supply curve, *S*, the equilibrium rental rate is $1,000 a day and 100 cranes are rented.

———— MyEconLab animation ————

the one that a household makes in deciding whether to rent or buy a home.

To make a rent-versus-buy decision, a firm must compare a cost incurred in the *present* with a stream of rental costs incurred over some *future* period. The Mathematical Note (pp. 334–335) explains how to make this comparison by calculating the *present value* of a future amount of money. If the *present value* of the future rental payments of an item of capital equipment exceeds the cost of buying the capital, the firm will buy the equipment. If the *present value* of the future rental payments of an item of capital equipment is less than the cost of buying the capital, the firm will rent (or lease) the equipment.

Land Rental Markets

The demand for land is based on the same factors as the demand for labor and the demand for capital—the *value of marginal product of land*. Profit-maximizing firms rent the quantity of land at which the value of marginal product of land is equal to the *rental rate of land.* The *lower* the rental rate, other things remaining the same, the *greater* is the quantity of land demanded.

But the supply of land is special: Its quantity is fixed, so the quantity supplied cannot be changed by people's decisions. The supply of each particular block of land is perfectly inelastic.

The equilibrium rental rate makes the quantity of land demanded equal to the quantity available. Figure 13.8 illustrates the market for a 10-acre block of land on 42nd Street in New York City. The quantity supplied is fixed and the supply curve is *S*. The value of marginal product and the demand curve is *VMP = D*. The equilibrium rental rate is $1,000 an acre per day.

The rental rate of land is high in New York because the willingness to pay for the services produced by that land is high, which in turn makes the *VMP* of land high. A Big Mac costs more at McDonald's on 42nd Street, New York, than at McDonald's on Jefferson Avenue, St. Louis, but not because the rental rate of land is higher in New York. The rental rate of land is higher in New York because of the greater willingness to pay for a Big Mac (and other goods and services) in New York.

FIGURE 13.8   A Rental Market for Land

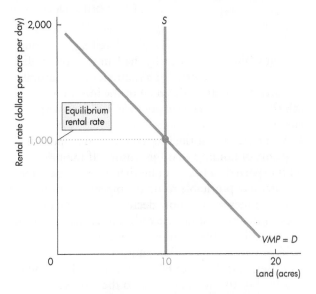

The value of marginal product of a 10-acre block, *VMP*, determines the rental demand, *D*, for this land. With the supply curve *S*, the block rents for $10,000 a day.

——————— MyEconLab animation ———————

Nonrenewable Natural Resource Markets

The nonrenewable natural resources are oil, gas, and coal. Burning one of these fuels converts it to energy and other by-products, and the used resource cannot be re-used. The natural resources that we use to make metals are also nonrenewable, but they can be used again, at some cost, by recycling them.

Oil, gas, and coal are traded in global commodity markets. The price of a given grade of crude oil is the same in New York, London, and Singapore. Traders, linked by telephone and the Internet, operate these markets around the clock every day of the year.

Demand and supply determine the prices and the quantities traded in these commodity markets. We'll look at the influences on demand and supply by considering the global market for crude oil.

The Demand for Oil   The two key influences on the demand for oil are

1. The *value of marginal product* of oil
2. The expected future price of oil

The value of marginal product of oil is the *fundamental* influence on demand. It works in exactly the same way for a nonrenewable resource as it does for any other factor of production. The greater the quantity of oil used, the smaller is the value of marginal product of oil. Diminishing value of marginal product makes the demand curve slope downward. The lower the price, the greater is the quantity demanded.

The higher the expected future price of oil, the greater is the present demand for oil. The expected future price is a *speculative* influence on demand. Oil in the ground and oil in storage tanks are inventories that can be held or sold. A trader might plan to buy oil to hold now and to sell it later for a profit. Instead of buying oil to hold and sell later, the trader could buy a bond and earn interest. The interest forgone is the opportunity cost of holding the oil. If the price of oil is expected to rise by a bigger percentage than the interest rate, a trader will hold oil and incur the opportunity cost. In this case, the return from holding oil exceeds the return from holding bonds.

The Supply of Oil   The three key influences on the supply of oil are

1. The known oil reserves
2. The scale of current oil production facilities
3. The expected future price of oil

Known oil reserves are the oil that has been discovered and can be extracted with today's technology. This quantity increases over time because advances in technology enable ever-less accessible sources to be discovered. The greater the size of known reserves, the greater is the supply of oil. But this influence on supply is small and indirect. It operates by changing the expected distant future price of oil. Even a major new discovery of oil would have a negligible effect on current supply of oil.

The scale of current oil production facilities is the *fundamental* influence on the supply of oil. Producing oil is like any production activity: It is subject to increasing marginal cost. The increasing marginal cost of extracting oil means that the supply curve of oil slopes upward. The higher the price of oil, the greater is the quantity supplied. When new oil wells are sunk or when new faster pumps are installed, the supply of oil increases. When existing wells run dry, the supply of oil decreases. Over time, the factors that increase supply are more powerful than those that decrease supply, so changes in the scale of current oil production facilities increase the supply of oil.

Speculative forces based on expectations about the future price also influence the supply of oil. The *higher* the expected future price of oil, the *smaller* is the present supply of oil. A trader with an oil inventory might plan to sell now or to hold and sell later. You've seen that interest forgone is the opportunity cost of holding the oil. If the price of oil is expected to rise by a bigger percentage than the interest rate, it is profitable to incur the opportunity cost of holding oil rather than selling it immediately.

The Equilibrium Price of Oil

The demand for oil and the supply of oil determine the equilibrium price and quantity traded. Figure 13.9 illustrates the market equilibrium.

The value of marginal product of oil, *VMP*, is the *fundamental determinant of demand*, and the marginal cost of extraction, *MC*, is the *fundamental determinant of supply*. Together, they determine the *market fundamentals price*.

If expectations about the future price are also based on fundamentals, the equilibrium price is the market fundamentals price. But if expectations about the future price of oil depart from what the market fundamentals imply, *speculation* can drive a wedge between the equilibrium price and the market fundamentals price.

FIGURE 13.9   A Nonrenewable Natural Resource Market

The value of marginal product of a natural resource, *VMP*, and the marginal cost of extraction, *MC*, determine the *market fundamentals* price. Demand, *D*, and supply, *S*, which determine the equilibrium price, are influenced by the expected future price. Speculation can bring a gap between the market fundamentals price and the equilibrium price.

MyEconLab animation

The Hotelling Principle

Harold Hotelling, an economist at Columbia University, had an incredible idea: Traders expect the price of a nonrenewable natural resource to rise at a rate equal to the interest rate. We call this idea the **Hotelling principle**. Let's see why it is correct.

You've seen that the interest rate is the opportunity cost of holding an oil inventory. If the price of oil is expected to rise at a rate that exceeds the interest rate, it is profitable to hold a bigger inventory. Demand increases, supply decreases, and the price rises. If the interest rate exceeds the rate at which the price of oil is expected to rise, it is not profitable to hold an oil inventory. Demand decreases, supply increases, and the price falls. But if the price of oil is expected to rise at a rate equal to the interest rate, holding an inventory of oil is just as good as holding bonds. Demand and supply don't change and the price does not change. Only when the price of oil is expected to rise at a rate equal to the interest rate is the price at its equilibrium.

Economics in Action
The World and U.S. Markets for Oil

The world produced about 87 million barrels of oil in 2011 and the price shot upward from $70 in 2010 to $100 in 2011.

Although the United States imports almost three quarters of its oil from other countries, much of it comes from close to home. Figure 1 provides the details: Only 14 percent of the U.S. oil supply comes from the Middle East and more than one third comes from Canada, Mexico, and other Western Hemisphere nations.

Even if the United States produced all its own oil, it would still face a fluctuating global price. U.S. producers would not willingly sell to U.S. buyers for a price below the world price. So energy independence doesn't mean an independent oil price.

The Hotelling principle tells us that we must expect the price of oil to rise at a rate equal to the interest rate. But expecting the price to rise at a rate equal to the interest rate doesn't mean that the price will rise at this rate. As you can see in Fig. 2, the price of oil over the past 50 or so years has not followed the path predicted by the Hotelling principle.

The forces that influence expectations are not well understood. The expected future price of oil depends on its expected future rate of use and the rate of discovery of new sources of supply. One person's expectation about a future price also depends on guesses about other people's expectations. These guesses can change abruptly and become self-reinforcing. When

Figure 2 The Price of Oil and Its Hotelling Path

Source of data: U.S. Energy Information Administration.

the expected future price of oil changes for whatever reason, demand and supply change, and so does the price. Prices in speculative markets are always volatile.

◆ REVIEW QUIZ

1 What determines demand and supply in rental markets for capital and land?
2 What determines the demand for a nonrenewable natural resource?
3 What determines the supply of a nonrenewable natural resource?
4 What is the market fundamentals price and how might it differ from the equilibrium price?
5 Explain the Hotelling principle.

You can work these questions in Study Plan 13.4 and get instant feedback.   MyEconLab

◆ *Reading Between the Lines* on pp. 332–333 contrasts the outcomes in competitive and union labor markets for teachers.

The next chapter looks more closely at the distribution of income and its trends. The chapter also looks at the efforts by governments to redistribute income and modify the market outcome.

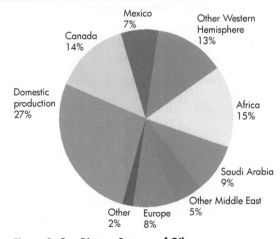

Figure 1 Our Diverse Sources of Oil

Source of data: U.S. Energy Information Administration.

Labor Markets in Action

Charter School Salaries Lower

The Journal Gazette
April 24, 2011

Fort Wayne—Allen County charter school teachers made $21,000 less on average than their regular public school counterparts in 2010, according to a *Journal Gazette* analysis.

The average public school teacher salary in Northwest Allen County Schools, Southwest Allen County Schools and Fort Wayne Community Schools was $49,987, while the average teacher salary in Fort Wayne's three charter schools was $28,584. ...

Charter school leaders said budget constraints make it difficult to match traditional public school salaries. Nevertheless, they said, teachers are drawn to charters out of an appreciation of their mission, a love for the kids they serve, and a desire for autonomy not granted in traditional public school environments. ...

Charter schools are public schools that are free from many of the regulations that govern traditional public schools; most do not have teachers unions. ...

According to a 2010 study by Vanderbilt University, charter schools tend to have higher teacher turnover rates than traditional schools. They also tend to have less-experienced, and therefore lower-paid, teachers.

Locally, teachers at Fort Wayne Community Schools had 14 years of experience on average, compared to 5 years or less at the city's charter schools. Those numbers are from the 2008–09 school year, the latest available on the Indiana Department of Education's website. ...

According to *The Journal Gazette's* analysis, the highest-paid traditional public school teacher in Allen County made about $49,000 more in 2010 than the highest-paid charter school teacher. ...

ESSENCE OF THE STORY

- In 2010 in an Indiana school district, charter school teachers made an average of $29,000 and traditional public school teachers made an average of $50,000, a gap of $21,000.

- The highest paid public school teacher made $49,000 more than the highest-paid charter school teacher.

- Charter school teachers have 5 years or less experience; public school teachers have 14 years on average.

- Charter schools have smaller budgets than public schools.

- Charter school teachers value greater autonomy.

- Charter schools have higher teacher turnover rates than traditional schools.

- Most charter schools do not have teachers' unions.

ECONOMIC ANALYSIS

- Teachers in charter schools are paid much lower salaries (wage rates), on average, than teachers in regular public schools for three main reasons:
  1. Charter school teacher are less experienced
  2. Charter schools have tighter budgets than regular public schools
  3. Charter school teachers are not (usually) unionized.

- Because charter school teachers are, on average, less experienced than regular public school teachers, they have a lower marginal product than regular public school teachers, which means they also have a lower *VMP* and a lower demand for their services.

- Because charter schools have tighter budgets than regular public schools, the market values their services at a lower (implicit) price, which further lowers the *VMP* and demand for charter school teachers.

- Some teachers say that they value the freedom and autonomy that a charter school gives them. This preference for working in a charter school increases the supply of charter school teachers (relative to what it would be without the autonomy.)

- The combination of a lower demand and greater supply lowers the equilibrium wage rate of charter school teachers.

- Figure 1 illustrates the influence of the factors you've just reviewed.

- If charter school teachers had the same experience as regular public school teachers and if charter school budgets were as big as regular public school budgets, the demand curve for teachers in charter schools would be D_P.

- If charter school teachers didn't have the autonomy they enjoy, the supply curve of charter school teachers would be S_P. The equilibrium wage rate would be $40,000 per year. (This wage rate is an assumption.)

- The factors discussed above decrease demand to D_C and increase supply to S_C and the equilibrium wage rate is only $30,000 per year.

- The fact that regular public school teachers are unionized and most charter school teachers are not, widens the wage gap even further.

- In Fig. 2, the teachers' union boosts demand by lobbying for bigger school budgets and restricts supply by raising qualification requirements.

- The demand for public school teachers increases from its competitive level, D_P, to D_U and supply decreases from its competitive level, S_P, to S_U.

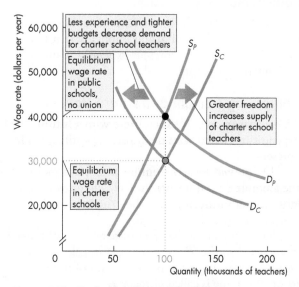

Figure 1 The Market for Charter School Teachers

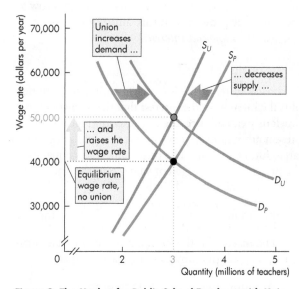

Figure 2 The Market for Public School Teachers with Union

- The equilibrium wage rate rises to $50,000 per year.

- When a regular public school is replaced by a charter school, the teachers who remain in the charter school take a very large wage cut.

- The wage cut explains the higher teacher turnover rate of charter schools. The wage cut is too big for some teachers, so they search for an alternative better paying job and quit teaching.

333

MATHEMATICAL NOTE
Present Value and Discounting

Rent-Versus-Buy Decision

To decide whether to rent an item of capital equipment or to buy the capital and implicitly rent it, a firm must compare the present expenditure on the capital with the future rental cost of the capital.

Comparing Current and Future Dollars

To compare a present expenditure with a future expenditure, we convert the future expenditure to its "present value."

The **present value** of a future amount of money is the amount that, if invested today, will grow to be as large as that future amount when the interest that it will earn is taken into account.

So the present value of a future amount of money is smaller than the future amount. The calculation that we use to convert a future amount of money to its present value is called **discounting**.

The easiest way to understand discounting and present value is to first consider its opposite: How a present value grows to a future amount of money because of *compound interest*.

Compound Interest

Compound interest is the interest on an initial investment plus the interest on the interest that the investment has previously earned. Because of compound interest, a present amount of money (a present value) grows into a larger future amount. The future amount is equal to the present amount (present value) plus the interest it will earn in the future. That is,

Future amount = Present value + Interest income.

The interest in the first year is equal to the present value multiplied by the interest rate, r, so

Amount after 1 year = Present value + ($r \times$ Present value).

or

Amount after 1 year = Present value $\times$ (1 + r).

If you invest $100 today and the interest rate is 10 percent a year ($r = 0.1$), 1 year from today you will have $110—the original $100 plus $10 interest. Check that the above formula delivers that answer:

$$\$100 \times 1.1 = \$110.$$

If you leave this $110 invested to earn 10 percent during a second year, at the end of that year you will have

Amount after 2 years = Present value $\times$ (1 + r)^2.

With the numbers of the previous example, you invest $100 today at an interest rate of 10 percent a year ($r = 0.1$). After 1 year, you will have $110—the original $100 plus $10 interest. And after 2 years, you will have $121. In the second year, you earned $10 on your initial $100 plus $1 on the $10 interest that you earned in the first year. Check that the above formula delivers that answer:

$$\$100 \times (1.1)^2 = \$100 \times 1.21 = \$121.$$

If you leave your $100 invested for n years, it will grow to

Amount after n years = Present value $\times$ (1 + r)^n.

With an interest rate of 10 percent a year, your $100 will grow to $195 after 7 years ($n = 7$)—almost double the present value of $100.

Discounting a Future Amount

We have just calculated future amounts 1 year, 2 years, and n years in the future, knowing the present value and the interest rate. To calculate the present value of these future amounts, we just work backward.

To find the present value of an amount 1 year in the future, we divide the future amount by (1 + r).

That is,

$$\text{Present value} = \frac{\text{Amount of money one year in future}}{(1 + r)}.$$

Let's check that we can use the present value formula by calculating the present value of $110 1 year from now when the interest rate is 10 percent a year.

You'll be able to guess that the answer is $100 because we just calculated that $100 invested today at 10 percent a year becomes $110 in one year. So the present value of $110 to be received 1 year from today is $100. But let's use the formula. Putting the numbers into the above formula, we have

$$\text{Present value} = \frac{\$110}{(1 + 0.1)}$$
$$= \frac{\$110}{1.1} = \$100.$$

To calculate the present value of an amount of money 2 years in the future, we use the formula:

$$\text{Present value} = \frac{\text{Amount of money two years in future}}{(1 + r)^2}$$

Use this formula to calculate the present value of $121 to be received 2 years from now at an interest rate of 10 percent a year. With these numbers, the formula gives

$$\text{Present value} = \frac{\$121}{(1 + 0.1)^2}$$
$$= \frac{\$121}{(1.1)^2}$$
$$= \frac{\$121}{1.21}$$
$$= \$100.$$

We can calculate the present value of an amount of money n years in the future by using the general formula

$$\text{Present value} = \frac{\text{Amount of money } n \text{ years in future}}{(1 + r)^n}$$

For example, if the interest rate is 10 percent a year, $100 to be received 10 years from now has a present value of $38.55. That is, if $38.55 is invested today at 10 percent a year it will accumulate to $100 in 10 years.

Present Value of a Sequence of Future Amounts

You've seen how to calculate the present value of an amount of money to be received 1 year, 2 years, and n years in the future. Most practical applications of present value calculate the present value of a sequence of future amounts of money that are spread over several years. An airline's payment of rent for the lease of airplanes is an example.

To calculate the present value of a sequence of amounts over several years, we use the formula you have learned and apply it to each year. We then sum the present values for all the years to find the present value of the sequence of amounts.

For example, suppose that a firm expects to pay $100 a year for each of the next 5 years and the interest rate is 10 percent a year ($r = 0.1$). The present value (PV) of these five payments of $100 each is calculated by using the following formula:

$$PV = \frac{\$100}{1.1} + \frac{\$100}{1.1^2} + \frac{\$100}{1.1^3} + \frac{\$100}{1.1^4} + \frac{\$100}{1.1^5},$$

which equals

$$PV = \$90.91 + \$82.64 + \$75.13 + \$68.30 + \$62.09$$
$$= \$379.07.$$

You can see that the firm pays $500 over 5 years. But because the money is paid in the future, it is not worth $500 today. Its present value is only $379.07. And the farther in the future the money is paid, the smaller is its present value. The $100 paid 1 year in the future is worth $90.91 today, but the $100 paid 5 years in the future is worth only $62.09 today.

The Decision

If this firm could lease a machine for 5 years at $100 a year or buy the machine for $500, it would jump at leasing. Only if the firm could buy the machine for less than $379.07 would it want to buy.

Many personal and business decisions turn on calculations like the one you've just made. A decision to buy or rent an apartment, to buy or lease a car, and to pay off a student loan or let the loan run another year can all be made using the above calculation.

SUMMARY

Key Points

The Anatomy of Factor Markets (p. 316)

- The factor markets are: job markets for labor; rental markets (often implicit rental markets) for capital and land; and global commodity markets for nonrenewable natural resources.
- The services of entrepreneurs are not traded on a factor market.

Working Problem 1 will give you a better understanding of the anatomy of factor markets.

The Demand for a Factor of Production

(pp. 317–319)

- The value of marginal product determines the demand for a factor of production.
- The value of marginal product decreases as the quantity of the factor employed increases.
- The firm employs the quantity of each factor of production that makes the value of marginal product equal to the factor price.

Working Problems 2 to 8 will give you a better understanding of the demand for a factor of production.

Labor Markets (pp. 320–327)

- The value of marginal product of labor determines the demand for labor. A rise in the wage rate brings a decrease in the quantity demanded.
- The quantity of labor supplied depends on the wage rate. At low wage rates, a rise in the wage rate increases the quantity supplied. Beyond a high enough wage rate, a rise in the wage rate decreases the quantity supplied—the supply curve eventually bends backward.

- Demand and supply determine the wage rate in a competitive labor market.
- A labor union can raise the wage rate by restricting the supply or increasing the demand for labor.
- A monopsony can lower the wage rate below the competitive level.
- A union or a minimum wage in a monopsony labor market can raise the wage rate without a fall in employment.

Working Problems 9 to 11 will give you a better understanding of labor markets.

Capital and Natural Resource Markets (pp. 328–331)

- The value of marginal product of capital (and land) determines the demand for capital (and land).
- Firms make a rent-versus-buy decision by choosing the option that minimizes cost.
- The supply of land is inelastic and the demand for land determines the rental rate.
- The demand for a nonrenewable natural resource depends on the value of marginal product and on the expected future price.
- The supply of a nonrenewable natural resource depends on the known reserves, the cost of extraction, and the expected future price.
- The price of nonrenewable natural resources can differ from the market fundamentals price because of speculation based on expectations about the future price.
- The price of a nonrenewable natural resource is expected to rise at a rate equal to the interest rate.

Working Problems 12 to 17 will give you a better understanding of capital and natural resource markets.

Key Terms

Bilateral monopoly, 325
Compound interest, 334
Derived demand, 317
Discounting, 334

Hotelling principle, 330
Labor union, 324
Monopsony, 325

Nonrenewable natural
  resources, 316
Present value, 334
Value of marginal product, 317

STUDY PLAN PROBLEMS AND APPLICATIONS

MyEconLab   You can work Problems 1 to 18 in Chapter 13 Study Plan and get instant feedback.

The Anatomy of Factor Markets (Study Plan 13.1)

1. Tim is opening a new online store. He plans to hire two people to key in the data at $10 an hour. Tim is also considering buying or leasing some new computers. The purchase price of a computer is $900 and after three years it is worthless. The annual cost of leasing a computer is $450.

   a. In which factor markets does Tim operate?

   b. What is the price of the capital equipment and the rental rate of capital?

The Demand for a Factor of Production

(Study Plan 13.2)

Use the following data to work Problems 2 to 7. Wanda owns a fish store. She employs students to sort and pack the fish. Students can pack the following amounts of fish:

Number of students	Quantity of fish (pounds)
1	20
2	50
3	90
4	120
5	145
6	165
7	180
8	190

The fish market is competitive and the price of fish is 50¢ a pound. The market for packers is competitive and their market wage rate is $7.50 an hour.

2. Calculate the marginal product of the students and draw the marginal product curve.

3. Calculate the value of marginal product of labor and draw the value of marginal product curve.

4. a. Find Wanda's demand for labor curve.

   b. How many students does Wanda employ?

Use the following additional information to work Problems 5 and 6.

The market price of fish falls to 33.33¢ a pound, but the packers' wage rate remains at $7.50 an hour.

5. a. How does the students' marginal product change?

   b. How does the value of marginal product of labor change?

6. a. How does Wanda's demand for labor change?

   b. What happens to the number of students that Wanda employs?

7. At Wanda's fish store, packers' wages increase to $10 an hour, but the price of fish remains at 50¢ a pound.

   a. What happens to the value of marginal product of labor?

   b. What happens to Wanda's demand for labor curve?

   c. How many students does Wanda employ?

8. **British Construction Activity Falls**

   Construction activity in Britain declined in June at the fastest rate in 11 years. A major home builder was unable to raise more capital—both signs of worsening conditions in the battered housing industry. Employment of construction labor declined in June after 23 months of growth. Average house prices fell 0.9 percent in June, the eighth consecutive month of declines, leaving the average 6.3 percent below June 2007.

   Source: *Forbes*, July 2, 2008

   a. Explain how a fall in house prices influences the market for construction labor.

   b. On a graph illustrate the effect of falling house prices in the market for construction labor.

Labor Markets (Study Plan 13.3)

Use the following news clip to work Problems 9 to 11.

In Modern Rarity, Workers Form Union at Small Chain

In New York's low-income neighborhoods, labor unions have virtually no presence. But after a year-long struggle, 95 workers at a chain of 10 sneaker stores have formed a union. After months of negotiations, the two sides signed a three-year contract that sets the wage rate at $7.25 an hour.

Source: *The New York Times*, February 5, 2006

9. Why are labor unions scarce in New York's low-income neighborhoods?

10. Who wins from this union contract? Who loses?

11. How can this union try to change the demand for labor?

Capital and Natural Resource Markets

(Study Plan 13.4)

12. Classify the following items as a nonrenewable natural resource, a renewable natural resource, or not a natural resource. Explain your answers.
    a. Trump Tower
    b. Lake Michigan
    c. Coal in a West Virginia coal mine
    d. The Internet
    e. Yosemite National Park
    f. Power generated by wind turbines

13. **Land Prices Reflect High Commodity Prices**
    As their family grows, the Steens are finding it more difficult for the next generation to stay in ranching. "The problem is they don't create any more land," Steen said. As the prices for cattle, corn, and other commodities climb, so does the value of land in South Dakota.
    Source: *Rapid City Journal*, January 30, 2012
    a. Why does the price of land in South Dakota keep rising? In your answer include a discussion of the demand for and supply of land.
    b. Use a graph to show why the price of land in South Dakota has increased over the past decade.
    c. Is the supply of land in South Dakota perfectly inelastic?

14. In the news clip in Problem 8,
    a. Explain how a fall in house prices influences the market for construction equipment leases.
    b. Draw a graph to illustrate the effect of a fall in house prices in the market for construction equipment leases.

Use the following news clip to work Problems 15 and 16.

Intensive Farming: Ecologically Sustainable?
According to the European Commission, global agricultural production needs to be doubled by 2050 to feed the world. But at the same time, it says this will have to be done with less water and fewer pesticides and greenhouse gas emissions, amid growing competition for land.
    Source: euractiv.com, August 16, 2011

15. a. Is farmland a renewable or nonrenewable resource?

b. Explain how the growing demand for farm products will affect the market for land and draw a graph to illustrate your answer.

16. How might farmers meet the growing demand for farm products without having to use a greater quantity of farmland?

17. **Copter Crisis**
    Helicopters are in short supply these days. You could blame a rise in military spending, a jump in disaster relief, even crowded airports pushing executives into private travel. But the fastest growth is coming from the offshore oil-and-gas industry, where helicopters are the only way to ferry crews to and from rigs and platforms. Hundred-dollar oil has pushed producers to work existing fields harder and to open new deep-sea wells in Brazil, India, and Alaska. The number of rigs and platforms has grown by 13% over the past decade. Oil companies are facing a two-year backlog in orders for the Sikorsky S92, a favorite of the oil industry, and a 40% rise in prices for used models.
    Source: *Fortune*, May 12, 2008
    a. Explain how high oil prices influence the market for helicopter leases and services (such as the Sikorsky S92).
    b. What happens to the value of marginal product of a helicopter as a firm leases or buys additional helicopters?

Mathematical Note (Study Plan 13.MN)

18. Keshia is opening a new bookkeeping service. She is considering buying or leasing some new laptop computers. The purchase price of a laptop is $1,500 and after three years it is worthless. The annual lease rate is $550 per laptop. The value of marginal product of one laptop is $700 a year. The value of marginal product of a second laptop is $625 a year. The value of marginal product of a third laptop is $575 a year. And the value of marginal product of a fourth laptop is $500 a year.
    a. How many laptops will Keshia lease or buy?
    b. If the interest rate is 4 percent a year, will Keshia lease or buy her laptops?
    c. If the interest rate is 6 percent a year, will Keshia lease or buy her laptops?

ADDITIONAL PROBLEMS AND APPLICATIONS

MyEconLab   You can work these problems in MyEconLab if assigned by your instructor.

The Anatomy of Factor Markets

19. Venus is opening a tennis school. She plans to hire a marketing graduate to promote and manage the school at $20 an hour. Venus is also considering buying or leasing a new tennis ball machine. The purchase price of the machine is $1,000 and after three years it is worthless. The annual cost of leasing the machine is $500.
    a. In which factor markets does Venus operate?
    b. What is the price of the capital equipment and the rental rate of capital?

The Demand for a Factor of Production

Use the following data to work Problems 20 to 23.
Kaiser's Ice Cream Parlor hires workers to produce milk shakes. The market for milk shakes is perfectly competitive, and the price of a milk shake is $4. The labor market is competitive, and the wage rate is $40 a day. The table shows the workers' total product schedule.

Number of workers	Quantity produced (milk shakes per day)
1	7
2	21
3	33
4	43
5	51
6	55

20. Calculate the marginal product of hiring the fourth worker and the fourth worker's value of marginal product.
21. How many workers will Kaiser's hire to maximize its profit and how many milk shakes a day will Kaiser's produce?
22. If the price of a milk shake rises to $5, how many workers will Kaiser's hire?
23. Kaiser's installs a new machine for making milk shakes that increases the productivity of workers by 50 percent. If the price of a milk shake remains at $4 and the wage rises to $48 a day, how many workers does Kaiser's hire?
24. **Detroit Oil Refinery Expansion Approved**
    Marathon Oil Saturday started work on a $1.9 billion expansion of its gasoline refinery in

Detroit. Marathon will employ 800 construction workers and add 135 permanent jobs to the existing 480 workers at the refinery.
    Source: *United Press International*, June 21, 2008
    a. Explain how rising gasoline prices influence the market for refinery labor.
    b. Draw a graph to illustrate the effects of rising gasoline prices on the market for refinery labor.

Labor Markets

Use the following news clip to work Problems 25 to 28.

Miner Sacks 17,000 Workers Over Pay Dispute
Impala Platinum has sacked 17,000 South African miners at its Rustenburg mine because they took part in an illegal strike. The miners refused to have their union negotiate in the two-week pay dispute with the world's second largest platinum producer. Mining provides a quarter of all jobs in Rustenburg.
    Source: abc.com.au, February 3, 2012

25. How would the wage rate and employment for the Rustenburg miners be determined in a competitive market?
26. a. Explain how it is possible that the mine workers were being paid less than the wage that would be paid in a competitive labor market.
    b. What would be the effect of a minimum wage law in the market for miners?
27. a. Explain how a miners' union would attempt to counteract Impala Mine's wage offers.
    b. Is it possible that the union officials might be acting in their own interest and not in the interest of the miners?
28. If the market for labor in mining is competitive, explain the potential effect of a union on the wage rate. Draw a graph to illustrate your answer.

Use the following news clip to work Problems 29 to 32.

The New War over Wal-Mart
Today, Wal-Mart employs more people—1.7 million—than any other private employer in the world. With size comes power: Wal-Mart's prices are lower and United Food and Commercial Workers International

Union argues that Wal-Mart's wages are also lower than its competitors. Last year, the workers at a Canadian outlet joined the union and Wal-Mart immediately closed the outlet. But does Wal-Mart behave any worse than its competitors? When it comes to payroll, Wal-Mart's median hourly wage tracks the national median wage for general retail jobs.

Source: *The Atlantic*, June 2006

29. a. Assuming that Wal-Mart has market power in a labor market, explain how the firm could use that market power in setting wages.

    b. Draw a graph to illustrate how Wal-Mart might use labor market power to set wages.

30. a. Explain how a union of Wal-Mart's employees would attempt to counteract Wal-Mart's wage offers (a bilateral monopoly).

    b. Explain the response by the Canadian Wal-Mart to the unionization of employees.

31. Based upon evidence presented in this article, does Wal-Mart function as a monopsony in labor markets, or is the market for retail labor more competitive? Explain.

32. If the market for retail labor is competitive, explain the potential effect of a union on the wage rates. Draw a graph to illustrate your answer.

Capital and Natural Resource Markets

33. New technology has allowed oil to be pumped from much deeper offshore oil fields than before. For example, 28 deep ocean rigs operate in the deep waters of the Gulf of Mexico.

    a. What effect do you think deep ocean sources have had on the world oil price?

    b. Who will benefit from drilling for oil in the Gulf of Mexico? Explain your answer.

34. Water is a natural resource that is plentiful in Canada but not plentiful in Arizona.

    a. If Canadians start to export bulk water to Arizona, what do you predict will be the effect on the price of bulk water?

    b. Will Canada eventually run out of water?

    c. Do you think the Hotelling principle applies to Canada's water? Explain why or why not.

Use the following news clip to work Problems 35 and 36.

Gas Prices Create Land Rush

There is a land rush going on across Pennsylvania, but buyers aren't interested in the land itself. Buyers

are interested in what lies beneath the earth's surface—mineral rights to natural gas deposits. Record high natural gas prices have already pushed up drilling activity across the state, but drilling companies have discovered a new technology that will enable deep gas-bearing shale to be exploited. Development companies, drilling companies, and speculators have been trying to lease mineral rights from landowners. The new drilling techniques might recover about 10 percent of those reserves, and that would ring up at a value of $1 trillion.

Source: *Erie Times-News*, June 15, 2008

35. a. Is natural gas a renewable or nonrenewable resource? Explain.

    b. Explain why the demand for land in Pennsylvania has increased.

36. a. If companies are responding to the higher prices for natural gas by drilling right now wherever they can, what does that imply about their assumptions about the future price of natural gas in relation to current interest rates?

    b. What could cause the price of natural gas to fall in the future?

Economics in the News

37. After you have studied *Reading Between the Lines* on pp. 434–435, answer the following questions.

    a. Is the average difference in the salaries of charter school and regular public school teachers greater or smaller than the difference at the top end of the pay scales?

    b. What are the influences on the demand for the highest paid teachers that explain their high wage rates?

    c. What are the influences on the supply of the highest paid teachers that explain their high wage rates?

    d. Draw a graph of the market for the highest-paid teachers.

    e. If all charter school teachers became unionized, how would the market for these teachers change? Illustrate your answer with a graph.

    f. How would you expect unionization of charter school teachers to influence the unionized market for regular public school teachers?

    g. If the public school systems were able to break the teachers' union, how would the market for regular public school teachers change? Illustrate your answer with a graph.

Absolute advantage A person has an absolute advantage if that person is more productive than another person. (p. 40)

Allocative efficiency A situation in which goods and services are produced at the lowest possible cost and in the quantities that provide the greatest possible benefit. We cannot produce more of any good without giving up some of another good that we *value more highly*. (p. 35)

Average cost pricing rule A rule that sets price to cover cost including normal profit, which means setting the price equal to average total cost. (p. 270)

Average fixed cost Total fixed cost per unit of output. (p. 210)

Average product The average product of a factor of production. It equals total product divided by the quantity of the factor employed. (p. 205)

Average total cost Total cost per unit of output. (p. 210)

Average variable cost Total variable cost per unit of output. (p. 210)

Barrier to entry A natural or legal constraint that protects a firm from potential competitors. (p. 254)

Behavioral economics A study of the ways in which limits on the human brain's ability to compute and implement rational decisions influences economic behavior—both the decisions that people make and the consequences of those decisions for the way markets work. (p. 168)

Benefit The benefit of something is the gain or pleasure that it brings and is determined by preferences. (p. 10)

Big tradeoff The tradeoff between efficiency and fairness. (p. 117)

Bilateral monopoly A situation in which a monopoly seller faces a monopsony buyer. (p. 325)

Black market An illegal market in which the equilibrium price exceeds the legally imposed price ceiling. (p. 128)

Budget line The limit to a household's consumption choices. It marks the boundary between those combinations of goods and services that a household can afford to buy and those that it cannot afford. (pp. 154)

Capital The tools, equipment, buildings, and other constructions that businesses use to produce goods and services. (p. 4)

Capital accumulation The growth of capital resources, including *human capital*. (p. 38)

Capture theory A theory that regulation serves the self-interest of the producer, who captures the regulator and maximizes economic profit. (p. 269)

Ceteris paribus Other things being equal—all other relevant things remaining the same. (p. 24)

Change in demand A change in buyers' plans that occurs when some influence on those plans other than the price of the good changes. It is illustrated by a shift of the demand curve. (p. 58)

Change in supply A change in seller's plans that occurs when some influence on those plans other than the price of the good changes. It is illustrated by a shift of the supply curve. (p. 63)

Change in the quantity demanded A change in buyers' plans that occurs when the price of a good changes but all other influences on buyers' plans remain unchanged. It is illustrated by a movement along the demand curve. (p. 61)

Change in the quantity supplied A change in sellers' plans that occurs when the price of a good changes but all other influences on sellers' plans remain unchanged. It is illustrated by a movement along the supply curve. (p. 64)

Command system A method of allocating resources by the order (command) of someone in authority. In a firm a managerial hierarchy organizes production. (pp. 106, 185)

Comparative advantage A person or country has a comparative advantage in an activity if that person or country can perform the activity at a lower opportunity cost than anyone else or any other country. (p. 40)

Competitive market A market that has many buyers and many sellers, so no single buyer or seller can influence the price. (p. 56)

Complement A good that is used in conjunction with another good. (p. 59)

Compound interest The interest on an initial investment plus the interest on the interest that the investment has previously earned. (p. 334)

Constant returns to scale Features of a firm's technology that lead to constant long-run average cost as output increases. When constant returns to scale are present, the *LRAC* curve is horizontal. (p. 218)

Consumer equilibrium A situation in which a consumer has allocated all his or her available income in the way that, given the prices of goods and services, maximizes his or her total utility. (p. 157)

Consumer surplus The excess of the benefit received from a good over the amount paid for it. It is calculated as the marginal benefit (or value) of a good minus its price, summed over the quantity bought. (p. 109)

Cross elasticity of demand The responsiveness of the demand for a good to a change in the price of a substitute or complement, other things remaining the same. It is calculated as the percentage change in the quantity demanded of the good divided by the percentage change in the price of the substitute or complement. (p. 92)

Deadweight loss A measure of inefficiency. It is equal to the decrease in total surplus that results from an inefficient level of production. (p. 113)

Demand The entire relationship between the price of the good and the quantity demanded of it when all other influences on buyers' plans remain the same. It is illustrated by a demand curve and described by a demand schedule. (p. 57)

Demand curve A curve that shows the relationship between the quantity demanded of a good and its price when all other influences on consumers' planned purchases remain the same. (p. 58)

Deregulation The process of removing regulation of prices, quantities, entry, and other aspects of economic activity in a firm or industry. (p. 269)

Derived demand Demand for a factor of production—it is derived from the demand for the goods and services produced by that factor. (p. 317)

Diminishing marginal returns The tendency for the marginal product of an additional unit of a factor of production to be less than the marginal product of the previous unit of the factor. (p. 207)

Diminishing marginal utility The tendency for marginal utility to decrease as the quantity consumed of a good increases. (p. 156)

Direct relationship A relationship between two variables that move in the same direction. (p. 18)

Discounting The calculation we use to convert a future amount of money to its present value. (p. 334)

Diseconomies of scale Features of a firm's technology that make average total cost rise as output increases—the *LRAC* curve slopes upward. (p. 218)

Doha Development Agenda (Doha Round) Negotiations held in Doha, Qatar, to lower tariff barriers and quotas that restrict international trade in farm products and services. (p. 307)

Dumping The sale by a foreign firm of exports at a lower price than the cost of production. (p. 308)

Economic depreciation The *fall* in the market value of a firm's capital over a given period. (p. 181)

Economic efficiency A situation that occurs when the firm produces a given output at the least cost. (p. 183)

Economic growth The expansion of production possibilities. (p. 38)

Economic model A description of some aspect of the economic world that includes only those features of the world that are needed for the purpose at hand. (p. 12)

Economic profit A firm's total revenue minus its total cost, with total cost measured as the opportunity cost of production. (p. 180)

Economic rent Any surplus—consumer surplus, producer surplus or economic profit. (p. 262)

Economics The social science that studies the *choices* that individuals, businesses, governments, and entire societies make as they cope with *scarcity* and the *incentives* that influence and reconcile those choices. (p. 2)

Economies of scale Features of a firm's technology that make average total cost fall as output increases—the *LRAC* curve slopes downward. (pp. 194, 218)

Economies of scope Decreases in average total cost that occur when a firm uses specialized resources to produce a range of goods and services. (p. 195)

Efficient Resource use is efficient if it is not possible to make someone better off without making someone else worse off. (p. 5)

Elastic demand Demand with a price elasticity greater than 1; other things remaining the same, the percentage change in the quantity demanded exceeds the percentage change in price. (p. 86)

Elasticity of supply The responsiveness of the quantity supplied of a good to a change in its price, other things remaining the same. (p. 94)

Entrepreneurship The human resource that organizes the other three factors of production: labor, land, and capital. (p. 4)

Equilibrium price The price at which the quantity demanded equals the quantity supplied. (p. 66)

Equilibrium quantity The quantity bought and sold at the equilibrium price. (p. 66)

Exports The goods and services that we sell to people in other countries. (p. 296)

Factors of production The productive resources used to produce goods and services. (p. 3)

Firm An economic unit that hires factors of production and organizes those factors to produce and sell goods and services. (pp. 44, 180)

Four-firm concentration ratio A measure of market power that is calculated as the percentage of the value of sales accounted for by the four largest firms in an industry. (p. 190)

General Agreement on Tariffs and Trade (GATT) An international agreement signed in 1947 to reduce tariffs on international trade. (p. 302)

Goods and services The objects that people value and produce to satisfy human wants. (p. 3)

Herfindahl–Hirschman Index A measure of market power that is calculated as the square of the market share of each firm (as a percentage) summed over the largest 50 firms (or over all firms if there are fewer than 50) in a market. (p. 190)

Hotelling Principle The idea that traders expect the price of a nonrenewable natural resource to rise at a rate equal to the interest rate. (p. 330)

Human capital The knowledge and skill that people obtain from education, on-the-job training, and work experience. (p. 3)

Implicit rental rate The firm's opportunity cost of using its own capital. (p. 180)

Import quota A restriction that limits the maximum quantity of a good that may be imported in a given period. (p. 304)

Imports The goods and services that we buy from people in other countries. (p. 296)

Incentive A reward that encourages an action or a penalty that discourages one. (p. 2)

Incentive system A method of organizing production that uses a market-like mechanism inside the firm. (p. 185)

Income elasticity of demand The responsiveness of demand to a change in income, other things remaining the same. It is calculated as the percentage change in the quantity demanded divided by the percentage change in income. (p. 91)

Inelastic demand A demand with a price elasticity between 0 and 1; the percentage change in the quantity demanded is less than the percentage change in price. (p. 85)

Inferior good A good for which demand decreases as income increases. (p. 60)

Interest The income that capital earns. (p. 4)

Inverse relationship A relationship between variables that move in opposite directions. (p. 19)

Labor The work time and work effort that people devote to producing goods and services. (p. 3)

Labor union An organized group of workers that aims to increase the wage rate and influence other job conditions. (p. 324)

Land The "gifts of nature" that we use to produce goods and services. (p. 3)

Law of demand Other things remaining the same, the higher the price of a good, the smaller is the quantity demanded of it; the lower the price of a good, the larger is the quantity demanded of it. (p. 57)

Law of diminishing returns As a firm uses more of a variable factor of production with a given quantity of the fixed factor of production, the marginal product of the variable factor of production eventually diminishes. (p. 207)

Law of supply Other things remaining the same, the higher the price of a good, the greater is the quantity supplied of it; the lower the price of a good, the smaller is the quantity supplied. (p. 62)

Legal monopoly A market in which competition and entry are restricted by the granting of a public franchise, government license, patent, or copyright. (p. 254)

Linear relationship A relationship between two variables that is illustrated by a straight line. (p. 18)

Long run The time frame in which the quantities of *all* factors of production can be varied. (p. 204)

Long-run average cost curve The relationship between the lowest attainable average total cost and output when the firm can change both the plant it uses and the quantity of labor it employs. (p. 217)

Macroeconomics The study of the performance of the national economy and the global economy. (p. 2)

Margin When a choice is made by comparing a little more of something with its cost, the choice is made at the margin. (p. 11)

Marginal benefit The benefit that a person receives from consuming one more unit of a good or service. It is measured as the maximum amount that a person is willing to pay for one more unit of the good or service. (pp. 11, 36)

Marginal benefit curve A curve that shows the relationship between the marginal benefit of a good and the quantity of that good consumed. (p. 36)

Marginal cost The *opportunity cost* of producing *one* more unit of a good or service. It is the best alternative forgone. It is calculated as the increase in total cost divided by the increase in output. (pp. 11, 35, 210)

Marginal cost pricing rule A rule that sets the price of a good or service equal to the marginal cost of producing it. (p. 269)

Marginal product The increase in total product that results from a one-unit increase in the variable input, with all other inputs remaining the same. It is calculated as the increase in total product divided by the increase in the variable input employed, when the quantities of all other inputs remain the same. (p. 205)

Marginal revenue The change in total revenue that results from a one-unit increase in the quantity sold. It is calculated as the change in total revenue divided by the change in quantity sold. (p. 228)

Marginal utility The *change* in total utility resulting from a one-unit increase in the quantity of a good consumed. (p. 155)

Marginal utility per dollar The marginal utility from a good that results from spending one more dollar on it. It is calculated as the marginal utility from the good divided by its price. (p. 158)

Market Any arrangement that enables buyers and sellers to get information and to do business with each other. (p. 44)

Market failure A situation in which a market delivers an inefficient outcome. (p. 113)

Microeconomics The study of the choices that individuals and businesses make, the way these choices interact in markets, and the influence of governments. (p. 2)

Minimum efficient scale The *smallest* quantity of output at which the long-run average cost reaches its lowest level. (p. 219)

Minimum wage A regulation that makes the hiring of labor below a specified wage rate illegal. The lowest wage at which a firm may legally hire labor. (p. 131)

Money Any commodity or token that is generally acceptable as the means of payment. (p. 44)

Money price The number of dollars that must be given up in exchange for a good or service. (p. 56)

Monopolistic competition A market structure in which a large number of firms make similar but slightly different products and compete on product quality, price, and marketing, and firms are free to enter or exit the market. (p. 189)

Monopoly A market structure in which there is one firm, which produces a good or service that has no close substitutes and in which the firm is protected from competition by a barrier preventing the entry of new firms. (pp. 189, 254)

Monopsony A market in which there is a single buyer. (p. 325)

Natural monopoly A market in which economies of scale enable one firm to supply the entire market at the lowest possible cost. (p. 254)

Negative relationship A relationship between variables that move in opposite directions. (p. 19)

Neuroeconomics The study of the activity of the human brain when a person makes an economic decision. (p. 169)

Normal good A good for which demand increases as income increases. (p. 60)

Normal profit The return to entrepreneurship is normal profit and it is the profit that an entrepreneur earns *on average*. (p. 181)

Offshore outsourcing A U.S. firm buys finished goods, components, or services from firms in other countries. (p. 309)

Oligopoly A market structure in which a small number of firms compete. (p. 189)

Opportunity cost The highest-valued alternative that we must give up to get something. (pp. 10, 33)

Perfect competition A market in which there are many firms each selling an identical product; there are many buyers; there are no restrictions on entry into the industry; firms in the industry have no advantage over potential new entrants; and firms and buyers are well informed about the price of each firm's product. (pp. 189, 228)

Perfectly elastic demand Demand with an infinite price elasticity; the quantity demanded changes by an infinitely large percentage in response to a tiny price change. (p. 85)

Perfectly inelastic demand Demand with a price elasticity of zero; the

quantity demanded remains constant when the price changes. (p. 85)

Perfect price discrimination Price discrimination that occurs when a firm sells each unit of output for the highest price that anyone is willing to pay for it. The firm extracts the entire consumer surplus. (p. 266)

Positive relationship A relationship between two variables that move in the same direction. (p. 18)

Preferences A description of a person's likes and dislikes and the intensity of those feelings. (pp. 10, 36, 155)

Present value The amount of money that, if invested today, will grow to be as large as a given future amount when the interest that it will earn is taken into account. (p. 334)

Price cap A regulation that makes it illegal to charge a price higher than a specified level. (p. 128)

Price ceiling A regulation that makes it illegal to charge a price higher than a specified level. (p. 128)

Price discrimination The practice of selling different units of a good or service for different prices. (p. 255)

Price elasticity of demand A units-free measure of the responsiveness of the quantity demanded of a good to a change in its price, when all other influences on buyers' plans remain the same. (p. 84)

Price floor A regulation that makes it illegal to trade at a price lower than a specified level. (p. 131)

Price taker A firm that cannot influence the price of the good or service it produces. (p. 228)

Principal–agent problem The problem of devising compensation rules that induce an *agent* to act in the best interest of a *principal*. (p. 185)

Producer surplus The excess of the amount received from the sale of a good or service over the cost of producing it. It is calculated as the price of a good minus the marginal cost (or minimum supply-price), summed over the quantity sold. (p. 111)

Product differentiation Making a product slightly different from the product of a competing firm. (p. 189)

Production efficiency A situation in which goods and services are

produced at the lowest possible cost. (p. 33)

Production possibilities frontier The boundary between the combinations of goods and services that can be produced and the combinations that cannot. (p. 32)

Production quota An upper limit to the quantity of a good that may be produced in a specified period. (p. 139)

Profit The income earned by entrepreneurship. (p. 4)

Property rights The social arrangements that govern the ownership, use, and disposal of anything that people value. Property rights are enforceable in the courts. (pp. 44)

Quantity demanded The amount of a good or service that consumers plan to buy during a given time period at a particular price. (p. 57)

Quantity supplied The amount of a good or service that producers plan to sell during a given time period at a particular price. (p. 62)

Rate of return regulation A regulation that requires the firm to justify its price by showing that its return on capital doesn't exceed a specified target rate. (p. 270)

Rational choice A choice that compares costs and benefits and achieves the greatest benefit over cost for the person making the choice. (p. 10)

Regulation Rules administered by a government agency to influence prices, quantities, entry, and other aspects of economic activity in a firm or industry. (p. 269)

Relative price The ratio of the price of one good or service to the price of another good or service. A relative price is an opportunity cost. (p. 56)

Rent The income that land earns. (p. 4)

Rent ceiling A regulation that makes it illegal to charge a rent higher than a specified level. (p. 128)

Rent seeking The lobbying for special treatment by the government to create economic profit or to divert consumer surplus or producer surplus away from others. The pursuit of wealth by capturing economic rent. (pp. 262)

Scarcity Our inability to satisfy all our wants. (p. 2)

Scatter diagram A graph that plots the value of one variable against the value of another variable for a number of different values of each variable. (p. 16)

Search activity The time spent looking for someone with whom to do business. (p. 128)

Self-interest The choices that you think are the best ones available for you are choices made in your self-interest. (p. 5)

Short run The time frame in which the quantity of at least one factor of production is fixed and the quantities of the other factors can be varied. The fixed factor is usually capital—that is, the firm uses a given plant. (p. 204)

Short-run market supply curve A curve that shows the quantity supplied in a market at each price when each firm's plant and the number of firms remain the same. (p. 234)

Shutdown point The price and quantity at which the firm is indifferent between producing the profit-maximizing output and shutting down temporarily. The shutdown point occurs at the price and the quantity at which average variable cost is a minimum. (p. 232)

Single-price monopoly A monopoly that must sell each unit of its output for the same price to all its customers. (p. 255)

Slope The change in the value of the variable measured on the *y*-axis divided by the change in the value of the variable measured on the *x*-axis. (p. 22)

Social interest Choices that are the best ones for society as a whole. (p. 5)

Subsidy A payment made by the government to a producer. (p. 140)

Substitute A good that can be used in place of another good. (p. 59)

Sunk cost The past expenditure on a plant that has no resale value. (p. 204)

Supply The entire relationship between the price of a good and the quantity supplied of it when all other influences on producers' planned sales remain the same. It is described by a supply schedule and illustrated by a supply curve. (p. 62)

Supply curve A curve that shows the relationship between the quantity supplied of a good and its price when all other influences on producers' planned sales remain the same. (p. 62)

Symmetry principle A requirement that people in similar situations be treated similarly. (p. 118)

Tariff A tax that is imposed by the importing country when an imported good crosses its international boundary. (p. 301)

Tax incidence The division of the burden of the tax between the buyer and the seller. (p. 133)

Technological change The development of new goods and of better ways of producing goods and services. (p. 38)

Technological efficiency A situation that occurs when the firm produces a given output by using the least amount of inputs. (p. 183)

Technology Any method of producing a good or service. (p. 182)

Total cost The cost of all the productive resources that a firm uses. (p. 209)

Total fixed cost The cost of the firm's fixed inputs. (p. 209)

Total product The maximum output that a given quantity of labor can produce. (p. 205)

Total revenue The value of a firm's sales. It is calculated as the price of the good multiplied by the quantity sold. (pp. 88, 228)

Total revenue test A method of estimating the price elasticity of demand by observing the change in total revenue that results from a change in the price, when all other influences on the quantity sold remain the same. (p. 88)

Total surplus The sum of consumer surplus and producer surplus. (p. 112)

Total utility The total benefit that a person gets from the consumption of all the different goods and services. (p. 155)

Total variable cost The cost of all the firm's variable inputs. (p. 209)

Tradeoff A constraint that involves giving up one thing to get something else. (p. 10)

Transactions costs The opportunity costs of making trades in a market. The costs that arise from finding someone with whom to do business, of reaching an agreement about the price and other aspects of the exchange, and of ensuring that the terms of the agreement are fulfilled. (pp. 115, 194, 320)

Unit elastic demand Demand with a price elasticity of 1; the percentage change in the quantity demanded equals the percentage change in price. (p. 85)

Utilitarianism A principle that states that we should strive to achieve "the greatest happiness for the greatest number of people." (p. 116)

Utility The benefit or satisfaction that a person gets from the consumption of goods and services. (p. 155)

Value of marginal product The value to the firm of hiring one more unit of a factor of prodeuction. It is calculated as the price of a unit of output multiplied by the marginal product of the factor of production. (p. 317)

Wages The income that labor earns. (p. 4)